# THE CONCISE HISTORY OF
# AVIATION

# THE CONCISE HISTORY OF
# AVIATION

## WITH OVER 1,000 SCALED PROFILES OF AIRCRAFT FROM 1903 TO THE PRESENT

Paolo Matricardi

Crescent Books
New York

Produced by ERVIN s.r.l., Rome
under the supervision of Adriano Zannino
editorial assistant Serenella Genoese Zerbi

Translated by S. M. Harris

Drawings by Egidio Imperi

Cutaway drawings on pages 13, 30, 34, 44, 62, 74,
78, 94, 112, 136, 148 and 154 by kind permission of
Pilot Press Limited

Published 1985 by Crescent Books, distributed by
Crown Publishers, Inc.

Library of Congress Cataloging in Publication Data

Matricardi, Paolo
    The concise history of aviation.

    1. Aeronautics—History. I. Title.
TL515.M29   1985       629.13'009       85-14980
ISBN   0-517-47137-X

Printed and bound in Italy by Officine Grafiche
Arnoldo Mondadori, Verona

# CONTENTS

The Wright Flyer 1, with Orville Wright on board. Wilbur Wright looks on - 1903

# INTRODUCTION

17 December 1903: the first flight of Flyer I. 14 April 1981: Columbia's first reentry into Earth's atmosphere – dates that encapsulate the evolution of the airplane in modern times. With the conquest of space by heavier-than-air craft, an era symbolically closed, one which had opened many years before with Orville and Wilbur Wright's experimental flights. The success of the Space Shuttle represented the culmination of over eighty years of aeronautical development, a history of machines and the men who made them, engaged in a constant search to extend the frontiers of science and technology.

Since it would take more than one book to cover all aspects of the history of aviation, our aim is to present an overall review of those eighty years, tracing the broad outlines of the fascinating journey towards man's conquest of the air – a journey characterized by setbacks and triumphs which, despite the fact that flight now extends well beyond the Earth's atmosphere, or the airplane's "natural" element, would appear to be only beginning.

The arrangement of material differs from the usual presentation in books of this type; the story is covered decade by decade, in seven chapters, from the pioneering days of aviation to the era of supersonic flight and the space age, with a "visual" review in the form of colour scale views of the most important aircraft. Every chapter is subdivided into sections, each of which covers a particular aspect of aviation with its own brief explanatory text. The introduction to each chapter serves to place the various parts in their historical context.

In addition to the 1,000 colour scale views, there are colour plates showing the military markings and liveries of the world's major airlines. The technical appendix gives the requisite data of the most important variants of the aircraft illustrated in the colour scale views, enabling rapid and easy reference to a particular aircraft or comparison between different types.

Two of the reasons for choosing this original format rather than the usual type of "history" of aviation are that the serious aviation enthusiast will find the volume a very handy general reference book, while the newcomer to the subject will have a clear, concise and technically reliable guide to the fascinating world of airplanes.

200.000F. de PRIX
Montaut
GRANDE SEMAINE
D'AVIATION DE LA
REIMS DU 22 AU 29 AOÛT 1909 CHAMPAGNE

# 1903 1910

## THE BIRTH OF AVIATION

Amazing as it may seem, anyone now enjoying a ripe old age was alive when aviation was born – just over eighty years ago, on 17 December 1903. So much has changed since then; the design, configuration and performance of today's aircraft are so far removed from the first flying machines, as to make that relatively recent era seem incredibly remote. It might almost be lost in the mists of time, as nebulous as the blurred photograph taken on that historic morning among the dunes of Kill Devil Hill, four miles south of Kitty Hawk in Dare County, North Carolina, showing Orville and Wilbur Wright, the two American pioneers, who with their Flyer, a clumsy contraption made of wood and fabric, had just the made the first powered flight in history, turning an ancient dream into reality.

Two contemporary documents bring the event vividly to life, conveying the emotions and tremendous tension of those thrilling hours. The first is a photograph, taken at 10.35 a.m. by John T. Daniels, a member of the local Kill Devil coastguard station personnel who, with four others, had been summoned by Orville and Wilbur Wright to witness their experiment. The second is a dispatch which the Wright brothers wrote themselves and sent to Associated Press on 5 January 1904 with the intention of spreading the news of their success to a waiting world.

The background in the photograph is partially obscured by the mist of a winter's day but in the foreground, right of center, two boxes, a shovel and a can lie on the sand; on the left towards the center is a long wooden rail and at its tip, about three feet in the air, is the Flyer I, its large pale wings tilting slightly towards the left-hand side; the propellers are whirring round and the pilot, Orville Wright, is lying face downwards in the center of the plane. To the right of the aircraft is Wilbur Wright, dressed in a jacket and cap, his whole being straining towards the aircraft as if willing it aloft. This first flight lasted just 12 seconds and the Wright brothers' own account shows why this was so.

"On the morning of December 17th, between the hours of 10.30 o'clock and noon, four flights were made, two by Orville Wright and two by Wilbur Wright. The starts were all made from a point on the level sand about two hundred feet [60 m] west of our camp, which is located a quarter of a mile [400 m] north of the Kill Devil sandhill, in Dare County, North Carolina. The wind at the time of the flights had a velocity of 27 miles [43.4 km] an hour at ten o'clock and 24 miles [38.6 km] an hour at noon, as recorded by the anemometer at the Kitty Hawk Weather Bureau Station. This anemometer is thirty feet [9 m] from the ground. Our own measurements, made with a hand anemometer at a height of four feet [1.22 m] from the ground, showed a velocity of about 22 miles [35 km/h] when the first flight was made, and 20½ miles [33 km/h] at the time of the last one. The flights were directly against the wind. Each time the machine started from the level ground by its own power alone with no assistance from gravity, or any other source whatever. After a run of about 40 feet [12 m] along a monorail track, which held the machine eight inches [20 cm] from the ground, it rose from the track and under the direction of the operator climbed upward on an inclined course till a height of eight or ten feet [2.4-3 m] from the ground was reached, after which the course was kept as near horizontal as the wind gusts and the limited skill of the operator would permit.

"Into the teeth of a December gale the 'Flyer' made its way forward with a speed of ten miles [16 km] an hour over the ground and thirty to thirty-five miles [48-56 km] through the air. It had previously been decided that for reasons of personal safety these first trials should be made as close to the ground as possible. The height chosen was scarcely sufficient for maneuvering in so gusty a wind and with no previous acquaintance with the conduct of the machine and its controlling mechanisms. Consequently the first flight was short. The succeeding flights rapidly increased in length and at the fourth trial a flight of fifty-nine seconds was made, in which time the machine flew a little more than a half mile [802 m] through the air, and a distance of 852 feet [260 m] over the ground."

The Wright brothers had written themselves into history: for the first time a machine carrying a man had raised itself by its own power into the air, had made a controlled flight and had landed at a point as high as that from which it started. Yet in spite of all the evidence and the Wrights' meticulously accurate and detailed official statement [which they had issued to correct the wildly inaccurate reports appearing in several newspapers] the news of their historic achievement met with scepticism and almost total indifference. It seemed that nobody, certainly in the United States, could accept what had happened as fact, mainly because this genuine breakthrough had been preceded by so many abortive attempts. For countless centuries man had been mesmerized by the dream of emulating the birds and conquering the sky; fantasy and speculation had always surrounded the enticement of flight; the challenge, it seemed, was as old as the human race.

Santos-Dumont 14 bis - 1906

This longing of men to be able to fly can be traced back to the earliest civilizations, with relics surviving in the form of winged figures from prehistoric times and from the Egyptian civilizations, as well as the flying bulls and horses of the Assyrians. Later on, the myths and legends of flight assume human shape, as in the story of Daedalus and Icarus and their flight towards the sun and the gods. In 2000 B.C. the Chinese Emperor Shin is said to have launched himself from a tower, using two very large straw hats to slow his rate of fall. The Persian king, Kai Kawus [1500 B.C.], travelled up to the heavens in a chariot drawn by eagles, while tradition has it that Alexander the Great was carried high into the sky by ferocious griffons. The legend of King Bladud of Brittany tells how this ruler wanted to harness magical powers to help him fly, and made an attempt with a pair of wings attached to his shoulders.

The first of a succession of disastrous, historically documented attempts took place in 852 when Armen Firman, a Muslim divine of Cordoba, leapt out into the air, convinced that he could copy the birds and fly.

Ellehammer IV - 1908

Far-fetched drawings of winged chariots and flying ships occur with increasing frequency down the centuries but Leonardo da Vinci [1452-1519] was the first to base his ideas on scientific reasoning rather than fantasy. Yet even he, all-round genius that he was, failed to approach the problem of flight from the correct standpoint; for most of his life he remained convinced that the solution lay in copying the mechanism of birds' wings and it was only latterly that he realized his mistake and guessed what the answer was: the fixed wing. Many of da Vinci's ideas and experiments foreshadowed inventions and methods which would only be tested hundreds of years later: structural details of machines, the parachute, numerous control systems and the "air-screw," the forerunner of the propeller.

Leonardo's Codex or research notes were, however, to be lost for nearly three hundred years and during this long lapse of time there was a resurgence of myth and fantasy; study and scientific analysis were ignored. When success did come it was achieved by a totally different method, using a relatively simple machine: the balloon. On 21 November 1783, an oval shaped hot air balloon, nearly 50 ft [15 m] wide and about 72 ft [22 m] high carried two men to a considerable height above ground for the first time ever. Although the protagonists of this historic ascent above Paris were Jean-François Pilâtre de Rozier and François d'Arlandes, the architects of this achievement, here again, were two brothers, Joseph Michel and Jacques Etienne Montgolfier, owners of a paper mill at Annonay. Their invention had been inspired by the observation that paper bags were pushed upwards into the air by hot smoke; they constructed a much larger balloon which was used in a successful test on 4 June 1783 at Versailles. They prudently refrained from travelling in it themselves but subjected three animals to the ordeal instead: a

Voisin-Farman - 1907

Voisin-Farman - 1907

June Bug - 1908

sheep, a goose and a rooster.

A new realm of exploration had been opened up, with fascinating possibilities. Many experimental flights took place and the concept of "lighter-than-air" flight was universally accepted [the French army being among the first to put it to practical use]. Further developments took place, using hydrogen instead of hot air, and another Frenchman, Jacques Alexandre César Charles, made the first ascent with a balloon of this type [called La Charlière] on 1 December 1783.

The new ballooning craze spread throughout Europe and America, and enthusiasm reached such a pitch that inventors were tempted to carry out experiments with powered flight. An Englishman, Sir George Cayley, was to prove one of the most influential figures in this field during the late eighteenth and early nineteenth centuries; his contribution is often considered to be comparable to that of Leonardo da Vinci. Cayley's crucial discoveries concerned the fundamental principles of flight – the relationship between weight, lift, drag and thrust which he expounded in his work *On Aerial Navigation*, published between 1809 and 1810. Cayley also carried out numerous experiments, beginning with scale models [in 1804 his small glider made a successful flight and this earned itself a place in history as the first real airplane ever constructed]. He then graduated to full-size machines with which he attempted manned flight in 1849 and 1853.

Cayley's experiments encouraged others. In 1842, another Englishman, William Samuel Henson, designed and patented a flying machine, "The Aerial Steam Carriage," which, although it was never built, had an enormous influence on later designs. Based on Cayley's working principles, the aircraft was to be powered by a 25-30 hp steam engine and was the first design for a fixed wing flying machine driven by propellers. The tangible results of the experiments which Henson carried out with his friend John Stringfellow, were in engine design: in 1868 another steam engine was built which was a gem of mechanical engineering and was widely acclaimed in the United States.

During the second half of the nineteenth century the search for an efficient propulsion unit was one of the main preoccupations of the Frenchmen, Alphonse Pénaud [1850-80] and Victor Tatin [1843-1913] and led to some significant progress in understanding the theory and practical application of aerodynamics. There was no shortage of volunteers willing to risk their lives for the potential thrill of experiencing powered flight and one of them, a French naval officer by the name of Félix du Temple, tested his steam-powered tractor [or "puller"] propeller monoplane in 1874 by launching himself down a ramp; his machine leapt into the air and made an uncontrolled flight or hop through the air, covering about 30 ft [10 m]. In 1881 an officer in the Imperial Russian Navy, Captain Alexander F. Mozhaiski, achieved much the same result with a similar machine. None of these attempts, however, could be described as true flight, much less controlled flight. Nevertheless two definite conclusions could be drawn from the results of these – and countless other – experiments: that the steam engine was not a suitable power unit for airplanes, whereas the propeller was an ideal means of propulsion.

It was to be some years before the internal combustion engine would be invented, consequently the first problem remained unsolved. Meantime the last remaining obstacle to mechanical flight was overcome and progress made in developing an efficient wing which also incorporated the concept of control surfaces. Among the most famous pioneers in this field was the German, Otto Lilienthal [1848-96], the first man to launch himself into the air in gliders with successful results. Other trailblazers included the Australian, Lawrence Hargrave [1850-1915], a Scot, Percy Sinclair Pilcher [1867-99] and a Frenchman, Octave Chanute, who acquired U.S. citizenship; these three must share the credit for developing volplaning theory to the extent that controlled flight became practicable and efficient. Chanute, in particular, greatly influenced and encouraged the activities of the Wright brothers.

There were to be two further unsuccessful attempts at flight before Orville and Wilbur Wright's breakthrough; one by a Frenchman, Clément Ader [1842-1925] the other by an American, Samuel Pierpont Langley [1834-1906]. Ader built and tried to fly two machines: the Eole and Avion III. Only the Eole went some way towards fulfilling his hopes when, on 9 October 1890, it rose about 4 in [10 cm] above the ground and travelled about 164 ft [50 m], driven by a steam-powered propeller. Langley tried to take off from a pontoon moored on the Potomac River on 7 October and 8 December 1903 in his Aerodrome, a tandem-winged monoplane with two propellers driven by a petrol engine, crashing on both occasions.

Wright R (Baby Wright) - 1910

Langley's experiments had been financed by Congress and these spectacular failures led to him being savagely attacked by the American press; this not only personally discouraged the elderly inventor and hastened his death from a heart attack, it also reinforced official scepticism with regard to claims by the Wright brothers. In May 1904, the aviation lobby suffered another blow to its credibility when, four months after their first flight, the Wrights invited the press along to see their improved model, Flyer II, being put through its paces at Hoffmann Prairie. The experimental flight never took place due to problems which developed in the engine. After this, the two pioneers wisely withdrew from the public gaze and continued their research and development while shunning publicity. On 16 October 1905 their new machine, Flyer III, flew for over half an hour, covering nearly 24 miles [39 m].

In spite of this the climate of opinion in the United States was such that the implications of these achievements could not be appreciated; if further proof of this were needed, it was forthcoming when the War Department turned down Orville and Wilbur Wright's offer to turn over the Flyer for tests and evaluation. The two brothers had to wait another three years before the time was right to demonstrate the results of their experiments to the world. This lapse of time provided Europe with a chance to catch up [which enthusiasts in France were particularly quick to seize] and regain some of the ground lost since Lilienthal's death in 1896, which had signalled a five-year standstill in European aeronautical progress.

In 1901, in fact, Ferdinand Ferber started to reexamine Lilienthal's theories and experimented with gliders. In 1904 this French pioneer's research culminated in the construction of a glider which was to influence subsequent designs: his brainchild was a biplane with fixed tail which was basically stable. Ferber's experimental flights proved breathtakingly successful, showing that he had solved nearly all the problems inherent in glider flight. Other enthusiasts who were later to become famous names in aviation, were also making considerable progress – among them Louis Blériot, Gabriel Voisin, Robert Esnault-Pelterie and Ernest Archdeacon.

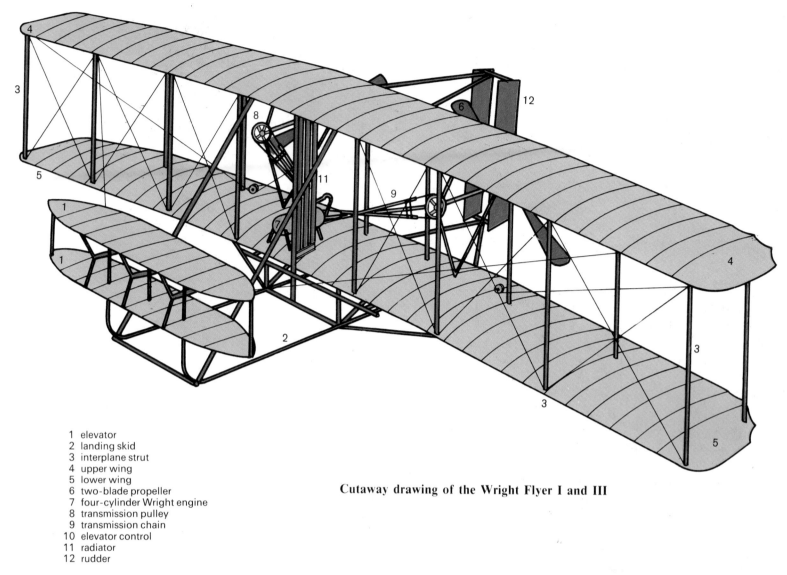

1 elevator
2 landing skid
3 interplane strut
4 upper wing
5 lower wing
6 two-blade propeller
7 four-cylinder Wright engine
8 transmission pulley
9 transmission chain
10 elevator control
11 radiator
12 rudder

**Cutaway drawing of the Wright Flyer I and III**

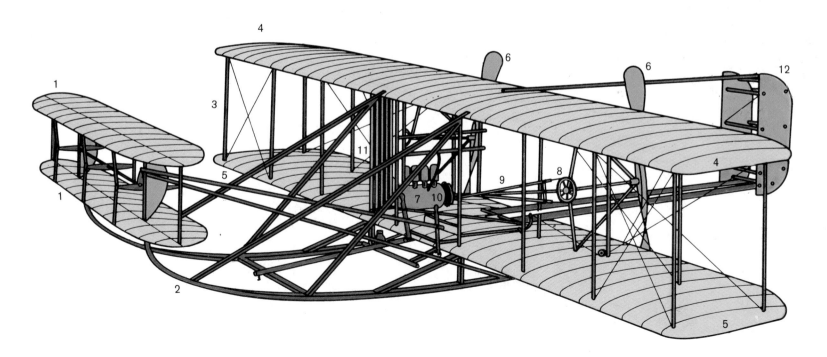

## 1903-1910
## The first flying machines

Europe's first successful flight took place nearly three years after the momentous winter morning at Kitty Hawk and the credit for this was largely due to the zeal and determination of Alberto Santos-Dumont, a Brazilian who had settled in Paris in 1898 and had become famous for his airship flights. When Santos-Dumont heard of the Wrights' achievements he set about building his first aircraft [which he named the 14 bis] and on 13 September 1906, at Bagatelle, near Paris, he managed a 23 ft [7 m] "hop" in the aircraft. On 23 October the flying machine flew 196 ft [60 m] and on 12 November it stayed airborne for 21 seconds, covering 656 ft [200 m], at one point reaching a height of over 19 ft [6 m]. His achievement did not equal that of the Wright brothers but Santos-Dumont's success won over public opinion and galvanized other aviation enthusiasts.

From then on the flying craze spread all over Europe like wildfire. On 9 November 1907 Henri Farman remained airborne for more than one minute. In Germany the era of the aircraft was inaugurated by a Dane, Jacob Christian Hansen Ellehammer, flying his Ellehammer IV in June 1980, while in Britain the breakthrough came on 23 July 1909 when Alliott Verdon Roe flew his Roe Triplane I.

The year 1908 was to prove crucial, when the U.S. and European aeronautical fraternity met and took each other's measure. By this time Orville and Wilbur Wright were confident that the right moment had come for them to make their achievements public. Orville took on the task of winning over an unreceptive U.S. government and the military establishment, while Wilbur travelled to Europe, taking with him their latest plane, the Wright A. From August to December Wilbur Wright's demonstration flights delighted and amazed European spectators in the fields near Le Mans. This led to an exchange of ideas from both sides of the Atlantic, which speeded up progress. Record flights were made by Henri Farman, Léon Delagrange and Louis Blériot and were in turn emulated by Cody and Roe in England. Back in the United States the work of the Aerial Experiment Association led to the construction of Glenn Curtiss's June Bug and J.A.D. McCurdy's Silver Dart.

Two events which took place in 1909 typified the unrelenting spirit of aeronautical endeavour: Louis Blériot's cross-Channel flight in his type XI monoplane on 25 July and the Reims air rally from 22-29 August. Blériot's flight demonstrated beyond doubt the airplane's capacity and potential, while the Reims meeting triggered a whole series of flying competitions which were to provide the most effective peacetime stimulus for the development of aeronautical technology.

**United States**

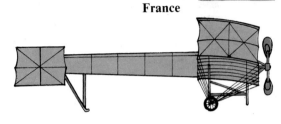

**France**

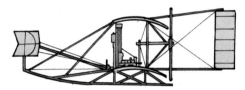

Wright Flyer I

Santos-Dumont 14 bis

Wright Flyer III

Vuia I

Demoiselle 20

Wright A

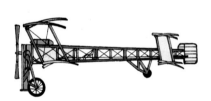

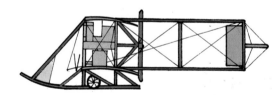

Goupy II

Wright B

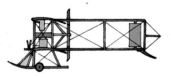

Blériot XI

Wright R

Curtiss Golden Flyer

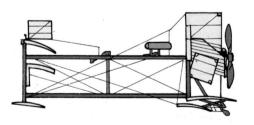

Hydravion Fabre

Voisin Farman

Phillips Multiplane 1

Roe Triplane II

Blériot VII

Dunne D.5

Blackburn Monoplane

Antoinette IV

de Havilland Biplane No. 1

Henri Farman III

Cody Michelin Cup

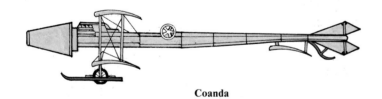

Coanda

Short No. 3

**Switzerland**

Dufaux 4

**Austria**

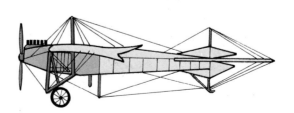

Etrich Taube

15

# 1910
# 1920

## PROGRESS
## IN PEACE
## AND WAR

The Reims International Meeting of August 1909 established the airplane's place in sporting competitions. It not only set an official seal of approval on aviation, by then widely accepted, but its main and most important function was to usher in an era of competitive flying which was to last for many years and which fostered rivalry in technological development. La Grande Semaine d'Aviation de la Champagne, to give it its full title, was sponsored by the French champagne industry, under the patronage of the President of the Republic with prizes worth 200,000 francs and was the setting for a large number of flying records. It also offered an effective proving ground for the best in contemporary aviation design, providing a means of "natural selection" by which the most outstanding and viable aircraft received praise and recognition while the last examples of aviation's "fantastic" phase were ruthlessly eliminated.

Before an enthusiastic crowd who had gathered from half the countries of Europe, a Henri Farman III aircraft won the coveted endurance prize, covering a distance of 112 miles [180 km] in 3 hours 4 minutes 56 seconds; a Curtiss Golden Flyer flew at 46 mph [76 km/h] beating all previous speed records; an Antoinette VII won the prize for the greatest altitude, reaching over 500 ft [155 m]; 87 flights were completed by 23 aircraft [out of a total of 38 participants], averaging distances of more than 3 miles [5 km]. Today these achievements may make us smile but at the time they almost defied belief; and these were only the most outstanding of the week's results.

The significance of the Reims meeting was far greater than the opportunity it provided for some determined and close-fought record beating; it resulted in many technical advances and improvements, and was notable for two spectacular innovations: Lucien Chauvière's propellers, the first rational and efficient types to be produced in Europe, and the Séguin brothers' Gnome rotary engines.

Laurent and Louis Séguin's rotary engine supplanted Léon Levavasseur's renamed Antoinette V-8 engine which is remembered as the propulsion unit without which many French pioneer aviators would have had to wait much longer for success, but the Gnome was the first of a series of engines which was to typify an entire era of aviation, the most highly developed versions being used to power aircraft up until the end of the First World War. Henri Farman was the first aviator to place his trust in the new rotary engine, despite its disconcerting habit of spluttering and irregular running while emitting spurts of oil and clouds of smoke. Only forty minutes before the Reims distance competition on 27 August, in the belief that it would improve his chances, he replaced the 8-cylinder Vivinus engine in his biplane with a Gnome rotary. In the event it did indeed give him the extra edge over his competitors, carrying him to victory.

The Reims meeting was the catalyst for the many sporting events which were organized during the years that followed, and aviators were encouraged to enter their aircraft in such important competitions as the Round-Britain race and the Circuit of Europe in 1911; the Gordon Bennett speed trophy [first held at the Reims meeting]; the Michelin Trophy for endurance, as well as countless air rallies; and the prestigious Schneider Trophy – a speed race for hydroplanes, inaugurated in 1912 and last flown in 1931. While these large, well-organized events [comparable to the Formula I car races of today] drew hundreds of enthusiasts and thousands of spectators, an equally powerful boost was given to the growth of air-mindedness by isolated achievements, often undertaken by lone aviators. Sometimes these ventures ended tragically, as when Géo Chavez, the Peruvian flyer, was killed on landing on 23 September 1910, after he had flown over the Alps in a Blériot monoplane. Between 17 September and 10 December 1911, the American Calbraith Rodgers flew 3,100 miles [5,000 km], from one side of the United States to the other in his little Baby Wright.

These and many other exploits showed what an important place the aircraft had won for itself in the industrialized world – all within the space of a few years in the early twentieth century – making its influence even more widely felt. But this novel and exciting pastime was no longer to be confined to the noble and harmless pursuit of sporting prowess and the conquest of records; the exaltation of the pioneering years, the feats and the prizes faded like the memories of a bygone era, as the harsh and brutal demands of nations at war preordained the airplane to another more deadly role.

Deperdussin Idrocorsa, 1913

The theory of the application of aircraft as a weapon was first put forward by an Italian, General [then Major] Giulio Douhet in 1909, the year of the Reims meeting. Douhet held that the use of aircraft must lead to a revolution in military tactics and in the traditional methods of waging war. He also realized the enormous strategic potential of air power, which he likened to the possession of a strong navy ["We are already aware," he wrote, "of the importance of sea power, in the near future it will be no less vital to achieve supremacy in the air."] The first practical applications of these theories were soon to follow. Two years later, when Italy invaded Libya, Italian aircraft were the first to be given a wartime role: the first reconnaissance flight in history was made on 23 October 1911 by Captain Carlo Piazza, and the first bombing mission was flown on 1 November by Second Lieutenant Giulio Guidotti. Piazza carried out the first photographic reconnaissance flight in March 1912. It was perhaps surprising that Italy should be the first to take the initiative, a nation that had been a late convert to the cause of aviation, although the first "heavier-than-air" flights took place there in the summer of 1908, when Léon Delagrange gave his flying exhibitions in a Voisin biplane; and in April 1909, when Wilbur Wright rekindled enthusiasm with a lengthy series of displays at the Centocelle field just outside Rome.

It was in 1909 that the Italians made their first hesitant attempts at designing aircraft of their own. The earliest original Italian projects were designed by Aristide Faccioli and Franz Miller for the Asteria company, in Turin; there were also those by Francesco Darbesio and Gianni Caproni. Italy did not keep her monopoly of the wartime employment of aircraft for long – other countries soon followed suit. As early as 1910 the French army had purchased some airplanes and trained sixty pilots; in 1911 France armed her reconnaissance planes. Meanwhile, in the United States, Glenn Curtiss had taken on the mantle of the Wright brothers. Having won a great many air races, he was the first to experiment with dropping bombs from aircraft [June 1910]. The following year another Curtiss biplane made the first take-off [and landing] from a platform constructed over the bows of a warship. On 13 April 1912 Britain's Royal Flying Corps was born, a joint services organization with an army and a navy wing and a combined flying school. In Imperial Russia the great aircraft designer, Igor Sikorsky, had managed to build the first giant of the air, the forerunner of the multi-engined strategic bombers of the First World War. Germany had strengthened her conventional armed forces with air units which came under the direct control of the army and which were thus answerable to the German High Command.

So the scene was set for heavier-than-air flying machines to play their part in the long, somber years of conflict which followed. As the war progressed and military operations widened in scope, the aircraft underwent great changes and assumed an increasingly important role. In August 1914, when hostilities broke out, the airplane was in the middle of its metamorphosis but was still slow, fragile and often unreliable and still a "pioneering" machine. By November 1918, military aviation had expanded and developed enormously, in terms both of structure and organization. More importantly, the airplane had evolved into a far more dependable and effective machine, so much progress had been made in terms of construction,

Curtiss Hydro A.1, 1911

Levy-Lepen R, 1917

Vickers Vimy Transatlantic, 1919

materials, engine technology and performance. By the last year of the war, the average fighter was powered by a 220 hp engine and could already reach speeds of 124–130 mph [200-210 km/h] with an operational ceiling of about 20,000 ft [6,100 m]. This was a far cry from the "scouts" which had duelled with each other in 1914, using rifles to fire at one another, or grappling hooks or steel darts to tear the canvas fabric of the enemy plane, or attempting to ram their adversary at a height of a few hundred meters.

War imposed its own brutal demands on the aircraft and supplanted the impetus of sporting competitions as the strongest influence on the airplane's development. Large-scale industrial production of aircraft started [in stark contrast to the small craftsmen's workshops in which the Wrights, Farmans, Blériots and so many others had toiled, building their flying machines slowly and laboriously], and no effort was spared to ensure that aircraft grew ever more efficient, capable of winning the air supremacy advocated by Douhet's theories.

The advantage in air power was to shift from one side to the other throughout the course of the war, altering the balance of power and determining strategy. The most significant progress was made in construction techniques and in engine development. During the war years a great many types of engines, which were specifically designed for aircraft, made their appearance: the German Mercedes-Benz inline engines, the British Rolls-Royce V-12, the French Hispano-Suiza and the American Liberty V-12 which could develop as much as 400 hp, were all landmarks in the technology of aircraft propulsion units. Such an increase in power and performance meant that structural changes had to be made, both in design and in the materials used. Fabric skins gave way to wooden coverings, followed by monocoque construction and later by the all-metal airplane. Aircraft of monoplane as well as biplane configuration were used during the war, although the prejudice against the former, on safety grounds, brought about the almost total supremacy of the biplane at least in the Allied airforces.

The effects of four and a half years of war did not stop there; a vast industrial infrastructure had grown up, employing large numbers of people and a great deal of expertise and money. A few figures suffice to show how sizeable this new industry had become: at the beginning of the war there were about 400 aircraft in front line service; on Armistice Day the number of combat planes had grown to nearly 13,000. Total 1914-18 production of aircraft of all types topped 177,000, nearly eighteen times the number of airplanes built worldwide during the years 1903-14.

It was obviously impossible either to dismantle or simply ignore this enormous industrial sector and, although the coming of peace meant that production was curbed, the momentum that had built up continued to have an effect on the growth of aviation. This acceleration was not confined to military aviation alone; civil transport was to expand rapidly from the unheralded and almost unremarked inauguration of the world's first passenger airline using heavier-than-air flying machines, which commenced operations in the United States on 1 January 1914, a venture launched by an enterprising industrialist from St. Louis, with a little Benoist XIV flying boat.

# 1910-1917
## The quest for speed. The first airliner

Speed seems always to have been the most exciting challenge in powered flight. In the early years of aviation, when airplanes and engines were in their infancy, to fly faster than anyone had done before, was not only a matter of prestige but also, and more importantly, evidence of progress. Each time a record was broken and higher speeds achieved [sometimes by only very small margins], presupposed almost incredible technological advances, some of which were the results of genius.

The best example of the first generation of "racers," thoroughly original in design and very advanced for its day, was the Deperdussin monoplane, conceived in early 1912 by Louis Béchereau specifically as a "speed-machine." It amply fulfilled his hopes by first winning the Gordon Bennett trophy in 1912 with a speed of 108.12 mph [174.01 km/h], and then went on to be the first aircraft to break the 124.27 mph [200 km] speed barrier when, on 29 September 1913 it set a new world speed record of 126.66 mph [203.85 km/h] at the Reims meeting. Maurice Prévost, who piloted the plane, was to achieve even greater fame at the controls of a floatplane version of the Deperdussin: on 16 April 1913 he won the first Schneider Trophy contest, held at Monaco, averaging a speed of 45.36 mph [73.63 km/h]. This was to be the only time that France won the Schneider race, which had been inaugurated on 5 December 1912 by the industrialist, Jacques Schneider, to encourage the development of seaplanes.

This type had first been built in France in 1910 by Henri Fabre who, while other aircraft designers in Europe and America vied with each other to produce effective machines which took off and landed on terra firma, was a lone pioneer, going against the current trend in deciding to use the surface of calm stretches of water for his aircraft's operations. Fabre's Hydravion, which had its maiden flight on 28 March 1910, was soon followed by other excellent designs, such as the American Curtiss A-1 in 1911, and the British Short S.41 and the Sopwith Bat Boat of 1912, which could claim to be valid alternatives to the more traditional landplanes.

Thus, on the eve of the First World War, floatplanes became the new vehicles for aviation advances and not only in competition flying (the second time the Schneider contest was held, on 20 April 1914, it was won by a British biplane, the Sopwith Tabloid, with a speed of 86.74 mph [139.60 km/h]), but also in the world of air transport. A flying boat was used that same year when the first passenger service was launched, operating an American Benoist XIV, between St. Petersburg and Tampa in Florida, a 21.43 mile [34.5 km]-flight. This was to prove the most important and far-reaching contribution made by this type of plane to the history of aviation.

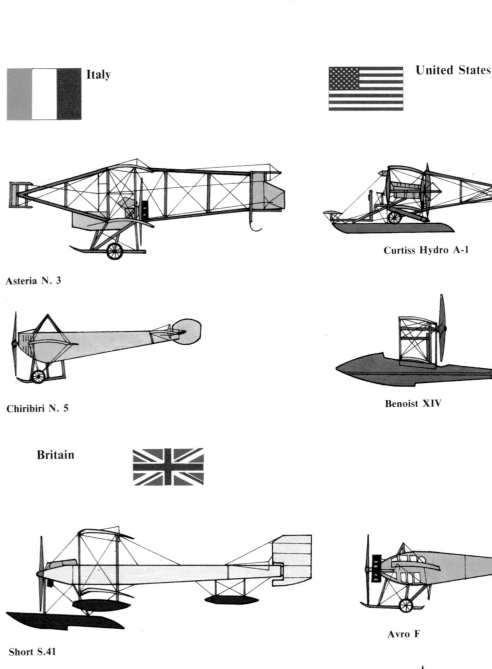

Italy

Asteria N. 3

Chiribiri N. 5

United States

Curtiss Hydro A-1

Benoist XIV

Britain

Short S.41

Avro F

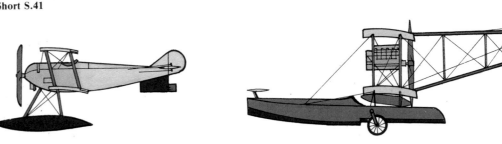

Sopwith Tabloid

Sopwith Bat Boat II

Netherlands

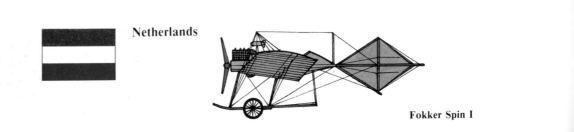

Fokker Spin I

France

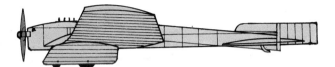

Antoinette Latham

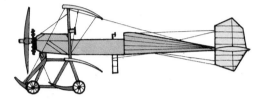

Breguet III

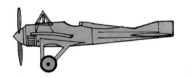

Deperdussin Monocoque

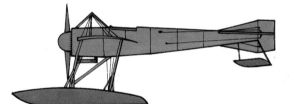

Deperdussin Monocoque

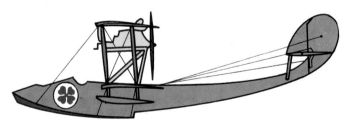

Lévy-Lepen R

# National markings of military aircraft in the first World War

Austro-Hungarian Empire – 1914

Austro-Hungarian Empire – 1915

Germany – 1915

Germany – 1916

Britain – Royal Naval Air Service – 1914

Britain – Royal Flying Corps – 1915

United States – 1917

United States – 1918

Imperial Russia – 1914

Imperial Russia – 1914 (navy)

Italy – 1915

Italy – 1915

Switzerland (neutral)

Sweden (neutral)

Austro-Hungarian Empire – 1916

Bulgaria – 1915

Germany – 1918

Germany – 1918

Britain – Royal Flying Corps – 1915

Britain – Royal Flying Corps – 1918 (night)

France

Belgium

Imperial Russia – 1916

Portugal

Japan

Turkey

China (neutral)

The Netherlands – 1916 (neutral)

France

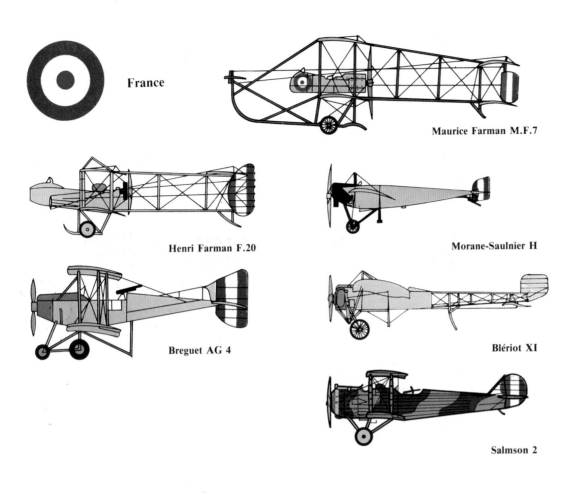

Maurice Farman M.F.7

Maurice Farman M.F.11

Henri Farman F.20

Morane-Saulnier H

R.E.P. N

Breguet AG 4

Blériot XI

Dorand AR.1

Salmson 2

Britain

R.A.F. B.E.8

R.A.F. B.E.2a

R.A.F. R.E.5

R.A.F. B.E.2c

Avro 504 A

R.A.F. R.E.8

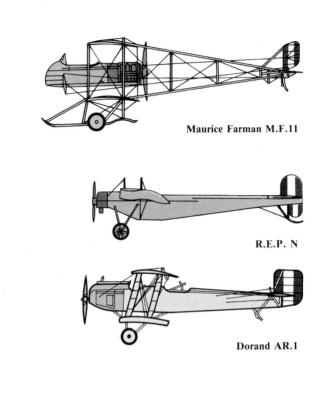

## 1913-1918
## Unarmed reconnaissance – the airplane's first role in war

When war broke out in August 1914, military aviation as such was unknown. The General Staffs of the combatant nations were extremely sceptical as to the value of aircraft in wartime; they put their faith in traditional military strategy, refusing to believe that this new invention could revolutionize warfare. To an extent this was understandable, for the aircraft at their disposal had been designed in the pioneering days of aviation and were ill-suited to fulfilling an offensive or defensive role, having been hastily adapted for military use. To begin with, the aircraft's contribution was limited to a highly predictable role: observation of enemy troop concentrations and movements and evaluation of their strength and preparedness. This could be done during slow, uneventful flights, well out of range of enemy fire and without aircraft venturing too far from their own lines.

Things were soon to change, however. Aircraft started to engage each other in aerial combat, extending the desperate and bloody daily battles of the ground forces to the skies. The only weapons at the disposal of the crews when they challenged each other, were their own hand-guns and rifles, and the duels which were fought out in the early stages of the war were usually decided by an aircraft running out of fuel rather than by a bullet finding its mark. Some resourceful expedients were introduced, such as steel

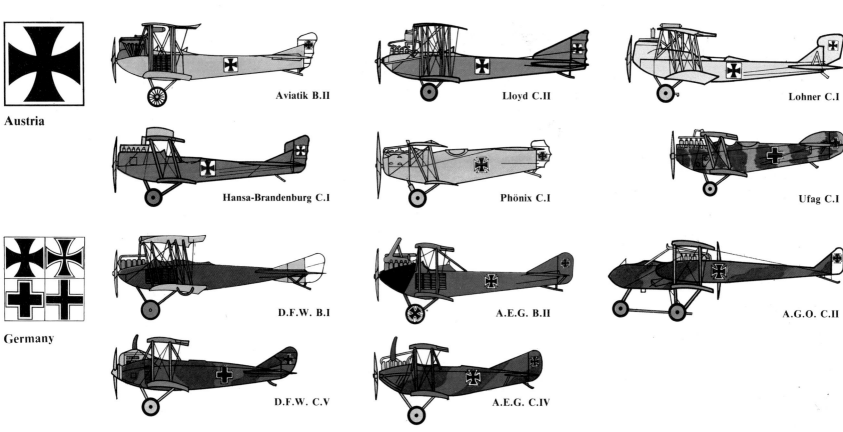

**Austria**

Aviatik B.II

Lloyd C.II

Lohner C.I

Hansa-Brandenburg C.I

Phönix C.I

Ufag C.I

**Germany**

D.F.W. B.I

A.E.G. B.II

A.G.O. C.II

D.F.W. C.V

A.E.G. C.IV

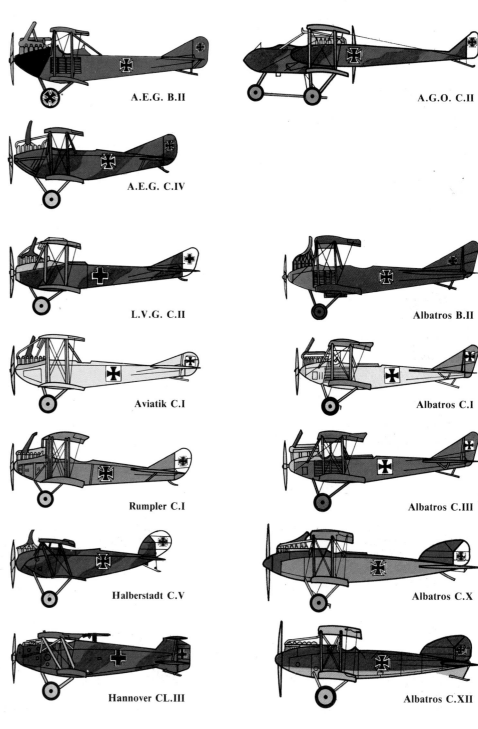

L.V.G. C.II

Albatros B.II

Aviatik C.I

Albatros C.I

Rumpler C.I

Albatros C.III

Halberstadt C.V

Albatros C.X

Hannover CL.III

Albatros C.XII

darts which were dropped with the intention of damaging the fabric covering of the fuselage and wings of the enemy aircraft, or hooks suspended on cables were swung in an attempt to grapple an opponent's aircraft and upset its stability [first to use this ploy was the Russian, Captain Alexander Alexandrovich Kazakov].

Towards the end of 1914 the introduction of the machine gun put an end to this era of heroic jousting in the skies and led to the birth of the warplane. Armed reconnaissance aircraft were put into service, equipped with a machine gun which could be easily aimed by the observer, a second machine gun being installed later in the nose of the plane for use by the pilot. A small bomb load could also be carried.

While this weaponry was being devised, great strides were being made in aircraft design and construction. Disbelief in the airplane's capabilities was replaced by an almost frenetic eagerness to exploit its potential to the full. All the warring nations, especially such advanced industrialized countries as Germany, France and Britain, which had been early converts to the cause of aviation, gave the greatest possible encouragement to aircraft designers and constructors, so that the aircraft industry expanded very rapidly as new companies were formed and quality control and quota coordination were introduced to meet specific technical demands as dictated by the General Staffs.

Although the reconnaissance plane, in its combat role, gave way to the fighter and the bomber, it continued to play its part throughout the war, and with ever-growing efficiency due to the advances which were made in every area of aircraft production.

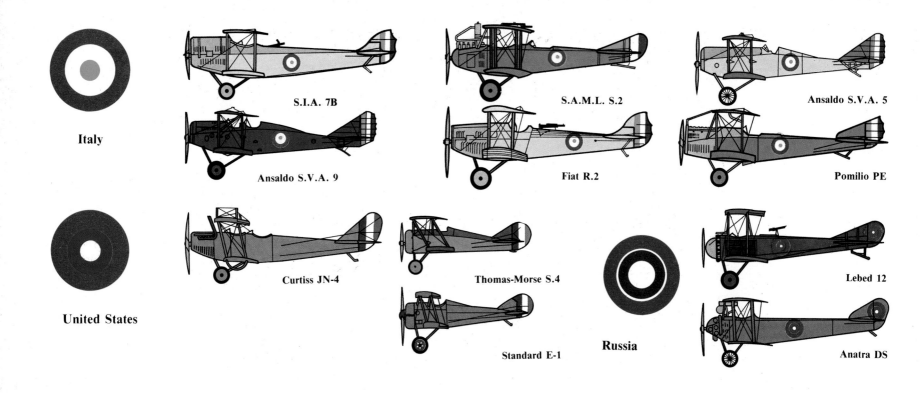

**Italy**

S.I.A. 7B

S.A.M.L. S.2

Ansaldo S.V.A. 5

Ansaldo S.V.A. 9

Fiat R.2

Pomilio PE

**United States**

Curtiss JN-4

Thomas-Morse S.4

Standard E-1

**Russia**

Lebed 12

Anatra DS

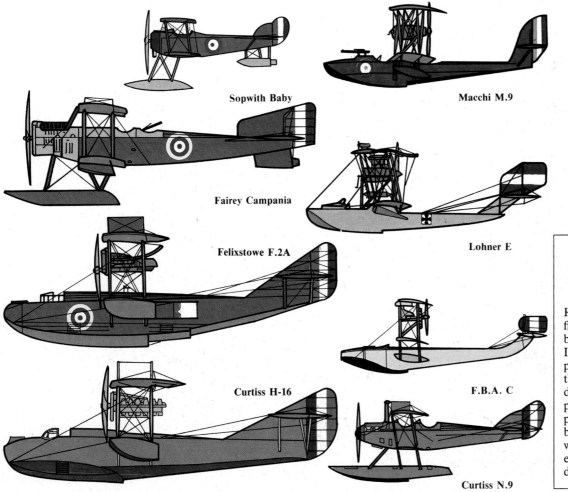

Sopwith Baby

Macchi M.9

Macchi L.1

Fairey Campania

Macchi M.5

Felixstowe F.2A

Lohner E

Curtiss H-16

F.B.A. C

Curtiss N.9

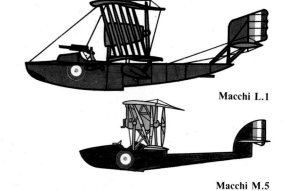

# 1912-1918
# Marine patrol aircraft

Reconnaissance aircraft played as vital a role at sea as fighters and bombers did over land. From the very beginning of the war both the Austrians and the Italians developed a variety of flying boats and float-planes which were in direct confrontation throughout the long years of conflict, besides carrying out such duties as maritime reconnaissance and anti-submarine patrols. While the Allies mainly limited their sea-planes' operations to the last two roles, the Germans built seaplanes which served as fighters, many of which proved outstanding, rivalling the landplanes in effectiveness, despite the aerodynamic and weight disadvantages imposed by floats.

# 1915-1918
# The first fighters appear in the skies over Europe

The purest, most revolutionary combat aircraft to emerge from the war years, was the fighter. A strategic weapon of immense potential in the achievement of air superiority, it had to be fast, maneuverable, powerful and well-armed.

At first, development of such an aircraft was hampered by the difficulty of perfecting a mechanism to allow a machine gun to be fired between the revolving propeller blades. Only when this problem was solved could the plane's armament be used to most effect. The first attempt at finding a solution was made in 1915 by the Frenchman Roland Garros who installed a fixed machine gun in a Morane-Saulnier L monoplane, the propeller blades protected by rudimentary metal deflecting plates on a level with the line of fire. This made it possible to fire forward, since bullets which did not pass between the blades were deflected by the plates. This system proved quite successful and the Morane-Saulnier L became the world's first fighter plane.

The German answer to this makeshift solution was not long in coming, and the first really efficient mechanism for synchronizing the machine gun and propeller was installed in one of the best monoplanes to be produced by the German aircraft industry, the Fokker E.1. In the summer of 1915, when this aircraft entered service, there was an immediate shift in the balance of air power and from then on, the struggle to regain or retain air superiority became a major war aim for both sides.

France and England were the two main challengers to the advantage which Germany had gained. By the beginning of 1916, "the Fokker scourge," as the Allies dubbed it, was on the wane; the British F.E.2b and Airco D.H.2. and the French Nieuport 11 and 17 fighters had won back air supremacy. They were reinforced towards the end of that year by the Spad S.VII, which represented the apex of airplane design at the time. The Germans were not to be outdone, however, putting into the skies an outstanding series of fighters: the Albatros D.I, D.II and D.III and the Halberstadt D.II and D.III, while at the same time reorganizing their squadrons. These moves resulted in a grave setback for the Allies and it was not until the spring-summer of 1917 that they managed to equip their units with aircraft which could master the enemy's fighters: the British Sopwith Camel and Triplane, the RAF S.E.5 and the Bristol Fighter and the French Spad S.XIII. The balance of air power altered dramatically and decisively in the Allies' favour and continued so until the end of the war, and Germany's last offensives [with the superlative Fokker D.VII and D.VIII, the Roland D.VI and the Pfalz D.XII] only succeeded in winning a temporary reprieve.

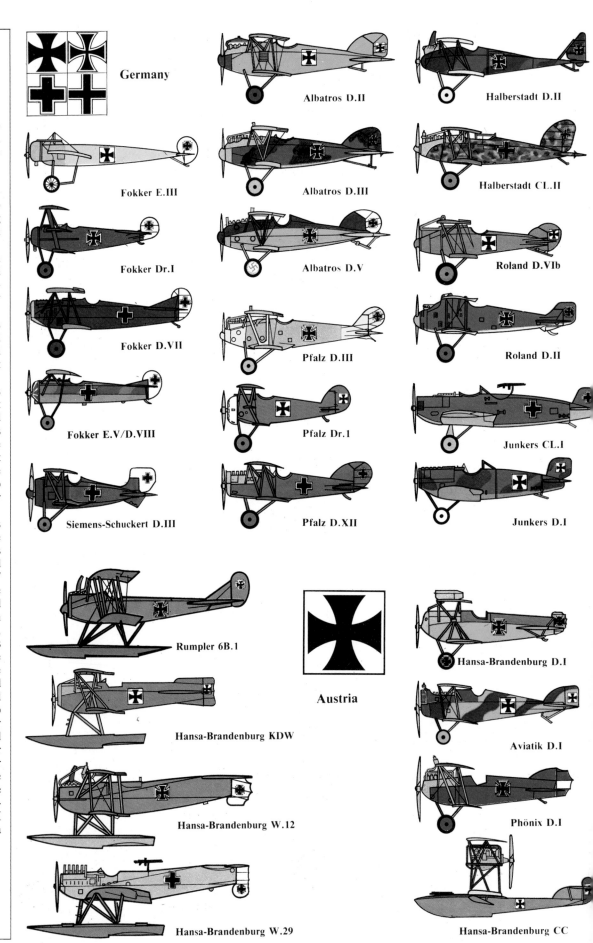

Germany

Albatros D.II

Halberstadt D.II

Fokker E.III

Albatros D.III

Halberstadt CL.II

Fokker Dr.I

Albatros D.V

Roland D.VIb

Fokker D.VII

Pfalz D.III

Roland D.II

Fokker E.V/D.VIII

Pfalz Dr.1

Junkers CL.I

Siemens-Schuckert D.III

Pfalz D.XII

Junkers D.I

Rumpler 6B.1

Austria

Hansa-Brandenburg D.I

Hansa-Brandenburg KDW

Aviatik D.I

Hansa-Brandenburg W.12

Phönix D.I

Hansa-Brandenburg W.29

Hansa-Brandenburg CC

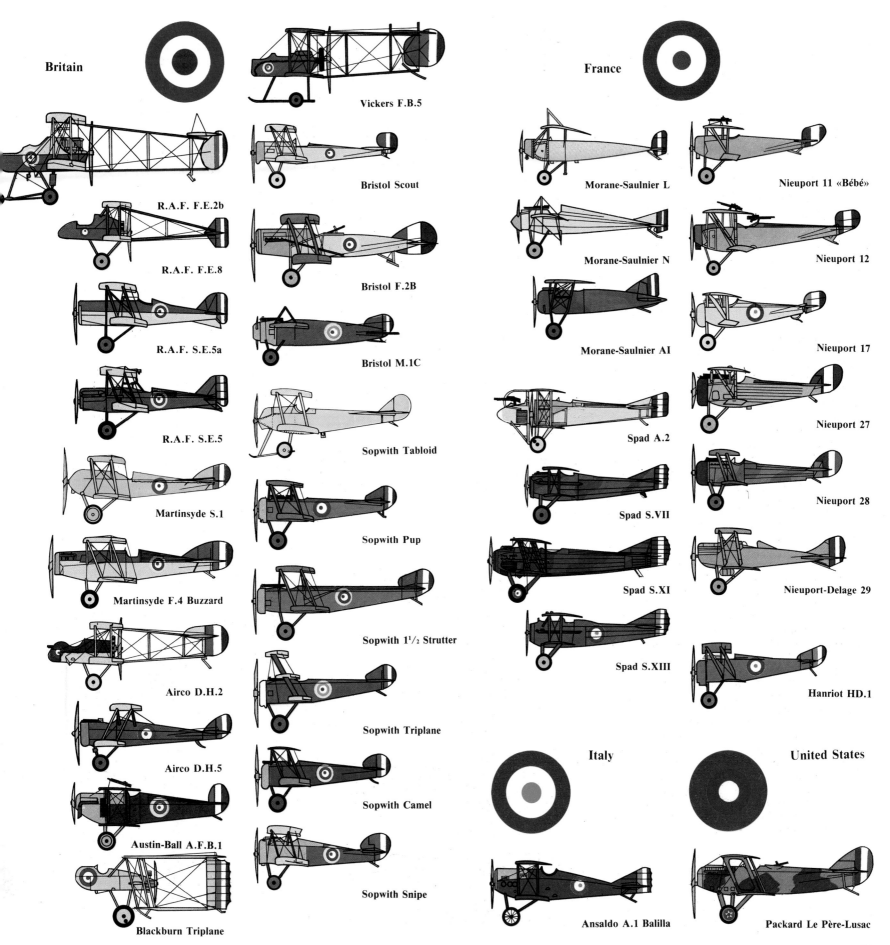

**Britain**

Vickers F.B.5

R.A.F. F.E.2b

Bristol Scout

R.A.F. F.E.8

Bristol F.2B

R.A.F. S.E.5a

Bristol M.1C

R.A.F. S.E.5

Sopwith Tabloid

Martinsyde S.1

Sopwith Pup

Martinsyde F.4 Buzzard

Sopwith 1½ Strutter

Airco D.H.2

Sopwith Triplane

Airco D.H.5

Sopwith Camel

Austin-Ball A.F.B.1

Sopwith Snipe

Blackburn Triplane

**France**

Morane-Saulnier L

Nieuport 11 «Bébé»

Morane-Saulnier N

Nieuport 12

Morane-Saulnier AI

Nieuport 17

Spad A.2

Nieuport 27

Spad S.VII

Nieuport 28

Spad S.XI

Nieuport-Delage 29

Spad S.XIII

Hanriot HD.1

**Italy**

**United States**

Ansaldo A.1 Balilla

Packard Le Père-Lusac

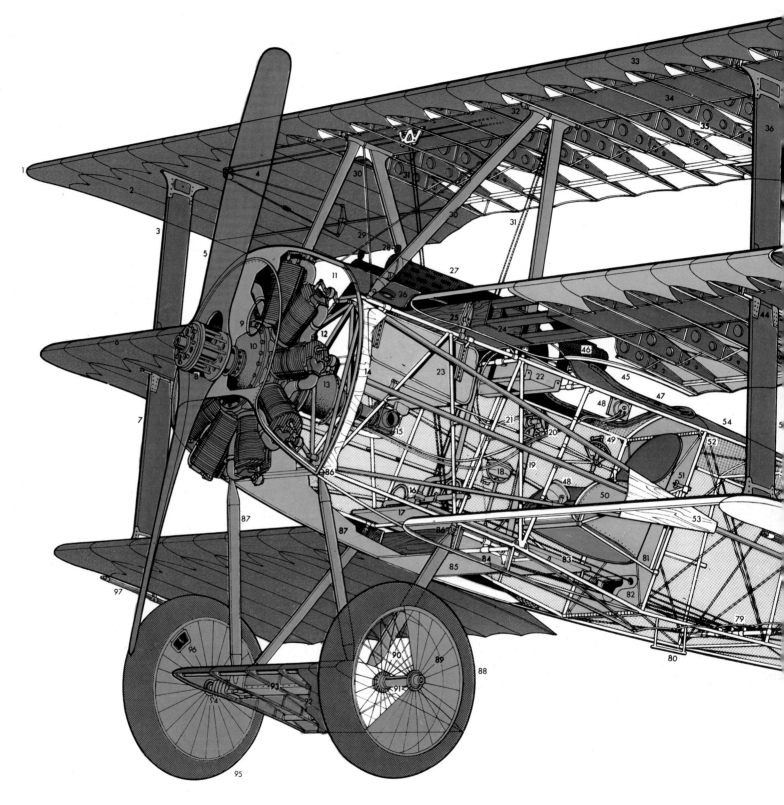

# Fokker Dr.1

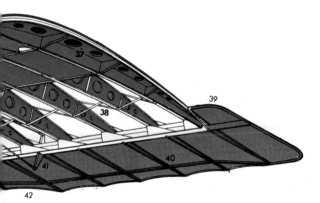

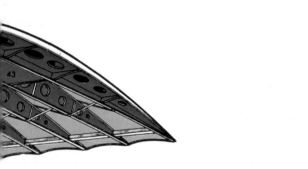

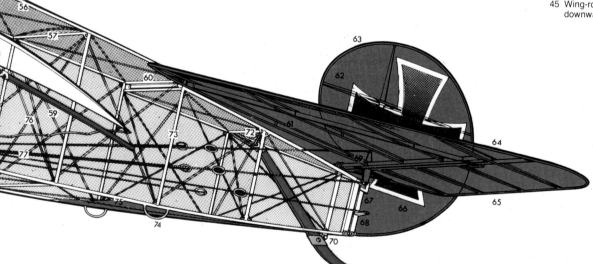

1 Starboard upper wing tip
2 Wing panel fabric covering
3 Starboard upper interplane strut
4 Aileron cable run
5 Two-bladed wooden propeller
6 Starboard center wing
7 Lower interplane strut
8 Propeller hub fixing bolts
9 Ventilated engine cowling
10 Oberursel Ur II (Le Rhône) nine-cylinder rotary engine
11 Engine compartment fireproof bulkhead
12 Engine bearer struts
13 Reduction gearbox
14 Plywood side fairing panel
15 Carburetor
16 Rudder pedal bar
17 Pilot's footboards
18 Compass mounting
19 Control column
20 Control column-mounted secondary throttle control
21 Gun firing cables
22 Ammunition boxes
23 Fuel tank (20-Imp gal/91-liter capacity)
24 Wing spar box construction
25 Center wing/fuselage attachments
26 Fuel filler cap
27 Twin 7.92 mm LMG 08/15 machine guns
28 Ring-and-bead gunsights
29 Diagonal wire bracing
30 Center section V-struts
31 Aileron cables
32 V-strut attachment
33 Plywood covered leading edge
34 Upper wing spar box
35 Wing ribs
36 Port upper interplane strut
37 Wing tip construction
38 Rib bracing tapes
39 Aileron horn balance
40 Welded steel tube aileron construction
41 Aileron control horn
42 Wire trailing edge
43 Port centre wing construction
44 Interplane strut attachment
45 Wing-root cut-out forward and downward visibility

46 Machine gun breaches
47 Padded cockpit coaming
48 Engine instruments
49 Engine throttle and fuel cock controls
50 Pilot's seat
51 Sliding seat adjustment
52 Welded steel-tube fuselage construction
53 Aft end of plywood side fairing panel
54 Plywood top decking
55 Port lower interplane strut
56 Fuselage top longeron
57 Horizontal spacers
58 Port lower wing tip
59 Wing tip skid
60 Tailplane center section mounting
61 Welded steel tube tailplane construction
62 Rudder horn balance
63 Steel tube leading edge
64 Elevator horn balance
65 Steel tube elevator construction
66 Rudder fabric covering
67 Sternpost
68 Rudder control horn
69 Elevator control horn
70 Tailskid hinge mounting
71 Steel-shod tailskid
72 Elastic cord shock absorbers
73 Fuselage vertical spacers
74 Lifting handles
75 Fuselage fabric covering
76 Diagonal wire bracing (double wires)
77 Tailplane control cables
78 Fuselage bottom longeron
79 Control cable guides
80 Mounting step
81 Seat support frame
82 Dust proof fabric bulkhead
83 Pilot's floor
84 Control column mounting shaft
85 Lower wing centre section spar box
86 Undercarriage strut attachments
87 Main undercarriage V-struts
88 Port mainwheel
89 Wheel disc fabric covering
90 Wheel spokes
91 Pivoted half-axle
92 Axle fairing construction
93 Axle spar box
94 Elastic cord shock absorbers
95 Starboard mainwheel
96 Tyre valve access
97 Starboard lower wing tip skid

# 1914-1920
## First-generation bombers

The bomber too came to play a vital role in the air war. Once armed reconnaissance planes were equipped to carry a small cache of bombs, it was obvious that they would be of great practical value, posing a direct threat to troops on the ground. Technical advances led inevitably to the purpose-built bombers: these were large, often multiengined aircraft, powerful enough to take the heaviest bomb loads, built for stability rather than speed or maneuverability. The French were alone in having formed special bombing squadrons before the outbreak of war, which were equipped with Voisin biplanes, typical examples of a generation of planes which had originally been intended to fulfil a less offensive role.

Surprisingly, the first "giants of the air" did not come from advanced aeronautical industries like those of France and Britain. In fact, a nation which had lagged behind in the aviation race, Imperial Russia, produced the forerunner of the heavy bomber as we know it. The credit for this achievement belongs to a young aircraft designer – Igor Ivanovich Sikorsky. His four-engined Ilya Mourometz bomber [which first flew in 1914] was the result of work which Sikorsky had begun in 1912 when he designed a large, multiengined transport. The Ilya Mourometz first saw action on 15 February 1915 and by the end of the war on the Eastern Front, these aircraft had flown over four hundred missions, carrying out bombing raids on targets inside Germany and Lithuania.

The second nation to put heavy bombers into service was Italy [with the Caproni Ca.32 on 20 August 1915] although development of these aircraft had commenced as early as 1913, at the same time that Sikorsky was carrying out his experiments. Britain soon caught up, however, followed by France and Germany. Twin-engine Handley Page bombers first saw action in November 1916, the first of a long line of heavy British bombers. About the same time, the German A.E.Gs appeared, to be followed by the Gothas and the Friedrichshafens and later the four-engine Zeppelin Staaken. The Germans lauched a form of warfare which was to become particularly devastating in the years to come: the prolonged strategic bombing of a particular target, which, in 1917 took the form of night bombing raids on London and southern England.

The last years of the war saw a tremendous increase in bomb-load capacity: the Handley Page V/1500 of 1918 could carry two bombs, each weighing 3,300 lb [1,497 kg], capable of causing devastating damage comparable to the large bombs used in the Second World War. The production V/1500s came too late, however, to have any effect on the war.

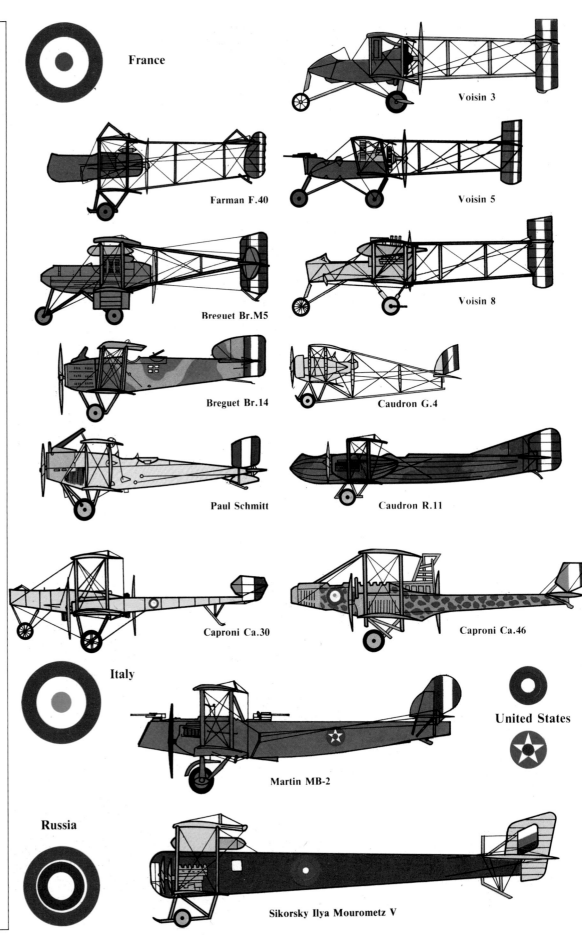

France

Voisin 3

Farman F.40

Voisin 5

Breguet Br.M5

Voisin 8

Breguet Br.14

Caudron G.4

Paul Schmitt

Caudron R.11

Caproni Ca.30

Caproni Ca.46

Italy

Martin MB-2

United States

Russia

Sikorsky Ilya Mourometz V

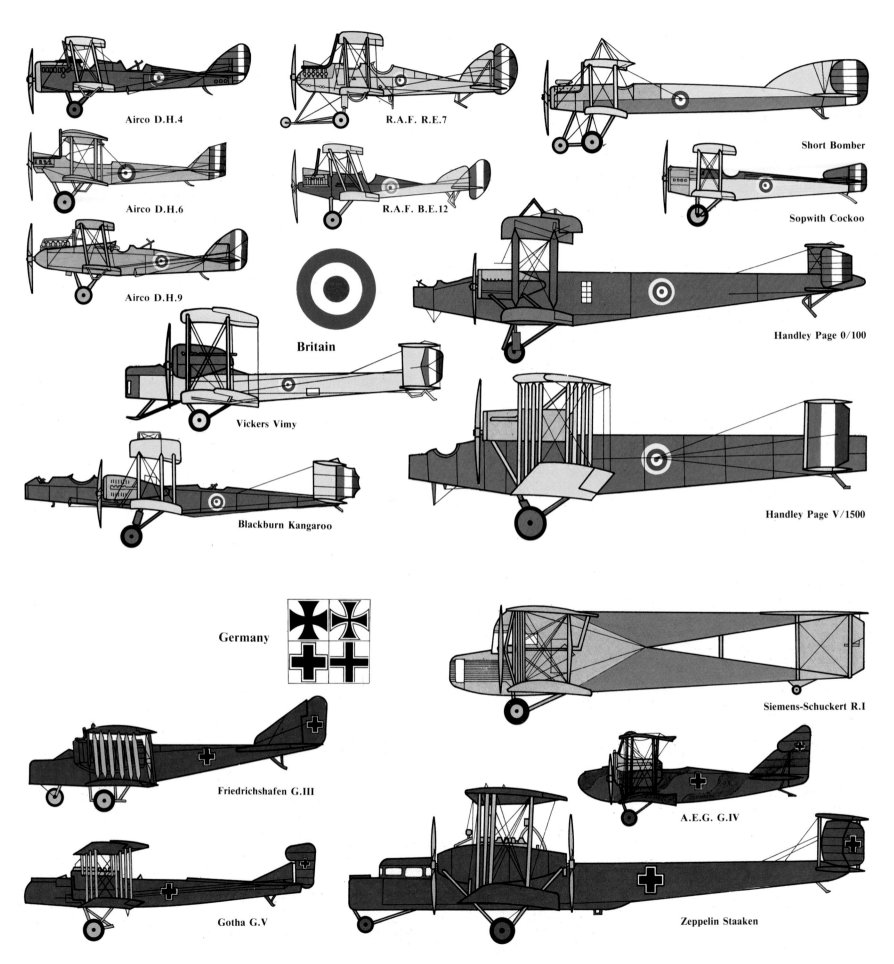

Airco D.H.4

R.A.F. R.E.7

Short Bomber

Airco D.H.6

R.A.F. B.E.12

Sopwith Cockoo

Airco D.H.9

Britain

Handley Page 0/100

Vickers Vimy

Handley Page V/1500

Blackburn Kangaroo

Germany

Siemens-Schuckert R.I

Friedrichshafen G.III

A.E.G. G.IV

Gotha G.V

Zeppelin Staaken

# Handley Page 0/400

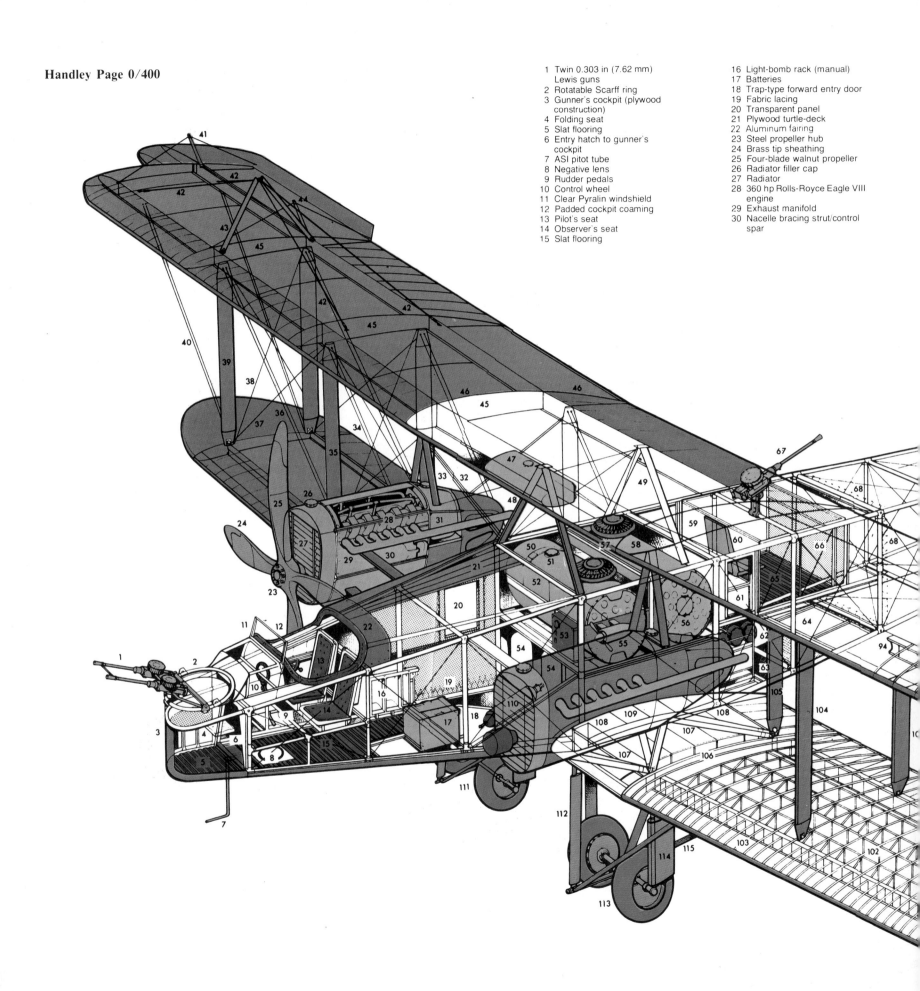

1 Twin 0.303 in (7.62 mm) Lewis guns
2 Rotatable Scarff ring
3 Gunner's cockpit (plywood construction)
4 Folding seat
5 Slat flooring
6 Entry hatch to gunner's cockpit
7 ASI pitot tube
8 Negative lens
9 Rudder pedals
10 Control wheel
11 Clear Pyralin windshield
12 Padded cockpit coaming
13 Pilot's seat
14 Observer's seat
15 Slat flooring
16 Light-bomb rack (manual)
17 Batteries
18 Trap-type forward entry door
19 Fabric lacing
20 Transparent panel
21 Plywood turtle-deck
22 Aluminum fairing
23 Steel propeller hub
24 Brass tip sheathing
25 Four-blade walnut propeller
26 Radiator filler cap
27 Radiator
28 360 hp Rolls-Royce Eagle VIII engine
29 Exhaust manifold
30 Nacelle bracing strut/control spar

31  Oil tank. 15 Imp gal (68 liter) in each nacelle
32  Rigging lines
33  Streamlined steel struts
34  Double flying cable braces
35  Spruce/plywood inner strut
36  Double flying cable braces
37  Single landing cable brace
38  Single stagger cables
39  Spruce/plywood outer strut
40  Double flying braces
41  Outer aileron control horn
42  Cabane braces (four point)
43  Steel cabane
44  Inner aileron control horn
45  Solid end ribs
46  Wing dihedral break-line

47  Gravity-feed fuel tanks in leading edge, two of 12-Imp gal (54.5 liter) capacity
48  Center-section streamlined forward cabane strut
49  Center-section streamlined aft cabane strut
50  Forward cylindrical fuel tank (held by web straps), capacity 130 Imp gal (581 litre)
51  Filler cap
52  Cross member
53  Engine control pulley cluster
54  Center-section main bomb-bay
55  Six volt wind-driven generator (port and starboard)
56  Perforated baffle plate

57  Air-driven fuel pumps
58  Aft fuel tank, capacity 130 Imp gal (59 litre)
59  Solid rib at dihedral break-line
60  Dorsal gunner's seat
61  Glazed panel
62  Lewis drum racks
63  Ventral gun position
64  Glazed panel
65  Gun compartment floor
66  Plywood bulkheads
67  Lewis gun
68  Fabric lacing
69  Cable pulley
70  Fuselage frame
71  Multi-strand cable bracing
72  Elevator control cable
73  Tail strut

74  Starboard rudder
75  Upper tail surface
76  Elevator control lever
77  Fixed surface centre-section
78  Upper elevator
79  Port rudder structure
80  Lower elevator
81  Lower tail surface
82  Rudder longeron
83  Tail ballast
84  Rear navigation light
85  Strut
86  Vertical stabilizer
87  Steel attachment point
88  Faired struts
89  Tail skid
90  Tail access panel
91  Lifting points (stations 10 & 12)
92  Port steel cabane
93  Main rear longeron
94  Main forward longeron
95  Plywood covering
96  Steel fitting
97  Solid drag strut
98  Wing structure
99  Port aileron structure
100 Port outer interplane struts (plywood-covered spruce)
101 Lower mainplane end rib
102 Wing structure
103 Leading-edge rib construction
104 Port inner interplane struts (plywood-covered spruce)
105 Hinge strut
106 Lower mainplane dihedral break-line
107 Steel tube engine nacelle support struts
108 Wing/fuselage attachment points
109 Wing root walkway
110 Fire extinguisher
111 Starboard undercarriage
112 Undercarriage forward strut
113 Port twin mainwheels
114 Faired rubber chord shock strut
115 Aft strut

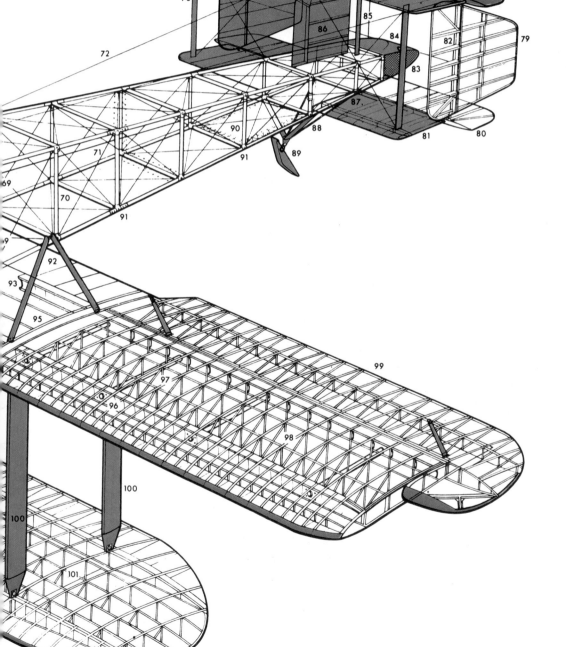

## 1919-1920
## Aviation in peacetime: the Atlantic challenge and the birth of civil aviation

By the end of the First World War, the airplane had become indispensable to the Military, but, although widely accepted as a thoroughly viable proposition, it had not yet become part of everyday life – a state of affairs that was soon to change.

It is perhaps surprising that the defeated power, Germany, should have inaugurated the first European airline [which was also the world's first regular passenger service with daily flights], just ahead of France, although the latter was, aeronautically speaking, more advanced. This historical event took place on 5 February 1919 when Deutsche Luft-Reederei inaugurated its Berlin-Weimar service [120 miles – 193 km] with A.E.G. biplanes.

There had, however, been an earlier commercial venture of this nature in Germany. In 1909 Count Ferdinand von Zeppelin, the father of the airship, founded DELAG, regarded as the world's first commercial air transport company, operating Zeppelin's rigid airships. In the years 1910-11 many experimental mail flights had been made in Britain, Italy and the U.S.A.: the first mail flight for which letters were conventionally postmarked, took place in England on 18 February 1911. In the U.S.A., Thomas Benoist's regular passenger service operated successfully for four months. As already mentioned, France was quick to follow the Germans' lead, and on 22 March 1919 a Farman F.60 Goliath, piloted by Lucien Bossoutrot, initiated the first European international route, inaugurating a regular service linking Paris and Brussels. Two months later Farman officially formed his air transport company [the first French operation, the second in Europe] which he named Lignes Aériennes Farman. A second French company, [La Compagnie des Messageries Aériennes, CMA] was founded on 1 May and a third, La Compagnie des Transports Aéronautiques du Sud-Ouest, in July. They were joined by others during 1919.

In Britain too the first airlines were springing up: after A.V. Roe & Co's short-lived venture into this market [194 commercial flights between 10 May and 30 September 1919], Air Transport and Travel [ATT] was the first airline in the world to operate daily international flights, between London and Paris, which started on 25 August. On 2 September a rival service, Handley Page Transport, joined ATT on this route.

These were the first stirrings in Europe of what was to become a huge air transport industry – ventures which were only possible because of the vast numbers of aircraft left over from the war, which were hastily converted to civil use until such time as the first purpose-built aircraft were produced [such as the German Junkers F.13 and the Dutch Fokker F.II]. Indeed, it was a converted Vickers Vimy bomber which inaugurated the fabulous era of long-distance flights. This historic transatlantic flight, from St. John's, Newfoundland, to Clifden in the west of Ireland [1,884 miles – 3,032 km] non-stop, on 14-15 June 1919, took 15 hours 57 minutes; at the controls were the Englishmen John Alcock and Arthur Whitten Brown.

A month earlier, on 18 May, two other Englishmen, Kenneth Mackenzie-Grieve and Harry Hawker, had been forced to abandon their attempt to cross the Atlantic in a Sopwith biplane; and on 16-31 May, an American Navy Curtiss NC-4 marine patrol flying boat made the first Atlantic crossing in stages, flying from Newfoundland to the Azores, thence to Portugal and on to England.

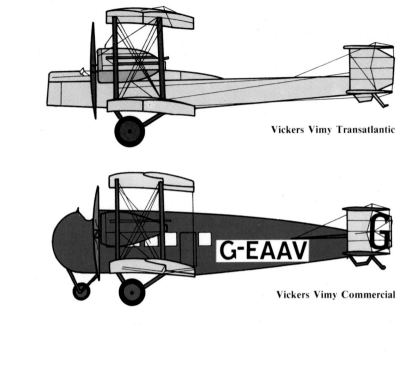

*Vickers Vimy Transatlantic*

*Vickers Vimy Commercial*

France

*Breguet 14T*

*Farman F.60 Goliath*

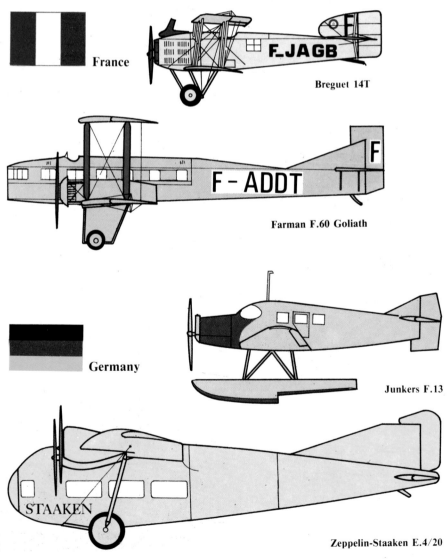

Germany

*Junkers F.13*

*Zeppelin-Staaken E.4/20*

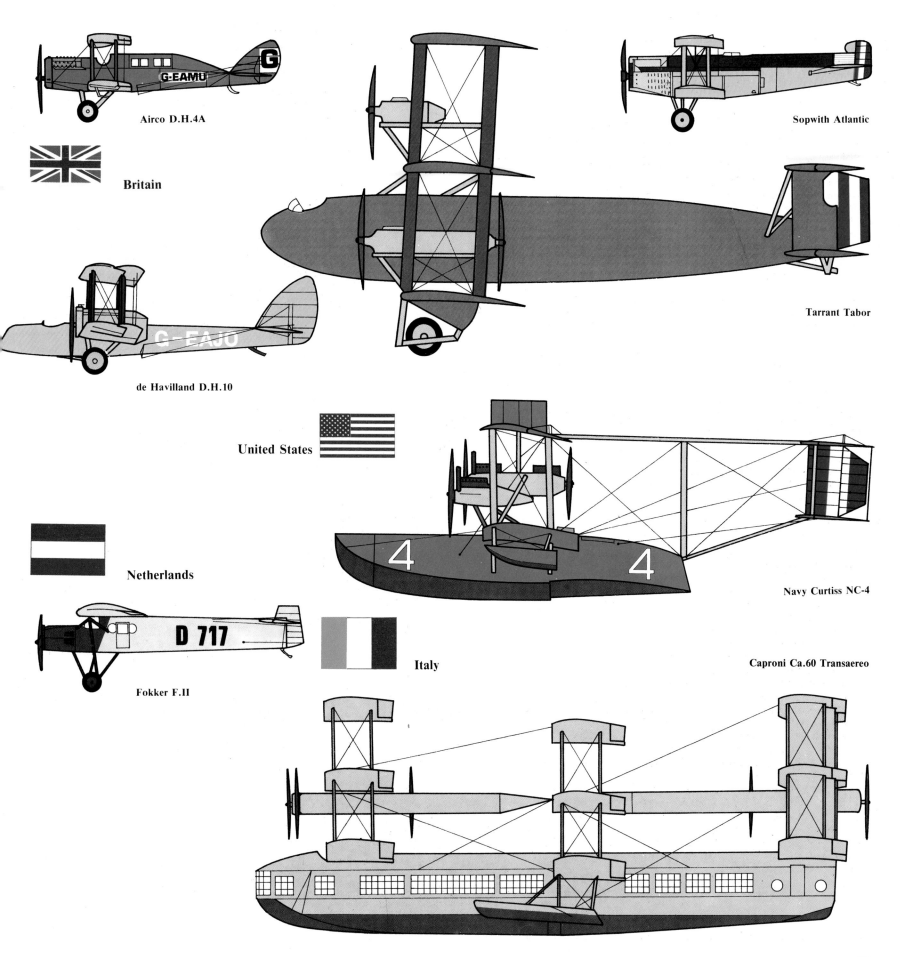

Airco D.H.4A

Britain

de Havilland D.H.10

Sopwith Atlantic

Tarrant Tabor

United States

Navy Curtiss NC-4

Netherlands

Fokker F.II

D 717

Italy

Caproni Ca.60 Transaereo

# 1920 1930

## THE DECADE OF PEACE AND LONG-DISTANCE FLIGHT

After the horrors of the war, the twenties represented a decade of peace and relative stability. Aviation reflected the spirit of recovery and reconstruction which was abroad, and was now set to reap the full benefits of the technological innovations brought about by the demands of war. The evolution of the airplane took on an entirely new dimension, affecting people's everyday lives, and involving the most powerful industrialized countries in commercial rivalry for markets of unimaginable potential. This was, of course, a gradually expanding process which continued throughout the years of peace between the First and Second World Wars. But the foundations had been laid in 1919 when the two former adversaries, France and Germany, ushered in the era of air transport.

For the first half of this decade, the two nations, fiercely competitive, were undisputed world leaders in commercial aviation.

The French government took a decisive step in January 1920 with the appointment of an undersecretary of state for aviation and air transport, with authority over several departments. State subsidies and concessions to commercial operators were authorized, and this official encouragement soon bore fruit. During the same year, 2,400 commercial flights were made, and routes linking France to the rest of Europe opened up. Among the most dynamic new companies was the Compagnie Franco-Roumaine de Navigation Aérienne [CFRNA, founded in April 1920, which flew to eastern Europe – eventually to Constantinople – a service inaugurated on 15 October 1922], and Lignes Aériennes Latécoère with services to North Africa. The latter company [which changed its name on 21 April, 1921 to Compagnie Générale d'Entreprises Aéronautiques, CGEA] had carried out the first experimental flights from Toulouse to Barcelona, Alicante and Rabat, flying Breguet 14 biplanes. Towards the end of 1922 came the first company mergers, with the aim of extending and consolidating the various companies' services: one of the most important was between the Compagnie des Grands Express Aériens and the Compagnie des Messageries Aériennes, which led eventually to the formation of a new company, Air Union, on 1 January 1923.

A few figures show how successful French commercial operators were in these early years: in 1920 a total of 942 passengers were carried; by 1925 this annual total had risen to 20,000.

The Germans spared no pains in building up a healthy civil aviation industry with intense rationalization of operations of the large number of companies. The result was that Germany captured the lead in air transport, both in Europe and worldwide for a good many years.

Following Deutsche Luft-Reederei's early operations, other small companies had been quick to profit from expanding demand [such as Lloyd Luftverkehr Sablatnig, Lloyd Luftdienst, Bayerischen Luftlloyd and Albatros] and by the spring of 1919 the whole of metropolitan Germany was served by commercial operators. These small airlines were extremely enterprising and keen to expand into such new ventures as the participation by Aero Union, in 1922, in collaboration with the Soviet government, in the creation of Deruluft, the first Russian airline, with a view to expanding international routes. Two large operators were to emerge as leaders in this field: Junkers Luftverkehr and Deutscher Aero Lloyd. By 1924 these two giants between them had a network which served the whole of Germany and most of Europe, operating concessions under agreements with the main foreign operators. Two years later the two companies decided to pool their resources and on 6 January 1926 Junkers and Aero Lloyd merged to form a single company which not only had government approval but benefited from massive state funding. The new company, Deutsche Luft Hansa, lost no time in acquiring a reputation for drive and efficiency, coupled with reliability and punctuality. The first commercial flight took place on 6 April and within a few months the network of routes extended beyond Germany and the rest of Europe. A year later DLH's fleet numbered 120 aircraft, the cream of the world's commercial aircraft.

Faced by this formidable competitor, Europe's other two leading exponents in the field of commercial aviation, Britain and Italy, were forced to bow the knee.

In Britain the first enthusiastic attempts to build up a network of air routes came to nought. A series of financial disasters caused a chain reaction which involved virtually all the small operators which had set up business since 1919 and even affected the largest companies [including Handley Page Transport and the Instone Air Line – the latter founded on 15 May 1920]. Unsuccessful appeals were made for government intervention. Only in early 1921, when the suspension of all Handley Page and Instone's services created a national furore was the government finally forced to act. The press had a field day and questions were asked in Parliament. Enough pressure was brought to bear on the government to prompt it to set up a special committee of inquiry to examine the airlines' problems. The outcome was a subsidy of £25,000 for each company, a modest sum even in those days; nonetheless it marked the first official recognition of government responsibility towards civil aviation – a step forward in formulating a policy for the industry.

The measures had an immediate effect. In the period 1922-23 four large airlines captured the market: Handley Page which flew the prestigious London – Paris route; Instone which operated flights to Brussels; Daimler Airways [founded in 1922] serving Amsterdam and other parts of the Netherlands; and British Marine Air Navigation [formed in 1923] which flew flights from the English to the French coast. This first reorganization was consolidated at the end of 1923, when a long-term plan for the future development of the civil transport industry was drawn up by the government. On 3 December an agreement was signed which outlined a merger of the four airlines into one company, and on 31 March 1924, Imperial Airways, the future giant of British civil aviation, started operations.

Lockheed Vega, 1927

The first Italian airlines were formed in 1923, Aero Espresso Italiana [AEI] and Società Italiana Servizi Aerei [SISA], followed in 1925 by S.A. Navigazione Aerea e Transadriatica, but the first scheduled commercial flights did not get under way until 1926 in spite of the fact that many experimental mail flights had been made from 1918 onwards; this delay was mainly due to the very grave economic and political crises in Italy after the First World War.

On 1 February 1926 Transadriatica inaugurated its Rome-Venice service; on 1 April SISA launched its Turin-Venice-Trieste route; on 7 April SANA commenced operations between Genoa, Rome and Naples; and on 1 August Aero Espresso opened the first air-link between Brindisi and Constantinople. During the next two years two other companies started up: Società Aerea Mediterranea [SAM] and Avio Linee Italiane [ALI] which began operating in February 1927 and October 1928 respectively. By the end of 1930 these six companies provided a comprehensive network of routes which stretched as far afield as Rhodes, Tripoli and Berlin.

Commercial aviation also got off to a slow start in the United States. In the months following the end of the war, official interest was monopolized by the need to catch up in military aviation, after revelations of U.S. weakness in this sector had caused an outcry during the war; as a result civil aviation was neglected for several years. The first steps were confined to the mail service and the government itself became involved, using obsolete military aircraft. On 15 May 1918 the first mail route was inaugurated, serving New York and Washington; from then on mail flights expanded very rapidly. On 15 May 1919 flights were extended to Chicago, followed by San Francisco on 8 September 1920. These were gruelling and often dangerous flights, involving six changes of aircraft [at Cleveland, Chicago, Omaha, Cheyenne, Salt Lake City and Reno], and a flying time of 34 hours 20 minutes travelling westwards and 29 hours 15 minutes travelling east.

Fokker F.VIIa/3m, 1926

SIAI Marchetti S.M.55A Santa Maria, 1927

Despite these inconveniences, the services were very successful, and in 1927 the U.S. Post Office handed over its airmail operations to private companies; Boeing Air Transport took over the Chicago-San Francisco mail flights and and National Air Transport operated the Chicago-New York run. On 1 April 1927 [when the Post Office granted licenses to carry mail], U.S. Mail aircraft had already flown 10 million miles [over 16 million kilometers] and had carried over six and a half million pounds [three million kilos] of mail.

The United States' first scheduled passenger service attracted little or no publicity when it started on 23 May 1926, operated by Western Air Press, a small company which had grown up as an offshoot of the vast mail network. It proved to be no more than an Indian summer, due to the prevailing lack of interest in air travel. What was needed was some stirring event which would ignite the public's interest in air travel – exactly what happened. A year later Charles Lindbergh's historic solo-crossing of the Atlantic inspired the entire nation with enthusiasm for airplanes and flying. Within a matter of days, it seemed, Americans had woken up to the potential of civil aviation. Commercial and industrial interests were suddenly alive to the fact that new opportunities beckoned in this fledgling industry. The changed climate of opinion led to the formation, on 16 May 1928, of the first large American airline, Transcontinental Air Transport [TAT], many of whose shareholders were highly influential. The nation's hero, Charles A. Lindbergh was appointed technical director. This was only one example, if perhaps the most spectacular, of how fortuitous events provided the fillip for further advances in aviation.

Among the more spectacular long-distance flights of those years were Ferrarin and Masiero's Rome-Tokyo flight in 1920; the round-the-world flight in stages by American Douglas DWC biplanes, in 1924; De Pinedo and Campanelli's flight from Rome to Australia and Japan and back [34,175 miles – 55,000 km]; and Byrd and Bennett's flight over the North Pole in May 1926. Speed competitions such as the Schneider Trophy gripped the public imagination. This was particularly so in the United States where flying competitions worked wonders for the technological advancement and popularity of the airplane.

From these happenings flowed a wealth of new ideas which were to see the light of day in the form of improved engines, airframes, instruments and equipment generally, the prelude to the next phase in the evolution of the airplane: the monoplane.

# 1920-1930
## Civil transport: France and Germany lead the pack

For many years France and Germany vied with one another for leadership in European civil aviation.

Expansion of French networks continued unabated. Once Air Union had consolidated its European routes during the early years, it began to extend its network southwards, to Corsica and North Africa, but never losing sight of what was still considered the most prestigious route of all – the Paris-London run.

In direct competition with British airlines, Air Union sprung a major coup on 30 July 1927, with the inauguration of a luxury service linking the two capitals, using for the purpose a Lioré et Olivier LeO 213, which offered passengers maximum comfort, top quality food and service. The British countered by introducing a similar service, with Armstrong-Whitworth Argosy trimotors.

Another leading airline, Lignes Aériennes Farman, newly rechristened Société Générale des Transports Aériens [SGTA], opened up a direct service between Paris and Berlin [26 May 1926], and in the following year, after an agreement with Deutsche Luft Hansa, extended its operations to Scandinavia. Meanwhile, the thrusting Compagnie Franco-Roumaine de Navigation Aérienne, [operating as Compagnie Internationale de Navigation Aérienne, CIDNA from 1 January 1925] started flights to eastern Europe, Turkey and Iran.

By the end of the 1920s, French airlines had expanded their operations in Europe, Africa, South America and Asia. German civil transport had undergone equally rapid expansion, if not, in fact, grown even faster, favoured by the existence of a single large state company [Deutsche Luft Hansa], and supported by an industry which was only too eager to supply the needs of German civil aviation while covertly laying the foundations of future military air power.

Dornier and Junkers were two of the most outstanding German aircraft manufacturers of the time and made the major contribution to the development of German commercial aviation. By the beginning of the 1930s Deutsche Luft Hansa had acquired a commanding lead over all the other European airlines in terms of passengers carried, accounting for a total of 110,000 in 1930. At the time Deutsche Luft Hansa had operating agreements with twelve European airlines, flying a comprehensive and busy network of international routes.

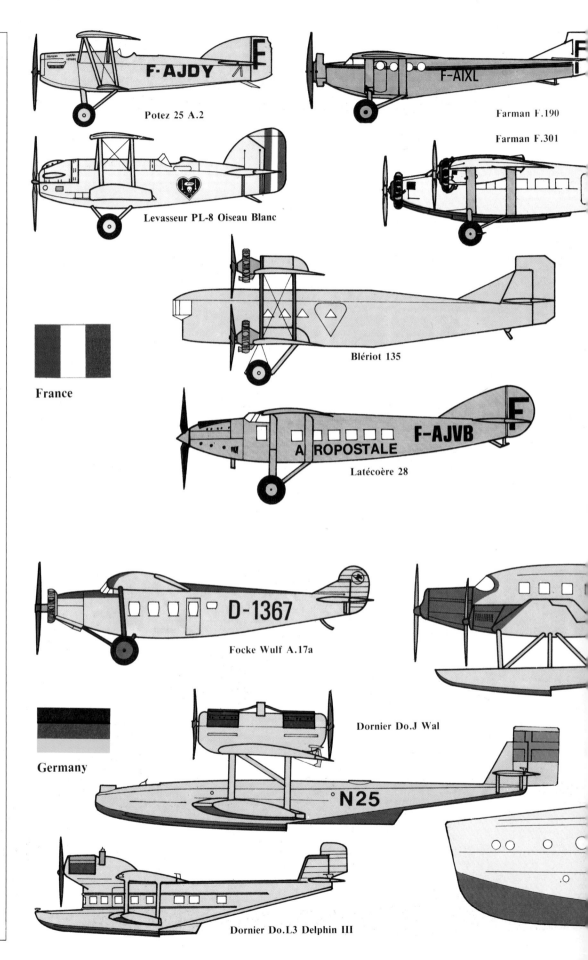

Potez 25 A.2

Farman F.190

Farman F.301

Levasseur PL-8 Oiseau Blanc

Blériot 135

France

Latécoère 28

Focke Wulf A.17a

Dornier Do.J Wal

Germany

Dornier Do.L3 Delphin III

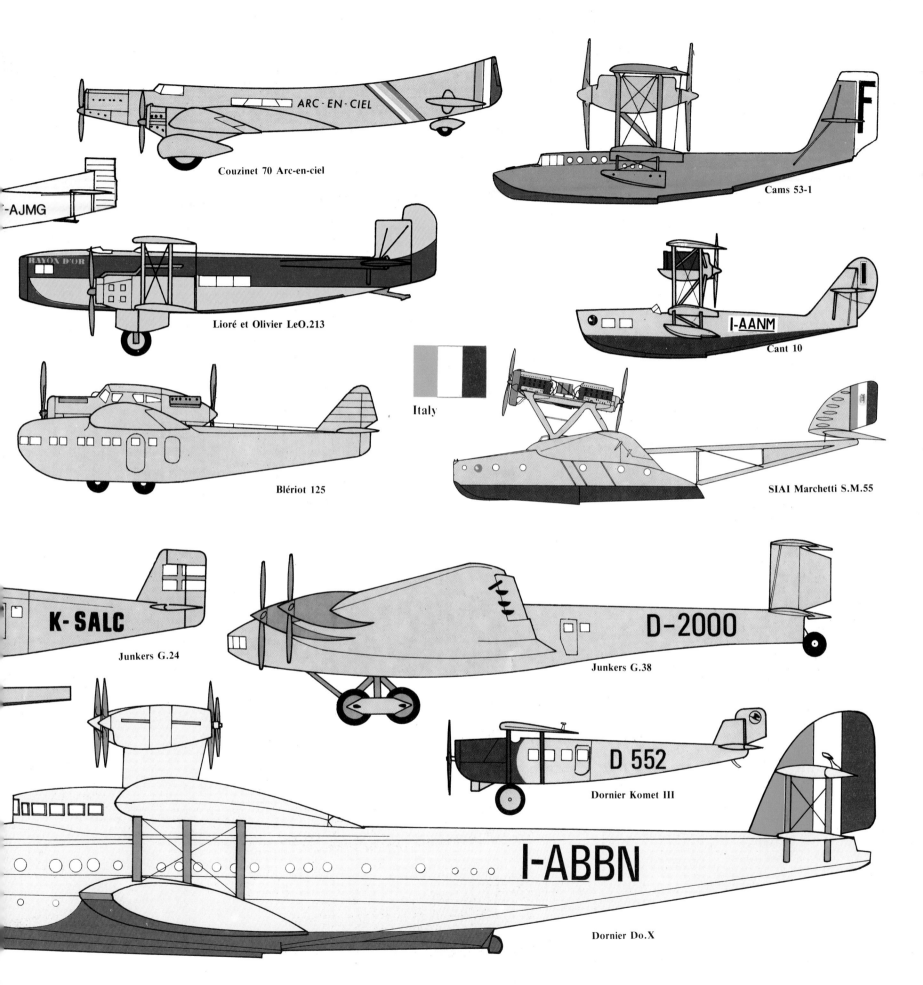

Couzinet 70 Arc-en-ciel

F-AJMG

Cams 53-1

Lioré et Olivier LeO.213

Cant 10
I-AANM

Italy

Blériot 125

SIAI Marchetti S.M.55

K-SALC
Junkers G.24

D-2000
Junkers G.38

D 552
Dornier Komet III

I-ABBN

Dornier Do.X

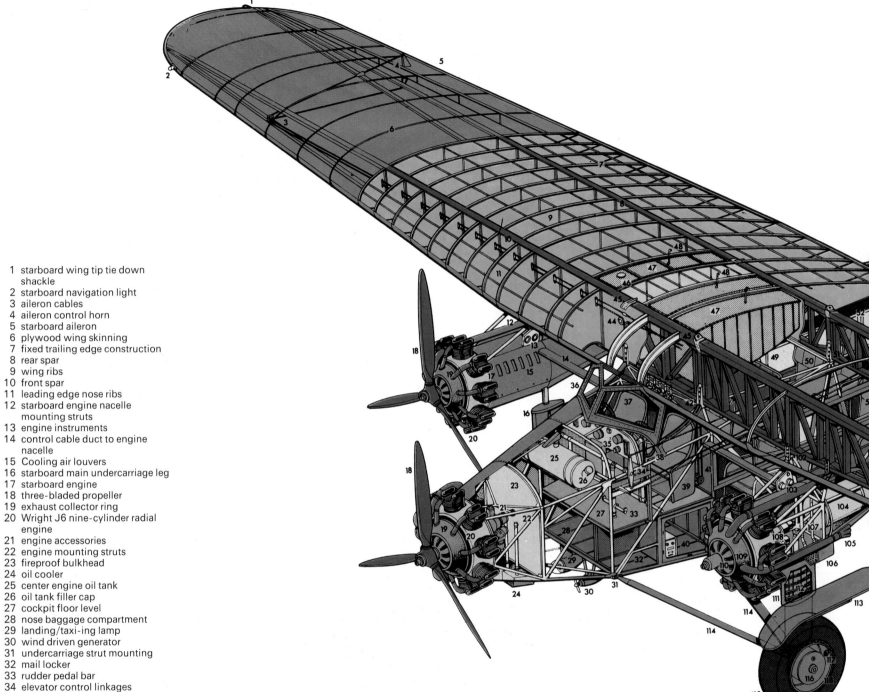

1 starboard wing tip tie down
  shackle
2 starboard navigation light
3 aileron cables
4 aileron control horn
5 starboard aileron
6 plywood wing skinning
7 fixed trailing edge construction
8 rear spar
9 wing ribs
10 front spar
11 leading edge nose ribs
12 starboard engine nacelle
   mounting struts
13 engine instruments
14 control cable duct to engine
   nacelle
15 Cooling air louvers
16 starboard main undercarriage leg
17 starboard engine
18 three-bladed propeller
19 exhaust collector ring
20 Wright J6 nine-cylinder radial
   engine
21 engine accessories
22 engine mounting struts
23 fireproof bulkhead
24 oil cooler
25 center engine oil tank
26 oil tank filler cap
27 cockpit floor level
28 nose baggage compartment
29 landing/taxi-ing lamp
30 wind driven generator
31 undercarriage strut mounting
32 mail locker
33 rudder pedal bar
34 elevator control linkages
35 instrument panel
36 windscreen panels
37 copilot's seat
38 control column handwheel
39 pilot's seat
40 radio
41 cockpit bulkhead
42 wing spar/fuselage attachment
43 fuel selector cocks
44 aileron cable runs
45 wing lifting lugs
46 fuel tank filler cap
47 fuel tanks
48 fuel vent pipes
49 starboard cabin window panel
50 passenger seats
51 rear spar/fuselage attachment

52 overhead luggage racks
53 cabin rear bulkhead
54 cabin doorway
55 toilet compartment
56 water tank
57 starboard baggage door
58 entry door
59 rear baggage compartment
60 steel tube upper longerons
61 fuselage stringers
62 control cable runs
63 horizontal spacers

64 starboard tailplane
65 elevator horn balance
66 starboard elevator
67 fin construction
68 rudder horn balance
69 sternpost
70 fabric covered rudder
   construction
71 tailplane bracing wire
72 elevator control horn
73 fabric covered port elevator
   construction

74 elevator horn balance
75 tailplane construction
76 rudder control horn
77 tailplane bracing strut
78 fuselage fabric covering
79 tailplane trim adjustment
80 tailskid
81 elastic cord shock absorber
82 vertical spacers
83 diagonal wire bracing
84 steel tube bottom longeron
85 welded fuselage construction

**Fokker F.VIIb-3m**

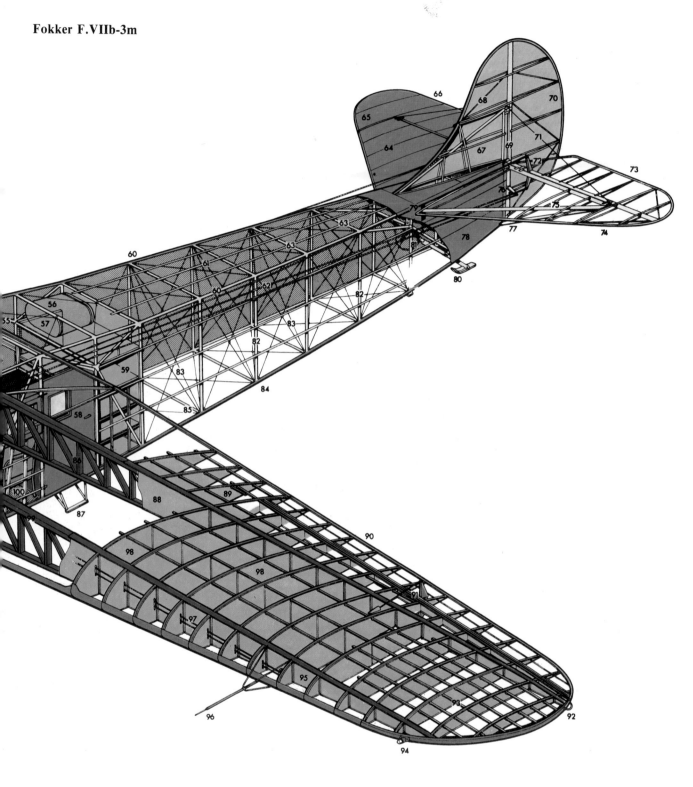

86 rear spar girder construction
87 step
88 spar plywood facing
89 trailing edge ribs
90 port aileron construction
91 aileron control horn
92 wing tip tie down shackle
93 wing tip stringer construction
94 port navigation light
95 leading edge construction
96 pitot tube
97 aileron cables

98 plywood ribs
99 front spar girder construction
100 passenger cabin floor level
101 engine nacelle rear struts
102 nacelle attachment joints
103 port engine instruments
104 oil tank
105 exhaust pipe
106 oil cooler
107 welded steel tube nacelle
     construction
108 port Wright J6 engine

109 exhaust collector ring
110 cooling air intake louvers
111 main undercarriage leg strut
112 elastic cord shock absorber
113 mudguard
114 undercarriage lower V-struts
115 port mainwheel
116 hydraulic brake
117 tire valve access
118 wheel disc cover/tire lacing

# 1920-1930
## British and Dutch compete for the first intercontinental routes

In its early years Imperial Airways had concentrated on consolidating the main European routes, but once this object had been achieved, the airline embarked on an ambitious plan to build up an intercontinental network linking Britain with its vast colonial possessions. This program was only completed in the 1930s and brought the British airline into direct competition with another European airline whose spectacular growth bears witness to the tremendous momentum of civil aviation expansion at the time. This was the Dutch airline, Koninklijke Luchtvaart Maatschapij, better known as KLM, which had been founded on 7 October 1919.

During the fifteen years which had elapsed between the birth of the airplane and the end of the First World War, the Netherlands had remained in the second division of aviation powers. When peace came, and brought Anthony Fokker, the great Dutch aircraft designer, back to his own country after working for the Germans, the way was clear for this small nation to take its place in the exclusive club of the "big boys" of aviation.

Until 1934, the story of KLM was to be the story of Anthony Fokker, the designer providing the airline with a succession of efficient commercial aircraft, starting with the single-engine F.II monoplane [with which KLM inaugurated its service to England, linking Amsterdam and Croydon on 30 September 1920], and ending when Fokker's large four-engined F.XX-XVI was turned down by KLM in favour of the American DC-2, ending the partnership which had produced a number of very successful airliners [among them the F.VII trimotors] which saw service all over the world.

It was during these fruitful years, when this collaboration was at its closest and busiest, that KLM made a bid to rival Imperial Airways, by opening up new intercontinental routes. In the autumn of 1924 both companies started to explore the feasibility of launching new routes to Asia. In 1926 the British airline inaugurated flights to Baghdad and, from 30 March 1929, to Karachi – then in India [different planes were used on this route: Argosy and Hercules trimotors and S.8 Calcutta flying boats].

KLM was not to be outdone; after a number of experimental flights, a mixed passenger and mail service to the Dutch East Indies was launched on 12 September 1929 [passengers as far as Sofia only]. On 2 October 1930 a second passenger route was opened, to Cairo via Athens. The Dutch company made its most ambitious move when scheduled passenger flights from Amsterdam to Batavia started on 1st October 1931. The journey lasted ten days, 81 hours flying time. Fokker F.12 trimotors which had been especially converted for long-distance flying were used, carrying only four passengers who travelled in luxury conditions, including a bar.

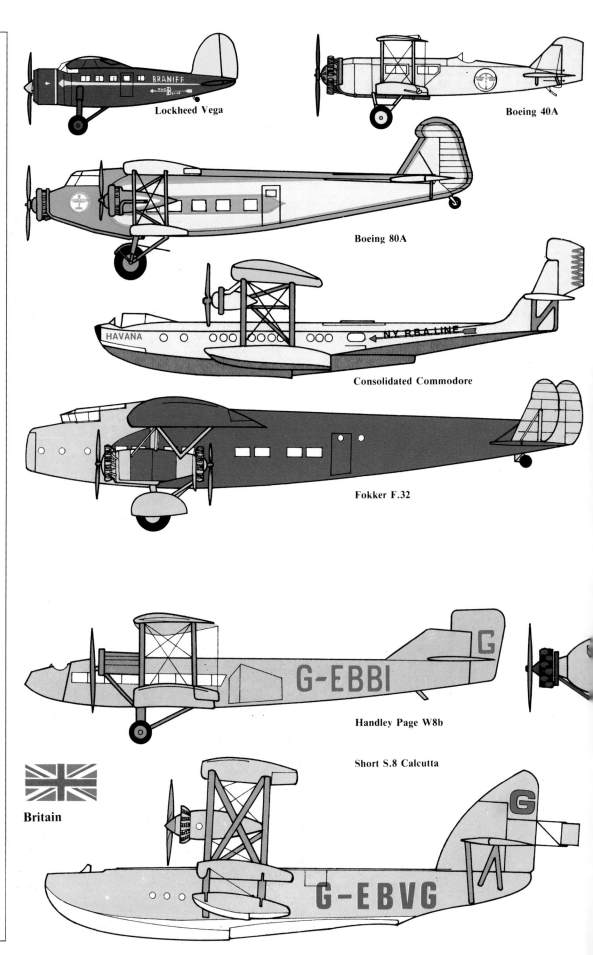

Lockheed Vega

Boeing 40A

Boeing 80A

Consolidated Commodore

Fokker F.32

Handley Page W8b

Short S.8 Calcutta

Britain

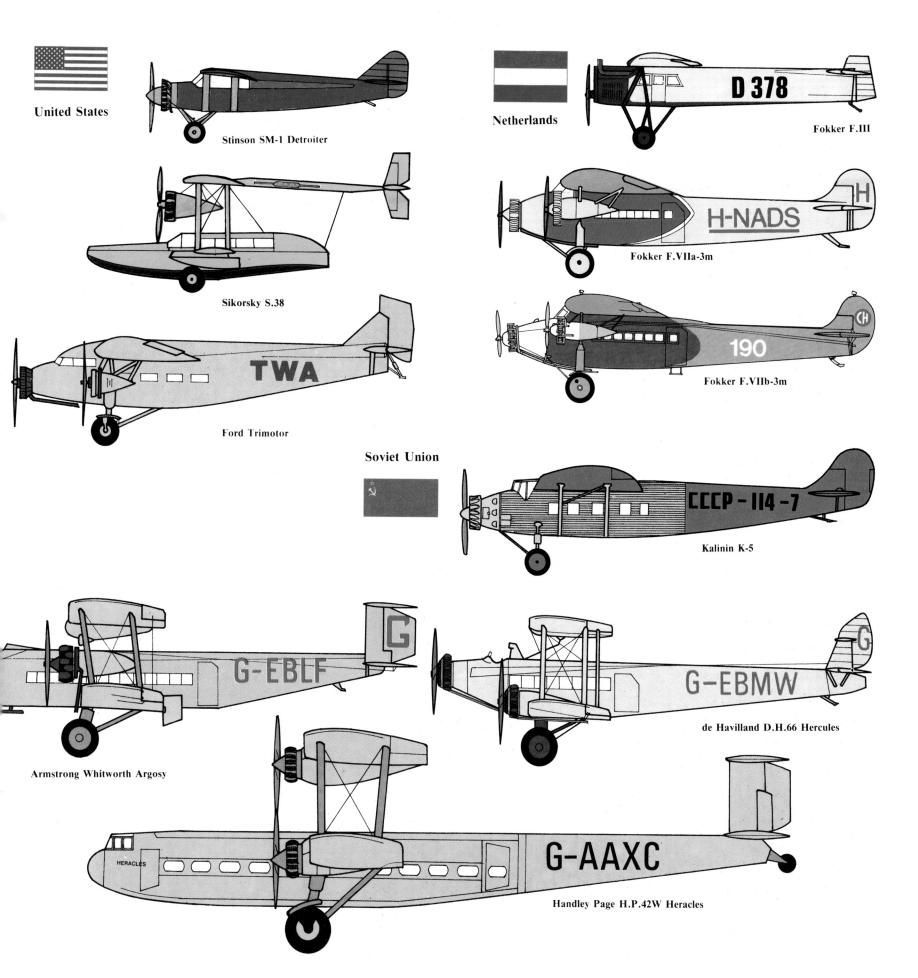

**United States**

Stinson SM-1 Detroiter

Sikorsky S.38

Ford Trimotor

**Netherlands**

Fokker F.III

D 378

Fokker F.VIIa-3m

H-NADS

Fokker F.VIIb-3m

190

**Soviet Union**

Kalinin K-5

CCCP-114-7

Armstrong Whitworth Argosy

G-EBLF

de Havilland D.H.66 Hercules

G-EBMW

Handley Page H.P.42W Heracles

G-AAXC

HERACLES

## 1919-1933
## The coming of long-distance flights

The first transatlantic flight had been achieved by Alcock and Brown in 1919; once again transoceanic flight was the subject of worldwide interest when, in 1927, Charles Lindbergh made the first solo crossing of the Atlantic in his Ryan NYP "Spirit of St. Louis." The story is part of aeronautical lore. Taking off at 07.52 hours on 20 May from Roosevelt Field [New York], the little aircraft covered the 3,523 miles [5,670 km] from New York to Paris in 33 hours 30 minutes and 28 seconds' flying time. Although it was not the first time an aircraft had flown across the Atlantic, nor the first non-stop flight, it was the first solo flight crossing.

The transatlantic flights which both preceded and followed Lindbergh's solo feat show the utter fascination in the idea of bridging the ocean which separated the old world from the new. The South Atlantic was flown for the first time in 1922 by the Portuguese Sacadura Cabral and Gago Coutinho in a Fairy III seaplane, flying from Lisbon to Rio de Janeiro in stages [30 March – 17 June]. The feat was repeated in 1926 by a Dornier Wal, suitably christened Plus Ultra, flown by Major Franco and his crew, who reached Buenos Aires on 10 February, having set off from Seville on 22 January. The first successful non-stop crossing did not take place until 1928, when the outstanding Italian S.M.64 flying boat, piloted by Arturo Ferrarin and Carlo Del Prete, captured the world non-stop distance record, flying 4,466 miles [7,188 km] from Montecelio to Natal, between 3-5 July.

A few days after Lindbergh's great adventure, two other Americans, Chamberlin and Levine, crossed the North Atlantic in a Bellanca W.B.2, the "Columbia," flying from New York to Berlin [3,910 miles – 6,294 km] on 4-6 June 1927. Later that month, Richard Byrd made an unsuccessful attempt in his Fokker C-2 "America." On 12-13 April 1928 a single-engine German Junkers W.33, the "Bremen," crewed by Herman Kohl, Günther von Huenefeld and James Fitzmaurice, made the first east-west crossing of the North Atlantic, from Dublin to Newfoundland, a distance of 2,175 miles [3,500 km].

The culmination of these daring transatlantic flights was reached with two Italian formation crossings, in 1930 and 1933, of the South Atlantic and the North Atlantic, the flight commander on both occasions being Italo Balbo. The first flight was made with fourteen twin-engine S.M.55A flying boats which took off from Orbetello on 17 December for Rio de Janeiro, a flight of 6,462 miles [10,400 km]. Twenty-five S.M.55X flying boats took part in the second flight, from Orbetello to New York and then back to Rome, a combined distance of 12,303 miles [19,800 km].

Apart from their contribution to technological progress, these flights provided a vital boost to the growth of air travel, as testing beds for the airworthiness of airplanes, and the feasibility of routes under widely differing flying conditions, all of which proved invaluable in creating a closely-woven network of routes linking the two continents.

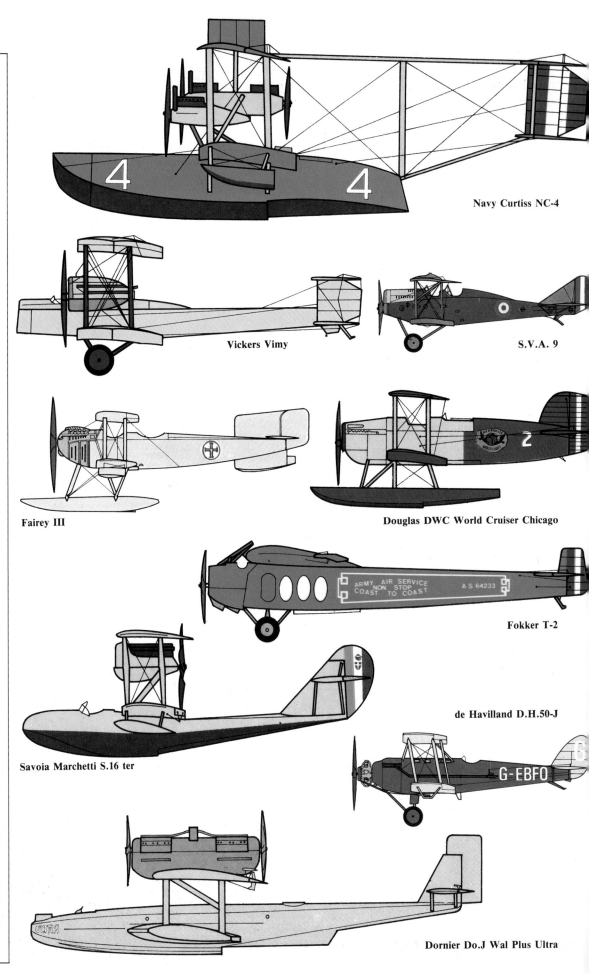

Navy Curtiss NC-4

Vickers Vimy

S.V.A. 9

Fairey III

Douglas DWC World Cruiser Chicago

Fokker T-2

de Havilland D.H.50-J

Savoia Marchetti S.16 ter

G-EBFO

Dornier Do.J Wal Plus Ultra

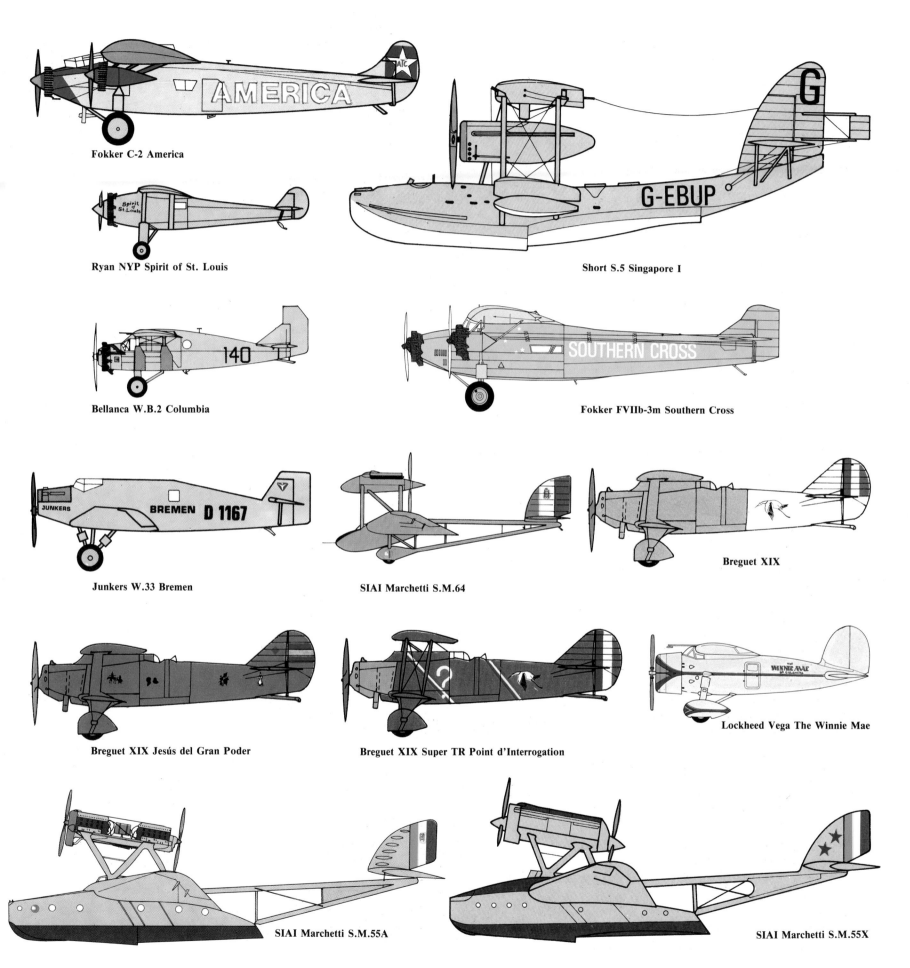

Fokker C-2 America

Ryan NYP Spirit of St. Louis

Short S.5 Singapore I

Bellanca W.B.2 Columbia

Fokker FVIIb-3m Southern Cross

Junkers W.33 Bremen

SIAI Marchetti S.M.64

Breguet XIX

Breguet XIX Jesús del Gran Poder

Breguet XIX Super TR Point d'Interrogation

Lockheed Vega The Winnie Mae

SIAI Marchetti S.M.55A

SIAI Marchetti S.M.55X

49

# 1920-1931
## The golden age of competitive flying

Speed has probably always been the most exciting facet of flying; it was certainly one of the main preoccupations of the aviation world between the two wars. What is now remembered as the golden age of the competition aircraft [or "racer"] was created by a tremendous wave of enthusiasm, unequalled since the very early pioneering days of aviation. All sorts of people seemed to be caught up in the racing fervour: pilots, enthusiasts, industrialists, businessmen and press barons – these last becoming the patrons of aviation.

All the time, waiting watchfully and monitoring developments, were government and military observers who saw the possibility of deriving increasingly effective military aircraft from competition "racers" as speed and performance increased dramatically. This obsession with air racing took hold in Europe and in the United States, reaching fever pitch during the second half of the 1920s, before gradually subsiding in the 1930s. Flying displays and competitions were organized all over Europe and the United States, some of which carried tremendous prestige from the very start.

Certain race meetings were revivals of competitions which had already drawn international participants during the pioneering days, such as the Gordon Bennett Aviation Cup which had generated so much excitement before the war and had led to the first records being established; others, like the Pulitzer Trophy which was first competed for in the United States in 1920, were to become such highly-charged and keenly fought events that both participants and spectators found them equally enthralling.

There was one competition, however, which outranked all the rest in terms of prestige and involved the national pride of four nations. This was the Schneider Trophy for seaplanes, a competition which marked the zenith, and by the time of the last meeting in the early thirties, the end of the great competitions in Europe. In the United States, however, a well-established tradition of major competitions [such as the National Air Races which were important aviation meetings, providing entertainment for mass audiences], remained popular until shortly before the Second World War, with highly prestigious prizes to be won, such as the Thompson and Bendix trophies.

After the two Schneider contests of 1913 and 1914, the competition was suspended during the war, to be resumed in 1919. The country which managed to win the Trophy three times within the time limit of five years, was adjudged the outright winner. The original French and British contenders were joined by a third, Italy, whose pilots and seaplanes were the center of attention in the three races held in the years 1919-21. On 10 September 1919, at Bournemouth, in the south of England, Guido Jannello, piloting a Savoia S.13 bis was the only competitor to cross the finishing line, at an average speed of 125 mph [201 km/h] but his victory was disallowed because of the prevailing fog and an allegedly incorrect route round the course. On

*continued on page 52*

**United States**

Dayton-Wright R.B. Racer

Verville VCP-R

Thomas-Morse MB-3

Curtiss CR-1

Curtiss-Cox Cactus Kitten

Curtiss R-6

Curtiss R2C-1

Curtiss CR-3

Verville-Sperry R-3

Curtiss R3C-1

Curtiss R3C-2

Travel Air R Mystery Ship

Laird LC-DW-300 Solution

**Italy**

Savoia S.12 bis

Fiat R700

Macchi M.7 bis

Macchi M.39

50

*continued from page 50*

21 September 1920, when the race was held in Venice, Luigi Bologna flew his Savoia S.12 bis to victory at an average speed of 105.97 mph [170.54 km/h]. Another Italian seaplane entry won the race the following year, also in Venice, on 7 August; this time a Macchi M.7, with Giovanni De Briganti at the controls, at an average speed of 117.85 mph [189.67 km/h]. The Italians appeared to be well on the way to winning the Trophy outright but the next year, at Naples, the Schneider Trophy passed to the British, after Henry C. Biard, the only British entrant, had a decisive victory over his three Italian adversaries, averaging 145.72 mph [234.51 km/h] in his Supermarine Sea Lion II.

Another formidable contender now entered the arena. The United States, with its wealth of outstanding racing planes, nurtured in the numerous national competitions, spared no expense to win the coveted trophy, partly perhaps in order to dispel a lingering sense of inferiority where the Europeans were concerned. The coming of the great recession, however, led the U.S. government to withdraw its support from this and all other competitive flying events. Before this happened, however, on 27-28 September 1923, when the race was held off the Isle of Wight, the British planes were soundly beaten by an American Navy Curtiss CR-3 [derived from an earlier racer, a winner of the Pulitzer Trophy], piloted by David Rittenhouse, at an average speed of 177.27 mph [285.30 km/h]; an identical machine came second.

The next time the race was held, on 26 October 1925 [no competition being held in the intervening year as the British and Italian entrants had not perfected their engines and aircraft], at Baltimore, the Americans won again, with a Curtiss R3C-2 flown by James H. Doolittle [average speed 232.57mph – 374.28 km/h].

The last challenge by the Americans before they withdrew from all international competitions was at Hampton Roads, Virginia [12-13 November 1926] when victory went to the Italians, with Mario De Bernardi in a Macchi M.39, averaging a speed of 246.496 mph [396.69 km/h]. The last three Schneider races [1927, 1929 and 1931] saw only two countries competing, Italy and Britain, and it was the British who were finally to win the Trophy outright with three successive victories: on 26 September 1927 at Venice, with Sidney N. Webster in a Supermarine S.5 [281.65 mph – 453.27 km/h], with H.R.D. Waghorn at Cowes on 6-7 September 1929 in a Supermarine S.6 [328.62 mph – 528.86 km/h], and on 13 September 1931, at Lee-on-Solent with John H. Boothman in another Supermarine S.6B, at a speed of 340.07 mph [547.30 km/h], setting a new world record for seaplanes.

The last Schneider race had its ridiculous side, since Boothman was the sole entrant [the French and Italians having failed to have their aircraft ready on time], and was therefore only flying against time. Italy made up for this missed opportunity [although the Schneider Trophy was no longer at stake] when, on 10 April 1933, a Macchi-Castoldi MC.72 [the last and best seaplane racer piloted by Francesco Agello], set a world seaplane record of 423.822 mph [682.078 km/h]. The following year, on 23 October, the same seaplane set a record speed of 442.081 mph [711.462 km/h], which still remains unbroken.

**Britain**

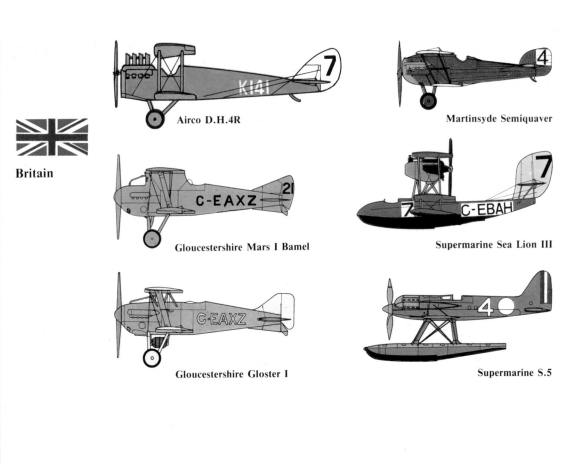

Airco D.H.4R

Martinsyde Semiquaver

Gloucestershire Mars I Bamel

Supermarine Sea Lion III

Gloucestershire Gloster I

Supermarine S.5

**France**

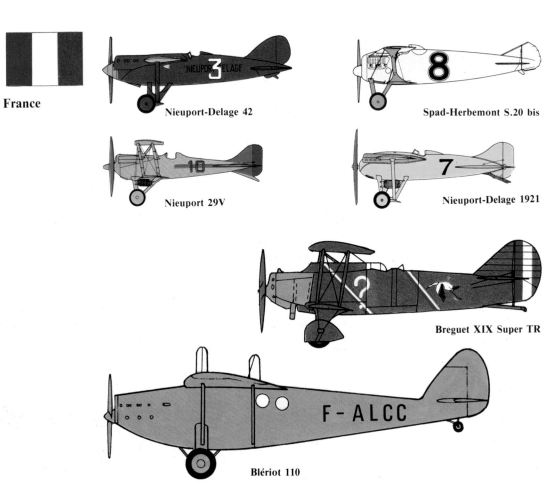

Nieuport-Delage 42

Spad-Herbemont S.20 bis

Nieuport 29V

Nieuport-Delage 1921

Breguet XIX Super TR

Blériot 110

# 1920-1930
## Peacetime development of the fighter

Until the early 1930s military aircraft had developed at a slow pace. Despite the powerful stimulus of the flying competitions, the continuous attempts to achieve ever higher records, and the technological advances accruing from long-distance flights in the development of both aircraft and engines, combat planes had not changed very much since the First World War. Significant improvements in overall performance had undoubtedly been achieved with the development of a new generation of engines, the V-12 liquid-cooled engines which had been adopted in Europe for the Schneider Trophy races, and the radial engines which found favour in the United States in the mid twenties after their success in the hotly contested National Air Races.

The fighter, however, had undergone few radical changes. The biplane formula was to remain in favour for many years [only very rarely was the high-wing monoplane configuration chosen], with a fixed under-carriage, open cockpit and two synchronized machine guns firing forward through the propeller arc. The main aeronautical powers thought this the best design for their fighters. One of the most significant combat planes to enter service in the 1920s was the Nieuport Delage NiD.29C.1; this French fighter had been developed during the closing months of the war but by the time it was operational the fighting was over.

In Britain, the Gloster Grebe, a small, maneuverable biplane which made its appearance in 1923, was the first of the new generation of warplanes but, again, was a throwback to the Sopwith Snipe of 1918. The first fighter designed and built in Italy, the Fiat C.R.1, went into service in 1923; while offering excellent performance, it differed little from the best wartime fighters.

It was a situation which was even more pronounced in the United States which had fallen far behind Europe's aviation industry and had to go through various phases of technological progress and experimentation which had already been completed and assimilated by the British, French and Italian industries. The Americans were, however, to succeed brilliantly in exploiting the innovations and advances which were the spin-offs of their major flying competitions. Until 1926 the U.S. Army and Navy not only participated directly in the Schneider Cup but were the main adversaries in U.S. national air race meetings. The main purpose of this participation was to speed up development of American engines and airframes to the maximum. The aircraft industry benefited greatly from this intervention and it was during these years that Curtiss and Boeing first made their mark as aircraft manufacturers, later to become such influential forces in the U.S. aviation world.

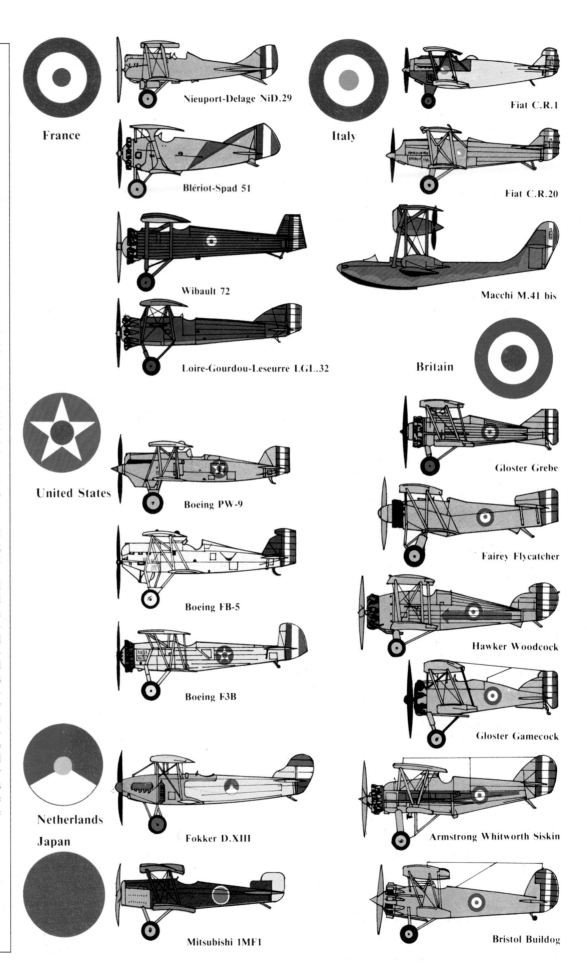

France

Nieuport-Delage NiD.29

Blériot-Spad 51

Wibault 72

Loire-Gourdou-Leseurre LGL.32

Italy

Fiat C.R.1

Fiat C.R.20

Macchi M.41 bis

United States

Boeing PW-9

Boeing FB-5

Boeing F3B

Netherlands

Fokker D.XIII

Japan

Mitsubishi 1MF1

Britain

Gloster Grebe

Fairey Flycatcher

Hawker Woodcock

Gloster Gamecock

Armstrong Whitworth Siskin

Bristol Buldog

# 1920-1930
## Bombers of the 1920s

The First World War also stimulated the development of another important category of front-line warplane: the bomber, the development of which did little more than mark time during the 1920s.

Ostensibly, Germany was no longer active in the field of military aviation as she was prohibited from building warplanes under the terms of the peace treaty. Following Hitler's rise to power, she was to flout these restrictions, at first surreptitiously, then blatantly after 1935. Only three European nations possessed the knowledge and expertise, as well as the financial strength, to develop this sector of military aviation – France, Britain and Italy, and they limited themselves to producing updated versions of the large, multiengined bombers, capable of carrying a considerable bomb load and thus ideal for strategic purposes. Also, technology of the time was simply not equal to developing anything radically different, and for many years these aircraft were to be little more than carbon copies of the bombers which sowed terror among troops and civilians alike in the First World War: huge biplanes, nearly always twin-engined, which were slow and vulnerable, held together by a web of struts and wires.

Among the most typical examples were the French Lioré et Olivier LeO 20 of 1928, the British Boulton Paul Sidestrand and the Handley Page Hinaidi, the prototypes of which first appeared in 1926 and 1927; the American Martin MB-2 and Keystone B-4 which were designed during the first half of the twenties to equip the U.S. Army with planes on a par with the best built in Europe during the war.

Another aircraft in this category, the light tactical bomber, evolved fairly rapidly, especially in England. Around 1925 military strategists became obsessed with the need to build a light bomber with an all-round performance superior to that of contemporary fighters. The ideal vehicle proved to be an elegant biplane, the Fox, designed by Fairey, which could out-maneuver any aircraft in service with the RAF or the Fleet Air Arm. Production was limited to an experimental run of twenty-eight airplanes but the foundations were laid for a long line of aircraft, culminating in the thirties in the Hawker Hart-Hind family of biplanes, an extremely successful group of hybrids which combined the performance of the fighter with some of the striking power of the bomber.

The man responsible for these aircraft was Sydney Camm, later to design another classic airplane, the Hurricane of the Second World War. The success of the basic design was mainly due to a very carefully selected engine and to the fact that great pains were taken to ensure that the plane was as aerodynamically efficient as possible. This combination of speed and offensive power was welcomed by the British Chiefs of Staff who saw to it that a succession of light bombers and attack aircraft for military and naval use, were posted to squadrons and updated as much as possible before design changed radically during the following decade.

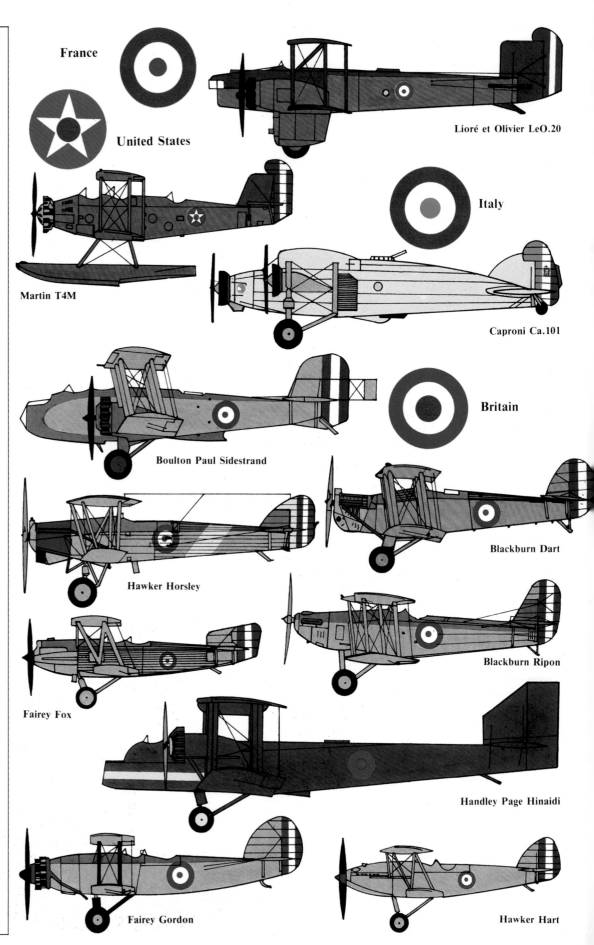

France

United States

Lioré et Olivier LeO.20

Martin T4M

Italy

Caproni Ca.101

Boulton Paul Sidestrand

Britain

Blackburn Dart

Hawker Horsley

Blackburn Ripon

Fairey Fox

Handley Page Hinaidi

Fairey Gordon

Hawker Hart

## 1920-1930
## Training and reconnaissance aircraft of the 1920s

Compared with the "thoroughbred" combat planes – the fighters and bombers – the evolution of trainers and reconnaissance aircraft in the 1920s was a more gradual process. With the exception of a few large marine patrol aircraft, most of these planes were fairly basic with no great sophistication, developed from designs already tried and tested. A particularly successful example was the Dutch Fokker C.V., a small but versatile biplane which, from 1924 until the eve of the Second World War, served with the air forces of a dozen countries, in many variants.

Reconnaissance aircraft were, more often than not, derived from light bombers; when it came to trainers it was recognized that the time had come to design aircraft exclusively for this role; this showed how thinking had changed in military aviation circles. The terrible loss of life during the First World War had shown clearly how vital it was to train pilots and crews properly and, once peace had returned, this conviction was translated into action. Both civilian and military flying schools proliferated during the years between the two world wars, not only as the natural reaction to the lessons learned during the last years of the war, but also to satisfy a new demand created by the reorganization and modernization of airforces.

This was very much the case in the United States which had yet to establish its own tradition of military aviation. Among the most widely-used trainers of these years were those built by Consolidated, designated PT by the Army and NY by the Navy. The prototype appeared in 1923 in response to a need for a reliable replacement for the obsolete Curtiss JN-4 Jenny of 1916. So satisfactory were the Consolidated trainers that they were periodically updated with engine changes and kept in service until 1939; although other, more modern types came on the scene during the intervening years, the Consolidated trainers continued to be eminently well suited to their tasks.

In the late 1920s, however, European manufacturers produced some outstanding trainers such as the French Morane-Saulnier M.S.230 [of which there were several variants, production totalling about 1,100 aircraft]; the Italian Breda Ba.25 [most of the Regia Aeronautica's pilots of the time saw training in one or other of the successive versions]; and the Russian Polikarpov Po.2, a tough and versatile biplane, of which a record number of over 20,000 were built between 1928 and 1952.

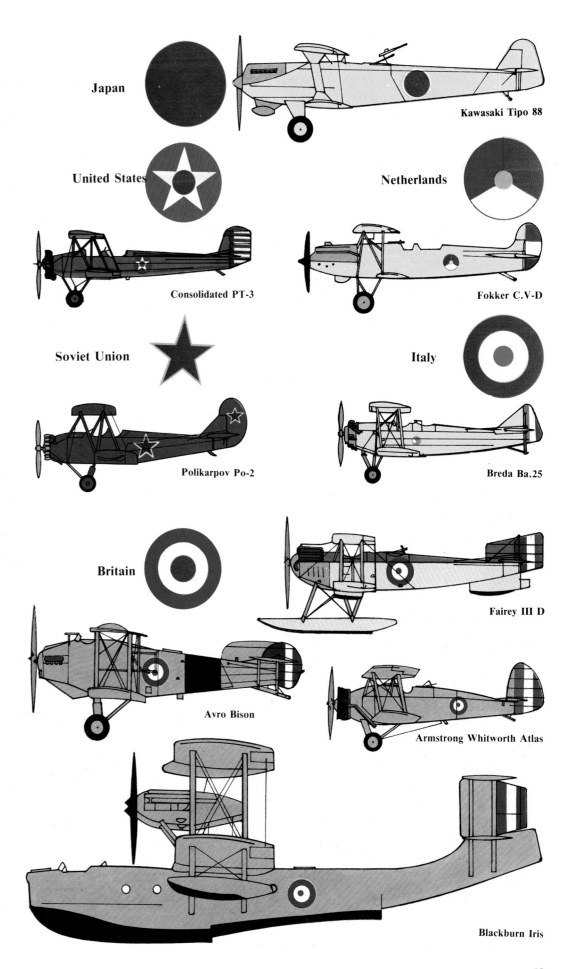

Japan
Kawasaki Tipo 88

United States
Consolidated PT-3

Netherlands
Fokker C.V-D

Soviet Union
Polikarpov Po-2

Italy
Breda Ba.25

Britain
Avro Bison

Fairey III D

Armstrong Whitworth Atlas

Blackburn Iris

# 1930
# 1940

## CIVIL AVIATION PRIOR TO THE SECOND WORLD WAR

Although enthusiasm for competition flying was to persist for some years, the most important phenomenon of the thirties was the boom in commercial transport. During the years which led up to another world war, air transport was gradually accepted as part of everyday life. This was the golden age of air travel when the foundations of modern civil aviation were laid. Keen competition developed between European and U.S. carriers, and although the European companies started out with more experience, their transatlantic rivals soon made up for the earlier lack of official interest in developing the commercial aviation sector.

Aided by their overall technological and industrial superiority, a vast and flourishing manufacturing base and a willingness to develop the necessary technology and design capability enabled the United States to catch up very quickly. This tremendous industrial strength, which was fully mobilized during the Second World War, was eventually to enable the United States to capture and keep the dominant role in western aviation, a position it shows no sign of relinquishing in the foreseeable future.

Competition to extend commercial networks and capture an increasing share of the market was fiercest on the transoceanic routes. The need for increased efficiency on long intercontinental flights led to a demand for more advanced aircraft thus stimulating technological progress. Competition had become particularly fierce by the time the Second World War threatened, nowhere more so than on the North Atlantic route, the most sought after, even to this day, on which scheduled services began at this time.

As the twenties gave way to the thirties, French commercial operators continued to expand and consolidate their already considerable share of the European market. With routes extending to Africa and Asia, their share of the air traffic for 1932 showed a healthy trading position: 5,779,000 miles [9,300,000 km] flown; 420,000 tonnes of cargo carried and 310,000 tonnes of mail. Air Union, one of the most go-ahead companies, had expanded its routes southwards and to Britain; Société Générale de Transport Aérien [SGTA], originally Farman air lines, ran services to northern Europe; CIDNA [which operated as the Compagnie Franco-Roumanie de Navigation Aérienne until 1924] served eastern Europe and the Middle East.

These companies were to the forefront in implementing the new French policy, adopted in 1933 of developing air transport, with a view to strengthening France's position in the face of increasingly keen competition, with the simultaneous aim of creating a coordinated and efficient French civil aviation industry. The government encouraged company mergers, in the hope of the eventual creation of a large state enterprise. On 30 August 1933, Air Orient, Air Union, CIDNA and SGTA amalgamated to form Air France. The establishment of the new company brought with it all the organizational and technical problems inherent in running a network covering nearly 23,600 miles [38,000 km] with a fleet of 259 airplanes of various types, many of them obsolete.

The changeover was carried through with great determination; the benefits were soon apparent. In 1934 the first commercial routes to South America were opened up [inaugurated on 28 May with the historic flight of the Couzinet Arc-en-Ciel trimotor]. Two years later a regular passenger service to Dakar in West Africa was started; 1937 brought route-proving flights across the North Atlantic, and by 1938, Air France's network had stretched to China and then to Hong Kong. Passenger traffic was also increasing: in 1930, 55,000 passengers travelled with the four main French airlines: Air Union, Farman, CIDNA and Aéropostale; by the end of 1939 the total had almost doubled.

Across the Channel, British civil aviation was undergoing a similar process of rationalization. Early in the 1930s a number of private companies, among them

Hillman's Airways [founded in 1932], Spartan Air Lines [1933], United Airways and British Continental Airways [1935], were set to challenge the monopoly of Imperial Airways. In the interests of all concerned, these smaller airlines merged in 1935 to form a new company, British Airways. The new airline [formed on 1 October] was eventually to take over the business once monopolized by Imperial Airways. The third main British operator was Scottish Airways, also the result of a merger which took place in 1937 between Highland Airways and Northern & Scottish Airways.

Both Imperial Airways and British Airways found themselves facing stiff international competition from the go-ahead Dutch airline KLM, and the formidable German state airline, Lufthansa. The ambitious expansion program which Imperial Airways had promoted from its earliest years, eventually spread the company's routes to the farthest limits of the Empire: Cape Town in South Africa, Hong Kong and Singapore in Asia, Brisbane and Sydney in Australia.

The Second World War had already started when Imperial Airways and British Airways merged to form a single, large state airline, British Overseas Airways Corporation. A year earlier, when the two companies had reached the peak of their expansion as separate entities, they had between them carried 200,000 passengers, placing Britain in third place in the European league table of airlines, behind Lufthansa and Aeroflot, and followed by KLM, Ala Littoria and Air France. The war put an abrupt stop to any further expansion.

Indisputably, the leader among the European airlines in the 1930s was Deutsche Lufthansa. On the strength of an extremely meticulous commercial organization and because of its very close ties with the German aeronautical industry's ambitious expansion policy [which meant that the airline had a supply of up-to-date and competitive aircraft at its disposal], this state airline reached the high point of its development shortly before the outbreak of the war. In 1938, 254,000 passengers and 7,000 tonnes of cargo were carried, a total of over 9 million miles [15 million km] flown. In 1939 the number of passengers was almost 280,000, about three times the total for 1930.

SIAI Marchetti S.M.83, 1937

Among the four "greats" of commercial aviation, one must include Italy. By 1930 the Italian civil aviation industry was third in order of importance [after France and Germany] with a total of 40,000 passengers carried, and during the second half of the decade, Italian airlines were subjected to far-reaching operational changes. In 1934 it was decided to form a national carrier, with the object of pooling resources and rationalizing networks. Thus the state airline Ala Littoria was formed, from a merger involving SISA, Aero Espresso, SANA and SAM [the latter having taken over Transadriatica in 1931]. The only remaining independent company was Avio Linee Italiane. With official approval, Ala Littoria embarked on an ambitious program of expansion, not only developing a comprehensive network of routes linking Italy with her colonies and extending European operations, but also opening up new intercontinental routes.

Just before the outbreak of the Second World War, the airline started flights to South America. LATI [Linee Aeree Transcontinentali Italiane] was formed [in 1939] for this purpose and the first Rome-Rio de Janeiro flight took off in December 1939. Because of the war, operations were soon suspended.

Another important operator which sought to make its mark on the European commercial aviation market was the Dutch company KLM, a large airline for so small a country. Dynamic and enterprising management made the airline the fourth most important operator in Europe [in 1939 170,000 passengers were carried]. In a shrewd move, following the ending of the partnership with Fokker in 1934, KLM was the first European airline to acquire the revolutionary DC-2, and later in 1936, the DC-3 for use on both the busy European routes and the intercontinental runs,

de Havilland D.H.89 Dragon Rapide, 1934

Wibault 283, 1934

Dornier Do.26, 1938

Douglas DC-3, 1936

thereby stealing a march on its rivals.

The rapid expansion in civil aviation in the U.S.S.R. during the thirties is the more surprising in view of the low-key development which had marked its progress up to then. An ineffectual attempt was made in 1924 to set up a national civil aviation infrastructure but the decisive step was taken in 1932, with the creation of the powerful state airline, Aeroflot. The airline soon achieved impressive operating results: in 1935, 111,000 passengers and over 11,000 tonnes of cargo were carried all over Soviet territory; in 1939 the number of passengers had risen to 270,000 and the state airline was the second biggest, after Lufthansa. In 1940, before the German invasion, Aeroflot operated a network covering 90,900 miles [146,300 km], carrying 395,000 passengers and 45,000 tonnes of cargo.

At the beginning of the decade, American airlines concentrated their activities mainly on establishing domestic networks. This vast potential market was effectively shared by four companies which came to be known as the "Big Four": American Air Lines, which emerged from the amalgamation of fifteen companies; United Air Lines [a six-company merger]; Eastern Air Lines, and Transcontinental & Western Air [TWA], both of these the product of a two-company merger. Besides these domestic operators, there was also Pan American Airways, a giant international operator, and no fewer than forty minor airlines which between them accounted for nearly five hundred aircraft and about 31,000 miles [50,000 km], a total to add to an already impressive statistic. The rapid expansion meant that the United States was soon the leader in world air transport. [As early as 1929 over 160,000 passengers travelled by American airlines.]

As domestic activity gathered pace, so did intercontinental expansion. Starting with flights to the Caribbean, Pan Am, in 1930, opened routes to the most far-flung points of South America; the inauguration of Trans-Pacific routes came in 1935 and direct flights to Alaska in 1938. In 1939 Pan Am launched scheduled flights across the North Atlantic and the following year opened a service to New Zealand. The outcome of such impressive enterprise was a vast commercial network, the largest in the world, operated with an imposing fleet of high-performance aircraft.

## 1930-1940
## British flying boats in the ascendancy

An already very active British civil aviation industry gained further impetus from the policy of expansion during the 1930s. Several of the main aircraft companies concentrated their efforts almost exclusively on supplying the commercial sector. De Havilland was to make its name as an outstanding light-aircraft manufacturer. In 1931 the company produced the versatile little D.H.82 Tiger Moth biplane; as the standard RAF trainer, 7,300 were built. In 1932 came the two-engine D.H.84 Dragon biplane designed to meet the demands of small operators. Next to follow, in 1934, was the D.H.86, the larger, four-engine plane, and then the D.H.89 Dragon Rapide which was effectively an improved version of the D.H.84. 737 Dragon Rapides were built over a ten-year period, a large production total for those days.

The most significant products of the British aircraft industry were the large airliners built for Imperial Airways to fly on their vast network of intercontinental routes. Four-engine planes proved particularly suitable, among the best being the Armstrong Whitworth A.W.15 Atalanta [1932, 8 built] which was designed specifically for service on Imperial's longest routes. The advanced A.W.27 Ensign was introduced in 1938, series production totalling thirteen. The de Havilland company also supplied large airliners like the elegant, clean-lined D.H.91 Albatross [1937, 5 built] which entered service in 1938. There followed de Havilland's last civil design to go into production before the war: the D.H.95 Flamingo, a modern, twin-engine metal construction monoplane which appeared in prototype in 1938 [23 built].

But the aircraft which best suited Imperial Airways' needs were the large flying boats, a succession of which were built by Short Brothers over several years. The most famous was the S.23, forty of which were built in three variants between 1935 and 1939.

The C-Class Empire boat service was inaugurated on Mediterranean routes in October 1936 and on Empire routes on 8 February the following year. They proved so popular that Shorts decided to develop other versions, one being the military S.25 Sunderland. Production culminated in the gigantic S.26 flying boat, constructed as a special order for Imperial in 1938 for its projected North Atlantic service. The first of three S.26s flew in June 1939 but the outbreak of war put an abrupt stop to any further development.

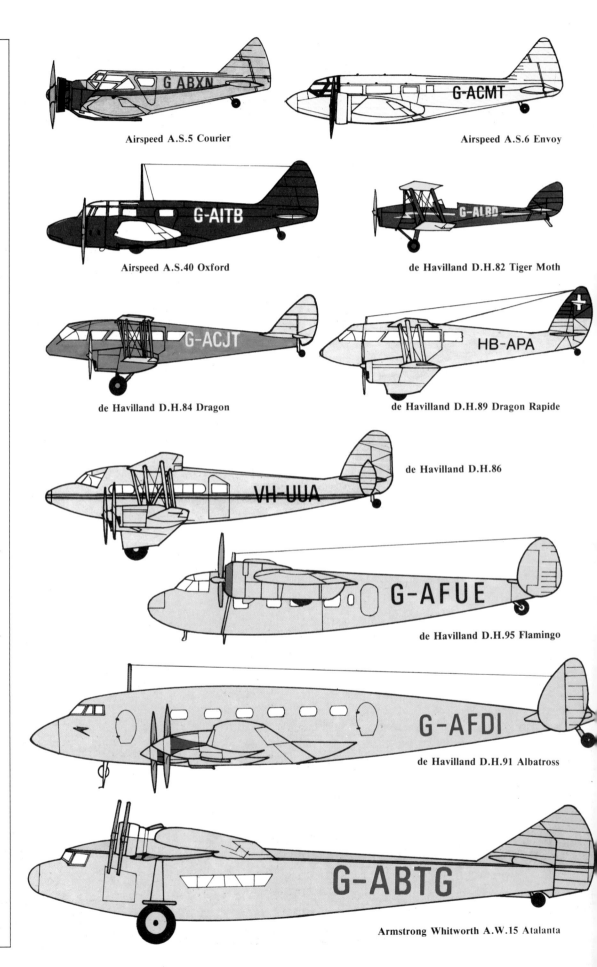

Airspeed A.S.5 Courier

Airspeed A.S.6 Envoy

Airspeed A.S.40 Oxford

de Havilland D.H.82 Tiger Moth

de Havilland D.H.84 Dragon

de Havilland D.H.89 Dragon Rapide

de Havilland D.H.86

de Havilland D.H.95 Flamingo

de Havilland D.H.91 Albatross

Armstrong Whitworth A.W.15 Atalanta

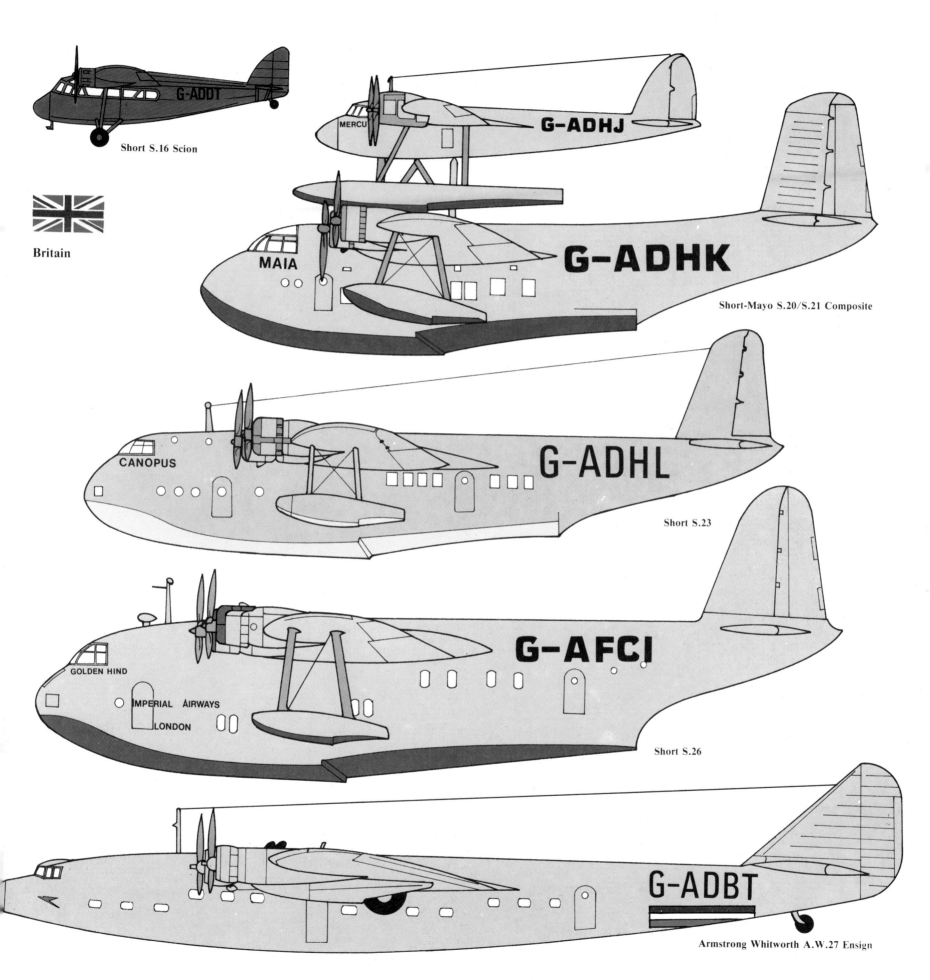

Short S.16 Scion

Britain

MERCU[RY] G-ADHJ

MAIA G-ADHK

Short-Mayo S.20/S.21 Composite

CANOPUS G-ADHL

Short S.23

GOLDEN HIND G-AFCI

IMPERIAL AIRWAYS
LONDON

Short S.26

G-ADBT

Armstrong Whitworth A.W.27 Ensign

1 starboard elevator
2 tailplane construction
3 elevator tab
4 tail navigation light
5 tailcone
6 rudder tabs
7 fabric covered rudder
8 fin girder construction
9 leading edge construction
10 aerial wire
11 port fabric covered elevator
12 port tailplane
13 rudder and elevator control levers
14 tailplane attachment double frames
15 fuselage frame and stringer construction
16 fuselage skin plating
17 rear bulkhead
18 baggage door
19 aft main baggage bay
20 cabin rear bulkhead
21 window panels
22 bilge keel construction
23 aft cabin, seating six passengers
24 cabin trim panels
25 overhead luggage racks
26 rear entry door
27 bulkhead doorway
28 wing root trailing edge fillet
29 cabin roof bedding stowage
30 window curtains
31 wing root rib
32 starboard dipole aerial mast
33 promenade cabin, eight passengers
34 starboard flap shroud
35 starboard gouge type flap
36 girder construction rear spar
37 trailing edge ribs
38 starboard aileron
39 fixed tab
40 aileron control horns
41 wing tip fairing
42 starboard navigation light
43 wire braced wing rib construction
44 front girder spar
45 leading edge nose ribs
46 float mounting struts
47 diagonal wire bracing
48 starboard wing tip float construction
49 landing/taxi-ing lamp
50 wing stringers
51 overwing exhaust outlet
52 carburetor air intake
53 starboard outer engine nacelle construction
54 engine mounting ring
55 exhaust collector ring
56 detachable engine cowlings
57 oil cooler radiators
58 hull planing bottom forward step
59 midships cabin, three passengers
60 midships window panel
61 starboard inner engine nacelle
62 cooling air flaps
63 nacelle tail fairing
64 heater intake duct
65 cabin heater/exhaust heat exchanger
66 wing/fuselage main spar attachments
67 root rib cut-outs

68 wing spar center section carry-through
69 port gouge-type trailing edge flap
70 flap screw jack
71 port dipole aerial mast
72 flap guide rails
73 port aileron
74 aileron control cables
75 fixed tab
76 port wing-tip fairing
77 port navigation light
78 landing/taxi-ing lamp
79 port outer engine nacelle
80 oil tank
81 Bristol Pegasus XC air cooled 9-cylinder radial engine
82 de Havilland three bladed propeller
83 propeller hub pitch change mechanism
84 port wing tip float
85 ram air intakes
86 oil radiators
87 outboard main fuel tanks
88 port inner engine nacelle
89 exhaust collector ring
90 cooling air flaps
91 overwing exhaust outlet
92 exhaust pipe heat exchanger
93 inboard main fuel tank, total tankage, 600 Imp gal (2,727 l)
94 engine cowl flaps and fuel cock controls
95 ship's clerk's station

96 upper deck crew entry door
97 access ladder between decks
98 steward's galley
99 port side toilet doors, two toilets
100 upper deck level
101 port mail and freight compartment
102 sliding door
103 forward entry door
104 smoking lounge, seven passengers
105 fuselage chine member
106 forward fuselage portholes
107 radio operator's seat
108 radio racks
109 aerial mast
110 pitot tubes
111 cockpit roof hatch
112 chart table
113 cockpit roof trim control cables
114 pilot's seat
115 sliding cockpit side windows
116 copilot's seat
117 control column
118 rudder pedals
119 instrument panel shroud
120 curved windscreen panels
121 mooring hatch
122 marine equipment compartment
123 mooring ladder
124 anchor winch
125 anchor stowage
126 retractable mooring bollard
127 towing cleat

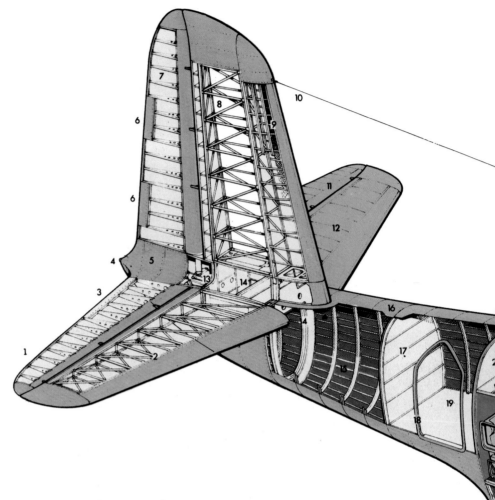

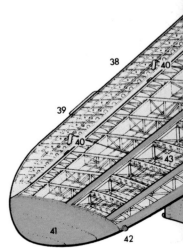

**Short S.23 Empire Class**

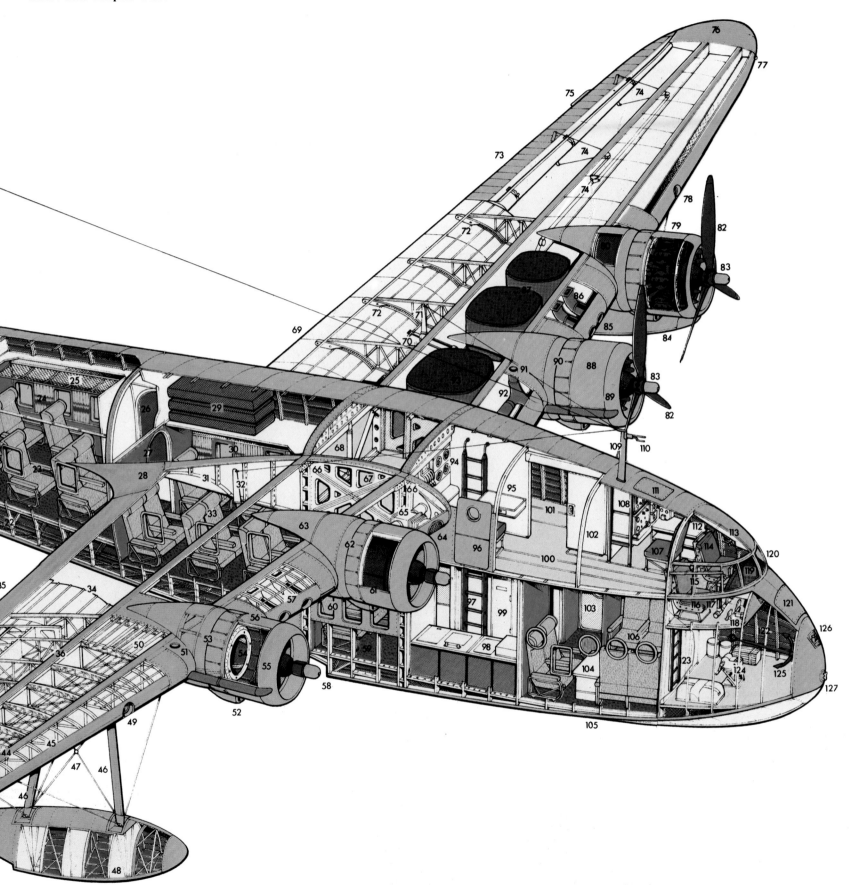

63

# 1930-1940
# French prominence in civil transport

France's aeronautical industry, like Britain's, flourished during this decade. Apart from light-aircraft manufacture, the most attractive market was in civil transport aircraft. The three-engine Wibault series 280T was an extremely versatile short-to-medium-range transport. First unveiled at the Paris Air Show in 1930, it remained in service with Air France's fleet on the main European routes for five years [1933 to 1938]. While the Wibault owed much to its advanced design, another trimotor which served on the demanding colonial routes for six gruelling years from 7 September 1934, the Bloch 120, was much more conventional. Seven of these aircraft were built and Régie Air Afrique found them invaluable as reliable workhorses operating sometimes under the most difficult conditions.

From 1937 onwards Air France flew another up-to-date twin-engine plane on its main European routes, the Bloch 220 [1935, 16 built]. How resilient this aircraft was, was shown when Air France up-rated the engines of five of these planes which had survived the war and put them back into service in 1949. The last, and best, conventional pre-war French transport was the Dewoitine D.338, a modern and sleek trimotor which made its maiden flight in 1935 [31 built]. Air France put its Dewoitines into service in 1936 on its most important routes: Europe, South America, the Far East and Africa. After the war, eight of nine surviving D.338s flew the Paris-Nice route for a while.

Long distance flight still held its fascination for the French imagination; many of the commercial aircraft built in France during the thirties were flying boats, then considered the best [certainly the safest] for long, transoceanic flights. The Latécoère 300 was one of the most famous, designed in 1931 in response to Air France's specification for an aircraft which could carry a tonne of mail on the South Atlantic route. This large, four-engine flying boat entered service on 31 December 1933 and started its career with a record-breaking flight from Marseilles to St. Louis, in Senegal [2,286 miles – 3,679 km in 24 hours]. The prototype was known as the "Croix du Sud" [Southern Cross] and had made about fifteen Atlantic crossings when it came down and was lost somewhere in the South Atlantic on 7 December 1936, with the famous Jean Mermoz at the controls. Six of these aircraft were built, three of which joined Air France's fleet. Another interesting project was the Latécoère 521, a giant multiengine aircraft built for the North Atlantic route. It only completed one flight to New York [23 August 1938] before the threatening storm-clouds of war began to close in.

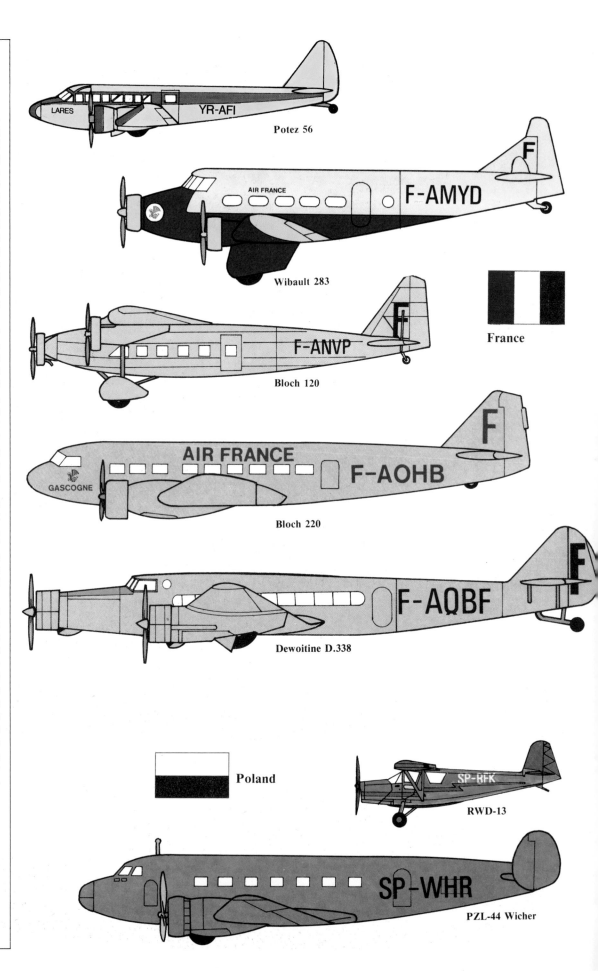

Potez 56

Wibault 283

Bloch 120

France

Bloch 220

Dewoitine D.338

Poland

RWD-13

PZL-44 Wicher

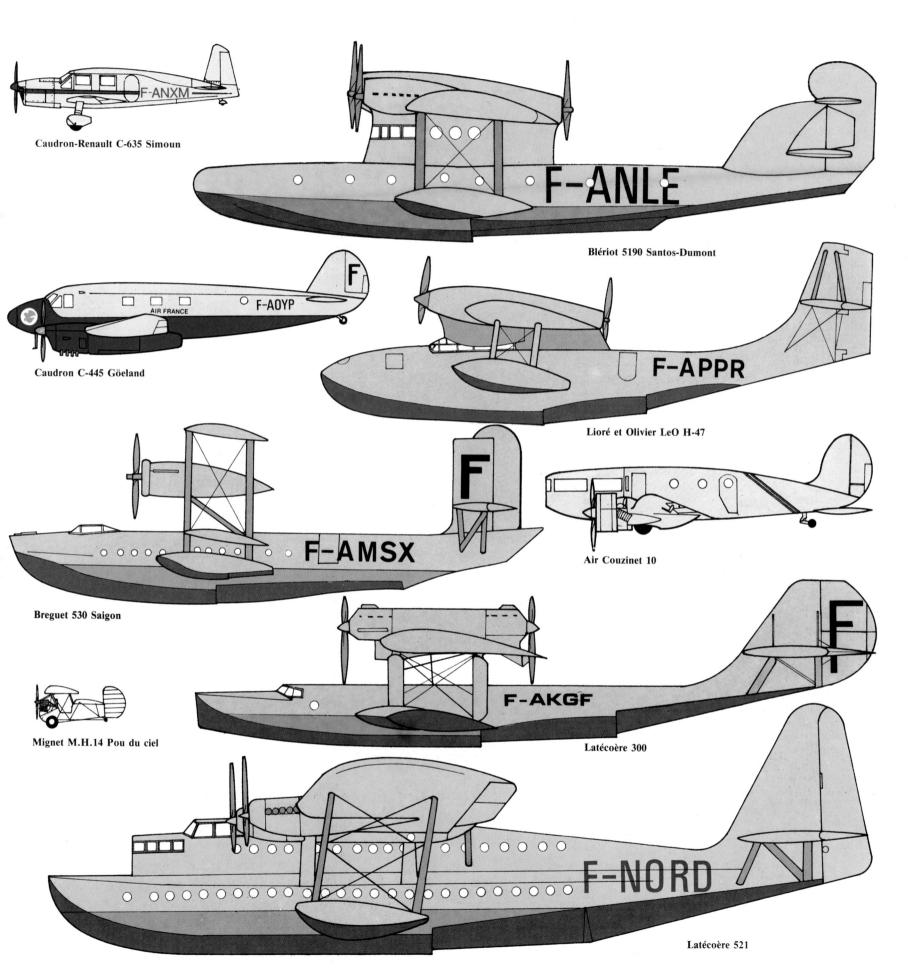

Caudron-Renault C-635 Simoun

Blériot 5190 Santos-Dumont

Caudron C-445 Göeland

Lioré et Olivier LeO H-47

Air Couzinet 10

Breguet 530 Saigon

Mignet M.H.14 Pou du ciel

Latécoère 300

Latécoère 521

# 1930-1940
## The rebirth of Germany's aviation industry

The growth of the German civil aviation industry followed a quite different pattern from that of other countries. The imposing structure set up by the state and managed with great efficiency by Lufthansa was in reality a screen to hide Germany's policy of rearmament and her determination to ensure that she had a powerful airforce to complement her growing military strength. This can be seen from the fact that the state airline put a number of very advanced transports into service during the 1930s which were nothing more than "civil" versions of the future bombers of the Luftwaffe.

The leading German manufacturers, Junkers, Heinkel, Focke Wulf, Dornier, each played an important role in ensuring that Deutsche Lufthansa retained its lead over other European carriers. In 1930 Junkers built its most famous transport, the Ju.52/3m, a tough and reliable trimotor which made a considerable contribution towards the development of German commercial aviation, before taking on an equally impressive role.

Between 1932 and 1939 a total of 200 civil Ju.52s were built and used by as many as thirty operators all over the world. Lufthansa alone had 78 in service in 1940. In 1934 the German advantage was further increased with the appearance of the Ju.86, a modern, twin-engine transport, later used as a bomber; about 1,000 were built, of which approximately 50 were in civil configuration and went into service with eight airlines including Lufthansa [16]. In 1938, the Ju.90 was unveiled: a large, up-to-date four-engine plane, of which Lufthansa ordered eight; they saw only limited service on European commercial routes before the war put an end to such activity.

Heinkel also produced some very important aircraft. Their first success came in 1933 with the He.70, an elegant monoplane, hailed as the fastest airliner in the world [28 civil and 296 military versions manufactured]. This was followed by a modern, twin-engine aircraft, the He.111 [10 were flown on European routes from 1936 onwards] which the Luftwaffe pressed into service as a bomber. Another Heinkel project, developed in 1936 in response to Lufthansa's requirement for a fast, high-altitude mailplane, to be designated He.116, failed for lack of a suitable engine.

Outstanding even among these thoroughbreds, was the Focke Wulf's Fw.200, the dreaded Condor of the war years. It had been developed in 1936 to provide Lufthansa with what it hoped would prove a rival to the Douglas DC-3 and 10 civil versions were in service from 1938 onwards. Among the route-proving flights made that year, one represented an outstanding achievement, a flight from Berlin to New York and back, starting on 10 August, the outward journey taking 24 hours 35 minutes and the return flight 19 hours 47 minutes.

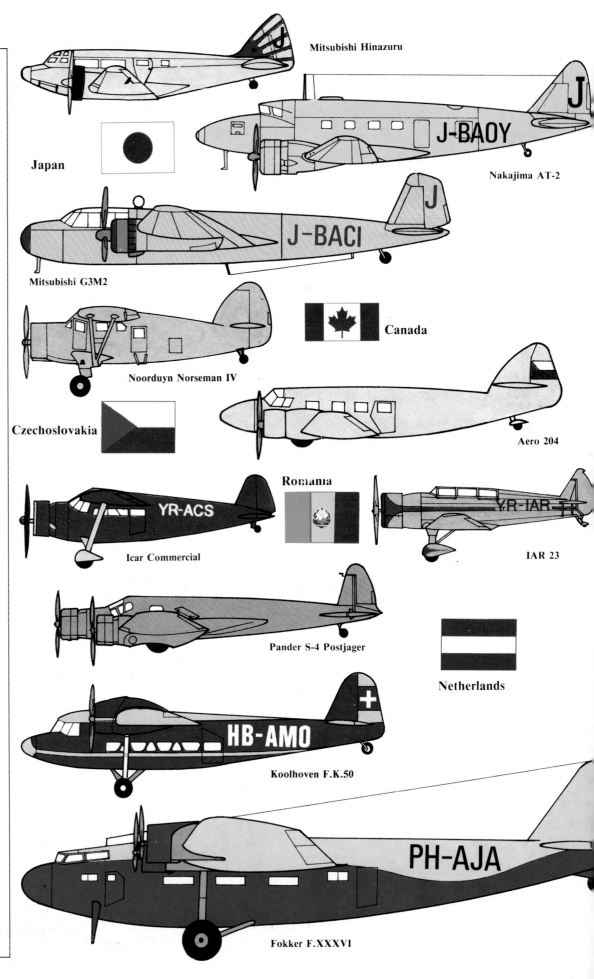

Mitsubishi Hinazuru

Japan

J-BAOY

Nakajima AT-2

J-BACI

Mitsubishi G3M2

Canada

Noorduyn Norseman IV

Czechoslovakia

Aero 204

Romania

YR-ACS

Icar Commercial

YR-IAR

IAR 23

Pander S-4 Postjager

Netherlands

HB-AMO

Koolhoven F.K.50

PH-AJA

Fokker F.XXXVI

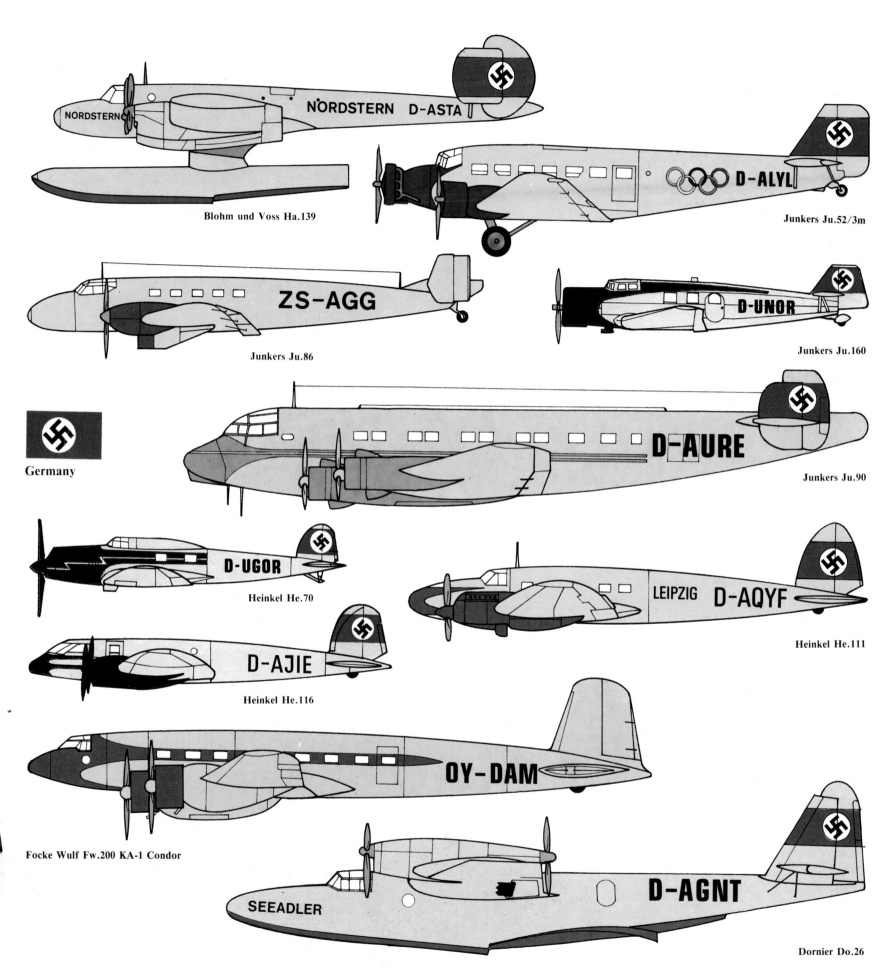

NORDSTERN D-ASTA

Blohm und Voss Ha.139

D-ALYL

Junkers Ju.52/3m

ZS-AGG

Junkers Ju.86

D-UNOR

Junkers Ju.160

Germany

D-AURE

Junkers Ju.90

D-UGOR

Heinkel He.70

LEIPZIG D-AQYF

Heinkel He.111

D-AJIE

Heinkel He.116

OY-DAM

Focke Wulf Fw.200 KA-1 Condor

SEEADLER D-AGNT

Dornier Do.26

# 1930-1940
## Italian civil aviation to the fore.
## The Soviet emergence

The Italian aviation industry was well equipped to meet the challenge of the burgeoning commercial sector. Italy retained her place among the leading aeronautical countries largely through her aircraft manufacturers' determination to compete with the best of foreign production and keep abreast of new technology. Particularly notable were the experiments carried out with the revolutionary Caproni Campini shortly before Italy's entry into war, with the aim of developing an alternative means of propulsion to the propeller.

SIAI Marchetti was certainly the most famous Italian civil aircraft manufacturer. Following the remarkable long-distance achievements of the S.M.55 and S.M.66 flying boats, the company decided to develop a series of landplanes which, it was hoped, would prove equally successful. The first of a succession of excellent trimotors was the S.M.71 of 1930. The S.M.73, a three-engine low-wing monoplane, which flew for the first time on 4 June 1934, was the first in a development line which was to lead to the more advanced S.M.75 and S.M.83 of 1937. The one exception to this basic design formula was the S.M.74, a large four-engine high-wing monoplane which appeared in prototype on 6 November 1934. The three aircraft which were built went into service with Ala Littoria on 18 July 1935.

Other interesting designs produced by Italy's flourishing aircraft industry were the Caproni Ca.101 and Ca.133 [1930 and 1935], high wing trimotors which saw long service on colonial routes; the outstanding Macchi M.C.94 and M.C.100 [1935 and 1939]; and the Fiat G.18 [1935], a modern twin-engine transport influenced by the American DC-1 and the DC-2; eight were built.

The 1930s saw the emergence of a country which was to become one of the giants of commercial aviation – the Soviet Union. Aeroflot's expansion was assured by the steady supply of dependable civil transports. Tupolev was only one of the outstanding designers working on large, multiengine aircraft around this time, reviving the design philosophy which had inspired Sikorsky's earlier experiments. The conventional ANT-29 of 1929 was followed in 1931 and 1934 by the giant ANT-14 and ANT-20 transports, remarkable for their size rather than design. Tupolev's ANT-35 of 1935 was the first of a new generation of planes which had originated with the American Boeing 247 two years earlier.

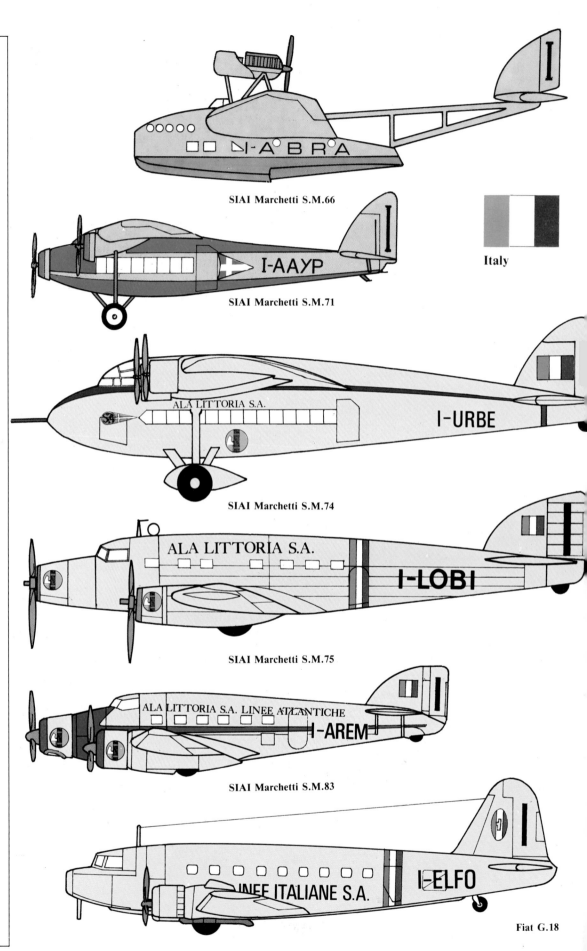

SIAI Marchetti S.M.66

SIAI Marchetti S.M.71

Italy

SIAI Marchetti S.M.74

SIAI Marchetti S.M.75

SIAI Marchetti S.M.83

Fiat G.18

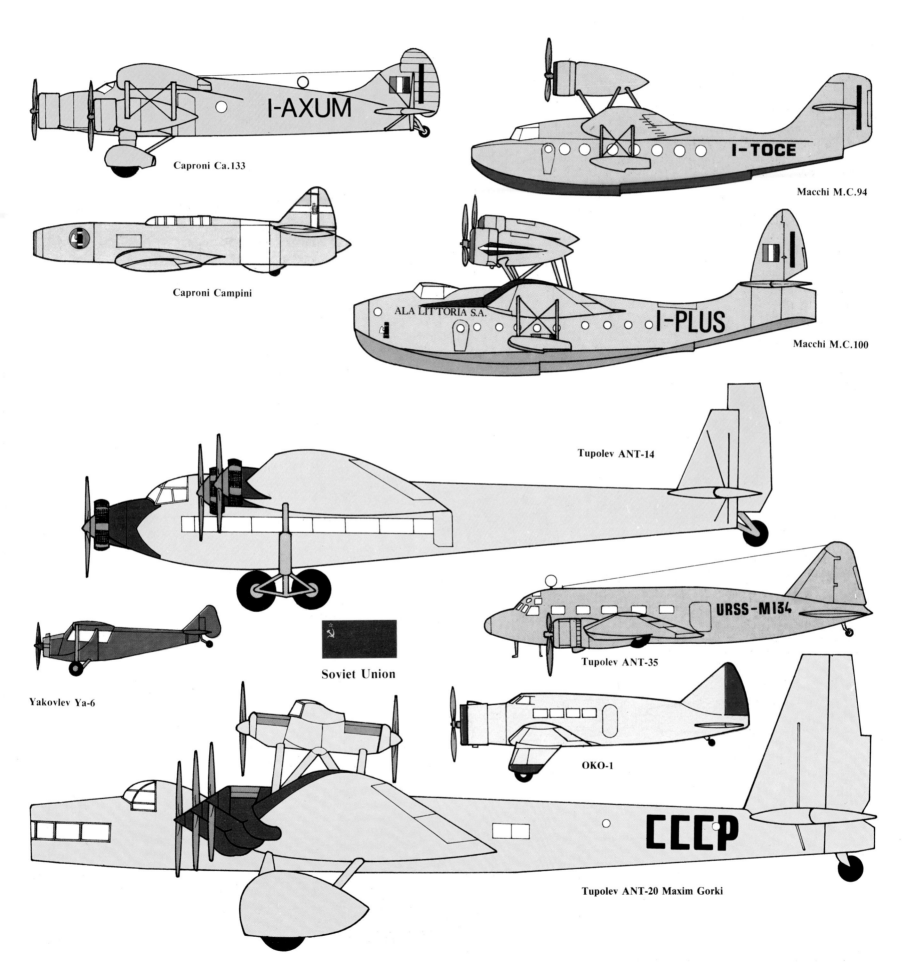

Caproni Ca.133

Caproni Campini

Macchi M.C.94

I-TOCE

ALA LITTORIA S.A.

I-PLUS

Macchi M.C.100

Tupolev ANT-14

Yakovlev Ya-6

Soviet Union

URSS-M134

Tupolev ANT-35

OKO-1

Tupolev ANT-20 Maxim Gorki

69

# 1930-1940
## The immortal DC-3 scores a first for the United States

The Boeing 247 signalled both the end of an era and the birth of the modern airliner. When this elegant twin-engine airplane was unveiled on 8 February 1933, the world of commercial aviation was shaken to its foundations. Tremendous technological advances had been incorporated in the new aircraft: all-metal structure, very advanced configuration [low-wing, with a retractable undercarriage], and such were the aerodynamic refinements, general level of performance and low-operating costs that the plane left all its contemporaries far behind.

Boeing had launched the project in 1931 in response to a military commitment which got no further than the prototype stage. One of the most dynamic airlines of the day, United Air Lines had the monopoly of the civil version, putting the first 247s into service on 30 March 1933, expanding its fleet as rapidly as the new aircraft came off the production lines, and as a result, capturing the lion's share of the market.

In 1932 TWA issued specifications for an airliner which could compete with the 247. Douglas, despite the fact that TWA had sought a conventional trimotor, was first in the field with an advanced twin-engine aircraft. The DC-1 prototype flew on 1 July 1933 and was accepted by TWA in September to initiate a series of proving flights on its main domestic routes.

The aircraft was an instantaneous success, with flight times so drastically reduced, that TWA captured the market lead from United. Having been guaranteed a monopoly of the first production aircraft, TWA took delivery of about 200 of the improved version, the DC-2, later to be joined by the definitive version, the DC-3, which went into production in 1936. By 1939 almost 90 per cent of world air traffic was operating with these aircraft.

Boeing and Douglas, however, were not to have everything their own way. In 1934 Lockheed introduced its Model 10 Electra, the first of a series of excellent, twin-engine aircraft. The years leading up to the outbreak of war saw tremendous progress in the evolution of aircraft. Among the most noteworthy were the Sikorsky S.40 and S.42, large, four-engine flying-boats built specially for Pan American for use on its medium-range flights. They were followed by the Martin M.130 with which Pan American inaugurated its San Francisco-Manila service in October 1936. Three aircraft were built [the famed China Clippers] and remained in service until the United States entered the war. From 1942 the two remaining Clippers were used as military transports.

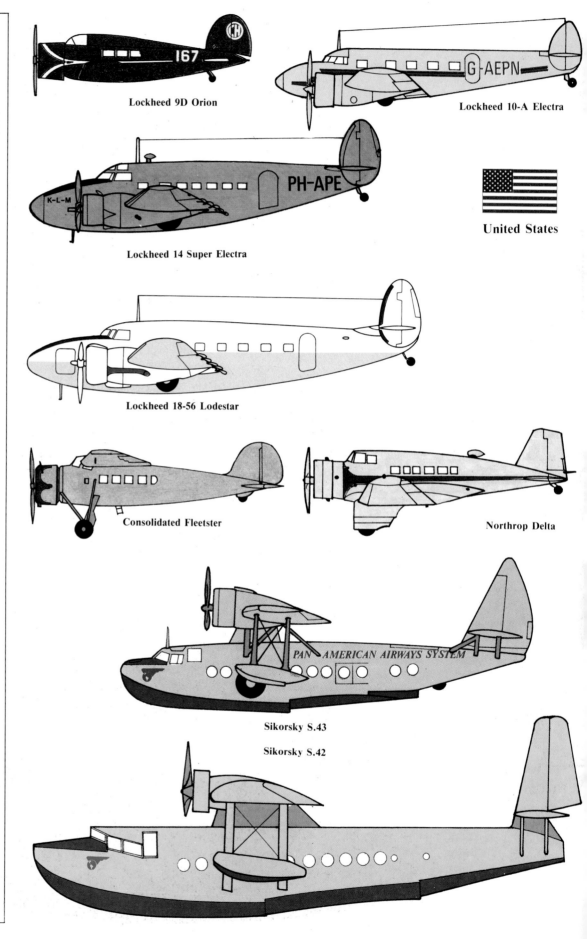

Lockheed 9D Orion

Lockheed 10-A Electra

Lockheed 14 Super Electra

United States

Lockheed 18-56 Lodestar

Consolidated Fleetster

Northrop Delta

Sikorsky S.43

Sikorsky S.42

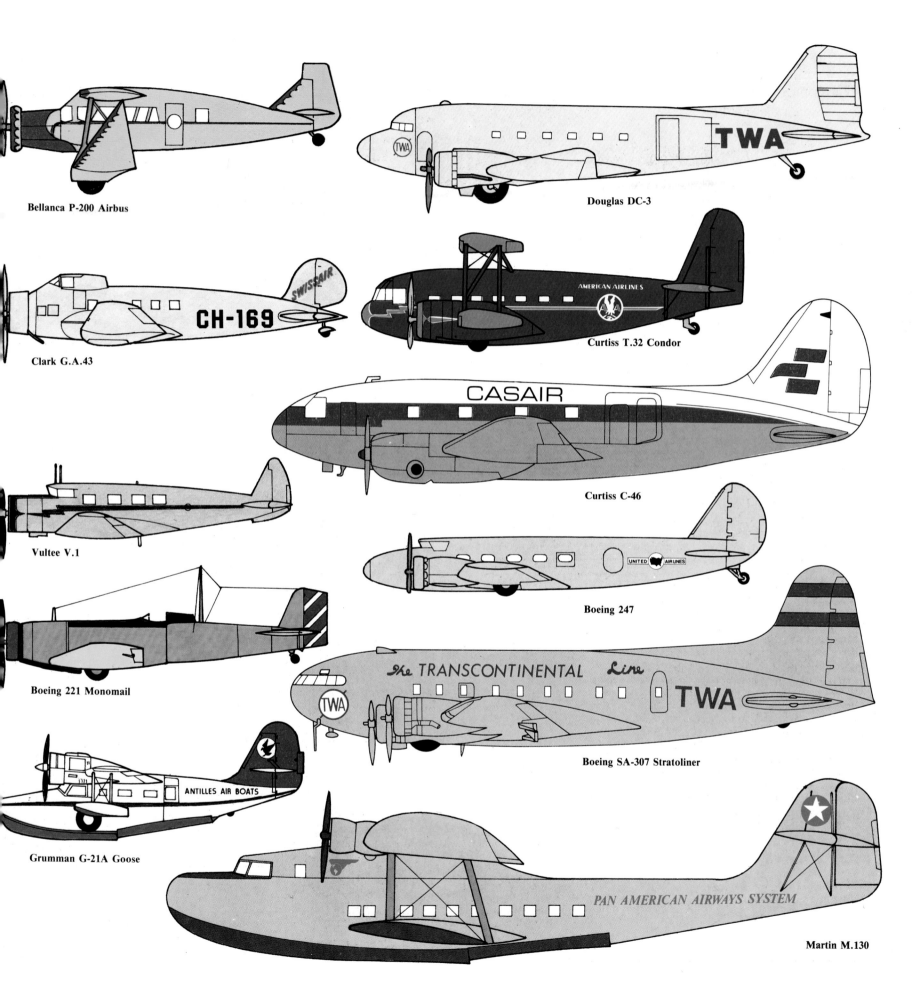

Bellanca P-200 Airbus

Douglas DC-3

Clark G.A.43

Curtiss T.32 Condor

Curtiss C-46

Vultee V.1

Boeing 247

Boeing 221 Monomail

Boeing SA-307 Stratoliner

Grumman G-21A Goose

Martin M.130

## 1930-1940
## The influence of the racing airplane on fighter design

While air transportation was expanding at an unprecedented rate, the aviation world was experiencing the last throes of one of its favourite pursuits – speed. The last Schneider Trophy race, held in 1931, virtually marked the end of organized competition flying in Europe. Though this is not to say that isolated record-breaking flights still did not have a part to play in the advancement of aircraft. In 1933 and 1934, in Italy, new records were set by the Macchi-Castoldi MC.72, the last floatplane racer to be built. In Britain, the de Havilland D.H.88 Comet [1934] and the little Percival Gull Six [1936] set new records for long-distance flight. In Germany, the competitiveness of the Messerschmitt was the technical breeding ground of the Luftwaffe's fighters. And in the U.S.S.R., the Tupolev ANT-25 set new distance records in 1934 and 1937.

It was altogether different in the United States. Enthusiasm for large-scale air races continued unabated and actually increased as the years went by, up to the outbreak of war. The flying craze still drew vast crowds to the National Air Races and there was no loss of interest in two other great prestige competitions: the Thompson Trophy and the Bendix Trophy. Many new aircraft were developed as a result of these very important competitions, such as the Wedell-Williams monoplane and the small, if extremely dangerous Gee-Bees of 1931 and 1932. There was also the sleek Howard DGA-6 Mr. Mulligan [1935], the Folkerts SK-3 Jupiter [1937] and the Laird-Turner L-RT Meteor of 1939, one of the last racing "thoroughbreds" of the air.

In 1934 Europe produced its first entry and winner in the National Air Races: the French Caudron C-460 which not only set a world speed record [313.8 mph – 505.33 km/h] but went on to win the Thompson Trophy in 1936. And, of course, the men who piloted these planes to victory also became famous: Robert Wedell, Ben Howard, Roscoe Turner and the millionaire Howard Hughes, to mention only the most celebrated. Hughes achieved his world speed record of 352 mph [566.49 km/h] in 1935 in his tiny H-1.

Such intense activity contributed greatly to the evolution of aeronautical technology. The stresses of competition flying led to the adoption of liquid-cooled V-engines in Europe and the development of the radial engine in the U.S.A., two schools of thought that were soon to be put to the test in the fiercest aerial contacts in the history of war. Airframe construction had also undergone great changes, the monoplane winning preference over the biplane; progress in control systems and equipment was equally impressive. Now that war was imminent, the fruits of all this experience were to be applied to aircraft militarization.

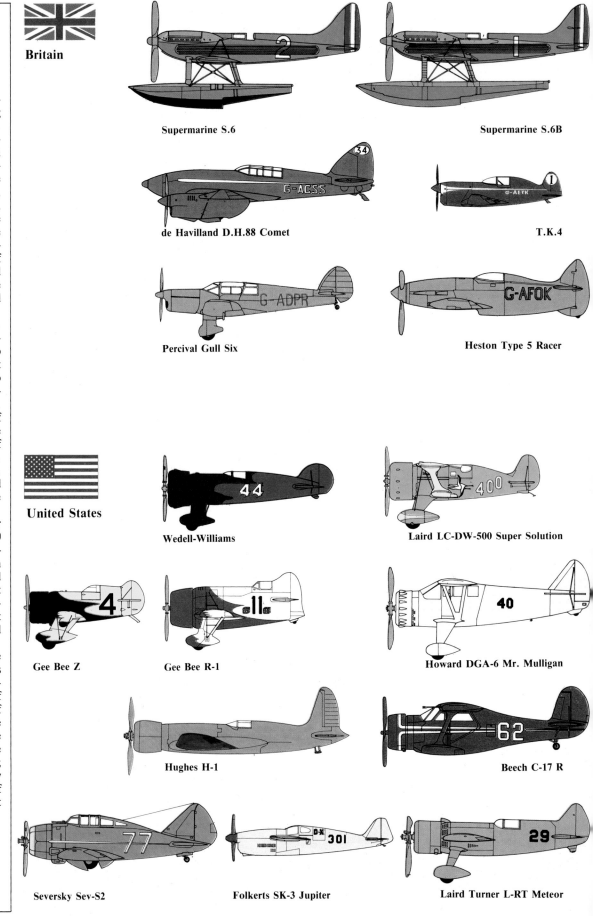

**Britain**

Supermarine S.6

Supermarine S.6B

de Havilland D.H.88 Comet

T.K.4

Percival Gull Six

Heston Type 5 Racer

**United States**

Wedell-Williams

Laird LC-DW-500 Super Solution

Gee Bee Z

Gee Bee R-1

Howard DGA-6 Mr. Mulligan

Hughes H-1

Beech C-17 R

Seversky Sev-S2

Folkerts SK-3 Jupiter

Laird Turner L-RT Meteor

**Italy**

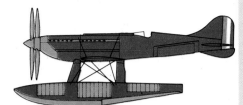

Macchi-Castoldi MC.72

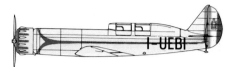

Nardi F.N.305D

**Germany**

Messerschmitt Bf.108B Taifun

**France**

Kellner-Béchereau 28 V.D.

Caudron C-460

**Soviet Union**

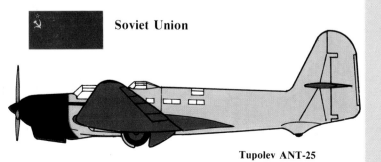

Tupolev ANT-25

"*Bristol*"

# de Havilland D.H.88 Comet

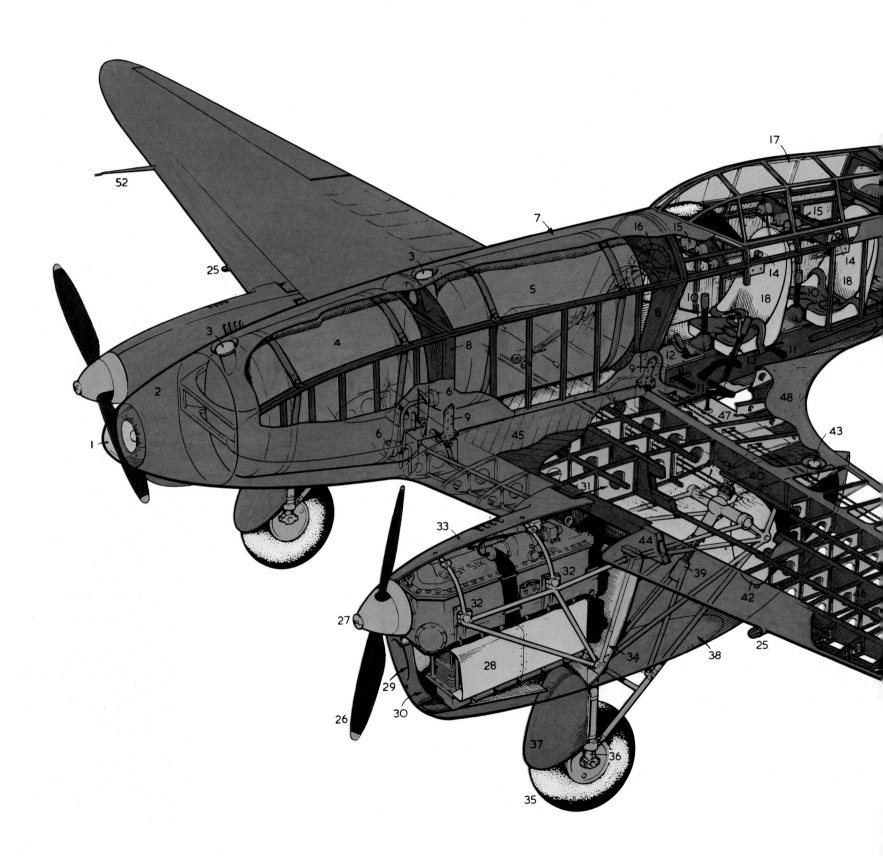

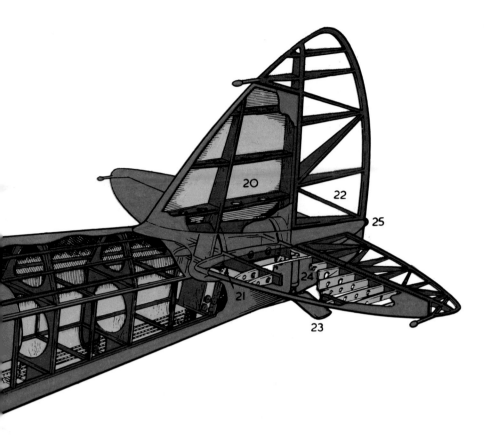

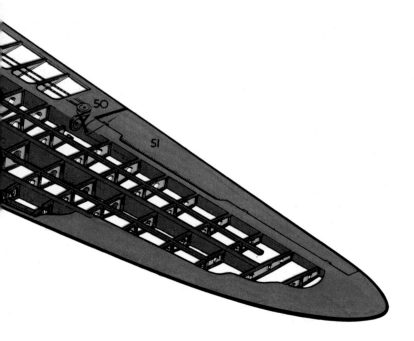

1 landing light
2 detachable nose cone
3 fuel tank fillers
4 front fuel tank, capacity 128 Imp gal (581 l)
5 midship fuel tank, capacity 110 Imp gal (500 l)
6 fuel jettison valves
7 fuselage skin, diagonally cross-laminated spruce
8 main bulkheads, plywood
9 fuselage/wing attachment points
10 control columns
11 rudder bars
12 wheel-brake lever
13 flap control lever
14 throttle controls
15 front and rear instrument panels
16 undercarriage retraction handwheel
17 one-piece canopy, hinged to starboard
18 fixed tandem seats, aluminum
19 rear fuel tank, capacity 20 Imp gal (91 l)
20 plywood-covered fin and tailplane
21 tailplane attachment points
22 rudder and elevators, plywood-covered
23 fully castoring tailskid
24 tailskid shock absorber
25 navigation lights
26 Ratier two-pitch propeller, 78.75-in (2-m) diameter
27 pitch control disc
28 230 hp de Havilland Gipsy Six R engine
29 carburetor air intake
30 cooling air intake
31 exhaust air outlet
32 four-point engine mounting
33 two-piece detachable aluminum engine cowling
34 aluminum and asbestos engine firewall
35 landing wheel, Dunlop 26.5 x 8.5
36 shock absorber, compressed rubber blocks
37 wheel fairing, retracts with wheel
38 one-piece rear aluminum fairing
39 retracting fork
40 screw-jack cable drum
41 screw-jack endless cable
42 oil tank, capacity 6.9 Imp gal (31 l)
43 oil tank filler
44 front, center and rear spars, plywood webs and spruce flanges
45 wing skins, diagonally cross-laminated spruce
46 wing ribs, birch plywood
47 split flaps
48 plywood-covered trailing edge
49 fabric-covered trailing edge
50 aileron control linkage
51 plywood-covered aileron, Frise type
52 pitot tube

# 1930-1940
## Luftwaffe the world's most powerful airforce at outbreak of the Second World War

The world did not have long to wait for the threatened storm to break. Germany signalled the start of the war when she launched her bombers and fighters against Poland on 1 September 1939 and took only a matter of hours to destroy Polish defenses in the first stage of Hitler's blitzkrieg.

Germany was the most advanced air power at the time since she had been preparing her military aviation throughout the thirties behind the smokescreen of a thriving commercial aviation industry. When Hitler lit the touchpaper of the Second World War he knew that he had the most formidable airforce in the world which had undergone invaluable battle training in the Spanish Civil War during the preceding three years. The Germans had 4,840 front-line aircraft, 1,750 of which were bombers and 1,200 fighters. This strength was constantly reinforced by aircraft production running at 1,000 planes a month; in 1939 alone a total of 8,300 military aircraft of all types were built.

Fighter planes had changed very little during the 1920s, having played an important part in deciding the outcome of the First World War; by the second half of the 1930s, Germany and Britain had reached a fairly well-matched confrontation. Both countries favoured the monoplane, whose high-level performance was the result of new, sophisticated engines and continual aerodynamic refinement, allied to powerful weaponry. In each of these areas the Messerschmitt Bf.109 [which was the standard German fighter developed for war purposes and which was to undergo little change during the conflict] could be compared with the contemporary Hawker Hurricane and Supermarine Spitfire. The main disparity between the two nations lay in the fact that Germany had been preparing for war for some years while Britain had to try to make up for lost time when it became clear in the late thirties that war was unavoidable.

While these two countries were very advanced aeronautical powers, the remaining European nations had lagged well behind and in some cases efforts to modernize came too late to stem the German advance. Prior to the German invasion, France's aviation industry had embarked upon an ambitious production program in an all-out effort to try to catch up. Some of the aircraft developed at that time were certainly a match for their German or British counterparts: the Morane-Saulnier M.S.406, the Bloch MB-152 and the Dewoitine D.520; but production got under way too late to save France from capitulation.

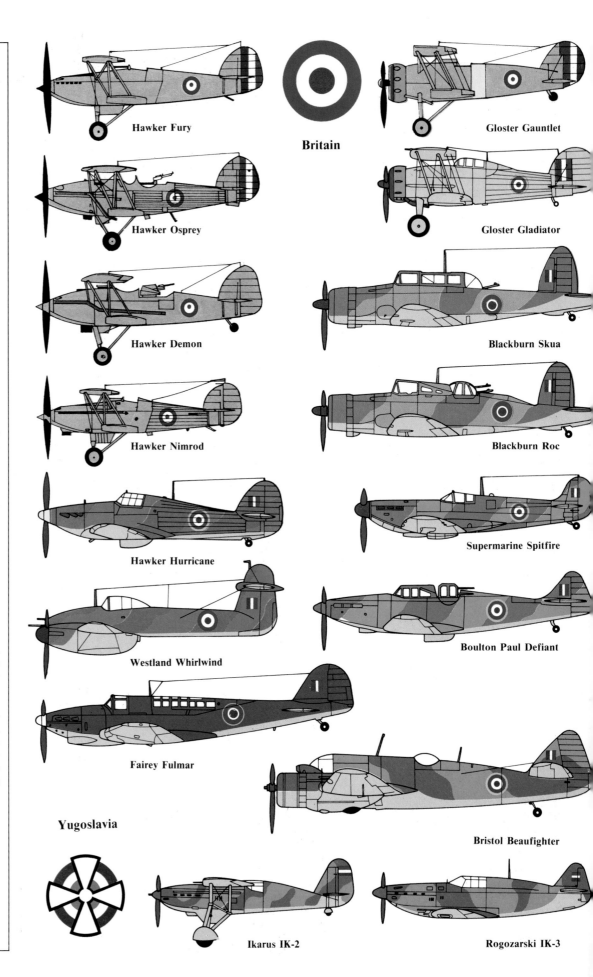

Hawker Fury

Gloster Gauntlet

**Britain**

Hawker Osprey

Gloster Gladiator

Hawker Demon

Blackburn Skua

Hawker Nimrod

Blackburn Roc

Hawker Hurricane

Supermarine Spitfire

Westland Whirlwind

Boulton Paul Defiant

Fairey Fulmar

Bristol Beaufighter

**Yugoslavia**

Ikarus IK-2

Rogozarski IK-3

Morane-Saulnier M.S.225

Loire 46

Germany

Henschel Hs.123

Morane-Saulnier M.S.406

Nieuport-Delage NID 622

Heinkel He.51

Dewoitine D.27

France

Blériot-Spad 510

Heinkel He.112

Dewoitine D.500

Arsenal VG-33

Arado Ar.68

Dewoitine D.520

Potez 630

Messerschmitt Bf.109

Hanriot NC-600

Caudron C.714

Messerschmitt Bf.110

Poland

Netherlands

Fokker D.XVII

Fokker D.XXI

Czechoslovakia

PZL P-7

Fokker G.1A

PZL P-24

Avia B-534

Fokker D.XXIII

77

# Supermarine Spitfire V B

1 Aerial stub attachment
2 Rudder upper hinge
3 Fabric-covered rudder
4 Rudder tab
5 Sternpost
6 Rudder tab hinge
7 Rear navigation light
8 Starboard elevator tab
9 Starboard elevator structure
10 Elevator balance
11 Tailplane front spar
12 IFF aerial
13 Castoring non-retractable tailwheel
14 Tailwheel strut
15 Fuselage double frame
16 Elevator control lever
17 Tailplane spar/fuselage attachment
18 Fin rear spar (fuselage frame extension)
19 Fin front spar (fuselage frame extension)
20 Port elevator tab hinge
21 Port elevator
22 IFF aerial
23 Port tailplane
24 Rudder control lever
25 Cross shaft
26 Tailwheel oleo access plate
27 Tailwheel oleo shock absorber
28 Fuselage angled frame
29 Battery compartment
30 Lower longeron
31 Elevator control cables
32 Fuselage construction
33 Rudder control cables
34 Radio compartment
35 Radio support tray
36 Flare chute
37 Oxygen bottle
38 Auxiliary long-range fuel tank (29 gal/132 liter)
39 Dorsal formation light
40 Aerial lead-in
41 HF aerial
42 Aerial mast
43 Cockpit aft glazing
44 Voltage regulator
45 Canopy track
46 Structural bulkhead
47 Headrest
48 Plexiglas canopy
49 Rear-view mirror
50 Entry flap (port)
51 Air bottles (alternative rear fuselage stowage)
52 Sutton harness
53 Pilot's seat (moulded Bakelite)
54 Datum longeron
55 Seat support frame
56 Wingroot fillet
57 Seat adjustment lever
58 Rudder pedal frame
59 Elevator control connecting tube
60 Control column spade grip
61 Trim wheel

62 Reflector gunsight
63 External windscreen armour
64 Instrument panel
65 Main fuselage fuel tank (48 gal/218 liter)
66 Fuel tank/longeron attachment fittings
67 Rudder pedals
68 Rudder bar
69 King post
70 Fuselage lower fuel tank (37 gal/168 liter)
71 Firewall/bulkhead

72 Engine bearer attachment
73 Steel tube bearers
74 Magneto
75 "Fishtail"/exhaust manifold
76 Gun heating "intensifier"
77 Hydraulic tank
78 Fuel filler cap
79 Air compressor intake
80 Air compressor
81 Rolls-Royce Merlin 45 engine
82 Coolant piping
83 Port cannon wing fairing
84 Flaps

85 Aileron control cables
86 Aileron push tube
87 Bellcrank
88 Aileron hinge
89 Port aileron
90 Machine gun access panels
91 Port wingtip
92 Port navigation light
93 Leading-edge skinning
94 Machine gun ports (protected)
95 20mm cannon muzzle
96 Three-blade constant-speed propeller

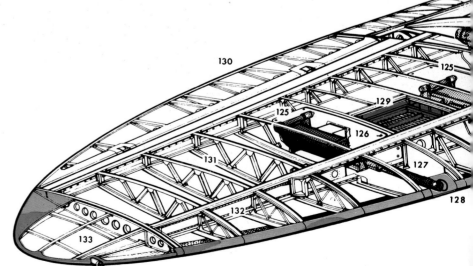

97 Spinner
98 Propeller hub
99 Coolant tank
100 Cowling fastening
101 Engine anti-vibration
    mounting pad
102 Engine accessories
103 Engine bearers
104 Main engine support member
105 Coolant pipe
106 Exposed oil tank
107 Port mainwheel
108 Mainwheel fairing

109 Carburettor air intake
110 Stub/spar attachment
111 Mainwheel leg pivot point
112 Main spar
113 Leading-edge ribs (diagonals
    deleted for clarity)
114 Mainwheel leg shock
    absorber
115 Mainwheel fairing
116 Starboard mainwheel
117 Angled axle
118 Cannon barrel support fairing
119 Spar cut-out

120 Mainwheel well
121 Gun heating pipe
122 Flap structure
123 Cannon wing fairing
124 Cannon magazine drum (120
    rounds)
125 Machine gun support brackets
126 Gun access panels
127 0.303 in machine gun barrels
128 Machine gun ports
129 Ammunition boxes (350 rpg)
130 Starboard aileron construction
131 Wing ribs

132 Single-tube outer spar section
133 Wingtip structure
134 Starboard navigation light

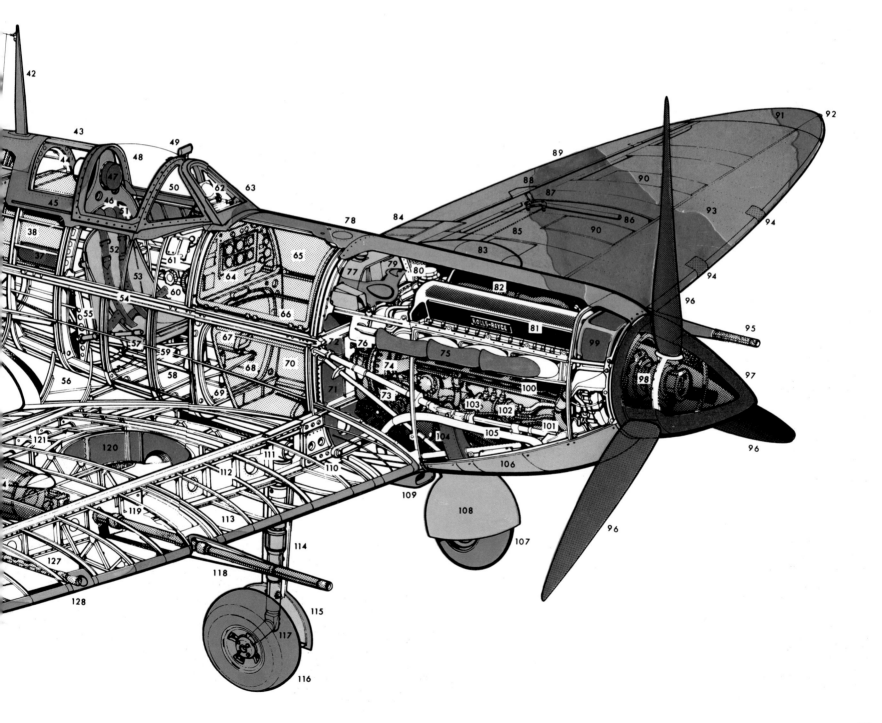

## 1930-1940
## The reality of war finds Italy unprepared

Italy was soon to find that facing hardened adversaries in a world war was very different from her easy victories in Ethiopia and Spain. The Regia Aeronautica had failed to move with the times; dazzled by the impressive show of strength of the early thirties and by the rhetoric of dictatorship, the military had failed to ensure that the Italian airforce was equipped with aircraft equal to fighting under such demanding conditions. On 10 June 1940 the Italian airforce had 3,296 aircraft but only 1,796 were front-line types, just over half the total strength. Of these 594 were fighters.

While other European nations had kept abreast of developments in aircraft construction, Italy had slipped behind and at the end of the thirties had still not wholeheartedly opted in favour of the monoplane fighter; in fact over half her front-line fighters were Fiat C.R.42 biplanes, among the best of their type but completely outclassed by the modern enemy fighters. The rest of her fighters were Fiat G.50 and Macchi M.C.200 monoplanes, the first of such to be built by the Italian aircraft industry.

The effectiveness of Italian combat planes was further hampered by the lack of really efficient and powerful engines in spite of all the efforts which had been made to develop the necessary technology. Only when the war was well under way were the Italians able to benefit from the engines developed by their German allies and develop really competitive aircraft.

In the case of the United States and Japan, late entrants to the conflict, an entirely different state of affairs prevailed. The United States underestimated Japanese strength to begin with, and was to find that although the American fighters were generally up-to-date, they were not quite a match for their enemies – and there were too few of them.

The disaster at Pearl Harbor produced a tremendous reaction and the whole of the United States' gigantic industrial might was directed towards retrieving lost time and missed opportunities. The result was that American military aircraft production caught up with the Japanese with relative ease and soon overtook the enemy in the quality and numbers of fighters manufactured. This same impetus was felt in all branches of aircraft production and Europe was also to benefit from this newly harnessed strength.

The other main combatant nation, the Soviet Union, also managed to overcome its technological backwardness relatively quickly and lay the foundations of its own powerful aviation industry. Among the best Soviet fighters to be developed in the war years were those designed by Mikoyan and Yakovlev.

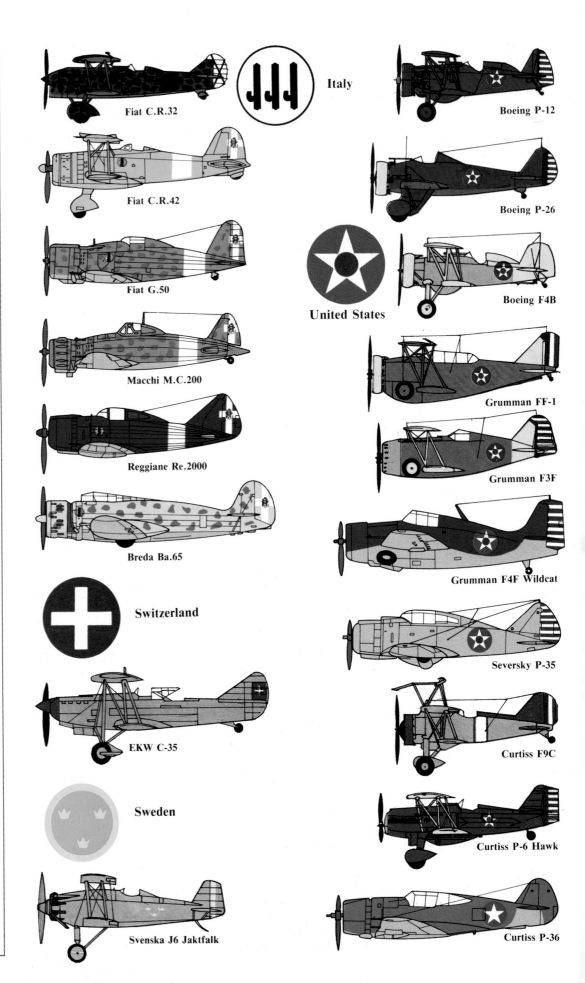

Fiat C.R.32

Italy

Fiat C.R.42

Fiat G.50

Macchi M.C.200

Reggiane Re.2000

Breda Ba.65

Switzerland

EKW C-35

Sweden

Svenska J6 Jaktfalk

Boeing P-12

Boeing P-26

United States

Boeing F4B

Grumman FF-1

Grumman F3F

Grumman F4F Wildcat

Seversky P-35

Curtiss F9C

Curtiss P-6 Hawk

Curtiss P-36

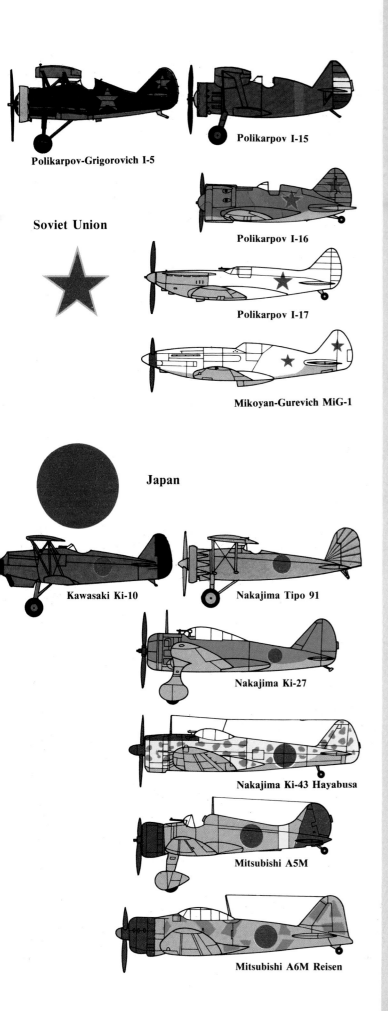

**Polikarpov-Grigorovich I-5**

**Polikarpov I-15**

Soviet Union

**Polikarpov I-16**

**Polikarpov I-17**

**Mikoyan-Gurevich MiG-1**

Japan

**Kawasaki Ki-10**

**Nakajima Tipo 91**

**Nakajima Ki-27**

**Nakajima Ki-43 Hayabusa**

**Mitsubishi A5M**

**Mitsubishi A6M Reisen**

**Nationalsozialistisches Fliegerkorps** (Arbeitsstab „Sudetenland", Sitz: Karlsbad, Parkstraße 41)

# 1930-1940
## British and German bombers: two design philosophies

The two countries had chosen to develop very different types of bombers; war would show which was the sounder policy. In the summer of 1940 the Luftwaffe was able to conduct its operations in an aura of invincibility, born of its victories in the Spanish Civil War. The German High Command had drawn certain inferences from the war in Spain and formulated very precise theories: they tended to think of the medium day bomber as their best strategic weapon and viewed their ground attack planes as their most efficient tactical weapon. When Britain came under direct attack, all these concepts were proved wrong.

During the Battle of Britain the Heinkel He.111 and Dornier Do.17 bombers, although fast, had insufficient range and were vulnerable to harassment by the well-piloted British fighter planes, making it necessary for bomber formations to have close and continuous protection by an escort of Messerschmitt Bf.109s. The escort fighters too, found their endurance range curtailed. While the Junkers Ju.87 Stuka had proved terrifyingly effective during the blitzkrieg in Europe, they were painfully slow and had insufficient armament to protect them from the Spitfires and Hurricanes. Even the Messerschmitt Bf.110 interceptor, Goering's "Zerstörer" [Destroyer] proved so unmaneuverable and slow that it had in turn to be escorted by other fighters. The Germans failed, however, to learn the lessons of the Battle of Britain and their continued lack of a heavy bomber which could stand up to wear and tear, put the Luftwaffe at a disadvantage.

Things turned out very differently for the British. The Battle of Britain vindicated the Royal Air Force's policy and signalled the start of a slow but unstoppable progress towards air supremacy with particularly obvious results in the bomber sector.

At the outbreak of war such front-line bombers as the twin-engine Bristol Blenheim, Handley Page Hampden, Vickers Wellington and Armstrong Whitworth Whitley, although effective and up-to-date when they first went into service, were not really suited to the strategic role they were called upon to play. They were soon joined, and then replaced, by the new generation of four-engine heavy bombers, the first of which, the Short Stirling, entered service in August 1940. It was soon followed by the Handley Page Halifax [in service from November 1940] and, in early 1942, by the Avro Lancaster. These two bombers, which far outstripped the Short Stirling showed that the RAF was on the right course and proved their strategic value. The Lancaster is still remembered as the RAF's most famous bomber.

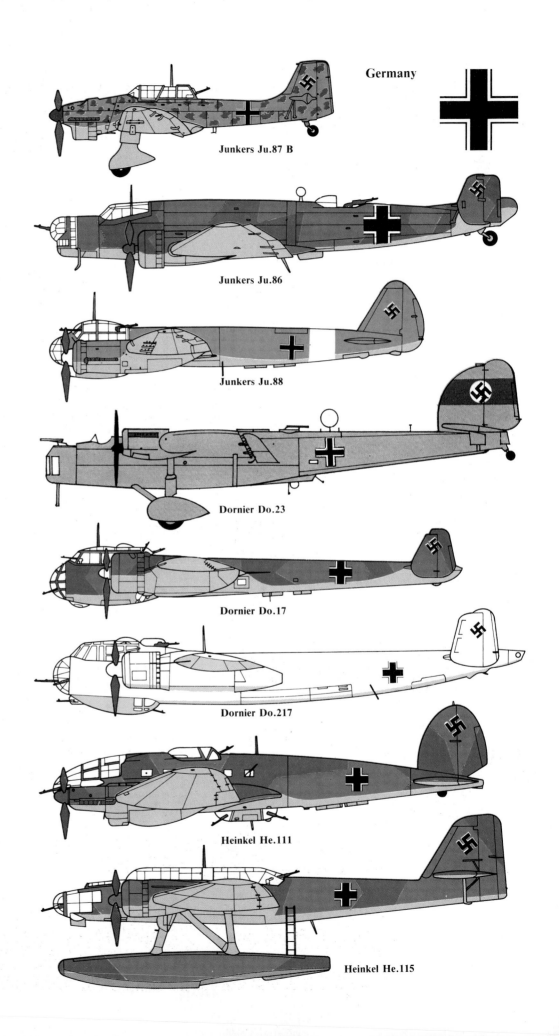

Germany

Junkers Ju.87 B

Junkers Ju.86

Junkers Ju.88

Dornier Do.23

Dornier Do.17

Dornier Do.217

Heinkel He.111

Heinkel He.115

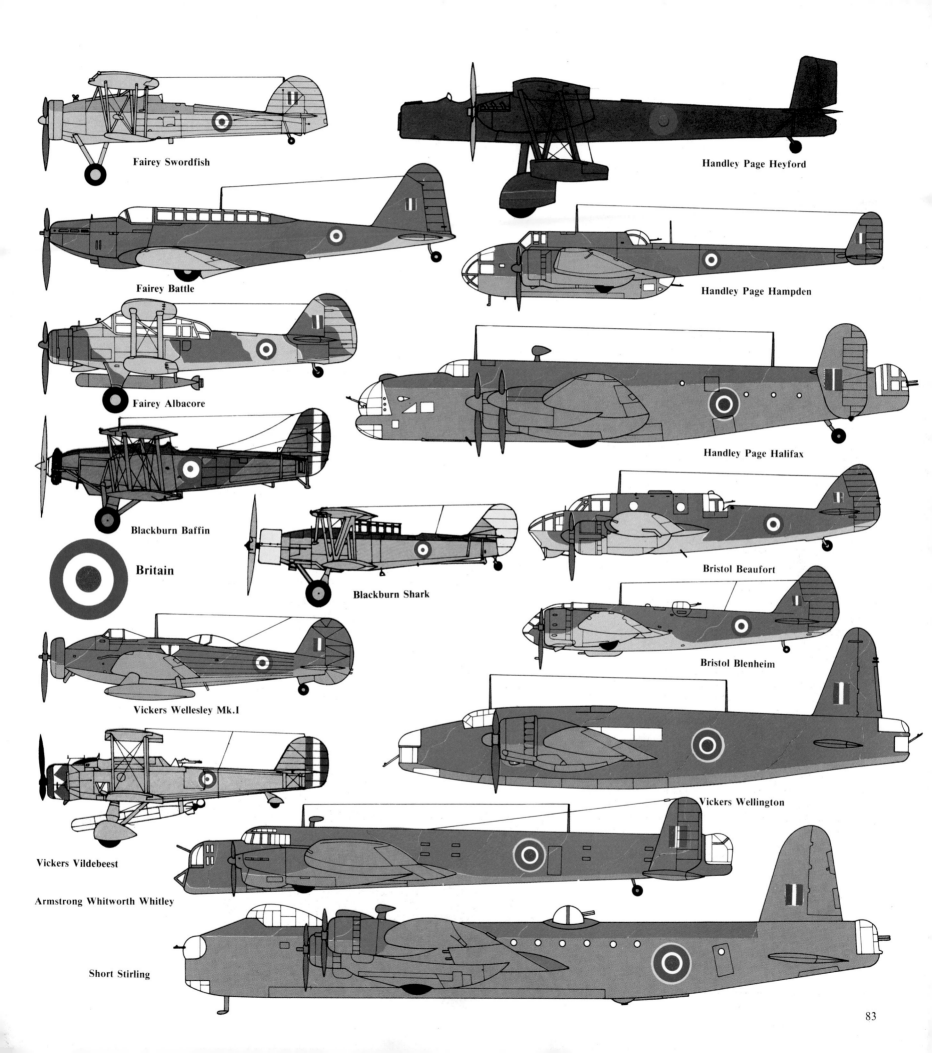

Fairey Swordfish

Handley Page Heyford

Fairey Battle

Handley Page Hampden

Fairey Albacore

Handley Page Halifax

Blackburn Baffin

Britain

Blackburn Shark

Bristol Beaufort

Bristol Blenheim

Vickers Wellesley Mk.1

Vickers Wellington

Vickers Vildebeest

Armstrong Whitworth Whitley

Short Stirling

83

## 1930-1940
## French, Dutch, Polish and Italian bombers at the outbreak of war

The Italians were also mistaken in their theories on strategy and in the conclusions they reached as to the best way to exploit air power; this inevitably influenced the choice of bombers for the Regia Aeronautica. Italy's production programs were planned along outdated guidelines, and bedevilled into the bargain by a general lack of efficient organization. The result was that Italy's front-line strength – made up mainly of Fiat B.R.20s, SIAI Marchetti S.M.79s and CANT Z.1007s and even, at the very beginning of the war, the old SIAI-Marchetti S.M.81 trimotors, was never anywhere near being on a par, in terms of quality or numbers, with the other Axis or Allied airforces.

Things never improved, not even after the Italian aircraft industry produced its one and only modern strategic bomber: the four-engine Piaggio P.108 which could be rated with the best of contemporary British and American production but which arrived too late to alter Italy's fortunes.

Because of France's early elimination from the war, it is more difficult to evaluate her combat planes. The Armée de l'Air's bomber wing was partly composed of totally obsolete aircraft like the Amiot 143, the Bloch 210 and the Farman F.222, but there were other, more up-to-date types which had been developed during the second half of the 1930s. These either reached the front line too late or were too mediocre to make any significant alteration to the course of the fighting.

The Bloch 131 was an example of the doubtful quality of many French bombers of the period, being immediately relegated to reconnaissance duties when it came into service in 1938. In contrast, the LeO 451 twin-engine medium bomber proved to be an excellent aircraft but was not ready in time to see war service. Another promising twin-engine bomber, the Amiot 354, had its maiden flight in prototype in January 1940 but only 89 reached squadrons before the armistice.

Two other interesting bombers, one Dutch, the other Polish, also had their operational lives curtailed in similar fashion: the Fokker T.VIII and the PZL P.37. The prototype of the former appeared in 1938, a twin-engine flying boat with good performance. Although about 40 were built, they were not to see combat before the Netherlands were overrun and were in fact used by the Germans in the Mediterranean and the North Sea.

The Polish PZL P.37 did see action; it had been designed in 1934 and started to go into squadron service in 1938. This modern twin-engine machine was considered one of the best combat planes ever produced by Poland.

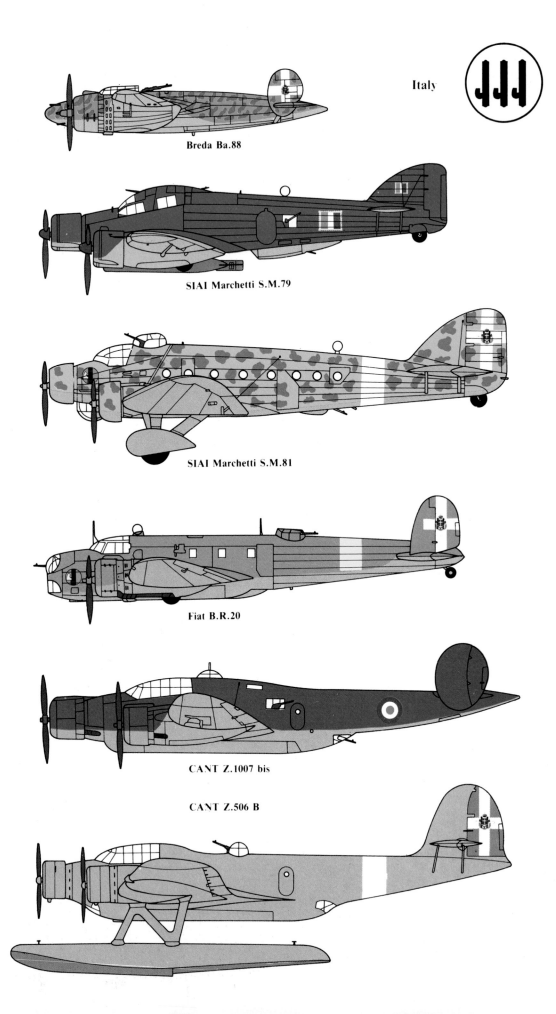

Italy

Breda Ba.88

SIAI Marchetti S.M.79

SIAI Marchetti S.M.81

Fiat B.R.20

CANT Z.1007 bis

CANT Z.506 B

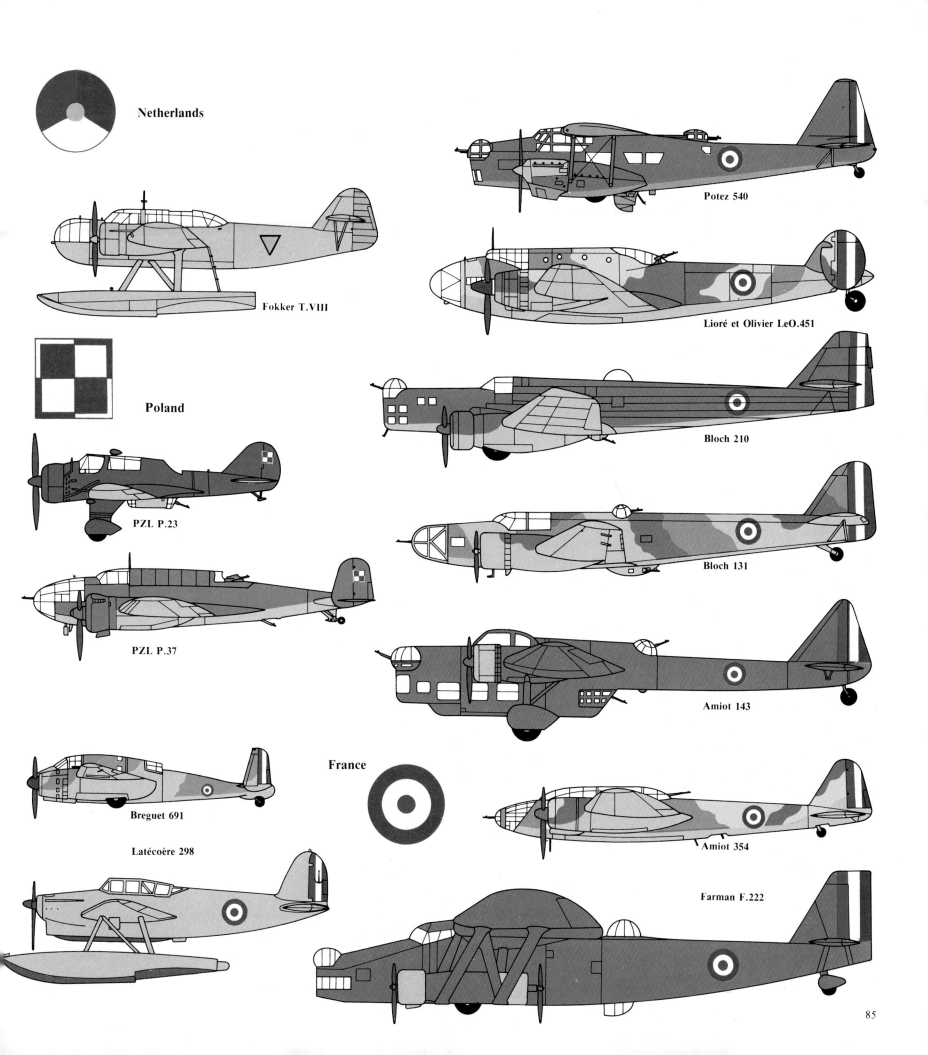

Netherlands

Fokker T.VIII

Poland

PZL P.23

PZL P.37

Breguet 691

Latécoère 298

France

Potez 540

Lioré et Olivier LeO.451

Bloch 210

Bloch 131

Amiot 143

Amiot 354

Farman F.222

85

## 1930-1940
## The United States, U.S.S.R. and Japan lag behind Europe in bomber development

The outbreak of war caught the Red Army's airforce short of bombers which could measure up to their German counterparts. As with fighters, it was some time before Soviet industry mobilized fully to supply front-line squadrons with planes capable of testing the Luftwaffe. One of the oldest bombers in service when the Germans invaded, was the Tupolev TB-3 [ANT-6], a relic of the twenties.

Another enormous aircraft which was still in service, was the Kalinin K-7, built in 1933, a gigantic multiengine specimen as useless as it was vulnerable. The most efficient bomber in the early stages of the war, was the twin-engine Tupolev SB-2 which had won its spurs in the Spanish Civil War. Progress in strategic bomber construction came with the development of the Ilyushin Il-4, a modern twin-engine airplane which went into service in 1940 and was to become the most widely-used Soviet bomber of the war.

The United States found itself in a somewhat similar, though not altogether analogous situation when Europe was plunged into war. Many of the bombers in service belonged to a bygone generation, and the early four-engine Boeing B-17s, which subsequently played such a decisive role in all the war theaters, were only just beginning to reach front-line squadrons.

Among U.S. operational medium bombers was the twin-engine Douglas B-18, a derivative of the DC-2, which replaced the obsolete Martin B-10, in service since 1934. The breathing space between the outbreak of war in Europe and Pearl Harbor proved vital, enabling the United States to start up-dating her military aviation, so when she entered the war it was immediately evident that the American industrial infrastructure could far outstrip that of any of her enemies [and allies].

Some of the most crucial air battles of the war took place in the Pacific theater with carrier-borne aircraft from the U.S. and Japanese fleets; at no time was this the case in the European battle zone.

Japan concentrated on developing her airforce until the time was ripe for attack and therefore began the war in better shape than her main adversary . The quality of Japanese aircraft was not particularly outstanding [they were generally inferior to contemporary European planes] but Japan had had time to accumulate very large fleets. The Mitsubishi G3M was typical of the standard Japanese front-line bomber at the outbreak of war [the prototype appeared in 1934] and underwent little modification throughout its long career.

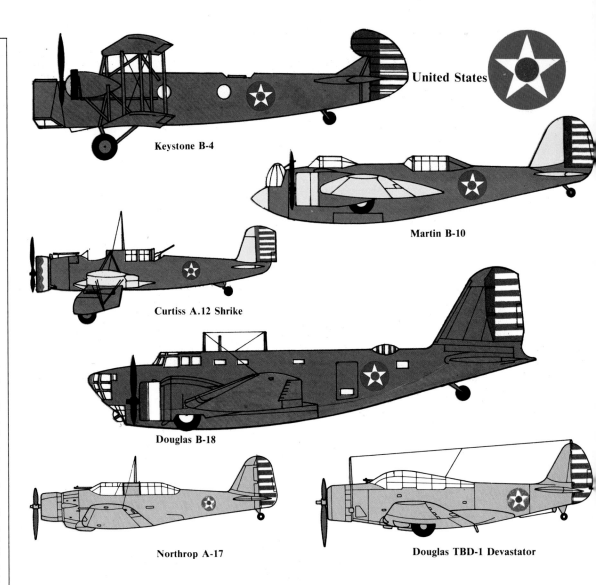

United States

Keystone B-4

Martin B-10

Curtiss A.12 Shrike

Douglas B-18

Northrop A-17

Douglas TBD-1 Devastator

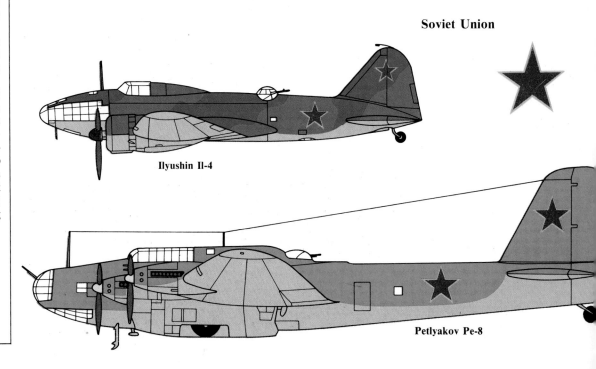

Soviet Union

Ilyushin Il-4

Petlyakov Pe-8

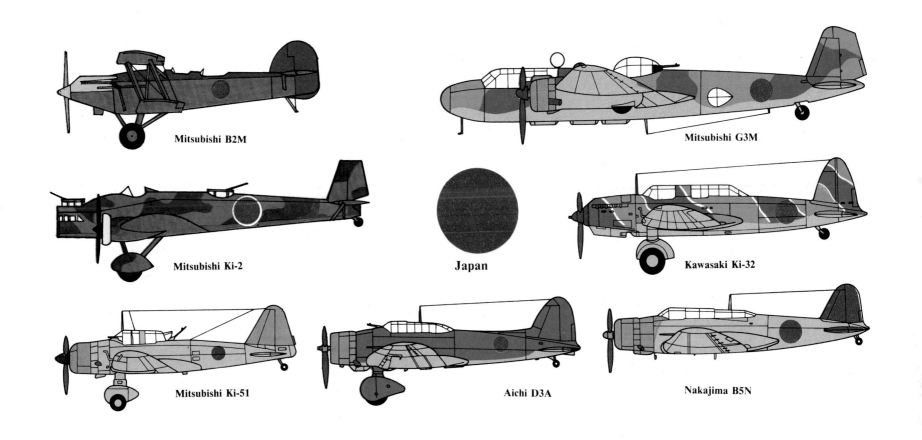

Mitsubishi B2M

Mitsubishi G3M

Mitsubishi Ki-2

Japan

Kawasaki Ki-32

Mitsubishi Ki-51

Aichi D3A

Nakajima B5N

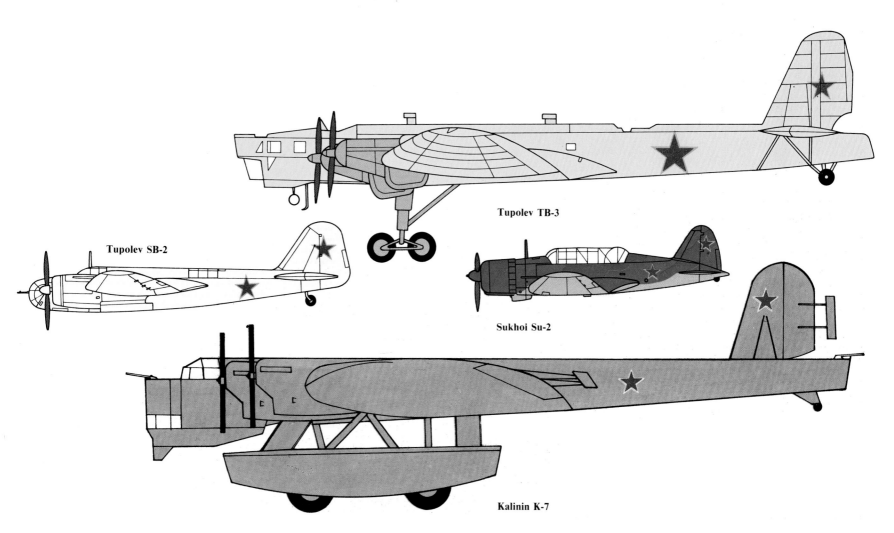

Tupolev TB-3

Tupolev SB-2

Sukhoi Su-2

Kalinin K-7

**National markings of military aircraft from 1936 to 1945**

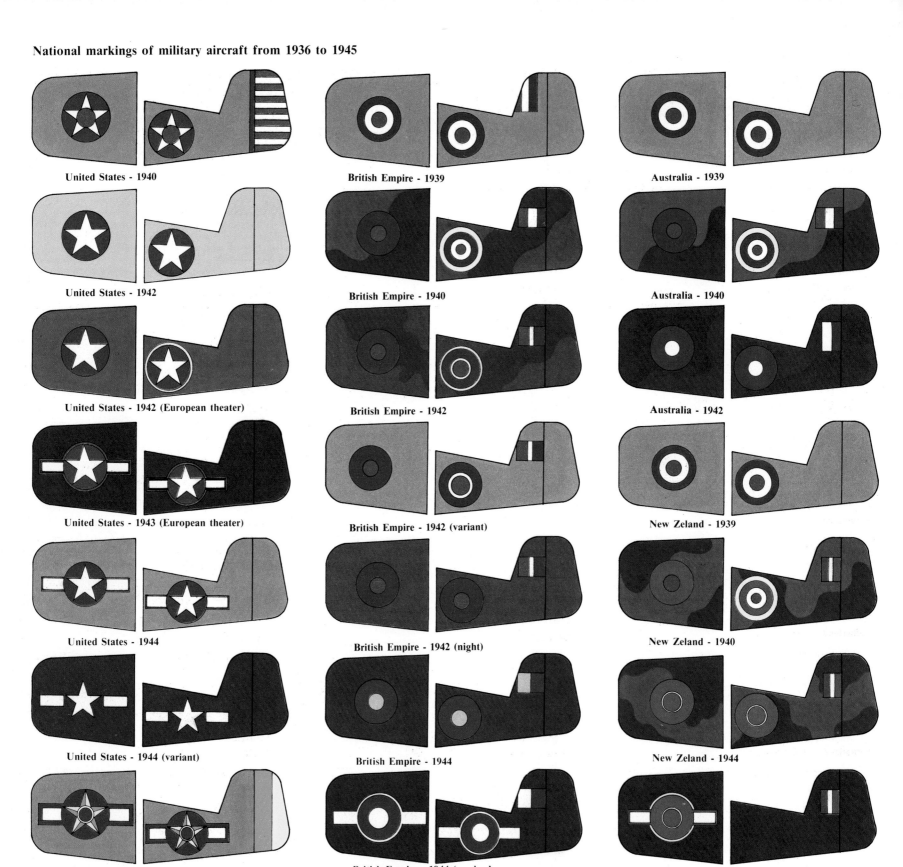

United States - 1940

United States - 1942

United States - 1942 (European theater)

United States - 1943 (European theater)

United States - 1944

United States - 1944 (variant)

Brazil - 1945 (European theater)

British Empire - 1939

British Empire - 1940

British Empire - 1942

British Empire - 1942 (variant)

British Empire - 1942 (night)

British Empire - 1944

British Empire - 1944 (carrier-borne
aircraft Pacific theater)

Australia - 1939

Australia - 1940

Australia - 1942

New Zeland - 1939

New Zeland - 1940

New Zeland - 1944

New Zeland - 1944 (carrier-borne aircraft)

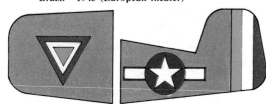

Mexico - 1945 (Pacific theater)

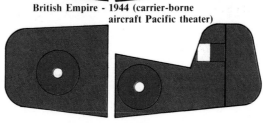

British Empire - 1944 (carrier-borne aircraft
Pacific theater - variant)

France - 1939

France - 1941 (Free French air force)

France - 1941 (Vichy air force)

Netherlands - 1939

Netherlands - 1940

Netherlands - 1942 (Far East theater)

Belgium - 1940

USSR

USSR (variant)

USSR (variant)

Poland - 1939

Denmark - 1940

Norway - 1940

Greece - 1940

Czechoslovakia - 1938

Slovakia - 1940

Slovakia - 1943

Yugoslavia - 1941

Croatia - 1942

Croatia - 1944

Yugoslavia - 1944

Yugoslavia - 1945

89

# National markings of military aircraft from 1936 to 1945

Germany – 1938

Germany – 1939

Germany – 1940

Germany – 1944

Germany – 1944 (alternative schemes)

Finland – 1939

Finland – 1944

Italy – 1936

Italy – 1939

Italy – 1940

Italy – 1944 (Co-belligerent Air Force)

Italy – 1944 (RSI)

Italy – 1945 (RSI)

Iraq

Bulgaria – 1939

Bulgaria – 1940

Bulgaria – 1944

Romania – 1941

Romania – 1944

Hungary – 1941

Hungary – 1944

Hungary – 1944 (variant)

Japan

Japan (variant)

Japan – 1944 (variant)

China

China   Nanking Government

Cochin China

Manchuria

Austria – 1938

Egypt

Estonia – 1937

Latvia – 1937

Lithuania – 1937

Philippines – 1941

Indonesia – 1945 (Provisional Government)

Spain – 1937 (Republican)

Spain – 1937 (Nationalist)

Spain – 1939

Portugal

Sweden

Switzerland

Turkey

# 1930-1940
## Allied and Axis reconnaissance, training and transport aircraft

In the Second World War far greater use was made of support aircraft than had been the case in the earlier conflict. Military transport and reconnaissance aircraft played every bit as vital a part in the tactical and strategic development of air warfare, as the fighter or the bomber. It is enough to recall the German airborne invasion of Crete or the crucial role of airborne troops in the Allied landings in Normandy. The war at sea could not have been won without the use of patrol aircraft in staking out the targets or controlling the deployment of whole fleets as they proved into battle formation. The highly specialized aircraft of today owe much to the technological advances made during the years of war.

At the outbreak of war many of the aircraft in operation harked back to the early thirties and were unsuited to the needs of modern warfare; a case in point were the French, for whom time ran out before the situation could be rectified. German aircraft, as was to be expected, showed up to advantage, none more so than the Junkers Ju.52/3m transport and the marine-patrol Focke Wulf Fw.200 Condor ["Scourge of the Atlantic"]. Outstanding on the British side were the Short Sunderland flying boat and the Supermarine Walrus.

There remain land-based reconnaissance aircraft and trainers, the latter of fundamental importance in the preparation, in the shortest possible time, of the enormous numbers of pilots and aircrew needed to carry on the war. Some reconnaissance aircraft made their mark immediately, for instance the "German Fieseler Fi.156 Storch, which served on all fronts throughout the war, the name "Stork" being descriptive of its short take-off capability, the first such aircraft of its kind.

Another outstanding reconnaissance plane was the Focke Wulf Fw.189, aptly called "Das fliegende Auge" – the Flying Eye – because of its exceptional qualities. The British Westland Lysander had much in common with the German Storch; it was used on many clandestine operations involving Resistance movements throughout Europe. Among the most outstanding biplane trainer aircraft were the German Bücker Bü.131 Jungmann and the British Avro Anson and de Havilland Tiger Moth, vast numbers of which were produced; even in the dangerous skies of wartime Europe, they carried a whiff of the carefree days of flying in the thirties.

As a basic trainer, the biplane remained unsurpassed over a long period of time. Over 10,000 Boeing-Stearman PT-17 Kaydets were in use with the USAAF and the U.S. Navy before production ceased in 1945. The Japanese equivalent, the Yokosuka K5Y, of which a total of 5,770 were built, was in production for ten years, from 1935.

*continued on page 96*

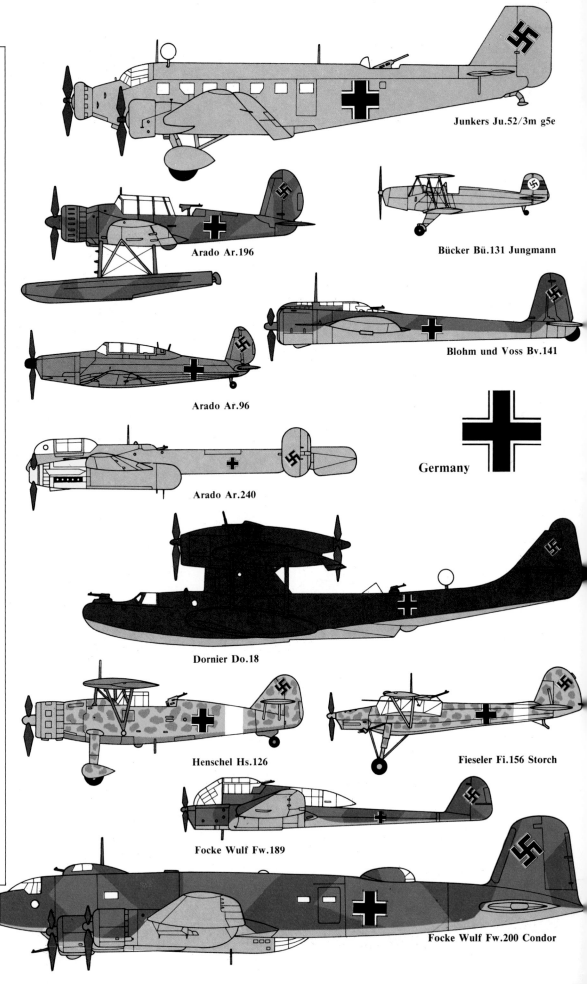

Junkers Ju.52/3m g5e

Arado Ar.196

Bücker Bü.131 Jungmann

Blohm und Voss Bv.141

Arado Ar.96

Arado Ar.240

Germany

Dornier Do.18

Henschel Hs.126

Fieseler Fi.156 Storch

Focke Wulf Fw.189

Focke Wulf Fw.200 Condor

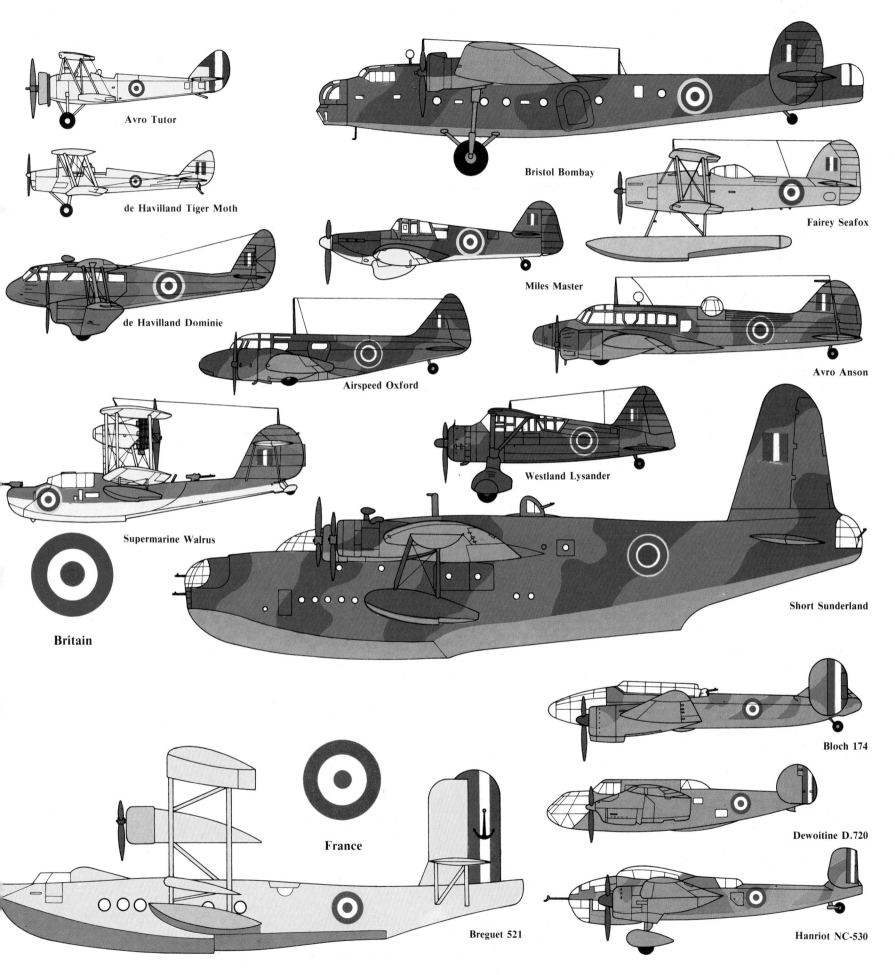

Avro Tutor

de Havilland Tiger Moth

de Havilland Dominie

Airspeed Oxford

Supermarine Walrus

Britain

Bristol Bombay

Miles Master

Westland Lysander

Fairey Seafox

Avro Anson

Short Sunderland

France

Breguet 521

Bloch 174

Dewoitine D.720

Hanriot NC-530

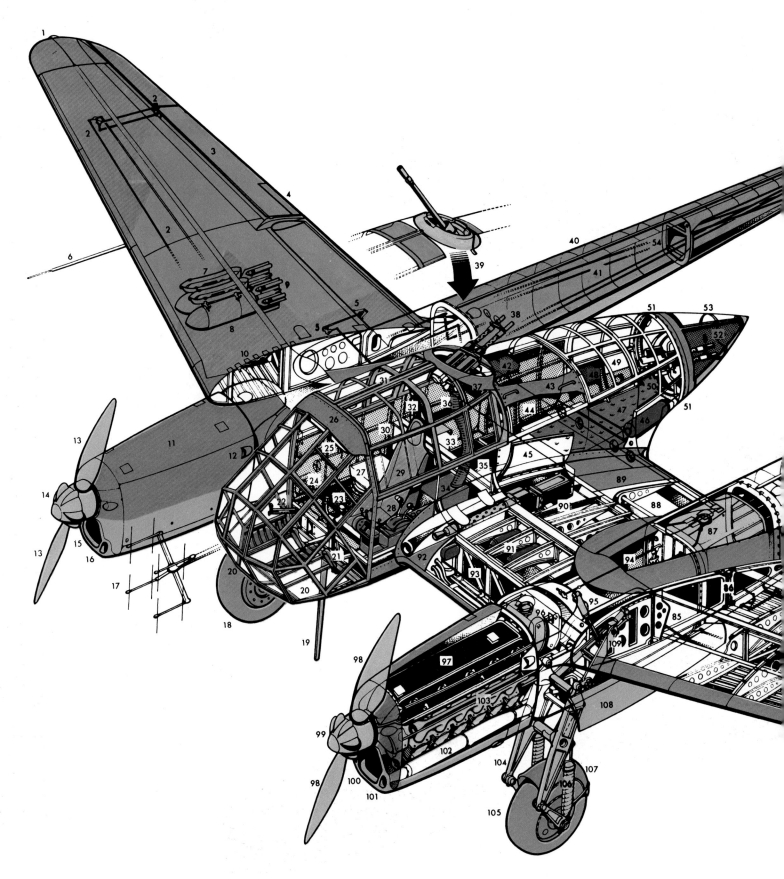

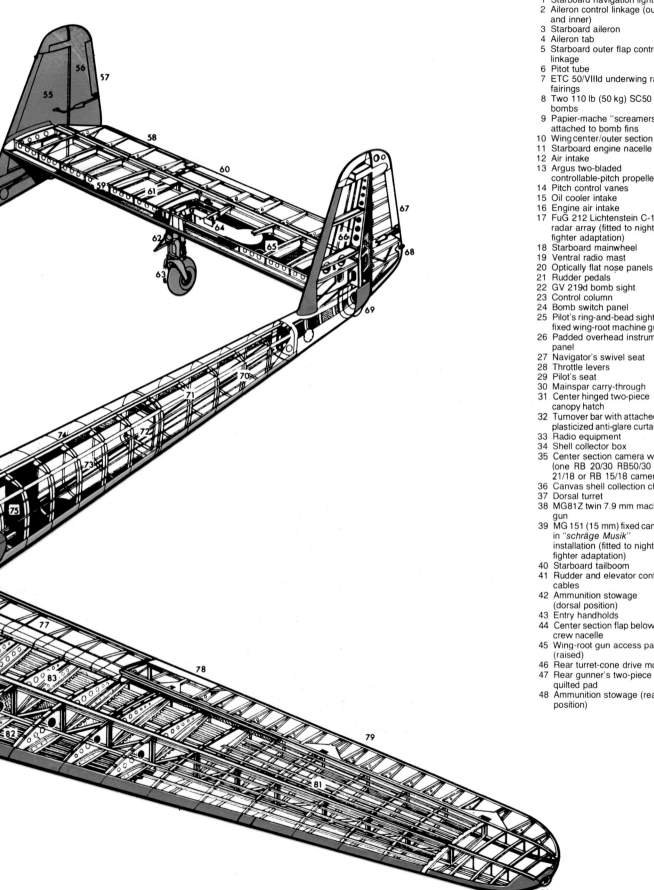

1 Starboard navigation light
2 Aileron control linkage (outer and inner)
3 Starboard aileron
4 Aileron tab
5 Starboard outer flap control linkage
6 Pitot tube
7 ETC 50/VIIId underwing rack fairings
8 Two 110 lb (50 kg) SC50 bombs
9 Papier-mache "screamers" attached to bomb fins
10 Wing center/outer section join
11 Starboard engine nacelle
12 Air intake
13 Argus two-bladed controllable-pitch propeller
14 Pitch control vanes
15 Oil cooler intake
16 Engine air intake
17 FuG 212 Lichtenstein C-1 radar array (fitted to night fighter adaptation)
18 Starboard mainwheel
19 Ventral radio mast
20 Optically flat nose panels
21 Rudder pedals
22 GV 219d bomb sight
23 Control column
24 Bomb switch panel
25 Pilot's ring-and-bead sight (for fixed wing-root machine guns)
26 Padded overhead instrument panel
27 Navigator's swivel seat
28 Throttle levers
29 Pilot's seat
30 Mainspar carry-through
31 Center hinged two-piece canopy hatch
32 Turnover bar with attached plasticized anti-glare curtain
33 Radio equipment
34 Shell collector box
35 Center section camera well (one RB 20/30 RB50/30 RB 21/18 or RB 15/18 camera)
36 Canvas shell collection chute
37 Dorsal turret
38 MG81Z twin 7.9 mm machine gun
39 MG 151 (15 mm) fixed cannon in "schräge Musik" installation (fitted to night fighter adaptation)
40 Starboard tailboom
41 Rudder and elevator control cables
42 Ammunition stowage (dorsal position)
43 Entry handholds
44 Center section flap below crew nacelle
45 Wing-root gun access panel (raised)
46 Rear turret-cone drive motor
47 Rear gunner's two-piece quilted pad
48 Ammunition stowage (rear position)

49 Rear canopy.opening
50 MG 81Z twin 7.9 mm machine guns (trunnion mounted)
51 Revolving Ikaria powered cone turret
52 Field-of-fire cut-out
53 Aft glazing
54 Tailboom mid-section strengthening frame
55 Starboard tailfin
56 Starboard rudder
57 Rudder tab
58 Elevator construction
59 Tailplane forward spar
60 Elevator tab
61 Tailplane construction
62 Tailwheel hinged (two-piece) door
63 Tailwheel (swivelling)
64 Tailwheel retraction mechanism
65 Tailwheel well (offset to port)
66 Tailfin construction
67 Rudder tab
68 Rear navigation light
69 Tail bumper
70 Tailboom frames
71 Tailboom upper longeron
72 Mid-section strengthening frame
73 Tail surface control cables
74 External stiffening strake (upper and lower)
75 Master compass
76 Wing-root fairing
77 Port outer flap construction
78 Aileron tab
79 Aileron construction
80 Port navigation light
81 Wing stringers (upper shell)
82 Lower shell wing inner skin stringers
83 Two-piece shaped wing ribs
84 Mainspar structure
85 Mainspar/boom attachment point
86 Rear spar/boom attachment point
87 Port fuel tank (24.2 Imp gal/ 110 liter of 87° A-2)
88 Center section one-piece flap
89 Wing walkway
90 Fixed 7.9 mm MG 17 machine gun
91 Pilot's oxygen (3.5 pint/2 liter) bottles in port wing with navigator's and gunner's supply (four 2 liter bottles) in starboard wing
92 Gun port
93 Forward spar structure (with warm-air and oil-pressure lines)
94 Wheel well
95 Mainwheel retraction jack
96 Oil tank (99 Imp gal/45 liter capacity)
97 Argus As 410A-1 12-cylinder inverted-V air-cooled engine
98 Two-blade controllable-pitch Argus propeller
99 Pitch control vanes
100 Oil cooler air intake
101 Engine air intake
102 Oil cooler trunking
103 Exhaust collector
104 H-section hydraulically-operated main undercarriage members
105 Port mainwheel
106 Shock absorbers
107 Mudguard
108 Mainwheel door
109 Mainwheel retraction mechanism

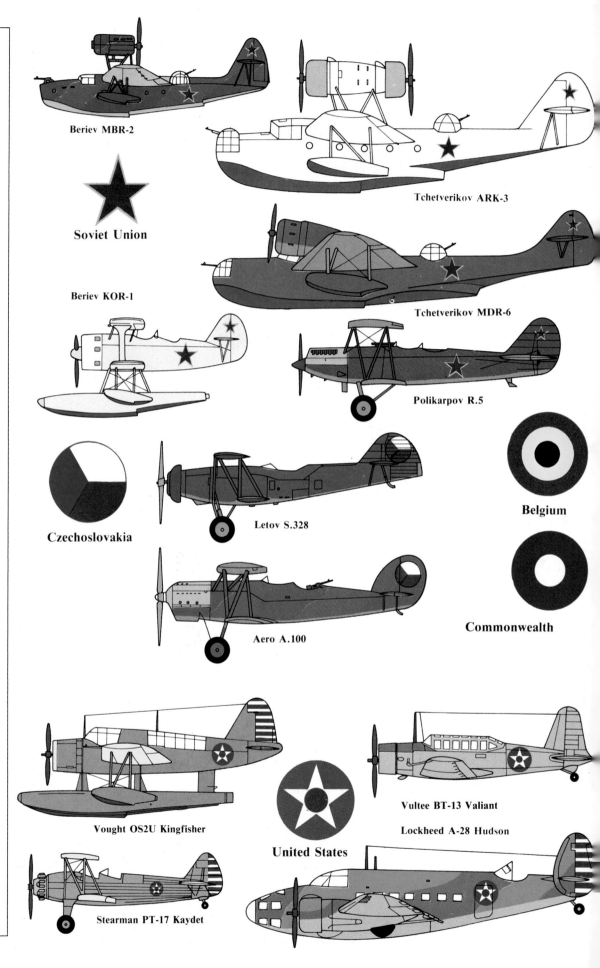

*continued from page 92*

Where advanced training for pilots and aircrew demanded more sophisticated types there were the British Airspeed Oxford and the Miles Master; the German Arado Ar.96 [total production of which topped 11,500]; the American Vultee BT-13 Valiant and Cessna AT-17; and the Australian Commonwealth CA-3 Wirraway, the first product [1939] of Australia's newly established aviation industry.

The Wirraway was a variant of the North American NA-33 [itself a descendant of the prolific and renowned AT-6 Texan series], which was built under license as the threat of a Japanese invasion of Australia seemed imminent. The Wirraway was assigned far more varied and demanding duties than its original manufacturers ever envisaged. In the hands of the versatile RAAF pilots, a trainer took on the protean roles of bomber, reconnaissance aircraft and even fighter, in each case with admirable results.

More than in any other theater of war, the conflict in the Pacific demonstrated the importance of maritime reconnaissance; large, multiengine marine patrol aircraft could stay airborne for hours on end, covering vast stretches of ocean. In the early stages of the war the Japanese employed the Kawanishi H6K for this purpose and the Americans the earlier PBY Catalina series; but small carrier-borne reconnaissance aircraft also flew countless patrol missions; the best known were the Vought OS2U Kingfisher and its Japanese equivalent, the Nakajima E8N.

The Italians used their IMAM Ro.43 for wartime reconnaissance duties [a navalized version of the Ro.37 landplane]. This elderly biplane had first flown in 1934. It was backed up by large numbers – a total of 1,693 aircraft made up of five main variants – of Caproni light twin-engine aircraft, manufactured from 1936 onwards. The Ca.309 Ghibli was followed in 1937 by the Ca.310 Libeccio and from 1939, by the improved and final series Ca.311, 313 and 314. These reconnaissance aircraft, which were to remain in service during the remainder of Italy's participation in the war, proved themselves versatile and reliable in a variety of roles.

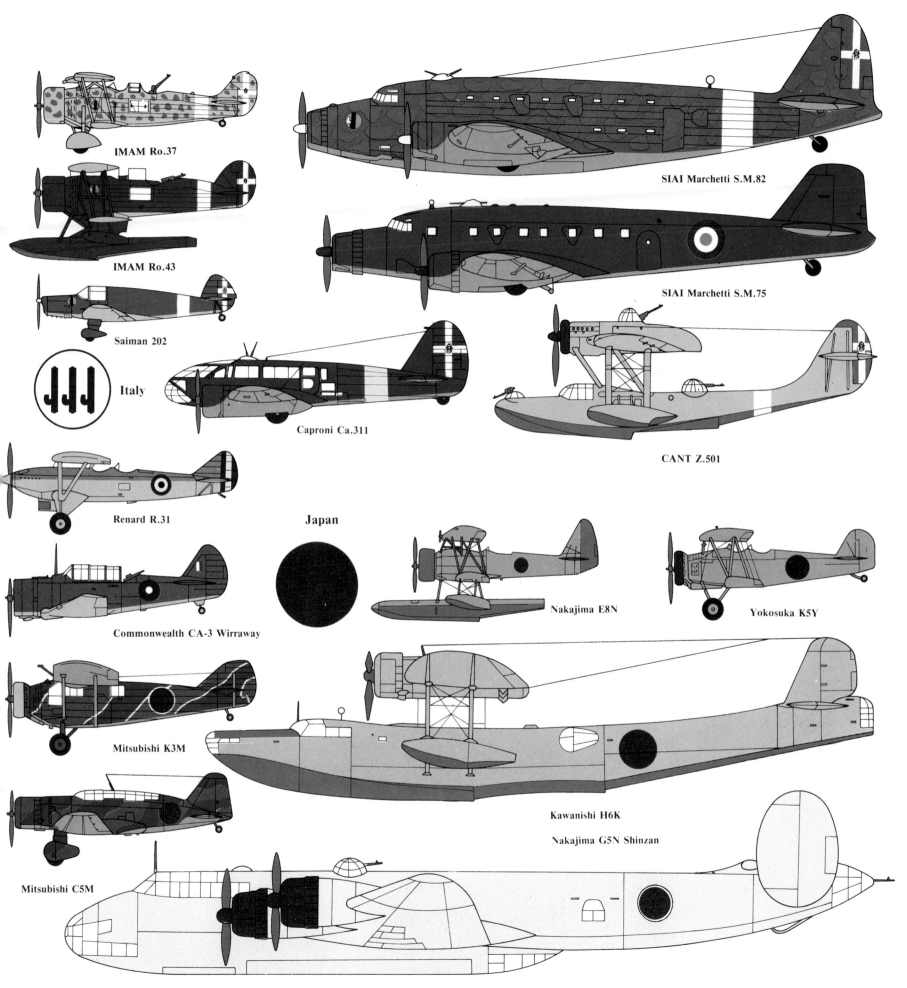

IMAM Ro.37

IMAM Ro.43

Saiman 202

Italy

Renard R.31

Commonwealth CA-3 Wirraway

Mitsubishi K3M

Mitsubishi C5M

SIAI Marchetti S.M.82

SIAI Marchetti S.M.75

Caproni Ca.311

CANT Z.501

Japan

Nakajima E8N

Yokosuka K5Y

Kawanishi H6K

Nakajima G5N Shinzan

Coming Right Up!

海軍飛行兵徴募

# 1940
# 1950

## THE SECOND WORLD WAR

When Germany invaded Poland in September 1939 many believed that the war would soon be over. Exactly six years later, in September 1945, the world found it hard to believe that Japan had finally capitulated [on board the U.S. battleship *Missouri,* anchored in the Bay of Tokyo] and that the most widespread and bloody conflict ever experienced was actually over. Both these events were brought about through the use of a relatively new but already indispensable means of fighting a war: the airplane. Hitler's use of wave-upon-wave of fighters and bombers which he unleashed on Poland on 1 September 1939 brought the Polish armed forces to their knees and vindicated the Führer's faith in his blitzkrieg theories. On 6 and 9 August 1945 two American bombers were to drop their atom bombs on Hiroshima and Nagasaki, the final, decisive blow which crushed any lingering Japanese resistance and put an end to her refusal to surrender.

Historians agree that in the long years of war which separated these two events, the whole course of the conflict and its shifting fortunes, first to one side, then the other, depended mainly on which country could muster the greatest number of technically superior aircraft and gain air superiority. Air power was the factor which decided the progress of hostilities in Europe, from the Battle of Britain to the strategic bombing raids on Germany and the Allied landings in Normandy. The same was true of the war in the Pacific, beginning with the Japanese attack on Pearl Harbor, to the battles of Midway and the great carrier-borne aircraft engagements, culminating in the American raids on Japanese territory.

Once more it was seen that nothing speeds up the evolution of aircraft as effectively as war. Between 1939 and 1945 the airplane underwent such changes that by the end of the conflict it was quite unlike any of the aircraft produced during the preceding twenty years of peace. The best piston-engine fighters could reach speeds in the region of 460 mph [750 km/h], nearly twice the speed of the last biplanes; of the bombers which were developed during the war years, the American B-29 proved the best and most effective aircraft of its category; its operational ceiling was so high, its speed so great and it was so well armed that it was practically invulnerable to enemy fire – whether from antiaircraft guns from below or enemy fighters in the sky.

Amazing technological progress was made both in materials and in engine design. The potential of the piston-engine had been exploited to the full and this type of power plant was gradually being replaced by jet propelled aircraft which the Germans and the British were the first to develop, racing against time and each other. Industrial activity reached fever pitch with record production levels, achieved and sustained by an unprecedented mobilization and organization of the work force. The developed world's economy was turned into a vast war machine, working flat out and depleting its reserves of manpower and materials faster than ever before. Under these conditions it was inevitable that the richest countries, those which could draw on unlimited stocks of raw materials and labour for a well organized war effort, should ultimately win the war.

It is therefore well worth examining how each great power developed and deployed its military aviation during the dark days of the war. One of the most significant developments came about when those countries which had no tradition of fostering the development of their military aviation [such as Japan and the Soviet Union] decided to establish themselves as air powers, and join the ranks of those nations which had long favored the possession of a strong airforce [as was the case with the U.S.A. and several European countries]. Another dominant trend was the gradual assumption by the United States of the leading role in aviation technology and production, supplanting the European aeronautical industries to a great extent. Whereas Japan's rise to a position of great strength in military aviation proved ephemeral [the war cost Japan her airforce], the Soviet Union's acquisition of air power was a gradual and inexorable process, fuelled by the postwar political groupings of the great world powers into two main opposing blocs.

When Europe was plunged into war, America's military aviation was ill-prepared for combat, especially as regards the caliber of its aircraft. Industry had not been encouraged by successive governments to gear itself to mass-producing aircraft of high quality. The first boost came in September 1939 with the suspension of the 1935 Neutrality Act [which had prohibited the export of any military equipment] and the adoption of a cash-and-carry policy which facilitated the sale of armaments. This meant that the U.S. aircraft industry could fulfil orders for military aircraft from France and Britain, the first two powers to make a concerted attempt to oppose the German advance.

It was some time, however, before the U.S. aviation industry moved into top gear; the war was already well under way, when in March 1941, the Lend-Lease Act was passed, a vital measure in view of Britain's straitened resources. In the two years preceding the United States' entry into the war [1940 and 1941] U.S. aircraft production totalled 6,028 and 19,445. Many of these aircraft went to strengthen the army and naval air forces: in 1939 the USAAF had a total of 2,400 aircraft of all types, by December 1941 this had risen to 3,305 serviceable planes. Over the same period of time the U.S. Navy Air Force's strength rose from 2,500 [600 being carrier-borne aircraft] to approximately 3,300. Organizational changes were also made: in June 1941 the USAAC [U.S. Army Air Corps] was given a greater degree of autonomy and renamed the USAAF [U.S. Army Air Force].

Hawker Typhoon, 1941

Obviously the real jolt which got things moving was the Japanese attack on Pearl Harbor; this disaster on 7 December 1941 meant, among other things, that the United States' war machine was boosted into top gear and revealed its awe-inspiring productivity. The U.S. aircraft industry not only met the growing needs of the USAAF and the U.S. Navy but also sent a sizeable proportion of its output to the Allies, mainly to Britain and the U.S.S.R. The statistics speak for themselves: in 1942, 47,836 aircraft were built in the United States [including 10,769 fighters and 12,627 bombers]; in 1943, 85,898 were manufactured [23,988 fighters and 29,355 bombers]; production rose to its highest level in 1944: 96,318 airplanes [38,873 fighters and 35,003 bombers]; in the last year of the war, 47,714 aircraft came off U.S. assembly lines [21,696 fighters and 16,492 bombers]. Total wartime military aircraft production, from 1941-45 reached 297,199: 99,742 fighters and 97,592 bombers, 35,743 of which were four-engine aircraft and 35,369 twin-engine. Besides this tremendous surge in quantity, the quality of U.S. aircraft also improved. By 1942 the early, transitional phase was over and the two American airforces had aircraft which were much better than those fielded by most of their enemies in the European and Pacific theaters of war. On 1 January 1945 the U.S. forces had a total of 86,000 combat planes.

Across the Atlantic, America's main ally, Britain, had been fighting since 3 September 1939 when she had declared war on Germany. The RAF seemed up to strength at the outbreak of war; in October 1939 front-line aircraft numbered 1,500 with as many again in support roles and production had reached a rate of 700 planes per month. Generally speaking, the aircraft in service with the RAF were a match for those fielded by the Luftwaffe. The end of the Battle of Britain [the first serious setback for German military might] triggered a phase of continuous acceleration in aircraft production, resulting in some of the most famous British planes of the war: the best versions of the Spitfire and the Mosquito; the Halifax and Lancaster – large strategic bombers which played such an important role in destroying the Third Reich's war industry. The first steps were taken toward the realization of one of aviation's most ambitious projects, the development and entry into service of a jet-engined warplane, the Gloster Meteor, which only saw combat in the last months

Messerschmitt Me.262, 1944

Supermarine Spitfire, 1940

Vought F4U, 1943

Mitsubishi J2M2, 1943

of the war and had been preceded by the German Me.262. Britain had the satisfaction, however, of knowing that she was the only one of the Allies to achieve this during the war.

Aircraft production rose very sharply, from 15,000 airplanes in 1940, to 20,100 in 1941; 23,671 in 1942; 26,263 in 1943 and to its maximum, 29,220 in 1944. The total number of all types of aircraft manufactured in Britain during the war was 125,254.

While the RAF soon felt the benefit of this massive boost, the Fleet Air Arm had to wait somewhat longer to have its strength increased: in September 1939 [the Fleet Air Arm had been constituted as a separate service in May of that year], it had 340 serviceable aircraft [225 of which were carrier-borne], and they were generally inferior to those flown by the RAF. It was not until 1942 that things began to improve, when a modernization program got under way and further planes started to arrive from the United States. By August 1945 the Fleet Air Arm had 1,300 front-line aircraft out of a total of 11,500.

The third major ally in the war against Germany was the Soviet Union. The weakness of her armed forces – and of her airforces in particular – was only too apparent from the very start of the German invasion [22 June 1941]. The Luftwaffe literally wiped out the Soviet airforce, which was equipped with planes dating well back into the thirties. The U.S.S.R. only started to recover in 1942, once her aviation industry had been reorganized and was working hard to produce more up-to-date types. Her allies made a very large contribution to her war effort: in the years 1942-44 the United States and Britain sent Russia a total of 14,833 aircraft of all types. Once the Russians were in less desperate straits, Soviet designers were able to make up for lost time and build some very good aircraft, many of them superior to contemporary German airplanes. Production of aircraft for the army and navy rose from 8,000 in 1942 to 18,000 in 1943 and then to 30,000 in 1944, reaching 25,000 in the first five months of 1945.

Events turned out very differently in France. During the ten-month period before France surrendered [3 September 1939 – 22 June 1940] the Armée de l'Air had no hope of retrieving the calamitous state of unpreparedness which had led to only 1,400 aircraft being in front-line service, two thirds of which were obsolescent. The reorganization of the French aircraft industry had been undertaken too late and there had been no attempt to launch efficient production programs. The situation was slightly improved as units started to receive some of the few new aircraft to go into squadron service and some help was forthcoming from France's allies, but this was far from being enough to change the course of the war. Time had already run out: two months before the armistice was signed, the total of front-line aircraft had risen to 1,501 of which 784 were fighters.

Of the Axis powers, Germany was, of course, the driving force in Europe while Japan took the initiative in Asia. In September 1939 the Third Reich had the world's most powerful airforce, successfully tried and tested in the Spanish Civil War which had ended only six months before. The Luftwaffe had 4,840 front-line aircraft – 1,750 of which were bombers and 1,200 fighters, all extremely modern – the most up-to-date in the world. This strength was being sustained at the rate of 1,000 new aircraft coming off the assembly lines each month.

The euphoria engendered by the Germans' early victories was soon tempered, however, by the first check to their advance, the defeat of the Battle of Britain. This proved a serious setback which revealed the failings of the German High Command's cherished theories as to what armaments were most effective: the Luftwaffe felt the lack of a heavy bomber. Decisions to develop such aircraft hung fire, however, and from then on Germany was to reap the consequences. A partially successful attempt was made to fill this gap by the sheer quantity of airplanes supplied to the Luftwaffe and by adapting existing types for varying operational roles. The German war machine responded well to the demands made of it: in 1940 aircraft manufacture of all types totalled 10,800; this rose to 11,800 the following year, and then to 15,600, 25,500 and 39,800 in 1942, 1943 and 1944 respectively, tailing off to 8,000 in the first five months of 1945. This desperate war effort also led to a milestone in aviation history: Germany built and put into service the world's first jet-powered combat plane: the Me.262 reached front-line units during the second half of 1944, followed shortly afterwards by the Arado Ar.234 bomber and the Heinkel He.162 interceptor.

Blohm und Voss Bv.222, 1942

Events followed a very similar pattern in Japan. When Japan triggered the war in the Pacific her airforce was extremely powerful and efficient; more importantly, the Western Powers were almost completely unaware of its strength. The day of the attack on Pearl Harbor, the Japanese Imperial Army's airforce had about 1,500 serviceable aircraft and the Naval airforce had a further 1,400. Their airplanes were very modern and flown by fanatically enthusiastic crews. Japan's early advantage was lost, first by the Navy in the great air-sea battles of 1942 and then by the Army, trapped into a desperate war of attrition. The reversal of Japan's fortunes was inexorable but right up to the very end of the war, Japan kept up an almost superhuman war effort. In 1940 aircraft production was 4,768; in 1941 this rose to 5,088 [1,080 fighters and 1,461 bombers], then to 8,861 in 1942 [2,953 fighters and 2,433 bombers]; soaring to 16,693 in 1943 [7,147 fighters and 4,189 bombers]; 28,180 in 1944 [13,811 and 5,100], dwindling to 11,066 [5,474 fighters and 1,934 bombers] in the eight months leading up to Japan's surrender in September 1945.

Italy was the third Axis power and certainly the weakest and the least well-prepared to engage in a full-scale war. On 10 June 1940, when Italy joined in the war, the Regia Aeronautica had 3,296 aircraft, 1,796 of which were combat planes [783 bombers, 594 fighters, 151 reconnaissance aircraft and 268 spotter planes]. This might appear satisfactory in terms of numbers but the aircraft were of very inferior quality and were ill-suited to modern warfare. This remained true of Italian wartime aircraft production and despite the help from the Germans [with engine development] and the valiant efforts of some outstanding designers, the situation did not materially improve. Some more advanced aircraft were produced [mainly fighters] but there was not the industrial infrastructure available to ensure a high, sustained level of production and Italy was soon desperately short of the raw materials needed for modern aircraft manufacture. A total of 3,257 aircraft were built in 1940; 3,503 in 1941; 2,818 in 1942 and 1,930 in the first eight months of 1943. By the time Italy surrendered, on 8 September 1943, only 887 aircraft had survived.

# 1940-1950
## Britain and Germany in race to field first jet combat planes

The evolution of the thoroughbred combat aircraft, the fighter, progressed along very similar lines in Germany and Britain, the two main European adversaries. Both nations had directed their efforts mainly towards developing increasingly efficient airplanes which each hoped would be able to outfly and outgun the enemy's aircraft. It was a desperate, unrelenting contest, in many ways reminiscent of the First World War, a struggle for survival.

Germany and Britain both achieved a similar aim at about the same time and that was to progress from the piston-engine to the jet-engine. Research and development work on this revolutionary means of propulsion were on parallel lines in both countries but the Germans were first past the post [the Me.262 saw action a few months before the rival Gloster Meteor, in the second half of 1944] and also produced more types of jet aircraft during the war [the Messerschmitt fighter was very soon joined by the Arado Ar.234 bomber and by two interceptors, the Heinkel He.162 and the Messerschmitt Me.163, the latter being the first rocket-powered combat aircraft in history]. The war, however, was ultimately to decide who was the real winner.

Germany and Britain were developing the jet-engine but the air battles were still being fought with propeller aircraft while the war lasted, and progress in development of such aircraft had been unflagging. The basic or standard German and British fighters [such as the Bf.109, the Fw.190 and the Spitfire] were continually updated and were flanked by other outstanding aircraft [such as the de Havilland Mosquito, the Hawker Typhoon and Tempest, and the German night fighters derived from the Ju.88], each making a considerable impact on the air war.

Italy was left way behind in this rivalry. The serious shortcomings of first-generation Italian fighters were partly rectified when the war was already well under way with the Germans coming to the aid of their allies, particularly with engines. This collaboration resulted in the Macchi MC.202 Folgore and the Reggiane Re.2002 of 1941, both powered by Daimler-Benz DB.601 engines; two years later the "Series 5" fighters [the Macchi M.C.205, the Fiat G.55 and the Reggiane Re.2005] were powered by Daimler's uprated engine, the DB.605. These were the best aircraft Italy produced during the war, but they went into service too late to have any effect on its outcome.

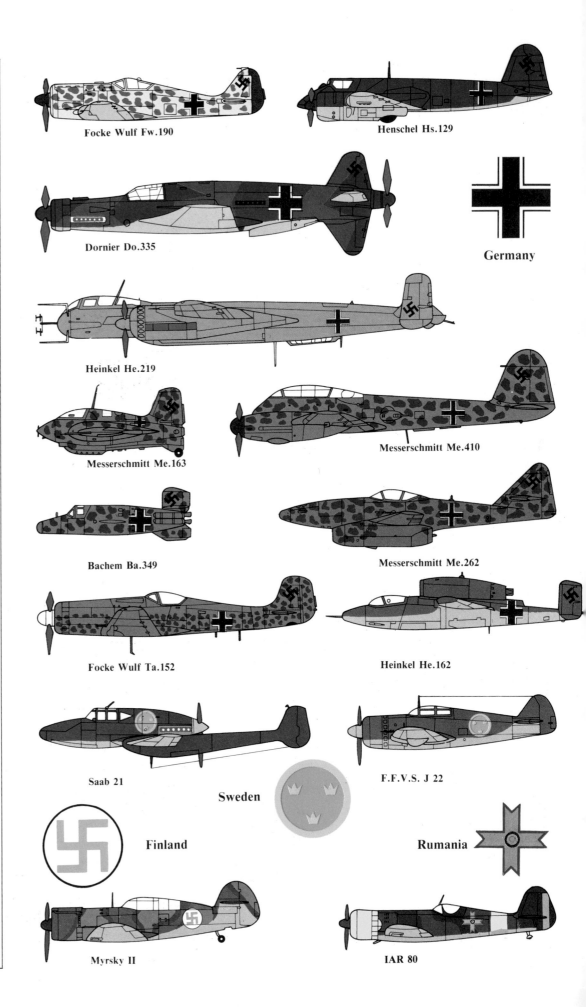

Focke Wulf Fw.190

Henschel Hs.129

Dornier Do.335

Germany

Heinkel He.219

Messerschmitt Me.163

Messerschmitt Me.410

Bachem Ba.349

Messerschmitt Me.262

Focke Wulf Ta.152

Heinkel He.162

Saab 21

F.F.V.S. J 22

Sweden

Finland

Rumania

Myrsky II

IAR 80

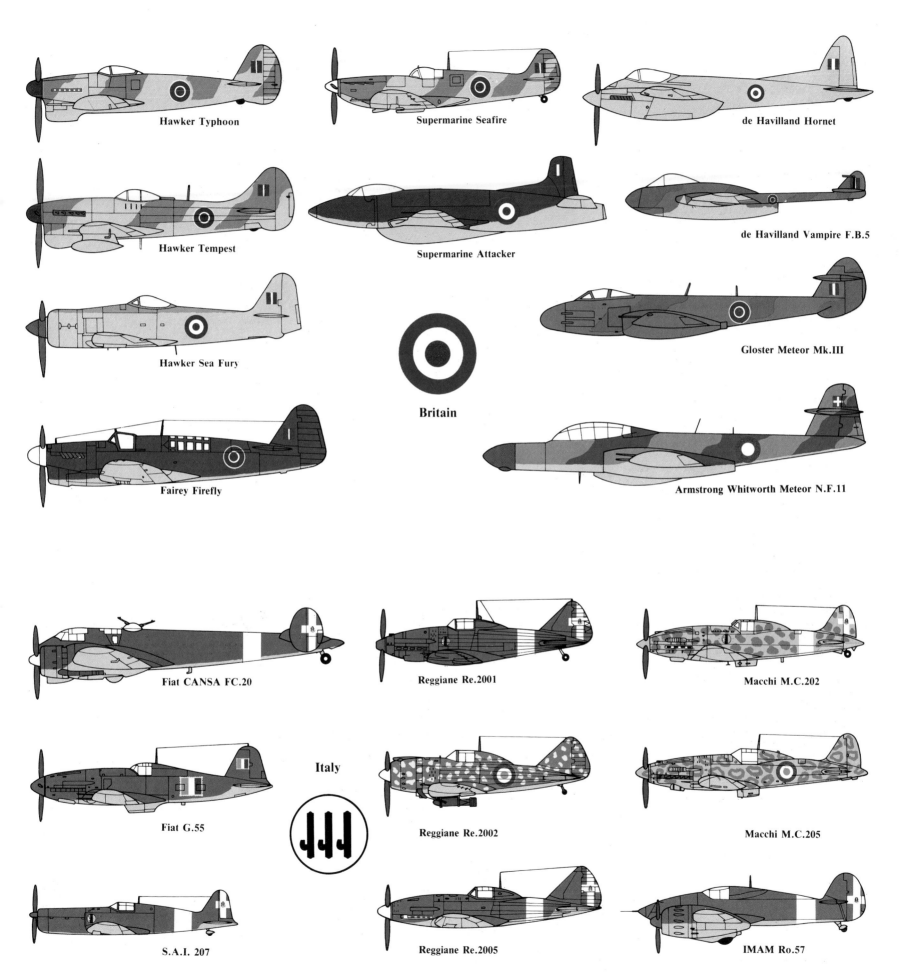

Hawker Typhoon

Supermarine Seafire

de Havilland Hornet

Hawker Tempest

Supermarine Attacker

de Havilland Vampire F.B.5

Hawker Sea Fury

Gloster Meteor Mk.III

**Britain**

Fairey Firefly

Armstrong Whitworth Meteor N.F.11

Fiat CANSA FC.20

Reggiane Re.2001

Macchi M.C.202

Fiat G.55

**Italy**

Reggiane Re.2002

Macchi M.C.205

S.A.I. 207

Reggiane Re.2005

IMAM Ro.57

# 1940-1950
## The U.S.S.R. unveils its new-generation fighters

The Soviet Union had traditionally been a second-tier aviation power but caught up during the war, setting in train a process of expansion which has continued to the present day. In view of later developments it was ironic that Stalin's allies [who were to become his bitterest enemies in 1945, when new boundaries had been drawn and new power groupings formed] helped to lay the foundations of this development by giving the U.S.S.R. vital help with technology and materials.

Without this assistance the Soviet Union would have taken far longer to convert to jet aircraft. Even after capturing a mass of scientific data, equipment and German technicians as its armies advanced westwards, the U.S.S.R. still did not manage to assimilate this material until after 1945. The German information and experts helped them to develop many prototypes, using engines derived from the BMW and Jumo turbojets, as a great effort was made to master the new technology.

The new aircraft were designed by the most famous Soviet designers, Mikoyan and Gurevich, Tupolev, Ilyushin, Yakovlev and Sukhoi. They belonged very much to the first generation of jets which were already no match for the jet engines which other aeronautical industries, particularly in Britain, had developed by that time. In 1946, the British government handed the Russians all the necessary technology when a license agreement was signed under which the Russians could build the most advanced turbojet, the Rolls-Royce Nene. Thus in one fell swoop the U.S.S.R. made up all the ground which had separated her from western aero-engine technology. A few months later the MiG-15 was unveiled, the Soviets' first second-generation jet fighter, powered by a copy of the British engine.

Before this great stride forward, however, the U.S.S.R. had developed her propeller-driven aircraft, producing planes of a very high standard. After winning air supremacy over the Luftwaffe in 1942, retaining it from then onwards only became possible when front-line units could rely on a steady supply of effective combat aircraft [such as the various versions of MiG, Yakovlev and Lavochkin fighters] to counter those fielded by the Germans.

Britain's influential position in the field of aero-engine technology was illustrated by another application of the Rolls-Royce Nene, when it was instrumental in reviving another country's postwar aeronautical industry. France had also been left behind but not for the same reasons as the Soviet Union, and the same turbojets as had been used to power the Russians' MiG fighters were installed in the first French jet fighter, the Dassault M.D.450 Ouragan, the prototype of which had its maiden flight on 28 February 1949.

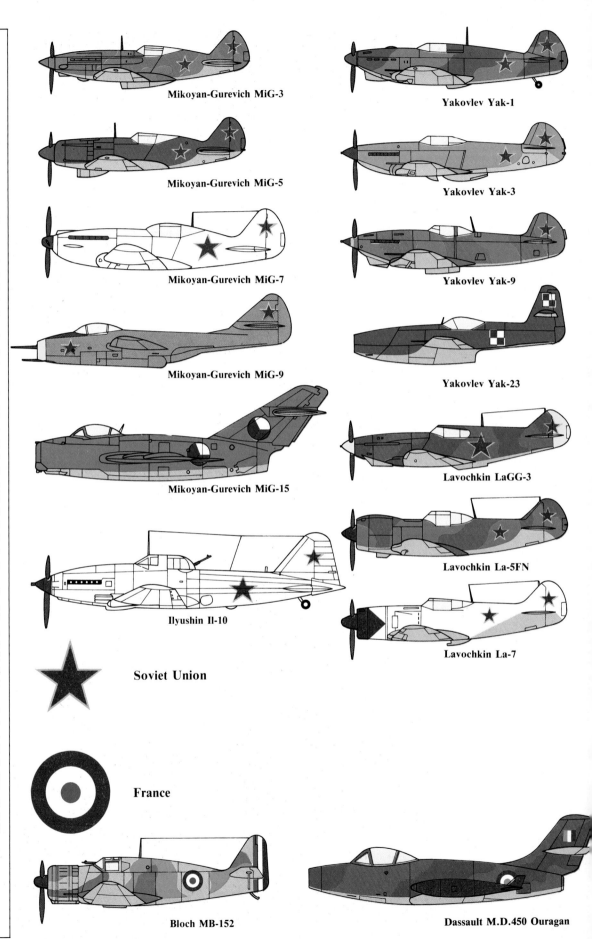

Mikoyan-Gurevich MiG-3

Yakovlev Yak-1

Mikoyan-Gurevich MiG-5

Yakovlev Yak-3

Mikoyan-Gurevich MiG-7

Yakovlev Yak-9

Mikoyan-Gurevich MiG-9

Yakovlev Yak-23

Mikoyan-Gurevich MiG-15

Lavochkin LaGG-3

Ilyushin Il-10

Lavochkin La-5FN

Lavochkin La-7

Soviet Union

France

Bloch MB-152

Dassault M.D.450 Ouragan

СЛАВА СОВЕТСКОМУ
ВОЗДУШНОМУ ФЛОТУ!

## 1940-1950
## Japan is faced with superior U.S. fighters

The U.S.A. did not have a jet combat plane in service at any time throughout the war [the Bell P-59 Airacomet, the United States' first venture in jet propulsion was almost immediately superseded by the more effective Lockheed F-80 Shooting Star which, in December 1945, became the first aircraft of its kind to see service with the USAAF. The U.S. Navy followed suit with the McDonnell FH-1 Phantom]. This in no way detracted from the decisive role played by American aircraft at all stages of the conflict.

After Pearl Harbor technological progress was rapid, stimulated by the determination to counter Axis aggression by every possible means. The United States entered the war with land-based and carrier-borne aircraft which were no match for the well-armed, more maneuverable Japanese planes. Up-to-date aircraft were developed, the Navy benefiting from various versions of the Grumman F6F Hellcat and Vought F4 Corsair [both of which had their first taste of combat in 1943].

Faced with the formidable fighters of the Luftwaffe, the U.S. developed such land-based fighters as the Lockheed P-38 Lightning, the Republic P-47 Thunderbolt and the North American P-51 Mustang. The Mustang was probably the best piston-engine fighter of the Second World War and owed its success to the combination of an extremely well-designed airframe with an outstanding British engine, the Rolls-Royce Merlin, which also powered the Spitfire fighters. Besides these exciting front-line combat planes, the American aircraft industry also manufactured such thoroughly reliable workhorses as the various versions of the Curtiss P-40 and Bell P-39, which contributed greatly to the effectiveness of allied air power on all fronts.

Faced with this impressive capability, Japan found, that despite frantic efforts to match U.S. production in quality and quantity, she was starting to slip well behind. While every effort was made constantly to update and improve the Mitsubishi A6M Reisen [the famous Zero fighter which in the early days of the war had come to be thought of as the symbol of the Land of the Rising Sun's air power], it could no longer meet its adversary's combat planes on equal terms and the same remained true of the best of its successors: the Mitsubishi J2M Raiden and the Kawanishi N1K1 Shiden.

The Imperial Army's airforce fared no better with the Nakajima Ki-84 and Ki-44 which entered service in 1943, and the Kawasaki Ki-61 and Ki-100. By then the result of the war in the Pacific was virtually certain, in spite of strenuous Japanese efforts which looked as if they might be successful, to develop a jet engine in close collaboration with their German allies during the final months. Massive American bombing raids on the Japanese homeland thwarted any hopes of achieving this aim.

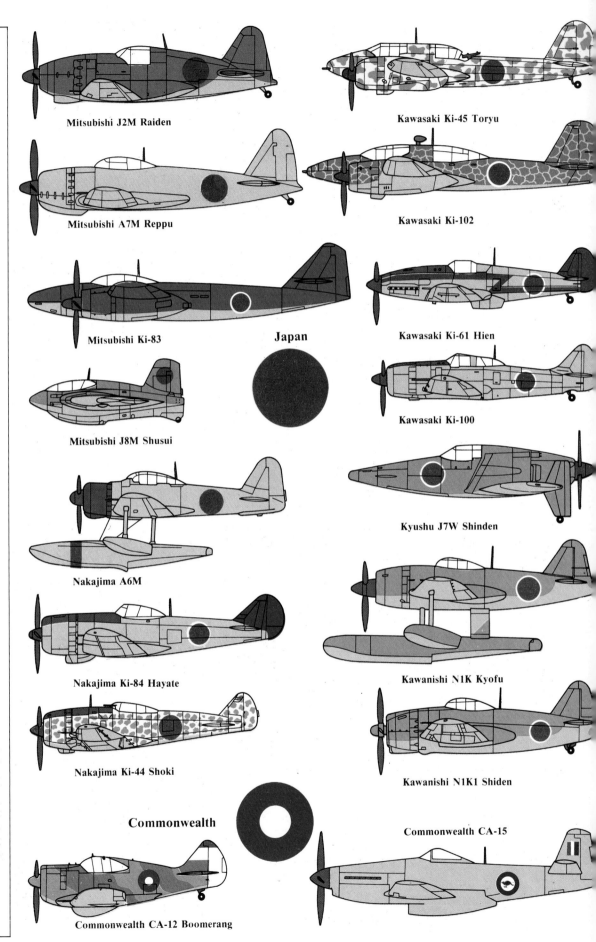

Mitsubishi J2M Raiden

Mitsubishi A7M Reppu

Mitsubishi Ki-83

Mitsubishi J8M Shusui

Nakajima A6M

Nakajima Ki-84 Hayate

Nakajima Ki-44 Shoki

Commonwealth

Commonwealth CA-12 Boomerang

Kawasaki Ki-45 Toryu

Kawasaki Ki-102

Kawasaki Ki-61 Hien

Japan

Kawasaki Ki-100

Kyushu J7W Shinden

Kawanishi N1K Kyofu

Kawanishi N1K1 Shiden

Commonwealth CA-15

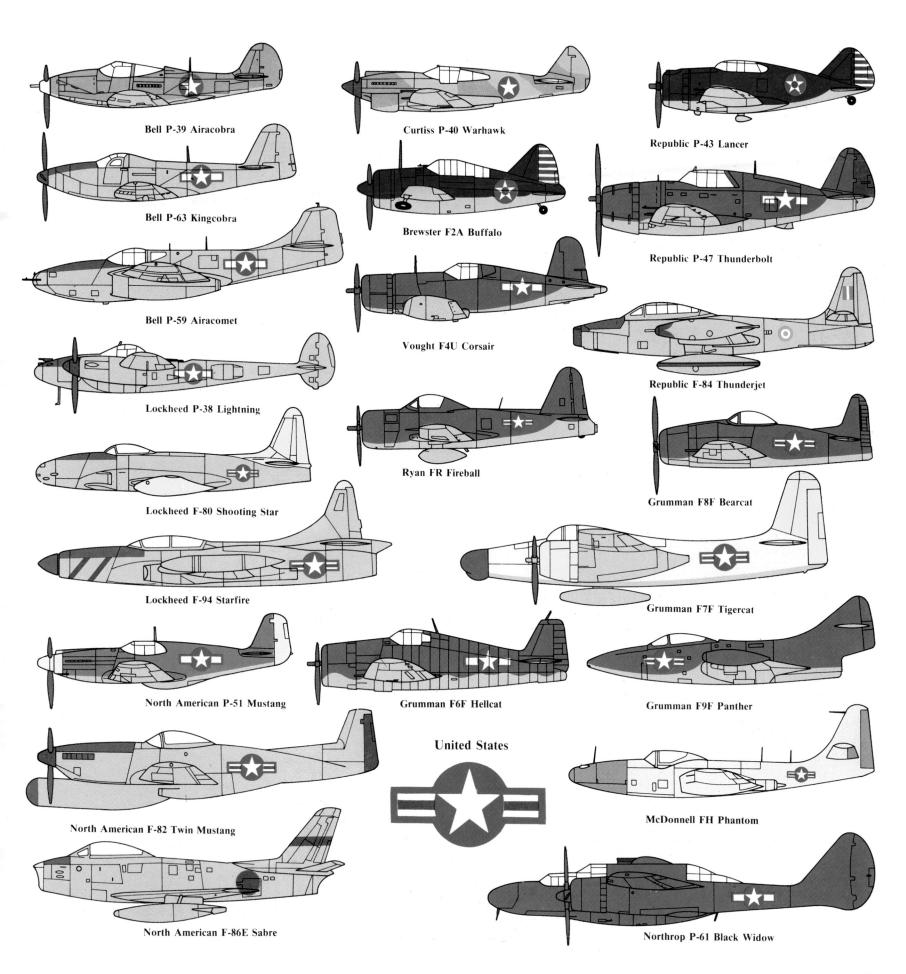

Bell P-39 Airacobra

Bell P-63 Kingcobra

Bell P-59 Airacomet

Lockheed P-38 Lightning

Lockheed F-80 Shooting Star

Lockheed F-94 Starfire

North American P-51 Mustang

North American F-82 Twin Mustang

North American F-86E Sabre

Curtiss P-40 Warhawk

Brewster F2A Buffalo

Vought F4U Corsair

Ryan FR Fireball

Grumman F6F Hellcat

**United States**

Republic P-43 Lancer

Republic P-47 Thunderbolt

Republic F-84 Thunderjet

Grumman F8F Bearcat

Grumman F7F Tigercat

Grumman F9F Panther

McDonnell FH Phantom

Northrop P-61 Black Widow

## 1940-1950
## The B-29 Superfortress – the final answer

The final stages of the war in the Pacific were marked by the appearance of a strategic bomber developed specifically to crush Japanese resistance: this was the Boeing B-29 Superfortress which symbolized both the end of one era of military aviation and the beginning of another – the atomic age. On 6 August 1945 at 09.15 hours 30 seconds local, Tinian time [a small island in the Marianas archipelago], a B-29 nicknamed "Enola Gay" piloted by Colonel Paul W. Tibbets, dropped an atomic bomb on Hiroshima from an altitude of 31,594 ft [9,630 m] while flying at 328 mph [528 km/h]. This was the first time such a weapon had been unleashed in a war and over 70,000 people were killed, a whole city destroyed in a split second. Three days later on 9 August, Nagasaki was to share the same terrible fate.

The B-29's role in the war went much further than just flying these two historic missions which finally forced the Japanese to surrender; a year earlier the large four-engine planes had launched a new phase in the Pacific war which was to prove crucial to U.S. success, when they were used for the first large-scale bombing raids over Japanese territory. The exceptional capabilities of the B-29 derived from the wealth of experience gained by the U.S. aviation industry during the war, experience which was also put to good use in the mass production of smaller types like the North American B-25, the Martin B-26, Douglas A-20 and A-26, the Boeing B-17 and Consolidated B-24 heavy bombers and carrier-borne assault aircraft such as the Grumman TBF Avenger and the Curtiss SB2C Helldiver. These aircraft were outstanding by any criteria.

Britain was the only other power to produce strategic bombers of the same caliber as those of her transatlantic ally and her excellent Avro Lancaster

continued on page 114

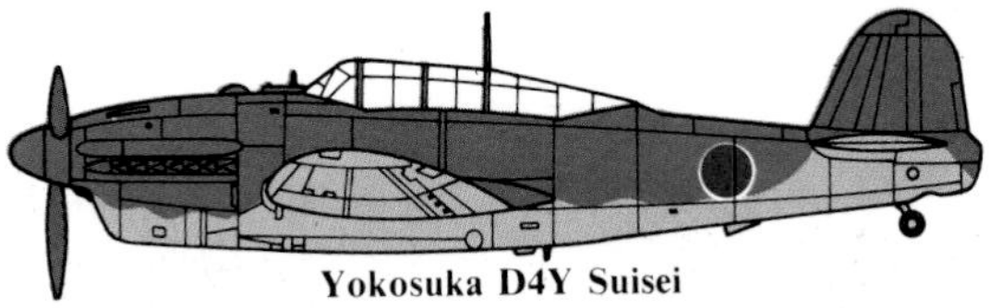

Yokosuka D4Y Suisei

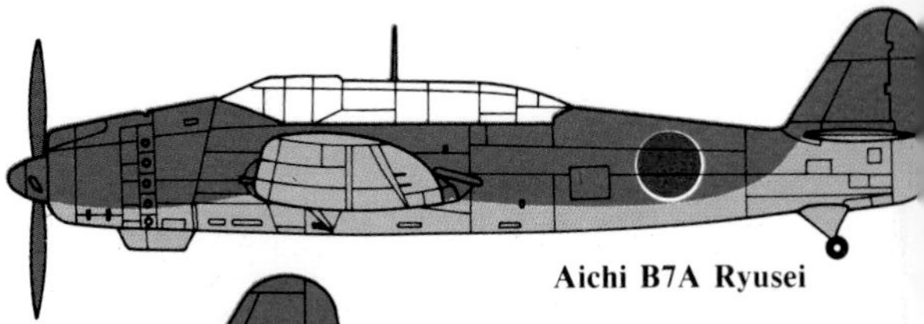

Aichi B7A Ryusei

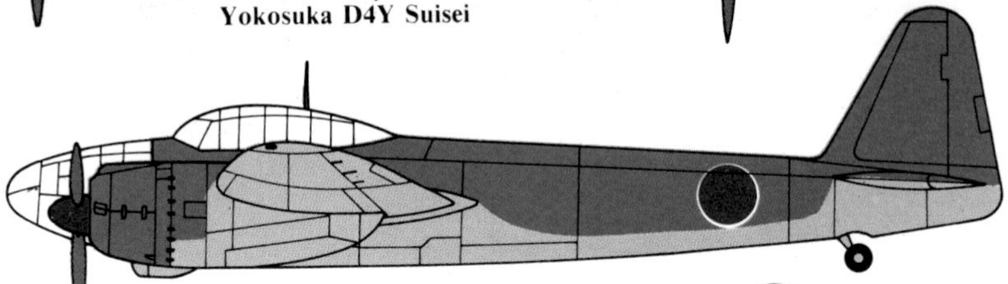

Yokosuka P1Y Ginga

Yokosuka Ohka 11

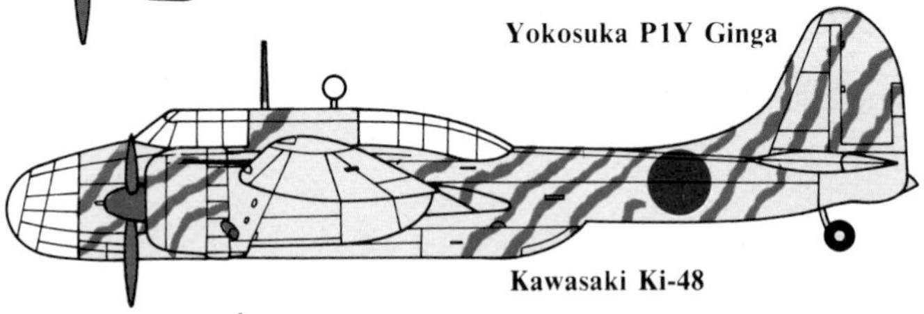

Kawasaki Ki-48

Japan

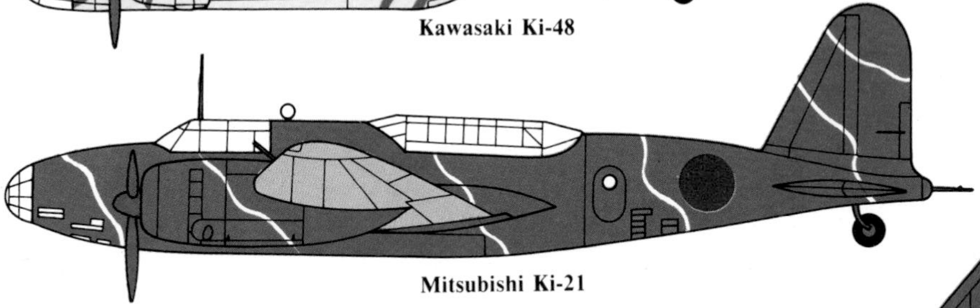

Mitsubishi Ki-21

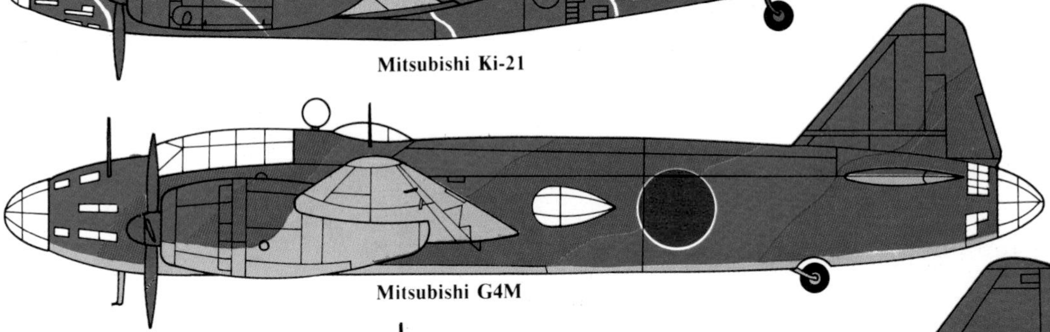

Mitsubishi G4M

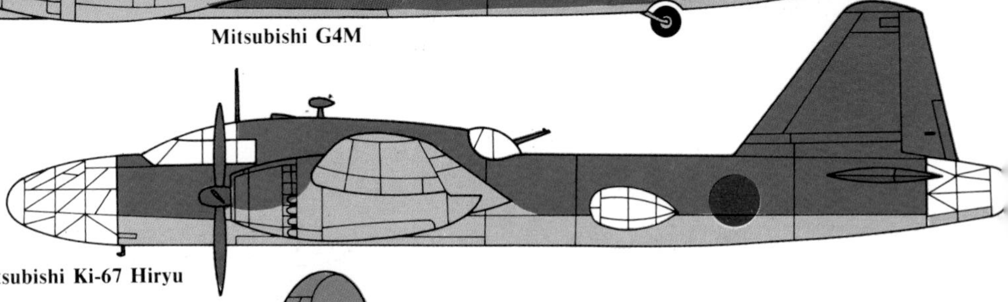

Mitsubishi Ki-67 Hiryu

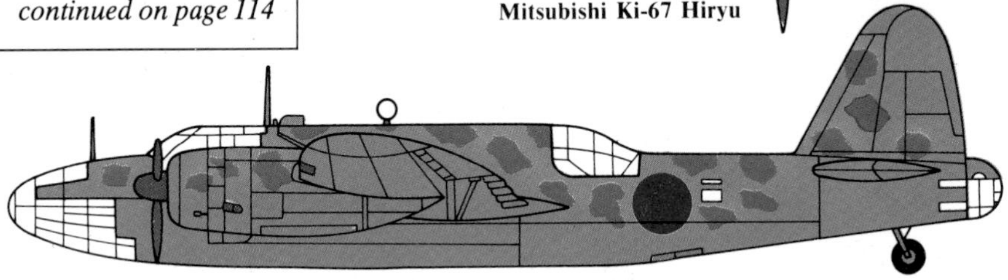

Nakajima Ki-49 Donryu

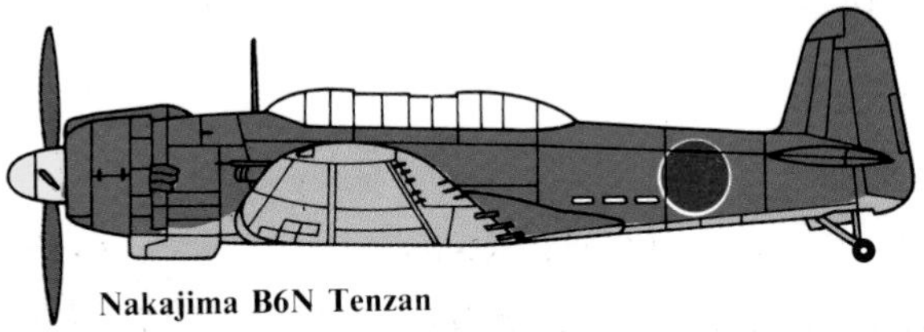

Nakajima B6N Tenzan

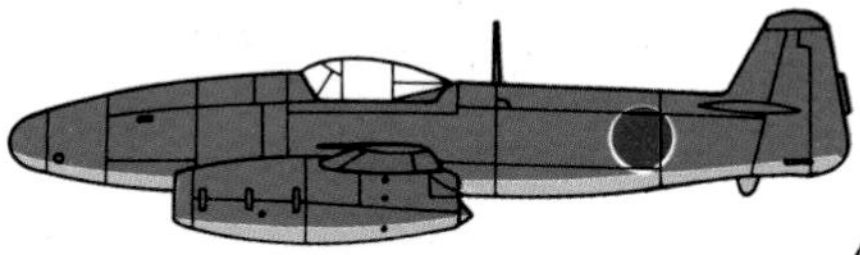

Nakajima Kikka

Nakajima G8N Renzan

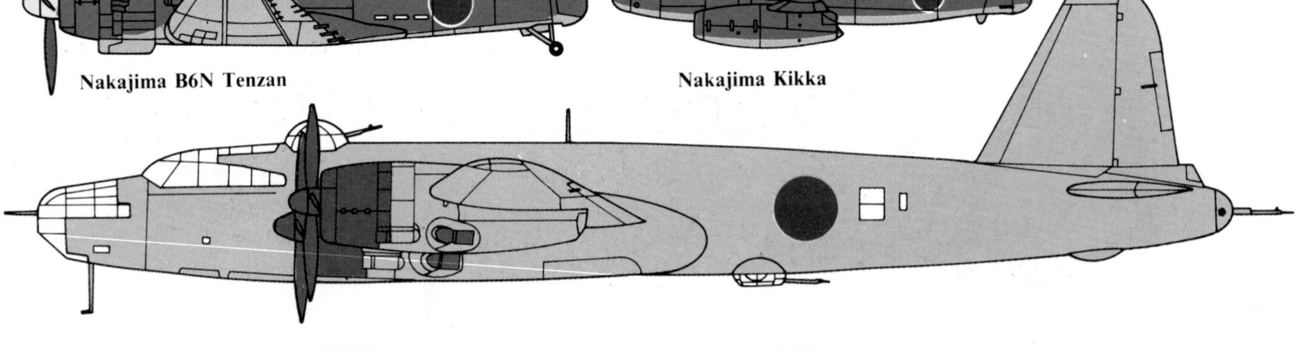

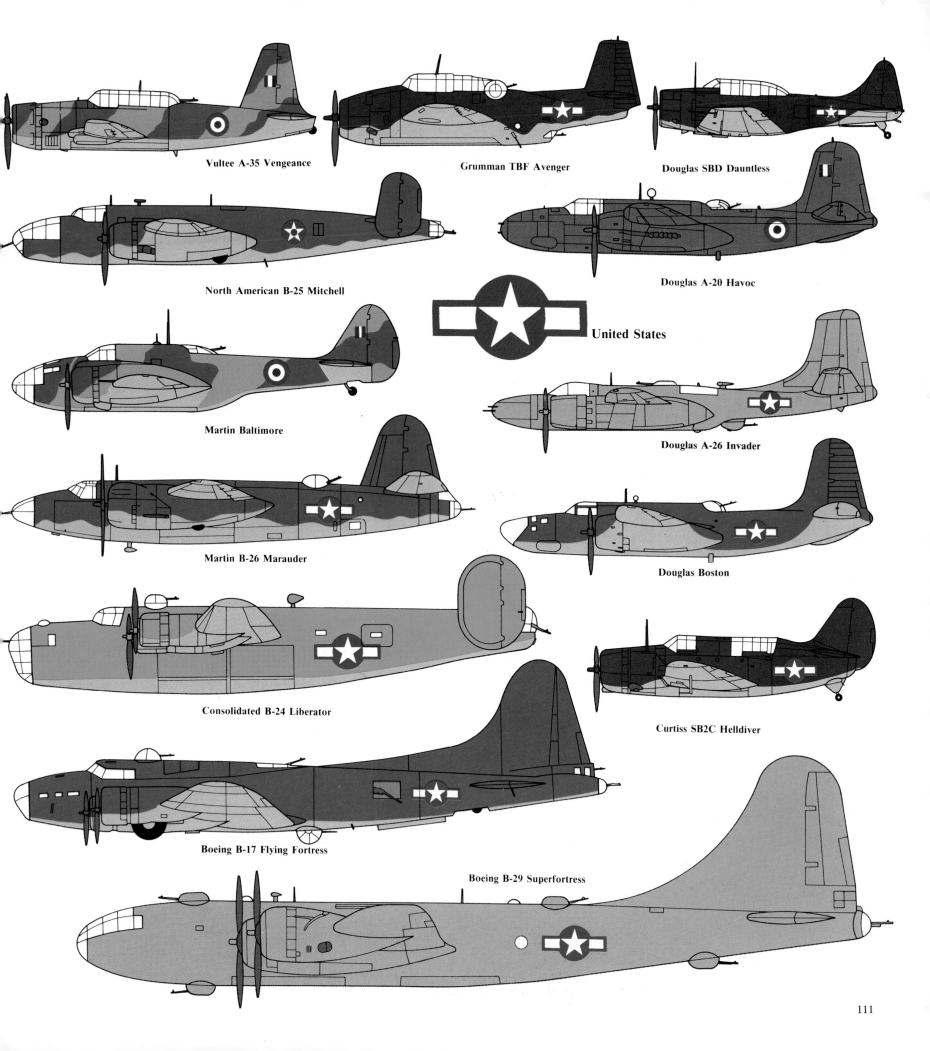

Vultee A-35 Vengeance

Grumman TBF Avenger

Douglas SBD Dauntless

North American B-25 Mitchell

Douglas A-20 Havoc

United States

Martin Baltimore

Douglas A-26 Invader

Martin B-26 Marauder

Douglas Boston

Consolidated B-24 Liberator

Curtiss SB2C Helldiver

Boeing B-17 Flying Fortress

Boeing B-29 Superfortress

111

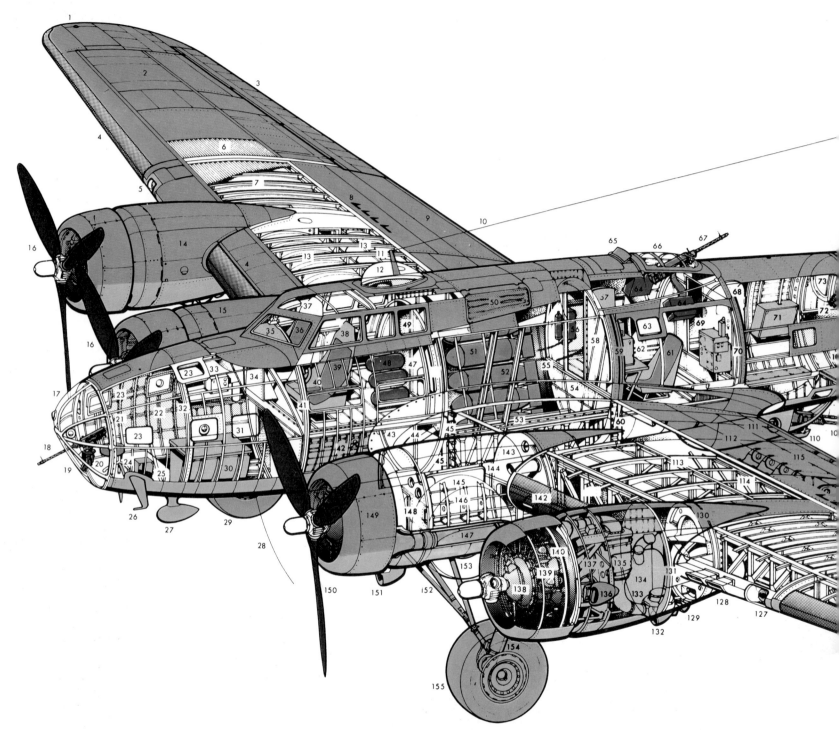

| | | | |
|---|---|---|---|
| 1 Starboard navigation light | 14 No 4 engine nacelle | 25 Bomb-aimer's panel | 40 Pilot's control column |
| 2 Wing skinning | 15 No 3 engine nacelle | 26 Pitot head | 41 No 3 fuselage frame bulkhead |
| 3 Starboard aileron | 16 Hamilton Standard | 27 D/F bullet fairing | 43 Underfloor control runs |
| 4 Leading-edge de-icing boot | three-bladed constant-speed | 28 Whip aerial | 43 Wingroot/fuselage fairing |
| 5 Starboard landing light | propellers | 29 Starboard mainwheel | 44 Battery access panels (in |
| 6 Wing corrugated inner skin | 17 Plexiglass nose-cone panels | 30 Navigator's table | wingroot) |
| 7 Starboard outer fuel tank | 18 0.30 in (7.62 mm) | 31 Window | 45 Main spar/fuselage |
| (9 inter-rib cells) | machine gun | 32 No 2 fuselage frame bulkhead | attachment |
| 8 Cooling air slots | 19 Optically flat bomb-aiming | 33 Navigation equipment | 46 No 4 fuselage frame bulkhead |
| 9 Starboard flaps | panel | 34 Central control pedestal | 47 Fire extinguisher |
| 10 Aerial | 20 Bombsight | 35 Windscreen | 48 Oxygen cylinders |
| 11 Aerial mast | 21 No 1 fuselage frame bulkhead | 36 Copilot's seat | 49 Flight-deck door |
| 12 Astrodome | 22 Forward fuselage structure | 37 Overhead control panel | 50 Dinghy stowage |
| 13 Starboard mid-wing tanks | 23 Nose windows | 38 Headrest/armour | 51 Horizontal bomb-load |
| (self-sealing) | 24 Bomb-aimer's seat | 39 Pilot's seat | (starboard shown) |

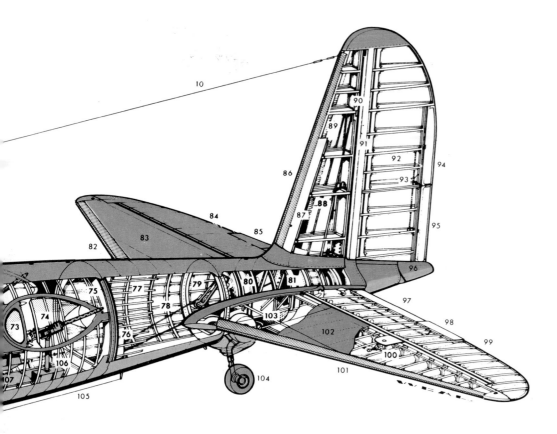

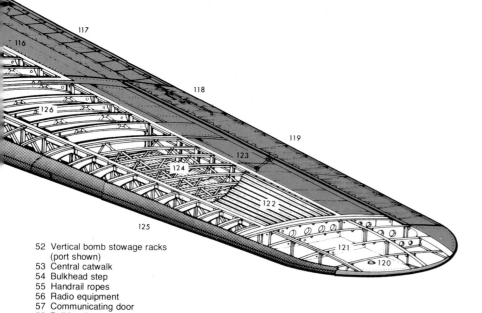

89 Tailfin construction
90 Rudder hinge (upper)
91 Rudder post
92 Rudder framework
93 Tab controls
94 Rudder tab (upper)
95 Rudder tab (lower)
96 Tail cone
97 Elevator tab (inner)
98 Elevator tab (outer)
99 Elevator construction
100 Elevator control linkage
101 Port tailplane de-icing boot
102 Tailplane skinning
103 Tailwheel
    (stowed/semi-retracted)
104 Tailwheel extended
105 Ventral aerial
106 Gun support mounting
107 Gunners catwalk
108 Ammunition box
109 Ventral gun position (twin
    0.50 in/12.7 mm machine
    guns)
110 Hinged lower section
111 Circular vision port
112 Ventral bath
113 Auxiliary mid spar
114 Rear spar
115 Flap profile
116 Cooling air slots
117 Flap construction
118 Aileron tab (port only)
119 Port aileron construction
120 Port navigation light
121 Wingtip structure
122 Wing corrugated inner skin
123 Aileron control linkage
124 Wing ribs
125 Leading-edge de-icing boot
126 Port outer fuel tank (nine
    inter-rib cells)
127 Port landing light
128 Supercharger intake
129 Supercharger waste-gate
130 Spar bulkhead
131 Intercooler intake
132 Intake
133 Supercharger
134 Oil tank (outboard nacelle
    wall)
135 Intercooler
136 Intake
137 Engine bearers
138 Propeller reduction gear
    casing
139 Wright R 1820-73 radial
    engine
140 Firewall
141 Front spar web structure
142 Oil radiator intake
143 Spar bulkhead
144 Intercooler pressure ducting
145 Oil tank (inboard nacelle wall)
146 Nacelle structure
147 Exhaust
148 Firewall
149 No 2 engine cowling
150 Three-blade propeller
151 Intake
152 Retraction struts
153 Mainwheel
    (stowed/semi-retracted)
154 Mainwheel oleo
155 Port mainwheel

65 Retractable wind deflector
66 Roof glazing
67 Dorsal gun position (0.50
   in/12.7 mm machine gun)
68 Crew entry door (starboard)
69 Bulkhead door
70 No 6 fuselage frame bulkhead
71 Ammunition box
72 Starboard waist gun (0.50
   in/12.7 mm machine gun)
73 Flush waist glazing
74 Port waist gun
   (0.50 in/12.7 mm machine
   gun)
75 Bulkhead
76 Toilet
77 Fuselage structure
78 Control cables
79 Tailwheel retraction
   mechanism
80 Fuselage frame
81 Tailfin/fuselage attachment
82 Starboard tailplane de-icing
   boot
83 Starboard tailplane
84 Starboard elevator
85 Elevator tab
86 Tailfin de-icing boot
87 Tailfin front spar
88 Rudder control linkage

52 Vertical bomb stowage racks
   (port shown)
53 Central catwalk
54 Bulkhead step
55 Handrail ropes
56 Radio equipment
57 Communicating door
58 Bulkhead
59 No 5 fuselage frame bulkhead
60 Rear spar/fuselage
   attachment
61 Radio operator's seat
62 Radio rack
63 Window
64 Ammunition boxes (dorsal
   position)

*continued from page 110*

and Handley Page Halifax night bombers joined the day-bombing B-17s and B-24s on massive, devastating raids during the later stages of the war, attacking key targets in the heart of the Third Reich. The British aviation industry managed to keep up with the United States in this sector for a while after the war had ended by developing one of the best of the first-generation jet bombers, the English Electric Canberra, a contemporary of North American's B-45 and Boeing's B-47.

Even the U.S.S.R., having failed to field a strategic bomber of comparable sophistication to those of her allies during the war, seized her newly-given opportunity to close the technological gap and embarked on production of first-generation jet bombers. The first of these was the twin-engine Ilyushin Il-28 which appeared in prototype in August 1948 and was manufactured in large numbers from 1950 onwards in the definitive version which had Russian-built copies of the Rolls-Royce Nene engines as did the MiG-15.

Throughout the war the Axis powers were to suffer from their lack of capacity to equal the Allies' vast armament production. Although Germany and Japan had some excellent medium bombers [the former had the world's first jet-powered bomber, the Arado Ar.234 in service by 1944] neither managed to build an effective strategic bomber. The Heinkel He.177 of 1939 and the Japanese Nakajima G5N and G8N of 1944 were not particularly effective.

It was not until the last, almost final stages of the war that the Germans came up with an answer to their failure to produce a strategic bomber capable of penetrating enemy defenses. It came in the form of the Mistel series of deadly flying bombs consisting of a large pilotless aircraft packed full of high explosive, launched at its target from a smaller guide plane.

Italy's front-line bombers were never to prove a serious threat to the Allies; the only design which could have given Italy an effective bomber – the Piaggio P.108 of 1942, the one modern Italian four-engine strategic bomber developed during these years, was ready too late to make any difference to the outcome of the war as far as Italy was concerned.

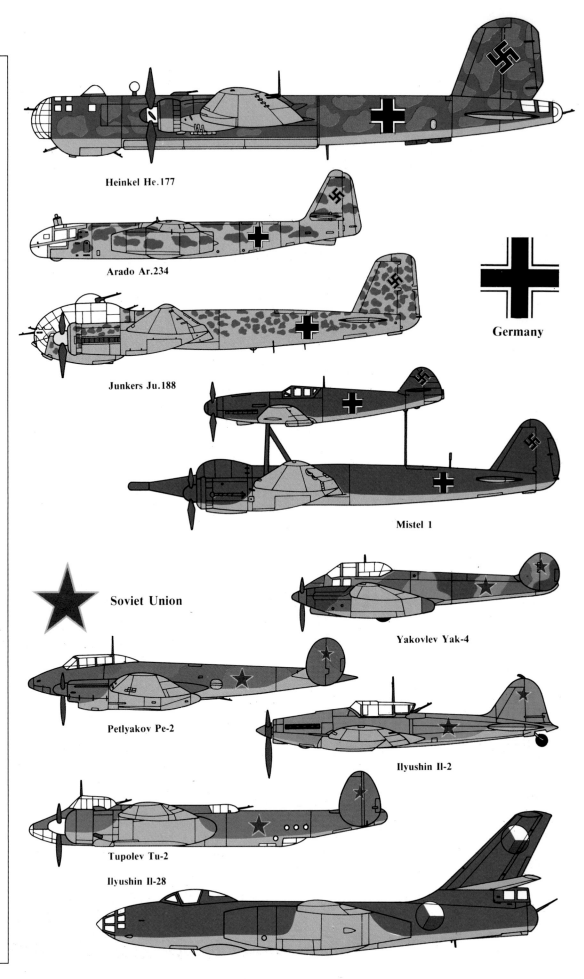

Heinkel He.177

Arado Ar.234

Junkers Ju.188

**Germany**

Mistel 1

**Soviet Union**

Yakovlev Yak-4

Petlyakov Pe-2

Ilyushin Il-2

Tupolev Tu-2

Ilyushin Il-28

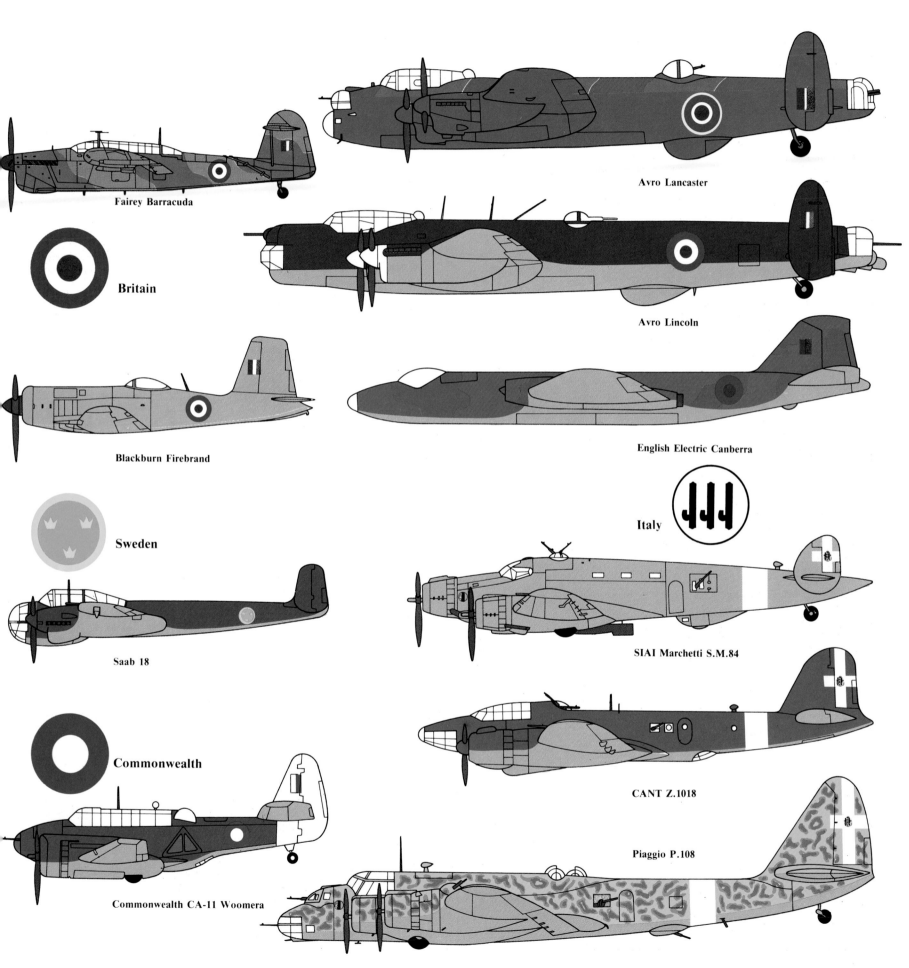

Fairey Barracuda

Avro Lancaster

Britain

Avro Lincoln

Blackburn Firebrand

English Electric Canberra

Sweden

Italy

Saab 18

SIAI Marchetti S.M.84

CANT Z.1018

Commonwealth

Piaggio P.108

Commonwealth CA-11 Woomera

## 1940-1950
## Reconnaissance, training and transport aircraft. Germany builds the largest wartime flying boat

Although the Luftwaffe never fielded a strategic bomber during the Second World War, it was not for lack of first-class designs with great potential. Work started on several projects which aimed to fill this gap in the German arsenal but neither the He.177 nor any of the others were officially sanctioned. This odd situation arose from the failure of the German High Command to adapt its theory of warfare according to new circumstances. Instead the generals looked back to the experience of the Spanish Civil War and maintained their belief that the medium-day bomber was the most effective strategic weapon and the ground-attack aircraft the best tactical weapon.

This thinking was epitomized by the fate of the Junkers Ju.290 of 1942: this was a large, four-engine plane, a derivative of the Ju.90 of 1936. About thirty aircraft in all were built, in seven main production variants which were first used as marine patrol aircraft and then as transports. A variant which had been developed specifically for high-altitude bombing, the B-1 of 1943, never went into production.

The largest marine patrol flying boat to be built during the war years, the Blohm und Voss Bv.222 Wiking, was originally designed for transport duties. Only seven of these gigantic multiengine aircraft went into service in 1942, but they were extensively used. In their first year of operations a total of 3,496 tonnes of material, 37,500 fully-equipped troops and 5,196 casualties were carried by the Bv.222s. Another giant transport was the Messerschmitt Me.323 of 1942, originally designed as a glider but modified for powered flight with six engines. Although this aircraft had serious limitations, 198 were built and proved invaluable in the Mediterranean theater and on the Russian front. Flying boats were ideally suited to one particular role – marine patrol. Nearly all the nations involved in the fighting used them in this role and some played a decisive part in determining the outcome of certain key battles of the war, such as the great naval battles between the Americans and the Japanese in the Pacific.

Land-based reconnaissance aircraft were just as vital, particularly since as strategic bombing was stepped up, photographs of target areas were needed – both to pinpoint the objective and to ascertain how successful the raids had been. Some of the best reconnaissance planes had been derived from aircraft already in production, special variants being developed for reconnaissance: the German Junkers Ju.388 and certain series of the British de Havilland Mosquito and Supermarine Spitfire were adapted for these duties.

It is very important not to lose sight of the tremendous boost to postwar civil aviation which was given by auxiliary aircraft built to meet wartime needs. Transport planes underwent great changes and these advances not only made for the availability of efficient

*continued on page 118*

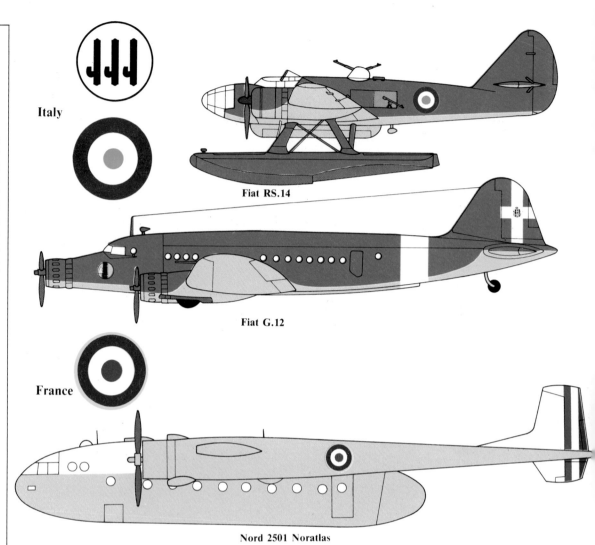

Italy

Fiat RS.14

Fiat G.12

France

Nord 2501 Noratlas

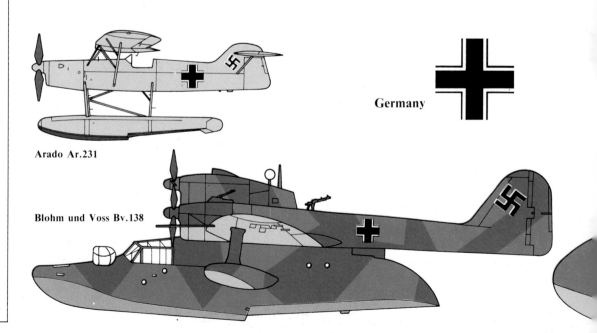

Arado Ar.231

Germany

Blohm und Voss Bv.138

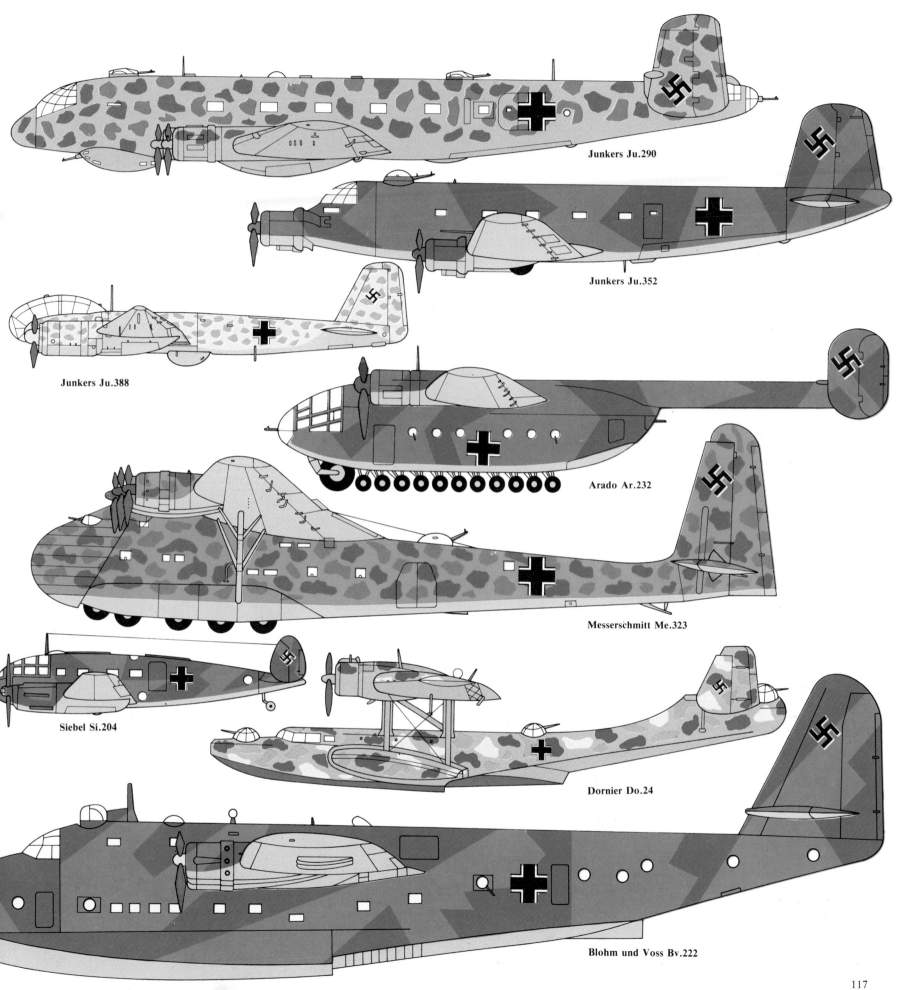

Junkers Ju.290

Junkers Ju.352

Junkers Ju.388

Arado Ar.232

Messerschmitt Me.323

Siebel Si.204

Dornier Do.24

Blohm und Voss Bv.222

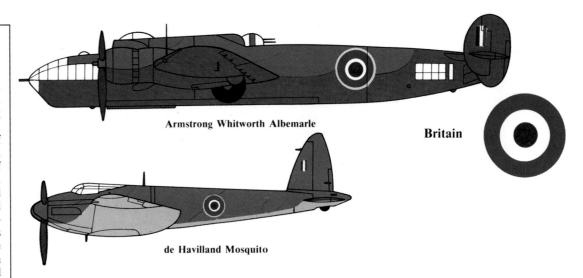

Armstrong Whitworth Albemarle

**Britain**

de Havilland Mosquito

*continued from page 116*

utility planes during the war but also laid the foundations of the future commercial sector once peace had returned. Nowhere was this more clearly illustrated than in the United States, which was the leading Allied nation in this field. The ground had been prepared for U.S. dominance during the second half of the thirties when Boeing's twin-engine 247 and Douglas's DC-2/DC-3 had revolutionized the world of commercial transport. The war served to strengthen this lead. Growing demands to provide improved logistical support in all operational theaters spurred the aircraft manufacturers to build new military transports, one of the earliest examples being the famous twin-engine Douglas C-47, thousands of which left the assembly lines. The U.S. domestic civil aviation market continued the expansion which had started during the previous decade.

Many postwar airliners were the direct descendants of wartime transport aircraft; the Douglas C-54 and the Lockheed C-69 were the military forerunners of a whole series of civil aircraft, the last piston-engine airliners to be developed before the introduction of the jet, among these the DC-4, DC-6 and DC-7 of which there were numerous variants, and the Constellation, also built in several versions, and the Super Constellation. In addition to its troop-transport requirements, the USAAF also procured such utility aircraft as the resilient and capacious twin-engine Curtiss C-46 Commando which, although produced in smaller numbers than its predecessor, the more famous C-47 [of which nearly 3,200 were built] was to meet with equal success, entering service in 1943.

Towards the end of the war, however, the USAAF found it needed purpose-built military transports. The first of this new-generation aircraft was the Fairchild C-119 Boxcar, 1,100 manufactured, many of which were kept in service with the U.S. forces until the late sixties while a considerable number went to equip America's allies. The last very large strategic transport to be powered by piston-engines, the Douglas C-124 Globemaster II, was a gigantic four-engine aircraft which could carry 200 troops or 31 tonnes of material. The prototype first flew in 1949 and production totalled 447, in two versions. The Globemaster II remained in front-line service until 1961.

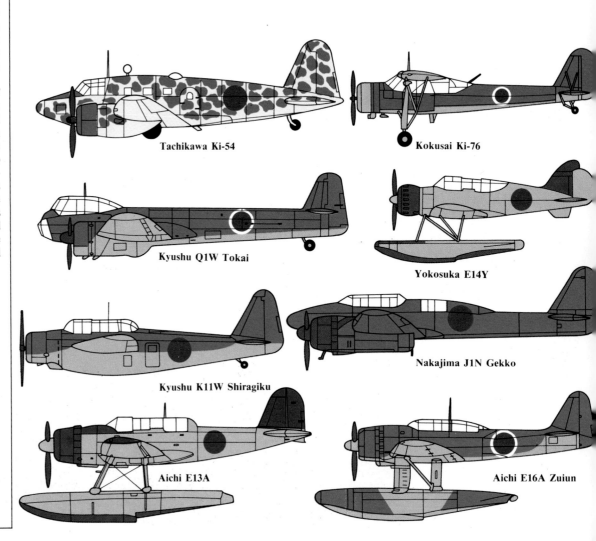

Tachikawa Ki-54

Kokusai Ki-76

Kyushu Q1W Tokai

Yokosuka E14Y

Kyushu K11W Shiragiku

Nakajima J1N Gekko

Aichi E13A

Aichi E16A Zuiun

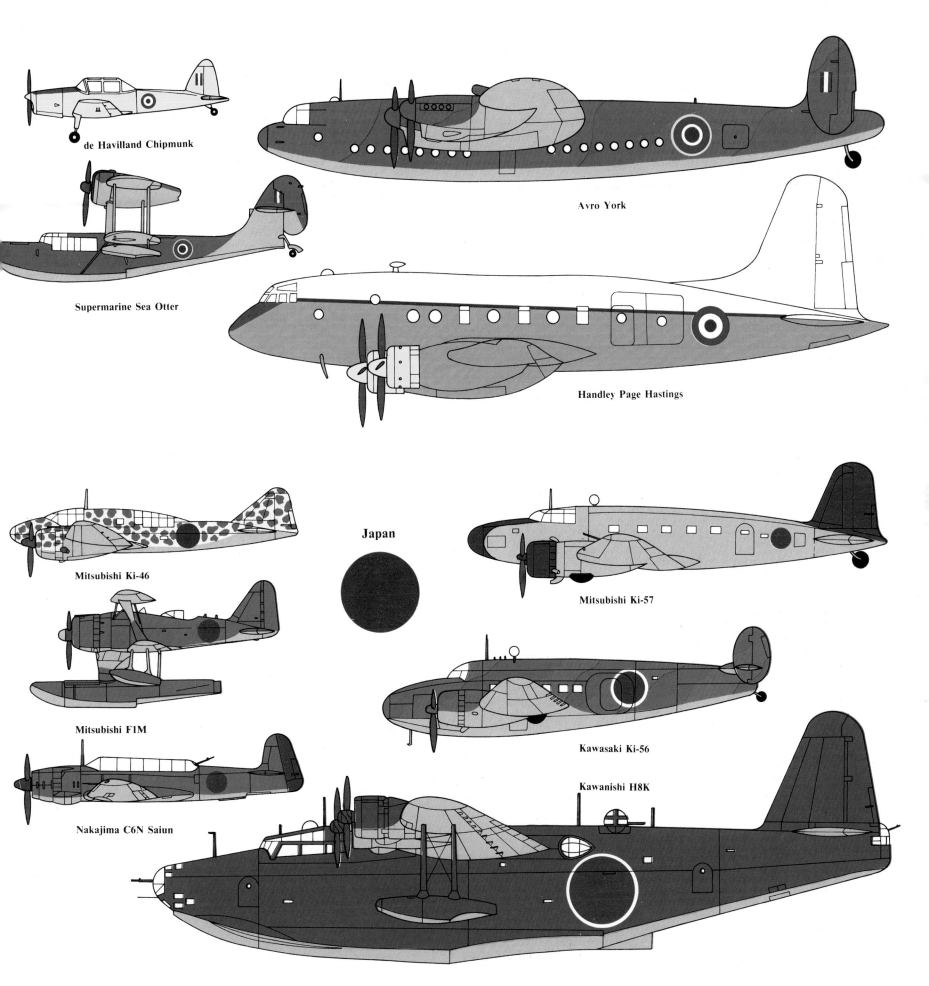

de Havilland Chipmunk

Avro York

Supermarine Sea Otter

Handley Page Hastings

Mitsubishi Ki-46

Japan

Mitsubishi Ki-57

Mitsubishi F1M

Kawasaki Ki-56

Nakajima C6N Saiun

Kawanishi H8K

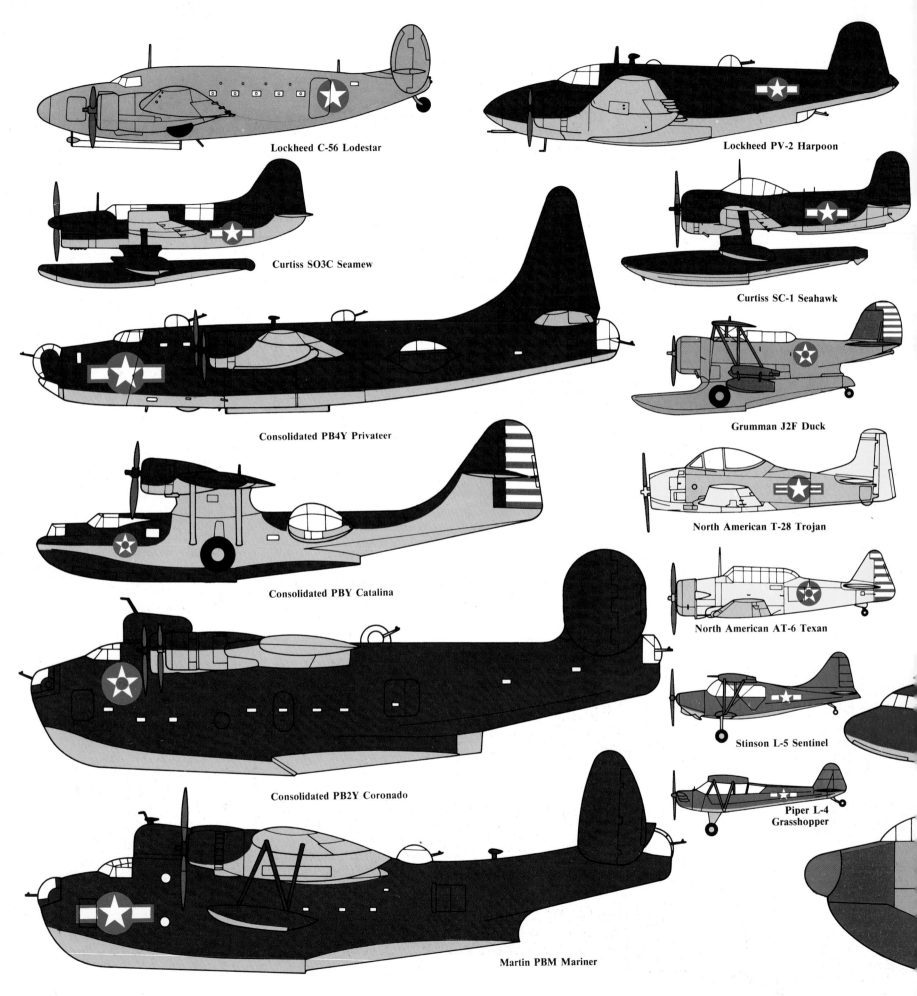

Lockheed C-56 Lodestar

Lockheed PV-2 Harpoon

Curtiss SO3C Seamew

Curtiss SC-1 Seahawk

Consolidated PB4Y Privateer

Grumman J2F Duck

North American T-28 Trojan

Consolidated PBY Catalina

North American AT-6 Texan

Stinson L-5 Sentinel

Consolidated PB2Y Coronado

Piper L-4 Grasshopper

Martin PBM Mariner

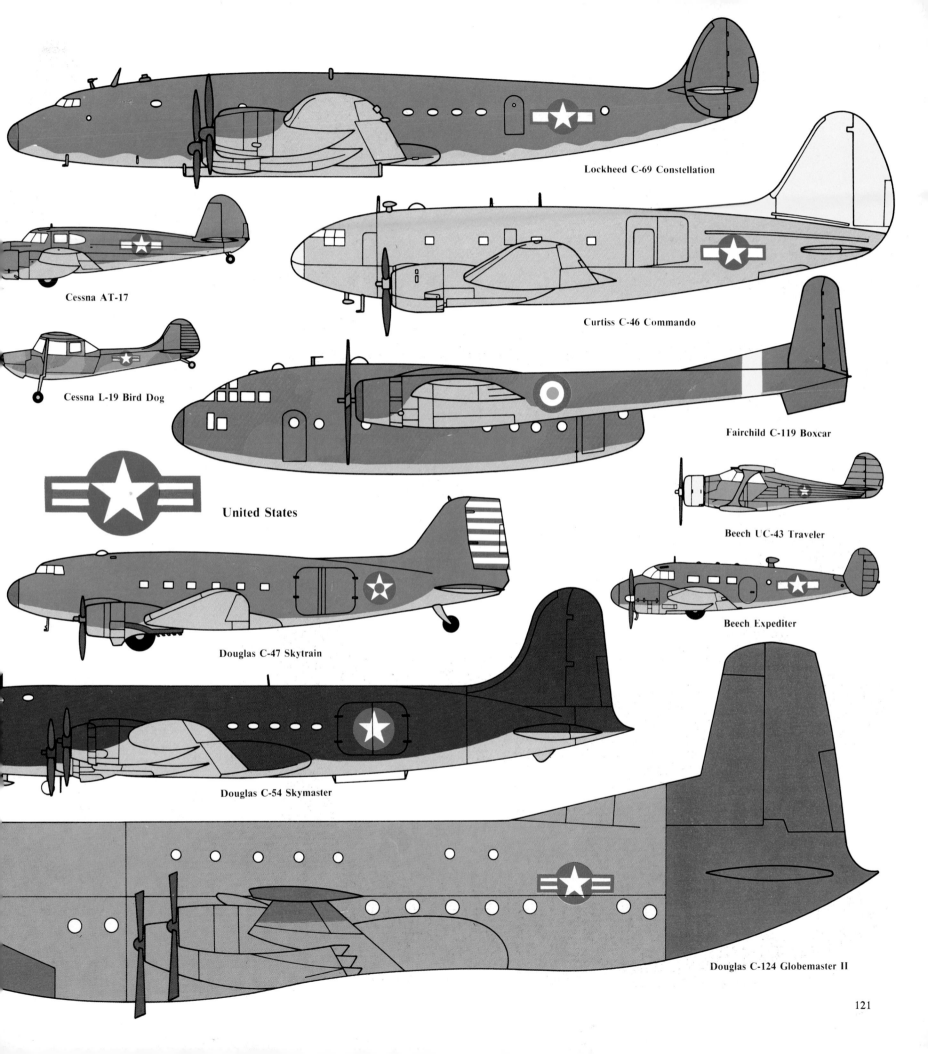

Lockheed C-69 Constellation

Cessna AT-17

Curtiss C-46 Commando

Cessna L-19 Bird Dog

Fairchild C-119 Boxcar

Beech UC-43 Traveler

United States

Beech Expediter

Douglas C-47 Skytrain

Douglas C-54 Skymaster

Douglas C-124 Globemaster II

# 1940-1950
## Peace brings upsurge in commercial aviation

The coming of peace signalled the beginning of a new surge of growth in civil aviation. All over the world both victors and vanquished felt the need to organize their air transport industries, although in each case the approach to the task and rate of progress varied. The United States, Britain and the Soviet Union were in the forefront of this expansion, having come through the war with flourishing aviation industries and manufacturing capacity intact. These three leaders were joined, somewhat surprisingly, by France whose defeat and occupation during the war had precluded any progress worthy of the name in aircraft production.

The French aviation industry had gone into a state of suspended animation during the years of German occupation but in 1945 it came to life once more and gradually started to make significant progress, resulting within a relatively short space of time in a strong, independent aeronautical industry, producing both military and civil aircraft.

The French drive to regain an important role in aviation resulted, in the second half of the decade, in the production of the large, four-engine Sud-Est SE-161 Languedoc and SE-2010 Armagnac airliners, aimed at retrieving some of the business captured by the American manufacturers, an ambitious objective considering the advanced technology and impressive capacity of the giant American aircraft companies whose output in the immediate postwar years covered the entire range of aircraft needed by the commercial aviation industry, from short-to-medium-range airliners. This market was catered for by Martin and Convair with the earlier versions of their twin-engine airliners, Convairs remaining in service for over twenty years as worthy successors to the DC-3. Long-range airliners offered to the airline companies included the four-engine Boeing 377 Stratocruiser and the Lockheed L-749 Constellation, which joined the DC-4 in the keen competition for business on the North Atlantic route. The American aircraft industry was to emerge as the clear winner in the fight to sell aircraft for this prestige route during the transitional phase prior to the introduction of jet engines.

Meanwhile, the Soviet Union was quietly but rapidly profiting from having been given the necessary technology to develop jet-powered aircraft, while continuing to build successful piston-engine airliners such as the Ilyushin Il-12 of 1946.

American dominance was only partially threatened by new British aircraft, some of which were built mainly for European markets and sold well, others being commercial failures [among them the Avro 688 and 689 Tudors of 1945-46] or meeting with only very modest success [Handley Page's H.P.81 Hermes of 1948]. Internationally competitive airliners had to wait until the 1950s when turboprop aircraft were introduced, the Vickers Viscount being the first of this new generation of aircraft.

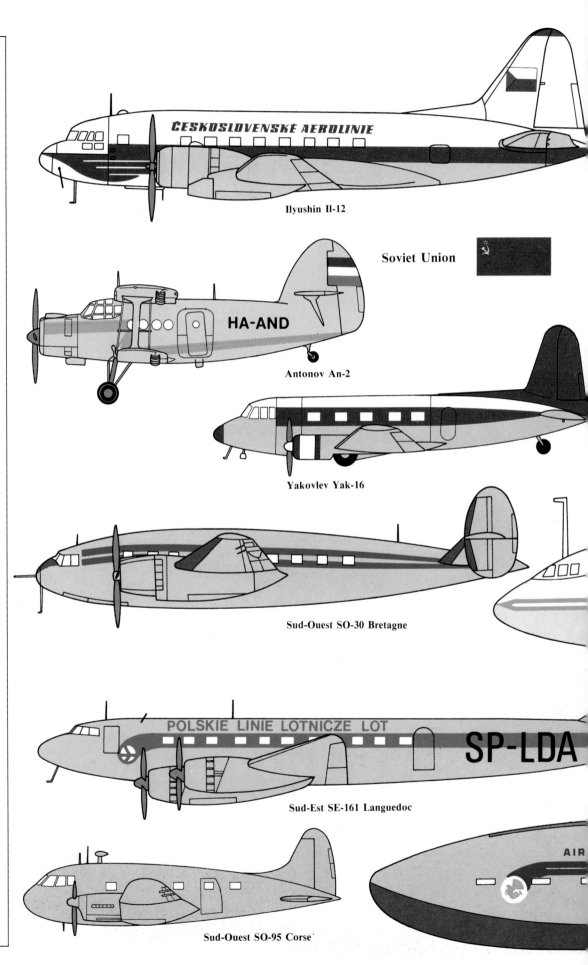

Ilyushin Il-12

Soviet Union

HA-AND

Antonov An-2

Yakovlev Yak-16

Sud-Ouest SO-30 Bretagne

POLSKIE LINIE LOTNICZE LOT

SP-LDA

Sud-Est SE-161 Languedoc

Sud-Ouest SO-95 Corse

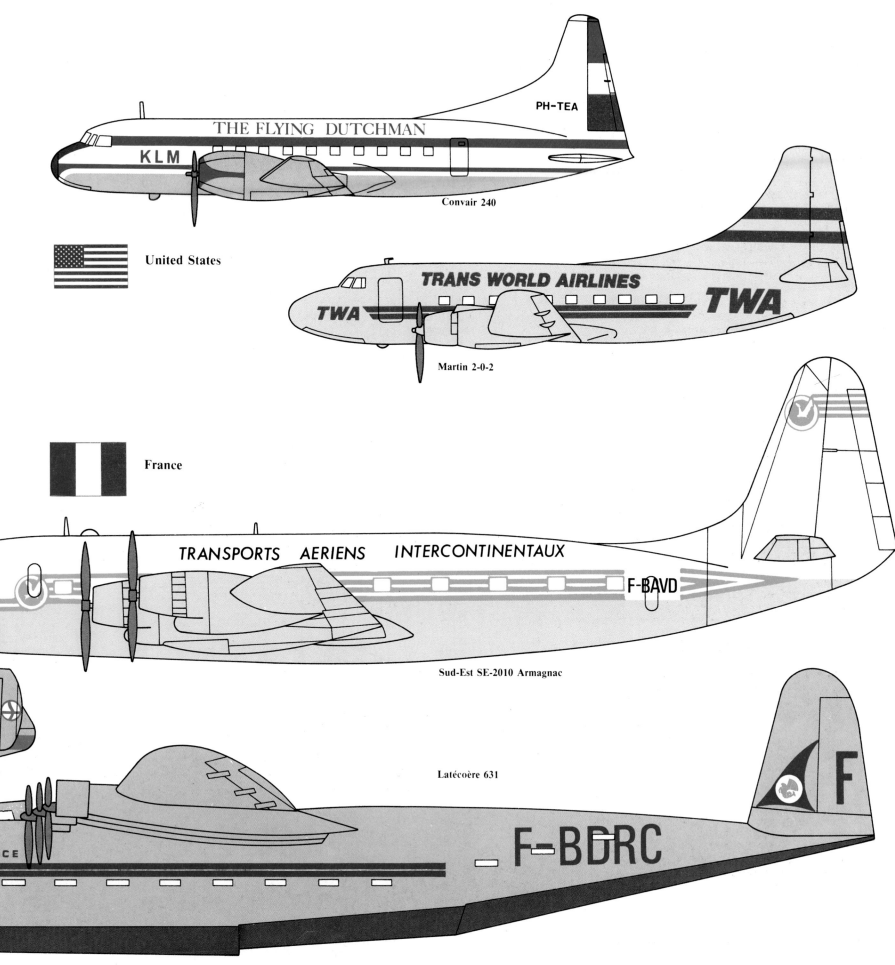

THE FLYING DUTCHMAN

PH-TEA

KLM

Convair 240

United States

TRANS WORLD AIRLINES

TWA

TWA

Martin 2-0-2

France

TRANSPORTS AERIENS INTERCONTINENTAUX

F-BAVD

Sud-Est SE-2010 Armagnac

Latécoère 631

F-BDRC

NCE

F

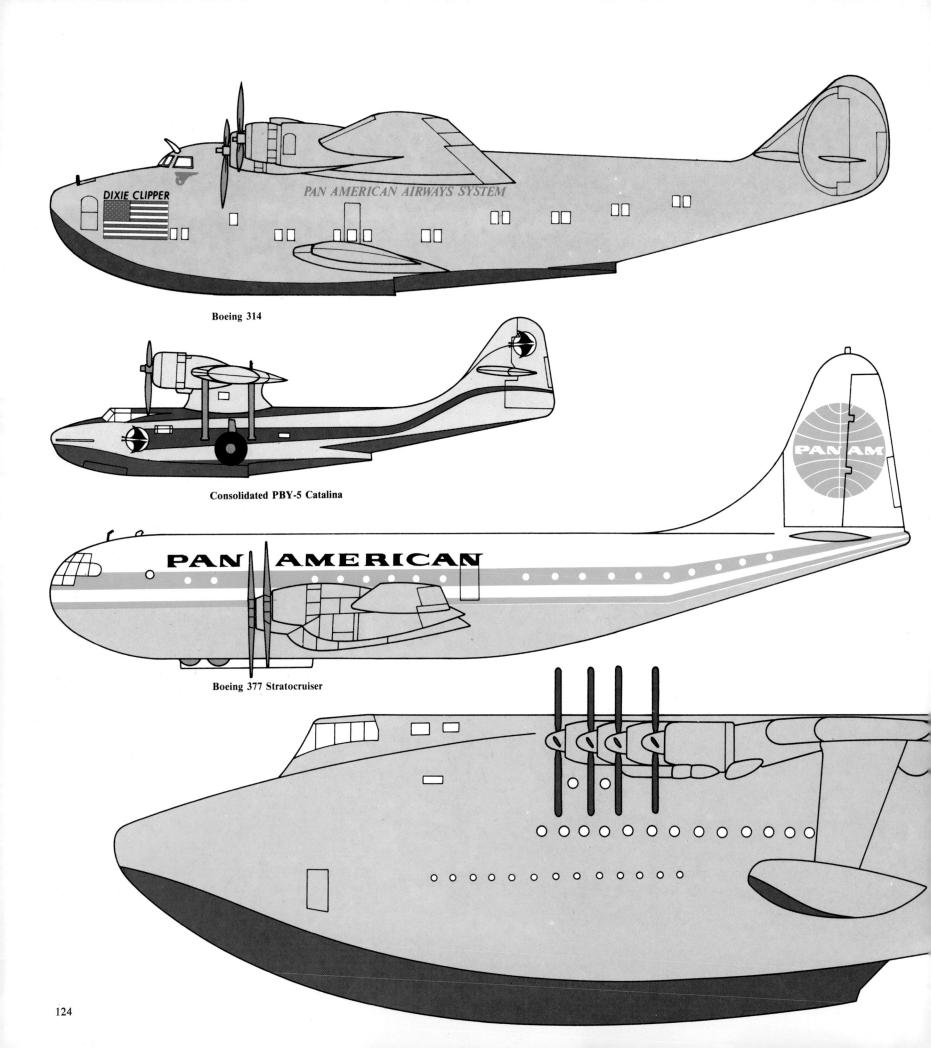

Boeing 314

Consolidated PBY-5 Catalina

Boeing 377 Stratocruiser

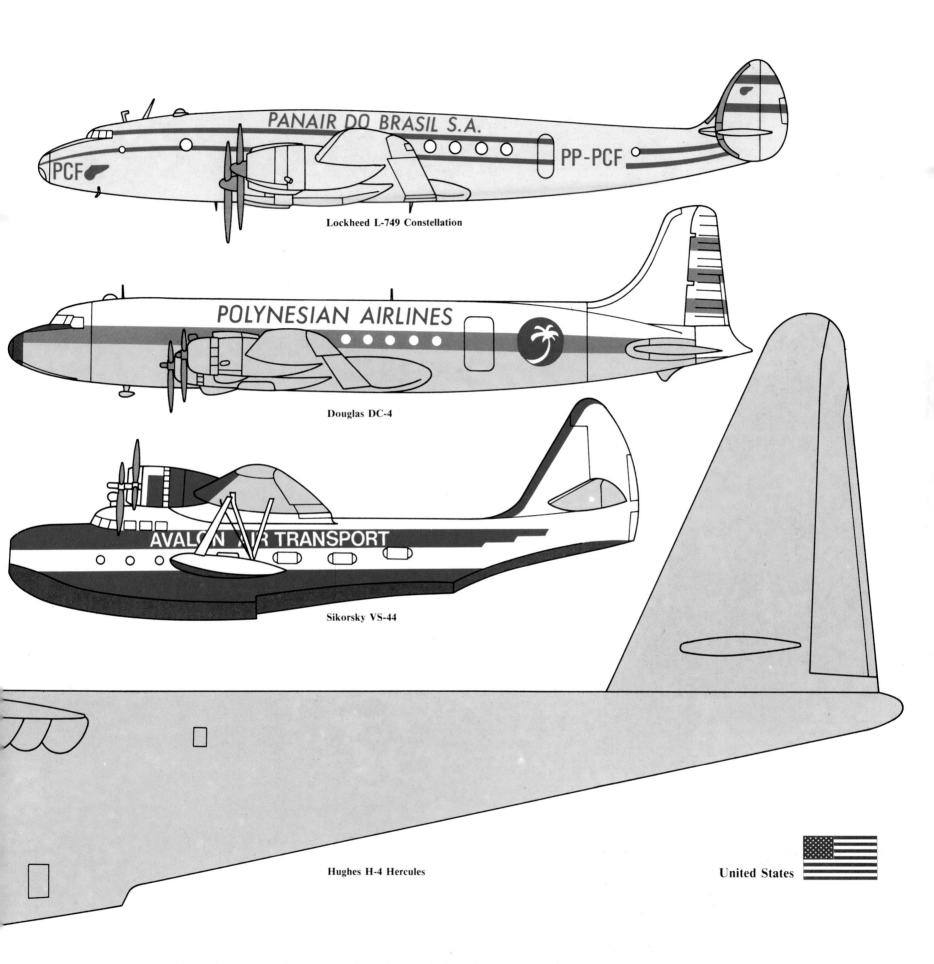

PANAIR DO BRASIL S.A.

PCF

PP-PCF

**Lockheed L-749 Constellation**

POLYNESIAN AIRLINES

**Douglas DC-4**

AVALON AIR TRANSPORT

**Sikorsky VS-44**

**Hughes H-4 Hercules**

**United States**

# 1940-1950
## The "Spruce Goose" and Brabazon – unsuccessful giants

This period of frenzied activity saw the launching of two of the most ambitious commercial projects ever undertaken, which, however, failed to realize their sponsors' expectations: the American Hughes H-4 Hercules [better known as "Spruce Goose"] and the British Bristol 167 Brabazon, enormous planes, both powered by eight engines.

The Hercules project dated back to 1942. Two of the most famous and colourful industrialists of the day, Henry J. Kaiser [the shipping magnate] and Howard Hughes, the millionaire flying enthusiast [already well known for his record-breaking flights] conceived the plan of constructing 5,000 gigantic flying boats to be used as military transports, which would replace whole fleets of merchant ships thereby robbing the German U-boats of their prey.

Although the idea met with considerable scepticism, it was thought sufficiently feasible by some members of the military staff for a contract to be signed in November 1942 for three prototypes. The procurement stipulated that construction was to be predominantly of wood in order to cut down on the use of strategic materials. The program got under way but serious delays built up due to the considerable technical difficulties inherent in the design.

With the war beginning to turn in favour of the Allies, the military authorities were no longer interested in developing the scheme and the program was cancelled in 1945. Howard Hughes was left with the first and only prototype, still unfinished. Nothing daunted, he completed it at his own expense, piloting the plane on its maiden flight in the Los Angeles roadstead on 2 November 1947. The "Spruce Goose" made only this one test flight, watched by thousands of excited and expectant onlookers. It was then towed back to its hangar where it remained for many years. The Hercules is now housed in a special museum at Long Beach.

The Brabazon project turned out much the same, having taken shape in 1943 on the recommendations of a special government committee which had been set the task of defining guidelines for development of postwar British commercial airplanes. The aim was to build an aircraft which could fly nonstop between London and New York, carrying at least 100 passengers. Progress on construction of the two prototypes was, however, very slow, plagued by continual technical hitches, mainly connected with cabin pressurization and with problems in the eight engines, each driving counter-rotating propellers.

The aircraft had its maiden flight on 4 September 1949, followed by a series of proving flights which dragged on for nearly two years. It was at this juncture that further difficulties arose during construction of the second prototype. In July 1953 the decision was finally taken to abandon the project and both the prototypes were scrapped.

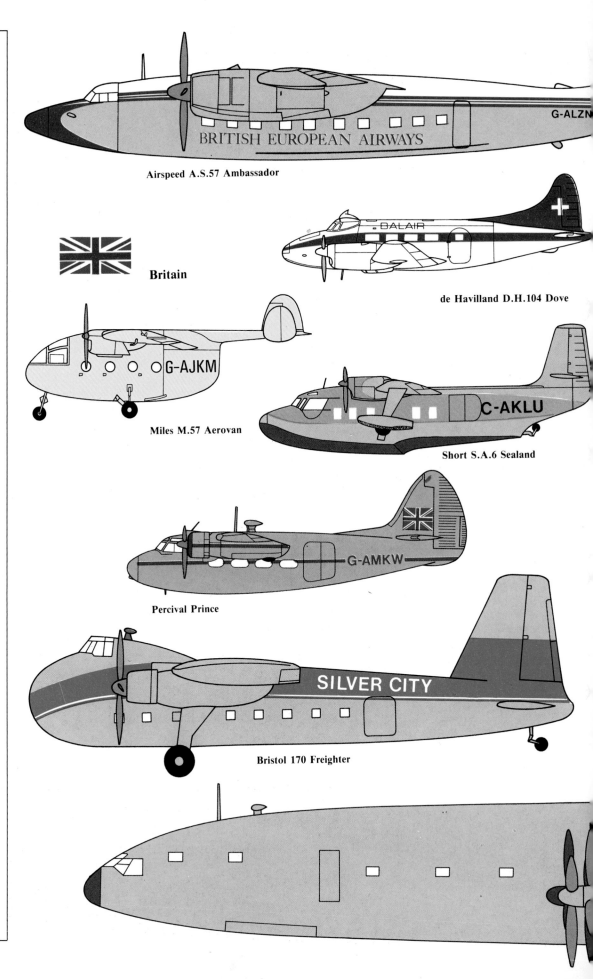

Airspeed A.S.57 Ambassador

Britain

de Havilland D.H.104 Dove

Miles M.57 Aerovan

Short S.A.6 Sealand

Percival Prince

Bristol 170 Freighter

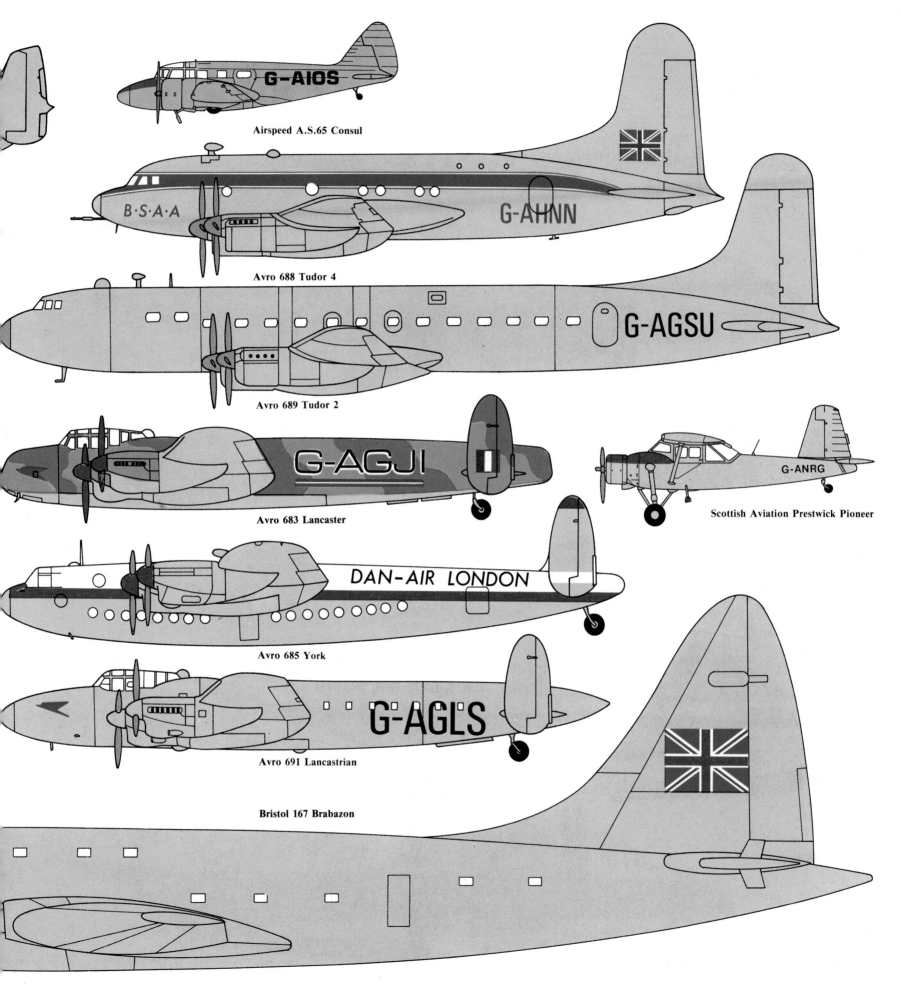

Airspeed A.S.65 Consul

Avro 688 Tudor 4

Avro 689 Tudor 2

Avro 683 Lancaster

Scottish Aviation Prestwick Pioneer

Avro 685 York

Avro 691 Lancastrian

Bristol 167 Brabazon

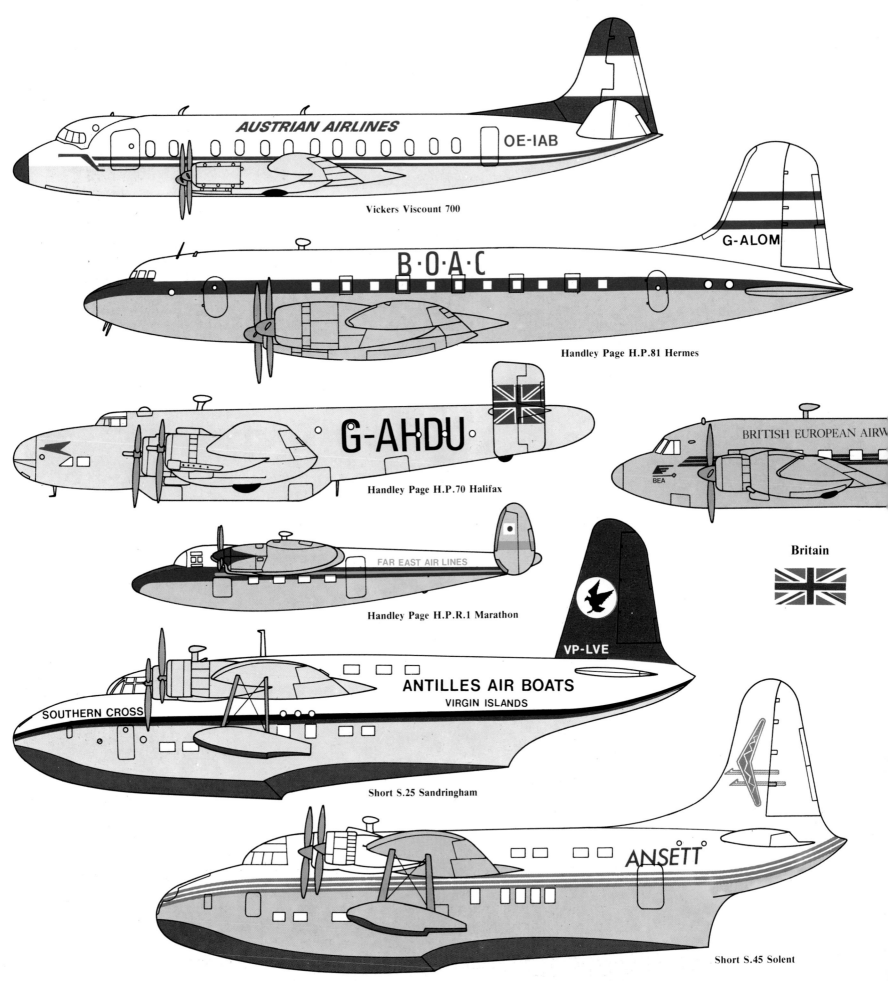

AUSTRIAN AIRLINES OE-IAB

Vickers Viscount 700

B·O·A·C G-ALOM

Handley Page H.P.81 Hermes

G-AHDU

Handley Page H.P.70 Halifax

BRITISH EUROPEAN AIRW

BEA

FAR EAST AIR LINES

Handley Page H.P.R.1 Marathon

Britain

VP-LVE

ANTILLES AIR BOATS
VIRGIN ISLANDS

SOUTHERN CROSS

Short S.25 Sandringham

ANSETT

Short S.45 Solent

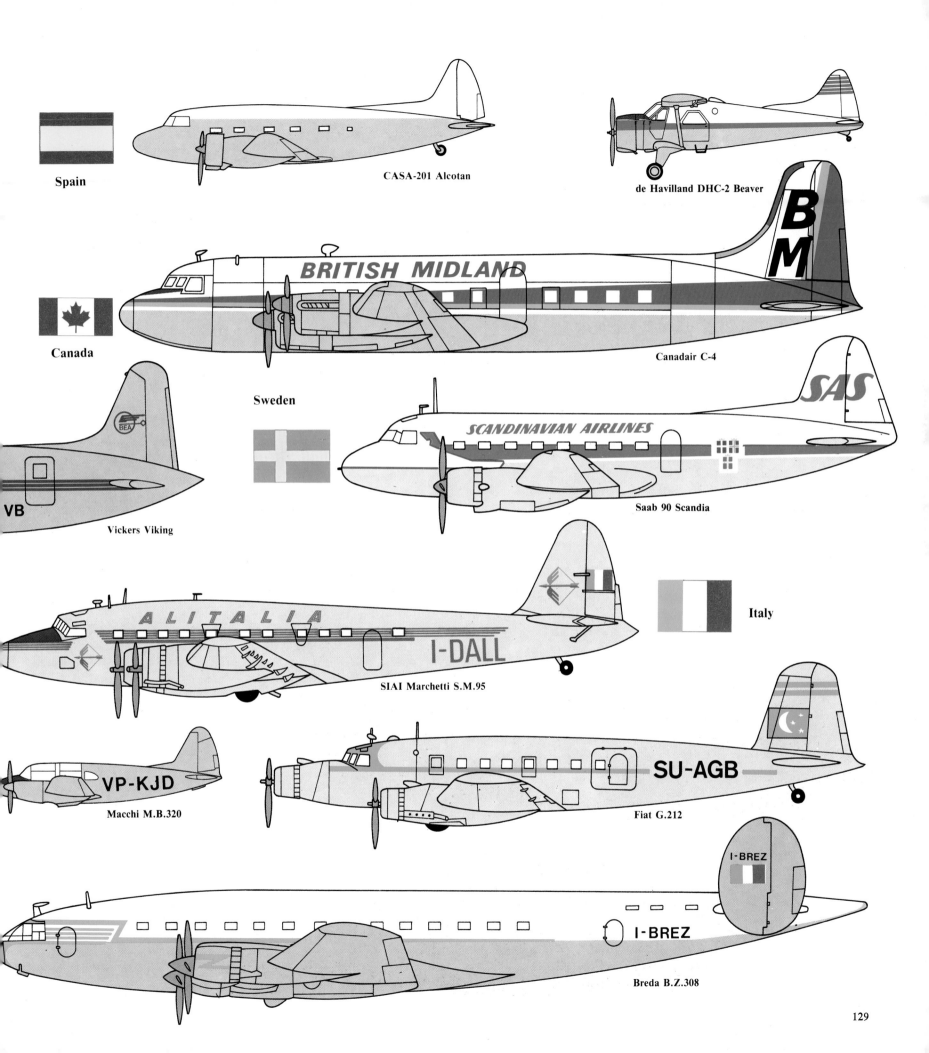

Spain

CASA-201 Alcotan

de Havilland DHC-2 Beaver

Canada

*BRITISH MIDLAND*

**B
M**

Canadair C-4

Sweden

VB

Vickers Viking

*SCANDINAVIAN AIRLINES*

**SAS**

Saab 90 Scandia

*ALITALIA*

**I-DALL**

Italy

SIAI Marchetti S.M.95

**VP-KJD**

Macchi M.B.320

**SU-AGB**

Fiat G.212

I-BREZ

**I-BREZ**

Breda B.Z.308

129

## Weather has its brighter side
### AND THAT'S WHERE TWA SKYLINERS FLY

Your whole picture of winter travel will change for the better
once you've flown TWA. For all thoughts of icy roads and snowbound
delays melt away when you travel at TWA's "fair-weather" level.
Up here sunshine knows no season; the stars light your way at night.
And while your TWA Skyliner makes time, you spend it
in leisurely fashion . . . enjoying the kind of service that's made TWA
first choice of more than two million passengers each year.

Where in the world do you want to go? For information
and reservations, call TWA or see your travel agent.

ACROSS THE U.S. AND OVERSEAS . . . FLY **TWA**
TRANS WORLD AIRLINES
U.S.A. · EUROPE · AFRICA · ASIA

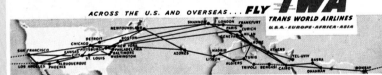

# 1950
# 1960

## THE JET AGE

The jet engine had been developed during the war and was to be the greatest influence on aircraft design in the 1950s. The enormous advances made in engine technology sparked off a new phase in the growth of aviation; while the effects of this technological revolution had already started to make themselves felt in the military sector in the first years of peace, it was not until the early 1960s that the full impact was felt in the civil transport market. When the time came, however, the effects were breathtaking. The changes which came about transformed a vast, worldwide industry which seemed capable of exponential growth and also presented designers and airlines with a new challenge, and competition became fiercer than ever.

Today this rivalry is still just as keen, although operating conditions have changed greatly since the early years of jet travel. Then, as now, the main protagonists were the United States, Britain and France in the West while the Soviet Union led the eastern bloc. The U.S.A. swiftly established a commanding lead, having achieved world air supremacy during the war. A few figures suffice to show just how vast the market had become. In 1960 the 92 airlines which belonged to IATA [the International Association of Travel Agents] reached the milestone of 100 million passengers carried; in that same year over fifty per cent of this volume was accounted for by American airlines, nearly forty per cent of which was carried by the five companies: United, Eastern, American, TWA and Pan Am, the remainder being shared by the other airlines – a total of about sixty running regular scheduled services.

This great surge of expansion had started to gather momentum in 1941 when America had yet to become embroiled in the war and this vast country with its large population was still isolated from the bloodshed which convulsed much of the rest of the world. In 1945 U.S. domestic airlines carried 6 million passengers [fifty per cent more than the total reached four years earlier]. In 1951 the totals revealed an even more impressive growth: American Airlines alone accounted for 4.9 million passengers; Eastern, 3.5 million; United, nearly 3 million; TWA, 2.2 million; Capital Airlines, almost 2 million; a further seven airlines each carried totals varying between 500,000 and one million.

In 1948, 240,000 passengers flew the North Atlantic route, the most hotly contested international service, with all the European airlines vying with each other to secure a good share of this lucrative business; of the 1948 transatlantic total, 148,000 passengers flew with TWA, Pan American and American Overseas; two years later [when these last two operators had merged] 174,000 passengers out of a total of 311,000 had travelled with an American airline. In 1960 the total of passengers carried reached 1,760,000; of these 368,000 flew Pan Am and 243,000 with TWA. In addition to this large share of passenger traffic, the U.S. aviation industry earned great prestige during this period through its commanding lead in aeronautical technology which was to influence every facet of civil aviation all over the world.

Although Britain, followed by the U.S.S.R., had put jet airliners into service before the United States, this ground was soon retrieved both in terms of numbers and the caliber of jet airliners coming off U.S. assembly lines. Much of the credit for this must go to Boeing: its 707 was not only the first commercial jet to be built in the U.S.A., it gave birth to a long line of airliners which were to prove immensely influential in the western world's civil aviation industry. The other two giant U.S. aircraft companies – Douglas and Lockheed – soon produced rival airliners and these three vast manufacturing concerns captured the lion's share of international markets, the only exception to this being the Eastern bloc, which the Soviet Union controlled and supplied.

Apart from the Soviet Union, two other countries were to play an influential role in postwar aviation: Britain and France. The daunting task of reorganizing the British airlines started on 1 August 1946 when BEA [British European Airways] was formed, taking over the entire European network from BOAC. This quickly led to improved efficiency but the British airlines had to await full recovery until the aircraft industry had adjusted itself to peacetime production and was able to exploit the commanding lead in engine development built up during the war.

The most important milestones in this process were the maiden flights of the Viscount [16 July 1948] and the Comet [27 July 1949], the former being the first turboprop airliner in the world and the latter the world's first commercial pure jet. The Comet suffered a grave setback early in its career [having made its inaugural flight on 2 May 1952] with two crashes on 10 January and 8 April 1954, near Elba and Stromboli, resulting in a four-and-a-half year delay to the aircraft's program, which very nearly cost Britain her lead.

Tupolev Tu-104, 1957

The Viscount, however, proved a great success from the outset. Once the first of the new turboprop airliners had gone into service [29 July 1950] and been enthusiastically received, BEA started to win a larger share of business: in 1955 it was the leading European airline, carrying one million passengers on European international routes and nearly 850,000 on domestic flights; by 1960 these totals had risen to two million and 1,700,000 respectively. BOAC's passenger traffic for these same two years was approximately 300,000 rising to 800,000 on its intercontinental routes, overtaking Air France by the end of the 1960s.

Air France, the French national carrier, had been reestablished on 1 January 1946 and reorganization and expansion had followed swiftly, encouraged by the government's vigorously pursued policy to put the country's aeronautical industry on a sound footing. Air France's success was also due in large part to the excellent airliners which the French aircraft industry was providing during this period, the most outstanding being the Caravelle, a twinjet which unexpectedly put French aircraft production on a par with U.S. manufacturers during the mid fifties. Air France had the biggest share of intercontinental business of all the European companies in 1955 [over 450,000 passengers] but was in second place in 1960, after BEA, with 700,000. On European and domestic routes, Air France was well behind BEA, with 650,000 European and 450,000 domestic in 1955 and over 1,250,000 and 950,000 in 1960.

Lockheed F-104 Starfighter, 1958

Since the war, Aeroflot has understandably retained its position as the largest rival to western commercial aviation as well as being the world's largest company. The Soviet state airline had reached second place in Europe by the eve of the Second World War and with the cessation of hostilities a program of recovery was launched in 1946, which led to very rapid expansion. The war had the effect of making the Soviet aircraft industry more efficient, which meant that Aeroflot could rely on a supply of competitive airliners; by the end of 1950 the state carrier served a network of over 186,000 miles [300,500 km], carrying 1,600,000 passengers and 181,000 tonnes of cargo and mail. By 1960 these totals had risen to nearly 200,000 miles [321,800 km], 2,500,000 passengers and nearly 259,000 tonnes of freight. Aircraft production was maintained at consistently high levels to satisfy the demand resulting from this growth. During a period of nearly two years Aeroflot was the only airline in the world to operate scheduled services with jet airliners. This historic step was taken on 15 September 1956 when the Tupolev Tu-104 made its inaugural flight and lasted until 4 October 1958 when the British Comets reentered service.

In the fifties, the "Big four" – those countries which then as now were in the forefront of aeronautical development, found themselves facing competition from literally hundreds of newly established airlines, a situation which was to bring about

Sud-Aviation SE-210 Caravelle, 1959

English Electric Lightning, 1961

Mikoyan-Gurevich MiG-21, 1958

drastic stages all over the world, within the contours of civil aviation. It was inevitable that some operators who had formerly enjoyed positions of prestige should lose their grip on the market when confronted by a new, harsh world of cut-throat competition. The two main defeated powers, Germany and Japan, rose to the challenge: Lufthansa and Japan Air Lines managed to claw their way back into the market and begin a process of recovery that eventually took them to the front rank.

In Italy civil aviation had to start again from scratch and in 1946 two state companies, Alitalia and Linee Aeree Italiane [LAI] were entrusted with the uphill task of winning back business. It proved a slow and difficult process and only started to meet with measurable success after the two airlines had merged in 1957 to form today's single state carrier, Alitalia.

During this first phase of the introduction of the jet engine the most widespread and rapidly developing changes were in the field of military aviation. The new postwar power groupings had resulted in the world being effectively split into two opposing blocs. Ironically, the most effective way of ensuring a lasting global peace seemed to lie in a finely tuned balance of military strength between both camps. This rationale fuelled the arms race as never before. The role of military aircraft was once again in the ascendant as each side strove to develop ever more deadly and sophisticated warplanes. As a result every aspect of aircraft design and construction came under scrutiny and reassessment: airframes, materials, equipment and avionics, primarily instigated by the enormous potential of jet propulsion and the possibility of extending the airplane's capability to limits which would have been inconceivable in the recent past.

Inevitably, the United States and the Soviet Union, set the pace. As leader of the Western powers, the United States had assumed the responsibility for protecting her allies and maintaining peace and no effort was spared to reorganize and strengthen her air power. The USAAF became a separate armed force on 18 September 1947 [its acronym changing to USAF] and together with the U.S. Navy's airforce exploited the great American industrial potential to the full, with demands for increasingly effective warplanes. The Soviet armed forces were no less demanding of their state industries.

A chance for these two superpowers to measure their strength in direct confrontation soon occurred in the guise of the Korean war, which broke out on 25 June 1950. In many ways this far-off conflict was a proving ground, in which modern military weapons [especially aircraft and their armament] were put to the test, and current tactical and strategic theories of warfare given practical application. This was the great powers' first opportunity of evaluating in the field what progress the enemy had made and the size and range of his armoury.

The Korean war triggered the second phase in postwar military aviation. The 1950s saw the birth of aircraft which were to be in front-line service for the next twenty years and the lessons of the war soon crystallized into the requirements for the world's airforces for the years to come: aircraft would be needed which could operate at speeds beyond the speed of sound, or even at twice the speed of sound, which called for new materials to be developed, new construction techniques and very sophisticated electronics. The most important American planes belonging to this new generation were the USAF's F-100, F-102, F-104 and the F-105, and the Navy's F-8 and F-4, as well as such strategic bombers as the powerful B-52. The U.S.S.R. fielded the family of MiG fighters, including the outstanding MiG-19 and MiG-21, while several excellent bombers were designed by the Yakovlev and Tupolev design bureaus.

## 1950-1960
## From Britain – the turboprop

One aircraft accounts for three historic dates in the history of civil aviation: the de Havilland D.H.106 Comet. On 27 July 1949 the prototype had its maiden flight, the first jet-powered airliner to take to the air; on 2 May 1952 the first scheduled jet passenger service was inaugurated [London-Johannesburg, with the Comet I registration G-ALYP]; on 4 October 1958 the first transatlantic service by jet aircraft [London-New York] was launched, after stiff competition between BOAC and Pan American, the latter flying Boeing 707-120s.

Besides the importance of these dates in the dramatic early stages of the development of the British four-engine jet airliner [interrupted by crashes leading to protracted enquiries into the causes, involving long delays in the Comet program] other events took place around these years which were also highly significant: on 15 September 1956 Aeroflot's first jet airliner, the Tupolev Tu-104 made its inaugural flight on the Moscow-Omsk-Irkutsk route; on 12 May 1959 Air France's Sud-Aviation SE-210 Caravelle entered service: this versatile and dependable twinjet was not only Europe's second alternative to the American jet challenge, it also introduced a highly successful new design formula which was soon adopted throughout the aircraft industry as the classic configuration for short-to-medium-range civil transports.

Once commercial jets had been introduced, progress was very swift and manufacturers competed aggressively for orders. The U.S. aircraft industry soon recovered its lead in the western world, with European companies trailing behind, and the two giant American manufacturers, Boeing and Douglas quickly proved their mettle. Boeing's first commercial jet had to fight hard for its market share against its direct [and equally attractive] rival, the DC-8, which Douglas had launched on 7 June 1955 [four months later Pan Am placed an order for 25 of these airliners, giving the first boost to its successful career]. Competition was fierce, with no quarter given. Some fine aircraft fell victim to this climate of merciless rivalry, such as the two projects developed by Convair in the late fifties: the 880 and the 990 [which had their maiden flights on 27 January 1959 and 24 January 1961 respectively]; in spite of being good designs, they failed to attract enough customers.

The jet engine was now to be teamed with aviation's earliest system of propulsion: the propeller. The British were once more first to introduce a new idea – redefining da Vinci's "airscrew" and endowing it with hitherto undreamt of possibilities when they developed the turbine engine. The Vickers Viscount [the world's first commercial turboprop] proved such a success that a succession of these aircraft was developed at the same time as pure jet airliners, evolving just as quickly and proving invaluable.

The long-awaited introduction of a nonstop scheduled London-New York service, for which many designers and manufacturers had developed aircraft

*continued on page 140*

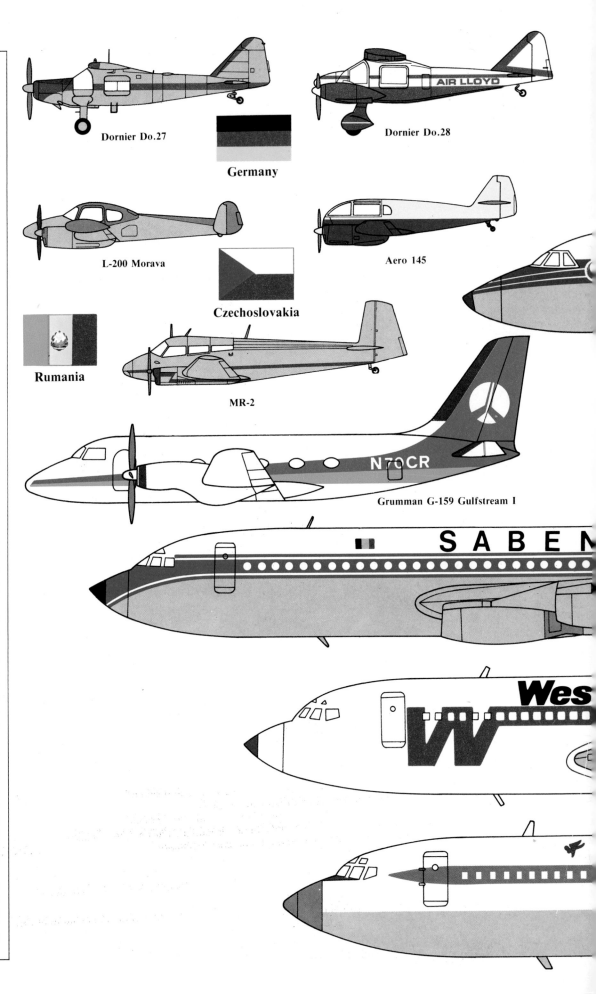

Dornier Do.27

Dornier Do.28

**Germany**

L-200 Morava

Aero 145

**Czechoslovakia**

**Rumania**

MR-2

Grumman G-159 Gulfstream I

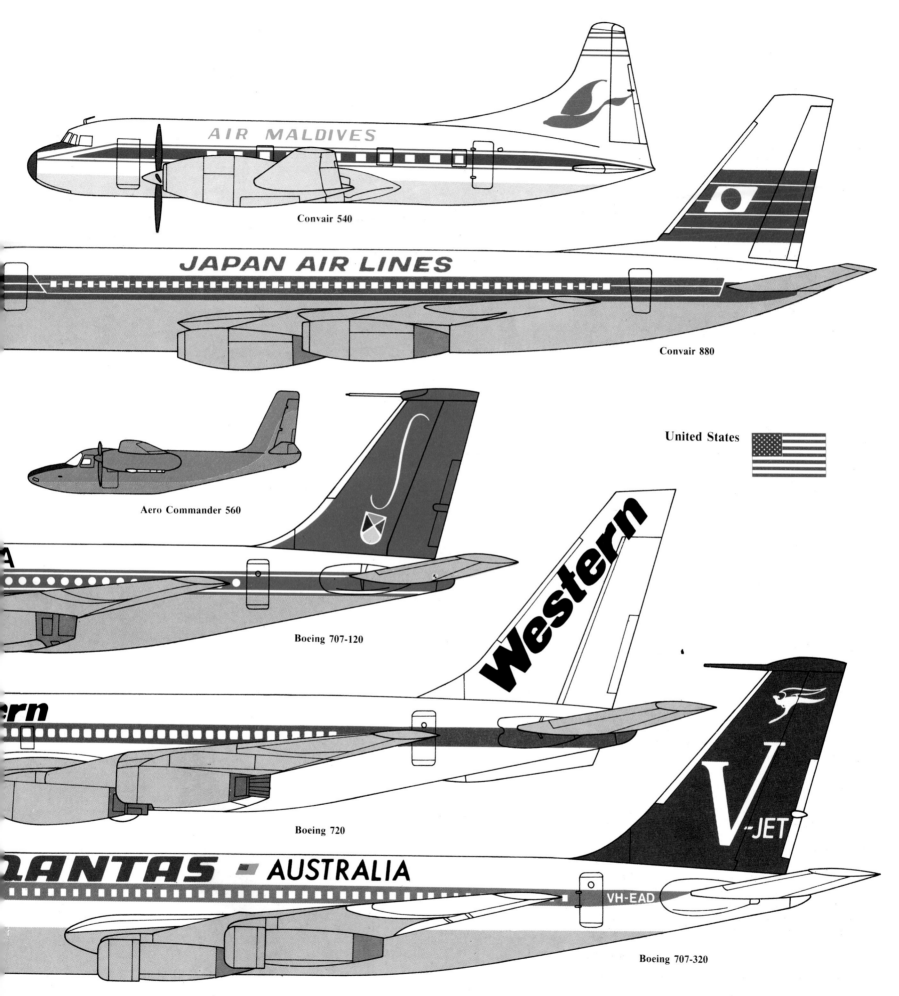

AIR MALDIVES

Convair 540

JAPAN AIR LINES

Convair 880

Aero Commander 560

United States

Boeing 707-120

Western

Boeing 720

QANTAS — AUSTRALIA

VH-EAD

V-JET

Boeing 707-320

1 nose cone
2 weather radar scanner
3 glide-slope aerial
4 forward pressure bulkhead
5 pitot head
6 nose frames
7 windscreen panels
8 eyebrow windows
9 overhead console
10 First Officer's seat
11 Captain's seat
12 forward frame
13 twin nosewheels
14 nosewheel doors
15 nosewheel box
16 drag struts
17 Navigator's table
18 Observer's seat
19 Navigator's seat
20 Navigator's overhead panel
21 Flight Engineer's seat
22 Flight Engineer's instrument panels
23 flight deck entry door
24 crew coat closet
25 crew toilet
26 crew galley/buffet
27 spare life vest stowage
28 radio (emergency) transmitter
29 life raft stowage (2)
30 VHF aerial
31 smoke and fume-proof curtain
32 forward entry door (24 × 72 ins)
33 escape slide stowage
34 forward underfloor freight hold
35 cabin floor level
36 six cargo pallets (total 4,424 cu ft)
37 ball transfer mat (five segments)
38 door actuator rams
39 main cargo door (raised)
40 engine intakes
41 secondary inlet doors
42 turbocompressor intakes
43 turbocompressor outlets
44 nacelle pylons
45 leading-edge wing flaps
46 main tank no. 3 (4,069 US gals)
47 fuel system dry bay
48 vortex generators
49 main tank no. 4 (2,323 US gals)
50 reserve tank (439 US gals)
51 vent surge tank
52 starboard wingtip
53 starboard outboard aileron
54 aileron balance tab
55 starboard outboard spoiler (extended)
56 starboard outboard flap
57 flap tracks
58 aileron/spoiler actuator linkage
59 starboard inboard aileron
60 control tab
61 starboard inboard flap
62 starboard inboard spoiler (extended)
63 life raft stowage (4)
64 escape straps
65 escape hatches/emergency exits (20 × 38 ins) (4)
66 life raft attachment clips
67 inter-cabin movable bulkhead
68 access door (port walkway)
69 fuselage frames
70 87-passenger Tourist Class cabin configuration (34 ins seat pitch)

71 4-abreast seating row (emergency exit stations)
72 ceiling air-conditioning
73 passenger amenities
74 rear cabin single-row seating
75 cabin windows
76 coat closet
77 life raft stowage (2)
78 spare life vests (and machete)
79 first aid kit
80 aft service door (starboard) (24 × 48 ins)
81 fin fillet
82 starboard tailplane
83 VOR antenna
84 removable fin leading edge
85 rudder control linkage
86 tail fin construction
87 rudder "Q" bellows
88 HF probe antenna
89 LORAN antenna
90 rudder
91 rudder control tab
92 rudder anti-balance tab
93 internal balance panel
94 rudder flutter damper
95 elevator torque tube
96 rudder trim tab
97 tail cone
98 tailplane actuator tab
99 elevator control tab
100 port elevator
101 port tailplane
102 internal balance panel
103 elevator linkage
104 crank assembly
105 elevator quadrant
106 autopilot elevator servo
107 tail fin spar/fuselage joints
108 rear pressure bulkhead
109 aft toilets (2)
110 coat closet
111 aft entry door
112 escape slide stowage
113 vestibule
114 fuselage skinning
115 aft underfloor freight hold
116 wingroot fairing
117 fillet flap
118 landing gear trunnion
119 undercarriage shock strut
120 main undercarriage well
121 side strut
122 torsion links
123 fuel tank end rib
124 wing rear spar/fuselage pick-up point
125 inboard wing stringers
126 wing front spar/fuselage pick-up point
127 fuselage center tank forward face
128 landing lights

129 front spar
130 four-wheel main landing gear
131 port inboard spoilers
132 port inboard flap
133 vortex generators
134 nacelle pylon
135 turbocompressor
136 engine intake
137 Pratt & Whitney JT3D turbofan
138 fan thrust reverser doors
139 engine fuel pump
140 starter
141 primary thrust reverser cascade vanes
142 wing anti-ice check valve
143 wing anti-ice shut-off valve
144 duct temperature sensor
145 leading-edge wing flap
146 dimpled inner skin
147 rear spar

148 leading-edge thermal anti-icing duct
149 integral wing fuel tanks
150 port inboard aileron
151 control tab
152 port outboard spoilers
153 port outboard flap
154 engine access doors (port and starboard)
155 nacelle nose cowl
156 nacelle structure
157 strut/pylon attachment
158 exhaust
159 pylon/wing joint
160 tab
161 leading-edge anti-ice supply manifold
162 port outboard aileron
163 wing skinning
164 port wingtip

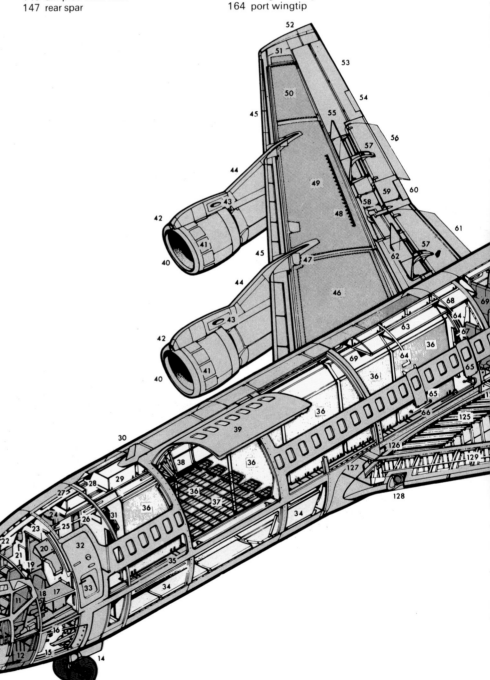

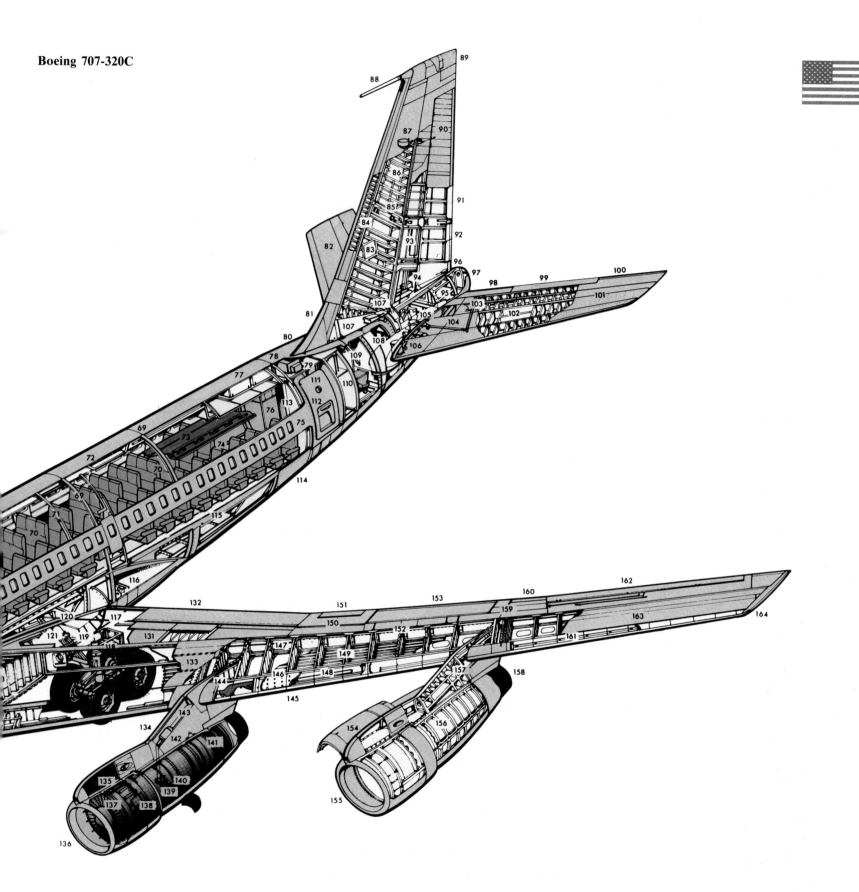

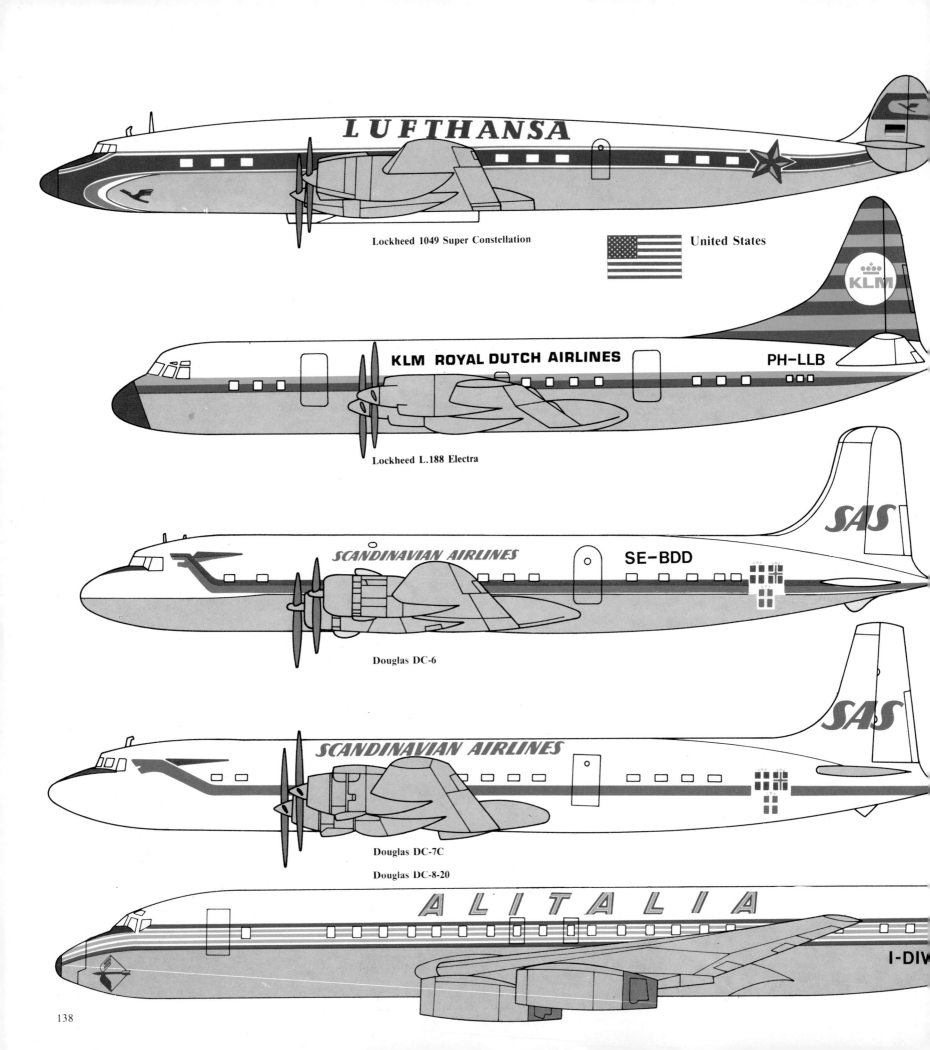

LUFTHANSA

Lockheed 1049 Super Constellation

United States

KLM ROYAL DUTCH AIRLINES

PH-LLB

Lockheed L.188 Electra

SAS

SCANDINAVIAN AIRLINES

SE-BDD

Douglas DC-6

SAS

SCANDINAVIAN AIRLINES

Douglas DC-7C

Douglas DC-8-20

ALITALIA

I-DIW

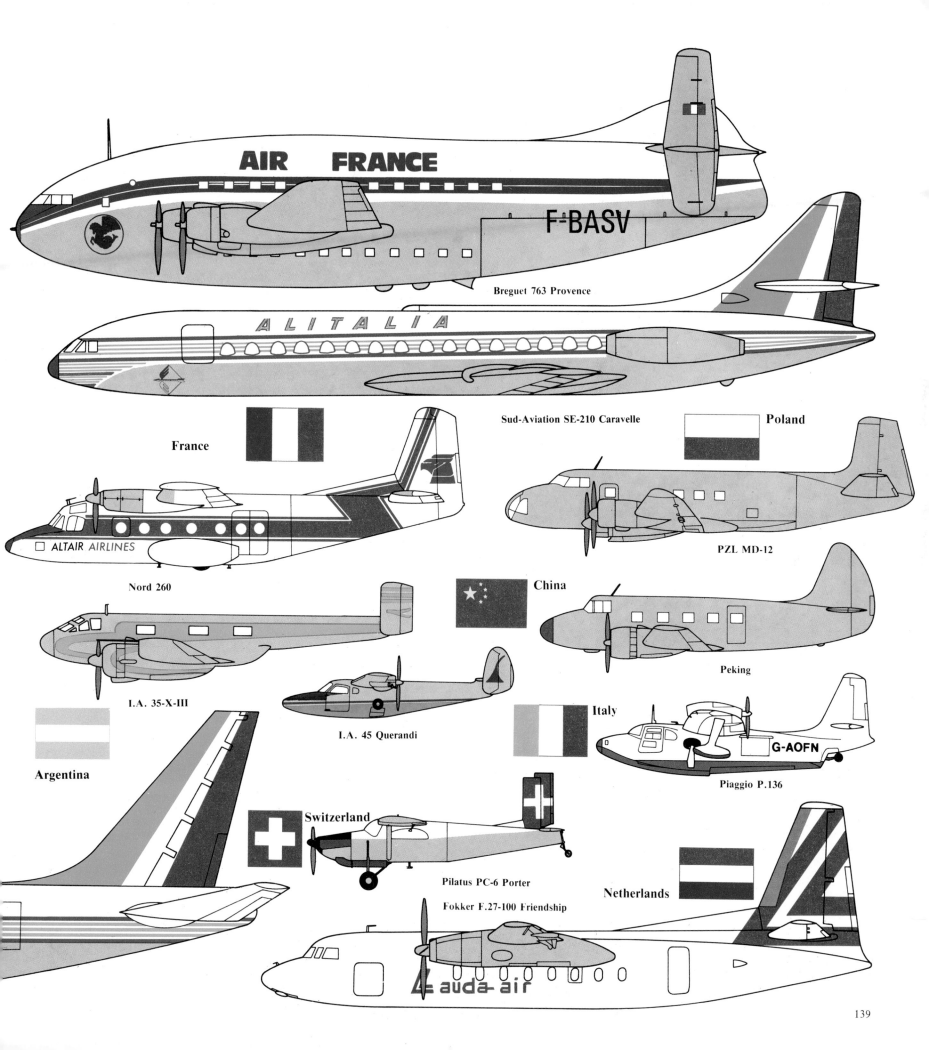

AIR FRANCE

F-BASV

Breguet 763 Provence

*ALITALIA*

Sud-Aviation SE-210 Caravelle

France

Poland

ALTAIR AIRLINES

PZL MD-12

Nord 260

China

I.A. 35-X-III

Peking

I.A. 45 Querandi

Italy

G-AOFN

Argentina

Piaggio P.136

Switzerland

Pilatus PC-6 Porter

Netherlands

Fokker F.27-100 Friendship

*auda-air*

139

*continued from page 134*

which never actually flew the route, was finally achieved by BOAC when the airline launched its service on 19 December 1957. The airliner which made this possible was the Bristol 175 Britannia, a clean-lined four-engine turboprop aircraft which was the first of its type to fly a regular nonstop route across the North Atlantic. Following in the wake of the Vickers Viscount's success, this plane marked another important achievement for the British aircraft industry and underlined its lead in this spectacular sector of aviation technology, ahead of the U.S. manufacturers.

The Britannia was soon followed by other aircraft using turboprop engines, [the first series Britannia having flown on 5 September 1954]. The United States and the Soviet Union designed and built their own turboprop airplanes; in the U.S.A. the Lockheed L.188 Electra went into service with Eastern Air Lines on 12 January 1959 [the prototype having had its maiden flight on 6 December 1957] while the U.S.S.R.'s Ilyushin Il-18 first flew on 4 July 1957, joining Aeroflot's fleet on 20 April 1959.

The Lockheed Electra was the only turboprop commercial transport developed during this era in the U.S.A. but in the U.S.S.R. others besides the Il-18 were built during the 1950s. The gigantic Tupolev Tu-144 was developed around this time [when the first of these outsize four-engine airliners made its appearance on 3 October 1957, it was the world's heaviest commercial aircraft] as was the Antonov An-10 and An-12 [which also saw a great deal of service with the military]. Toward the end of the decade these aircraft were joined by the smaller Antonov An-24 [first flight 20 December 1959], a short-to-medium-range twin-engine airliner which was on a par with the best of contemporary European production, such as the British Handley Page H.P.R.7 Herald and the Dutch Fokker F.27 Friendship, the latter proving one of the greatest success stories among turboprop airliners marketed at that time.

Soviet ventures into the construction of giant turboprop transports were conspicuously successful. An ambitious British project which had been initiated many years earlier, before turbines had been introduced for commercial airplanes was, however, to prove abortive. Only one prototype of the Saunders Roe S.R.45 Princess was ever completed, the intention being to revive the use of flying boats which had proved so successful in the days of the luxuriously appointed Empire Boats in the 1930s. The construction program for the Princess was first commenced in 1945 and kept alive until 1952, but the last very large commercial flying boat, with its ten engines and planned capacity for 105 passengers, intended for the North Atlantic route, never progressed beyond the prototype stage; it was an anachronism which its designers hoped to market well after its era had passed. The maiden flight on 22 August 1952 was followed by a series of test flights, after which all work on the project was halted.

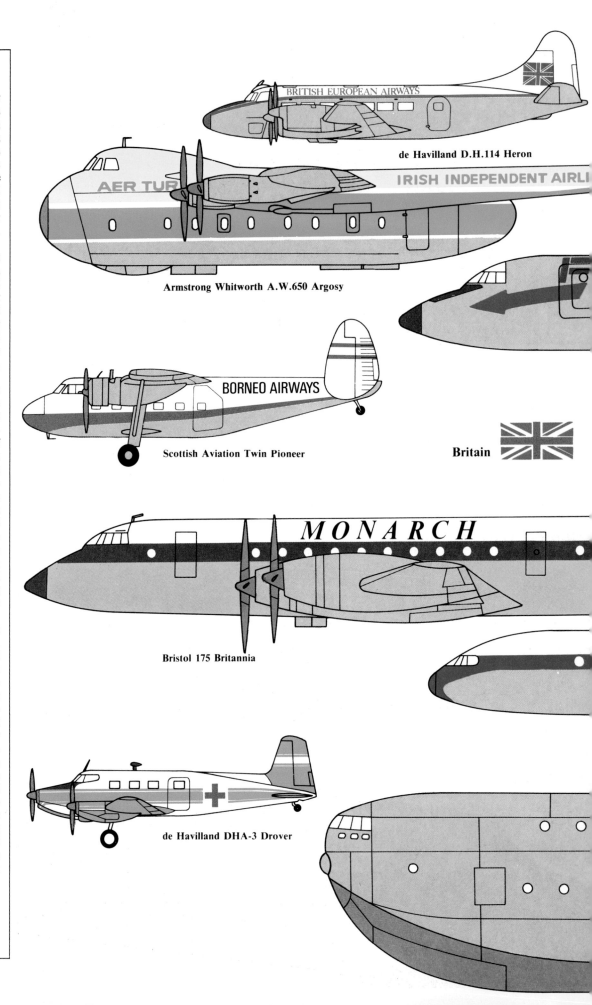

de Havilland D.H.114 Heron

Armstrong Whitworth A.W.650 Argosy

Scottish Aviation Twin Pioneer

**Britain**

Bristol 175 Britannia

de Havilland DHA-3 Drover

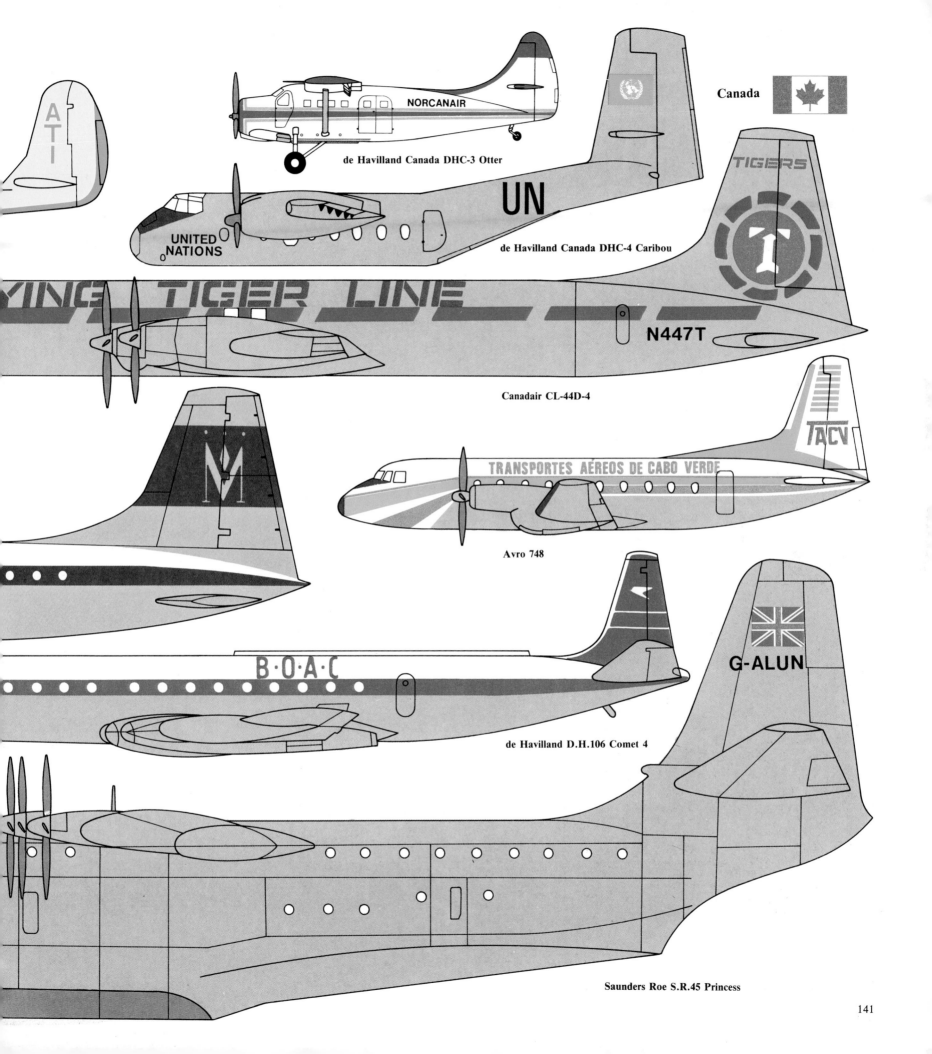

ATI

de Havilland Canada DHC-3 Otter

NORCANAIR

Canada

UN

UNITED NATIONS

de Havilland Canada DHC-4 Caribou

TIGERS

FLYING TIGER LINE

N447T

Canadair CL-44D-4

TACV

TRANSPORTES AÉREOS DE CABO VERDE

Avro 748

B·O·A·C

G-ALUN

de Havilland D.H.106 Comet 4

Saunders Roe S.R.45 Princess

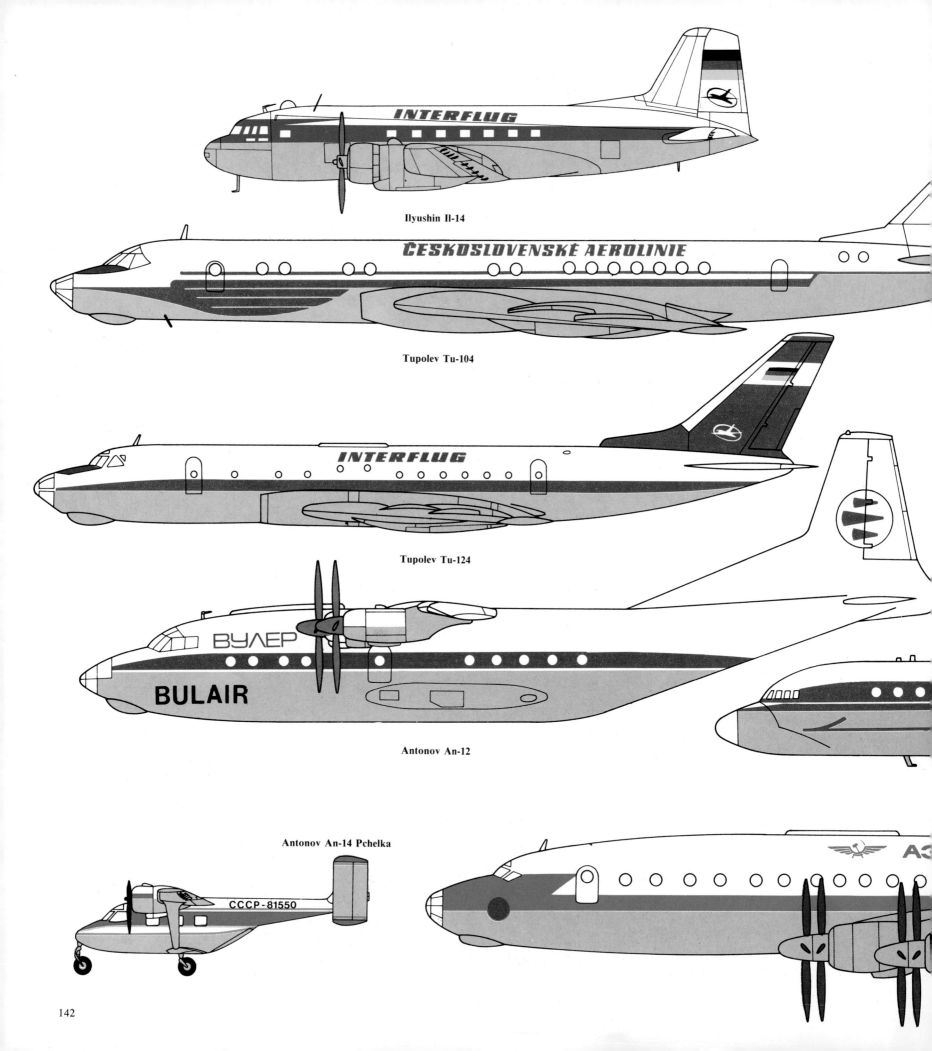

Ilyushin Il-14

Tupolev Tu-104

Tupolev Tu-124

Antonov An-12

Antonov An-14 Pchelka

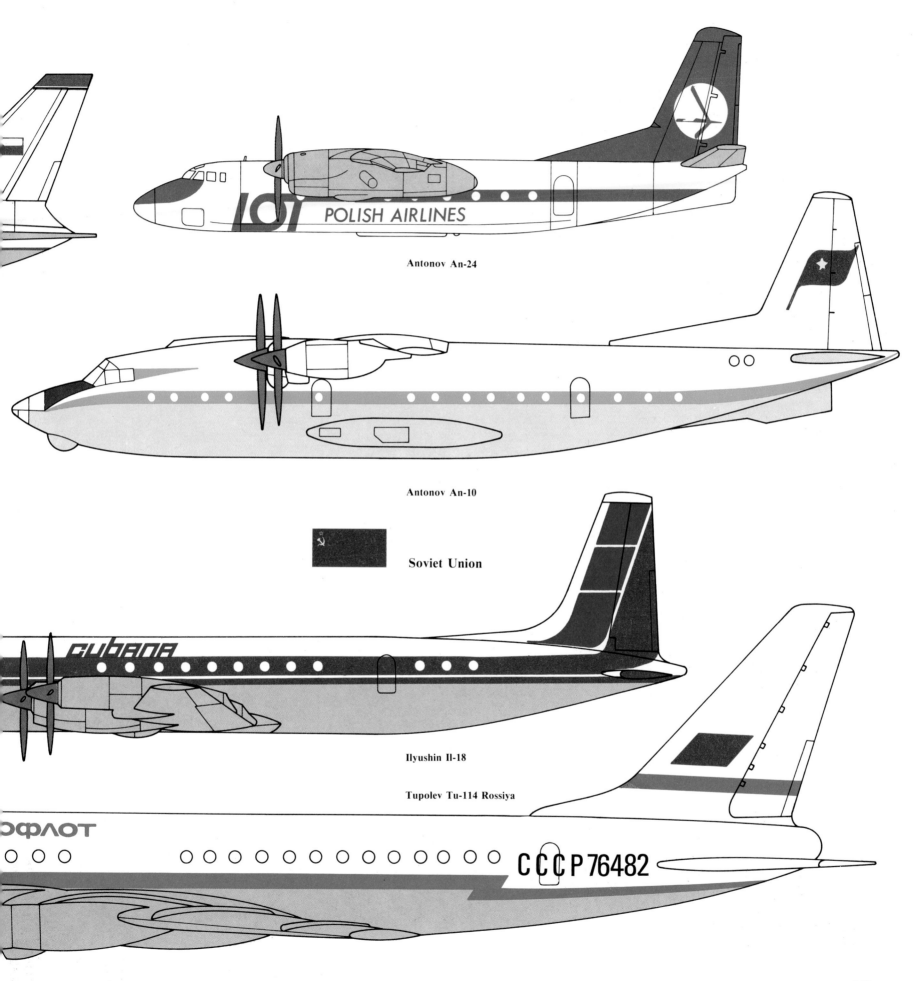

POLISH AIRLINES

Antonov An-24

Antonov An-10

Soviet Union

Ilyushin Il-18

Tupolev Tu-114 Rossiya

СССР 76482

# National markings of military aircraft since 1945

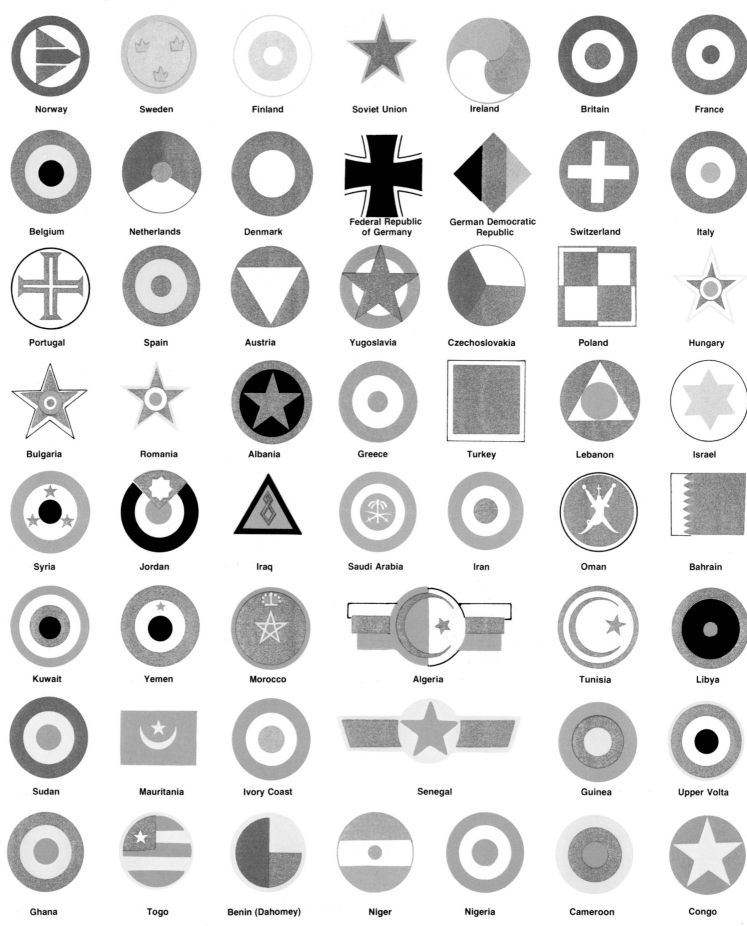

| | | | | | | |
|---|---|---|---|---|---|---|
| Norway | Sweden | Finland | Soviet Union | Ireland | Britain | France |
| Belgium | Netherlands | Denmark | Federal Republic of Germany | German Democratic Republic | Switzerland | Italy |
| Portugal | Spain | Austria | Yugoslavia | Czechoslovakia | Poland | Hungary |
| Bulgaria | Romania | Albania | Greece | Turkey | Lebanon | Israel |
| Syria | Jordan | Iraq | Saudi Arabia | Iran | Oman | Bahrain |
| Kuwait | Yemen | Morocco | Algeria | | Tunisia | Libya |
| Sudan | Mauritania | Ivory Coast | Senegal | | Guinea | Upper Volta |
| Ghana | Togo | Benin (Dahomey) | Niger | Nigeria | Cameroon | Congo |

| | | | | | |
|---|---|---|---|---|---|
| Ethiopia | Somalia | Kenya | Uganda | Zimbabwe | South Africa | Canada |

United States of America · Mexico · Guatemala · Cuba · Dominican Republic

Honduras · El Salvador · Haiti · Panama · Nicaragua · Colombia

Ecuador · Venezuela · Peru · Bolivia · Brazil · Paraguay

Uruguay · Chile · Argentina · Australia · New Zealand · India · Japan

People's Republic of China · Taiwan · Mongolia · Afghanistan · Pakistan · DPR Korea (North)

Republic of Korea · Sri Lanka · Nepal · Burma · Thailand

Laos · Kampuchea · Vietnam · Philippines · Indonesia · Malaysia

# 1950-1960
## The multirole combat plane takes over

The speed with which the fighter developed in the 1950s owed a great deal to the advances which had been made in engine technology and electronics. With the lessons of the Korean war fresh in mind, the two superpowers were the first to develop second-generation jet fighters. They both arrived at similar choices of fighter design: new engines gave impressive increase in speed and performance and, in time, solutions were found to the aerodynamic and structural problems which had first to be overcome. The introduction of new hardware in the shape of missiles transformed the traditional fighter into an even deadlier weapon, with an electronic nerve center which not only allowed the pilot to maneuver his aircraft much more easily and fulfil its combat role far more effectively but also enabled the aircraft to carry out a wide variety of duties – the multirole combat plane had arrived.

While the United States and the Soviet Union were maintaining such high levels of production, European aircraft manufacture was also forging ahead. Two countries with an illustrious aeronautical tradition, Britain and France, developed some outstanding aircraft. Meanwhile competition was forthcoming from an unexpected source – Sweden.

The growth of the Swedish aeronautical industry had no parallel elsewhere in the world but was a logical development of Sweden's policy of neutrality, supported by a very strong capability for national self-defense. The Saab 32 Lansen which went into service in 1955 was an effective multirole aircraft and on 25 October that same year the prototype of a very advanced and powerful airplane, the Saab 35 Draken was unveiled, later acknowledged to be one of the best interceptors of its day.

The Korean war also led the British to reexamine their air capability, and the military authorities soon realized the need for aircraft renewal; this gave a stimulus to the aviation industry after a lull following the end of the Second World War. The transition to second-generation fighters was swiftly accomplished, best illustrated by the RAF's powerful Mach 2 interceptor, the English Electric Lightning, which went into service in 1960, and by the Fleet Air Arm's sophisticated Supermarine Scimitar and Hawker Siddeley Sea Vixen.

The fifties saw the successful development of France's new aviation industry, towards which one man, Marcel Dassault, contributed so much. After the Ouragan had proved so satisfactory [France's first jet fighter, it appeared in 1949] this enterprising industrialist introduced the supersonic Mystère and Super Mystère fighters and the carrier-borne Etendard. Expertise gained during the building of these planes led to the development of what was to be far and away Dassault's most famous combat aircraft, the Mirage, the basic version of which [Mirage III] flew for the first time on 17 November 1956 and went into series production in 1960.

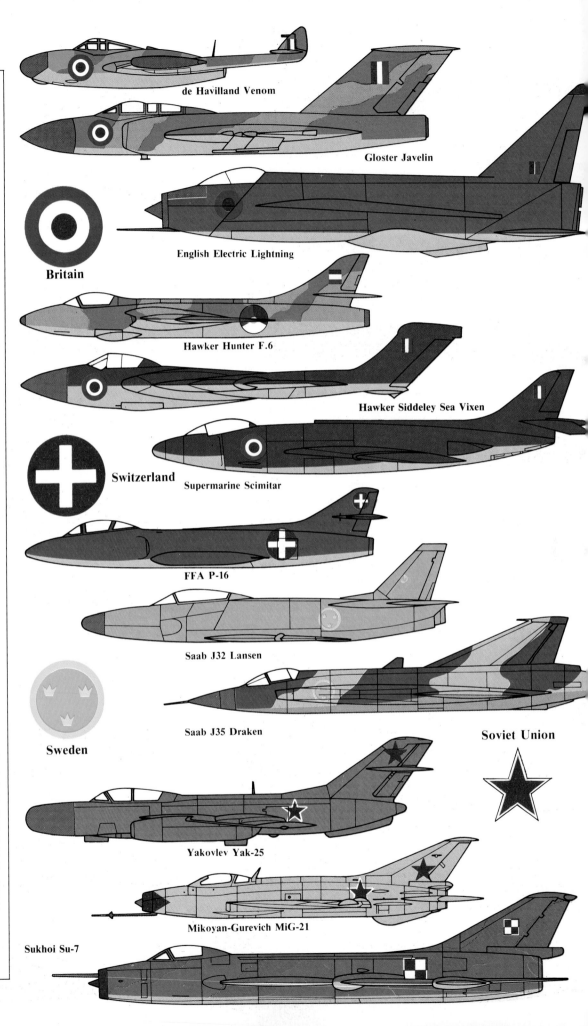

de Havilland Venom

Gloster Javelin

Britain

English Electric Lightning

Hawker Hunter F.6

Hawker Siddeley Sea Vixen

Switzerland

Supermarine Scimitar

FFA P-16

Saab J32 Lansen

Sweden

Saab J35 Draken

Soviet Union

Yakovlev Yak-25

Mikoyan-Gurevich MiG-21

Sukhoi Su-7

North American F-86K Sabre

North American F-100 Super Sabre

United States

Convair F-102 Delta Dagger

North American FJ Fury

Northrop F-89 Scorpion

Vought F7U Cutlass

LTV F-8 Crusader

Douglas F4D Skyray

McDonnell F2H Banshee

Douglas F3D Skynight

Republic F-105 Thunderchief

France

Dassault Mystère IV-A

McDonnell F3H Demon

Dassault Super Mystère B-2

Dassault Etendard

McDonnell F-4 Phantom II

Dassault Mirage III-C

Lockheed F-104 Super Starfighter

147

1 Pitot-static boom
2 Pitch vanes
3 Yaw vanes
4 Conical three-position intake centerbody
5 "Spin Scan" search-and-track radar antenna
6 Boundary layer slot
7 Engine air intake
8 Radar ("Spin Scan")
9 Lower boundary layer exit
10 Antennae
11 Nosewheel doors
12 Nosewheel leg and shock absorbers
13 Castoring nosewheel
14 Anti-shimmy damper
15 Avionics bay access
16 Attitude sensor
17 Nosewheel well
18 Spill door
19 Nosewheel retraction pivot
20 Bifurcated intake trunking
21 Avionics bay
22 Electronics equipment
23 Intake trunking
24 Upper boundary layer exit
25 Dynamic pressure probe for g-feel
26 Semi-elliptical armour-glass windscreen
27 Gunsight mounting
28 Fixed quarterlight
29 Radar scope
30 Control column (with tailplane trim switch and two firing buttons)
31 Rudder pedals
32 Underfloor control runs
33 KM-1 two-position zero-level ejection seat
34 Port instrument console
35 Undercarriage handle
36 Seat harness
37 Canopy release/lock
38 Starboard wall switch panel
39 Rear-view mirror fairing
40 Starboard-hinged canopy
41 Ejection seat headrest
42 Avionics bay
43 Control rods
44 Air conditioning plant
45 Suction relief door
46 Intake trunking
47 Wingroot attachment fairing
48 Wing/fuselage spar-lug attachment points (four)
49 Fuselage ring frames

50 Intermediary frames
51 Main fuselage fuel tank
52 RSIU radio bay
53 Auxiliary intake
54 Leading-edge integral fuel tank
55 Starboard outer weapons pylon
56 Outboard wing construction
57 Starboard navigation light
58 Leading-edge suppressed aerial
59 Wing fence
60 Aileron control jack
61 Starboard aileron
62 Flap actuator fairing
63 Starboard blown flap – SPS (sduva pogranichnovo sloya)
64 Multispar wing structure
65 Main integral wing fuel tank
66 Undercarriage mounting/pivot point
67 Starboard mainwheel leg
68 Auxiliaries compartment
69 Fuselage fuel tanks Nos 2 and 3
70 Mainwheel well external fairing
71 Mainwheel (retracted)
72 Trunking contours
73 Control rods in dorsal spine
74 Compressor face
75 Oil tank
76 Avionics pack
77 Engine accessories
78 Tumansky R-13 turbojet (rated at 14,550 lb/6,600 kg with full reheat)
79 Fuselage break/transport joint
80 Intake
81 Tail surface control linkage
82 Artificial feel unit
83 Tailplane jack
84 Hydraulic accumulator
85 Tailplane trim motor
86 Tailfin spar attachment plate
87 Rudder jack
88 Rudder control linkage
89 Tailfin structure
90 Leading-edge panel
91 Radio cable access
92 Magnetic detector
93 Tailfin mainspar
94 RSIU (radio-stantsiya istrebitelnaya ultrakorot-kykh vol'n – very short-wave fighter radio) antenna plate
95 VHF/UHF aerials
96 IFF antennae
97 Formation light

98 Tail warning radar
99 Rear navigation light
100 Fuel vent
101 Rudder construction
102 Rudder hinge
103 Braking parachute hinged bullet fairing
104 Braking parachute stowage
105 Tailpipe (variable convergent nozzle)
106 Afterburner installation
107 Afterburner bay cooling intake
108 Tailplane linkage fairing
109 Nozzle actuating cylinders
110 Tailplane torque tube
111 All-moving tailplane
112 Anti-flutter weight
113 Intake
114 Afterburner mounting
115 Fixed tailplane root fairing
116 Longitudinal lap joint
117 External duct (nozzle hydraulics)

118 Ventral fin
119 Engine guide rail
120 JATO assembly canted nozzle
121 JATO assembly thrust plate forks (rear mounting)
122 JATO assembly pack
123 Ventral airbrake (retracted)
124 Trestle point
125 JATO assembly release solenoid (front mounting)
126 Underwing landing light
127 Ventral stores pylon
128 Mainwheel inboard door
129 Splayed link chute
130 Twin 23 mm GSh-23 cannon installation
131 Cannon muzzle fairing
132 Debris deflector plate
133 Auxiliary ventral drop tank
134 Port forward air brake (extended)
135 Leading-edge integral fuel tank

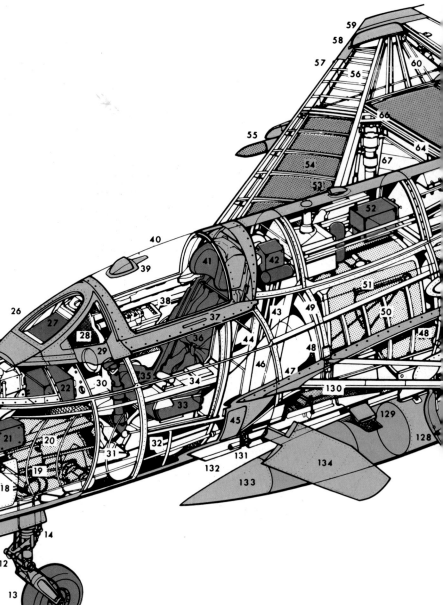

148

# Mikoyan-Gurevich MiG-21 MF

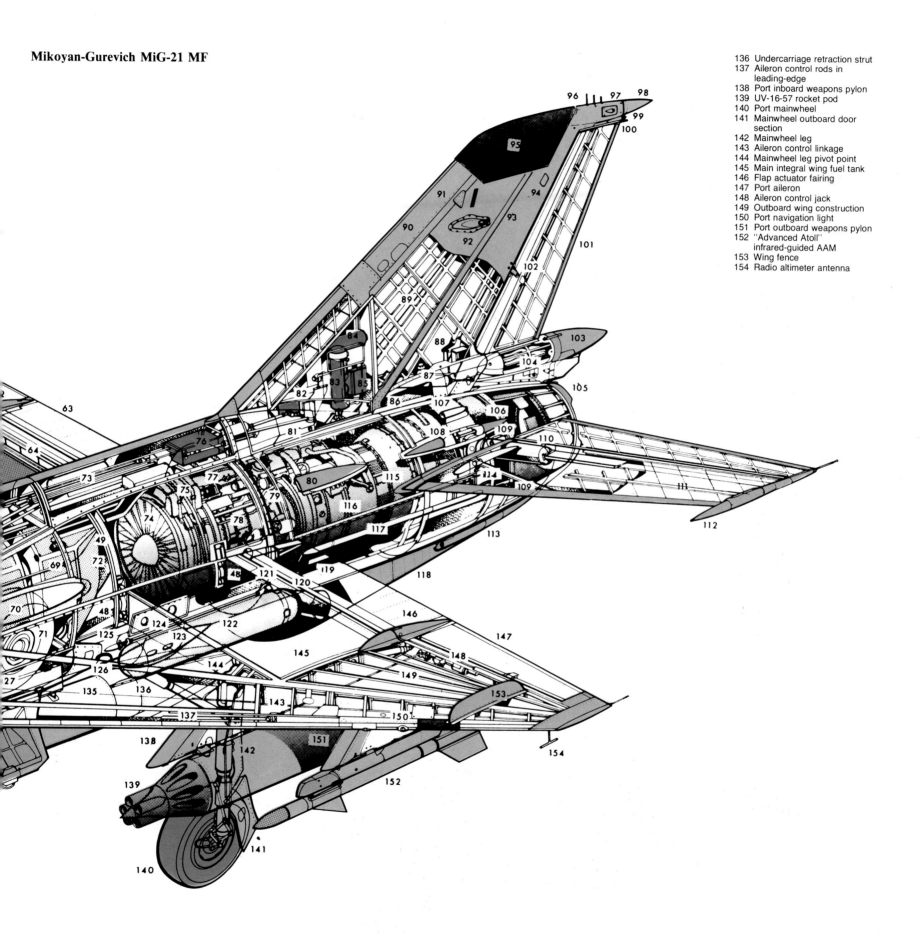

136 Undercarriage retraction strut
137 Aileron control rods in
    leading-edge
138 Port inboard weapons pylon
139 UV-16-57 rocket pod
140 Port mainwheel
141 Mainwheel outboard door
    section
142 Mainwheel leg
143 Aileron control linkage
144 Mainwheel leg pivot point
145 Main integral wing fuel tank
146 Flap actuator fairing
147 Port aileron
148 Aileron control jack
149 Outboard wing construction
150 Port navigation light
151 Port outboard weapons pylon
152 "Advanced Atoll"
    infrared-guided AAM
153 Wing fence
154 Radio altimeter antenna

# 1950-1960
## Evolution of the bomber – the first delta-wing aircraft

The importance of the strategic bomber had been recognized during the Second World War and was exploited to the fullest possible extent during the 1950s, before the advent of intercontinental ballistic missiles made these aircraft obsolescent. The countries most committed to the evolution of the big bomber were the U.S.A., U.S.S.R. and Britain. The United States could draw on such battle-proven aircraft as the B-29 bombers as prototypes for developing new strategic aircraft while more advanced versions of the atom bombs which had been dropped on Hiroshima and Nagasaki were perfected.

Since the USAF had long since identified its most likely adversary in the event of war, it concentrated on improving the performance of these long-range bombers and on increasing the destructive power of the weapons they carried, remaining faithful to this policy for many years. The Convair B-36, the last in the line of large, piston-engine military aircraft, which had featured the B-29 and B-50 was a monster which could carry 36 tonnes of material, with a range exceeding 6,300 miles [10,000 km]. The first series production aircraft entered service in 1947.

The transition to jet propulsion is well illustrated by the later development of the B-36: the D variant of 1949 and subsequent versions were given an extra power boost by the installation of four Pratt & Whitney J47 turbojets in addition to the six 3,800 hp Pratt & Whitney piston-engines which powered earlier versions.

From then on the pace of progress accelerated, by the end of 1950 units were taking delivery of the first of a total of 1,800 of the new Boeing B-47 Stratojets [the USAF's first satisfactory all-jet strategic bomber]. Some seven years later Strategic Air Command found its strength greatly enhanced when it took delivery of the aircraft which was to symbolize the conventional strategic bomber until the end of the 1970s: the Boeing B-52 Stratofortress, an aircraft which proved so impressive that it was not made obsolescent by the more modern [Mach 2] Convair B-58 Hustler which reached squadrons in late 1959.

In the U.S.S.R. aircraft evolved along similar lines, leading to the development of giant bombers, also favoured by the Russians, before their strategic role was taken over by missiles. The most noteworthy aircraft in this category were the Myasishchev Mya-4 [the prototype of which was unveiled in 1953 but the type was subsequently relegated to reconnaissance]; the Tupolev Tu-20 turboprop and the twinjet Tu-16 [both of 1954] and the supersonic Tu-22 which was put into service in 1960 to counter the B-58 Hustler which had just reached USAF bomber squadrons.

Britain also made her mark in this field, with three strategic bombers [the so-called "V" class], built during a phase of concentrated effort to strengthen Britain's air capability in the early fifties; the first of these was the Vickers Valiant [unveiled at the end of 1953]; then came the Avro Vulcan [February 1959] and the Handley Page Victor [February 1956]. The best of these was the Vulcan, the world's first delta-wing bomber, which was only taken out of service in the early 1980s.

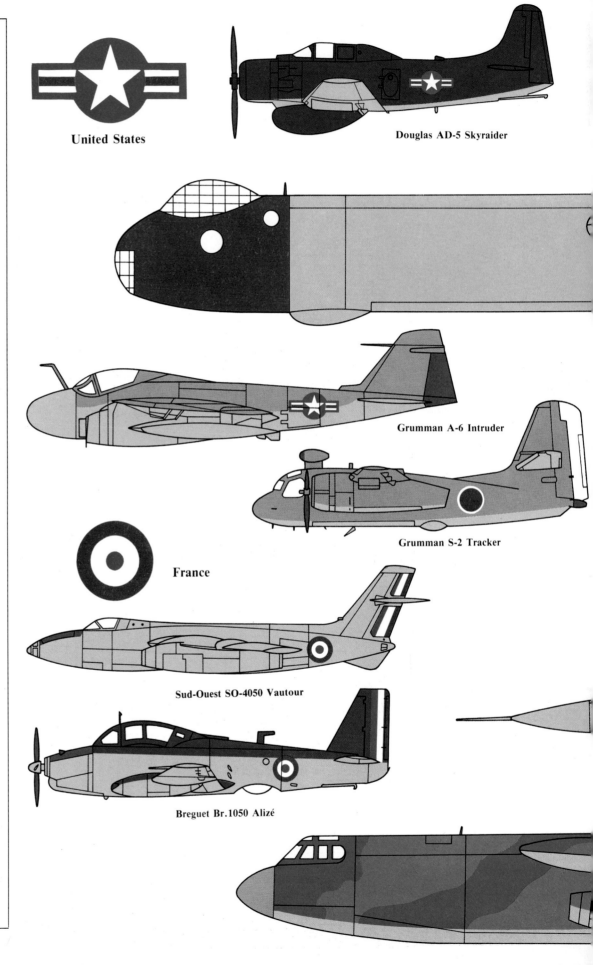

**United States**

Douglas AD-5 Skyraider

Grumman A-6 Intruder

Grumman S-2 Tracker

**France**

Sud-Ouest SO-4050 Vautour

Breguet Br.1050 Alizé

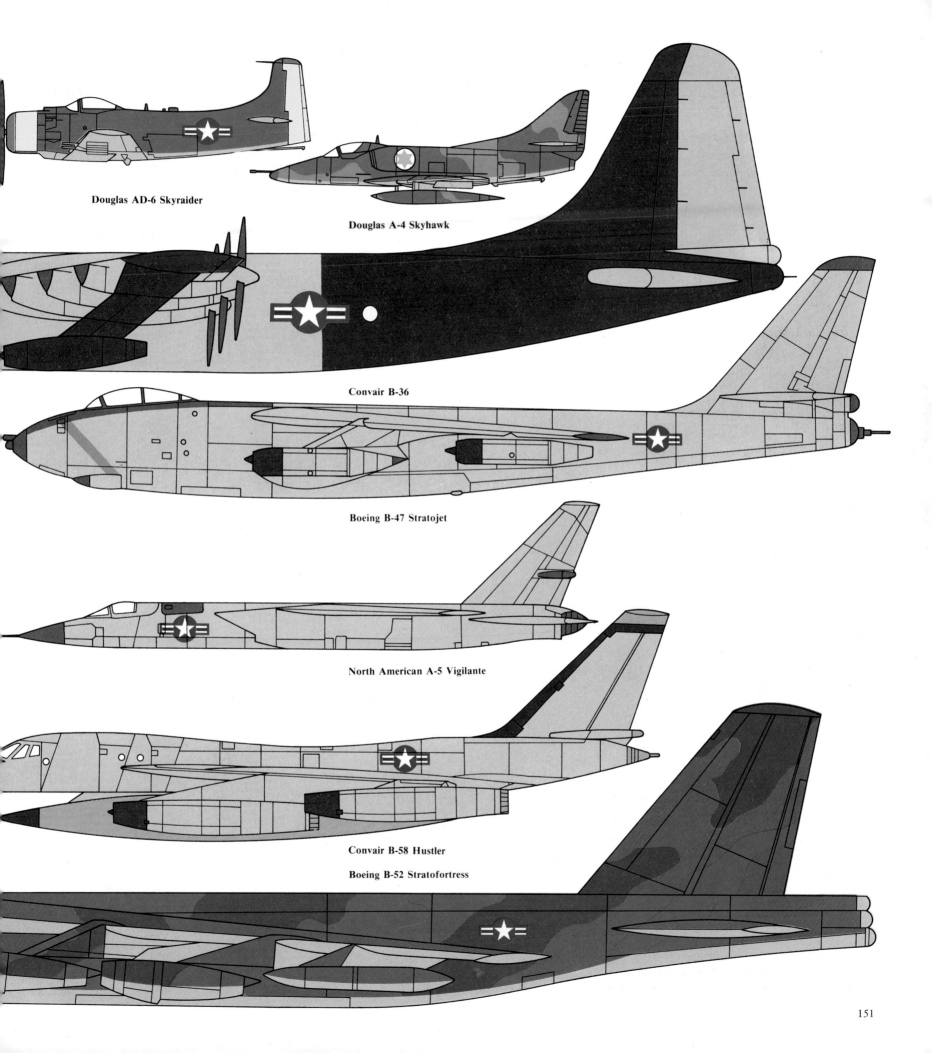

Douglas AD-6 Skyraider

Douglas A-4 Skyhawk

Convair B-36

Boeing B-47 Stratojet

North American A-5 Vigilante

Convair B-58 Hustler

Boeing B-52 Stratofortress

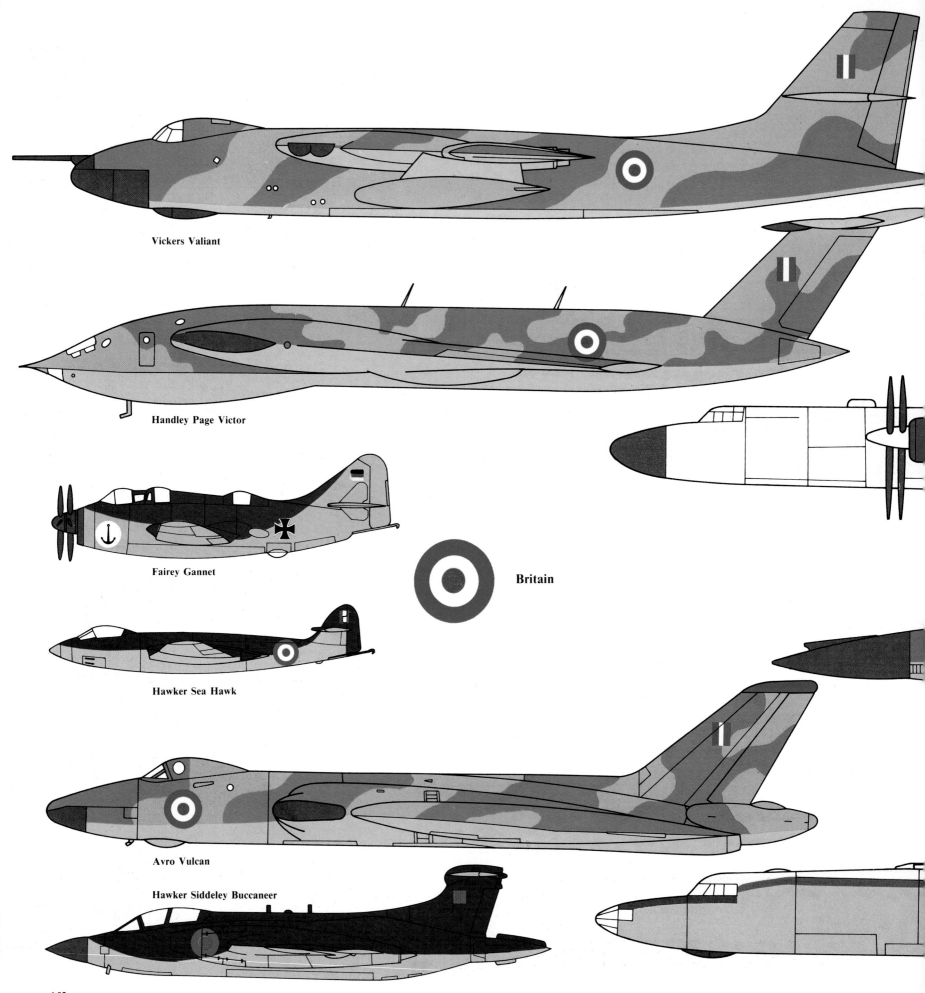

Vickers Valiant

Handley Page Victor

Fairey Gannet

Britain

Hawker Sea Hawk

Avro Vulcan

Hawker Siddeley Buccaneer

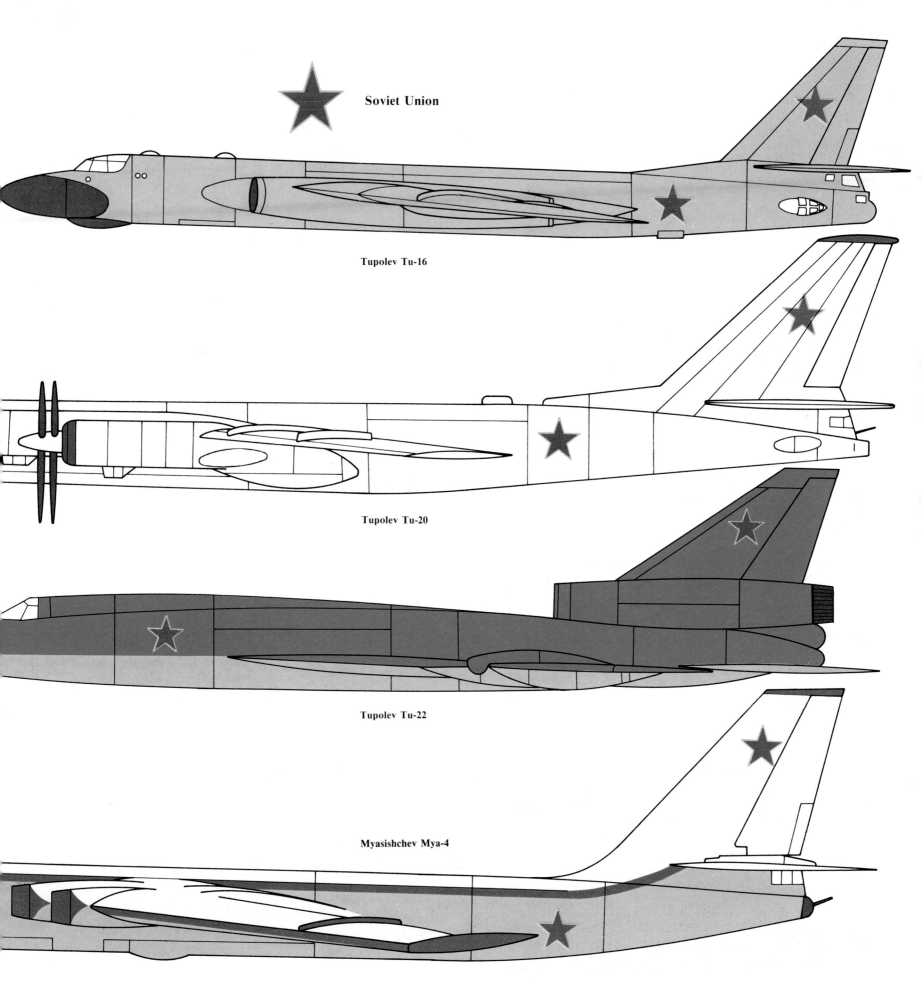

**Soviet Union**

Tupolev Tu-16

Tupolev Tu-20

Tupolev Tu-22

Myasishchev Mya-4

1 Wing tip antennae
2 Starboard navigation light
3 Starboard wing tip construction
4 Outboard aileron
5 Inboard aileron
6 Rear spar
7 Outboard wing panel ribs
8 Front spar
9 Leading edge ribs
10 Cranked leading edge
11 Corrugated leading-edge inner skin
12 Retractable landing and taxying lamp
13 Fuel tank fire extinguisher bottles
14 Outer wing panel joint rib
15 Honeycomb skin panel
16 Outboard elevator
17 Inboard elevator
18 Elevator hydraulic jacks
19 No 7 starboard fuel tank
20 No 5 starboard fuel tank
21 Diagonal rib
22 Leading edge de-icing air duct
23 Wing stringer construction
24 Parallel chord wing skin panels
25 No 6 starboard fuel tank
26 No 4 starboard fuel tank
27 No 3 starboard fuel tank
28 Main undercarriage leg
29 Eight-wheel bogie
30 Mainwheel well door
31 Fuel tank fire extinguishers
32 Inboard leading edge construction
33 De-icing air supply pipe
34 Fuel collectors and pumps
35 Main undercarriage wheel bay
36 Retracting mechanism
37 Airborne auxiliary power plant (AAPP)
38 Electrical equipment bay
39 Starboard engine bays
40 Rolls-Royce (Bristol) Olympus 301 engines
41 Air system piping
42 Engine bay dividing rib
43 Engine fire extinguishers
44 Jet pipes
45 Fixed trailing edge construction
46 Jet pipe nozzles
47 Rear equipment bay
48 Oxygen bottles
49 Batteries
50 Rudder power control unit
51 Rear electronics bay
52 Electronic countermeasures system equipment
53 Cooling air intake
54 Tail warning radar scanner

55 Tail radome
56 Twin brake parachute housing
57 Brake parachute door
58 Rudder construction
59 Rudder balance weights and seals
60 Fin de-icing air outlet
61 Di-electric fin tip fairing
62 Passive electronic countermeasures (ECM) antennae
63 Fin construction
64 Fin leading edge
65 Corrugated inner skin
66 Communications aerial
67 Fin de-icing air supply
68 Bomb-bay rear bulkhead
69 Bomb-bay roof arch construction
70 Flush air intake
71 Communications aerial
72 Port Olympus 301 engines
73 Engine bay top panel construction
74 Port jet pipe fairing
75 Electrical equipment bay
76 Chaff dispenser
77 "Green Satin" navigational radar bay
78 Elevator balance weights and seals
79 Elevator hydraulic jacks
80 Inboard elevator
81 Outboard elevator
82 Inboard aileron
83 Aileron balance weights
84 Control rods
85 Aileron power control jacks
86 Jack fairings
87 Outboard aileron
88 Port wing tip antennae
89 Retractable landing and taxying lamp

90 Cranked leading edge
91 Fuel tank fire extinguishers
92 Cambered leading edge profile
93 No 7 port fuel tank
94 No 5 port fuel tank
95 Leading edge de-icing air duct
96 No 6 port fuel tank
97 No 4 port fuel tank
98 No 3 port fuel tank
99 Port main undercarriage bay
100 Wing stringer construction
101 Port airbrakes

102 Airbrake drive mechanism
103 Intake ducts
104 Front wing spar attachment joints
105 Center section front spar frame
106 Suppressed aerial
107 Anti-collision light
108 Bomb bay longerons
109 Forward limit of bomb bay
110 Starboard airbrake housings
111 Boundary layer bleed air duct
112 Starboard intake ducts

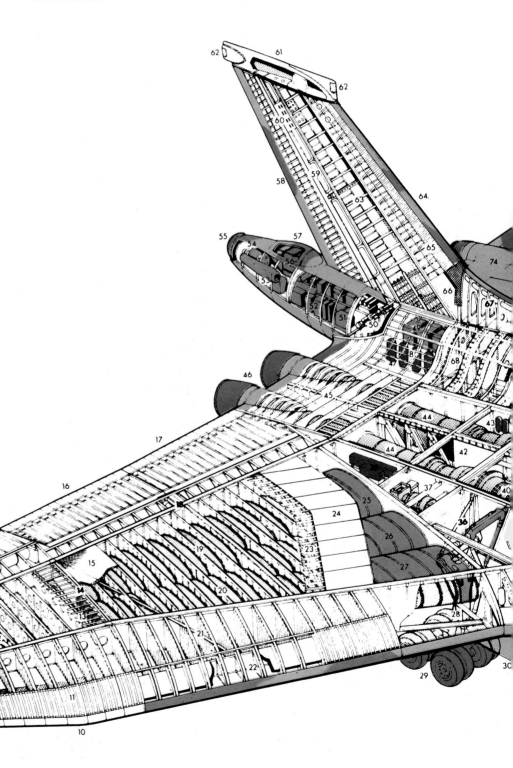

# Avro Vulcan B Mk.2

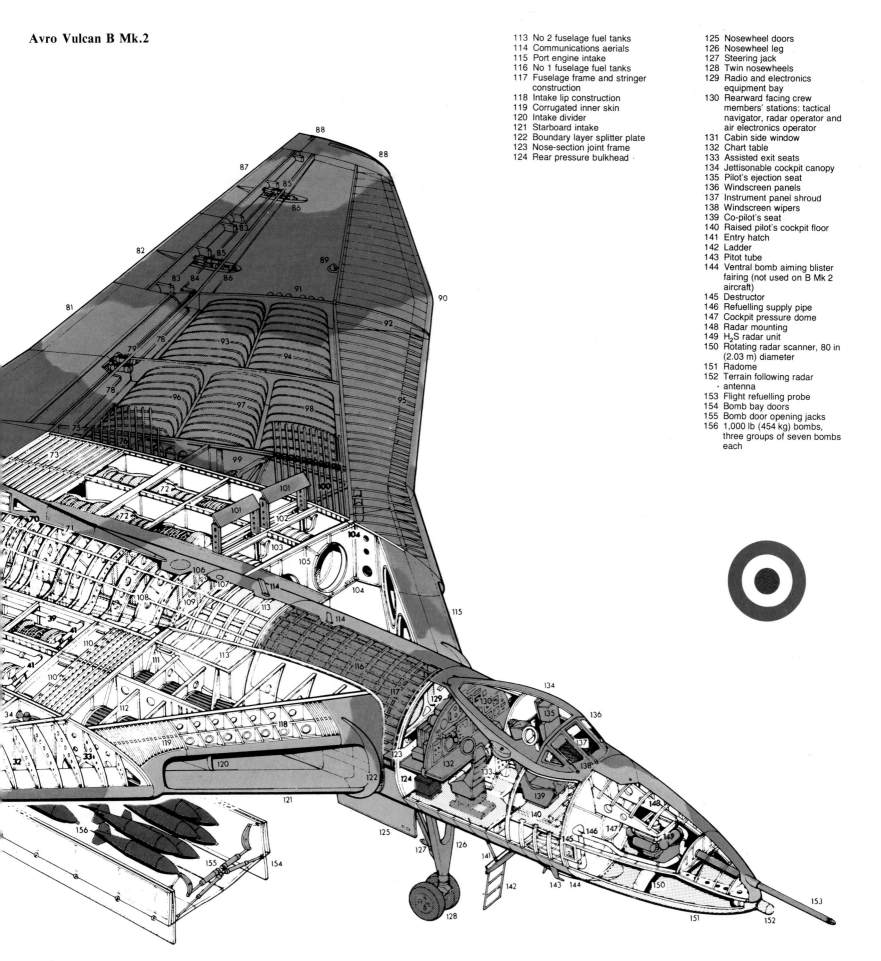

113 No 2 fuselage fuel tanks
114 Communications aerials
115 Port engine intake
116 No 1 fuselage fuel tanks
117 Fuselage frame and stringer construction
118 Intake lip construction
119 Corrugated inner skin
120 Intake divider
121 Starboard intake
122 Boundary layer splitter plate
123 Nose-section joint frame
124 Rear pressure bulkhead ·
125 Nosewheel doors
126 Nosewheel leg
127 Steering jack
128 Twin nosewheels
129 Radio and electronics equipment bay
130 Rearward facing crew members' stations: tactical navigator, radar operator and air electronics operator
131 Cabin side window
132 Chart table
133 Assisted exit seats
134 Jettisonable cockpit canopy
135 Pilot's ejection seat
136 Windscreen panels
137 Instrument panel shroud
138 Windscreen wipers
139 Co-pilot's seat
140 Raised pilot's cockpit floor
141 Entry hatch
142 Ladder
143 Pitot tube
144 Ventral bomb aiming blister fairing (not used on B Mk 2 aircraft)
145 Destructor
146 Refuelling supply pipe
147 Cockpit pressure dome
148 Radar mounting
149 $H_2S$ radar unit
150 Rotating radar scanner, 80 in (2.03 m) diameter
151 Radome
152 Terrain following radar antenna
153 Flight refuelling probe
154 Bomb bay doors
155 Bomb door opening jacks
156 1,000 lb (454 kg) bombs, three groups of seven bombs each

# 1950-1960
## Advances in reconnaissance, training and transport aircraft

The first use of aircraft in the military sphere was reconnaissance; this role was to prove of the most vital significance in the prevailing conditions of the Cold War.

In May 1960 news broke which both alarmed and intrigued the world, causing a buildup in international tension such as had not been experienced for many years: Francis Gary Powers, a USAF pilot, was shot down over the U.S.S.R. while flying his Lockheed U-2, sophisticated and top secret spy plane, on a reconnaissance mission. Up till then, the plane's very existence had been a well-kept secret: now the facts were blazoned in the international press: Powers' aircraft had been brought down by a Soviet missile while flying at very high altitude on a photographic reconnaissance mission in Russian airspace, well over 1,240 miles [2,000 km] inside Soviet territory. Powers was eventually put on trial amid great publicity, accused of spying.

For several months the uneasy peace of the Cold War seemed threatened. Just over two years later the world seemed to teeter on the brink of war again, when in October 1962 another U-2 brought back photographic evidence that the U.S.S.R. had installed missiles on sites in Cuba. The ensuing confrontation between the U.S.A. and her powerful adversary brought the two superpowers closer to nuclear war than ever before.

At that time the Lockheed U-2 stood for the state of the art in modern strategic reconnaissance: a fast and powerful aircraft which had the extremely high service ceiling necessary to avoid interception, unarmed, but with an impressive array of sophisticated electronic devices to ensure maximum efficiency.

Progress in such surveillance equipment technology meant that its application spread to other branches of reconnaissance, albeit on a less sophisticated level. The tactical reconnaissance sector certainly placed fewer demands on designers and manufacturers. During the 1950s many of these tactical reconnaissance planes were derived from fighters or other existing combat planes [such as the American Republic RF-84F Thunderflash, a specialized variant of the prolific family of Thunderjet/Thunderstreak aircraft]. Another example was the Italian Fiat G.91, a tactical fighter which had won a NATO competition in 1953, the first operational version of which, the Series R, was a close support/reconnaissance plane. Some reconnaissance planes were, however, purpose-built: in 1959 the U.S. Army and Marines issued a specification which called for a small twin-engine plane which could operate in close liaison with ground forces and this led to the development of the Grumman OV-1 Mohawk. The aircraft was more like a helicopter than airplane in terms of performance, and was to prove its value in the Vietnam war.

A great effort was made during the 1950s to improve marine reconnaissance. The Western Powers

*continued on page 158*

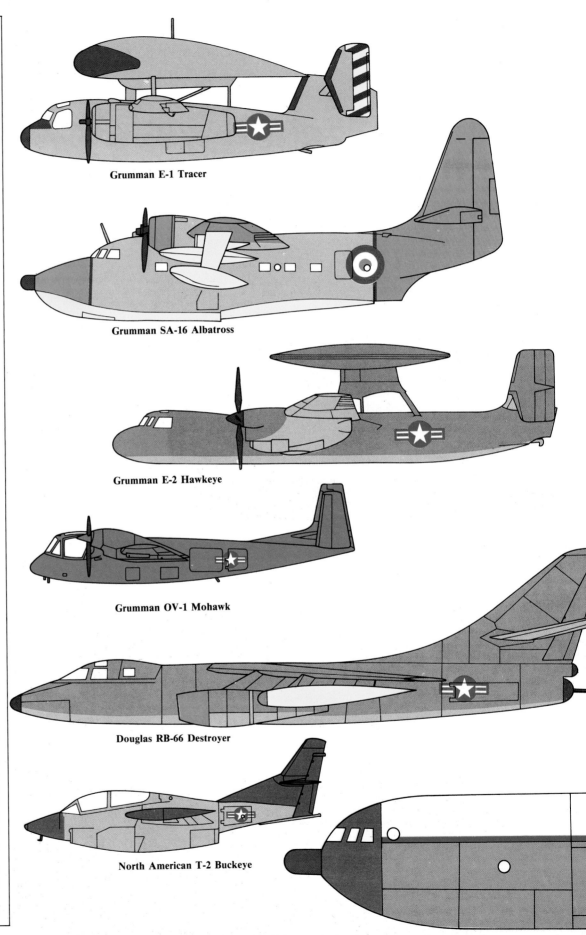

Grumman E-1 Tracer

Grumman SA-16 Albatross

Grumman E-2 Hawkeye

Grumman OV-1 Mohawk

Douglas RB-66 Destroyer

North American T-2 Buckeye

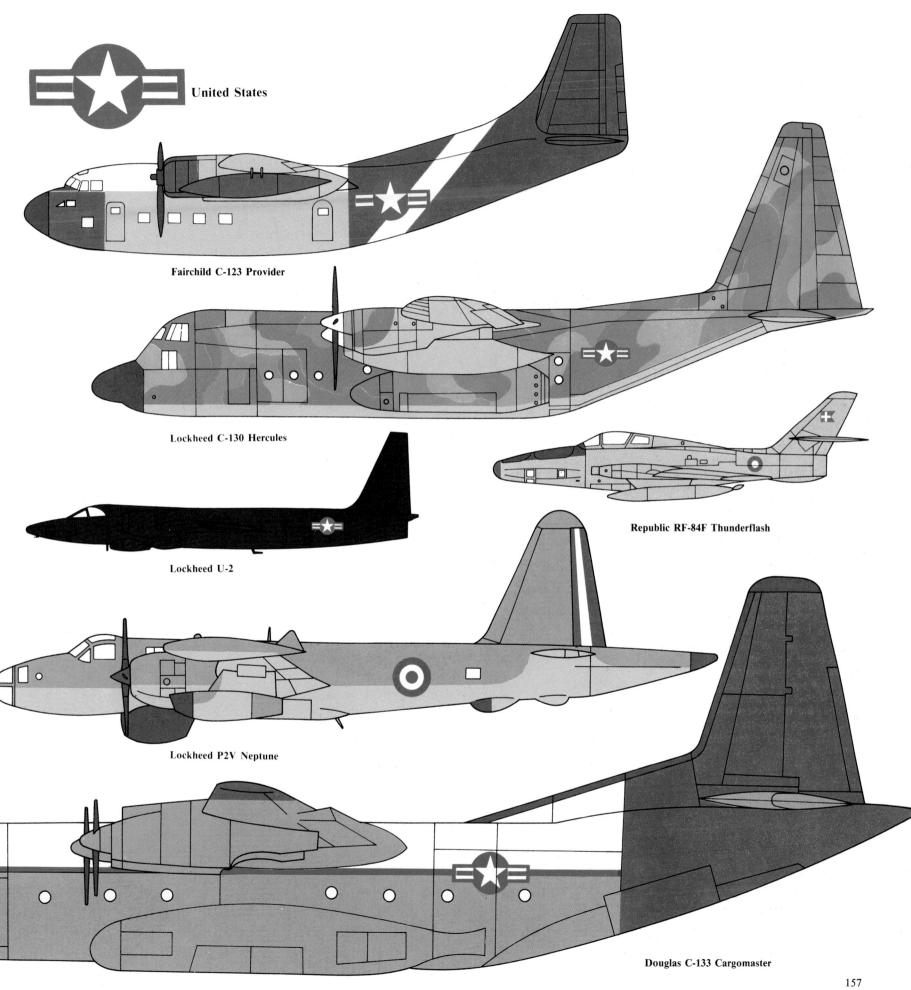

**United States**

Fairchild C-123 Provider

Lockheed C-130 Hercules

Lockheed U-2

Republic RF-84F Thunderflash

Lockheed P2V Neptune

Douglas C-133 Cargomaster

157

*continued from page 156*

had traditionally assigned flying boats to these duties [the last big U.S. aircraft in this category being the Martin P5M Marlin, which entered service in 1952], but land-based marine patrol aircraft were now taking over. Such reliable workhorses as the American Lockheed P2V Neptune were introduced, a versatile twin-piston-engine aircraft, over 1,200 of which were built in seven basic versions, seeing service in no fewer than eleven countries; there were the British four-engine Avro Shackleton, several variants of which were flown from 1951 to the early 1980's and the Canadian Canadair CL-28 Argus, developed in 1954 from the British Britannia transport, which entered service four years later.

The traditional method of carrying out photographic or electronic reconnaissance was extended during the second half of the fifties, with the introduction of airborne information-gathering platforms, the new strategic command posts which could feed tactical forces with information and coordinate movements. The United States was first, with the introduction of highly-specialized aircraft for this task and to begin with the Navy assumed responsibility for testing carrier-based surveillance aircraft. One of the earliest to be put into service was the Grumman E-1 Tracer [derived from the twin-engine carrier-borne S-2 Tracker] which went into service in early 1958. The plane's function was betrayed by the distinctive fairing which housed its main radar. The Tracer resulted from the adaptation of an existing aircraft, but the next in line of these ultrasophisticated planes, the Grumman E-2 Hawkeye, which first appeared in prototype in October 1960, was designed from scratch as an airborne command post and proved invaluable, monitoring and processing information with great efficiency.

Increased efficiency was also the watchword in two other support sectors of military aviation: transport and training. Where transports were concerned, manufacturers concentrated their efforts on meeting the military's demand for increased capacity and endurance; in the case of training, straightforward reliable aircraft were required which trainee pilots could learn to fly easily but which could also prepare them for conversion to the more complex flying of frontline combat aircraft. Turboprop transports proved thoroughly satisfactory and the Soviets were by no means alone in exploiting this type of transport. In the U.S.A. it led to the development in the mid 1950s of one of the most widely used transports, the Lockheed C-130 Hercules [which had its maiden flight on 23 August 1954]. This versatile four-engine aircraft has seen service with the airforces of thirty countries and is still flying in the mid eighties.

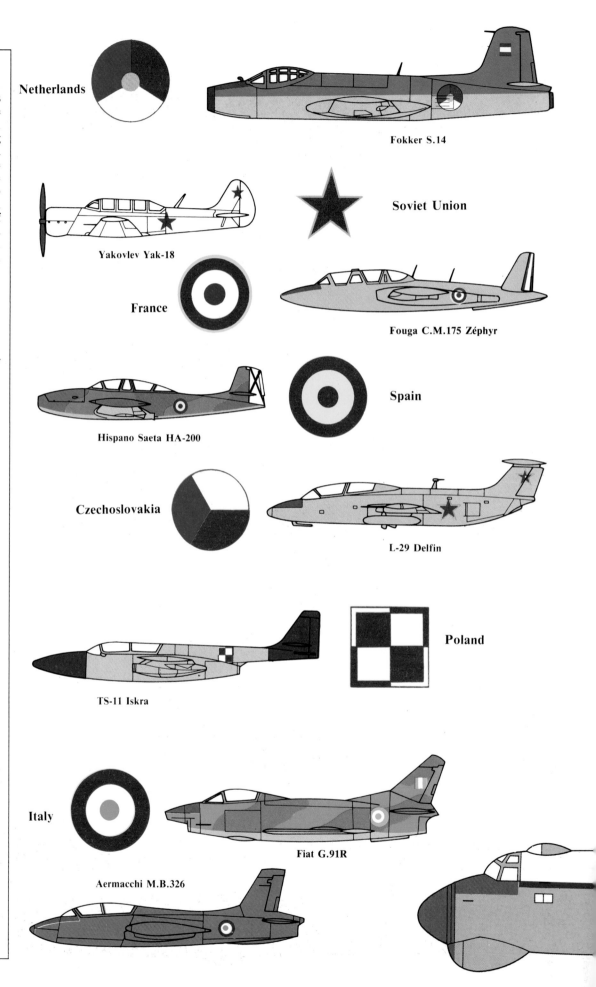

Netherlands

Fokker S.14

Yakovlev Yak-18

Soviet Union

France

Fouga C.M.175 Zéphyr

Spain

Hispano Saeta HA-200

Czechoslovakia

L-29 Delfin

Poland

TS-11 Iskra

Italy

Fiat G.91R

Aermacchi M.B.326

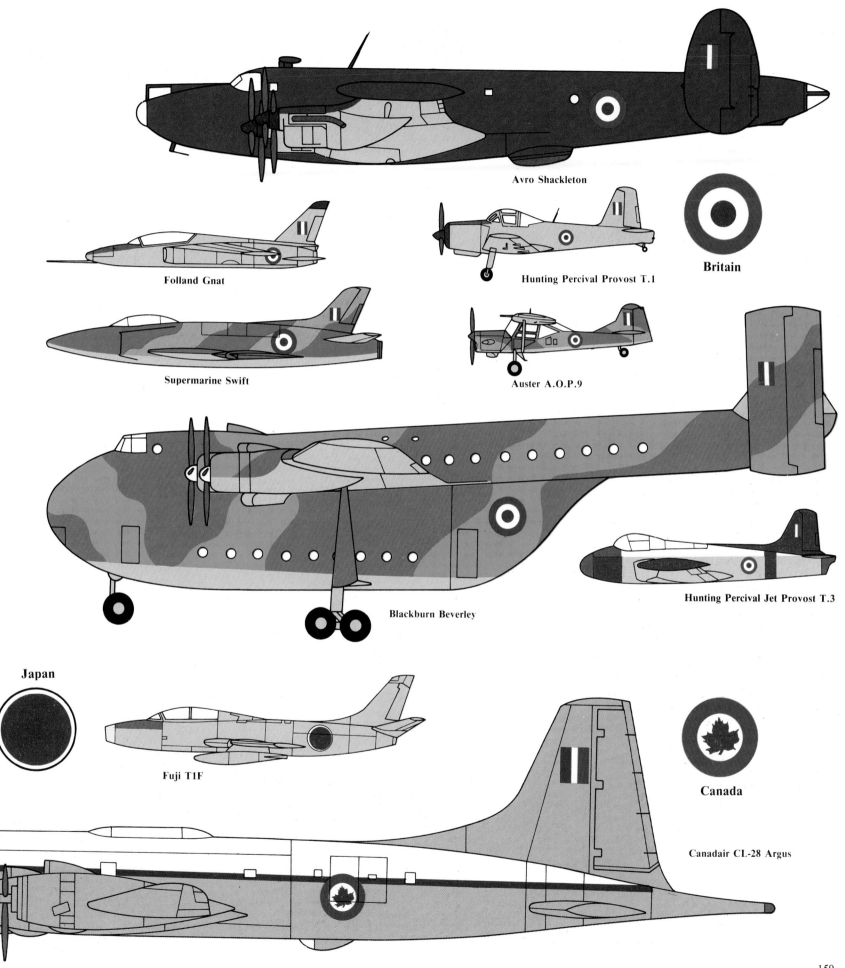

Avro Shackleton

Folland Gnat

Hunting Percival Provost T.1

Britain

Supermarine Swift

Auster A.O.P.9

Blackburn Beverley

Hunting Percival Jet Provost T.3

Japan

Fuji T1F

Canada

Canadair CL-28 Argus

159

# 1960
# 1985

## THE PERILOUS YEARS – BUT TECHNOLOGICAL PROGRESS KNOWS NO FRONTIERS

The dual role which the airplane continues to play in the history of our times was never more apparent than it is today – as part of our consumer-oriented economy on the one hand, and as one of the most awesome instruments in preserving the balance of power on the other. These two roles certainly appear contradictory but are inevitable.

So far the theory of maintaining a balance of power by counterbalancing arsenals has averted a third world war. The great powers seem more than ever committed to upholding such global equilibrium, their first priority being to ensure that the opposing power grouping does not grow stronger, to which end increasingly deadly weapons are continually being developed, bringing with them the threat of widespread destruction – possibly total annihilation.

This is not a static balance; the means of maintaining it are undergoing continual change and this dynamic process has meant that during the last twenty-five years stockpiles of weapons have grown at an incredible rate and armaments have evolved with breathtaking speed. The role of the airplane has been extended to complement the use of missiles and to form part of the developing space program, all of which has led to an unprecedented acceleration in its evolution. Progress in aviation still relies mainly on military imperatives but when new technology is applied by the civil sector, the effects are just as important and far-reaching.

The Soviet Union and the United States still have a commanding lead over the rest of the world in these spheres, both benefiting from the incalculably valuable spin-offs from their space programs. The United States can, however, be considered as the most influential, since it is willing to let much of the Western world's aeronautical industry share in its resources, both financial and technical, whilst the same is not necessarily true of the Soviet Union vis à vis its allies.

Against this background, what part is left for the European aviation industry to play? Faced by the prospect of being left far behind by its superpower ally, the trend since the 1970s has been towards reliance on joint ventures – where several countries agree to pool their technological, financial and industrial resources and capacity; this represents the only hope left to them if they are ever successfully to challenge the U.S. preeminence in aircraft production. The most ambitious projects involving international cooperation to be launched during recent years in the West have precisely that object in mind: to try to win business away from the giant American aircraft companies. Many programs along these lines have proved successful, especially those involving airliners.

Viewed from a purely technological point of view, Concorde was an epoch-making triumph for the European aviation industry – and for British and French expertise in particular, for once stealing a march on their transatlantic rivals. A more commercially successful example of cooperation, the Airbus, captured a large share of the international market from such vast concerns as Boeing, McDonnell-Douglas and Lockheed who were somewhat belated in taking up the challenge. In the military sector, only France and Sweden have nationally produced combat aircraft in recent years which can be compared with their U.S. and Soviet equivalents. The outstanding example of European cooperation in the eighties is the Tornado, a sophisticated multirole combat aircraft, developed by Britain, Germany and Italy, which can hold its own with the cream of the world's military aircraft.

While military aviation seems destined to achieve increasingly ambitious objects [given the enormous expenditure on arms], the advances in civil aviation during recent years have been just as impressive. While the revolution in air travel brought about by the SuperSonic Transports [SST] was both won and lost by the Europeans [today Concorde is practically obsolete, like its ill-fated rival the Tupolev Tu-144, while the United States continues working on second-generation SSTs], two other major developments have been dominated by the U.S. aircraft industry: the advent of the wide-bodied airplane and conversion to less fuel-hungry, quieter aircraft. Boeing was the first manufacturer to identify and meet both needs, beginning in the 1970s with the 747 "Jumbo" and then, in the early 1980s, offering the 767 and the 757, two airliners which marked turning points in civil transport as regards fuel economy and maximum efficiency of operation.

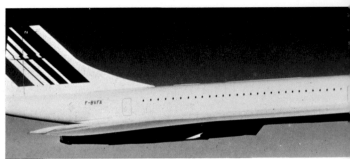

BAC-Aérospatiale Concorde, 1969

These developments were forced on commercial aviation by one of the gravest crises the industry has ever had to face: the energy shock of 1979-81. Just as the commercial operators thought they were on the crest of a wave of unparalleled expansion with prospects of unlimited growth and an enormous increase in capacity, they were plunged into an extremely precarious position, hammered by a very severe recession throughout the industrialized world.

An outline of the state of the industry as the 1970s drew to a close [a decade during which air traffic had soared, achieving an average yearly growth rate of 8.1 per cent] shows the scale of the crisis. In 1979 the airlines of the 145 countries belonging to the ICAO [International Civil Aviation Organization] carried 747 million passengers on scheduled flights, an increase of 10 per cent over the previous year, and 11,200,000 tonnes of cargo, representing a 5.7 per cent increase. Passenger traffic on international routes increased by 10.6 per cent and by 9.9 per cent on domestic routes; international traffic, when measured in terms of tonne/kilometers had risen by 12.1 per cent, as against 10.6 per cent for domestic traffic. The United States and the Soviet Union accounted for about 51 per cent of the total volume of scheduled traffic on domestic and international routes, their shares being 37 per cent and 14 per cent respectively. These two countries alone accounted for nearly 80 per cent of the world's domestic traffic [56 and 24 per cent]. The United States and Britain between them attracted approximately 27 per cent of international traffic [17 and 10 per cent]. When listed in order of traffic volume handled, the United States, the Soviet Union and Britain were followed by Japan, France, Canada, West Germany and Australia.

The challenge which faced this gigantic industry was to adapt to different operating conditions, while still remaining competitive and economically viable, even when faced with an enormous increase in costs and parallel drop in traffic. This was the problem which brought about three years of turmoil in the world's airlines, during which time a remedy was desperately being sought for the industry's over-capacity. The solutions ranged from price wars [in defiance of international agreements on fare structures; the busiest routes such as those over the North Atlantic, saw fares being slashed in an attempt to attract the largest possible numbers of passengers], to leasing or selling off airliners to compensate for disastrous operating losses in an attempt to make the balance sheet look healthier.

The outcome was not a happy one. Many airlines [the most unscrupulous] went out of business, sometimes in a blaze of publicity, owing millions of dollars; others accumulated enormous deficits, while some only survived by carrying out ruthless cost-cutting measures, reducing staff and aircraft numbers drastically. Other, new companies were formed in the hope of filling the gap left by the failed operators. These dark days in the world of civil transport lasted from 1980-83 and are summed up by a few bald figures issued by IATA: in 1980 the total indebtedness of its 112 member airlines amounted to $1,100 million; in 1981 this rose to $1,200 million; in 1982 it reached $1,800 million, while in 1983 [the year in which the first signs of recovery were discernible as the major industrialized countries started to recover from the recession, led by the United States] the worldwide airline deficit had fallen back to $1,200 million.

Tupolev Tu-144, 1968

At this point air traffic started to pick up, having averaged zero growth in 1981 and a 0.9 per cent drop the following year, showing a slight rise at long last in the

second half of 1983, suggesting that the forecast of an annual growth rate of 2.3 per cent was correct. According to IATA's estimates released in 1983, there should have been an increase of 4.6 per cent in 1984; 5.2 per cent in 1985 and growth should average 4.7 per cent during the years 1986-88. These are encouraging figures, although a far cry from those for the previous decade. Airlines were expected to break even across the board in 1985.

This reversal of trends was accompanied by a complete reorganization of the whole structure of the business, with the aim of reducing capacity and drastically cutting operating and management costs. As in the past, the commercial aviation industry responded to the demands of a changed market, launching a new era of fierce competition. Now that some of the first-generation of less fuel-hungry aircraft have started to join the airlines' fleets, the largest international aircraft companies are already planning for the 1990s and projects are being put in train for the next generation of airliners, expected to be even more competitive than those now entering service; today's requirements are for economy of operation, low noise and very high efficiency.

McDonnell-Douglas is now offering sophisticated developed versions of its "old" DC-9, announced in late 1983 [the MD-80 series with up-dated engines] which should be delivered from 1987-88 onwards [the Long Beach company has, however, had to put certain other construction programs on ice because of the prolonged crisis in the airline industry, among them their latest derivative, the MD-90 and the MD-100 trijet, planned as a very advanced version of the DC-10]. Boeing is also making sure of its market with its new 737, 757 and 767 aircraft. The same aim has motivated the Airbus consortium to build the A-320, the 150-seat aircraft which is Europe's hope of repeating the success of the A-300 and the A-310 [in the face of many setbacks] as a challenge to the U.S. equivalents.

Whatever may be the outcome of developments in the near future in commercial aviation, with the winners and losers being decided by their ability or failure to apply up-to-date technology and interpret the state of the market, the eighties have shown that in the most prestigious area of development there is no longer any question of rivalry between the Old World and the New. The aircraft has been transformed into a vehicle which can now travel outside its traditional element into a new dimension, that of space. The United States has achieved this with its Space Shuttle, a hybrid which cannot satisfactorily be described as an aircraft or as a winged-rocket, but however it is defined, it is certainly the embodiment of a long-held dream. Not only have the frontiers between aviation and space travel become blurred but we have had a glimpse of the immense potential of the flying machines of the future. This potential could be exploited constructively or destructively. It is to be hoped that man's conscience will prompt him to use it to work for peace and progress.

Space Shuttle, 1981

# Insignia of the world's airlines

 Icelandair

 Scandinavian Airlines System

 Scanair

 Transair Sweden

 Finnair O/Y

 Aeroflot

 Air France

 Air Littoral

 Air Inter

 Air Alpes

 Touraine Air Transport

Union de Transports Aériens

 Sabena-Belgian World Airlines

 Condor Flugdienst

 Luftransport-Unternehmen

 Bavaria Germanair

 Interflug

 LOT - Polskie Linie Lotnicze

 Ceskoslovenske Aerolinie

 Swissair

 Aviaco-Aviacion Y Comercio

 Alitalia - Linee Aeree Italiane

 Aero Trasporti Italiani

 Air Malta

 Jugoslovenski Aerotransport

 Inex Adria Airways

 Egyptair

 Air Mali

 Air Niger

 Sudan Airways

 Ethiopian Airlines

 Air-Guinnée

 Air Zaire

 Air Tanzania

 Air Kenya

 TAAG - Linhas Aéreas de Angola

 Zambia Airways

 Air Malawi

 LAM Lineas Aereas de Mocambique

 MEA - Middle East Airlines Air Liban

 Trans Mediterranean Airways

 Syrian Arab Airlines

 Iraqi Airways

 El Al Israel Airlines

 Arkia Israel Inland Airways

 Air-India

 Indian Airways

 Airlanka

 MIAT Air Mongol

CAAC - Civil Aviation Administration of China

Cathay Pacific Airways

Aer Lingus Irish Airlines
 British Airways
 Air UK
 Britannia Airways
 British Caledonian Airways
 Laker Airways
 Dan-Air Services
 Monarch Airlines
Sterling Airways A/S

 Sobelair - Société Belge de Transports Par Air
 Trans European Airways
 Luxair
 Koninklijke Luchtvaart Maatschapij NV
 Martinair Holland
 Transavia Holland
 Lufthansa

 Balair
 Crossair
 Austrian Airlines
 TAROM - Transporturite Aeriene Romane
 TAP - Transportes Aereos Portugueses
 Iberia
 Spantax Trasportes Aereos

 Aviogenex
 Olympic Airways
 Balkan Bulgarian Airlines
 Royal Air Maroc
 Air Algerie
Tunis Air
 Libyan Arab Airlines

 Air Afrique
 Air Ivoire
 Ghana Airways
 Nigeria Airways
 Cameroon Airlines
 Air Gabon

 Direccao de Exploracao dos Transportes Aéreos
 Air Madagascar
 South African Airways
 Safair Freighters
 Cyprus Airways
 Turk Hava Yollari

 Alia-Royal Jordanian Airlines
 Saudia
 Kuwait Airways
 Gulf Air
 Yemenia
 Iran Air
PIA Pakistan International Airlines

 China Airlines
 Korean Air Lines
 Japan Air Lines
 All Nippon Airways
 Japan Asia Airways
 TDA - Domestic Airlines
 Southwest Air Lines

# Insignia of the world's airlines

 Royal Nepal Airlines

 Bangladesh Biman

 Burma Airways

 Thai Airways International

 Thai Airways

 MAS Malaysian Airlines System

 PAL Philippine Airlines

 Wardair International

 Nordair

 Okanagan Helicopters

 Trans World Airlines

 Pan American World Airways

 American Airlines

 United Airlines

 Pacific Southwest Airlines

 Northwest Orient

 National Airlines

 Alaska International Air

 Air California

 Aeroamerica

 Seaboard World Airlines

 SMB Stage Line

 World Airways

 Wien Air Alaska

 Western Airlines

 Texas International Airlines

 Piedmont Airlines

 Ozark Air Lines

 Transamerica Airlines

 Aeromech Airlines

 Golden West Airlines

 Alaska Airlines

 Frontier Airlines

 Federal Express

 Belize Airlines

 Lineas Aereas Costaricenses

 Air Panama Internacional

 Empresa Consolidada Cubana de Aviacion

Bahamasair

 Air Jamaica

 Ecuatoriana

 Antilles Air Boats

 British West Indian Airways

 AeroPeru

Cruzeiro do Sul

 VOTEC Servicos Aéreos Regionais

 VARIG - Viacao Aérea Rio Gradense

 PLUNA Primeras Lineas Uruguayas de Navegacion Aérea

 Air Calédonie

 Air Niugini

Talair TPY

Surinam Airways

Qantas Airways

 **Sterling Philippine Airways**

 **SIA**
**Singapore Airlines**

 **Royal Brunei Airlines**

 **Garuda**
**Indonesian Airways**

 **Air Canada**

 **CP Air**
**Canadian Pacific Airlines**

 **Quebecair**

 **Braniff International**

 **Flying Tiger Line**

 **Continental Airlines**

 **USAIR**

 **Capitol International Airways**

 **Eastern Air Lines**

 **Delta Air Lines**

 **Air Florida**

 **Republic Airlines**

 **Cochise Airlines**

 **Evergreen International Airlines**

 **Rio Airways**

 **Sierra Pacific Airlines**

 **Hughes Airwest**

 **Hawaiian Airlines**

 **Aloha Airlines**

 **Sea Airmotive**

 **Zantop International Airlines**

 **Trans Continental Airlines**

 **Aspen Airways**

 **Southern Airways**

 **Aeromexico**

 **Mexicana**

 **SAHSA**
**Servicio Aereo de Honduras SA**

 **Aviateca**
**Aerolineas de Guatemala**

 **Dominicana**

 **Caribbean Airways**

 **Aerovias Nacionales de Colombia**

 **Aerocondor**
**Aerovias Condor de Colombia**

 **Venezolana International**
**de Aviacion SA**

 **Lloyd Aereo Boliviano**

 **Viacao Aérea Sao Paulo**

 **Transbrasil S/A**
**Linhas Aereas**

 **Rio-Sul**

 **LADECO**
**Linea Aerea del Cobre**

 **Lan Chile**

 **Aerolineas Argentinas**

 **Austral Lineas Aereas**

 **East-West Airlines**

 **Ansett Airlines of Australia**

 **Trans-Australia Airlines**

 **Polynesian Airlines**

 **Air New Zealand**

 **IATA - International Air**
**Transport Association**

# 1960-1980
## The "wide-body" makes its appearance

Perhaps no innovation since the introduction of the jet engine has changed civil aviation as much as the high-capacity aircraft which started to join commercial fleets in the 1960s. At a time when traffic was increasing particularly swiftly, airlines saw that it was in their best interests to transport as many passengers as possible on each flight in order to achieve optimum profitability. As usual, the most energetic commercial and industrial initiative came from the U.S.A., and Boeing once more led the way: the era of the wide-bodied jet was inaugurated on 8 February 1969 when the Boeing 747 first took to the air, a giant airliner which could accommodate over 400 passengers and which was immediately dubbed the Jumbo Jet.

The impact which the 747 had on the market [it is still the largest commercial aircraft in service] is illustrated by a few facts: in 1966, two years before the prototype's maiden flight, Boeing had already taken orders worth $1.8 billion; during this famous airliner's first six months of operation on scheduled routes it carried over a million passengers; in December 1980 the 500th 747 came off the assembly line; by late 1983 orders for the airliner totalled 613.

This was not the only wide-bodied aircraft to be offered by U.S. aircraft companies; McDonnell-Douglas also came up with their own high-capacity airliner, the DC-10. Work started on this very large trijet in response to American Airlines' requirement [in 1966] for a wide-bodied airplane which could operate from airports which did not have the very long runways which were essential for the 747. The first DC-10 flew on 29 August 1970 and the first series aircraft entered service on 5 August the following year, on the Los Angeles-Chicago route, in American Airlines livery. The DC-10's career was not, however, such a resounding success as its direct rival's [in part due to some serious accidents which fuelled suspicions of structural weakness] and in the early 1980s the assembly lines were closed down, with the exception of those needed for the military version, the KC-10 advanced tanker.

The third U.S. company to enter the lists was Lockheed, with its L-1011 TriStar, another high capacity trijet developed from June 1968 onwards to meet the demand from U.S. airlines operating domestic routes. The prototype's first flight took place on 16 November 1970; scheduled services with the TriStar were inaugurated on 26 April 1972 by Eastern Airlines. This aircraft also has not sold as well as had been hoped.

In the wake of the Americans, the Russians had also decided to build their own wide-bodied type. The Ilyushin Il-86 project was launched in 1970 and the prototype [a cross between the 747 and the 707] flew on 22 December 1976. On 24 October the following year the first series aircraft was unveiled and commenced scheduled flights with Aeroflot on 26 December 1980.

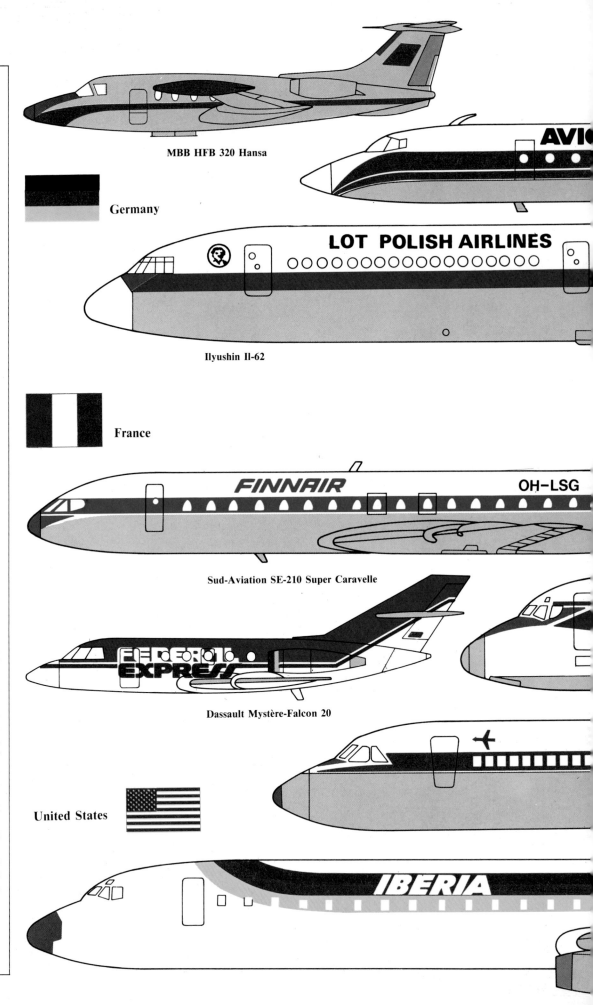

MBB HFB 320 Hansa

Germany

Ilyushin Il-62

France

Sud-Aviation SE-210 Super Caravelle

Dassault Mystère-Falcon 20

United States

GENEX

Soviet Union

Tupolev Tu-134

SP-LAA

F-BPUH

Fokker F.27-500 Friendship

Netherlands

DELTA

DELTA AIR LINES

DELTA

N330/L

McDonnell-Douglas DC-9-10

SWISSAIR

HB-ICB

Convair 990 Coronado

EC-BMY

Douglas DC-8-63

Swearingen Metro II

S A B E N A   🔲 belgian world airlines                    OO-SDA

Boeing 737

TWA

Cessna Citation

Lear Jet 24

AERO SPAC

AIRBUS INDUSTRIE

Alitalia

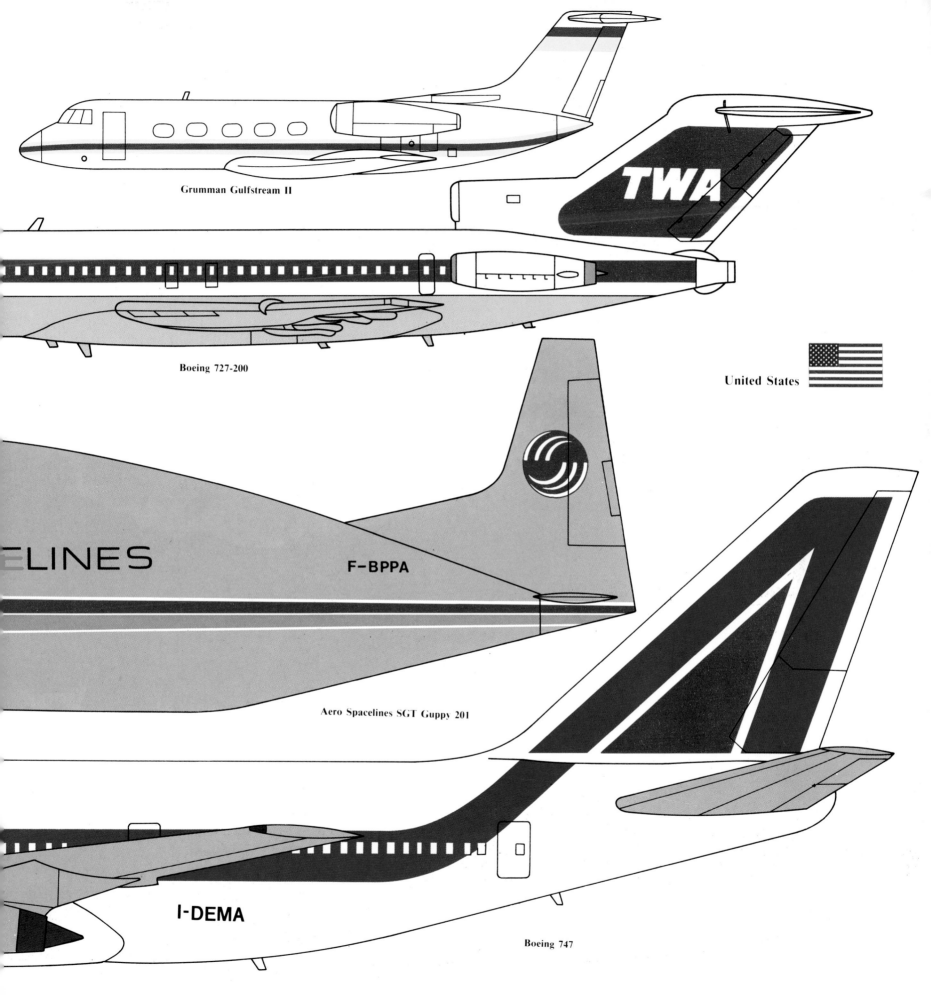

Grumman Gulfstream II

Boeing 727-200

United States

ELINES

F–BPPA

Aero Spacelines SGT Guppy 201

I-DEMA

Boeing 747

171

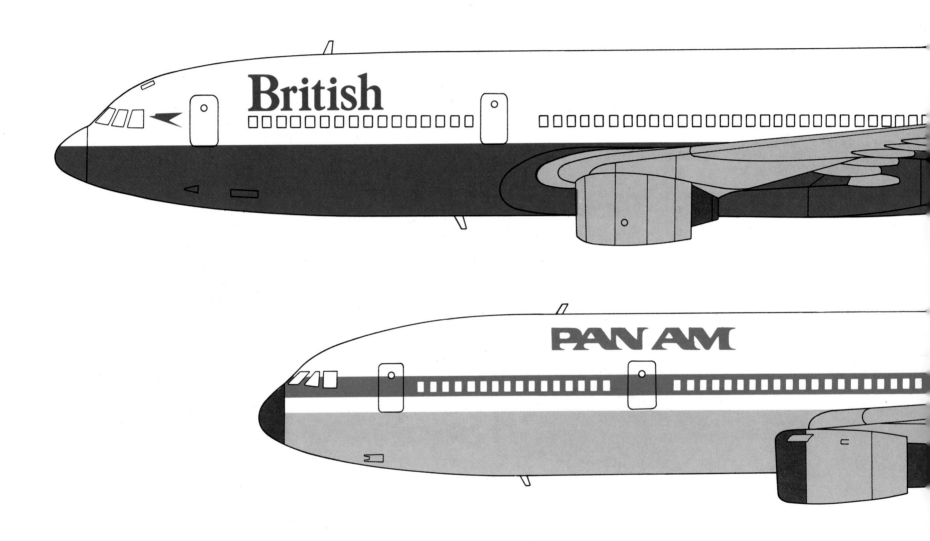

British

PAN AM

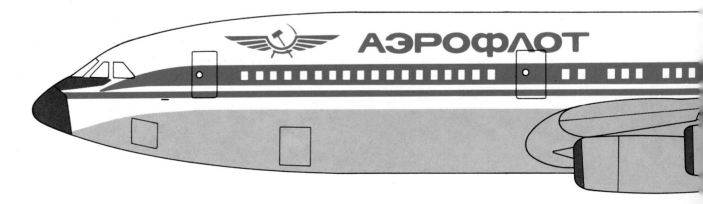

АЭРОФЛОТ

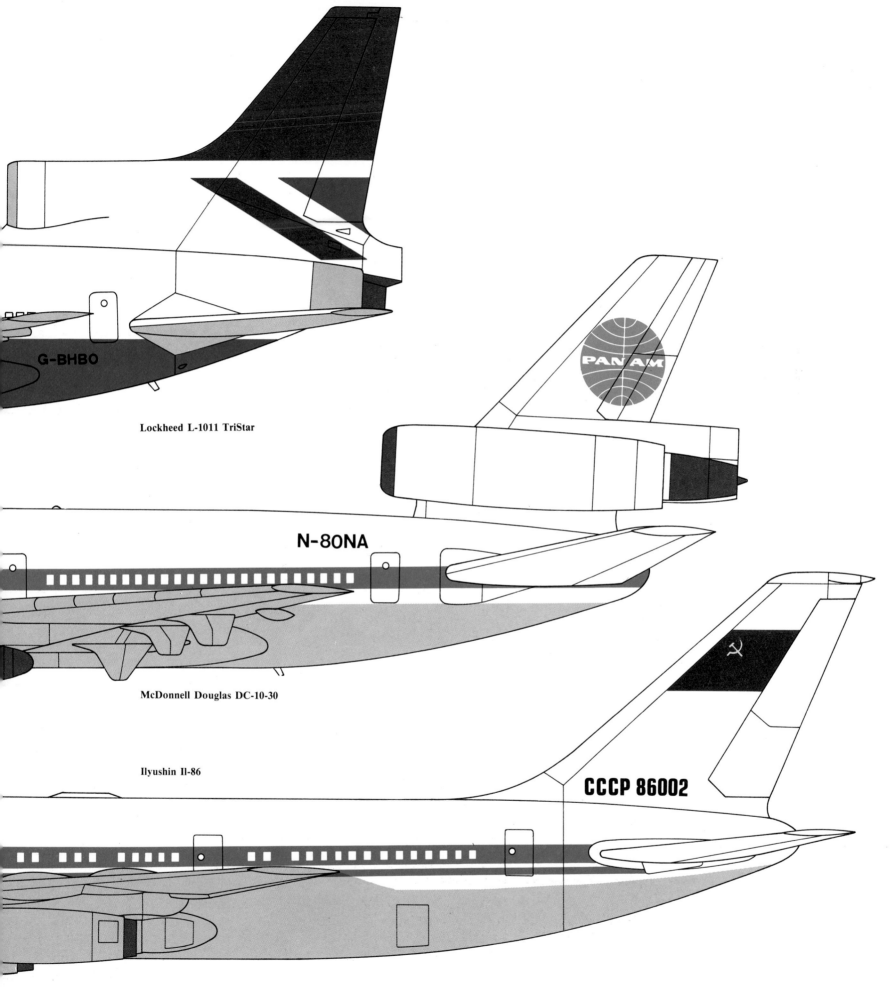

G-BHBO

Lockheed L-1011 TriStar

PAN AM

N-80NA

McDonnell Douglas DC-10-30

Ilyushin Il-86

CCCP 86002

# 1960-1980
## Supersonic civil transport – a story of travail

Besides being in competition for the wide-bodied jet market, U.S. aircraft manufacturers also vied with each other to capture orders for short-to-medium-range and medium-capacity aircraft, where the possible rewards were just as substantial and tempting. During the 1960s the most important airliners of this class were produced by Boeing and McDonnell-Douglas. The McDonnell-Douglas DC-9 [first flight 25 February 1965] and Boeing's B-727 [9 February 1963] and B-737 [9 April 1967] have proved amazingly profitable [and their production continues well into the 1980s]. The 727 has the enviable distinction of being the best-selling aircraft in the Western world, with production ending in mid 1984 after the completion of 1,832 aircraft; the final versions of the 737 and the DC-9 will be developed into advanced variants as the 1980s progress.

Manufacturers from outside the United States were tempted to compete for a share of this market, often with encouraging results, like the British BAC One-Eleven [first flight 20 August 1963] and the Hawker Siddeley Trident [9 January 1962] as well as the Soviet's Tupolev Tu-134 [1964] and Tu-154 [1968]. The most recent short-to-medium-range aircraft to emerge from behind the Iron Curtain is the Antonov An-72, a twin jet with STOL [Short Take-off and Landing] capability, the prototype of which was unveiled on 22 December 1972 and destined to replace the twin-engine An-26 turboprop in Aeroflot's fleet and with the Soviet airforces.

But the most thrilling contest was fought out during the 1960s between the world's four leading air powers [U.S.A., U.S.S.R., France and Britain] in a race to be first with a supersonic civil transport. This was a daunting objective, involving not only the mastery of new technology, necessitating long and costly research and development programs in order to open up another phase in the airplane's evolution, but with the added incentive of a tremendous boost in national prestige for the country which won. The question was, whether such kudos were worth the incredibly high costs involved. In the event there were two starters and one nonstarter.

The Soviets' Tupolev Tu-144 was the first SST to fly [on 31 December 1968] but the aircraft progressed little further than the experimental stage over a period of ten years before being mothballed. The Anglo-French Concorde [maiden flight 2 March 1969, 18 built] had to wait for some time before finding its niche in the market; on 21 January 1976 it finally entered service with Air France and British Airways but by the end of 1983 this aircraft was already fighting for its life, because of very high operating costs and insufficient demand for these very fast but very expensive flights. The American project for an SST, launched by Boeing in October 1968, was dropped when, on 24 March 1971, the U.S. Senate voted against allocating the huge sums needed if such a construction program were to continue.

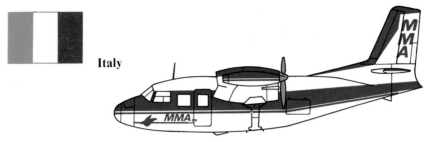

Italy

Piaggio P.166 Portofino

Canada

de Havilland Canada DHC-6 Twin Otter 300

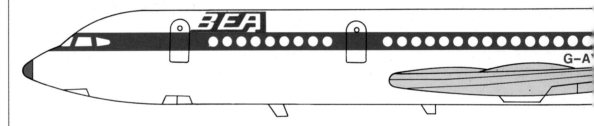

Hawker Siddeley Trident 2E

BAC One-Eleven 500

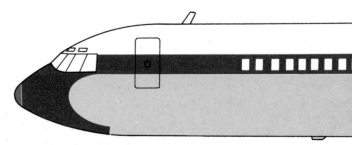

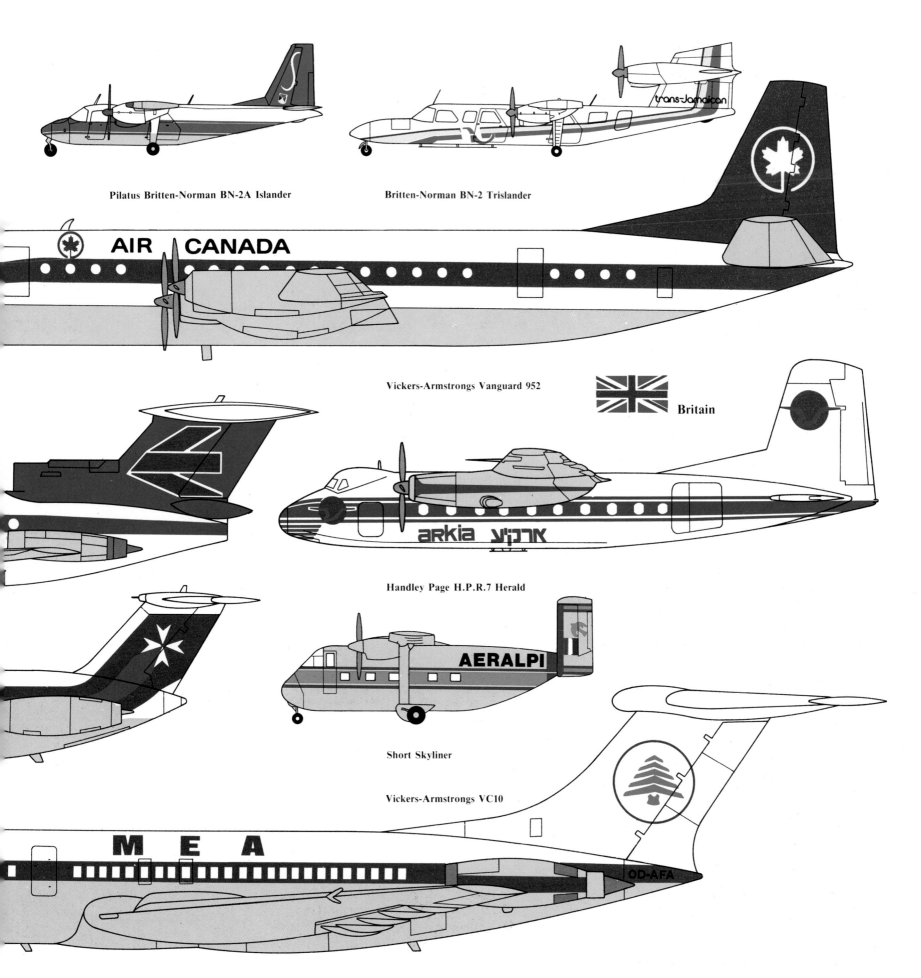

Pilatus Britten-Norman BN-2A Islander

Britten-Norman BN-2 Trislander

AIR CANADA

Vickers-Armstrongs Vanguard 952

Britain

arkia אַרקיע

Handley Page H.P.R.7 Herald

AERALPI

Short Skyliner

Vickers-Armstrongs VC10

M E A

OD-AFA

France

Britain

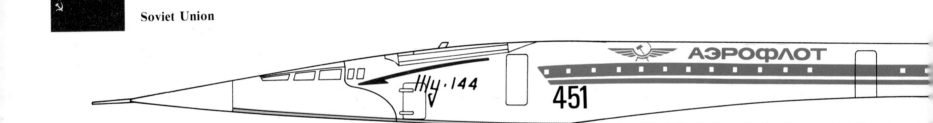

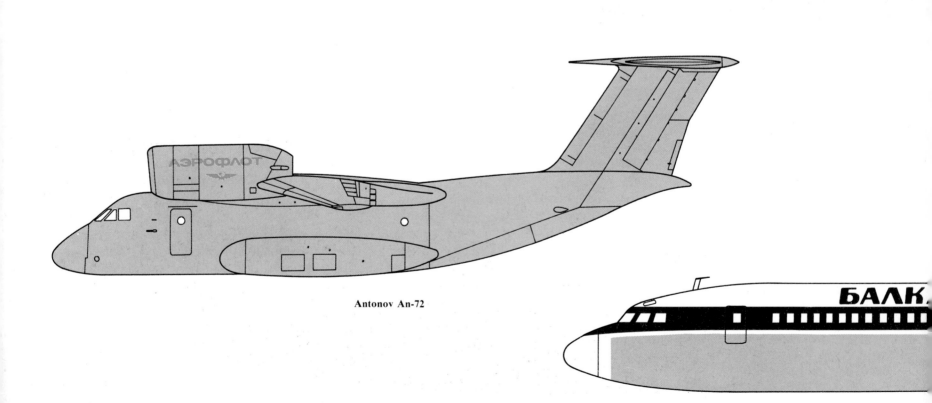

Antonov An-72

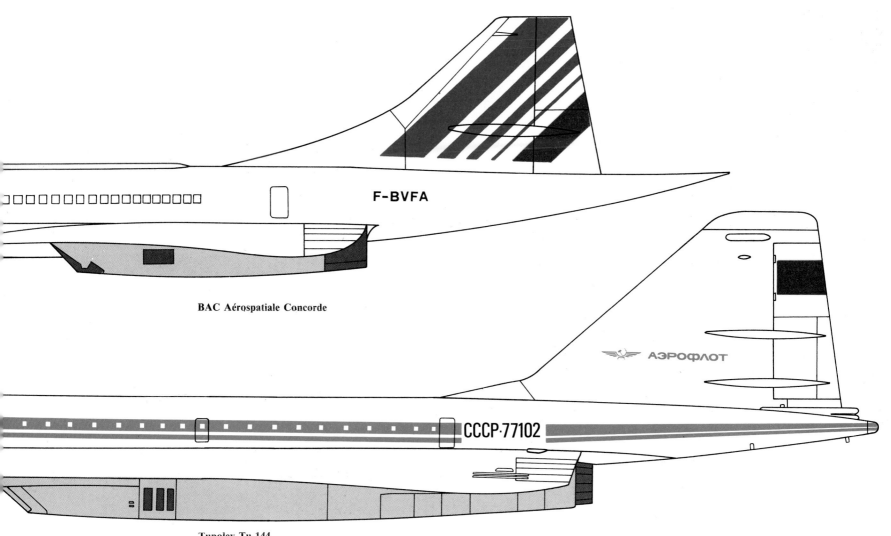

F-BVFA

**BAC Aérospatiale Concorde**

CCCP·77102

**Tupolev Tu-144**

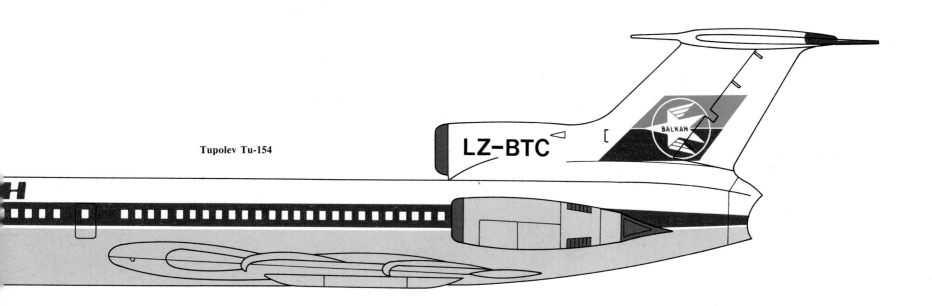

**Tupolev Tu-154**

LZ-BTC

## 1960-1985
## The continuing quest for deadlier warplanes

From the late 1960s onwards a near-frenzied struggle for air superiority between the two superpowers has led to the development of increasingly sophisticated, fast and deadly warplanes, veritable weapon systems controlled by advanced computer technology.

The U.S. Navy had the edge in carrier-based aircraft, having gained a head start with the Grumman F-14 Tomcat [maiden flight 24 May 1971], a powerful and sophisticated variable geometry interceptor, and with the McDonnell-Douglas F-18 Hornet [the prototype first flew towards the end of 1978], a combat/strike aircraft destined to replace the F-4 Phantom. The USAF put two equally impressive combat planes into service: the McDonnell-Douglas F-15 Eagle interceptor [first flight 27 July 1972], and the General Dynamics F-16 multirole combat aircraft [first flight 13 December 1973].

The Soviet Union's combat planes of the eighties are in some respects less sophisticated than the latest U.S. types but equally powerful and battle-prepared. The most important belong to the prolific families of MiG and Sukhoi, among the most outstanding being the variable geometry MiG-23 [1967], the [Mach 3] MiG-25, the Su-15 interceptor [1967] and the powerful, multirole Su-24 [1974].

The best of Europe's combat planes still in use were built by France, Britain and Sweden. They include the most recent variants of the Mirage jets [the series 2000 which appeared in March 1978 and the Super Mirage 4000 – the prototype of which first flew on 9 March 1979]; the Saab 37 Viggen [maiden flight 8 February 1967]; and the variable geometry MRCA Tornado built by the three nation consortium [Panavia] formed by Britain, Germany and Italy, which first took to the air on 14 August 1974. Italy and Brazil have collaborated in developing the AMX tactical fighter for their airforces; the prototype had its maiden flight on 15 May 1984 but an accident a fortnight later led to the interruption of the test program.

The British aircraft industry earned great prestige with the vertical take-off Harrier fighter. This ambitious project first took shape as long ago as 1957 and it was ten years before the first series aircraft came off the assembly lines. The Harrier was such a success that an order was forthcoming from the U.S. Marines and a license agreement was concluded with McDonnell-Douglas who developed an advanced, more powerful variant [the AV-8B Harrier II]. The Soviets' answer to the Harrier was the carrier-based Yakovlev Yak-36 [1976].

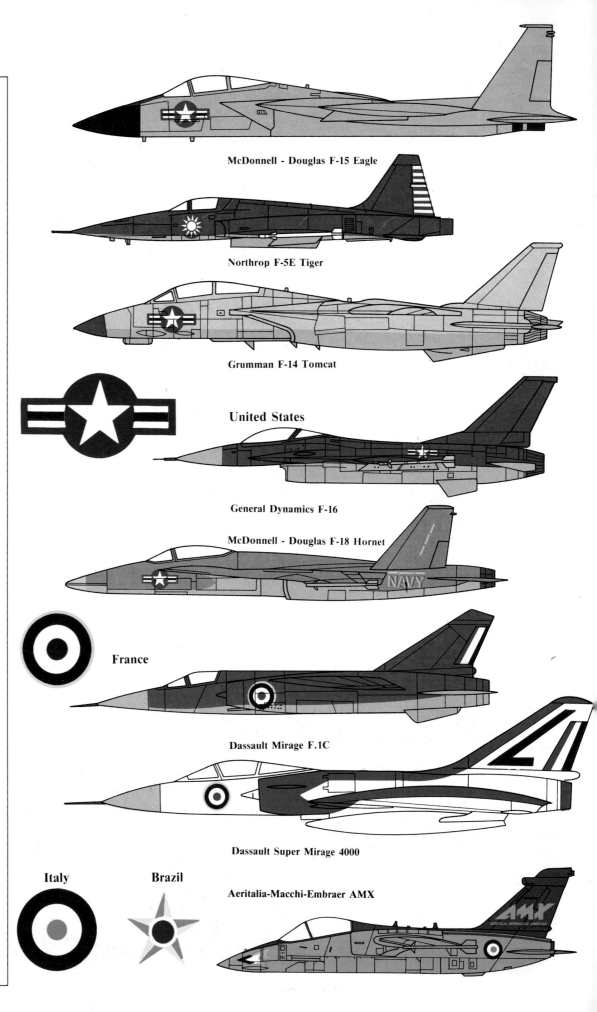

McDonnell - Douglas F-15 Eagle

Northrop F-5E Tiger

Grumman F-14 Tomcat

United States

General Dynamics F-16

McDonnell - Douglas F-18 Hornet

France

Dassault Mirage F.1C

Dassault Super Mirage 4000

Italy

Brazil

Aeritalia-Macchi-Embraer AMX

Yakovlev Yak-36

Sukhoi Su-15

Soviet Union

Sukhoi Su-19

Mikoyan-Gurevich MiG-23

Mikoyan-Gurevich MiG-25

Sweden

Israel

Saab AJ37 Viggen

IAI Kfir C2

Britain

India

Hawker Siddeley Harrier

HAL HF-24 Marut

Germany    Britain    Italy

Britain

France

Sepecat Jaguar

MRCA Tornado

179

## 1960-1985
## Death of the strategic bomber

The strategic bomber which played a key role in two world wars, had been developed to the limit of its capacity during the fifties and sixties. During the following decade its traditional role gradually became less and less relevant, supplanted firstly by the new and deadly intercontinental ballistic missiles and then by the equally formidable Cruise missiles, ultrasophisticated nuclear weapons which in themselves are autonomous and "intelligent" aircraft.

This tend was to be briefly interrupted in the United States at the beginning of the 1980s, when the Reagan administration's policies led to the U.S. stepping up her arms development and production. This was not a new departure, simply a marked acceleration of an existing policy. Some of the most advanced weapons systems were to be integrated into the overall arms planning; one such was the Rockwell International B-1, one of the most controversial aircraft ever designed.

This sophisticated strategic bomber [designated B-1B in its definitive configuration] which can carry as many as 22 Cruise missiles, was first developed in the late sixties as a replacement for the B-52 bomber. The program was cancelled by President Carter in 1977 and revived four years later by Ronald Reagan. The relaunch of the project was approved on 2 October 1981: a procurement for 100 aircraft was issued with deliveries to commence in 1986.

Other examples of how the strategic bomber's tasks have been taken over [the B-1B is more correctly described as a Cruise missile carrier rather than as a traditional strategic bomber] are provided by assault/ground attack aircraft and multirole combat planes, a great many of which are in service with airforces all over the world. One of the most effective, still in service with western airforces, is the General Dynamics F-111, a large, powerful twinjet flying at speeds in excess of Mach 2, which originated as long ago as 1962 in response to a specification for a strike aircraft. The Mirage IV-A is another survivor, developed by the French in the late 1950s as a carrier of nuclear weapons.

Two assault aircraft especially conceived to carry out tactical duties must not be omitted: the carrier-based Lockheed S-3A Viking and its land-based equivalent, the Fairchild Republic A-10A Thunderbolt II. The former was designed in the late sixties in response to a requirement from the U.S. Navy which needed a replacement for its obsolescent Grumman S-2 Tracker aircraft. Work first started on the Thunderbolt in 1967, to meet a USAF specification for an advanced antitank attack aircraft. The Viking had its maiden flight on 21 January 1972 and has been in service from 1974 on U.S. aircraft carriers; the Thunderbolt II [the prototype of which first flew on 10 May 1972] reached squadrons from March 1977 onwards.

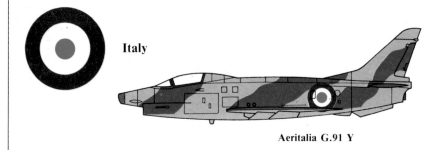

Italy

Aeritalia G.91 Y

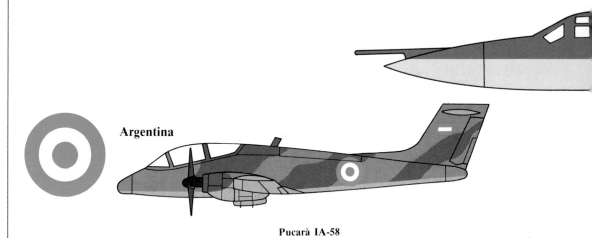

Argentina

Pucarà IA-58

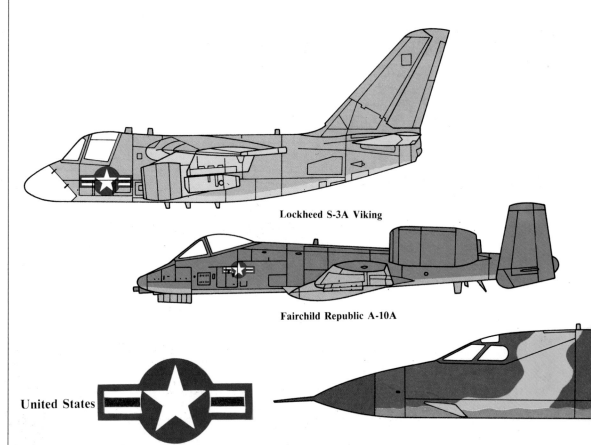

Lockheed S-3A Viking

Fairchild Republic A-10A

United States

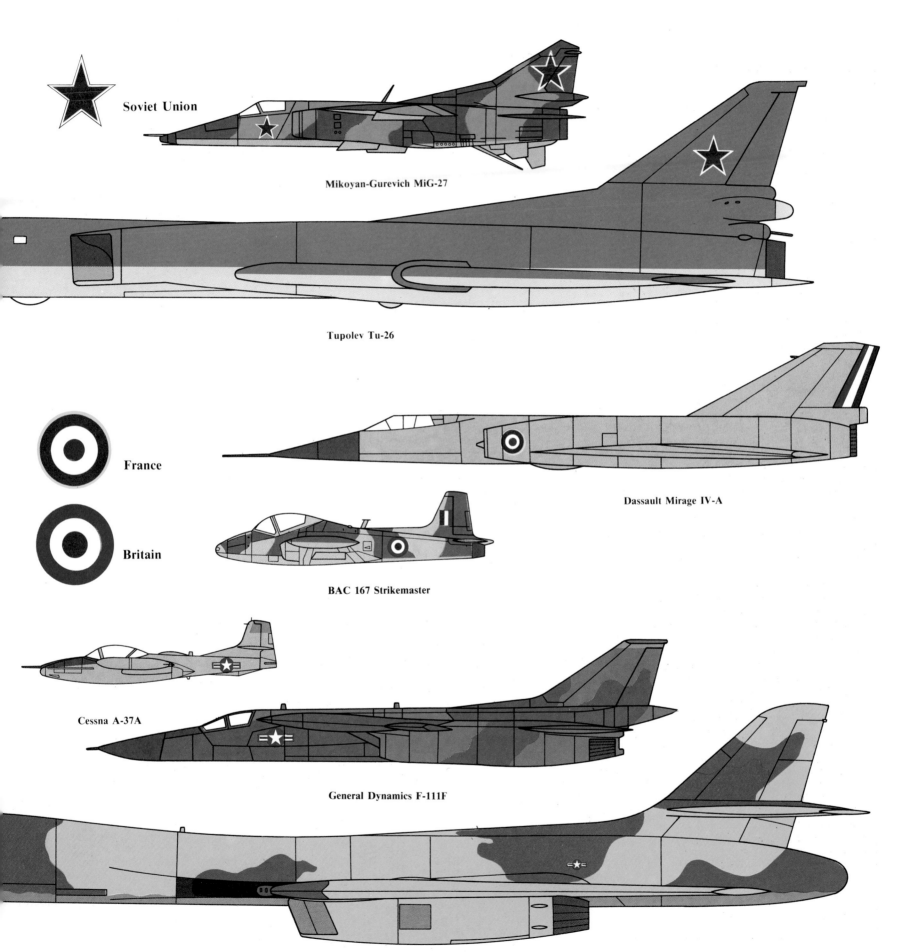

Soviet Union

Mikoyan-Gurevich MiG-27

Tupolev Tu-26

France

Britain

Dassault Mirage IV-A

BAC 167 Strikemaster

Cessna A-37A

General Dynamics F-111F

Rockwell International B-1B

181

# 1960-1985
## Modern reconnaissance – the all-seeing eye

From the 1960s onwards reconnaissance aircraft have had to play a far more specialized role, the emphasis increasingly tending toward strategic reconnaissance. The installation of sophisticated electronics systems has been a determining influence both on the development of these aircraft and the highly skilled crews needed to operate them.

Today's reconnaissance aircraft are veritable airborne intelligence centers, packed with complicated equipment for observation of the territories they overfly. Increasingly selective and powerful radar can "see" from the highest altitudes, while automatic long-focus cameras scan the terrain far below, where not many years earlier pilots and observers had to rely on their own eyes and binoculars. Photographs taken by these modern reconnaissance planes and by satellites are capable of depicting the minutest objects from several kilometers away, with the clearest of definition. Where the traditional role of the reconnaissance aircraft has changed most is perhaps in the sphere of maritime patrol. The Western powers' best aircraft in this field include the Lockheed P-3 Orion [a four-engine turboprop derived from the Electra civil transport] which entered service in 1962 and has since been continually updated; the French Breguet Atlantic [which first flew on 21 October 1961] and has been part of Europe's front-line forces since the late sixties; and the British BAe Nimrod, derived from the four-engine Comet airliner, the first prototype having flown on 23 May 1967.

At the end of the 1960s, these land-based aircraft were joined by what is now the world's only four-engine reconnaissance flying boat, whose ancestors belonged to the golden age of flying: the Japanese Shin Meiwa, which had its maiden flight on 5 October 1967 and was especially developed for service with the Japanese Maritime Self-Defense Force. For self-defense on land, Japan's growing aircraft industry also produced the highly successful Kawasaki C-1, an up-to-date twinjet transport, first planned in 1966, the prototype of which appeared on 12 November 1970.

From aircraft such as these have come the infinitely more sophisticated "Airborne Command Posts," of our day such as the Boeing E-3 Sentry [first flight 1970], the British BAe Nimrod A.E.W. Mk.3 [which evolved from the earlier maritime patrol aircraft and had its maiden flight on 28 June 1977], the

*continued on page 184*

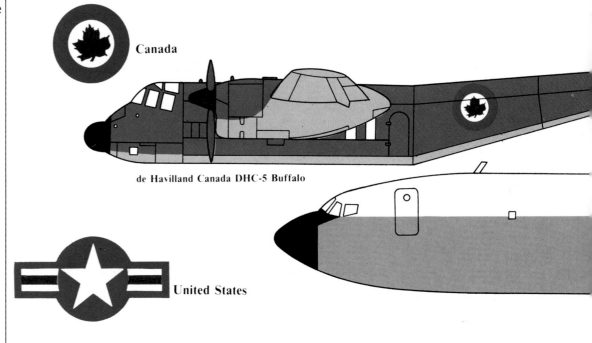

Canada

United States

de Havilland Canada DHC-5 Buffalo

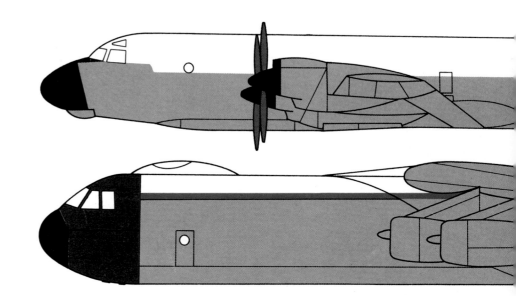

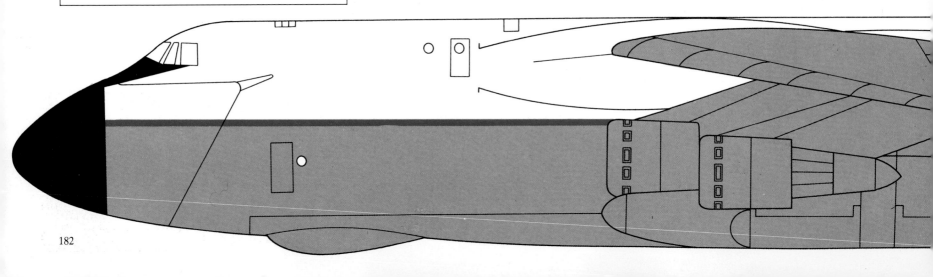

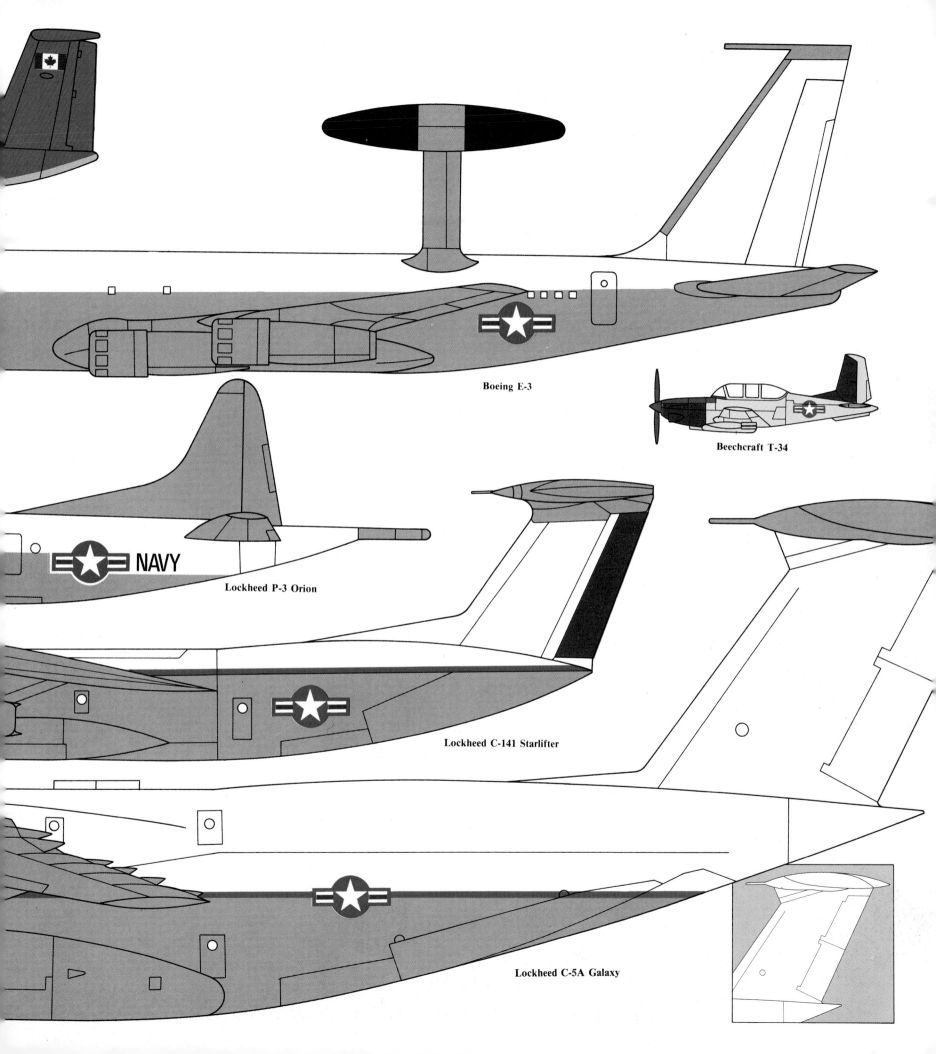

Boeing E-3

Beechcraft T-34

Lockheed P-3 Orion

Lockheed C-141 Starlifter

Lockheed C-5A Galaxy

NAVY

continued from page 182

Soviets' Tupolev Tu-126 [derived from the gigantic four-engine Tupolev Tu-144 civil turboprop airliner] which was unveiled in 1968 – all these aircraft belong to the same category [known in the West under the acronym of AWACS – Airborne Warning And Control System]; all have advanced avionics which enable them to coordinate many different operations simultaneously.

The Boeing E-3 was based on the four-engine B-707-320 commercial transport in response to a USAF program launched in the early 1970s and went into service with the specially created 552 Airborne Warning and Control Wing, based in Oklahoma, in March 1977. The aircraft proved so satisfactory that a requirement was issued for an even more sophisticated strategic command post which Boeing met by modifying the B-747, but without the distinctive overfuselage rotodome housing the main radar. The first E-4 [the military designation for the Jumbo-Jet] was delivered in 1973.

Even the E-4/747 is dwarfed by an aircraft which is by far the largest strategic transport operated by western airforces: the Lockheed Galaxy is an enormous four-engine aircraft with a very large front-loading ramp, which can carry a payload of over 100 tonnes [or 345 fully-equipped troops] over 3,700 miles [6,000 km] at speeds of about 620 mph [nearly 1,000 km/h]. Work started on the project in 1963 when the USAF issued a specification for a strategic transport which would supersede the Lockheed C-141 Starlifter's already considerable capacity. Lockheed won the contract and the first C-5A flew on 30 June 1968. Since 1982, all 77 of the Galaxies still operational have undergone important structural modification [replacement of the wings] aimed at prolonging their then operation life.

Among other giant military transports deserving of mention are the Soviet Antonov An-22 Antei [which first appeared in 1965] and the British Short Belfast [maiden flight, 5 January 1964]. In the early 1970s the Ilyushin Il-76 [which first flew on 25 March 1971] was chosen as a more modern successor to the An-22; this robust four-engine jet transport can operate from short, semiprepared runways; some also went into operation with Aeroflot. Of the medium transports built in Europe, the most noteworthy are the Transall C-160 [built by France and Germany], which first flew on 25 February 1963, and the Aeritalia G.222 [18 July 1970].

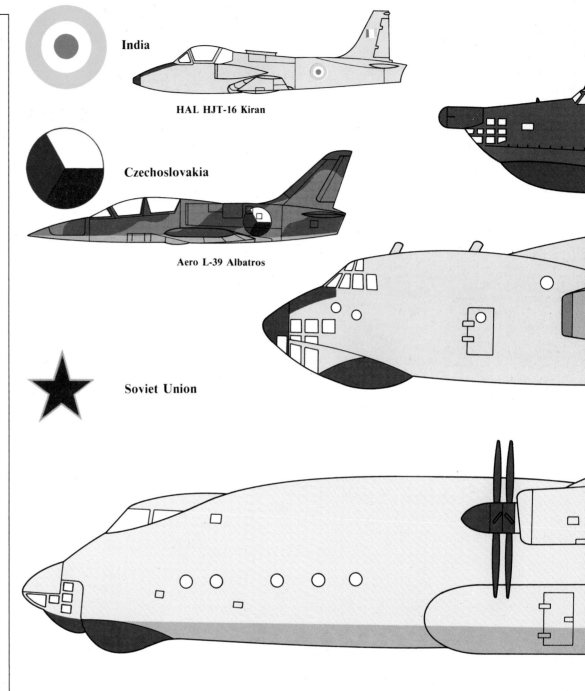

India

HAL HJT-16 Kiran

Czechoslovakia

Aero L-39 Albatros

Soviet Union

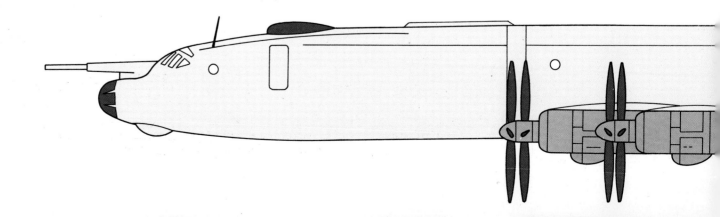

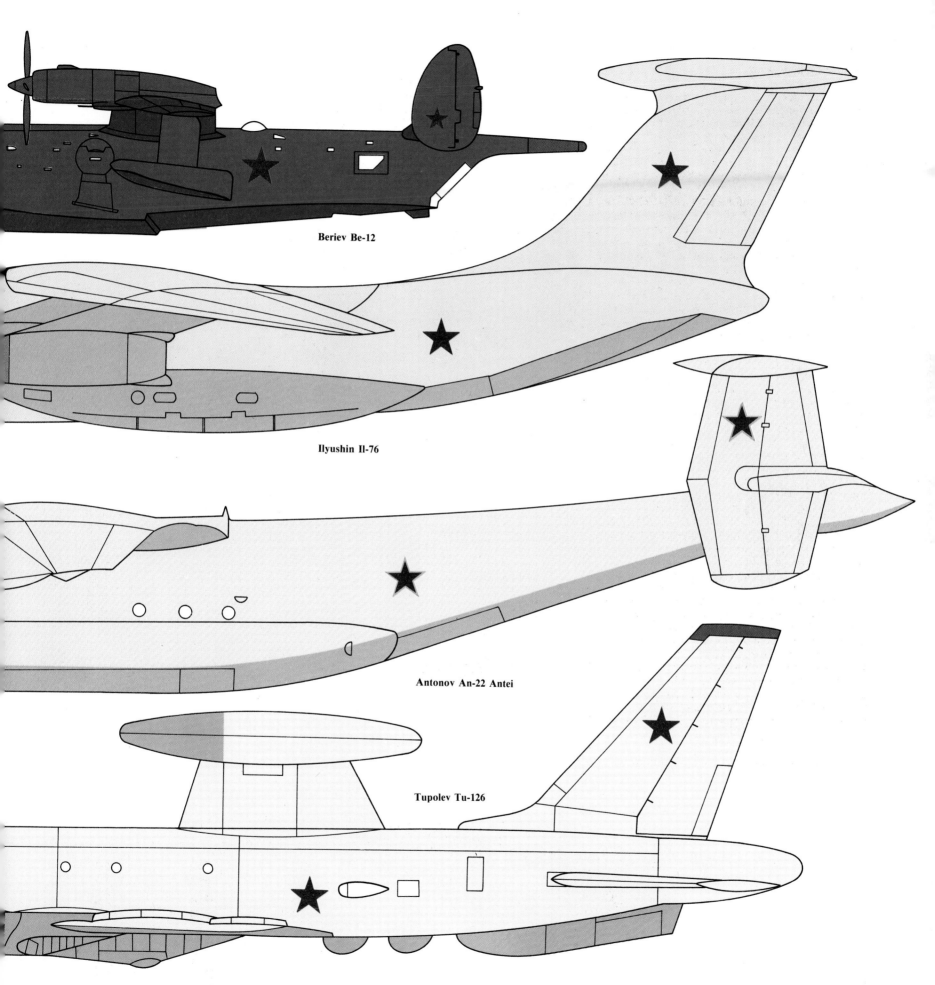

**Beriev Be-12**

**Ilyushin Il-76**

**Antonov An-22 Antei**

**Tupolev Tu-126**

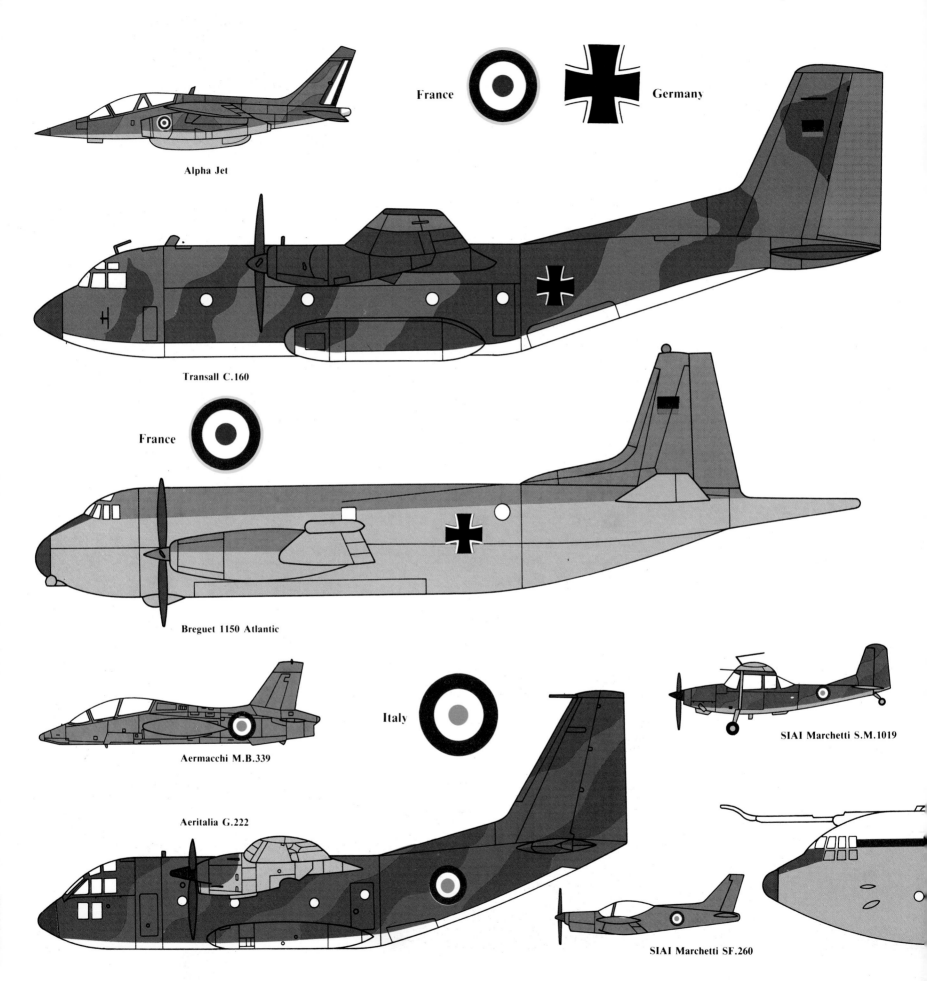

Alpha Jet

France

Germany

Transall C.160

France

Breguet 1150 Atlantic

Aermacchi M.B.339

Italy

SIAI Marchetti S.M.1019

Aeritalia G.222

SIAI Marchetti SF.260

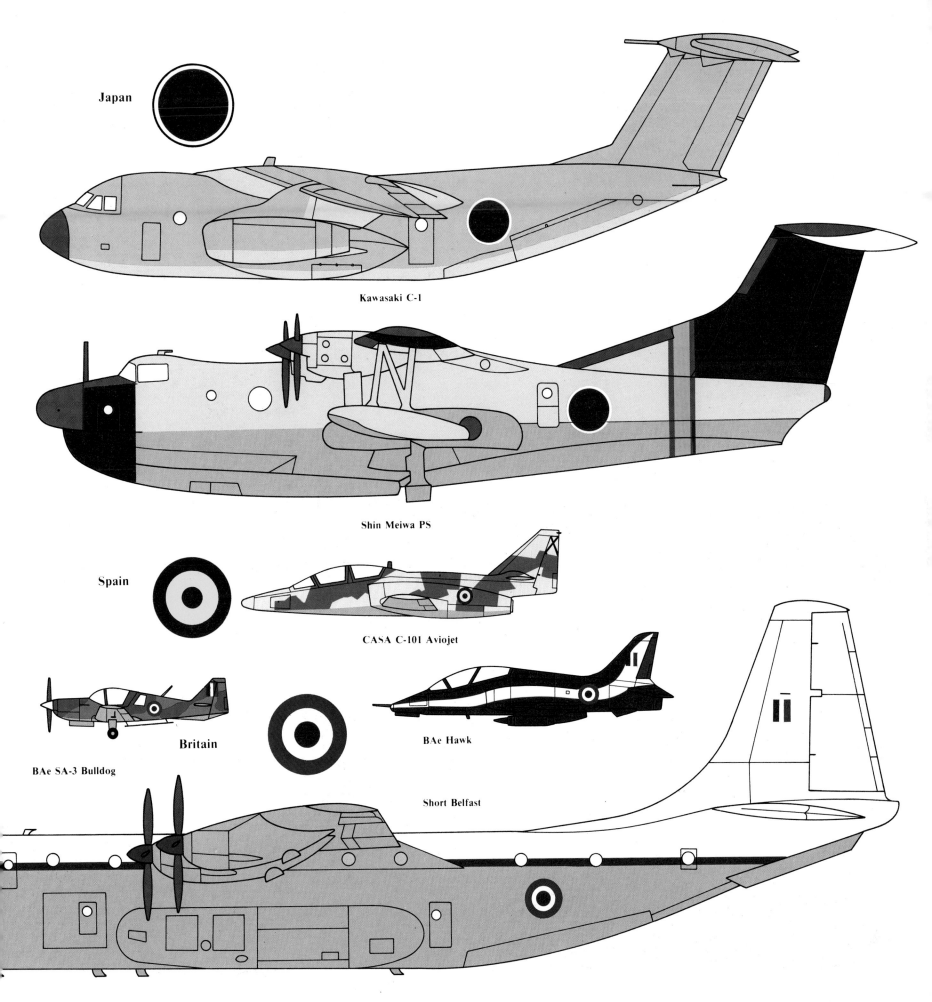

Japan

Kawasaki C-1

Shin Meiwa PS

Spain

CASA C-101 Aviojet

BAe SA-3 Bulldog

Britain

BAe Hawk

Short Belfast

# 1960-1985
## Large capacity short-to-medium-range airliners

The design formula introduced with France's twin-jet Caravelle was the magnet for many imitators in the 1950s. One of the more recent examples of this particular construction is the Dutch Fokker F.28 Fellowship, aimed at the short-haul market and built in the hope of repeating the success of the F.27 Friendship turboprop.

The F.28 prototype had its maiden flight on 9 May 1967 and production was characterized by continual updating [as was the case with the DC-9], as the makers strove for increased capacity and greater versatility. The modifications which were made included fuselage stretches, more efficient wing design and more powerful engines. By mid 1981 a total of 182 had been ordered [consisting of six basic variants] by 43 operators from 27 countries and the construction program was expected to reach a total of 230 aircraft by 1985.

Less fortunate was another project launched by VFW-Fokker in Germany in 1968 and subsidized by the Federal German Government. This was to be a small short-range twinjet, the Model 614. The first prototype flew on 14 July 1971 and was certificated in November 1976. Although early problems were overcome, the aircraft failed to attract many buyers; by late 1979 only 12 of the 614s were in airline service and an empty order book had already led to the termination of the program.

A recent project undertaken by the British aircraft industry is the BAe 146, a small and very fuel-efficient, medium-capacity four-engine airliner, which has proved very popular with small operators. The prototype was unveiled on 3 September 1981 and the first series aircraft, the 146-100, entered service in 1982. Towards the end of 1983 a large order from the U.S. company Pacific Southwest for 20 of the series 200 brought total sales of this little jet to 30, with options on a further 45.

A breakthough by the European aircraft industry in a sector which had come to be regarded as a U.S. preserve – the large capacity medium-range market, came in the mid seventies with the brilliant achievements of the Airbus consortium. Unlike an earlier attempt to enter this market at the end of the previous decade [the very large capacity Dassault-Breguet Mercure twinjet seating 162 passengers had its maiden flight on 28 May 1971, but only 10 were built], this new challenge was successful. The two basic A-300 variants first flew on 28 October 1972 and the smaller A-310 had its rollout on 16 February 1982, first deliveries, to Lufthansa and Swissair, were made in March 1983: 13 A-310s were in service by October. By the beginning of the 1980s the A-300 and the A-310 had captured about half world market for this type of airliner; by mid 1983 total sales to 46 airlines in 23 countries had reached 350.

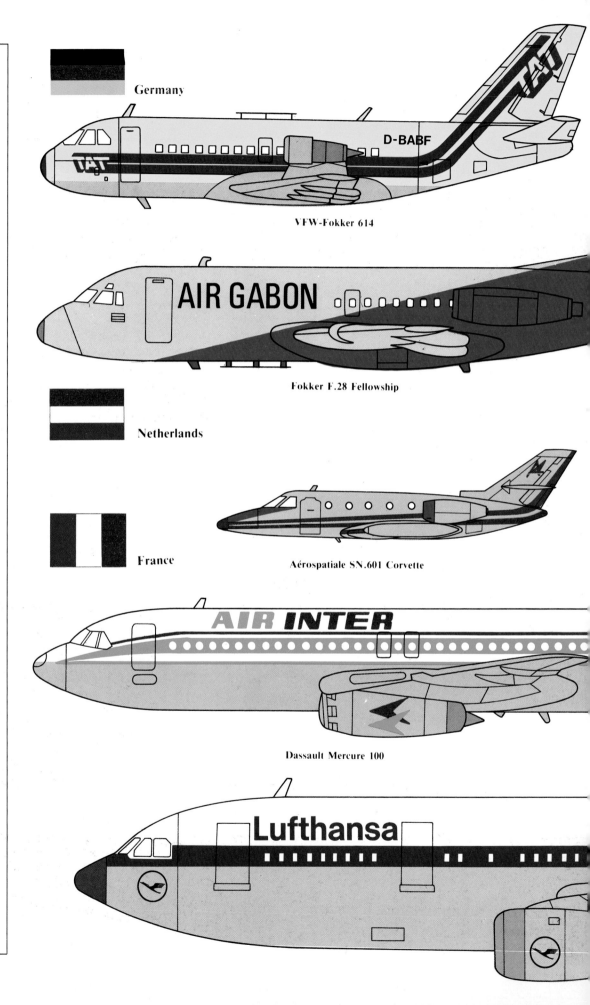

Germany

VFW-Fokker 614

Fokker F.28 Fellowship

Netherlands

France

Aérospatiale SN.601 Corvette

Dassault Mercure 100

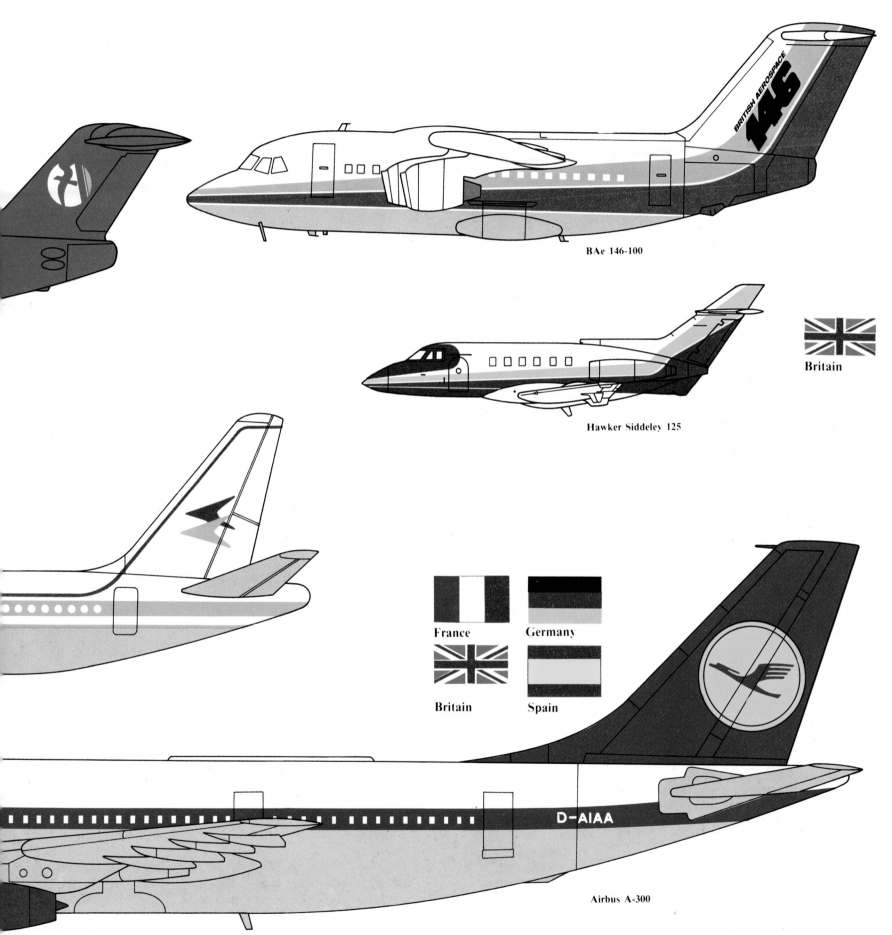

BAe 146-100

Hawker Siddeley 125

Britain

France    Germany

Britain    Spain

D-AIAA

Airbus A-300

189

# 1980-1985
# The energy crisis

The success of the Airbus Industrie consortium [involving the French company Aérospatiale; two German companies, MBB and VFW; British Aerospace and CASA, the Spanish aircraft manufacturer, joined for the A-310 project by the Dutch Fokker company and the Belgian Belairbus] appeared threatened when already well on course. The cause was twofold: the fuel crisis which hit the air transport industry at the beginning of the 1980s and the reaction of U.S.A. aircraft manufacturers to the challenge from the other side of the Atlantic.

The energy crisis plus high inflation meant that operating costs rocketed and world recession brought airlines growth to an abrupt stop as business contracted. Aircraft manufacturers were confronted by a new challenge: the need to develop extremely fuel-efficient civil transports with very low operating costs.

Boeing, the world's largest aircraft company, led the way by offering two new-generation airliners designed specifically with these requirements in mind: the B-767 and the B-757. The 767 prototype was unveiled on 26 September 1981 and entered service with the American airline, United, on 9 August 1982. By March 1984 a total of 182 orders had been placed for the 767. The 757 first flew on 19 February 1982 and commenced airline service on 1 January 1983 [Eastern Airlines was the first to fly the new aircraft, followed by British Airways]. By February 1984, orders had totalled 140. The cost-effectiveness of these two aircraft is revealed by two figures: the B-767 achieves a fuel saving estimated at around 35 per cent, while the B-757 is 47 per cent less fuel-hungry than the aircraft it was designed to replace, the B-727 trijet.

McDonnell-Douglas was the next manufacturer to develop a fuel-efficient airliner which, while being promoted as a totally new airplane, was actually a very sophisticated and updated development of the early DC-9 series. The DC-9 Super 80 [redesignated MD-80 in 1983] originated at the end of the 1970s in response to a Swissair specification and the program was launched on 18 October 1979 when the prototype had its maiden flight [deliveries to the Swiss airline commenced on 12 September 1982].

The new aircraft was well received: by 1 September 1983 orders and options had reached a total of 275. That same year McDonnell-Douglas was sufficient encouraged by the MD-80's success to plan an entire family of derivatives, each one more sophisticated and efficient than its predecessor, resulting in the MD-83 and the MD-90, which together with a similar development of the DC-10 trijet, [redesignated MD-100] were to anticipate the market's probable needs during the second half of the eighties.

Towards the end of 1983, however, the old-established Long Beach company was forced to lower its ceiling of ambitions for these projects, since the crisis in civil aviation proved more long-enduring than anticipated. The MD-90 and MD-100 programs were suspended since no firm interest was shown by any

*continued on page 192*

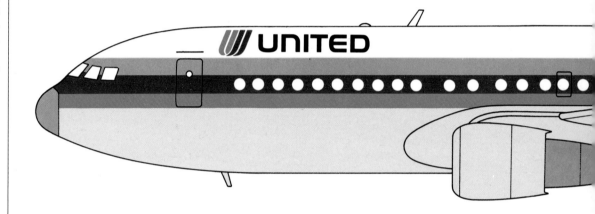

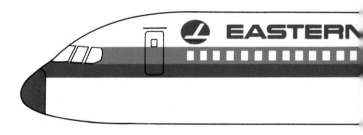

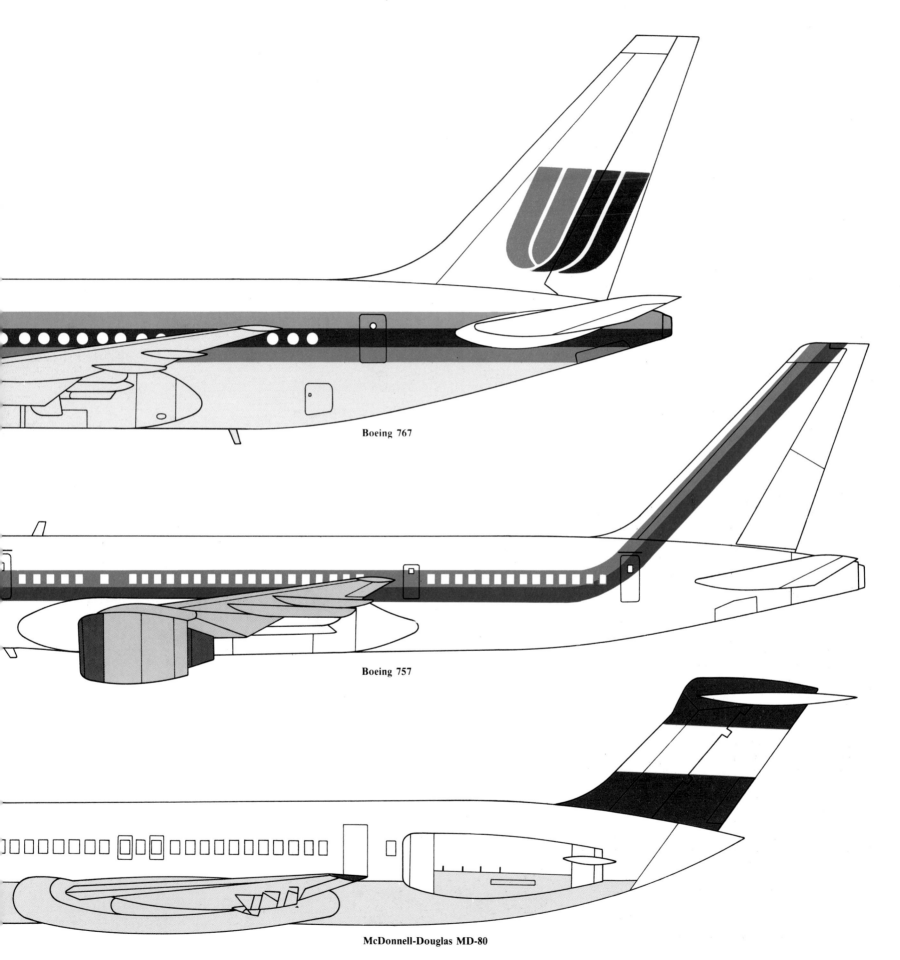

Boeing 767

Boeing 757

McDonnell-Douglas MD-80

191

*continued from page 190*

airline. The program for the MD-80 series was continued, however, and there was a strong probability that the 150-seat version would be built, scheduled for the late 1980s to compete with its European rival.

The perilous state of the airline industry was not the only reason for McDonnell-Douglas's shelving of some projects: a more decisive factor was the rapid progress made by the Company's old rival, Boeing, with its most recent airliner, the B-737-300, one of the Seattle-based company's more competitive aircraft, which first took to the air on 24 February 1984, with first deliveries scheduled for November to the American airline USAir. Boeing plans to develop other, improved versions of the 737, such as the series 400. This is the shrewdly exploited market in which the European challenger, the Airbus A-320 which is designed to use 43 per cent less fuel than the B-727 on short hauls [575 miles – 925 km] has to compete.

While Boeing and McDonnell-Douglas [offering their B-7-7 and MD-3300] were convinced in early 1984 that a new-generation aeroengine, which would not be perfected before 1988-89, was necessary to power the next generation of civil passenger aircraft, the Airbus consortium members hoped that their aircraft would be ready for the airlines rather earlier. In March 1984, after months of debate and uncertainty occasioned by the airline industry's lack of interest and by the knowledge that very substantial investment would be needed to launch the program, the A-320 received official backing from the British and German governments; at that time there were 51 firm orders as well as 45 options.

Deliveries are scheduled to begin in 1988 and early series aircraft will be powered by the "transitional" CFM-56-4 engine, a joint Franco-American development. The A-320 is only one of several programs mooted by the Airbus consortium in the early 1980s which could come to fruition if the market proves favourable, such are the longer range series planned for 1985: the A-310-300, the A-300-600 which has an improved passenger:cost ratio, and, looking further forward into the future, the TA-11 [a four-engine long-range airliner], and the TA-9 300- seat twinjet and its long-range version, the TA-12.

Competition for sales of this new generation of airliners which combine fuel economy with low operating costs promises to be very keen during the whole of the present decade. The same is true of the so-called third-level airliners: medium-capacity civil transports which are designed to give the best possible return on short-range domestic routes. One of the best contemporary planes in this category is the ATR-42 twin turboprop, developed as a joint Franco-Italian venture by Aeritalia and Aérospatiale. Rollout was scheduled for August 1984 and the aircraft will go into service on feeder routes. Seating 50, with a 124-808-mile [200-1,300 km] range and 310 mph [500 km/h] cruising speed, the ATR-42 achieves remarkably low fuel consumption and dramatically reduced operating costs. By late 1983, when the project was still on the drawing board, 13 airlines [including five U.S. operators] had shown interest in the ATR-42, with firm orders totalling 46 and options on a further 13.

A new executive plane, planned for 1988 promises to be one of the more impressive solutions to today's high fuel costs: the GP-180 is a very sophisticated 7-9 seat twin-engine turboprop designed by Rinaldo Piaggio and developed as a joint venture for the international market by two partners, the Genoa-based Piaggio company and the American aircraft manufacturer, Gates Learjet [the agreement between the two parties for production and marketing the plane having been announced in October 1983]. The GP-180 boasts an original design formula with super-critical winglets and sophisticated aerodynamics giving the plane a considerable edge on its pure-jet equivalents: a cruising speed of 460 mph [740 km/h] at 41,000 ft [12,500m] and a maximum range of 2,485 miles [4,000 km], while fuel consumption is almost unbelievably low – amounting to 7 U.S. gallons/U.K. 6 Imperial gallons/27 litres per 62 miles [100 km]. This works out at just under 2½ miles to 0.264 U.S. gallon/0.220 Imperial gallon [4 km/litre]: the same consumption as a powerful automobile engine.

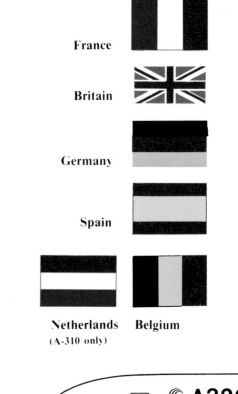

France

Britain

Germany

Spain

Netherlands (A-310 only)    Belgium

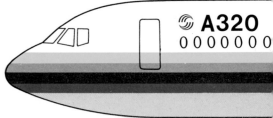

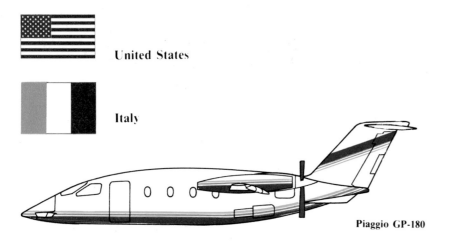

United States

Italy

Piaggio GP-180

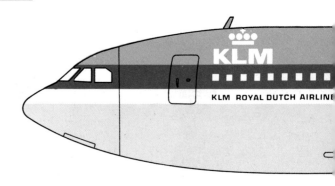

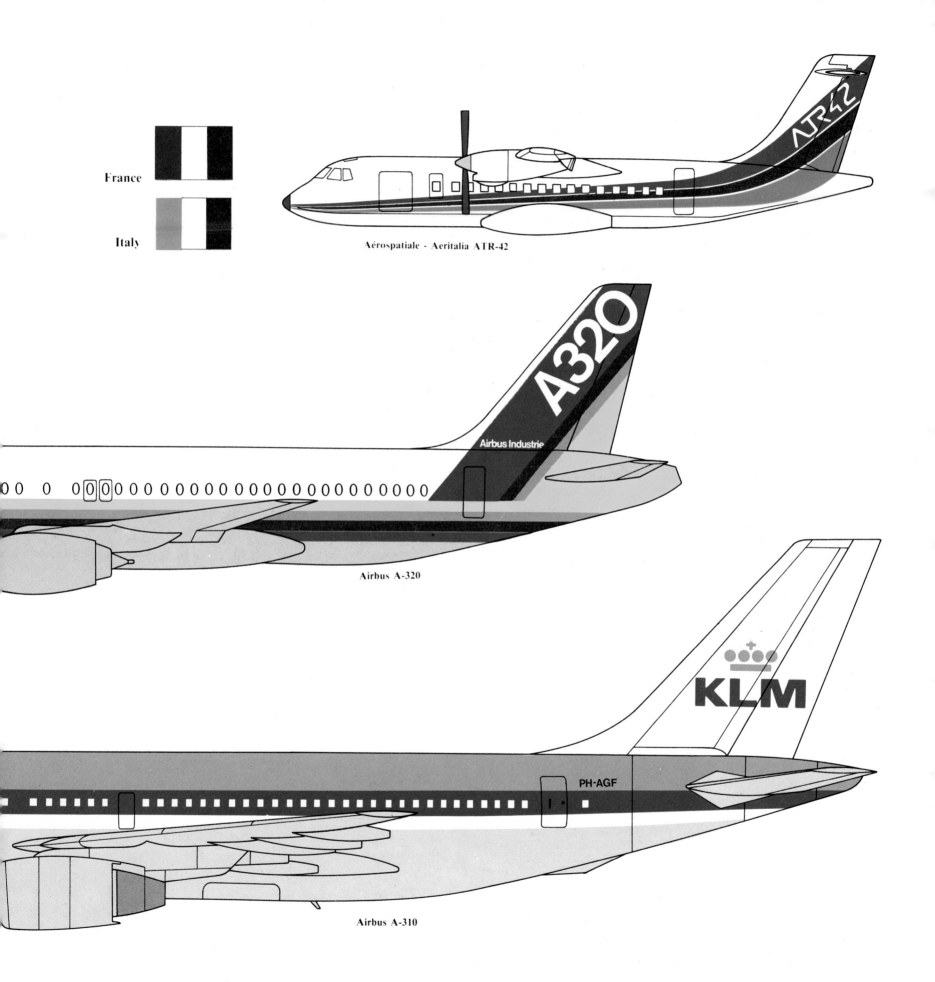

France

Italy

Aérospatiale - Aeritalia ATR-42

Airbus A-320

KLM

PH-AGF

Airbus A-310

193

## 1950-1985
## Supersonic and space flight

The first phase of aeronautical development spans less than eighty years – from the Wright brothers' conquest of the air with their first powered flight on the morning of 17 December 1903, to 14 April 1981 when man's entry into a new dimension, that of space, was witnessed by hundreds of millions of people on their television screens all over the world as the first Space Shuttle, Columbia, returned to earth [in stark contrast to the five witnesses of Orville and Wilbur Wright's first "public" demonstration of their epoch-making achievement]. On that day in 1981 a new era was born: the merging of aviation and space travel, using "hybrid" flying machines.

There is a strong case for maintaining that aviation is now the dominant strain in this fusion of two disciplines which has given us the Space Shuttle, since the philosophy underlying its development concerned the contruction of an aircraft which could make hundreds of trips back and forth between earth and space, in much the same way as conventional airplanes which operate between airports all over the world.

In practice, the scientists have created a shuttle which is launched like a rocket and goes into orbit like a satellite but completes the most demanding phase of its mission, reentry into the earth's atmosphere and landing back on earth, as an airplane or, more accurately, a glider. Its amazingly sophisticated systems and controls do not alter the fact that it is still governed by the mechanics of flight which baffled the early pioneers a century ago.

The Space Shuttle represents the apex of the art: the practical application of the very latest research and development programs, and this has only been made possible by years of experimentation as the airplane and aeronautical technology evolved slowly but surely.

From the very early years of aviation, war has always provided the strongest stimulus for growth and change. Shortly after the end of the Second World War, however, this impetus was to be shared by another, equally strong: the interest to explore and exploit space. It is difficult, if not impossible, to quantify the influence of space programs on aviation as compared with "traditional" aeronautical research and development; during the last forty years both realms have benefited from costly and lengthy scientific studies and design projects and are now very closely interlinked.

Development of these experimental aircraft is another, enthralling branch of aviation history and its milestones chart the achievement of increasingly

*continued on page 196*

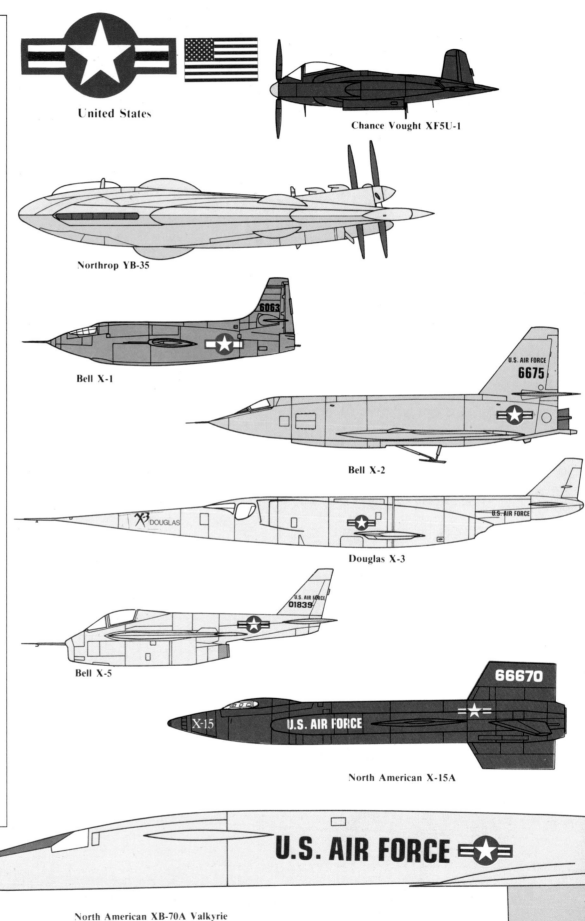

United States

Chance Vought XF5U-1

Northrop YB-35

Bell X-1

Bell X-2

Douglas X-3

Bell X-5

North American X-15A

North American XB-70A Valkyrie

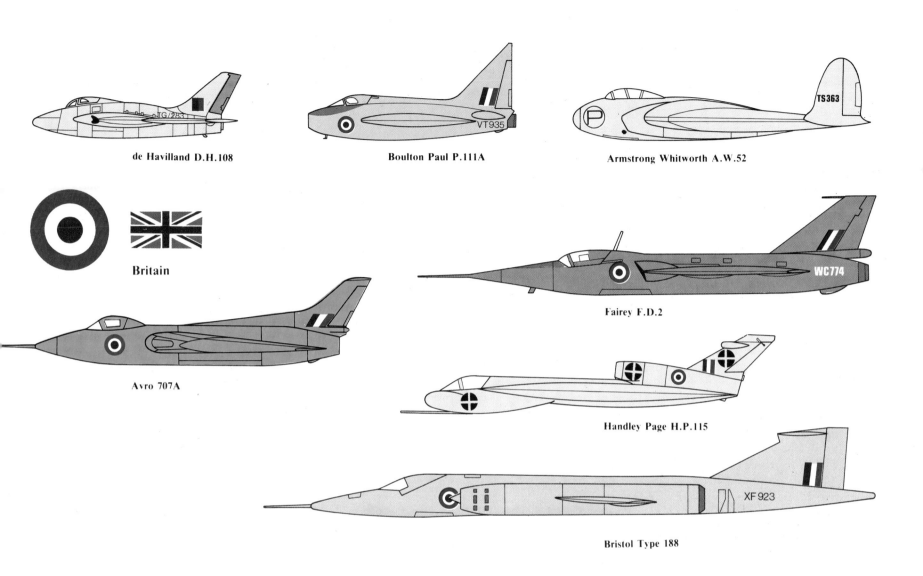

de Havilland D.H.108

Boulton Paul P.111A

Armstrong Whitworth A.W.52

Britain

Avro 707A

Fairey F.D.2

Handley Page H.P.115

Bristol Type 188

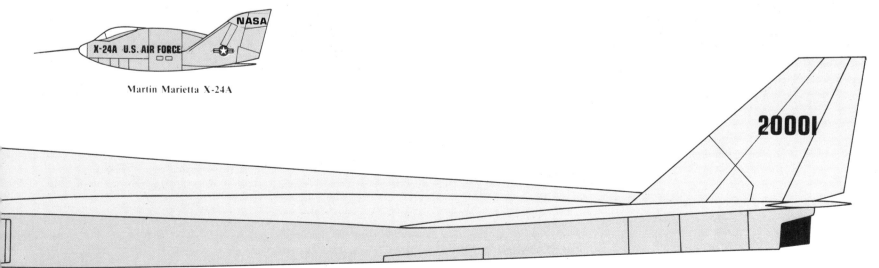

Martin Marietta X-24A

*continued from page 194*

ambitious targets. The contribution of all this work to the evolution of the airplane has, of course, not only proved of great value in military aviation but has also had an enormous influence on the civil sector which in turn today carries far more weight than ever before when decisions are taken as to the development of new aircraft, since the financial interests involved have grown to such huge proportions.

Charting the entire course of research and experimental aircraft and itemizing all the dates, places and people involved would fill a large volume, but the broad outlines can be traced by mentioning some of the more important "X-aircraft," a famous family of experimental aircraft which were built in the U.S.A. from the 1940s onwards as part of the Experimental Research Aircraft Program [launched in 1942]. This program is probably unique in the history of aviation – for continuity and for the scale of changes it brought about in aircraft development.

Experimental aircraft of the modern era have been the means of reaching all the most important aviation milestones of postwar years: an X-aircraft made the first supersonic flight; another was the first to test variable geometry wings; first to fly at altitudes above 328,000 ft [100,000m]; the first to fly at six times the speed of sound. New, sophisticated alloys were also first used in the construction of experimental aircraft, as were rocket engines and revolutionary new designs for more efficient aerodynamics.

The first in this line of epoch-making aircraft was America's first rocket-powered plane, the Bell X-1, developed in order to enable scientists to study problems which occurred in supersonic flight. The aim of breaking the sound barrier was achieved on 14 October 1947, when the first of three prototypes, piloted by Charles Yeager was air-launched at 29,500 ft [approx. 9,000m] from a B-29 and reached a speed of 670 mph [1,078 km/h] in level flight. Other historic flights were made on 12 December 1953, when a speed of 1,650 mph [2,655 km/h] was recorded and on 4 June 1954, an altitude record of 90,000 ft [27,435m] was set.

The main function of the next experimental aircraft, the Bell X-2, was to test the swept wing and powered test flights started on 11 November 1955. The most significant records set by this aircraft were recorded on 7 September 1956, when an altitude of 120,200 ft [36,637m] was reached, with Iven Kincheloe at the controls, and on 27 September, when Milburn Apt achieved a speed of 2,094 mph [3,370 km/h].

The X-3 was built by Douglas in order to gather information on aerodynamic and structural behaviour during prolonged flights at supersonic speeds. Dubbed Stiletto on account of its sharp clean lines, the plane first flew on 20 October 1952 and underwent a three-year test cycle, but the project was finally abandoned for want of a suitable jet engine.

The most famous of all the "X-aircraft" was undoubtedly the X-15, which far exceeded the achievements of the X-1 and X-2, reaching to the very edges of the stratosphere, the borderline between aerial and space flight. The first of three North American X-15s took to the air suspended beneath the wing of a specially modified B-52 on 10 March 1959. Flight testing began on 15 November 1960 and a staggering number of records were broken between then and 24 October 1968, when the last of a total of 199 test flights by the three aircraft was complete. In his X-15, on 9 November 1961, pilot Bob White achieved a speed of 4,092 mph [6,586 km/h]; on 30 April 1962, Joe Walker took his plane to an altitude of 265,541 ft [80,938m]; on 22 April 1963, the same pilot reached 354,195 ft [107,960m].

The fastest X-15 of all reached a speed of 4,519 mph [7,273 km/h] on 3 October 1967, piloted by William Knight. This particular aircraft had been provided with larger capacity fuel tanks to increase

**NASA/Rockwell International Space Shuttle Orbiter**

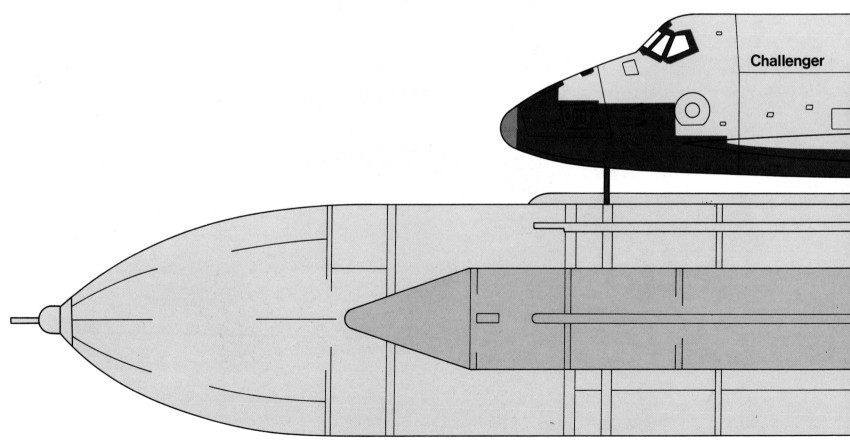

the operating time of its rocket engine.

Worth remembering too are the experiments carried out by NASA to prepare the way for development of the Space Shuttle and in particular to analyze the characteristics and behaviour of a vehicle designed to reenter the Earth's atmosphere from space and make a controlled landing at an exact spot on the map. The program began in the 1960s when two "lifting-body" projects were launched for wingless research vehicles which achieved lift through the design of their fuselages: the HL-10 and the M2-F2. The former commenced its test program on 22 December 1966 and by the end of 1971 had made 37 flights; the latter was used from 12 July, 1966 until 20 December 1972 when the test series ended, during the course of which the craft was modified and redesignated M2-F3 [1970].

These two projects were succeeded by another experimental vehicle, the X-24 [first flight April 1969] with which NASA concluded the preparatory work for the space program itself. From a strictly aeronautical standpoint the X-24 was the true forerunner of the Space Shuttle; its operational proving trials ended on 23 September 1975, a year before rollout of the first Space Shuttle.

United States

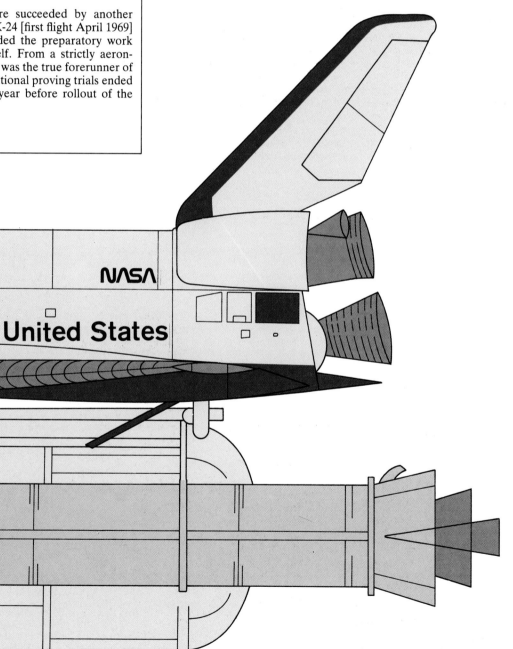

## Abbreviations used in data tables

| | | | | | |
|---|---|---|---|---|---|
| **A** | = attack/assault | **Fr** | = fighter | **p** | = passengers |
| **a.a.** | = anti-aircraft | **g** | = gun | **r** | = radial |
| **a.c.** | = air-cooled | **HB** | = heavy bomber | **Rc** | = reconnaissance |
| **AS** | = anti-submarine | **Ic** | = interceptor | **Rp** | = racer/competition plane |
| **a.t.** | = antitank | **LB** | = light bomber | **rp** | = rocket projectile |
| **b** | = bombs | **l.c.** | = liquid-cooled | **t** | = torpedo |
| **B** | = bomber | **Li** | = liaison | **T** | = trainer |
| **CIS** | = close support | **LT** | = light transport | **TB** | = torpedo bomber |
| **cl** | = cylinders | **mg** | = machine gun | **tf** | = turbofan |
| **CTr** | = civil transport | **Mr** | = marine reconnaissance | **tj** | = turbojet |
| **Ex** | = experimental | **mr** | = multirole | **tp** | = turboprop |
| **FB** | = fighter bomber | **msl** | = missile | **Tr** | = transport |
| | | **NF** | = night fighter | **w.c.** | = water-cooled |
| | | **Os** | = observation | **\*** | = estimated |

| Page | Aircraft | Nation | Manufacturer | Type | Year | Engine | Wingspan m | ft |
|---|---|---|---|---|---|---|---|---|
| 14 | Wright Flyer I | USA | Wright Brothers | — | 1903 | Wright 12 hp (4 cl) w.c. | 12.29 | 40.4 |
| 14 | Wright Flyer III | USA | Wright Brothers | — | 1905 | Wright 20 hp (4 cl) w.c. | 12.34 | 40.6 |
| 14 | Wright A | USA | Wright Brothers | — | 1908 | Wright 30 hp (4 cl) w.c. | 11.13 | 36.5 |
| 14 | Wright B | USA | Wright Brothers | — | 1910 | Wright 30 hp (4 cl) w.c. | 11.90 | 39.0 |
| 14 | Wright R | USA | Wright Brothers | — | 1910 | Wright 30 hp (4 cl) w.c. | 8.07 | 26.4 |
| 14 | Curtiss Golden Flyer | USA | Herring-Curtiss Co. | — | 1909 | Curtiss 50 hp (8 cl) w.c. | 8.76 | 28.9 |
| 14 | Santos-Dumont 14 bis | F | Alberto Santos-Dumont | — | 1906 | Antoinette 50 hp (8 cl) w.c. | 11.20 | 36.9 |
| 14 | Vuia N. 1 | F | Trajan Vuia | — | 1906 | Serpollet 25 hp | 8.68 | 28.6 |
| 14 | Demoiselle 20 | F | Alberto Santos-Dumont | — | 1909 | Dutheil-Chalmers 35 hp (2 cl) w.c. | 5.10 | 16.7 |
| 14 | Goupy II | F | Louis Blériot | — | 1909 | R.E.P. 24 hp (7 cl) a.c. | 6.10 | 20.0 |
| 14 | Blériot XI | F | Louis Blériot | — | 1909 | Anzani 25 hp (3 cl) a.c. | 7.80 | 25.6 |
| 14 | Hydravion Fabre | F | Henri Fabre | — | 1910 | Gnome 50 hp (7 cl) | 14 | 45.9 |
| 15 | Voisin Farman | F | Voisin Frères | — | 1907 | Antoinette 50 hp (8 cl) w.c. | 10.20 | 33.5 |
| 15 | Blériot VII | F | Louis Blériot | — | 1907 | Antoinette 50 hp (8 cl) w.c. | 11 | 36.1 |
| 15 | Antoinette IV | F | Société Antoinette | — | 1909 | Antoinette 50 hp (8 cl) w.c. | 12.80 | 42.0 |
| 15 | Henri Farman III | F | Henri Farman | — | 1909 | Gnome 50 hp (7 cl) | 9.95 | 32.8 |
| 15 | Coanda | F | Henri Coanda | — | 1910 | Clerget 50 hp (4 cl) w.c. | 10.08 | 33.1 |
| 15 | Dufaux 4 | CH | Armand Dufaux | — | 1910 | Antoinette 50 hp (8 cl) w.c. | 8.50 | 27.8 |
| 15 | Phillips Multiplane 1 | GB | Horatio Phillips | — | 1904 | Phillips 22 hp (4 cl) w.c. | 5.41 | 17.7 |
| 15 | Roe Triplane I | GB | A.V. Roe | — | 1909 | J.A.P. 20 hp (4 cl) a.c. | 6.10 | 20.0 |
| 15 | Dunne D.5 | GB | Short Brothers | — | 1910 | Green 60 hp (4 cl) w.c. | 14.02 | 46.0 |

# TECHNICAL DATA

Below and on the following pages are the principal data referring to the most important variants of the aircraft illustrated in the colour scale views.

Figures have been adjusted to the nearest decimal point in accordance with current practice.

| Length | | Height | | Take-off weight | | Speed | | Ceiling | | Range | | Crew | Payload/armament |
|---|---|---|---|---|---|---|---|---|---|---|---|---|---|
| m | ft | m | ft | kg | lb | km/h | mph | m | ft | km | ml | | |
| 6.43 | 21.1 | 2.44 | 8.0 | 340 | 750 | 48 | 30 | | | | | 2 | 2 mg; 1 g.; 900 kg (1,000 lb) |
| 8.53 | 28.0 | 2.44 | 8.0 | 380 | 855 | 56 | 35 | | | | | | |
| 8.81 | 28.9 | 2.46 | 8.0 | 544 | 1,200 | 71 | 44 | | | | | | |
| 9.45 | 31.0 | — | — | 567 | 1,250 | 75 | 46 | | | | | | |
| 5.94 | 19.4 | — | — | 390 | 859 | 80 | 49 | | | | | | |
| 8.66 | 28.5 | 2.74 | 9.0 | 376 | 830 | 72 | 44 | | | | | | |
| 9.70 | 31.8 | 3.40 | 11.2 | 300 | 661 | 40 | 25 | | | | | | |
| 2.99 | 9.10 | 3.28 | 10.9 | 241 | 531 | — | — | | | | | | |
| 8 | 26.3 | 2.40 | 7.9 | 143 | 315 | 90 | 56 | | | | | | |
| 7.01 | 23.0 | 2.44 | 8.0 | — | — | 97 | 60 | | | | | | |
| 8 | 26.3 | 2.59 | 8.6 | 300 | 661 | 58 | 36 | | | | | | |
| 8.50 | 27.9 | 3.66 | 12.0 | 475 | 1,047 | 89 | 55 | | | | | | |
| 10.50 | 34.4 | 3.35 | 11.0 | 522 | 1,150 | 55 | 34 | | | | | | |
| 8 | 26.3 | 2.75 | 9 | 425 | 937 | 80 | 49 | | | | | | |
| 11.46 | 37.7 | 2.99 | 9.10 | 590 | 1,300 | 70 | 43 | | | | | | |
| 11.97 | 39.3 | 3.50 | 11.6 | 550 | 1,213 | 60 | 37 | | | | | | |
| 12.70 | 41.6 | 2.74 | 9.0 | 420 | 926 | — | — | | | | | | |
| 9.50 | 31.1 | 2.70 | 8.8 | 485 | 1,069 | 78 | 48 | | | | | | |
| 4.19 | 13.9 | 3.05 | 10.0 | 272 | 600 | 55 | 34 | | | | | | |
| 7.01 | 23.0 | 3.35 | 11.0 | 204 | 450 | 40 | 25 | | | | | | |
| 6.21 | 20.4 | 3.50 | 11.6 | 703 | 1,550 | 72 | 45 | | | | | | |

# Technical Data

| Page | Aircraft | Nation | Manufacturer | Type | Year | Engine | Wingspan m | ft |
|------|----------|--------|--------------|------|------|--------|-----------|-----|
| 15 | Blackburn Monoplane | GB | Blackburn Aeroplane Co. | — | 1909 | Green 35 hp (4 cl) w.c. | 9.14 | 30 |
| 15 | de Havilland N° 1 | GB | de Havilland-Hearle | — | 1910 | de Havilland 45 hp (4 cl) w.c. | 10.97 | 36 |
| 15 | Cody Michelin Cup | GB | Cody | — | 1910 | E.N.V. 60 hp (8 cl) w.c. | 14.02 | 46 |
| 15 | Short N° 3 | GB | Short Brothers | — | 1910 | Green 35 hp (4 cl) w.c. | 10.7 | 35.2 |
| 15 | Etrich Taube | A | — | — | 1910 | Mercedes 100 hp (6 cl) w.c. | 14.35 | 47.1 |
| 20 | Asteria N° 3 | I | Soc. Aeronautica Asteria | — | 1911 | Gnome 50 hp (7 cl) | 15 | 49.3 |
| 20 | Chiribiri N° 5 | I | A. Chiribiri & Co. | — | 1912 | Chiribiri 50 hp (4 cl) w.c. | 9.45 | 31 |
| 20 | Curtiss Hydro A-1 | USA | Glenn Curtiss | — | 1911 | Curtiss 75 hp (8 cl) w.c. | 11.28 | 37 |
| 20 | Benoist XIV | USA | Thomas Benoist | — | 1914 | Roberts 75 hp (6 cl) l.c. | 13.72 | 26 |
| 20 | Short S.41 | GB | Short Brothers | — | 1912 | Gnome 100 hp | 15.24 | 50 |
| 20 | Avro F | GB | A.V. Roe & Co. | — | 1912 | Viale 35 hp (r 5 cl) | 8.53 | 28 |
| 20 | Sopwith Tabloid | GB | Sopwith Aviation Co. Ltd. | — | 1914 | Gnome 100 hp (r 9 cl) a.c. | 7.77 | 25.6 |
| 20 | Sopwith Bat Boat N° 2 | GB | Sopwith Aviation Co. Ltd. | — | 1914 | Sunbeam 225 hp (8 cl) l.c. | 16.76 | 55 |
| 20 | Fokker Spin I | NL | Anthony Fokker | — | 1911 | Argus 50 hp (4 cl) w.c. | 11 | 36.1 |
| 21 | Antoinette Latham | F | Société Antoinette | — | 1911 | Antoinette 50 hp (8 cl) w.c. | 15.90 | 52.2 |
| 21 | Breguet III | F | Louis Breguet | — | 1912 | Canton-Unné 80 hp (7 cl) w.c. | 13.61 | 44.8 |
| 21 | Deperdussin Monocoque Racer | F | Deperdussin Co. | — | 1912 | Gnome 160 hp (r 14 cl) a.c. | 6.60 | 21.6 |
| 21 | Deperdussin Monocoque Idro | F | Deperdussin Co. | — | 1913 | Gnome 160 hp (r 14 cl) | 13.49 | 44.2 |
| 21 | Lévy-Lepen R | F | Hydravions Georges Lévy | CTr | 1917 | Renault 300 hp (12 cl V) l.c. | 18.49 | 60.7 |
| 24 | Maurice Farman M.F. 7 | F | Farman Frères | Rc | 1913 | Renault 70 hp (8 cl) a.c. | 15.54 | 51 |
| 24 | Maurice Farman M.F. 11 | F | Farman Frères | Rc/LB | 1914 | Renault 100 hp (8 cl) a.c. | 16.15 | 53 |
| 24 | Henri Farman H.F. 20 | F | Farman Frères | Rc | 1914 | Gnome 7A 80 hp | 15.54 | 51 |
| 24 | Morane-Saulnier H | F | Société Anonyme des Aéroplanes M-S | Rc | 1913 | Gnome 80 hp | 9.12 | 29.9 |
| 24 | R.E.P.N | F | Robert Esnault-Pelterie | Rc | 1914 | Gnome 80 hp | 10.97 | 36 |
| 24 | Breguet AG 4 | F | Louis Breguet | Rc | 1914 | Gnome 160 hp | 15.35 | 50.4 |
| 24 | Blériot XI | F | Louis Blériot | Rc | 1914 | Gnome 7A 70 hp | 10.33 | 33.11 |
| 24 | Dorand AR.1 | F | Section Technique de L'Aéronautique | Rc/T | 1917 | Renault 190 hp (8 cl) w.c. | 13.29 | 43.7 |
| 24 | Salmson 2 | F | Société des Moteurs Salmson | Rc | 1918 | Salmson (Canton-Unné) 260 hp (9 cl) l.c. | 11.80 | 38.8 |
| 24 | R.A.F. B.E.8 | GB | Royal Aircraft Factory | Rc | 1913 | Gnome 80 hp | 12.03 | 39.6 |
| 24 | R.A.F. B.E.2a | GB | Royal Aircraft Factory | Rc/LB | 1913 | Renault 70 hp (8 cl) a.c. | 10.68 | 35.03 |
| 24 | R.A.F. R.E. 5 | GB | Royal Aircraft Factory | Br/Rc | 1913 | Beardmore 120 hp (6 cl) l.c. | 13.56 | 44.6 |
| 24 | R.A.F. B.E. 2c | GB | Royal Aircraft Factory | Rc/LB | 1914 | R.A.F. 1a 90 hp (8 cl V) a.c. | 11.28 | 37 |
| 24 | Avro 504/A | GB | A.V. Roe & Co. Ltd. | Rc/LB | 1914 | Gnome 80 hp (r 7 cl) a.c. | 10.97 | 36 |
| 24 | R.A.F. R.E. 8 | GB | Royal Aircraft Factory | Rc/Br | 1916 | R.A.F. 4a 150 hp (12 cl) a.c. | 12.98 | 42.7 |
| 25 | Aviatik B.II | A | Oesterreichishe-Ungarische Flugzeugfabrik Aviatik | Rc | 1915 | Austro-Daimler 120 hp (6 cl) l.c. | 14.02 | 46 |
| 25 | Lloyd C.II | A | Ungarische Lloyd Flugzeug AG. | Rc | 1915 | Hiero 145 hp (6 cl) l.c. | 14 | 45.9 |
| 25 | Lohner C.I | A | Jacob Lohner Werke & Co. | Rc | 1916 | Austro-Daimler 160 hp (6 cl) l.c. | 13.46 | 44.15 |
| 25 | Hansa-Brandenburg C.I | A | Hansa und Brandenburgische Werke GmbH | Rc | 1916 | Austro-Daimler 160 hp (6 cl) l.c. | 12.25 | 40.18 |
| 25 | Phönix C.I | A | Phönix Flugzeug-Werke AG. | Rc | 1918 | Hiero 230 hp (6 cl) l.c. | 10.99 | 36.1 |
| 25 | Ufag C.I | A | Ungarische Flugzeugfabrik AG. | Rc | 1918 | Hiero 230 hp (6 cl) l.c. | 10.69 | 35.2 |
| 25 | D.F.W. B.I | D | Deutsche Flugzeug-Werke AG. | Rc | 1914 | Mercedes 100 hp (6 cl) l.c. | 13.97 | 45.8 |
| 25 | A.E.G. B.II | D | Allgemeine Elektrizitäts Gesellschaft | Rc | 1914 | Mercedes 110 hp (6 cl) l.c. | 12.98 | 42.7 |
| 25 | A.G.O. C.II | D | Ago-Flugzeugwerke | Rc | 1916 | Benz 220 hp (6 cl) l.c. | 14.48 | 47.7 |
| 25 | D.F.W. CV | D | Deutsche Flugzeug-Werke AG. | Rc | 1916 | Benz Bz.IV 200 hp (6 cl) l.c. | 13.29 | 43.6 |
| 25 | A.E.G. C.IV | D | Allgemeine Elektrizitäts Gesellschaft | Rc | 1916 | Mercedes D.III 160 hp (6 cl) l.c. | 13.46 | 44.2 |
| 25 | L.V.G. C.II | D | Luft-Verkehrs-Gesellschaft | Rc | 1915 | Mercedes 160 hp (6 cl) l.c. | 12.85 | 42.2 |
| 25 | Aviatik C.I | D | Automobil und Aviatikwerke AG. | Rc | 1915 | Mercedes 160 hp (6 cl) l.c. | 12.50 | 41 |
| 25 | Albatros B.II | D | Albatros Flugzeug-Werke GmbH | Rc | 1914 | Mercedes 100 hp (6 cl) l.c. | 12.80 | 42 |
| 25 | Albatros C.I | D | Albatros Flugzeug-Werke GmbH | Rc | 1915 | Mercedes D.III 160 hp (6 cl) l.c. | 12.90 | 42.4 |
| 25 | Albatros C.III | D | Albatros Flugzeug-Werke GmbH | Rc | 1916 | Mercedes D.III 160 hp (6 cl) l.c. | 11.70 | 38.4 |
| 25 | Albatros C.X | D | Albatros Flugzeug-Werke GmbH | Rc | 1917 | Mercedes D.IVa 260 hp (6 cl) l.c. | 14.36 | 47.1 |
| 25 | Albatros C.XII | D | Albatros Flugzeug-Werke GmbH | Rc | 1917 | Mercedes D.IVa 260 hp (6 cl) l.c. | 14.37 | 47.2 |
| 25 | Rumpler C.I | D | E. Rumpler Flugzeug-Werke GmbH | Rc | 1915 | Mercedes D.III 160 hp (6 cl) l.c. | 12.15 | 39.8 |
| 25 | Halberstadt C.V | D | Halberstädter Flugzeug-Werke GmbH | Rc | 1918 | Benz Bz.IV 220 hp (6 cl) l.c. | 13.62 | 44.8 |
| 25 | Hannover CL.IIIa | D | Hannoversche Waggonfabrik AG. | Rc | 1918 | Argus As.III 180 hp (6 cl) l.c. | 11.70 | 38.5 |
| 26 | S.I.A. 7.B1 | I | Società Italiana Aviazione | Rc | 1917 | Fiat A-12 260 hp (6 cl) l.c. | 13.32 | 43.8 |
| 26 | S.A.M.L. S.2 | I | Società Aeronautica Meccanica Lombarda | Rc | 1917 | Fiat A-12 300 hp (6 cl) l.c. | 12.10 | 39.8 |
| 26 | Ansaldo S.V.A. 5 | I | Giovanni Ansaldo & C. | Rc | 1918 | S.P.A. 6A 220 hp (6 cl) l.c. | 9.45 | 31 |
| 26 | Ansaldo S.V.A. 9 | I | Giovanni Ansaldo & C. | Rc | 1918 | S.P.A. 6A 220 hp (6 cl) l.c. | 9.45 | 31 |
| 26 | Fiat R.2 | I | Fiat Aviazione | Rc | 1918 | Fiat A-12 bis 300 hp (6 cl) l.c. | 12.30 | 40.4 |
| 26 | Pomilio PE | I | Fabbrica Aeroplani Ing. O. Pomilio & C. | Rc | 1918 | Fiat A12 260 hp (6 cl) l.c. | 11.78 | 38.8 |
| 26 | Curtiss JN-4 | USA | Curtiss Aeroplane and Motor Co. | T | 1916 | Curtiss OX-5 90 hp (8 cl) l.c. | 13.29 | 43.7 |
| 26 | Thomas-Morse S.4C | USA | Thomas Morse Aircraft Co. | T | 1917 | Le Rhône 9C 80 hp | 8.07 | 26.4 |
| 26 | Standard E-1 | USA | Standard Aircraft Co. | A | 1918 | Le Rhône 80 hp | 7.32 | 24 |
| 26 | Lebed 12 | Russia | V.A. Lebedev Aeronautics Ltd. | Rc | 1916 | Salmson 150 hp (9 cl) a.c. | 13.14 | 43.1 |
| 26 | Anatra DS | Russia | Zavod A.A. Anatra | Rc | 1917 | Salmson 150 hp (9 cl) a.c. | 11.43 | 37.5 |

| Length | | Height | | Take-off weight | | Speed | | Ceiling | | Range | | Crew | Payload/armament |
|---|---|---|---|---|---|---|---|---|---|---|---|---|---|
| m | ft | m | ft | kg | lb | km/h | mph | m | ft | km | ml | | |
| 7.92 | 26 | 2.90 | 9.6 | — | — | 97 | — | — | — | — | — | — | — |
| 8.84 | 29 | 3 | 9.10 | — | — | — | — | — | — | — | — | — | — |
| 11.73 | 38.6 | 3.96 | 13 | 1,138 | 2.950 | 105 | 65 | — | — | — | — | — | — |
| 9.45 | 31 | 2.64 | 8.8 | 389 | 860 | — | — | — | — | — | — | — | — |
| 9.85 | 32.4 | 3.15 | 10.4 | 870 | 1.918 | 115 | 71.5 | — | — | — | — | — | — |
| 10.50 | 34.5 | — | — | — | — | — | — | — | — | — | — | — | — |
| 7.32 | 24 | — | — | — | — | 90 | 56 | — | — | — | — | — | — |
| 8.43 | 27.6 | 2.84 | 9.3 | 714 | 1.575 | 105 | 65 | — | — | — | — | — | — |
| 7.92 | 26 | — | — | 680 | 1.499 | 105 | 65 | — | — | — | — | 1 | 1p |
| 11.88 | 39 | 3.58 | 11.9 | 771 | 1.700 | 96 | 60 | — | — | 5h | — | — | — |
| 7.01 | 23 | 2.31 | 7.6 | 363 | 800 | 105 | 65 | — | — | — | — | — | — |
| 7.32 | 24 | 2.57 | 8.4 | 650 | 1.433 | 148 | 92 | — | — | — | — | — | — |
| 10.97 | 36 | — | — | 1,442 | 3.180 | 120 | 74 | — | — | 5h | — | — | — |
| 7.75 | 25,5 | 3 | 9.10 | 400 | 882 | 90 | 56 | — | — | — | — | — | — |
| 11.50 | 37.8 | 2.50 | 8.2 | 1,350 | 2.976 | — | — | — | — | — | — | — | — |
| 8.84 | 29 | 2.99 | 9.10 | 949 | 2.095 | 100 | 62 | — | — | 7h | — | 2-3 | — |
| 6.10 | 20 | 2.78 | 7.6 | 612 | 1.350 | 209 | 130 | — | — | — | — | — | — |
| 9.98 | 32.7 | — | — | 1,200 | 2.645 | 210 | 130 | — | — | — | — | 2 | — |
| 12.39 | 40.8 | 3.85 | 12.7 | 2,450 | 5.400 | 145 | 90 | — | — | — | — | 1 | 1p |
| 11.35 | 37 | 3.45 | 11.4 | 855 | 1.885 | 95 | 59 | 4,000 | 13,123 | 3h30' | — | 2 | — |
| 9.45 | 31 | 3.18 | 10.5 | 928 | 2.045 | 106 | 66 | 3,800 | 12,500 | 3h45' | — | 2 | 1 mg; b (130 kg - 288 lb) |
| 8.79 | 27.9 | 3.10 | 10.2 | 710 | 1.565 | 100 | 65 | 2,750 | 9,000 | 3h30' | — | 2 | 1 mg |
| 6.28 | 20.7 | 2.30 | 7.6 | 470 | 1.034 | 135 | 85 | 1,000 | 3,280 | 3h | — | 1 | 1 mg |
| 7.92 | 26 | — | — | — | — | 116 | 72 | — | — | — | — | 2 | — |
| 8.25 | 27.1 | 3.30 | 10.10 | 1,350 | 2.970 | 100 | 65 | 1,500 | 4,290 | — | — | 2 | 1 mg |
| 8.48 | 27.10 | 2.65 | 8.5 | 834 | 1.838 | 106 | 66 | 1,000 | 3,280 | 3h30' | — | 2 | — |
| 9.14 | 30 | 3.30 | 10.10 | 1,247 | 2.750 | 152 | 94.5 | 5,500 | 18,045 | 3h | — | 2 | 2-3 mg; b (82 kg - 181 lb) |
| 8.50 | 27.10 | 2.90 | 9.6 | 1,269 | 2.797 | 185 | 115 | 6,250 | 20,505 | 3h | — | 2 | 2-3 mg |
| 8.30 | 27.3 | 2.84 | 9.4 | — | — | 113 | 70 | — | — | — | — | 2 | b (45 kg - 100 lb) |
| 9 | 29.6 | 3.10 | 10.2 | 726 | 1.600 | 112.6 | 70 | 3,048 | 10,000 | 3h | — | 2 | b (45 kg - 100 lb) |
| 7.98 | 26.2 | 2.94 | 9.8 | — | — | 125 | 77.6 | — | — | — | — | 2 | b (27 kg - 60 lb) |
| 8.31 | 27.3 | 3.38 | 11.1 | 972 | 2.142 | 116 | 72 | 3,048 | 10,000 | 3h15' | — | 2 | 1 mg; b (102 kg - 224 lb) |
| 8.97 | 29.5 | 3.18 | 10.5 | 713 | 1.574 | 132 | 82 | 3,950 | 12,960 | 3h | — | 2 | 1 mg; b (45 kg - 100 lb) |
| 8.48 | 27.10 | 3.45 | 11.3 | 1,215 | 2.678 | 164 | 101.9 | 4,115 | 13,500 | 4h15' | — | 2 | 2 mg; b (118 kg - 260 lb) |
| 8 | 26.2 | 3.20 | 10.6 | 870 | 1.917 | 109 | 68 | 2,500 | 8,140 | 4h | — | 2 | b (20 kg - 44 lb) |
| 9 | 29.6 | 3.40 | 11.2 | 1,350 | 2.976 | 128 | 79.5 | 3,000 | 9,842 | 2h30' | — | 2 | 1 mg |
| 9.22 | 30.3 | 3.25 | 10.8 | 1,360 | 2.998 | 137 | 85 | 3,500 | 11,482 | 3h | — | 2 | 1 mg |
| 8.45 | 27.8 | 3.32 | 10.11 | 1,310 | 2.888 | 140 | 87 | 5,800 | 19,028 | 3h | — | 2 | 2 mg; b (60 kg - 132 lb) |
| 7.52 | 24.8 | 2.95 | 9.8 | 1,105 | 2.436 | 177 | 110 | 5,400 | 17,715 | 3h30' | — | 2 | 2 mg; b (50 kg - 110 lb) |
| 7.30 | 23.8 | 2.92 | 9.7 | 1,050 | 2.315 | 190 | 118 | 4,900 | 16,075 | 3h | — | 2 | 2-3 mg |
| 8.38 | 27.5 | 2.99 | 9.10 | 1,019 | 2.246 | 120 | 75 | 3,000 | 9,842 | 4h | — | 2 | — |
| 7.80 | 25.7 | 3.10 | 10.2 | — | — | — | — | — | — | — | — | 2 | — |
| 9.84 | 32.3 | 3.18 | 10.5 | 1,360 | 2.998 | 135 | 83.8 | 4,500 | 14,764 | 4h | — | 2 | 1 mg |
| 7.87 | 25.10 | 3.25 | 10.8 | 1,427 | 3.146 | 155 | 97 | 5,000 | 16,405 | 4h30' | — | 2 | 2 mg; b (100 kg - 220 lb) |
| 7.15 | 23.5 | 3.35 | 11 | 1,120 | 2.464 | 158 | 99 | 5,000 | 16,405 | 4h | — | 2 | 2 mg; b (90 kg - 198.4 lb) |
| 8.10 | 25.7 | 2.92 | 9.6 | 1,402 | 3.091 | 130 | 81 | 5,030 | 16,502 | 4h | — | 2 | 1-2 mg |
| 8 | 26.2 | 3.25 | 10.8 | 1,286 | 2.835 | 120 | 74.5 | 4,000 | 13,123 | 3h30' | — | 2 | 1-2 mg |
| 7.62 | 24.9 | 3.15 | 10.4 | 1,069 | 2.357 | 105 | 66 | 3,000 | 9,842 | 4h | — | 2 | — |
| 7.85 | 25.9 | 3.14 | 10.3 | 1,190 | 2.618 | 132 | 82 | 3,050 | 10,006 | 2h30' | — | 2 | 1 mg |
| 8 | 26.2 | 3.10 | 10.2 | 1,352 | 2.977 | 140 | 87.5 | 3,380 | 11,089 | 4h | — | 2 | 2-3 mg; b (90 kg - 198.4 lb) |
| 9.15 | 30.01 | 3.40 | 11.2 | 1,668 | 3.669 | 175 | 109 | 5.000 | 16.405 | 3h25' | — | 2 | 2 mg |
| 8.85 | 29 | 3.25 | 10.8 | 1,639 | 3.606 | 175 | 109 | 5,000 | 16,405 | 3h15' | — | 2 | 2 mg |
| 7.85 | 25.9 | 3.08 | 10.1 | 1,330 | 2.687 | 152 | 95 | 5,030 | 16,502 | 4h | — | 2 | 2 mg; b (90 kg - 198.4 lb) |
| 6.92 | 22.8 | 3.36 | 11.01 | 1,365 | 2.730 | 170 | 106 | 5,000 | 16,405 | 3h30' | — | 2 | 2 mg |
| 7.58 | 24.10 | 2.80 | 9.2 | 1,081 | 2.378 | 165 | 103 | 7,500 | 24,600 | 3h | — | 2 | 3 mg |
| 9.06 | 29.8 | 3 | 9.10 | 1,567 | 3.455 | 187 | 116 | 7,000 | 22,965 | 4h | — | 2 | 2 mg; b (60 kg - 132 lb) |
| 8.50 | 27.10 | 2.98 | 9.9 | 1,395 | 3.075 | 162 | 101 | 5,000 | 16,405 | 3h30' | — | 2 | 2 mg |
| 8.10 | 26.6 | 2.94 | 9.7 | 948 | 2.090 | 230 | 143 | 6,700 | 21,980 | 6h | — | 1 | 2 mg |
| 8.10 | 26.6 | 2.92 | 9.7 | 1,040 | 2.293 | 218.8 | 137 | 5,000 | 16,405 | 4h | — | 2 | — |
| 8.80 | 29.10 | 3.30 | 10.10 | 1,720 | 3.792 | 175 | 109 | 4,800 | 15,750 | 3h30' | — | 2 | 2-3 mg |
| 8.94 | 29.4 | 3.35 | 11 | 1,538 | 3.391 | 194 | 120 | 5,000 | 16,405 | 3h30' | — | 2 | — |
| 8.33 | 27.4 | 3.01 | 9.8 | 966 | 2.130 | 121 | 75 | 3,350 | 11,000 | 2h | — | — | — |
| 5.64 | 18.5 | 2.47 | 8.1 | 622 | 1.371 | 152.9 | 95 | 4,572 | 15,000 | 2h30' | — | 1 | 1 mg |
| 5.74 | 18.10 | 2.38 | 7.10 | 523 | 1.153 | 161 | 100 | 4,511 | 14,800 | 2h30' | — | 1 | — |
| 7.95 | 26.1 | — | — | 1,213 | 2.674 | 134 | 83 | 3,505 | 11,499 | 3h | — | 2 | 2 mg; b (90 kg - 198.4 lb) |
| 8.10 | 26.6 | 2.79 | 9.15 | 1,164 | 2.566 | 144 | 89.5 | 4,298 | 14,100 | 3h30' | — | 2 | 2 mg |

# Technical Data

| Page | Aircraft | Nation | Manufacturer | Type | Year | Engine | Wingspan m | ft |
|------|----------|--------|--------------|------|------|--------|------------|-----|
| 26 | Sopwith Baby | GB | Sopwith Aviation Company | Rc | 1917 | Clerget 110 or 130 hp | 7.82 | 25.8 |
| 26 | Fairey Campania | GB | Fairey Aviation Co. Ltd. | Rc | 1917 | Rolls-Royce Eagle VIII, 345 hp (12 cl) l.c. | 18.78 | 61.7 |
| 26 | Felixstowe F.2A | GB | Aircraft Manifacturing Co. | Rc | 1917 | 2 x Rolls-Royce Eagle VIII, 700 hp (12 cl) l.c. | 29.15 | 95.7 |
| 26 | Curtiss H-16 | USA | Naval Aircraft Factory | Rc/AS | 1918 | 2 x Liberty 400 hp (12 cl) l.c. | 31.70 | 104 |
| 26 | Curtiss N.9 | USA | Curtiss Aeroplane and Motor Co. | A | 1917 | Curtiss OX-6 100 hp (8 cl) l.c. | 16.25 | 53.3 |
| 26 | Macchi M.9 | I | S.A. Nieuport-Macchi | Rc | 1918 | Fiat A-12 bis 280 hp (6 cl) l.c. | 15.40 | 50.6 |
| 26 | Macchi L.1 | I | S.A. Nieuport-Macchi | Rc | 1915 | Isotta-Fraschini V.4A, 150 hp (6 cl) l.c. | 16.40 | 53.8 |
| 26 | Macchi M.5 Mod | I | S.A. Nieuport-Macchi | Fr/Rc | 1918 | Isotta-Fraschini V6B 250 hp (6 cl) l.c. | 9.70 | 31.8 |
| 26 | Lohner E | A | Jacob Lohner Werke & Co. | Rc | 1914 | Hiero 85 hp (6 cl) l.c. | 16.20 | 53.2 |
| 26 | F.B.A. Type C | F | Franco-British Aviation | Rc | 1915 | Clerget 130 hp | 13.70 | 44.9 |
| 28 | Fokker E.III | D | Fokker Flugzeug-Werke GmbH | Fr | 1915 | Oberursel 100 hp | 9.40 | 30.8 |
| 28 | Fokker Dr.I | D | Fokker Flugzeug-Werke GmbH | Fr | 1917 | Le Rhône 9J-Thulin 110 hp | 7.19 | 23.7 |
| 28 | Fokker D.VII | D | Fokker Flugzeug-Werke GmbH | Fr | 1918 | Mercedes D.III 160 hp (6 cl) l.c. | 8.92 | 29.3 |
| 28 | Fokker E.V/D.VIII | D | Fokker Flugzeug-Werke GmbH | Fr | 1918 | Oberursel U.R.II 110 hp | 8.40 | 27.6 |
| 28 | Albatros D.II | D | Albatros Flugzeug-Werke GmbH | Fr | 1916 | Mercedes D.III 160 hp (6 cl) l.c. | 8.50 | 27.8 |
| 28 | Albatros D.III | D | Albatros Flugzeug-Werke GmbH | Fr | 1917 | Mercedes D.IIIa 176 hp (6 cl) l.c. | 9.04 | 29.8 |
| 28 | Albatros D.Va | D | Albatros Flugzeug-Werke GmbH | Fr | 1917 | Mercedes D.IIIa 180 hp (6 cl) l.c. | 9.04 | 29.8 |
| 28 | Pfalz D.III | D | Pfalz Flugzeug-Werke GmbH | Fr | 1917 | Mercedes D.III 160 hp (6 cl) l.c. | 9.39 | 30.8 |
| 28 | Pfalz Dr.1 | D | Pfalz Flugzeug-Werke GmbH | Fr | 1917 | Siemens-Halske 160 hp | 8.53 | 28 |
| 28 | Pfalz D.XII | D | Pfalz Flugzeug-Werke GmbH | Fr | 1918 | Mercedes D.IIIa 180 hp (6 cl) l.c. | 9 | 29.5 |
| 28 | Halberstadt D.II | D | Halberstädter Flugzeug-Werke GmbH | Fr | 1916 | Mercedes D.II 120 hp (6 cl) l.c. | 8.81 | 28.8 |
| 28 | Halberstadt CL.II | D | Halberstädter Flugzeug-Werke GmbH | Fr | 1917 | Mercedes D.III 160 hp (6 cl) l.c. | 10.77 | 35.4 |
| 28 | Roland D.VIb | D | Luftfahrzeug GmbH | Fr | 1918 | Benz Bz.IIIa 200 hp (6 cl) l.c. | 9.39 | 30.8 |
| 28 | Roland D.II | D | Luftfahrzeug GmbH | Fr | 1917 | Mercedes D.III 160 hp (6 cl) l.c. | 8.91 | 29.3 |
| 28 | Junkers CL.I | D | Junkers Flugzeug-Werke AG. | Fr/A | 1918 | Mercedes D.IIIa 180 hp (6 cl) l.c. | 12.05 | 39.6 |
| 28 | Junkers D.I | D | Junkers Flugzeug-Werke AG. | Fr | 1918 | B.M.W. IIIa 185 hp (6 cl) l.c. | 8.88 | 29.6 |
| 28 | Rumpler 6B.1 | D | E. Rumpler Flugzeug-Werke GmbH | Fr | 1916 | Mercedes D.III 160 hp (6 cl) l.c. | 12.05 | 40 |
| 28 | Hansa-Brandenburg KDW | D | Hansa und Brandenburgische Flugzeug-Werke GmbH | Fr | 1916 | Benz 150 hp (6 cl) l.c. | 9.22 | 30.4 |
| 28 | Hansa-Brandenburg W.12 | D | Hansa und Brandenburgische Flugzeug-Werke GmbH | Fr | 1917 | Benz Bz.III 150 hp (6 cl) l.c. | 11.20 | 36.9 |
| 28 | Hansa-Brandenburg W.29 | D | Hansa und Brandenburgische Flugzeug-Werke GmbH | Fr | 1918 | Benz Bz.III 150 hp (6 cl) l.c. | 13.50 | 44.4 |
| 28 | Phönix D.I | A | Phönix Flugzeug-Werke AG. | Fr | 1918 | Hiero 200 hp (6 cl) l.c. | 9.88 | 32 |
| 28 | Aviatik D.I | A | Oesterreichische-Ungarische Flugzeugfabrik Aviatik | Fr | 1917 | Austro-Daimler 200 hp (6 cl) l.c. | 8 | 26.2 |
| 28 | Hansa-Brandenburg D.I | A | Phönix Flugzeug-Werke AG. | Fr | 1916 | Austro-Daimler 160 hp (6 cl) l.c. | 8.51 | 27.9 |
| 28 | Hansa-Brandenburg CC | A | Phönix Flugzeug-Werke AG. | Fr | 1916 | Benz Bz.III 150 hp (6 cl) l.c. | 9.30 | 30.6 |
| 29 | Vickers F.B.5 | GB | Vickers Ltd. | Fr | 1914 | Gnome Monosoupape 100 hp | 11.13 | 36.6 |
| 29 | R.A.F. F.E.2b | GB | Royal Aircraft Factory | Fr/Rc | 1915 | Beardmore 160 hp (6 cl) l.c. | 14.56 | 47.9 |
| 29 | R.A.F. F.E.8 | GB | Royal Aircraft Factory | Fr | 1916 | Gnome Monosoupape 100 hp | 9.60 | 31.6 |
| 29 | R.A.F. S.E.5a | GB | Royal Aircraft Factory | Fr | 1917 | Wolseley W.4A Viper 200 hp (8 cl) l.c. | 8.10 | 26.7 |
| 29 | R.A.F. S.E.5 | GB | Royal Aircraft Factory | Fr | 1917 | Hispano-Suiza 150 hp (8 cl) l.c. | 8.10 | 26.7 |
| 29 | Bristol Scout D | GB | British & Colonial Aeroplane Co. Ltd. | Fr | 1915 | Gnome 80 hp | 7.50 | 24.7 |
| 29 | Bristol F.2B | GB | British & Colonial Aeroplane Co. Ltd. | Fr | 1917 | Rolls-Royce Falcon III 275 hp (12 cl) l.c. | 11.97 | 39.3 |
| 29 | Bristol M.1C | GB | British & Colonial Aeroplane Co. Ltd. | Fr | 1917 | Le Rhône 9J 110 hp | 9.37 | 30.9 |
| 29 | Sopwith Tabloid | GB | Sopwith Aviation Company | Fr | 1914 | Gnome 80 hp | 7.77 | 25.6 |
| 29 | Sopwith Pup | GB | Sopwith Aviation Company | Fr | 1916 | Le Rhône 9C 90 hp | 8.08 | 26.6 |
| 29 | Sopwith 1½ Strutter | GB | Sopwith Aviation Company | Fr/Br | 1916 | Clerget 9Z 110 hp | 10.21 | 33.6 |
| 29 | Sopwith Triplane | GB | Sopwith Aviation Company | Fr | 1917 | Clerget 9B 130 hp (9 cl) a.c. | 8.07 | 26.6 |
| 29 | Sopwith F1 Camel | GB | Sopwith Aviation Company | Fr | 1917 | Clerget 9B 130 hp | 8.53 | 28 |
| 29 | Sopwith 7 F.1 Snipe | GB | Sopwith Aviation Company | Fr | 1918 | Bentley B.R.2 230 hp | 9.14 | 30 |
| 29 | Martinsyde F.4 Buzzard | GB | Martinsyde Ltd. | Fr | 1918 | Hispano-Suiza 8F 300 hp (8 cl) l.c. | 9.99 | 32.9 |
| 29 | Martinsyde S.1 | GB | Martinsyde Ltd. | Fr | 1914 | Gnome 80 hp | 8.43 | 27.8 |
| 29 | Airco D.H.2 | GB | Aircraft Manifacturing Co. | Fr | 1916 | Gnome Monosoupape 100 hp | 8.61 | 28.3 |
| 29 | Airco D.H. 5 | GB | Aircraft Manifacturing Co. | Fr | 1917 | Le Rhône 9J 110 hp | 7.82 | 25.8 |
| 29 | Austin-Ball A.F.B.1 | GB | Austin Motor Co. Ltd. | Fr | 1918 | Hispano-Suiza 200 hp (8 cl) l.c. | 9.14 | 30 |
| 29 | Blackburn Triplane | GB | Blackburn Aeroplane & Motor Co. | Fr | 1917 | Clerget 9Z 110 hp | 7.32 | 24 |
| 29 | Morane-Saulnier L | F | Société Anonyme des Aéroplanes Morane-Saulnier | Fr | 1913 | Gnome 80 hp | 10.30 | 33.8 |
| 29 | Morane-Saulnier N | F | Société Anonyme des Aéroplanes Morane-Saulnier | Fr | 1914 | Le Rhône 9J 110 hp | 8.30 | 27.2 |
| 29 | Morane-Saulnier A.I | F | Société Anonyme des Aéroplanes Morane-Saulnier | Fr | 1917 | Gnome Monosoupape 9N 160 hp | 8.50 | 27.9 |
| 29 | Spad A.2 | F | S.P.A.D. | Fr | 1915 | Le Rhône 80 hp | 9.55 | 31.4 |
| 29 | Spad S.VII | F | S.P.A.D. | Fr | 1916 | Hispano-Suiza 8Aa 150 hp (8 cl) l.c. | 7.77 | 25.6 |
| 29 | Spad S.XI | F | S.P.A.D. | Rc/LB | 1916 | Hispano-Suiza 235 hp (8 cl) | 11.23 | 36.9 |
| 29 | Spad S.XIII | F | S.P.A.D. | Fr | 1917 | Hispano-Suiza 8 Bec 235 hp (8 cl) l.c. | 8.20 | 26.9 |
| 29 | Nieuport 11 «Bébé» | F | Société Anonyme des Etablissement Nieuport | Fr | 1915 | Le Rhône 9C 80 hp (9 cl) a.c. | 7.55 | 24.9 |
| 29 | Nieuport 12 | F | Société Anonyme des Etablissements Nieuport | Fr | 1915 | Clerget 9B 130 hp | 9.03 | 29.7 |

| Length | | Height | | Take-off weight | | Speed | | Ceiling | | Range | | Crew | Payload/armament |
| --- | --- | --- | --- | --- | --- | --- | --- | --- | --- | --- | --- | --- | --- |
| m | ft | m | ft | kg | lb | km/h | mph | m | ft | km | ml | | |
| 7.01 | 23 | 3.05 | 10 | 778 | 1,715 | 157.6 | 97.9 | 2,316 | 7,600 | 2h | — | 1 | 1 mg |
| 3.12 | 43.1 | 4.60 | 15.1 | 2,566 | 5,675 | 129 | 80 | 1,680 | 5,500 | 3h | — | 2 | 1 mg |
| 4.10 | 46.3 | 5.33 | 17.6 | 4,980 | 10.978 | 153 | 95 | 2,930 | 9,600 | 6h | — | 4 | 4-7 mg; b (208 kg - 460 lb) |
| 4.05 | 46.1 | 5.39 | 17.8 | 5,889 | 12,983 | 139.9 | 86.9 | 3,810 | 12,500 | 11h | — | 4 | 5-6 mg; b (420 kg - 926 lb) |
| 9.09 | 29.8 | 3.33 | 10.9 | 1,093 | 2,409 | 113 | 70.2 | 2,743 | 8,999 | 2h | — | 2 | — |
| 9.50 | 31.2 | 3.15 | 10.4 | 1,800 | 3,968 | 187 | 116 | 5,500 | 18,050 | 4h | — | 2 | 1 mg |
| 0.25 | 33.8 | 3.85 | 12.8 | 1,700 | 3,747 | 110 | 68 | 5,000 | 16,405 | 4h | — | 2 | 1 mg |
| 8 | 26.2 | 2.85 | 9.3 | 1,081 | 2,383 | 205 | 127.3 | 5,990 | 19,652 | 3h40' | — | 1 | 2 mg |
| 0.26 | 33.8 | 3.85 | 12.8 | 1,700 | 3,747 | 105 | 65 | 4.000 | 13,120 | 4h | — | 2 | — |
| 8.79 | 28.8 | 3.40 | 11.2 | 940 | 2,072 | 110 | 68 | 3,500 | 11,480 | 3h | — | 2 | 1 mg |
| 7.29 | 23.9 | 2.79 | 9.1 | 608 | 1,340 | 141 | 87.5 | 3,660 | 12,007 | 1h30' | — | 1 | 2 mg |
| 5.77 | 18.9 | 2.95 | 9.8 | 585 | 1,289 | 165 | 102.5 | 6,100 | 20,013 | 1h30' | — | 1 | 2 mg |
| 6.95 | 22.8 | 2.75 | 9.2 | 877 | 1,940 | 189 | 117.4 | 6,000 | 19,685 | 1h30' | — | 1 | 2 mg |
| 5.86 | 19.4 | 2.82 | 9.3 | 562 | 1,238 | 185 | 115 | 6,300 | 20,670 | 1h30' | — | 1 | 2 mg |
| 7.40 | 24.3 | 2.74 | 8.9 | 886 | 1,953 | 175 | 109 | 5,180 | 17,060 | 1h30' | — | 1 | 2 mg |
| 7.32 | 24.01 | 2.97 | 9.7 | 884 | 1,949 | 176 | 109.3 | 5,500 | 18,050 | 2h | — | 1 | 2 mg |
| 7.32 | 24.01 | 2.85 | 9.4 | 935 | 2,061 | 187 | 116 | 6,250 | 20,505 | 2h | — | 1 | 2 mg |
| 6.96 | 22.8 | 2.67 | 8.7 | 928 | 2,046 | 165 | 102.5 | 5,180 | 16,995 | 2h30' | — | 1 | 2 mg |
| 5.48 | 18 | 2.69 | 8.8 | 703 | 1,551 | 201 | 125 | 6,000 | 19,685 | 1h30' | — | 1 | 2 mg |
| 6.35 | 20.8 | 2.70 | 8.8 | 902 | 1,989 | 180 | 111.8 | 5,640 | 18,537 | 2h30' | — | 1 | 2 mg |
| 7.29 | 23.9 | 2.67 | 8.7 | 728 | 1,605 | 145 | 90 | 4,000 | 13,123 | 1h30' | — | 1 | 1-2 mg |
| 7.29 | 23.9 | 2.74 | 9 | 1,133 | 2,493 | 165 | 102.5 | 5,100 | 16,732 | 3h | — | 2 | 2-3 mg; b (50 kg - 110 lb) |
| 6.36 | 20.8 | 2.80 | 9.2 | 860 | 1,892 | 183 | 114 | 5,800 | 19,029 | 2h | — | 1 | 2 mg |
| 6.91 | 22.8 | 2.82 | 9.3 | 739 | 1,794 | 169 | 105 | 5,000 | 16,405 | 2h | — | 1 | 2 mg |
| 7.90 | 25.9 | 2.65 | 7.9 | 1,055 | 2,310 | 169 | 105 | 6,000 | 19,685 | 2h | — | 2 | 3 mg |
| 6.70 | 21.9 | 2.25 | 7.4 | 835 | 1,835 | 186 | 119 | 6,000 | 19,685 | 1h30' | — | 1 | 2 mg |
| 9.40 | 30.8 | 3.60 | 11.6 | 1,140 | 2,508 | 153 | 95 | 5,000 | 16,405 | 4h | — | 1 | 1 mg |
| 8 | 26.2 | 3.30 | 10.8 | 1,045 | 2,304 | 172 | 106.8 | 4,000 | 13,123 | 3h | — | 1 | 1-2 mg |
| 9.65 | 31.6 | 3.30 | 10.8 | 1,460 | 3,199 | 161 | 100 | 5,000 | 16,405 | 3h30' | — | 2 | 2-3 mg |
| 9.38 | 30.8 | 3 | 9.9 | 1,494 | 3,285 | 175 | 109 | — | — | 4h | — | 2 | 3 mg |
| 6.63 | 21.7 | 2.79 | 9.2 | 803 | 1,775 | 180 | 112.5 | 6,000 | 19,685 | 2h | — | 1 | 2 mg |
| 6.95 | 22.9 | 2.49 | 8.2 | 881 | 1,942 | 185 | 115 | 6,220 | 20,406 | 2h30' | — | 1 | 2 mg |
| 6.35 | 20.8 | 2.79 | 9.2 | 917 | 2,024 | 187 | 116 | 5,000 | 16,405 | 2h30' | — | 1 | 1 mg |
| 7.65 | 25.1 | 3.20 | 10.6 | 1,356 | 2,989 | 175 | 109 | — | — | 3h30' | — | 1 | 1 mg |
| 8.28 | 27.2 | 3.50 | 11.6 | 930 | 2,050 | 113 | 70 | 2,743 | 9,000 | 4h | — | 2 | 1-2 mg |
| 9.83 | 32.3 | 3.85 | 12.7 | 1,378 | 3,037 | 146 | 92 | 3,350 | 11,000 | 2h30' | — | 2 | 2 mg |
| 7.21 | 23.8 | 2.79 | 9.2 | 611 | 1,346 | 151.3 | 94 | 4,420 | 14,500 | 4h | — | 1 | 1 mg |
| 6.38 | 20.9 | 2.89 | 9.6 | 902 | 1,988 | 222 | 138 | 5,944 | 19,500 | 3h | — | 1 | 2 mg |
| 6.38 | 20.9 | 2.87 | 9.5 | 877 | 1,940 | 196.3 | 122 | 5,791 | 18,999 | 2h30' | — | 1 | 2 mg |
| 6.30 | 20.8 | 2.59 | 8.6 | 567 | 1,250 | 161 | 100 | 4,900 | 16,076 | 2h | — | 1 | 1 mg |
| 7.87 | 25.8 | 2.97 | 9.9 | 1,261 | 2,779 | 196 | 123 | 6,096 | 20,000 | 3h | — | 2 | 3 mg; b (109 kg - 240 lb) |
| 6.24 | 20.5 | 2.37 | 7.9 | 611 | 1,348 | 209 | 130 | 6,096 | 20,000 | 1h45' | — | 1 | 1 mg |
| 6.20 | 20.4 | 2.56 | 8.5 | 508 | 1,120 | 148 | 92 | 4,572 | 15,000 | 3h30' | — | 1 | 1 mg |
| 5.89 | 19.3 | 2.87 | 9.5 | 556 | 1,225 | 179 | 111 | 5,334 | 17,500 | 3h | — | 1 | 1 mg |
| 7.70 | 25.3 | 3.12 | 10.3 | 1,062 | 2,341 | 162 | 100 | 3,962 | 13,000 | 4h | — | 1 | 2 mg |
| 5.98 | 19.6 | 3.20 | 10.6 | 699 | 1,541 | 181 | 112 | 6,248 | 20,500 | 2h45' | — | 1 | 1 mg |
| 5.72 | 18.9 | 2.59 | 8.6 | 659 | 1,453 | 185 | 115 | 5,791 | 19,000 | 2h30' | — | 1 | 2 mg |
| 5.84 | 19.1 | 2.89 | 9.6 | 916 | 2,020 | 195 | 121 | 5,944 | 19,500 | 3h | — | 1 | 2 mg |
| 7.76 | 25.6 | 2.69 | 8.8 | 1,087 | 2,398 | 213 | 140 | 7,315 | 24.000 | — | — | 1 | 2 mg |
| 6.40 | 21 | 2.49 | 8.2 | — | — | 135 | 84 | — | — | — | — | 1 | 1 mg |
| 7.67 | 25.2 | 2.81 | 9.6 | 654 | 1,441 | 150 | 93 | 4,420 | 14,501 | 2h45' | — | 1 | 1 mg |
| 6.71 | 22 | 2.78 | 9.1 | 677 | 1,492 | 164 | 102 | 4,877 | 16,000 | 2h45' | — | 1 | 1 mg |
| 6.55 | 21.6 | 2.82 | 9.3 | 942 | 2,007 | 222 | 138 | 6,700 | 22,000 | 2h15' | — | 1 | 2 mg |
| 6.53 | 21.5 | — | — | 680 | 1,500 | — | — | — | — | 3h | — | 1 | 1 mg |
| 6.32 | 20.7 | 3.15 | 10.3 | 680 | 1,500 | 115 | 72 | 4,000 | 13,123 | 2h30' | — | 2 | 1 mg |
| 6.70 | 21.9 | 2.50 | 8.2 | 510 | 1,225 | 165 | 102.5 | 4,000 | 13,123 | 1h30' | — | 1 | 1 mg |
| 5.63 | 18.6 | 2.41 | 7.9 | 650 | 1,433 | 208 | 129 | 7,000 | 22,965 | 2h30' | — | 1 | 1-2 mg |
| 7.29 | 23.9 | 2.60 | 8.8 | 708 | 1,562 | 130 | 80 | — | — | — | — | 2 | 1 mg |
| 6.13 | 20.1 | 2.33 | 7.8 | 703 | 1,550 | 192 | 119 | 5,334 | 17,500 | 2h15' | — | 1 | 1 mg |
| 7.75 | 25.5 | 2.59 | 8.6 | 1,048 | 2,310 | 176 | 109 | 7,000 | 22,965 | 2h15' | — | 2 | 2-3 mg; b (70 kg - 154 lb) |
| 6.30 | 20.8 | 2.42 | 7.9 | 820 | 1,801 | 222 | 138 | 6,650 | 21,820 | 2h | — | 1 | 2 mg |
| 5.80 | 19 | 2.45 | 8 | 480 | 1,060 | 156 | 97 | 4,600 | 15,090 | 2h30' | — | 1 | 1 mg |
| 7.30 | 23.9 | 2.67 | 8.8 | 920 | 2,028 | 155 | 97 | 4,700 | 15,420 | 2h45' | — | 1-2 | 1-2 mg |

# Technical Data

| Page | Aircraft | Nation | Manufacturer | Type | Year | Engine | Wingspan m | ft |
|---|---|---|---|---|---|---|---|---|
| 29 | Nieuport 17 | F | Société Anonyme des Etablissements Nieuport | Fr | 1916 | Le Rhône 9J 110 hp | 8.17 | 26.8 |
| 29 | Nieuport 27 | F | Société Anonyme des Etablissements Nieuport | Fr | 1917 | Le Rhône 9JB 120 hp | 8.18 | 26.8 |
| 29 | Nieuport 28 | F | Société Anonyme des Etablissements Nieuport | Fr | 1917 | Gnome Mosoupape 9N 160 hp | 8.15 | 26.7 |
| 29 | Nieuport-Delage 29 | F | Société Anonyme des Etablissements Nieuport | Fr | 1918 | Hispano-Suiza 300 hp (8 cl) l.c. | 9.75 | 32 |
| 29 | Hanriot HD.1 | F | Société Anonyme des Appareils d'Aviation Hanriot | Fr | 1917 | Le Rhône 9J 110 hp | 8.68 | 28.6 |
| 29 | Ansaldo A.1 Balilla | I | Giovanni Ansaldo & C. | Fr | 1918 | S.P.A. 6A 220 hp (6 cl) l.c. | 7.68 | 25.2 |
| 29 | Packard Le Père-Lusac 11 | USA | Packard Motor Car Co. | Fr | 1918 | Liberty 12-A 400 hp (12 cl) l.c. | 12.68 | 41.7 |
| 32 | Farman F.40 | F | Farman Frères | Rc/LB | 1915 | Renault 160 hp l.c. | 17.62 | 57.8 |
| 32 | Voisin 3 | F | Gabriel Voisin | LB | 1914 | Canton-Unné 120 hp l.c. | 14.75 | 48.4 |
| 32 | Voisin 5 | F | Gabriel Voisin | LB | 1915 | Salmson 150 hp l.c. | 14.75 | 48.4 |
| 32 | Voisin 8 | F | Gabriel Voisin | Br | 1916 | Peugeot 220 hp (8 cl) l.c. | 18.80 | 61.7 |
| 32 | Breguet Br. M5 | F | Louis Breguet | Br | 1915 | Renault 220 hp l.c. | 17.60 | 57.9 |
| 32 | Breguet Br. 14B2 | F | Louis Breguet | Br | 1917 | Renault 12 FCX 300 hp (12 cl) l.c. | 14.36 | 47.1 |
| 32 | Caudron G.4 | F | Caudron Frères | Br | 1915 | 2 x Le Rhône 80 hp or 2 x Anzani 100 hp | 17.20 | 56.5 |
| 32 | Caudron R.11 | F | Caudron Frères | Br | 1918 | 2 x Hispano-Suiza 8B 220 hp l.c. | 17.90 | 58.7 |
| 32 | Paul Schmitt 7 | F | Paul Schmitt | Br | 1917 | Renault 200 hp (8 cl) l.c. | 17.65 | 57.9 |
| 32 | Caproni Ca.30 | I | Società di Aviazione Ing. Caproni | Br | 1914 | 3 x Gnome 80 hp | 22.20 | 72.8 |
| 32 | Caproni Ca. 46 | I | Società di Aviazione Ing. Caproni | Br | 1918 | 3 x Fiat A-12bis 300 hp (6 cl) l.c. | 23.40 | 76.9 |
| 32 | Martin MB-2 | USA | Glenn L. Martin Co. | Br | 1920 | 2 x Liberty 12 420 hp (12 cl) l.c. | 22.60 | 74.2 |
| 32 | Sikorsky Ilya Mourometz V | Russia | R.B.V.Z. | Br | 1915 | 4 x Sunbeam 150 hp (6 cl V) l.c. | 29.80 | 97.9 |
| 33 | Airco D.H.4 | GB | Aircraft Manufacturing Co. | Br | 1917 | Rolls-Royce Eagle VII 375 hp (12 cl V) l.c. | 12.93 | 42.4 |
| 33 | Airco D.H.6 | GB | Aircraft Manufacturing Co. | Br | 1917 | R.A.F. 1a 90 hp (8 cl V) l.c. | 10.95 | 35.9 |
| 33 | Airco D.H.9 | GB | Aircraft Manufacturing Co. | Br | 1918 | B.H.P. 230 hp (6 cl) l.c. | 12.92 | 42.4 |
| 33 | R.A.F. R.E.7 | GB | Royal Aircraft Factory | Br | 1915 | R.A.F.4a 150 hp (12 cl V) a.c. | 17.37 | 57 |
| 33 | R.A.F. B.E.12 | GB | Royal Aircraft Factory | Fr/Br | 1916 | R.A.F.4a 150 hp (12 cl V) a.c. | 11.28 | 37 |
| 33 | Short Bomber | GB | Short Brothers | HB | 1916 | Rolls-Royce Eagle III 250 hp (12 cl V) l.c. | 25.91 | 85 |
| 33 | Sopwith Cockoo | GB | Sopwith Aviation Company | TB | 1917 | Hispano-Suiza 200 hp (8 cl V) l.c. | 14.25 | 46.9 |
| 33 | Vickers Vimy | GB | Vickers Ltd. | HB | 1918 | 2 x Rolls-Royce Eagle VIII 360 hp (12 cl V) l.c. | 20.73 | 68 |
| 33 | Blackburn Kangaroo | GB | Blackburn Aeroplane & Co. Ltd. | Br | 1918 | 2 x Rolls-Royce Falcon II 255 hp (12 cl) l.c. | 22.82 | 74.9 |
| 33 | Handley Page 0/100 | GB | Handley Page Ltd. | HB | 1916 | 2 x Rolls-Royce Eagle II 250 hp (12 cl) l.c. | 30.48 | 100 |
| 33 | Handley Page V/1500 | GB | Handley Page Ltd. | HB | 1918 | 4 x Rolls-Royce Eagle VIII 375 hp (12 cl) l.c. | 38.40 | 126 |
| 33 | Friedrichshafen G.III | D | Flugzeugbau Friedrichshafen AG. | Br | 1917 | 2 x Mercedes DVIa 260 hp (6 cl) l.c. | 23.75 | 77.9 |
| 33 | Gotha G.V | D | Gothaer Waggonfabrik AG. | Br | 1917 | 2 x Mercedes DVIa 260 hp (6 cl) l.c. | 23.70 | 77.9 |
| 33 | Siemens-Schuckert R.I | D | Siemens-Schuckert Werke AG. | Br | 1915 | 3 x Benz 150 hp (6 cl) l.c. | 28.04 | 92 |
| 33 | A.E.G. GIV | D | Allgemeine Elektrizitäts-Gesellschaft | Br | 1916 | 2 x Mercedes D.IVa 260 hp (6 cl) l.c. | 18.34 | 60.4 |
| 33 | Zeppelin Staaken R.6 | D | Zeppelin-Werke Staaken | Br | 1917 | 4 x Mercedes D.IVa 260 hp (6 cl) l.c. | 42.20 | 138.5 |
| 36 | Vickers Vimy Transatlantic | GB | Vickers Ltd. | Rp | 1919 | 2 x Rolls-Royce Eagle VIII 360 hp (12 cl) l.c. | 20.47 | 67.2 |
| 36 | Vickers Vimy Commercial | GB | Vickers Ltd. | CTr | 1920 | 2 x Rolls-Royce Eagle VIII 360 hp (12 cl V) l.c. | 20.47 | 67.2 |
| 36 | Breguet 14 T | F | Société Anonyme des Ateliers d'Aviation L. Breguet | CTr | 1919 | Renault 12 FCX 300 hp (12 cl V) l.c. | 14.36 | 47.1 |
| 36 | Farman F.60 Goliath | F | Avions H. et M. Farman | CTr | 1919 | 2 x Salmson C.M.9 260 hp (r 9 cl) l.c. | 26.46 | 86.8 |
| 36 | Junkers F.13 | D | Junkers Flugzeuge und Motorenwerke AG. | CTr | 1919 | B.M.W. IIIa 185 hp (6 cl) l.c. | 17.75 | 58.2 |
| 36 | Zeppelin-Staaken E.4/20 | D | Zeppelin-Werke GmbH | CTr | 1920 | 4 x Maybach Mb.IVa 260 hp (6 cl V) l.c. | 30.98 | 101.8 |
| 37 | Airco D.H.4A | GB | Aircraft Manufacturing Co. Ltd. | CTr | 1919 | Rolls-Royce Eagle VIII 350 hp (12 cl V) l.c. | 12.93 | 42.5 |
| 37 | de Havilland D.H. 10 | GB | Aircraft Manufacturing Co. Ltd. | Br | 1919 | 2 x Liberty 400 hp (12 cl V) l.c. | 19.96 | 65.6 |
| 37 | Sopwith Atlantic | GB | Sopwith Aviation Co. | Rp | 1919 | Rolls-Royce Eagle VIII 350 hp (12 cl V) l.c. | 14.18 | 46.6 |
| 37 | Tarrant Tabor | GB | W.G. Tarrant Ltd. | HB | 1919 | 6 x Napier Lion 500 hp (12 cl V) l.c. | 40 | 131. |
| 37 | Navy Curtiss NC-4 | USA | Curtiss Aeroplane and Motor Co. | Rc | 1919 | 4 x Liberty 12 400 hp (12 cl V) l.c. | 38.40 | 126 |
| 37 | Fokker F.II | NL | Fokker | CTr | 1920 | B.M.W. 185 hp (6 cl) l.c. | 17.24 | 56.5 |
| 37 | Caproni Ca.60 Transaereo | I | Società Aviazione Ing. Caproni | CTr | 1921 | 8 x Liberty 400 hp (12 cl V) l.c. | 30 | 98.5 |
| 42 | Potez 25A.2 | F | Société des Aéroplanes Potez H. | CTr | 1925 | Lorraine-Dietrich 450 hp (12 cl V) l.c. | 14.19 | 46.7 |
| 42 | Levasseur PL-8 Oiseau Blanc | F | Société Pierre Levasseur | — | 1927 | Lorraine-Dietrich 450 hp (12 cl V) l.c. | 14.63 | 48 |
| 42 | Farman F.190 | F | Avions H. & M. Farman | CTr | 1928 | Gnome-Rhône 5 Ba 230 hp (r 5 cl) a.c. | 14.40 | 47.3 |
| 42 | Farman F.301 | F | Avions H. & M. Farman | CTr | 1930 | 3 x Salmson 9Ab 230 hp (r 9 cl) a.c. | 19.08 | 62.7 |
| 42 | Blériot 135 | F | Blériot Aéronautique | CTr | 1924 | 4 x Salmson 6Ab 230 hp (r 9 cl) a.c. | 24.99 | 82 |
| 42 | Latécoère 28 | F | Forges et Atelier de Construction Latécoère | CTr | 1929 | Hispano-Suiza 12 Hbr 600 hp (12 cl V) l.c. | 19.25 | 63.1 |
| 42 | Focke Wulf A.17a | D | Focke Wulf Flugzeugbau GmbH | CTr | 1927 | Siemens-Jupiter VI 480 hp (r 9 cl) a.c. | 19.99 | 65.7 |
| 42 | Dornier Do.J Wal | D | C.M.A.S.A. | CTr | 1923 | 2 x Rolls-Royce Eagle IX 360 hp (12 cl V) l.c. | 22.50 | 73.8 |
| 42 | Dornier Do.L2 Delphin | D | Dornier Werke GmbH | CTr | 1924 | B.M.W. IV 300 hp (6 cl) l.c. | 17.10 | 56.1 |
| 43 | Dornier Do.X | D | Dornier Werke GmbH | CTr | 1929 | 12 x Curtiss Conquerors 600 hp (12 cl V) l.c. | 48 | 157. |
| 43 | Dornier Komet III | D | Dornier Werke GmbH | CTr | 1925 | Rolls-Royce Eagle IX 360 hp (12 cl) l.c. | 19.59 | 64.2 |
| 43 | Junkers G.24 | D | Junkers Flugzeuge und Motorenwerke AG. | CTr | 1925 | 3 x Junkers L.5 310 hp (6 cl) l.c. | 29.90 | 98. |
| 43 | Junkers G.38 | D | Junkers Flugzeuge und Motorenwerke AG. | CTr | 1930 | 4 x Junkers L 88a 800 hp (12 cl V) l.c. | 44 | 144. |
| 43 | Blériot 125 | F | Blériot Aéronautique | CTr | 1930 | 2 x Hispano-Suiza 12Hbr 500 hp (12 cl V) l.c. | 29.40 | 96. |
| 43 | Lioré et Olivier LeO 213 | F | Etablissements Lioré et Olivier | CTr | 1928 | 2 x Renault 12JA 450 hp (12 cl V) l.c. | 23.43 | 76. |
| 43 | Couzinet 70 Arc en Ciel | F | Société des Avions René Couzinet | CTr | 1929 | 3 x Hispano-Suiza 12Nb 650 hp (12 cl V) l.c. | 30 | 98. |
| 43 | Cams 53-1 | F | Chantiers Aéronautiques Maritimes de la Seine | CTr | 1929 | 2 x Hispano-Suiza 12 Lbr 580 hp (12 cl V) l.c. | 20.40 | 66. |
| 43 | Cant 10 ter | I | Cantieri Navali Triestini | CTr | 1926 | Lorraine 400 hp (12 cl V) l.c. | 15.30 | 50. |

| Length | | Height | | Take-off weight | | Speed | | Ceiling | | Range | | Crew | Payload/armament |
|---|---|---|---|---|---|---|---|---|---|---|---|---|---|
| m | ft | m | ft | kg | lb | km/h | mph | m | ft | km | ml | | |
| 5.77 | 18.9 | 2.44 | 8 | 565 | 1,246 | 177 | 110 | 5,300 | 17,390 | 2h | — | 1 | 2 mg |
| 6.35 | 20.8 | 2.43 | 8 | 585 | 1,289 | 187 | 116 | 5,550 | 18,210 | 1h30' | — | 1 | 2 mg |
| 6.40 | 21 | 2.50 | 8.1 | 737 | 1,627 | 196 | 122 | 5,182 | 16,995 | 1h30' | — | 1 | 2 mg |
| 6.50 | 21.5 | 2.77 | 9.1 | 1,096 | 2,420 | 237 | 148 | 8,200 | 26,900 | 2h | — | 1 | 2 mg |
| 5.85 | 19.2 | 2.55 | 8.3 | 605 | 1,334 | 183 | 115 | 6,300 | 20,670 | 2h30' | — | 1 | 1 mg |
| 6.84 | 22.5 | 2.53 | 8.3 | 885 | 1,951 | 220 | 137 | 5,000 | 16,405 | 1h30' | — | 1 | 2 mg |
| 7.70 | 25.6 | 2.89 | 9.6 | 1,699 | 3,746 | 212 | 132 | 6,517 | 21,200 | 2h | — | 2 | 4 mg |
| 9.24 | 30.4 | 3.89 | 12.8 | 1,120 | 2,475 | 135 | 84 | 4,900 | 16,076 | 2h20' | — | 2 | 1 mg; b (50 kg - 110 lb) |
| 9.50 | 31.2 | 3.80 | 12.6 | 1,370 | 3,025 | 120 | 74 | 3,500 | 11,485 | 4h | — | 2 | 1 mg |
| 9.53 | 31.3 | 3.63 | 11.9 | 1,140 | 2,516 | 105 | 65 | 3,500 | 11,485 | 3h30' | — | 2 | 1 mg or 1 g; b (60 kg - 132 lb) |
| 11.02 | 36.2 | 3.50 | 11.5 | 1,860 | 4,100 | 132 | 82 | 4,300 | 14,110 | 4h | — | 2 | 1-2 mg; b (180 kg - 379 lb) |
| 9.90 | 32.6 | 3.89 | 12.9 | 1,921 | 4,235 | 142 | 88 | 4,300 | 14,110 | 5h | — | 2 | 1-2 mg; b (300 kg - 661 lb) |
| 8.87 | 29 | 3.30 | 10.9 | 1,765 | 3,892 | 177 | 110 | 5,800 | 19,030 | 2h45' | — | 2 | 2-3 mg; b (300 kg - 661 lb) |
| 7.16 | 23.6 | 2.60 | 8.5 | 1,330 | 2,932 | 132 | 82 | 4,300 | 14,110 | 3h30' | — | 2 | 1 mg; b (113 kg - 249 lb) |
| 11.25 | 36.9 | 3 | 9.9 | 2,165 | 4,775 | 183 | 114 | 5,950 | 19,520 | 3h | — | 3 | 5 mg; b (120 kg - 265 lb) |
| 9.60 | 31.3 | 3.58 | 11.9 | 2,093 | 4,615 | 135 | 84 | 4,300 | 14,110 | 5h | — | 2 | 2-3 mg; b (150 kg - 330 lb) |
| 10.90 | 35.9 | 3.70 | 12.2 | 3,810 | 8,400 | 137 | 85 | 4,100 | 13,451 | 3h30' | — | 4 | 2-4 mg; b (453 kg - 1,000 lb) |
| 12.62 | 41.4 | 4.40 | 14.8 | 5,300 | 11,684 | 152 | 95 | 4,500 | 14,760 | 4h | — | 4 | 2 mg; b (540 kg - 1,190 lb) |
| 13 | 42.8 | 4.47 | 14.8 | 5,465 | 12,064 | 160 | 100 | 2,590 | 8,500 | 900 | 560 | 4 | 5 mg; b (1,360 kg - 3,000 lb) |
| 17.10 | 56.1 | 4.72 | 15.6 | 4,589 | 10,117 | 121 | 75 | 3,000 | 9,840 | 5h | — | 4-7 | 3-7 mg; b (521 kg - 1,150 lb) |
| 9.34 | 30.8 | 3.55 | 11.6 | 1,575 | 3,472 | 230 | 143 | 6,700 | 21,981 | 3h30' | — | 2 | 2-4 mg; b (210 kg - 460 lb) |
| 8.32 | 27.3 | 3.27 | 10.9 | 920 | 2,027 | 106 | 66 | — | — | — | — | 1 | b (45 kg - 100 lb) |
| 9.30 | 30.5 | 3.40 | 11.1 | 1,662 | 3,664 | 180 | 112 | 4,724 | 15,498 | 4h | — | 2 | 2-3 mg; b (210 kg - 463 lb) |
| 9.72 | 31.9 | 3.84 | 12.7 | 1,564 | 3,449 | 137 | 85 | 1,981 | 6,500 | 2h | — | 2 | 1 mg; b (152 kg - 336 lb) |
| 8.31 | 27.3 | 3.39 | 11.1 | 1,067 | 2,352 | 164 | 102 | 3,810 | 12,500 | 2h30' | — | 1 | 1-2 mg |
| 13.72 | 45 | 4.57 | 15 | 3,084 | 6,800 | 125 | 75 | 2,896 | 9,500 | 6h | — | 2 | 1 mg; b (410 kg - 920 lb) |
| 8.69 | 28.6 | 3.35 | 10.9 | 1,620 | 3,572 | 166 | 103 | 4,755 | 15,600 | 4h | — | 1 | 1 t |
| 13.27 | 43.6 | 4.57 | 15 | 5,670 | 12,500 | 165 | 103 | 2,134 | 7,001 | 8h | — | 3 | 4 mg; b (2,180 kg - 4,806 lb) |
| 14.02 | 46 | 5.13 | 16.8 | 3,636 | 8,017 | 161 | 100 | 3,200 | 10,500 | 8h | — | 4 | 2 mg; b (416 kg - 917 lb) |
| 19.15 | 62.8 | 6.71 | 22 | 6,352 | 14,003 | 153 | 95 | 2,134 | 7,001 | 6h | — | 4 | 4-5 mg; b (700 kg - 1,543 lb) |
| 19.51 | 64 | 7.01 | 23 | 13,608 | 30,000 | 146 | 90 | 3,353 | 11,000 | 6h | — | 4 | 4-6 mg; b (3,390 kg - 7,474 lb) |
| 12.85 | 42 | 3.66 | 12 | 3,940 | 8,646 | 141 | 88 | 4,510 | 14,765 | 5h | — | 3 | 2-4 mg; b (1,000 kg - 2,205 lb) |
| 12.36 | 40 | 4.30 | 14.1 | 3,967 | 8,745 | 140 | 88 | 6,500 | 21,325 | 6h | — | 3 | 3-4 mg; b (600 kg - 1,323 lb) |
| 17.48 | 57.5 | 4.90 | 16.1 | 5,402 | 11,910 | 130 | 81 | 3,800 | 12,500 | 4h | — | 7 | 2 mg; b (376 kg - 830 lb) |
| 9.85 | 32.3 | 3.89 | 12.9 | 3,630 | 7,986 | 166 | 103 | 4,000 | 13,123 | 4h30' | — | 3 | 3 mg; b (360 kg - 794 lb) |
| 22.10 | 72.6 | 6.30 | 20.8 | 11,824 | 26,067 | 135 | 84 | 4,320 | 14,173 | 7-10h | — | 7 | 4-7 mg; b (2,000 kg - 4,409 lb) |
| 13.26 | 43.6 | 4.65 | 15.3 | 6,025 | 13,285 | 161 | 100 | 3,200 | 10,500 | 3,926 | 2,440 | 2 | — |
| 13 | 42.8 | 4.65 | 15.3 | 5,663 | 12,485 | 135 | 84 | 3,200 | 10,500 | 724 | 450 | 2 | 10 p |
| 8.99 | 29.6 | 3.30 | 10.8 | 1,984 | 4,374 | 125 | 78 | 4,500 | 14,770 | 460 | 285 | 1 | 2 p |
| 14.33 | 47 | — | — | 4,774 | 10,515 | 120 | 75 | 4,000 | 13,123 | 400 | 250 | 2 | 12 p |
| 9.60 | 31.6 | 4.50 | 14.7 | 1,730 | 3,810 | 140 | 87 | 4,000 | 13,123 | 560 | 350 | 2 | 4 p |
| 16.49 | 54.1 | — | — | 8,500 | 18,739 | 211 | 124 | — | — | 1,200 | 740 | 3 | 12-18 p |
| 9.29 | 30.6 | 3.35 | 11 | 1,685 | 3,720 | 195 | 121 | — | — | — | — | 1 | 2 p |
| 12.03 | 39.7 | 4.41 | 14.6 | 4,077 | 8,989 | 181 | 112 | 5,000 | 16,405 | 1,000 | 621.4 | 3-4 | — |
| 9.60 | 31.6 | 3.38 | 11.1 | 2,780 | 6,130 | — | — | 3,960 | 12,988 | 3,000 | 1,860 | 2 | — |
| 23.30 | 76.4 | 11.35 | 37.3 | 20,385 | 44,941 | 177 | 110 | 3,962 | 12,998 | 1500-1900 | 900-1,200 | 5 | b (2,100 kg - 4,650 lb) |
| 20.80 | 68.2 | 7.46 | 24.5 | 12,422 | 27,386 | 146 | 91 | 1,372 | 4,501 | 2,366 | 1,470 | 6 | — |
| 10.28 | 33.7 | 3.17 | 10.5 | 1,894 | 4,188 | 150 | 93 | — | — | — | — | 2 | 4 p |
| 23.45 | 77 | 9.15 | 30 | 26,000 | 55,100 | 130 | 80 | — | — | 660 | 410 | 8 | 100 p or 5,445 kg (12,000 lb) |
| 9.19 | 30.2 | 3.65 | 12 | 1,965 | 4,338 | 170 | 106 | — | — | 500 | 310 | 2 | 507 kg (1,119 lb) |
| 9.75 | 32 | 3,96 | 13 | 4,954 | 10,924 | 193 | 120 | — | — | 6,000 | 3,725 | 2 | — |
| 10.45 | 34.3 | — | — | 1,800 | 3,968 | 160 | 100 | 5,150 | 16,900 | 850 | 530 | 1 | 4 p |
| 13.35 | 43.9 | 3.50 | 11.6 | 4,530 | 9,987 | 190 | 118 | 4,500 | 14,760 | 850 | 530 | 2 | 8 p |
| 14.45 | 47.5 | 4.93 | 16.2 | 5,492 | 12,125 | 135 | 84 | 4,200 | 13,780 | 600 | 370 | 2 | 10 p |
| 13.64 | 44.4 | — | — | 5,017 | 11,061 | 200 | 124 | 5,500 | 18,004 | 3,200 | 1,988 | 2 | 299 kg (659 lb) |
| 12.95 | 42.5 | 3.99 | 13.1 | 4,000 | 8,818 | 167 | 104 | 4,500 | 14,760 | 800 | 500 | 2 | 8 p |
| 17.25 | 56.7 | 5.20 | 17 | 5,700 | 12,566 | 140 | 87 | 3,500 | 11,480 | 2,200 | 1,350 | 2 | 8-14 p |
| 11.99 | 39.4 | — | — | 2,525 | 5,566 | 125 | 78 | 3,000 | 9,800 | — | — | 1 | 6-7 p |
| 40.05 | 131.4 | 10.10 | 33.1 | 52,000 | 114,640 | 190 | 118 | 500 | 1,640 | 1,700 | 1,056 | 10 | 72 p |
| 12.29 | 40.3 | 3.45 | 11.4 | 3,220 | 7,099 | 155 | 96 | 3,500 | 11,480 | 1,050 | 650 | 2 | 6 p |
| 15.69 | 51.6 | — | — | 6,500 | 14,330 | 182 | 113 | 4,700 | 15,400 | 1,300 | 800 | 3 | 9 p |
| 23.20 | 76.1 | 7.20 | 23.6 | 24,000 | 52,911 | 180 | 112 | 2,500 | 8,200 | 3,500 | 2,175 | 7 | 4 p |
| 13.80 | 45.3 | 4 | 13.1 | 7,140 | 15,741 | 180 | 112 | 4,500 | 14,760 | 800 | 500 | 3 | 1,920 kg (4,233 lb) |
| 15.95 | 52.4 | 4.30 | 14.1 | 5,692 | 12,566 | 175 | 108 | 4,500 | 14,760 | 560 | 350 | 2-3 | 12 p |
| 16.15 | 53 | — | — | 16,790 | 37,015 | 236 | 147 | — | — | 6,800 | 4,225 | 4 | 600 kg (1,322 lb) |
| 14.82 | 48.7 | — | — | 6,900 | 15,212 | 170 | 106 | 4,500 | 14,760 | 1,125 | 700 | 2 | 4 p |
| 11.50 | 37.7 | 4.06 | 13.4 | 3,000 | 6,600 | 150 | 93 | 4,200 | 13,700 | 595 | 370 | 1 | 4 p |

## Technical Data

| Page | Aircraft | Nation | Manufacturer | Type | Year | Engine | Wingspan m | ft |
|------|----------|--------|--------------|------|------|--------|-----------|-----|
| 43 | SIAI Marchetti S.M. 55 P | I | SIAI Marchetti | CTr | 1926 | 2 x Isotta-Fraschini 400 hp (12 cl V) l.c. | 24 | 78.9 |
| 46 | Lockheed Vega | USA | Lockheed Aircraft Company | CTr | 1927 | Wright Whirlwind J-5 220 hp (r 9 cl) a.c. | 12.50 | 41 |
| 46 | Boeing 40-A | USA | Boeing Aircraft Company | CTr | 1927 | Pratt & Whitney Wasp 420 hp (r 9 cl) a.c. | 13.46 | 44.2 |
| 46 | Boeing 80-A | USA | Boeing Airplane Co. | CTr | 1928 | 3 x Pratt & Whitney Hornet 525 hp (r 9 cl) a.c. | 24.38 | 80 |
| 46 | Consolidated Commodore | USA | Consolidated Aircraft Co. | CTr | 1929 | 2 x Pratt & Whitney Hornet B 575 hp (r 9 cl) a.c. | 30.48 | 100 |
| 46 | Fokker F.32 | USA | Fokker Aircraft Co. | CTr | 1929 | 4 x Pratt & Whitney Hornet 575 hp (r 9 cl) a.c. | 30.18 | 99 |
| 46 | Short S.8 Calcutta | GB | Short Brothers Ltd. | CTr | 1928 | 3 x Bristol Jupiter XIF 540 hp (r 9 cl) a.c. | 28.34 | 93 |
| 46 | Handley Page W8b | GB | Handley Page Ltd. | CTr | 1922 | 2 x Rolls-Royce Eagle VIII 360 hp (12 cl) l.c. | 22.86 | 75 |
| 47 | Handley Page H.P.42E | GB | Handley Page Ltd. | CTr | 1930 | 4 x Bristol Jupiter XIF 500 hp (r 9 cl) a.c. | 39.62 | 130 |
| 47 | de Havilland D.H.66 Hercules | GB | The de Havilland Aircraft Co. Ltd. | CTr | 1926 | 3 x Bristol Jupiter VI 420 hp (r 9 cl) a.c. | 24.23 | 79.6 |
| 47 | Armstrong Whitworth A.W. 155 Argosy | GB | Armstrong Whitworth Aircraft Ltd. | CTr | 1926 | 3 x Armstrong Siddeley Jaguar III 385 hp (r 14 cl) a.c. | 27.43 | 90 |
| 47 | Kalinin K-5 | USSR | State Industries | CTr | 1930 | M.15 450 hp (r 9 cl) a.c. | 20.50 | 67.3 |
| 47 | Stinson SM.1 Detroiter | USA | Stinson Aircraft Co. | CTr | 1929 | Wright J-6 300 hp (r 9 cl) a.c. | 14.22 | 46.8 |
| 47 | Sikorsky S.38 | USA | Sikorsky Aircraft | CTr | 1928 | 2 x Pratt & Whitney Wasp 420 hp (r 9 cl) a.c. | 21.84 | 71.8 |
| 47 | Ford Trimotor | USA | Ford Motor Company | CTr | 1926 | 3 x Wright J-6 Whirlwind 300 hp (r 9 cl) a.c. | 22.56 | 74 |
| 47 | Fokker F.III | NL | Fokker | CTr | 1921 | Siddeley Puma 230 hp (6 cl) l.c. | 17.60 | 57.2 |
| 47 | Fokker F.VIIa-3m | NL | Fokker | CTr | 1926 | 3 x Wright Whirlwind 240 hp (r 9 cl) a.c. | 19.30 | 63.4 |
| 47 | Fokker F.VIIb-3m | NL | Fokker | CTr | 1928 | 3 x Wright Whirlwind 300 hp (r 9 cl) a.c. | 21.71 | 71.2 |
| 48 | Navy Curtiss NC-4 | USA | Curtiss Aeroplane and Motor Co. | Rc | 1919 | 4 x Liberty 12 400 hp (12 cl) l.c. | 38.40 | 126 |
| 48 | Douglas DWC/0-5 World Cruiser | USA | Douglas Aircraft Co. | Rp | 1924 | Liberty 12A 420 hp (12 cl V) l.c. | 15.24 | 50 |
| 48 | Vickers Vimy | GB | Vickers Ltd. | Rp | 1918 | 2 x Rolls-Royce Eagle VIII 360 hp (12 cl V) l.c. | 20.73 | 68 |
| 48 | Fairey III C | GB | Fairey Aviation Co. | Rc | 1919 | Rolls-Royce Eagle 350 hp (12 cl V) l.c. | 14.05 | 46 |
| 48 | de Havilland D.H.50-J | GB | de Havilland Aircraft Ltd. | Rp | 1925 | Armstrong Siddeley Jaguar 390 hp (r 14 cl) a.c. | 13.03 | 42.7 |
| 48 | Fokker T.2 | NL | Fokker | Tr | 1921 | Liberty 12-A 420 hp (12 cl V) l.c. | 24.79 | 81.4 |
| 48 | Savoia Marchetti S.16 ter | I | Società Idrovolanti Alta Italia | CTr | 1923 | Lorraine 400 hp (12 cl V) l.c. | 15.50 | 50.9 |
| 48 | S.V.A. 9 | I | Giovanni Ansaldo & C. | Rc | 1918 | S.P.A. 6A 220 hp (6 cl) l.c. | 9.45 | 31 |
| 48 | Dornier Do.J Wal Plus Ultra | D | C.M.A.S.A. | CTr | 1923 | 2 x Rolls-Royce Eagle IX 360 hp (12 cl V) l.c. | 22.50 | 73.8 |
| 49 | Fokker C-2 America | USA | Atlantic Aircraft Corp. | Rp | 1927 | 3 x Wright R-730 Whirlwind 220 hp (r 9 cl) a.c. | 21.70 | 71.2 |
| 49 | Ryan NYP Spirit of St. Louis | USA | Ryan Airlines Inc. | — | 1927 | Wright Whirlwind J-5-C 220 hp (r 9 cl) a.c. | 14.02 | 46 |
| 49 | Bellanca W.B.2 Columbia | USA | Bellanca Aircraft Corp. | Rp | 1927 | Wright Whirlwind J-5 220 hp (r 9 cl) a.c. | 14.12 | 46.4 |
| 49 | Lockheed Vega The Winnie Mae | USA | Lockheed Aircraft Co. | CTr | 1927 | Wright Whirlwind J-5 220 hp (r 9 cl) a.c. | 12.50 | 41 |
| 49 | Junkers W.33 Bremen | D | Junkers Flugzeuge und Motorenwerke AG. | CTr | 1927 | Junkers L.5 310 hp (6 cl) l.c. | 17.75 | 58.2 |
| 49 | Breguet XIX Jesús del Gran Poder | E | Soc. Anon. des Ateliers d'Aviation L. Breguet | — | 1929 | Hispano-Suiza 500 hp | 18.30 | 60 |
| 49 | Short S.5 | GB | Short Brothers | Rc | 1926 | 2 x Rolls-Royce Condor IIIA 650 hp (12 cl V) l.c. | 28.35 | 93 |
| 49 | Fokker FVIIb-3m Southern Cross | NL | Fokker | CTr | 1928 | 3 x Wright Whirlwind 300 hp (r 9 cl) a.c. | 21.71 | 71.2 |
| 49 | SIAI Marchetti S.M. 64 | I | SIAI Marchetti | Rp | 1928 | Fiat A22T 590 hp (12 cl V) l.c. | 21.49 | 70.6 |
| 49 | SIAI Marchetti S.M. 55A | I | SIAI Marchetti | Rp | 1927 | 2 x Isotta-Fraschini 500 hp (12 cl V) l.c. | 24 | 78.9 |
| 49 | SIAI Marchetti S.M. 55X | I | SIAI Marchetti | Rp | 1933 | 2 x Isotta-Fraschini Asso 800 hp (12 cl V) l.c. | 24 | 78.9 |
| 49 | Breguet XIX | F | Société Anonyme des Ateliers d'Aviation L. Breguet | — | 1929 | Lorraine Dietrich 450 hp | 18.30 | 60 |
| 49 | Breguet XIX Super TR Point d'Interrogation | F | Société Anonyme des Ateliers d'Aviation L. Breguet | Rp | 1929 | Hispano-Suiza 12Nb 650 hp (12 cl V) l.c. | 18.30 | 60 |
| 50 | Dayton-Wright R.A. | USA | Dayton-Wright Airplane Corp. | Rp | 1920 | Hall-Scott 250 hp (6 cl) l.c. | 6.45 | 21.2 |
| 50 | Verville VCP-R | USA | Verville | Rp | 1920 | Packard 1A-2025 635 hp (12 cl V) l.c. | 8.38 | 27.6 |
| 50 | Verville Sperry | USA | Verville | Rp | 1924 | Curtiss D-12A 500 hp (12 cl V) l.c. | 9.19 | 30.1 |
| 50 | Thomas-Morse MB-3 | USA | Thomas-Morse Aircraft Co. | Rp | 1920 | Wright H-2 385 hp (8 cl V) l.c. | 7.92 | 26 |
| 50 | Curtiss CR-1 | USA | Curtiss Aeroplane and Motor Co. | Rp | 1921 | Curtiss CD-12 405 hp (12 cl V) l.c. | 6.91 | 22.7 |
| 50 | Curtiss-Cox Cactus Kitten | USA | Curtiss Aeroplane and Motor Co. | Rp | 1921 | Curtiss C-12 435 hp (12 cl V) l.c. | 6.10 | 20 |
| 50 | Curtiss R-6 | USA | Curtiss Aeroplane and Motor Co. | Rp | 1922 | Curtiss D-12 468 hp (12 cl V) l.c. | 5.79 | 19 |
| 50 | Curtiss R2-C1 | USA | Curtiss Aeroplane and Motor Co. | Rp | 1923 | Curtiss D-12A 520 hp (12 cl V) l.c. | 6.70 | 22 |
| 50 | Curtiss CR-3 | USA | Curtiss Aeroplane and Motor Co. | Rp | 1923 | Curtiss D-12 450 hp (12 cl V) l.c. | 6.91 | 22.8 |
| 50 | Curtiss R3C-1 | USA | Curtiss Aeroplane and Motor Co. | Rp | 1925 | Curtiss V-1400 610 hp (12 cl V) l.c. | 6.70 | 22 |
| 50 | Curtiss R3C-2 | USA | Curtiss Aeroplane and Motor Co. | Rp | 1925 | Curtiss V-1400 610 hp (12 cl V) l.c. | 6.71 | 22 |
| 50 | Travel Air Mystery Ship | USA | Travel Air | Rp | 1929 | Wright R-975 400 hp (9 cl) a.c. | 8.89 | 29.2 |
| 50 | Laird LC-DW-300 Solution | USA | Laird | Rp | 1930 | Pratt & Whitney Wasp Jr. 470 hp (r 9 cl) a.c. | 6.40 | 21 |
| 50 | Savoia S.12 bis | I | Idrovolanti Savoia | Rp | 1920 | Ansaldo V-12 500 hp (12 cl V) l.c. | 11.72 | 38.5 |
| 50 | Fiat R700 | I | Fiat S.A. | Rp | 1921 | Fiat A.14 650 hp (12 cl V) l.c. | 10.60 | 34.9 |
| 50 | Macchi M.7 bis | I | Società Aeronautica Nieuport Macchi | Rp | 1921 | Isotta-Fraschini V6bis 280 hp (6 cl) l.c. | 7.75 | 25.5 |
| 50 | Macchi M.39 | I | Aeronautica Macchi | Rp | 1926 | Fiat A.S.2 800 hp (12 cl V) l.c. | 9.26 | 30.4 |
| 52 | Airco D.H.4R | GB | Aircraft Manufacturing Co. | Rp | 1919 | Napier Lion II 450 hp (12 cl W) l.c. | 12.93 | 42.5 |
| 52 | Gloucestershire Mars I Bamel | GB | Gloucestershire Aircraft Ltd. | Rp | 1921 | Napier Lion III 450 hp (12 cl W) l.c. | 6.70 | 22 |
| 52 | Gloucestershire Gloster I | GB | Gloucestershire Aircraft Ltd. | Rp | 1923 | Napier Lion III 480 hp (12 cl W) l.c. | 6.09 | 20 |
| 52 | Martinsyde Semiquaver | GB | Martinsyde Ltd. | Rp | 1920 | Hispano-Suiza 8Fb 320 hp (8 cl V) l.c. | 6.15 | 20.2 |
| 52 | Supermarine Sea Lion III | GB | The Supermarine Aviation Works Ltd. | Rp | 1922 | Napier Lion 450 hp (12 cl W) l.c. | 9.75 | 32 |
| 52 | Supermarine S.5/25 | GB | The Supermarine Aviation Works Ltd. | Rp | 1927 | Napier Lion VIIB 875 hp (12 cl W) l.c. | 7.77 | 25.5 |
| 52 | Nieuport-Delage 42 | F | Société Anonyme des Etablissements Nieuport | Rp | 1924 | Hispano-Suiza 51 545 hp (12 cl V) l.c. | 9.50 | 31.2 |
| 52 | Nieuport-Delage 1921 | F | Société Anonyme des Etablissements Nieuport | Rp | 1921 | Hispano-Suiza 8Fb 320 hp (8 cl V) l.c. | 8 | 26.8 |
| 52 | Nieuport 29V | F | Société Anonyme des Etablissements Nieuport | Rp | 1920 | Hispano-Suiza 8Fb 300 hp (8 cl V) l.c. | 5.46 | 17.9 |
| 52 | Spad S.20bis | F | S.P.A.D. | Rp | 1920 | Hispano-Suiza 8Fb (8 cl V) l.c. | 6.47 | 21.2 |

| Length | | Height | | Take-off weight | | Speed | | Ceiling | | Range | | Crew | Payload/armament |
| --- | --- | --- | --- | --- | --- | --- | --- | --- | --- | --- | --- | --- | --- |
| m | ft | m | ft | kg | lb | km/h | mph | m | ft | km | ml | | |
| 16.50 | 54.1 | 5 | 16.5 | 7,200 | 15,873 | 170 | 106 | 3,800 | 12,467 | 1,100 | 684 | 3 | 9-11 p |
| 8.38 | 27.6 | 2.59 | 8.4 | 1,574 | 3,470 | 190 | 118 | 4,570 | 15,000 | 1,450 | 900 | 1 | 4 p |
| 10.10 | 33.2 | 3.73 | 12.3 | 2,718 | 6,000 | 169 | 105 | 4,420 | 14,500 | 1,046 | 650 | 1 | 2 p; 544 kg (1,200 lb) |
| 17.22 | 56.6 | 4.65 | 15.3 | 7,928 | 17,478 | 201 | 125 | 4,270 | 14,000 | 740 | 460 | 2-3 | 18 p |
| 18.79 | 61.8 | 4.77 | 15.6 | 7,983 | 17,600 | 174 | 108 | 3,430 | 11,253 | 1,610 | 1,000 | 3 | 18-22 p |
| 21.28 | 70.2 | 5.03 | 16.6 | 10,985 | 24,217 | 198 | 123 | 4,115 | 13,500 | 1,191 | 740 | 2 | 32 p |
| 20.34 | 66.7 | 7.24 | 23.9 | 10,190 | 22,465 | 156 | 97 | 4,100 | 13,451 | 1,050 | 652 | 3 | 15 p |
| 18.31 | 60.1 | 5.18 | 17 | 5,346 | 11,984 | 145 | 90 | 3,200 | 10,498 | 644 | 400 | 2 | 12 p |
| 27.36 | 89.7 | 8.23 | 27 | 12,701 | 28,000 | 161 | 100 | — | — | 400 | 249 | 2 | 24 p |
| 16.91 | 55.6 | 5.56 | 18.3 | 7,067 | 15,600 | 177 | 110 | 3,960 | 12,992 | — | — | 3 | 7 p |
| 19.66 | 64.5 | 5.79 | 19 | 8,154 | 17,976 | 145 | 90 | — | — | 650 | 404 | 2 | 20 p |
| 15.87 | 51.6 | — | — | 3,750 | 8,267 | 157 | 98 | 4,780 | 15,680 | 950 | 590 | 2 | 8 p |
| 9.95 | 32.8 | 2.74 | 9 | 1,950 | 4,300 | 182 | 113 | 4,900 | 16,076 | 1,095 | 680 | 1 | 5 p |
| 12.27 | 40.3 | 4.21 | 13.1 | 4,747 | 10,465 | 166 | 103 | 4,877 | 16,000 | 965 | 600 | 2 | 8 p |
| 15.19 | 49.8 | 3.58 | 11.7 | 4,598 | 10,100 | 172 | 107 | 5,030 | 16,502 | 917 | 570 | 2 | 11-14 p |
| 11.07 | 36.7 | 3.58 | 11.7 | 1,900 | 4,188 | 135 | 84 | — | — | 675 | 420 | 1 | 5 p |
| 14.57 | 47.8 | 3.91 | 12.8 | 3,896 | 8,787 | 190 | 118 | — | — | 2,575 | 1,600 | 2 | 8 p |
| 14.50 | 47.7 | 3.90 | 12.8 | 5,000 | 11,023 | 198 | 123 | 6,000 | 19,685 | 1,200 | 745 | 2 | 8-10 p |
| 20.80 | 68.2 | 7.46 | 24.5 | 12,422 | 27,386 | 146 | 91 | 1,372 | 4,501 | 2,366 | 1,470 | 6 | — |
| 10.72 | 35.6 | 4.60 | 15.1 | 3,998 | 8,814 | 161 | 100 | 2,134 | 7,000 | 3,540 | 2,200 | 2 | — |
| 13.27 | 43.5 | 4.57 | 15 | 5,670 | 12,500 | 165 | 102 | 2,134 | 7,000 | 1,450 | 901 | 3 | — |
| 10.97 | 36 | 3.70 | 12.1 | 2,290 | 5,049 | 162 | 101 | 2,775 | 9,104 | 5h | — | 2 | — |
| 9.07 | 29.8 | 3.35 | 11 | 1,770 | 3,902 | 180 | 112 | 4,550 | 14,928 | — | — | 1 | — |
| 14.79 | 49.1 | 3.60 | 11.8 | 4,880 | 10,759 | 155 | 96 | — | — | — | — | 2 | 10 p |
| 13.50 | 44.3 | 3.66 | 12 | 2,652 | 5,732 | 175 | 109 | 3,000 | 9,845 | 1,000 | 621 | 1 | 4 p |
| 8.10 | 26.6 | 2.92 | 9.6 | 1,040 | 2,293 | 219 | 136 | 5,000 | 16,405 | 4h | — | 2 | — |
| 17.25 | 56.7 | 5.20 | 17 | 5,700 | 12,566 | 140 | 87 | 3,500 | 11,480 | 2,200 | 1,350 | 2 | 8-14 p |
| 14.80 | 48.6 | 3.69 | 12.1 | 3,360 | 7,408 | 177 | 110 | 5,000 | 16,405 | — | — | 3 | — |
| 8.36 | 27.5 | 2.44 | 8 | 2,379 | 5,245 | 180 | 112 | 5,000 | 16,405 | 6,600 | 4,100 | 1 | — |
| 8.23 | 27 | 2.57 | 8.5 | 2,450 | 5,400 | 170 | 105 | 3,960 | 12,990 | — | — | 2 | — |
| 8.38 | 27.6 | 2.59 | 8.5 | 1,574 | 3,470 | 190 | 118 | 4,570 | 15,000 | 1,450 | 900 | 1 | 4 p |
| 10.50 | 34.5 | 3.56 | 11.8 | 2,500 | 5,511 | 150 | 93 | 4,300 | 14,100 | 1,000 | 621 | 2-3 | 6 p |
| 10.72 | 35.1 | 4.06 | 13.3 | 6,700 | 14,771 | 245 | 152 | 6,700 | 21,981 | 9,500 | 5,903 | 2 | — |
| 19.96 | 65.4 | — | — | 9,525 | 20,999 | 206 | 128 | — | — | — | — | 6 | — |
| 14.50 | 47.7 | 3.90 | 12.8 | 5,000 | 11,023 | 198 | 123 | 6,000 | 19,685 | 1,200 | 745 | 2 | 8-10 p |
| 8.99 | 29.6 | 3.68 | 12.1 | 7,000 | 15,432 | 235 | 146 | — | — | 11,505 | 7,148 | 2-3 | — |
| 16.50 | 54.1 | 5 | 16.5 | 6,506 | 14,341 | 165 | 103 | 3,000 | 9,845 | 1,000 | 621 | 4 | 1,770 kg (3,750 lb) |
| 16.50 | 54.1 | 5 | 16.5 | 10,000 | 22,000 | 240 | 149 | 5,000 | 16,405 | 4,000 | 2,400 | 4 | 5,000 kg (11,000 lb) |
| 10.72 | 35.1 | 4.06 | 13.3 | 6,700 | 14,771 | 245 | 152 | 6,700 | 21,981 | 9,500 | 5,903 | 2 | — |
| 10.72 | 35.1 | 4.06 | 13.3 | 6,700 | 14,771 | 245 | 152 | 6,700 | 21,981 | 9,500 | 5,903 | 2 | — |
| 6.91 | 22.8 | 2.44 | 8 | 839 | 1,850 | 322 | 200 | — | — | — | — | 1 | — |
| 7.36 | 24.2 | 2.64 | 8.8 | 1,451 | 3,200 | 299 | 186 | — | — | 300 | 186 | 1 | — |
| 7.16 | 23.6 | 2.16 | 7.1 | 1,124 | 2,478 | 378 | 235 | 6,980 | 22,900 | — | — | 1 | — |
| 6.10 | 20 | 2.56 | 8.5 | 950 | 2,095 | 264 | 164 | 5,945 | 19,500 | 790 | 491 | 1 | — |
| 6.40 | 21 | 2.44 | 8 | 982 | 2,165 | 322 | 200 | 7,315 | 24,000 | 378 | 235 | 1 | — |
| 5.87 | 19.3 | 2.59 | 8.5 | 1,091 | 2,405 | 306 | 190 | — | — | — | — | 1 | — |
| 5.74 | 18.8 | 2.31 | 7.6 | 962 | 2,121 | 386 | 240 | — | — | 455 | 283 | 1 | — |
| 6.02 | 19.8 | 2.06 | 6.8 | 963 | 2,123 | 428 | 266 | 9,700 | 31,800 | 192 | 119 | 1 | — |
| 7.63 | 25 | 3.15 | 10.3 | 1,246 | 2,746 | 314 | 195 | 5,852 | 19,200 | 840 | 522 | 1 | — |
| 6.12 | 20 | 2.06 | 6.9 | 989 | 2,180 | 458 | 285 | 8,050 | 26,410 | 299 | 142 | 1 | — |
| 6.15 | 20.2 | 3.15 | 10.3 | 1,242 | 2,738 | 426 | 264 | 8,047 | 26,400 | 402 | 250 | 1 | — |
| 6.15 | 20.2 | 2.67 | 8.7 | 879 | 1,940 | 336 | 209 | — | — | 845 | 525 | 1 | — |
| 5.94 | 19.6 | — | — | 860 | 1,985 | 325 | 202 | — | — | — | — | 1 | — |
| 9.95 | 32.8 | 3.81 | 12.5 | 1,740 | 3,836 | 222 | 138 | — | — | — | — | 1 | — |
| 7.85 | 25.9 | 2.90 | 9.6 | 2,250 | 4,960 | 336 | 209 | — | — | 430 | 267 | 1 | — |
| 6.78 | 22.3 | 2.99 | 9.9 | 1,030 | 2,270 | 257 | 160 | 6,500 | 21,325 | 770 | 478 | 1 | — |
| 6.73 | 22.1 | 3.06 | 10 | 1,575 | 3,472 | 416 | 259 | — | — | — | — | 1 | — |
| 8.65 | 28 | 3.55 | 11.6 | 1,447 | 3,191 | 241 | 150 | — | — | — | — | 1 | — |
| 7.01 | 23 | 2.84 | 9.4 | 1,134 | 2,500 | 325 | 202 | — | — | — | — | 1 | — |
| 7.01 | 23 | 2.84 | 9.4 | 1,202 | 2,650 | 354 | 220 | — | — | — | — | 1 | — |
| 5.86 | 19.3 | 2.17 | 7.2 | 919 | 2,026 | 260 | 165 | — | — | — | — | 1 | — |
| 7.54 | 24.9 | — | — | 1,291 | 2,850 | 257 | 160 | — | — | 3h | — | 1 | — |
| 7.06 | 23.1 | 3.38 | 11.1 | 1,474 | 3,242 | 499 | 310 | — | — | — | — | 1 | — |
| 7.30 | 23.9 | 2.50 | 8.2 | 1,440 | 3,174 | 312 | 194 | — | — | — | — | 1 | — |
| 6.10 | 20 | 2.02 | 6.7 | 1,014 | 2,236 | 375 | 233 | — | — | 560 | 349 | 1 | — |
| 6.20 | 20.4 | 2.50 | 8.2 | 936 | 2,063 | 302 | 188 | — | — | — | — | 1 | — |
| 7.18 | 23.6 | 2.50 | 8.2 | 1,050 | 2,315 | 309 | 192 | — | — | — | — | 1 | — |

# Technical Data

| Page | Aircraft | Nation | Manufacturer | Type | Year | Engine | Wingspan m | ft |
|---|---|---|---|---|---|---|---|---|
| 52 | Breguet XIX Super TR | F | Société Anonyme des Ateliers d'Aviation L. Breguet | Rp | 1929 | Hispano-Suiza 12Nb 650 hp (12 cl V) l.c. | 18.30 | 60 |
| 52 | Blériot 110 | F | Blériot Aéronautique | Rp | 1930 | Hispano-Suiza 600 hp (12 cl V) l.c. | 26.50 | 86.9 |
| 53 | Nieuport-Delage NiD.29 | F | Société Anonyme des Etablissements Nieuport | Fr | 1922 | Hispano-Suiza 8FB 300 hp (8 cl V) l.c. | 9.70 | 31.8 |
| 53 | Blériot-Spad 51 | F | Blériot Aéronautique | Fr | 1924 | Gnome-Rhône Jupiter 380 hp (r 9 cl) a.c. | 9.47 | 31.1 |
| 53 | Wibault 72C1 | F | Chantiers Aéronautiques Wibault | Fr | 1926 | Gnome-Rhône Jupiter 9Ac 420 hp (r 9 cl) a.c. | 10.95 | 35.9 |
| 53 | Loire-Gourdou-Leseurre LGL32 C.1 | F | Loire-Gourdou-Leseurre | Fr | 1927 | Gnome-Rhône Jupiter 9Ac 420 hp (r 9 cl) a.c. | 12.20 | 40 |
| 53 | Fiat C.R.1 | I | Fiat S.A. | Fr | 1924 | Hispano-Suiza 300 hp l.c. | 8.95 | 29.4 |
| 53 | Fiat C.R. 20 | I | Fiat S.A. | Fr | 1926 | Isotta-Fraschini Asso 450 hp (12 cl V) a.c. | 9.80 | 32.2 |
| 53 | Macchi M.41 bis | I | Aeronautica Macchi | Fr | 1929 | Fiat A.20 420 hp (12 cl V) l.c. | 11.12 | 36.6 |
| 53 | Boeing PW-9C | USA | Boeing Airplane Co. | Fr | 1926 | Curtiss D-12 435 hp (12 cl V) l.c. | 9.75 | 32 |
| 53 | Boeing FB-5 | USA | Boeing Airplane Co. | Fr | 1927 | Packard 2A-1500 520 hp (12 cl V) l.c. | 9.75 | 32 |
| 53 | Boeing F3B-1 | USA | Boeing Airplane Co. | Fr | 1928 | Pratt & Whitney Wasp 425 hp (r 9 cl) a.c. | 10.06 | 33 |
| 53 | Fokker D.XIII | NL | Fokker | Fr | 1925 | Napier Lion XI 450 hp (12 cl W) l.c. | 11 | 36.1 |
| 53 | Mitsubishi 1MF1 | J | Mitsubishi Jukogyo K.K. | Fr | 1923 | Hispano-Mitsubishi 300 hp (8 cl V) l.c. | 9.30 | 30.6 |
| 53 | Gloster Grebe Mk II | GB | Gloucestershire Aircraft Co. | Fr | 1924 | Armstrong Siddeley Jaguar IV 400 hp (r 14 cl) a.c. | 8.94 | 29.4 |
| 53 | Fairey Flycatcher | GB | Fairey Aviation Co. | Fr | 1923 | Armstrong Siddeley Jaguar III 400 hp (r 14 cl) a.c. | 8.84 | 29 |
| 53 | Hawker Woodcock Mk II | GB | H. G. Hawker Engineering Co. | Fr | 1925 | Bristol Jupiter IV 420 hp (r 9 cl) a.c. | 9.91 | 32.6 |
| 53 | Gloster Gamecock Mk.I | GB | Gloucestershire Aircraft Co. | Fr | 1926 | Bristol Jupiter VI 425 hp (r 9 cl) a.c. | 9.08 | 29.9 |
| 53 | Armstrong Whitworth Siskin Mk.IIIA | GB | Armstrong Whitworth Aircraft Ltd. | Fr | 1927 | Armstrong Siddeley Jaguar IV 425 hp (r 14 cl) a.c. | 10.11 | 33.2 |
| 53 | Bristol Bulldog Mk.IIA | GB | Bristol Aeroplane Co. | Fr | 1929 | Bristol Jupiter VIIF 490 hp (r 9 cl) a.c. | 10.33 | 33.9 |
| 54 | Lioré et Olivier LeO 20 Bn3 | F | Etablissements Lioré et Olivier | Br | 1928 | 2 x Gnome-Rhône 9 Ady 420 hp (r 9 cl) a.c. | 22.25 | 73 |
| 54 | Martin T4M | USA | Glenn L. Martin Co. | TB | 1928 | Pratt & Whitney R-1960-24 Hornet 525 hp (r 9 cl) a.c. | 16.15 | 53 |
| 54 | Caproni Ca.101 | I | Società Italiana Caproni | Br | 1930 | 3 x Alfa Romeo D.2 270 hp (r 9 cl) a.c. | 19.68 | 64.6 |
| 54 | Boulton Paul Sidestrand Mk.III | GB | Boulton Paul Aircraft Ltd. | Br | 1928 | 2 x Bristol Jupiter VIIIF 460 hp (r 9 cl) a.c. | 21.92 | 71.9 |
| 54 | Hawker Horseley | GB | H. G. Hawker Engineering Co. Ltd. | Br | 1927 | Rolls-Royce Condor IIIA 665 hp (12 cl V) l.c. | 17.22 | 56.6 |
| 54 | Hawker Hart | GB | H. G. Hawker Engineering Co. Ltd. | Br | 1930 | Rolls-Royce Kestrel IB 525 hp (12 cl V) l.c. | 11.35 | 37.3 |
| 54 | Fairey Fox Mk.I | GB | Fairey Aviation Co. Ltd. | Br | 1926 | Curtiss D.12 480 hp (12 cl V) l.c. | 11.58 | 38 |
| 54 | Fairey Gordon Mk.I | GB | Fairey Aviation Co. Ltd. | Br | 1930 | Armstrong Siddeley Panther IIA 525 hp (14 cl) a.c. | 13.94 | 45.9 |
| 54 | Handley Page Hinaidi Mk.II | GB | Handley Page Ltd. | Br | 1929 | 2 x Bristol Jupiter VIII 440 hp (r 9 cl) a.c. | 22.86 | 75 |
| 54 | Blackburn Ripon Mk.II | GB | Blackburn Aeroplane and Motor Co. Ltd. | TB | 1929 | Napier Lion XIA 570 hp (12 cl W) l.c. | 13.66 | 40.8 |
| 54 | Blackburn Dart Mk.II | GB | Blackburn Aeroplane and Motor Co. Ltd. | TB | 1923 | Napier Lion IIB 450 hp (12 cl V) l.c. | 13.86 | 45.6 |
| 55 | Kawasaki Tipo 88 | J | Kawasaki Kokuki Kogyo K.K. | Rc | 1928 | B.M.W. - Kawasaki 500 hp (12 cl V) l.c. | 15.20 | 49.8 |
| 55 | Consolidated PT-3 | USA | Consolidated Aircraft Co. | T | 1928 | Wright R-790 220 hp (r 9 cl) a.c. | 10.52 | 34.6 |
| 55 | Fokker CV-D | NL | Fokker | Rc | 1926 | Bristol Jupiter 450 hp (r 9 cl) a.c. | 12.50 | 41 |
| 55 | Polikarpov Po-2 | USSR | State Industries | T | 1928 | M.11 110 hp (r 5 cl) a.c. | 11.50 | 37.5 |
| 55 | Breda Ba.25 | I | Società Italiana Ernesto Breda | T | 1930 | Alfa Romeo Lynx 220 hp (r 7 cl) a.c. | 10 | 32.8 |
| 55 | Fairey III D | GB | Fairey Aviation Co. Ltd. | Br/Rc | 1924 | Napier Lion IIB 450 hp (12 cl W) l.c. | 14.05 | 46.1 |
| 55 | Avro-Bison Mk.II | GB | A.V. Roe & Co. Ltd. | Rc | 1923 | Napier Lion 480 hp (12 cl W) l.c. | 14.02 | 46 |
| 55 | Armstrong Whitworth Atlas | GB | Armstrong Whitworth Aircraft Ltd. | Rc | 1927 | Armstrong Siddeley Jaguar IV 450 hp (14 cl) a.c. | 12.04 | 39.6 |
| 55 | Blackburn Iris Mk.III | GB | Blackburn Aeroplane and Motor Co. | Rc | 1930 | 3 x Rolls-Royce Condor IIIB 675 hp (12 cl V) l.c. | 29.57 | 97 |
| 60 | Airspeed A.S.5A Courier | GB | Airspeed Ltd. | LT | 1933 | Armstrong Siddeley Lynx IVC 240 hp (r 7 cl) a.c. | 14.33 | 47 |
| 60 | Airspeed A.S.6 Envoy II | GB | Airspeed Ltd. | LT | 1934 | 2 x Armstrong Siddeley Lynx IV-C 220 hp (r 7 cl) a.c. | 15.95 | 52.4 |
| 60 | Airspeed A.S.40 Oxford | GB | Airspeed Ltd. | LT | 1937 | 2 x Armstrong Siddeley Cheetah X 370 hp (r 7 cl) a.c. | 16.25 | 53.4 |
| 60 | de Havilland D.H.82A Tiger Moth | GB | de Havilland Aircraft Co. | T | 1931 | de Havilland Gipsy Major 190 hp (4 cl) a.c. | 8.94 | 29.4 |
| 60 | de Havilland D.H.84 Dragon | GB | de Havilland Aircraft Ltd. | CTr | 1933 | 2 x de Havilland Gipsy Major 130 hp (4 cl) a.c. | 14.42 | 47.4 |
| 60 | de Havilland D.H. 86 | GB | de Havilland Aircraft Ltd. | CTr | 1934 | 4 x de Havilland Gipsy Six I 200 hp (6 cl) a.c. | 19.66 | 64.6 |
| 60 | de Havilland D.H. 89 Dragon Rapide | GB | de Havilland Aircraft Ltd. | CTr | 1934 | 2 x de Havilland Gipsy Six I 200 hp (6 cl) a.c. | 14.63 | 48 |
| 60 | de Havilland D.H. 95 Flamingo | GB | de Havilland Aircraft Co. Ltd. | CTr | 1938 | 2 x Bristol Perseus XVI 930 hp (9 cl) a.c. | 21.33 | 70 |
| 60 | de Havilland D.H.91 Albatross | GB | de Havilland Aircraft Co. Ltd. | CTr | 1937 | 4 x de Havilland Gipsy Twelve I 525 hp (12 cl V) a.c. | 32 | 104.9 |
| 60 | Armstrong Whitworth A.W.15 Atalanta | GB | Armstrong Whitworth Ltd. | CTr | 1932 | 4 x Armstrong Siddeley Serval III 340 hp (r 10 cl) a.c. | 27.43 | 90 |
| 61 | Armstrong Whitworth A.W.27 Ensign | GB | Armstrong Whitworth Aircraft Ltd. | CTr | 1938 | 4 x Armstrong Siddeley Tiger IX 850 hp (r 14 cl) a.c. | 37.49 | 123 |
| 61 | Short S.16 Sion | GB | Short Brothers Ltd. | LT | 1935 | 2 x Pobjov Niagara III 90 hp (r 7 cl) a.c. | 12.80 | 42 |
| 61 | Short Mayo S.20/S.21 Composite | GB | Short Brothers Ltd. | CTr | 1938 | — | — | — |
| 61 | Short S.23 | GB | Short Brothers Ltd. | CTr | 1936 | 4 x Bristol Pegasus XC 920 hp (r 9 cl) a.c. | 34.74 | 114 |
| 61 | Short S.26 | GB | Short Brothers Ltd. | CTr | 1939 | 4 x Bristol Hercules IV 1380 hp (r 14 cl) a.c. | 40.95 | 134.4 |
| 64 | Potez 56 | F | Société des Aéroplanes Henry Potez | CTr | 1934 | 2 x Potez 9Ab 185 hp (r 9 cl) a.c. | 16 | 52.6 |
| 64 | Wibault 283T | F | Chantiers Aéronautiques Wibault | CTr | 1934 | 3 x Gnome-Rhône Titany Major 7Kd 350 hp (r 7 cl) a.c. | 22.60 | 74.2 |
| 64 | Bloch 120 | F | Avions Marcel Bloch | CTr | 1934 | 3 x Lorraine Algol 9Na 300 hp (r 9 cl) a.c. | 20.54 | 67.4 |
| 64 | Bloch 220 | F | Avions Marcel Bloch | CTr | 1935 | 2 x Gnome-Rhône 14N16 915 hp (r 14 cl) a.c. | 22.82 | 74.9 |
| 64 | Dewoitine D.338 | F | Société Aéronautique Française | CTr | 1935 | 3 x Hispano-Suiza 9V 16/17 650 hp (r 9 cl) a.c. | 29.35 | 96.3 |
| 64 | RWD-13 | PL | Doswiadczalne Warsztaty Lotnicze | LT | 1935 | Walter Major 130 hp (4 cl) a.c. | 11.50 | 37.9 |
| 64 | PZL-44 Wicher | PL | Pantswowe Zakiady Lotnicze | CTr | 1938 | 2 x Wright GR-1820-G2 Cyclone 1000 hp (r 9 cl) a.c. | 23.80 | 78.1 |
| 65 | Caudron C-445 Goéland | F | Société Anonyme des Avions Caudron | CTr | 1935 | 2 x Renault 6Q-01 Bengali 220 hp (6 cl) a.c. | 17.60 | 57.9 |

| Length | | Height | | Take-off weight | | Speed | | Ceiling | | Range | | Crew | Payload/armament |
|---|---|---|---|---|---|---|---|---|---|---|---|---|---|
| m | ft | m | ft | kg | lb | km/h | mph | m | ft | km | ml | | |
| 10.72 | 35.1 | 4.06 | 13.3 | 6,700 | 14,771 | 245 | 152 | 6,700 | 21,981 | 9,500 | 5,903 | 2 | — |
| 14.57 | 47.9 | 4.90 | 16.1 | 7,250 | 15,980 | 210 | 130 | — | — | 10,601 | 6,588 | 2 | — |
| 6.50 | 21.4 | 2.50 | 8.2 | 1,192 | 2,628 | 213 | 132 | 7,700 | 25,260 | 580 | 360 | 1 | 2 mg |
| 6.45 | 21.2 | 3.10 | 10.2 | 1,631 | 3,595 | 231 | 143 | 9,000 | 29,530 | — | — | 1 | 2 mg |
| 7.45 | 24.5 | 2.96 | 9.8 | 1,444 | 3,183 | 227 | 141 | 8,100 | 26,575 | 600 | 373 | 1 | 2 mg |
| 7.55 | 24.9 | 2.95 | 9.1 | 1,376 | 3,033 | 237 | 147 | 8,750 | 28,700 | 500 | 310 | 1 | 4 mg |
| 6.24 | 20.6 | 2.40 | 7.8 | 1,155 | 2,546 | 270 | 168 | 7,450 | 24,440 | 650 | 405 | 1 | 2 mg |
| 6.71 | 22 | 2.79 | 9.2 | 1,480 | 3,263 | 275 | 171 | 7,500 | 24,606 | 750 | 460 | 1 | 2 mg |
| 8.66 | 28.5 | 3.12 | 10.3 | 1,600 | 3,257 | 256 | 159 | 7,500 | 24,606 | 700 | 435 | 1 | 2 mg; b (60 kg - 132 lb) |
| 7.04 | 23.1 | 2.64 | 8.8 | 1,438 | 3,170 | 265 | 165 | 6,150 | 20,175 | 2h35' | — | 1 | 2 mg |
| 7.14 | 23.5 | 2.49 | 8.2 | 1,286 | 2,835 | 256 | 159 | 5,770 | 18,925 | 628 | 390 | 1 | 2 mg |
| 7.57 | 24.9 | 2.79 | 9.2 | 1,336 | 2,945 | 253 | 157 | 6,550 | 21,500 | 547 | 340 | 1 | 2 mg |
| 7.90 | 25.9 | 2.90 | 9.6 | 1,610 | 3,549 | 265 | 164 | 8,000 | 26,246 | 600 | 373 | 1 | 2 mg |
| 6.71 | 22 | 2.95 | 9.8 | 1,140 | 2,510 | 237 | 147 | 7,000 | 22,965 | 2h30' | — | 1 | 2 mg |
| 6.17 | 20.3 | 2.82 | 9.3 | 1,185 | 2,614 | 252 | 157 | 7,000 | 22,965 | 2h45' | — | 1 | 2 mg |
| 7.01 | 23 | 3.45 | 11.3 | 1,350 | 2,976 | 214 | 133 | 5,800 | 19,029 | 420 | 260 | 1 | 2 mg; b (36 kg - 80 lb) |
| 7.98 | 26.2 | 3.02 | 9.9 | 1,351 | 2,979 | 222 | 138 | 6,100 | 20,000 | 435 | 270 | 1 | 2 mg |
| 5.99 | 19.8 | 2.94 | 9.8 | 1,299 | 2,863 | 249 | 155 | 6,700 | 22,000 | 587 | 365 | 1 | 2 mg |
| 7.72 | 25.4 | 3.10 | 10.2 | 1,366 | 3,012 | 251 | 156 | 8,230 | 27,000 | 450 | 280 | 1 | 2 mg |
| 7.62 | 25.2 | 2.99 | 9.8 | 1,587 | 3,503 | 280 | 174 | 8,230 | 27,000 | 440 | 274 | 1 | 2 mg; b (36 kg - 80 lb) |
| 13.87 | 45.4 | 5.05 | 16.7 | 5,300 | 11,684 | 200 | 124 | 5,750 | 18,865 | 1,000 | 621 | 4-5 | 4 mg; b (1,040 kg - 2,300 lb) |
| 10.85 | 35.7 | 4.50 | 14.9 | 3,661 | 8,071 | 183 | 114 | 3,095 | 10,150 | 583 | 363 | 3 | 2 mg; 1 t |
| 13.80 | 45.3 | 3.89 | 12.7 | 4,975 | 10,968 | 165 | 102 | 6,100 | 20,000 | 1,000 | 621 | 3 | 2-3 mg; b (500 kg - 1,100 lb) |
| 14.05 | 46 | 4.52 | 14.8 | 4,626 | 10,200 | 225 | 140 | 7,315 | 24,000 | 805 | 500 | 4 | 3 mg; b (476 kg - 1,050 lb) |
| 11.84 | 38.8 | 4.16 | 13.8 | 3,538 | 7,800 | 203 | 126 | 4,270 | 14,000 | 10h | — | 2 | 2 mg; b (272 kg - 600 lb) |
| 8.94 | 29.4 | 3.17 | 10.5 | 2,063 | 4,554 | 296 | 184 | 6,500 | 21,300 | 756 | 470 | 2 | 2 mg; b (226 kg - 500 lb) |
| 9.50 | 31.2 | 3.25 | 10.8 | 1,867 | 4,117 | 251 | 156 | 5,180 | 17,000 | 805 | 500 | 2 | 2 mg; b (208 kg - 460 lb) |
| 11.17 | 36.8 | 4.31 | 14.2 | 2,675 | 5,900 | 233 | 143 | 6,700 | 22,000 | 965 | 600 | 2 | 2 mg; b (208 kg - 460 lb) |
| 18.03 | 59.2 | 5.18 | 17 | 6,568 | 14,480 | 197 | 122 | 4,419 | 14,498 | 1,370 | 850 | 4 | 3 mg; b (656 kg - 1,446 lb) |
| 10.97 | 36.9 | 4.06 | 13.4 | 3,359 | 7,405 | 203 | 126 | 3,050 | 10,000 | 1,310 | 815 | 2 | 2 mg; 1 t |
| 10.77 | 35.4 | 3.94 | 12.9 | 2,895 | 6,370 | 172 | 107 | 3,870 | 12,700 | 460 | 285 | 1 | 1 t |
| 12.28 | 40.3 | 3.40 | 11.2 | 3,100 | 6,800 | 210 | 130 | 5,200 | 17,000 | 5h | — | 2 | 2-3 mg; b (200 kg - 440 lb) |
| 8.50 | 27.9 | 3.02 | 9.9 | 1,192 | 2,627 | 157 | 98 | 4,630 | 15,200 | 482 | 300 | 2 | — |
| 9.55 | 31.4 | 3.50 | 11.6 | 1,915 | 4,222 | 322 | 200 | 6,000 | 19,600 | 1,200 | 740 | 2 | 2 mg |
| 8.15 | 26.9 | 3.02 | 9.9 | 981 | 2,167 | 146 | 93 | 4,000 | 13,120 | 430 | 267 | 2 | 1 mg; b (250 kg - 550 lb) |
| 8 | 26.3 | 2.90 | 9.6 | 1,000 | 2,204 | 205 | 127 | 4,900 | 16,075 | 400 | 248 | 2 | — |
| 11.28 | 37 | 3.45 | 11.4 | 2,231 | 4,918 | 171 | 105 | 5,180 | 17,000 | 885 | 550 | 3 | 2 mg |
| 10.97 | 36 | 4.32 | 14.2 | 2,781 | 6,132 | 177 | 110 | 3,660 | 12,000 | 580 | 360 | 3-4 | 2 mg |
| 8.68 | 28.6 | 3.20 | 10.6 | 1,823 | 4,018 | 229 | 142 | 5,120 | 16,800 | 770 | 480 | 2 | 2 mg; b (137 kg - 302 lb) |
| 20.54 | 67.5 | 7.77 | 25.6 | 13,154 | 29,000 | 190 | 118 | 3,050 | 10,000 | 756 | 470 | 5 | 3 mg; b (907 kg - 2,000 lb) |
| 8.69 | 28.6 | 2.67 | 8.9 | 1,769 | 3,900 | 212 | 132 | 4,115 | 13,500 | 1,020 | 634 | 1 | 5 p |
| 10.52 | 34.6 | 2.90 | 9.6 | 2,645 | 5,831 | 246 | 153 | 5,030 | 16,502 | 1,045 | 650 | 1 | 6-8 p |
| 10.51 | 34.6 | 3.38 | 11.1 | 3,447 | 7,600 | 266 | 166 | 5,790 | 18,996 | 1,450 | 900 | 1-2 | 4 p |
| 7.29 | 23.9 | 2.66 | 8.9 | 826 | 1,825 | 176 | 109 | 5,180 | 16,994 | 483 | 300 | 2 | — |
| 10.51 | 34.6 | 3.07 | 10.1 | 1,902 | 4,200 | 175 | 109 | 3,810 | 12,500 | 740 | 460 | 1 | 6 p; 122 kg (269 lb) |
| 13.38 | 43.9 | 3.96 | 13 | 4,170 | 9,132 | 233 | 145 | 6,250 | 20,500 | 725 | 450 | 2 | 10 p |
| 10.52 | 34.6 | 3.12 | 10.3 | 2,495 | 5,500 | 214 | 133 | 5,090 | 16,699 | 930 | 578 | 1 | 6-8 p |
| 15.72 | 51.7 | 4.65 | 15.3 | 7,983 | 17,599 | 296 | 184 | 6,370 | 20,900 | 1,950 | 1,212 | 3 | 12-17 p |
| 21.79 | 71.5 | 6.78 | 22.2 | 13,381 | 29,500 | 338 | 210 | 5,455 | 17,900 | 1,670 | 1,040 | 4 | 22 p |
| 21.79 | 71.5 | 4.57 | 15 | 9,525 | 21,000 | 209 | 130 | 2,135 | 7,004 | 645 | 400 | 2 | 17 p |
| 34.75 | 114 | 7.01 | 23 | 22,226 | 49,000 | 274 | 170 | 5,500 | 18,044 | 1,290 | 802 | 4 | 27-40 p |
| 9.60 | 31.6 | 3.15 | 10.4 | 1,452 | 3,200 | 187 | 116 | 3,960 | 13,000 | 628 | 390 | 1 | 6 p |
| — | — | — | — | 22,000 | 48,502 | 314 | 195 | — | — | 6,276 | 3,900 | — | 450 kg (922 lb) |
| 26.82 | 88 | 9.72 | 31.9 | 18,371 | 40,500 | 265 | 164 | 6,100 | 20,000 | 1,225 | 760 | 5 | 24 p |
| 30.89 | 101.4 | 11.46 | 37.6 | 33,340 | 73,502 | 290 | 180 | 6,100 | 20,000 | 5,150 | 3,200 | 5-7 | 40 p |
| 11.84 | 38.8 | — | — | 2,980 | 6,569 | 250 | 155 | 6,000 | 19,685 | 1,100 | 683 | 2 | 6 p |
| 16.99 | 55.9 | — | — | 6,342 | 13,981 | 230 | 143 | 5,200 | 17,060 | 1,050 | 652 | 2 | 10 p |
| 15.30 | 50.2 | — | — | 6,000 | 13,227 | 230 | 143 | 6,300 | 20,670 | — | — | 3 | 3-4 p; 800 kg (1,760 lb) |
| 19.25 | 63.1 | 3.90 | 12.9 | 9,500 | 20,943 | 280 | 174 | 7,000 | 22,965 | 1,400 | 870 | 4 | 16 p |
| 22.13 | 72.7 | 5.57 | 2.75 | 11,150 | 24,581 | 260 | 162 | 4,900 | 16,075 | 1,950 | 1,210 | 3 | 22 p |
| 7.85 | 25.9 | 2.05 | 6.9 | 930 | 2.050 | 180 | 112 | 4,200 | 13,800 | 900 | 560 | 1 | 2 p |
| 18.45 | 60.6 | 4.80 | 15.9 | 9,500 | 20,943 | 280 | 174 | 6,850 | 22,850 | 1,840 | 1,144 | 3-4 | 14 p |
| 13.80 | 45.3 | 3.50 | 11.6 | 3,500 | 7,716 | 260 | 162 | 5,600 | 18,370 | 560 | 348 | 2 | 6 p |

# Technical Data

| Page | Aircraft | Nation | Manufacturer | Type | Year | Engine | Wingspan m | Wingspan ft |
|------|----------|--------|--------------|------|------|--------|------------|-------------|
| 65 | Caudron-Renault C-635 Simoun | F | Société Anonyme des Avions Caudron | LT | 1934 | Renault 6 Pri Bengali 180 hp (6 cl) a.c. | 10.40 | 34.1 |
| 65 | Blériot 5190 Santos-Dumont | F | Blériot Aéronautique | CTr | 1934 | 4 x Hispano-Suiza 12Nbr 650 hp (12 cl V) l.c. | 43 | 141.1 |
| 65 | Lioré et Olivier LeO H-47 | F | SNCASE | CTr | 1936 | 4 x Hispano-Suiza 12Ydrs 880 hp (12 cl V) l.c. | 31.80 | 104.4 |
| 65 | Breguet 530 Saigon | F | Société Anonyme des Ateliers d'Aviation L. Breguet | CTr | 1934 | 3 x Hispano-Suiza 12Ybr 785 hp (12 cl V) l.c. | 35.06 | 115 |
| 65 | Air Couzinet 10 | F | Société des Avions René Couzinet | Rp | 1937 | 2 x Hispano-Suiza 9V16 606 hp (r 9 cl) a.c. | 18 | 59 |
| 65 | Mignet M.H.14 Pou du Ciel | F | Société des Aeronefs Mignet | — | 1933 | Aubier & Dunne 22 hp (2 cl) a.c. | 5.18 | 17 |
| 65 | Latécoère 300 | F | Forges et Ateliers de Construction Latécoère | CTr | 1932 | 4 x Hispano-Suiza 12Nbr 650 hp (12 cl V) l.c. | 44.19 | 145 |
| 65 | Latécoère 521 | F | Forges et Ateliers de Construction Latécoère | CTr | 1935 | 6 x Hispano-Suiza 12Ybrs 860 hp (12 cl V) l.c. | 49.31 | 161.9 |
| 66 | Mitsubishi Hinazuru | J | Mitsubishi Jukogyo K.K. | CTr | 1934 | 2 x Mitsubishi Lynx-IV-C 240 hp (r 7 cl) a.c. | 15.95 | 52.4 |
| 66 | Mitsubishi G3M2 | J | Mitsubishi Jukogyo K.K. | CTr | 1938 | 2 x Mitsubishi Kinsel 41 1075 hp (r 14 cl) a.c. | 25 | 82 |
| 66 | Nakajima AT-2 | J | Nakajima Hikoki K.K. | CTr | 1936 | 2 x Nakajima Kotobuki 41 710 hp (r 9 cl) a.c. | 19.91 | 65.4 |
| 66 | Noorduyn Norseman IV | CDN | Noorduyn Aviation Ltd. | CTr | 1937 | Pratt & Whitney R-1340-S3H1 Wasp 600 hp (r 9 cl) a.c. | 15.75 | 56.1 |
| 66 | Aero 204 | CS | Aero Tovarna Letadel | CTr | 1937 | 2 x Walter Pollux IIR 360 hp (r 9 cl) a.c. | 19 | 62.4 |
| 66 | Icar Commercial | R | ICAR | CTr | 1934 | Armstrong Siddeley Serval Mk.I 940 hp (r 9 cl) a.c. | 15.40 | 50.6 |
| 66 | IAR 23 | R | Industria Aeronautica Romena | Rp | 1934 | Hispano-Suiza 9Qa 340 hp (r 9 cl) a.c. | 12 | 39.4 |
| 66 | Pander S-4 Postjager | NL | Pander | CTr | 1933 | 3 x Wright R-975-E2 Whirlwind 420 hp (r 9 cl) a.c. | 16.60 | 54.5 |
| 66 | Koolhoven F.K.50 | NL | N. V. Koolhoven Vllegtulgen | CTr | 1935 | 2 x Pratt & Whitney R-985-T1B Wasp Junior 400 hp (r 9 cl) a.c. | 18 | 59 |
| 66 | Fokker XXXVI | NL | Fokker | CTr | 1934 | 4 x Wright Cyclone 750 hp (r 9 cl) a.c. | 33 | 108.3 |
| 67 | Blohm und Voss Ha. 139A | D | Blohm und Voss Schiffswert Abteilung Flugzeugbau | CTr | 1936 | 4 x Junkers Jumo 205C 600 hp (6 cl) l.c. | 27 | 88.7 |
| 67 | Junkers-Ju.52/3m | D | Junkers Flugzeuge und Motorenwerke AG. | CTr | 1932 | 3 x B.M.W. Hornet 525 hp (r 9 cl) a.c. | 29.25 | 95.9 |
| 67 | Junkers Ju.86 | D | Junkers Flugzeuge und Motorenwerke AG. | CTr | 1934 | 2 x Rolls-Royce Kestrel XVI 745 hp (12 cl V) l.c. | 22.50 | 73.8 |
| 67 | Junkers Ju.160 | D | Junkers Flugzeuge und Motorenwerke AG. | CTr | 1934 | B.M.W 132E 660 hp (r 9 cl) a.c. | 14.32 | 46.9 |
| 67 | Junkers Ju.90B | D | Junkers Flugzeuge und Motorenwerke AG. | CTr | 1938 | 4 x B.M.W. 132H 830 hp (r 9 cl) a.c. | 35.02 | 114.8 |
| 67 | Heinkel He.70G | D | Ernst Heinkel AG. | CTr | 1933 | B.M.W. VI 630 hp (12 cl V) l.c. | 14.80 | 48.6 |
| 67 | Heinkel He.111C | D | Ernst Heinkel AG. | CTr | 1935 | 2 x B.M.W. VIu 720 hp (12 cl V) l.c. | 22.60 | 74.1 |
| 67 | Heinkel He.116 | D | Ernst Heinkel AG. | CTr | 1937 | 4 x Hirth HM508B 240 hp (8 cl V) l.c. | 22 | 72.2 |
| 67 | Focke Wulf Fw. 200 Condor PKA-1 | D | Focke Wulf Flugzeugbau GmbH | CTr | 1937 | 4 x B.M.W. 132G 720 hp (r 9 cl) a.c. | 33 | 108.3 |
| 67 | Dornier Do.26A | D | Dornier Werke AG. | CTr | 1938 | 4 x Junkers Jumo 205C 600 hp (6 cl) l.c. | 30 | 98.5 |
| 68 | SIAI Marchetti S.M.66 | I | SIAI Marchetti | CTr | 1932 | 3 x Fiat A24R 750 hp (12 cl V) l.c. | 33 | 108.3 |
| 68 | SIAI Marchetti S.M.71 | I | SIAI Marchetti | CTr | 1932 | 3 x Piaggio Stella VII 370 hp (r 7 cl) a.c. | 21.20 | 69.6 |
| 68 | SIAI Marchetti S.M.7G | I | SIAI Marchetti | CTr | 1935 | 4 x Piaggio Stella X.R.C. 700 hp (r 9 cl) a.c. | 29.68 | 97.4 |
| 68 | SIAI Marchetti S.M.75 | I | SIAI Marchetti | CTr | 1937 | 3 x Alfa Romeo A.R.126 RC34 750 hp (r 9 cl) a.c. | 29.68 | 97.4 |
| 68 | SIAI Marchetti S.M.83 | I | SIAI Marchetti | CTr | 1937 | 3 x Alfa Romeo A.R.126 RC34 750 hp (r 9 cl) a.c. | 21.20 | 69.6 |
| 68 | Fiat G.18V | I | Fiat S.A. | CTr | 1937 | 2 x Fiat A.80 RC 41 1000 hp (r 18 cl) a.c. | 25 | 82 |
| 69 | Caproni Ca.133 | I | Società Italiana Caproni | CTr | 1935 | 3 x Piaggio PVII C16 160 hp (r 7 cl) a.c. | 21.44 | 70.3 |
| 69 | Caproni Campini CC2 | I | Società Italiana Caproni | CTr | 1940 | Isotta-Fraschini L121 MC 40 Asso 900 hp (12 cl V) l.c. | 14.63 | 48 |
| 69 | Macchi M.C.94 | I | Aeronautica Macchi | CTr | 1935 | 2 x Wright SGR-1280 Cyclone 770 hp (r 9 cl) a.c. | 22.79 | 74.7 |
| 69 | Macchi M.C.100 | I | Aeronautica Macchi | CTr | 1939 | 3 x Alfa Romeo A.R.126RC10 800 hp (r 9 cl) a.c. | 26.71 | 87.6 |
| 69 | Tupolev ANT-14 | USSR | State Industries | CTr | 1931 | 5 x M.22 480 hp (r 9 cl) a.c. | 40.40 | 132.7 |
| 69 | Tupolev ANT-35 | USSR | State Industries | CTr | 1936 | 2 x M.85 850 hp (r 14 cl) a.c. | 20.80 | 68.3 |
| 69 | Tupolev ANT-20 Maxim Gorki | USSR | State Industries | CTr | 1934 | 8 x AM.34RN 900 hp (12 cl V) l.c. | 63 | 206.9 |
| 69 | Yakovlev Ya-6 | USSR | State Industries | CTr | 1932 | M.11 110 hp (r 5 cl) a.c. | 12 | 39.4 |
| 69 | OKO-1 | USSR | State Industries | LT | 1937 | M.25A 730 hp (r 9 cl) a.c. | 15.40 | 50.6 |
| 70 | Lockheed 9D Orion | USA | Lockheed Aircraft Co. | CTr | 1931 | Pratt & Whitney Wasp 500 hp (r 9 cl) a.c. | 13.05 | 42.9 |
| 70 | Lockheed 10 Electra | USA | Lockheed Aircraft Co. | CTr | 1934 | 2 x Pratt & Whitney Wasp Jr. 420 hp (r 9 cl) a.c. | 16.76 | 55 |
| 70 | Lockheed 14 Super Electra | USA | Lockheed Aircraft Co. | LT | 1937 | 2 x Wright GR-1820-F62 Cyclone 760 hp (r 9 cl) a.c. | 19.96 | 65.6 |
| 70 | Lockheed 18-56 Lodestar | USA | Lockheed Aircraft Co. | LT | 1940 | 2 x Wright R-1820 G205A Cyclone 1200 hp (r 9 cl) a.c. | 19.96 | 65.6 |
| 70 | Consolidated Fleetster | USA | Consolidated Aircraft Co. | CTr | 1932 | Pratt & Whitney Hornet B1 575 hp (r 9 cl) a.c. | 15.24 | 49.9 |
| 70 | Northrop Delta | USA | Northrop Co. | CTr | 1934 | Wright R-1820-F52 Cyclone 775 hp (r 9 cl) a.c. | 14.51 | 47.9 |
| 70 | Sikorsky S.43 | USA | Sikorsky Aircraft | CTr | 1935 | 2 x Pratt & Whitney S1EG Hornet 750 hp (r 9 cl) a.c. | 26.71 | 86 |
| 70 | Sikorsky S.40 | USA | Sikorksy Aircraft | CTr | 1935 | 4 x Pratt & Whitney Hornet 750 hp (r 9 cl) a.c. | 36.02 | 118 |
| 71 | Bellanca P-200 Airbus | USA | Bellanca Aircraft Co. | CTr | 1931 | Wright R-1820-E Cyclone 575 hp (r 9 cl) a.c. | 19.81 | 65 |
| 71 | Douglas DC-3 | USA | Douglas Aircraft Co. | CTr | 1936 | 2 x Pratt & Whitney 1200 hp (r 9 cl) a.c. | 28.96 | 95 |
| 71 | Clark G.A.43 | USA | General Aviation Corp. | CTr | 1933 | Wright R-1820-F1 Cyclone 715 hp (r 9 cl) a.c. | 16.15 | 53 |
| 71 | Curtiss T.32 Condor | USA | Curtiss Aeroplane and Motor Co. | CTr | 1933 | 2 x Wright Cyclone 760 hp (r 9 cl) a.c. | 24.99 | 82 |
| 71 | Curtiss C.46 | USA | Curtiss-Wright Corp. | CTr | 1940 | 2 x Pratt & Whitney R-2800-51 Double Wasp 2000 hp (r 18 cl) a.c. | 32.94 | 108 |
| 71 | Vultee V.1 | USA | Vultee Aircraft | CTr | 1934 | Wright R-1825-F2 Cyclone 735 hp (r 9 cl) a.c. | 15.24 | 50 |
| 71 | Boeing 221 Monomail | USA | Boeing Airplane Co. | CTr | 1931 | Pratt & Whitney Hornet B 575 hp (r 9 cl) a.c. | 18.03 | 59.1 |
| 71 | Boeing 247 | USA | Boeing Airplane Co. | CTr | 1934 | 2 x Pratt & Whitney Wasp 550 hp (r 9 cl) a.c. | 22.56 | 74 |
| 71 | Boeing SA-307 Stratoliner | USA | Boeing Aircraft Co. | CTr | 1940 | 4 x Wright GR-1820 Cyclone 900 hp (r 9 cl) a.c. | 32.69 | 107.3 |
| 71 | Grumman G-21 | USA | Grumman Aircraft Engineering Corp. | LT | 1937 | 2 x Pratt & Whitney R-385-AN6 Wasp Jr. 450 hp (r 9 cl) a.c. | 14.95 | 49 |

| Length | | Height | | Take-off weight | | Speed | | Ceiling | | Range | | Crew | Payload/armament |
|---|---|---|---|---|---|---|---|---|---|---|---|---|---|
| m | ft | m | ft | kg | lb | km/h | mph | m | ft | km | ml | | |
| 8.70 | 28.6 | 2.25 | 7.4 | 1,230 | 2,712 | 280 | 174 | 7,300 | 23,950 | 1,260 | 783 | 2 | 150 kg (331 lb) |
| 26 | 85.3 | — | — | 22,000 | 48,502 | 190 | 118 | — | — | 3,200 | 1,988 | 8 | 600 kg (1,323 lb) |
| 21.18 | 69.6 | 7.20 | 23.7 | 17,900 | 39,463 | 290 | 180 | 7,000 | 22,965 | 4,000 | 2,485 | 5 | 1,320 kg (2,910 lb) |
| 20.30 | 66.7 | 7.51 | 24.7 | 15,000 | 33,069 | 200 | 124 | 5,000 | 16,400 | 1,100 | 680 | 2 | 20 p |
| 12.60 | 41.4 | — | — | 8,400 | 18,518 | 350 | 217 | — | — | 7,000 | 4,350 | 3 | — |
| 3.60 | 11.9 | 1.68 | 5.6 | 250 | 550 | 100 | 62 | — | — | 322 | 200 | 1 | — |
| 26.18 | 85.9 | — | — | 23,000 | 50,706 | 160 | 99 | 4,600 | 15,090 | 4,800 | 2,982 | 4 | 100 kg (2,204 lb) |
| 31.62 | 103.9 | 9.07 | 29.9 | 37,933 | 83,627 | 210 | 167 | 6,300 | 20,669 | 4,100 | 2,547 | 8 | 30-70 p |
| 10.52 | 34.6 | 2.90 | 9.5 | 2,656 | 5,850 | 240 | 149 | 5,030 | 16,502 | 1,045 | 650 | 1 | 8 p |
| 16.45 | 53.9 | 3.68 | 12.1 | 8,000 | 17,637 | 280 | 174 | 8,000 | 26,240 | 3,500 | 2,175 | 2 | 8 p |
| 15.30 | 50.2 | 4.15 | 13.7 | 5,250 | 11,574 | 310 | 193 | 7,000 | 22,965 | 1,200 | 746 | 2 | 10 p |
| 9.68 | 31.7 | 3.07 | 10 | 3,356 | 7,399 | 238 | 148 | 6,705 | 22,000 | 1,850 | 1,150 | 1 | 9 p; 270 kg (596 lb) |
| 13 | 42.8 | 3.40 | 11.2 | 4,300 | 9,480 | 286 | 178 | 5,800 | 19,029 | 900 | 560 | 2 | 8 p |
| 9.80 | 32.2 | 2.80 | 9.2 | 2,250 | 4,960 | 220 | 137 | 4,500 | 14,764 | 700 | 435 | 2 | 6 p |
| 8.35 | 27.5 | 2.70 | 8.8 | 1,920 | 4,233 | 245 | 152 | 4,100 | 13,100 | 2,300 | 1,429 | 2 | — |
| 12.50 | 41 | 3.30 | 10.8 | 5,700 | 12,566 | 300 | 186 | 6,050 | 19,850 | — | — | 2-3 | — |
| 14 | 45.9 | 3.70 | 12.1 | 4,100 | 9,039 | 260 | 162 | 5,200 | 17,060 | 1,000 | 621 | 2 | 8 p |
| 23.60 | 77.5 | 5.99 | 19.8 | 16,500 | 36,376 | 240 | 149 | 4,400 | 14,435 | 1,350 | 838 | 4 | 32 p |
| 19.50 | 64 | 4.50 | 14.7 | 17,500 | 38,581 | 260 | 162 | 3,500 | 11,480 | 5,300 | 3,293 | 4 | 480 kg (1,058 lb) |
| 18.90 | 62 | 5.54 | 18.1 | 9,200 | 20,282 | 245 | 152 | 5,200 | 17,000 | 914 | 568 | 2 | 15-17 p |
| 17.42 | 57.2 | 4.80 | 15.9 | 7,700 | 16,975 | 255 | 158 | 6,100 | 20,012 | 1,100 | 680 | 2 | 10 p |
| 12 | 39.4 | 3.92 | 13.1 | 3,550 | 7,826 | 315 | 196 | 5,400 | 17,716 | 1,000 | 621 | 2 | 6 p |
| 26.30 | 86.3 | 7.30 | 24.7 | 23,000 | 50,706 | 320 | 200 | 5,500 | 18,045 | 2,092 | 1,300 | 4 | 40 p |
| 12 | 39.4 | 3.10 | 10.2 | 3,460 | 7,628 | 305 | 190 | 5,600 | 18,370 | 1,000 | 621 | 1 | 4 p |
| 17.50 | 57.5 | 4.39 | 14.4 | 7,870 | 17,350 | 305 | 190 | 4,800 | 15,750 | 1,000 | 621 | 2 | 10 p |
| 13.70 | 44.9 | 3.30 | 10.8 | 6,930 | 15,278 | 300 | 186 | 4,400 | 14,435 | 4,500 | 2,795 | 4 | 550 kg (1,212 lb) |
| 23.85 | 78.3 | 6.30 | 20.6 | 14,600 | 32,000 | 325 | 202 | 6,700 | 21,980 | 1,250 | 775 | 4 | 26 p |
| 24.60 | 80.8 | 6.85 | 22.6 | 20,000 | 44,092 | 310 | 193 | 4,800 | 15,750 | 9,000 | 5,592 | 4 | 500 kg (1,102 lb) |
| 16.63 | 54.6 | 4.89 | 16 | 11,600 | 27,574 | 222 | 138 | 5,500 | 18,045 | 1,290 | 800 | 3 | 14-18 p |
| 14 | 45.9 | — | — | 5,060 | 11,600 | 229 | 142 | 5,900 | 19,357 | 1,200 | 745 | 3 | 8-10 p |
| 21.36 | 70.1 | 5.50 | 18.1 | 14,000 | 30,865 | 300 | 186 | 7,000 | 22,965 | 2,000 | 1,242 | 4 | 27 p |
| 21.60 | 70.8 | 5.10 | 16.7 | 14,500 | 31,967 | 325 | 202 | 7,000 | 22,965 | 2,280 | 1,416 | 4 | 18-24 p |
| 16.20 | 53.1 | 4.60 | 15 | 10,400 | 22,928 | 400 | 248 | 7,000 | 22,965 | 4,800 | 2,983 | 4 | 10 p |
| 18.81 | 61.8 | 5.01 | 16.5 | 10,800 | 23,809 | 340 | 211 | 8,700 | 28,543 | 1,675 | 1,041 | 3 | 18 p |
| 15.45 | 50.6 | 4 | 13.2 | 6,700 | 14,771 | 230 | 143 | 5,500 | 18,045 | 1,350 | 840 | 2 | 16 p |
| 12.10 | 39.8 | 4.70 | 15.5 | 4,217 | 9,300 | 360 | 224 | 4,000 | 13,120 | — | — | 2 | — |
| 15.52 | 50.9 | 5.45 | 17.8 | 7,800 | 17,196 | 250 | 155 | 5,800 | 19,029 | 1,375 | 850 | 3 | 12 p |
| 17.69 | 58 | 6.12 | 20 | 13,200 | 29,100 | 263 | 163 | 6,500 | 21,325 | 1,400 | 870 | 3 | 26 p |
| 26.48 | 86.9 | 5.40 | 17.9 | 17,143 | 37,800 | 195 | 121 | 4,220 | 13,845 | 1,200 | 746 | 6 | 36 p |
| 14.96 | 49.2 | 5.91 | 19.5 | 6,620 | 14,594 | 349 | 217 | 8,500 | 27,887 | 2,000 | 1,242 | 2 | 10 p |
| 32.47 | 106.6 | 11.25 | 36.9 | 42,000 | 92,595 | 220 | 137 | 6,000 | 19,684 | 2,000 | 1,242 | 8 | 43 p |
| 7.10 | 23.3 | 2.26 | 7.5 | 993 | 2,189 | 140 | 87 | 4,500 | 14,764 | 600 | 373 | 1 | 2 p |
| 11.60 | 38.2 | — | — | 3,500 | 7,716 | 280 | 174 | 6,740 | 22,110 | 700 | 435 | 2 | 6 p |
| 8.38 | 27.4 | 2.95 | 9.6 | 2,450 | 5,401 | 293 | 182 | — | — | 901 | 560 | 1 | 4 p |
| 11.76 | 38.7 | 3.05 | 10.1 | 4,763 | 10,300 | 327 | 203 | 6,100 | 20,012 | 1,207 | 750 | 2 | 12 p |
| 13.40 | 44.4 | 3.49 | 11.5 | 7,838 | 17,278 | 362 | 225 | 6,558 | 21,515 | 2,558 | 1,590 | 2-3 | 12 p |
| 15.18 | 49.8 | 3.37 | 11 | 7,938 | 17,500 | 404 | 251 | 8,230 | 27,000 | 2,671 | 1,660 | 3 | 17 p |
| 10.28 | 33.7 | 3.65 | 11.9 | 3,084 | 6,799 | 257 | 160 | 5,500 | 18,045 | 1,290 | 801 | 1-2 | 7 p |
| 10.08 | 33 | 2.74 | 8.9 | 3,334 | 7,350 | 322 | 200 | 7,130 | 23,392 | 3,106 | 1,930 | 2 | 7 p |
| 15.60 | 51.2 | 5.38 | 17.8 | 8,485 | 19,500 | 267 | 166 | 6,100 | 20,012 | 1,250 | 775 | 2-3 | 16-25 p |
| 20.73 | 68 | 5.28 | 17.4 | 19,051 | 42,000 | 274 | 170 | 4,572 | 15,000 | 1,931 | 1,200 | 5 | 32 p |
| 13.03 | 42.9 | 3.15 | 10.4 | 4,344 | 9,590 | 196 | 122 | 4,270 | 14,000 | 1,160 | 720 | 1 | 12 p |
| 19.65 | 64.5 | 5.15 | 49.2 | 11,415 | 25,166 | 290 | 180 | 7,070 | 23,195 | 2,091 | 1,299 | 2 | 14-32 p |
| 13.13 | 43.1 | 3.81 | 12.6 | 3,964 | 8,739 | 274 | 170 | 5,490 | 18,012 | 684 | 425 | 1-2 | 10-11 p |
| 14.81 | 48.7 | 4.98 | 16.4 | 7,927 | 17,476 | 233 | 145 | 7,011 | 23,000 | 1,045 | 649 | 2 | 15 p |
| 23.27 | 76.4 | 6.63 | 21.9 | 21,772 | 48,000 | 314 | 195 | 7,470 | 24,500 | 2,896 | 1,799 | 4 | 36-50 p |
| 11.28 | 37 | 2.80 | 9.1 | 3,850 | 8,500 | 346 | 215 | 6,100 | 20,012 | 1,610 | 1,000 | 2 | 8 p |
| 12.55 | 41.1 | 3.81 | 12.4 | 3,629 | 8,000 | 220 | 135 | 4,480 | 14,700 | 869 | 540 | 1 | 8 p |
| 15.72 | 51.7 | 4.69 | 15.4 | 6,192 | 13,650 | 249 | 154 | 7,742 | 25,400 | 840 | 521 | 2-3 | 10 p |
| 22.66 | 74.4 | 6.33 | 20.9 | 19,051 | 42,000 | 357 | 222 | 7,985 | 26,200 | 3,700 | 2,299 | 5 | 33 p |
| 11.70 | 38.4 | 3.66 | 12 | 3,629 | 8,000 | 306 | 191 | 6,700 | 21,981 | 1,287 | 800 | 2 | 6-7 p |

# Technical Data

| Page | Aircraft | Nation | Manufacturer | Type | Year | Engine | Wingspan m | ft |
|------|----------|--------|--------------|------|------|--------|------------|-----|
| 71 | Martin M.130 China Clipper | USA | Glenn L. Martin Co. | CTr | 1935 | 4 x Pratt & Whitney Twin Wasp 830 hp (r 14 cl) a.c. | 39.70 | 130.2 |
| 72 | Supermarine S.6 | GB | The Supermarine Aviation Works Ltd. | Rp | 1929 | Rolls-Royce R 1900 hp (12 cl V) l.c. | 9.14 | 30 |
| 72 | Supermarine S.6B | GB | The Supermarine Aviation Works Ltd. | Rp | 1931 | Rolls-Royce R 2350 hp (12 cl V) l.c. | 9.14 | 30 |
| 72 | de Havilland D.H.88 Comet | GB | de Havilland Aircraft Ltd. | Rp | 1934 | 2 x de Havilland Gipsy Six R 230 hp (6 cl) | 13.41 | 44 |
| 72 | T.K.4 | GB | de Havilland Aeronautical Technical School | Rp | 1937 | de Havilland Gipsy Major III 137 hp (4 cl) a.c. | 5.84 | 19.1 |
| 72 | Percival P.3 Gull Six | GB | Percival Aircraft Co. Ltd. | Rp | 1934 | de Havilland Gipsy Six 200 hp (6 cl) a.c. | 11.02 | 36.2 |
| 72 | Heston Type 5 Racer | GB | Heston Aircraft Co. | Rp | 1940 | Napier Sabre 2560 hp (24 cl H) l.c. | 9.78 | 32 |
| 72 | Wedell-Williams | USA | Wedell-Williams | Rp | 1931 | Pratt & Whitney Wasp Jr. 550 hp (r 9 cl) a.c. | 7.92 | 35.9 |
| 72 | Laird LC-DW-500 Super Solution | USA | Laird | Rp | 1931 | Pratt & Whitney Wasp Jr. 535 hp (r 9 cl) a.c. | 6.40 | 21 |
| 72 | Laird Turner L-RT Meteor | USA | Laird | Rp | 1939 | Pratt & Whitney S1B3G Twin Wasp 1000 hp (r 14 cl) a.c. | 7.62 | 25 |
| 72 | Gee Bee Z | USA | Granville Brothers Aircraft | Rp | 1931 | Pratt & Whitney Wasp Jr. 535 hp (r 9 cl) a.c. | 7.16 | 23.6 |
| 72 | Gee Bee R-1 | USA | Granville Brothers Aircraft | Rp | 1932 | Pratt & Whitney Wasp Jr. 800 hp (r 9 cl) a.c. | 7.62 | 25 |
| 72 | Howard DGA-6 Mr. Mulligan | USA | Howard | Rp | 1935 | Pratt & Whitney Wasp 830 hp (r 9 cl) a.c. | 9.65 | 31.8 |
| 72 | Hughes H-1 | USA | Hughes Aircraft Corp. | Rp | 1935 | Pratt & Whitney Twin Wasp 1000 hp (r 14 cl) a.c. | 9.75 | 31.9 |
| 72 | Beech C-17 R | USA | Beech Aircraft Corp. | Rp | 1936 | Wright Cyclone 450 hp (r 9 cl) a.c. | 9.75 | 31.9 |
| 72 | Seversky Sev-S2 | USA | Republic Aviation Corp. | Rp | 1937 | Pratt & Whitney RK30 Twin Wasp 1000 hp (r 14 cl) a.c. | 10.97 | 36 |
| 72 | Folkerts SK-3 Jupiter | USA | Folkerts | Rp | 1937 | Menasco C-654 400 hp (6 cl) a.c. | 5.08 | 16.8 |
| 73 | Macchi-Castoldi MC-72 | I | Aeronautica Macchi | Rp | 1933 | Fiat A.S.6 3000 hp (24 cl V) l.c. | 9.48 | 31.1 |
| 73 | Nardi F.N.305D | I | Fratelli Nardi | Rp | 1938 | Walter Bora 200 hp (r 9 cl) a.c. | 8.47 | 27.9 |
| 73 | Messerschmitt Bf. 108B | D | Messerschmitt AG. | Rp | 1935 | Argus As10c 240 hp (8 cl V) a.c. | 10.49 | 34.5 |
| 73 | Kellner-Bechereau 28V.D. | F | Kellner-Bechereau | Rp | 1933 | Delage 370 hp (12 cl V) l.c. | 6.65 | 21.8 |
| 73 | Caudron C-460 | F | Caudron | Rp | 1934 | Renault Bengali 340 hp (6 cl) a.c. | 6.73 | 22.1 |
| 73 | Tupolev ANT 25 | USSR | State Industries | Rp | 1934 | M 34 R 950 hp (12 cl V) l.c. | 33.98 | 111.6 |
| 76 | Hawker Fury | GB | Hawker Aircraft Ltd. | Fr | 1931 | Rolls-Royce Kestrel IIS 525 hp (12 cl V) l.c. | 9.14 | 30 |
| 76 | Hawker Osprey Mk.I | GB | Hawker Aircraft Ltd. | Fr | 1932 | Rolls-Royce Kestrel IIMS 630 hp (12 cl V) l.c. | 11.28 | 37 |
| 76 | Hawker Demon | GB | Hawker Aircraft Ltd. | Fr | 1933 | Rolls-Royce Kestrel V 584 hp (12 cl V) l.c. | 11.35 | 37.3 |
| 76 | Hawker Nimrod Mk.II | GB | Hawker Aircraft Ltd. | Fr | 1934 | Rolls-Royce Kestrel IIS 590 hp (12 cl V) l.c. | 10.21 | 33.6 |
| 76 | Hawker Hurricane Mk.I | GB | Hawker Aircraft Ltd. | Fr | 1937 | Rolls-Royce Merlin II 1030 hp (12 cl V) l.c. | 12.19 | 40 |
| 76 | Westland Whirlwind Mk.I | GB | Westland Aircraft Ltd. | FB | 1940 | 2 x Rolls-Royce Peregrine I 885 hp (12 cl V) l.c. | 13.71 | 45 |
| 76 | Fairey Fulmar Mk.I | GB | Fairey Aviation Co. Ltd. | Fr | 1940 | Rolls-Royce Merlin VIII 1080 hp (12 cl V) a.c. | 14.13 | 46.4 |
| 76 | Gloster Gauntlet Mk.I | GB | Gloster Aircraft Co. | Fr | 1935 | Bristol Mercury VIS2 645 hp (r 9 cl) a.c. | 9.99 | 32.9 |
| 76 | Gloster Gladiator Mk.II | GB | Gloster Aircraft Co. Ltd. | Fr | 1938 | Bristol Mercury VIIIA 840 hp (r 9 cl) a.c. | 9.83 | 32.3 |
| 76 | Blackburn Skua Mk.II | GB | Blackburn Aircraft Ltd. | FB | 1938 | Bristol Perseus XII 890 hp (r 9 cl) a.c. | 14.07 | 46.2 |
| 76 | Blackburn Roc | GB | Boulton Paul Aircraft Ltd. | Fr | 1938 | Bristol Perseus XII 890 hp (r 9 cl) a.c. | 14.02 | 46 |
| 76 | Supermarine Spitfire Mk.1 | GB | Supermarine Division of Vickers-Armstrongs Ltd. | Fr | 1938 | Rolls-Royce Merlin II 1030 hp (12 cl V) l.c. | 11.22 | 36.8 |
| 76 | Boulton Paul Defiant Mk.I | GB | Boulton Paul Aircraft Ltd. | Fr | 1940 | Rolls-Royce Merlin III 1030 (12 cl V) l.c. | 11.99 | 39.4 |
| 76 | Bristol Beaufighter Mk.iF | GB | Bristol Aeroplane Co. Ltd. | Fr | 1940 | 2 x Bristol Hercules XI 1400 hp (r 14 cl) a.c. | 17.63 | 57.8 |
| 76 | Ikarus IK-2 | YU | Ikarus A.D. | Fr | 1937 | Hispano-Suiza 12 Ycrs 860 hp (12 cl V) l.c. | 11.40 | 37.5 |
| 76 | Rogozarski IK-3 | YU | Rogozarski A.D. | Fr | 1940 | Avia-Hispano-Suiza 12 Ycrs 920 hp (12 cl V) l.c. | 10.28 | 33.9 |
| 77 | Morane-Saulnier M.S.225 C1 | F | Morane-Saulnier | Fr | 1933 | Gnome-Rhône 9Kbrs 440 hp (r 9 cl) a.c. | 10.56 | 34.5 |
| 77 | Morane-Saulnier M.S.406 | F | SNCAO | Fr | 1938 | Hispano-Suiza 12Y 850 hp (12 cl V) l.c. | 10.60 | 34.7 |
| 77 | Dewoitine D.27 | F | EKW | Fr | 1931 | Hispano-Suiza 12 Mc 500 hp (12 cl V) l.c. | 9.80 | 32.2 |
| 77 | Dewoitine D.500C1 | F | Société Aéronautique Française | Fr | 1935 | Hispano-Suiza 12Xbrs 690 hp (12 cl V) l.c. | 12 | 39.5 |
| 77 | Dewoitine D.520 | F | SNCAM | Fr | 1940 | Hispano-Suiza 12Y 910 hp (12 cl V) l.c. | 10.18 | 33.5 |
| 77 | Hanriot NC-600 | F | SNCAC | Fr | 1939 | 2 x Gnome-Rhône MO/01 700 hp (r 14 cl) a.c. | 12.77 | 41.9 |
| 77 | Loire 46 C.1 | F | SNCAO | Fr | 1936 | Gnome-Rhône 14KFS 930 hp (r 14 cl) a.c. | 11.80 | 38.9 |
| 77 | Nieuport-Delage NID 622 C.1 | F | Société Anonyme des Etablissements Nieuport | Fr | 1931 | Hispano-Suiza 12Md 500 hp (12 cl V) l.c. | 12 | 39.5 |
| 77 | Blériot-Spad 510 C.1 | F | Blériot Aéronautique | Fr | 1937 | Hispano-Suiza 12 Xbrs 690 hp (12 cl V) l.c. | 8.84 | 29 |
| 77 | Arsenal VG-33 | F | Arsenal de l'Aéronautique | Fr | 1940 | Hispano-Suiza 12Y 860 hp (12 cl V) l.c. | 10.80 | 35.5 |
| 77 | Potez 630 | F | SNCAN | Fr | 1938 | 2 x Hispano-Suiza 14 Hbs 640 hp (r 14 cl) a.c. | 16 | 52.6 |
| 77 | Caudron C.714 | F | Caudron | Fr | 1939 | Renault 12 RO-3 450 hp (12 cl V) a.c. | 8.96 | 29.5 |
| 77 | Henschel Hs.123 A-1 | D | Henschel Flugzeugwerke AG. | Fr/A | 1936 | B.M.W. 132Dc 880 hp (r 9 cl) a.c. | 10.50 | 34.5 |
| 77 | Heinkel He.51 | D | Ernst Heinkel A.G. | Fr | 1935 | B.M.W. VI 750 hp (12 cl V) l.c. | 10.99 | 36.1 |
| 77 | Heinkel He.112 B-O | D | Ernst Heinkel AG. | Fr | 1938 | Junkers Jumo 210 Ea 680 hp (12 cl V) l.c. | 9.10 | 29.8 |
| 77 | Arado Ar. 68E-1 | D | Arado Flugzeugwerke GmbH | Fr | 1937 | Junkers Jumo 210 Ea 680 hp (12 cl V) l.c. | 11 | 36.1 |
| 77 | Messerschmitt Me (Bf) 109 E-1 | D | Messerschmitt AG. | Fr | 1939 | Daimler Benz DB 601A 1050 hp (12 cl V) l.c. | 9.87 | 32.4 |
| 77 | Messerschmitt Me (Bf) 110 C-1 | D | Messerschmitt AG. | Fr | 1939 | 2 x Daimler Benz DB 601 A-1 1050 hp (12 cl V) l.c. | 16.25 | 53.4 |
| 77 | PZL P.7 | PL | Pantswowe Zaklady Lotnicze | Fr | 1932 | Bristol Jupiter VIIF (Skoda) 485 hp (r 9 cl) a.c. | 10.31 | 33.8 |
| 77 | PZL P.24 | PL | Pantswowe Zaklady Lotnicze | Fr | 1935 | Gnome-Rhône 14 N7 970 hp (r 14 cl) a.c. | 10.71 | 35.2 |
| 77 | Avia B-534 | CS | Avia | Fr | 1935 | Avia-Hispano-Suiza 12Ydrs 860 hp (12 cl V) l.c. | 9.40 | 30.8 |
| 77 | Fokker D.XVII | NL | Fokker | Fr | 1932 | Rolls-Royce Kestrel IIS 595 hp (12 cl V) | 9.60 | 31.6 |
| 77 | Fokker D.XXI | NL | Fokker | Fr | 1938 | Bristol Mercury VIII 760 hp (r 9 cl) a.c. | 11 | 36.1 |
| 77 | Fokker G.1A | NL | Fokker | Fr | 1937 | 2 x Bristol Mercury VIII 830 hp (r 9 cl) a.c. | 17.15 | 56.3 |
| 77 | Fokker D.XXIII | NL | Fokker | Fr | 1939 | 2 x Walter Sagitta I-SR 540 hp (12 cl) a.c. | 11.50 | 37.9 |

| Length | | Height | | Take-off weight | | Speed | | Ceiling | | Range | | Crew | Payload/armament |
|---|---|---|---|---|---|---|---|---|---|---|---|---|---|
| m | ft | m | ft | kg | lb | km/h | mph | m | ft | km | ml | | |
| 27.31 | 89.5 | 7.30 | 23.9 | 23,587 | 52,000 | 266 | 165 | 5,150 | 18,896 | 5,150 | 3,200 | 5 | 48 p |
| 8.73 | 28.6 | 3.73 | 12.3 | 2,618 | 5,772 | 576 | 358 | — | — | — | — | 1 | — |
| 8.78 | 28.9 | 3.73 | 12.3 | 2,761 | 6,087 | 656 | 408 | — | — | — | — | 1 | — |
| 8.83 | 29 | 3.05 | 10 | 2,410 | 5,313 | 381 | 237 | 5,790 | 19,000 | 4,700 | 2,925 | 2 | — |
| 4.83 | 15.8 | — | — | 615 | 1,357 | 393 | 244 | 6,400 | 21,000 | 724 | 450 | 1 | — |
| 7.54 | 24.9 | 2.24 | 7.4 | 1,111 | 2,450 | 286 | 178 | 6,100 | 20,000 | 1,030 | 640 | 1 | — |
| 7.49 | 24.7 | 3.61 | 11.9 | 3,266 | 7,200 | 772 | 480 | — | — | — | — | 1 | — |
| 6.48 | 21.3 | 2.44 | 8 | 1,001 | 2,206 | 491 | 305 | — | — | — | — | 1 | — |
| 5.94 | 19.6 | — | — | 1,126 | 2,482 | 426 | 265 | — | — | — | — | 1 | — |
| 7.11 | 23.4 | 3.05 | 10 | 2,238 | 4,933 | 496 | 308 | — | — | — | — | 1 | — |
| 4.60 | 15.1 | — | — | 1,034 | 2,284 | 460 | 286 | — | — | 1,600 | 1,000 | 1 | — |
| 5.41 | 17.9 | 2.47 | 8.1 | 1,395 | 3,075 | 477 | 296 | — | — | — | — | 1 | — |
| 7.64 | 25.1 | 3.35 | 11 | 1,909 | 4,210 | 470 | 292 | 7,925 | 26,000 | 2,815 | 1,750 | 2 | — |
| 8.58 | 28.1 | — | — | 2,500 | 5,500 | 587 | 365 | 6,100 | 20,000 | 4,006 | 2,490 | 1 | — |
| 7.98 | 26.2 | 3.12 | 10.3 | 1,769 | 3,900 | 325 | 202 | 6,700 | 21,981 | 1,125 | 700 | 2 | — |
| 7.77 | 25.6 | 2.97 | 9.9 | 2,899 | 6,390 | 491 | 305 | 9,050 | 29,685 | — | — | 1 | — |
| 6.40 | 21 | 1.22 | 4 | 628 | 1,385 | 413 | 257 | — | — | — | — | 1 | — |
| 8.33 | 27.3 | 3.30 | 10.8 | 2,907 | 6,409 | 712 | 442 | — | — | — | — | 1 | — |
| 7.90 | 25.9 | 2.10 | 6.8 | — | — | 340 | 211 | 6,000 | 19,684 | 4,500 | 2,800 | 2 | — |
| 8.28 | 27.2 | 2.29 | 7.6 | 1,383 | 3,050 | 302 | 187 | — | — | 1,000 | 621 | 1 | — |
| 7.16 | 23.6 | 2.65 | 8.7 | 1,600 | 3,527 | 400 | 249 | — | — | — | — | 1 | — |
| 7.11 | 23.4 | — | — | 948 | 2,090 | 505 | 314 | — | — | — | — | 1 | — |
| 13.18 | 43.8 | 5.49 | 18 | 11,226 | 24,749 | 240 | 149 | 7,000 | 23,000 | 13,000 | 8,078 | 3 | — |
| 8.12 | 26.8 | 3.09 | 10.2 | 1,580 | 3,490 | 333 | 207 | 8,535 | 28,000 | 490 | 305 | 1 | 2 mg |
| 8.94 | 29.4 | 3.17 | 10.5 | 2,245 | 4,950 | 270 | 169 | 7,160 | 23,500 | — | — | 2 | 2 mg |
| 9.01 | 29.7 | 3.17 | 10.5 | 2,022 | 4,464 | 293 | 182 | 8,380 | 27,493 | 2h30' | — | 2 | 3 mg |
| 8.23 | 27 | 2.97 | 9.9 | 1,944 | 4,258 | 314 | 195 | 7,925 | 26,000 | 2h5' | — | 1 | 2 mg; b (36 kg - 80 lb) |
| 9.55 | 31.5 | 3.99 | 13.1 | 2,816 | 6,208 | 518 | 322 | 10,180 | 33,398 | 845 | 525 | 1 | 8 mg |
| 9.98 | 32.9 | 3.53 | 11.7 | 4,652 | 10,356 | 579 | 360 | 9,150 | 30,000 | — | — | 1 | 4 g; b (453 kg - 1,000 lb) |
| 12.26 | 40.3 | 4.26 | 14 | 4,440 | 9,800 | 426 | 265 | 7,900 | 26,000 | 1,290 | 800 | 2 | 8 mg |
| 8.05 | 26.2 | 3.12 | 10.4 | 1,801 | 3,970 | 370 | 230 | 10,210 | 33,497 | 740 | 460 | 1 | 2 mg |
| 8.36 | 27.5 | 3.10 | 10.2 | 2,200 | 4,850 | 414 | 257 | 10,210 | 33,497 | 715 | 444 | 1 | 4 mg |
| 10.85 | 35.7 | 3.81 | 12.6 | 3,727 | 8,228 | 362 | 225 | 5,820 | 19,100 | 1,220 | 761 | 2 | 5 mg; b (335 kg - 740 lb) |
| 10.85 | 35.7 | 3.68 | 12.1 | 3,600 | 7,950 | 359 | 223 | 5,500 | 18,000 | 1,300 | 810 | 2 | 4 mg |
| 9.12 | 29.9 | 3.48 | 11.5 | 2,415 | 5,332 | 571 | 355 | 10,360 | 34,000 | 805 | 500 | 1 | 8 mg |
| 10.77 | 35.4 | 3.70 | 12.2 | 3,785 | 8,350 | 487 | 303 | 9,250 | 30,350 | 748 | 465 | 2 | 4 mg |
| 12.50 | 41.4 | 4.83 | 15.8 | 9,500 | 21,000 | 516 | 321 | 8,000 | 26,240 | 1,890 | 1,170 | 2 | 4 g; 6 mg |
| 7.88 | 25.8 | 3.84 | 12.7 | 1,930 | 4,255 | 428 | 266 | 10,500 | 34,450 | 400 | 248 | 1 | 1 g; 2 mg |
| 8.35 | 27.5 | 3.25 | 10.8 | 2,400 | 5,291 | 526 | 327 | 8,000 | 26,240 | 500 | 310 | 1 | 1 g; 2 mg |
| 7.24 | 23.6 | 3.30 | 10.8 | 1,581 | 3,484 | 333 | 207 | 10,000 | 32,808 | 700 | 435 | 1 | 2 mg |
| 8.15 | 26.9 | 2.82 | 9.3 | 2,720 | 6,000 | 486 | 302 | 9,400 | 30,840 | 800 | 497 | 1 | 1 g; 2 mg |
| 6.50 | 21.4 | 2.79 | 9.2 | 1,382 | 3,046 | 312 | 194 | 9,200 | 30,185 | 600 | 373 | 1 | 2 mg |
| 7.74 | 25.5 | 3.63 | 11.9 | 1,710 | 3,770 | 359 | 223 | 11,000 | 36,100 | 860 | 535 | 1 | 4 mg |
| 8.76 | 28.7 | 2.56 | 8.5 | 2,780 | 6,144 | 529 | 329 | 11,000 | 36,100 | 998 | 620 | 1 | 1 g; 4 mg |
| 8.78 | 28.8 | 3.12 | 10.3 | 3,995 | 8,818 | 542 | 337 | 8,000 | 26,250 | 860 | 534 | 2 | 3 g; 2 mg |
| 7.76 | 25.6 | 4.18 | 13.9 | 1,985 | 4,376 | 410 | 255 | 10,500 | 34,450 | 750 | 465 | 1 | 4 mg |
| 7.63 | 25 | 3 | 9.8 | 1,838 | 4,052 | 248 | 154 | 7,700 | 25,260 | 650 | 404 | 1 | 2 mg |
| 7.10 | 23.4 | 3.41 | 11.2 | 1,795 | 3,957 | 372 | 231 | 9,950 | 32,645 | 700 | 435 | 1 | 4 mg |
| 8.64 | 28.4 | 3.30 | 10.8 | 2,896 | 6,393 | 558 | 347 | 11,000 | 36,100 | 1,200 | 745 | 1 | 1 g; 4 mg |
| 11.07 | 36.4 | 3.61 | 11.9 | 3,845 | 8,488 | 370 | 230 | 10,000 | 32,808 | 1,225 | 760 | 3 | 2 g; 1 mg |
| 8.50 | 27.9 | 2.87 | 9.5 | 1,748 | 3,858 | 487 | 303 | 9,100 | 30,000 | 900 | 559 | 1 | 4 mg |
| 8.33 | 27.4 | 3.21 | 10.6 | 2,200 | 4,888 | 317 | 212 | 9,000 | 29,525 | 860 | 534 | 1 | 2 mg; b (200 kg - 440 lb) |
| 8.38 | 27.6 | 3.20 | 10.6 | 1,900 | 4,200 | 330 | 205 | 7,700 | 25,260 | 570 | 350 | 1 | 2 mg |
| 9.30 | 30.6 | 3.84 | 12.7 | 2,250 | 4,960 | 510 | 317 | 8,500 | 27,890 | 1,100 | 683 | 1 | 4 mg; b (60 kg - 132 lb) |
| 9.50 | 31.2 | 3.30 | 10.8 | 2,020 | 4,453 | 335 | 208 | 8,100 | 26,575 | 500 | 310 | 1 | 2 mg |
| 8.65 | 28.4 | 2.50 | 8.2 | 2,010 | 4,431 | 550 | 342 | 10,500 | 34,450 | 660 | 410 | 1 | 2 mg; 2 g |
| 12.07 | 39.7 | 4.12 | 13.6 | 6,028 | 13,289 | 540 | 336 | 10,000 | 32,808 | 1,125 | 699 | 2-3 | 5 mg; 2 g |
| 7.46 | 24.8 | 2.74 | 9 | 1,380 | 3,050 | 327 | 203 | 10,000 | 32,808 | 700 | 435 | 1 | 2 mg |
| 7.49 | 24.8 | 2.70 | 8.8 | 1,917 | 4,226 | 430 | 267 | — | — | 800 | 497 | 1 | 2 mg; 2 g |
| 8.20 | 26.9 | 2.79 | 9.2 | 1,980 | 4,365 | 394 | 245 | 10,600 | 34,875 | 600 | 373 | 1 | 4 mg |
| 7.20 | 23.7 | 3 | 9.8 | 1,480 | 3,262 | 335 | 208 | 8,750 | 28,710 | 850 | 528 | 1 | 2 mg |
| 8.20 | 26.9 | 2.95 | 9.8 | 2,050 | 4,519 | 460 | 286 | 11,000 | 36,100 | 950 | 590 | 1 | 4 mg |
| 11.50 | 37.9 | 3.40 | 11.2 | 4,790 | 10,560 | 475 | 295 | 9,300 | 30,500 | 1,520 | 944 | 3 | 9 mg; b (400 kg - 881 lb) |
| 11.70 | 38.4 | 3.34 | 10.9 | 2,990 | 6,600 | 524 | 326 | 9,000 | 29,525 | 900 | 559 | 1 | 4 mg |

# Technical Data

| Page | Aircraft | Nation | Manufacturer | Type | Year | Engine | Wingspan m | ft |
|------|----------|--------|--------------|------|------|--------|------------|-----|
| 80 | Fiat C.R.32 | I | Fiat S.A. | Fr | 1935 | Fiat A.30 RA 600 hp (12 cl V) l.c. | 9.50 | 31.2 |
| 80 | Fiat C.R.42 | I | Fiat S.A. | Fr | 1939 | Fiat A.74 RC38 840 hp (r 14 cl) a.c. | 9.70 | 31.8 |
| 80 | Fiat G.50 | I | Fiat S.A. | Fr | 1939 | Fiat A.74 RC38 840 hp (r 14 cl) a.c. | 10.98 | 36 |
| 80 | Macchi M.C. 200 | I | Aeronautica Macchi S.p.A. | Fr | 1939 | Fiat A.74 RC38 840 hp (r 14 cl) a.c. | 10.68 | 35 |
| 80 | Reggiane Re. 2001 | I | Officine Meccaniche Reggiane S.p.A. | Fr/A | 1941 | Daimler Benz 601/A1 1175 hp (12 cl V) l.c. | 11 | 36.1 |
| 80 | Breda Ba. 65 | I | Società Italiana Ernesto Breda | Fr/A | 1935 | Fiat A.80RC41 1000 hp (r 18 cl) a.c. | 12.10 | 39.8 |
| 80 | EKW C.35 | CH | EKW | Fr | 1937 | Hispano-Suiza 12Ycrs 860 hp (12 cl V) l.c. | 13 | 42.8 |
| 80 | Svenska J6 Jaktfalk | S | Svenska Aero A.B. | Fr | 1931 | Bristol Jupiter VIIF 500 hp (r 9 cl) a.c. | 8.80 | 28.8 |
| 80 | Boeing P-12E | USA | Boeing Airplane Co. | Fr | 1931 | Pratt & Whitney Wasp 500 hp (r 9 cl) a.c. | 9.14 | 30 |
| 80 | Boeing P-26A | USA | Boeing Airplane Co. | Fr | 1934 | Pratt & Whitney Wasp 500 hp (r 9 cl) a.c. | 8.52 | 27.9 |
| 80 | Boeing F4B-4 | USA | Boeing Airplane Co. | Fr | 1932 | Pratt & Whitney Wasp 550 hp (r 9 cl) a.c. | 9.14 | 30 |
| 80 | Grumman FF-1 | USA | Grumman Aircraft Engineering Co. | Fr | 1933 | Wright Cyclone 700 hp (r 9 cl) a.c. | 10.51 | 34.6 |
| 80 | Grumman F3F-1 | USA | Grumman Aircraft Engineering Co. | Fr | 1936 | Pratt & Whitney Twin Wasp Jr. 700 hp (r 14 cl) a.c. | 9.75 | 32 |
| 80 | Grumman F4F-4 Wildcat | USA | Grumman Aircraft Engineering Corp. | Fr | 1941 | Pratt & Whitney R-1830-86 Twin Wasp 1200 hp (r 14 cl) a.c. | 11.58 | 38 |
| 80 | Seversky P-35 | USA | Republic Aviation Corp. | Fr | 1937 | Pratt & Whitney R-1830-9 Twin Wasp 950 hp (r 14 cl) a.c. | 10.97 | 36 |
| 80 | Curtiss F9C-2 | USA | Curtiss Aeroplane and Motor Co. | Fr | 1932 | Wright Whirlwind 438 hp (r 9 cl) a.c. | 7.74 | 25.6 |
| 80 | Curtiss P-6E Hawk | USA | Curtiss Aeroplane and Motor Co. | Fr | 1932 | Curtiss V-1750-23 700 hp (12 cl V) l.c. | 9.60 | 31.6 |
| 80 | Curtiss P-36-C | USA | Curtiss-Wright Corp. | Fr | 1939 | Pratt & Whitney R-1830-17 Twin Wasp 1200 hp (r 14 cl) a.c. | 11.38 | 37.4 |
| 81 | Polikarpov-Grigorowitsh | USSR | State Industries | Fr | 1931 | M.22 480 hp (r 9 cl) a.c. | 10.24 | 33.7 |
| 81 | Polikarpov I-15 | USSR | States Industries | Fr | 1934 | M.25 (Wright Cyclone) 700 hp (r 9 cl) a.c. | 9.15 | 30 |
| 81 | Polikarpov I-16/10 | USSR | State Industries | Fr | 1937 | M.25B 775 hp (r 9 cl) a.c. | 9 | 29.6 |
| 81 | Polikarpov I-17 | USSR | State Industries | Fr | 1937 | Klimov M.100 860 hp (12 cl V) l.c. | 10.10 | 33.1 |
| 81 | Mikoyan-Gurevich MiG-1 | USSR | State Industries | Fr | 1940 | Mikulin AM.35 1200 hp (12 cl V) l.c. | 10.28 | 33.9 |
| 81 | Kawasaki Ki-10 | J | Kawasaki Kokuki Kogyo K.K. | Fr | 1935 | Kawasaki Ha.911a 850 hp (12 cl V) l.c. | 9.55 | 31.4 |
| 81 | Nakajima Tipo 91 | J | Nakajima Hikoki K.K. | Fr | 1931 | Bristol Jupiter-Nakajima 500 hp (r 9 cl) a.c. | 10.97 | 36 |
| 81 | Nakajima Ki-27b | J | Nakajima Hikoki K.K. | Fr | 1939 | Nakajima Ha-1b 710 hp (r 9 cl) a.c. | 11.31 | 37.1 |
| 81 | Nakajima Ki-43 Hayabusa-Ia | J | Nakajima Hikoki K.K. | Fr | 1940 | Nakajima Ha-25 980 hp (r 14 cl) a.c. | 11.43 | 37.6 |
| 81 | Mitsubishi A5M4 | J | Mitsubishi Jukogyo K.K. | Fr | 1939 | Nakajima Kotobuki 41 710 hp (r 9 cl) a.c. | 11 | 36.1 |
| 81 | Mitsubishi A6M2 Reisen | J | Mitsubishi Jukogyo K.K. | Fr | 1940 | Nakajima NK1C Sakae 12 950 hp (r 14 cl) a.c. | 12 | 39.3 |
| 82 | Junkers Ju.87B-1 | D | Junkers Flugzeuge und Motorenwerke AG. | A | 1938 | Junkers Jumo 211 Da 1200 hp (12 cl V) l.c. | 13.79 | 45.3 |
| 82 | Junkers Ju.86E-1 | D | Junkers Flugzeuge und Motorenwerke AG. | Br | 1937 | 2 x B.M.W. 132F 810 hp (r 9 cl) a.c. | 22.47 | 73.8 |
| 82 | Junkers Ju.88A-1 | D | Junkers Flugzeuge und Motorenwerke AG. | Br | 1939 | 2 x Junkers Jumo 211B 1200 hp (12 cl V) l.c. | 18.38 | 60.3 |
| 82 | Dornier Do.23G | D | Dornier Werke GmbH | Br | 1935 | 2 x B.M.W. VI U 750 hp (12 cl V) l.c. | 25.60 | 84 |
| 82 | Dornier Do.17Z-2 | D | Dornier Werke GmbH | Br | 1939 | 2 x B.M.W. Bramo 323P 100 hp (r 9 cl) a.c. | 18 | 59 |
| 82 | Dornier Do.217 E-1 | D | Dornier Werke GmbH | Br | 1940 | 2 x B.M.W. 801 MA 1580 hp (r 14 cl) a.c. | 19 | 62.4 |
| 82 | Heinkel He.111H-2 | D | Ernst Heinkel AG. | Br | 1939 | 2 x Junkers Jumo 211A-3 1100 hp (r 14 cl) a.c. | 22.60 | 74.1 |
| 82 | Heinkel He.115B-1 | D | Ernst Heinkel AG. | TB | 1939 | 2 x B.M.W. 132K 960 hp (r 9 cl) a.c. | 22.20 | 72.2 |
| 83 | Fairey Swordfish Mk.I | GB | Fairey Aviation Co. Ltd. | TB | 1936 | Bristol Pegasus III M.3 690 hp (r 9 cl) a.c. | 13.87 | 45.6 |
| 83 | Fairey Battle Mk.I | GB | Fairey Aviation Co. Ltd. | Br | 1937 | Rolls-Royce Merlin Mk-1 1030 hp (12 cl V) l.c. | 16.46 | 54 |
| 83 | Fairey Albacore | GB | Fairey Aviation Co. Ltd. | TB | 1940 | Bristol Taurus II 1065 hp (r 14 cl) a.c. | 15.24 | 50 |
| 83 | Blackburn Baffin | GB | Blackburn Aeroplane and Motor Co. Ltd. | TB | 1934 | Bristol Pegasus IM3 565 hp (r 9 cl) a.c. | 13.86 | 45.6 |
| 83 | Blackburn Shark Mk.III | GB | Blackburn Aeroplane and Motor Co. Ltd. | TB | 1937 | Armstrong Siddeley Tiger VI 760 hp (r 14 cl) a.c. | 14.02 | 46 |
| 83 | Handley Page Heyford Mk.IA | GB | Handley Page Ltd. | Br | 1933 | 2 x Rolls-Royce Kestrel IIIS 525 hp (12 cl V) l.c. | 22.86 | 75 |
| 83 | Handley Page Hampden Mk.I | GB | Handley Page Ltd. | Br | 1938 | 2 x Bristol Pegasus XVIII 1000 hp (r 9 cl) a.c. | 21.08 | 69.2 |
| 83 | Handley Page Halifax Mk.I | GB | Handley Page Ltd. | Br | 1940 | 4 x Rolls-Royce Merlin X 1280 hp (12 cl V) l.c. | 30.12 | 98.8 |
| 83 | Bristol Beaufort Mk.I | GB | Bristol Aeroplane Co. Ltd. | TB | 1939 | 2 x Bristol Taurus VI 1130 hp (r 14 cl) a.c. | 17.62 | 57.8 |
| 83 | Bristol Blenheim Mk.I | GB | Bristol Aeroplane Co. Ltd. | Br | 1937 | 2 x Bristol Mercury VIII 840 hp (r 9 cl) | 17.17 | 56.4 |
| 83 | Vickers Wellesley Mk.I | GB | Vickers Ltd. | Br | 1937 | Bristol Pegasus XX 925 hp (r 9 cl) a.c. | 22.73 | 74.7 |
| 83 | Vickers Vildebeest Mk.IV | GB | Vickers Ltd. | TB | 1937 | Bristol Perseus VIII 825 hp (r 9 cl) a.c. | 14.93 | 49 |
| 83 | Vickers Wellington Mk.I | GB | Vickers-Armstrongs Ltd. | Br | 1938 | 2 x Bristol Pegasus XVIII 1000 hp (r 9 cl) a.c. | 26.26 | 86.2 |
| 83 | Armstrong Whitworth Whitley Mk.V | GB | Armstrong Whitworth Aircraft | Br | 1939 | 2 x Rolls-Royce Merlin X 1145 hp (12 cl V) l.c. | 25.60 | 84 |
| 83 | Short Stirling Mk.I | GB | Short Brothers Ltd. | Br | 1940 | 4 x Bristol Hercules XI 1590 hp (r 14 cl) a.c. | 31.21 | 99.1 |
| 84 | Breda Ba.88 | I | Società Italiana Ernesto Breda | A | 1938 | 2 x Piaggio P.XI RC40 1000 hp (r 14 cl) a.c. | 15.60 | 51.2 |
| 84 | SIAI Marchetti S.M.79III | I | SIAI Marchetti | Br/TB | 1937 | 3 x Alfa Romeo A.R.126RC34 750 hp (r 9 cl) a.c. | 21.20 | 69.7 |
| 84 | SIAI Marchetti S.M.81 | I | SIAI Marchetti | Br | 1935 | 3 x Alfa Romeo A.R.125RC35 680 hp (r 9 cl) a.c. | 24 | 78.9 |
| 84 | Fiat B.R.20 | I | Fiat S.A. | Br | 1937 | 2 x Fiat A.80RC41 1000 hp (r 18 cl) a.c. | 21.56 | 70.8 |
| 84 | CANT Z.1007 bis | I | Cantieri Riuniti dell'Adriatico | Br | 1938 | 3 x Piaggio P.XI RC40 1000 hp (r 14 cl) a.c. | 24.80 | 81.4 |
| 84 | CANT Z.506B | I | Cantieri Riuniti dell'Adriatico | Br | 1937 | 3 x Alfa Romeo A.R.126RC34 750 hp (r 9 cl) a.c. | 26.50 | 86.9 |
| 85 | Fokker T.VIII | NL | Fokker | Br | 1940 | 2 x Wright Whirlwind 450 hp (r 9 cl) a.c. | 17.98 | 59 |
| 85 | PZL P.23B | PL | Pantswowe Zaklady Lotnicze | A | 1937 | PZL-Bristol Pegasus VIII 680 hp (r 9 cl) a.c. | 13.95 | 45.9 |
| 85 | PZL P.37B | PL | Pantswowe Zaklady Lotnicze | Br | 1938 | 2 x PZL-Bristol Pegasus XIIB 873 hp (r 9 cl) a.c. | 17.93 | 58.8 |
| 85 | Breguet 691 | F | Breguet | A | 1939 | 2 x Hispano-Suiza A4 Ab 700 hp (r 14 cl) a.c. | 15.36 | 50.5 |
| 85 | Latécoère 298 | F | Latécoère | Br | 1938 | Hispano-Suiza 12 Ycrs 880 hp (12 cl V) l.c. | 15.50 | 50.8 |
| 85 | Potez 540M4 | F | Société des Aéroplanes Henry Potez | Br | 1934 | 2 x Hispano-Suiza 12Kirs 690 hp (12 cl V) l.c. | 22.10 | 72.6 |
| 85 | Lioré et Olivier LeO 451 | F | SNCASE | Br | 1935 | 2 x Gnome-Rhône 14N 1140 hp (r 14 cl) a.c. | 22.50 | 73.8 |

| Length | | Height | | Take-off weight | | Speed | | Ceiling | | Range | | Crew | Payload/armament |
|---|---|---|---|---|---|---|---|---|---|---|---|---|---|
| m | ft | m | ft | kg | lb | km/h | mph | m | ft | km | ml | | |
| 7.45 | 24.5 | 2.63 | 8.8 | 1,850 | 4,080 | 375 | 233 | 8,800 | 28,900 | 750 | 466 | 1 | 2 mg |
| 8.26 | 27 | 3.30 | 10.8 | 2,295 | 5,060 | 440 | 273 | 10,500 | 34,450 | 785 | 490 | 1 | 2 mg |
| 7.80 | 25.7 | 2.95 | 9.8 | 2,395 | 5,280 | 473 | 294 | 10,730 | 35,200 | 675 | 420 | 1 | 2 mg |
| 8.19 | 26.9 | 3.51 | 11.6 | 2,208 | 4,874 | 512 | 318 | 8,750 | 28,700 | 870 | 540 | 1 | 2 mg |
| 8.36 | 27.5 | 3.15 | 10.4 | 3,170 | 6,989 | 563 | 349 | 11,000 | 36,100 | 1,100 | 684 | 1 | 4 mg |
| 9.30 | 30.6 | 3.20 | 10.6 | 3,490 | 7,695 | 430 | 267 | 8,300 | 27,230 | 550 | 342 | 1 | 4 mg |
| 9.25 | 30.4 | 3.75 | 12.4 | 3,122 | 6,882 | 335 | 208 | 10,000 | 32,800 | 620 | 385 | 2 | 1 g; 3 mg; b (100 kg - 220 lb) |
| 7.50 | 24.7 | 3.46 | 11.4 | 1,740 | 3,836 | 310 | 193 | 8,000 | 26,200 | 550 | 342 | 1 | 2 mg |
| 6.17 | 20.3 | 2.74 | 9 | 1,220 | 2,690 | 304 | 189 | 8,020 | 26,300 | 941 | 585 | 1 | 2 mg |
| 7.26 | 23.8 | 3.17 | 10.4 | 1,340 | 2,955 | 377 | 235 | 8,352 | 27,401 | 1,022 | 635 | 1 | 2 mg; b (50 kg - 110 lb) |
| 6.12 | 20.1 | 2.84 | 9.4 | 1,635 | 3,611 | 302 | 188 | 8,200 | 26,900 | 941 | 585 | 1 | 2 mg |
| 7.46 | 24.6 | 3.63 | 11.1 | 2,187 | 4,830 | 333 | 207 | 6,400 | 21,000 | 1,481 | 920 | 2 | 3 mg |
| 7.06 | 23.1 | 2.84 | 9.4 | 1,867 | 4,121 | 372 | 231 | 8,687 | 28,500 | 853 | 530 | 1 | 2 mg; b (50 kg - 110 lb) |
| 8.76 | 28.9 | 3.60 | 11.8 | 3,360 | 7,408 | 512 | 318 | 10,640 | 34,900 | 1,240 | 770 | 1 | 6 mg; b (91 kg - 200 lb) |
| 8.17 | 25.2 | 2.97 | 9.9 | 2,855 | 6,195 | 453 | 281 | 9,330 | 30,600 | 1,850 | 1,150 | 1 | 2 mg; b (136 kg - 300 lb) |
| 6.27 | 20.5 | 3.32 | 10.8 | 1,255 | 2,767 | 284 | 176 | 5,852 | 19,199 | 589 | 366 | 1 | 2 mg |
| 7.06 | 23.1 | 2.72 | 8.8 | 1,538 | 3,392 | 319 | 198 | 7,530 | 24,700 | 460 | 285 | 1 | 2 mg |
| 8.68 | 28.6 | 3.70 | 12.2 | 2,790 | 6,150 | 500 | 331 | 10,300 | 33,700 | 1,320 | 825 | 1 | 4 mg |
| 6.78 | 22.3 | 2.98 | 9.9 | 1,355 | 2,767 | 278 | 173 | 7,300 | 23,950 | 660 | 410 | 1 | 2 mg |
| 6.30 | 20.6 | 2.92 | 9.7 | 1,420 | 3,130 | 360 | 223 | 10,000 | 32,808 | 725 | 450 | 1 | 4 mg |
| 6.07 | 19.9 | 2.46 | 8 | 1,678 | 3,699 | 464 | 288 | 9,000 | 29,525 | 800 | 497 | 1 | 4 mg |
| 7.40 | 24.2 | 2.56 | 8.5 | 1,912 | 4,215 | 490 | 305 | 11,000 | 36,100 | 800 | 497 | 1 | 1 g; 2 mg |
| 8.15 | 26.9 | 2.59 | 8.6 | 3,095 | 6,823 | 627 | 390 | 12,000 | 39,370 | 580 | 360 | 1 | 3 mg; b (200 kg - 440 lb) |
| 7.20 | 23.7 | 3 | 9.8 | 1,650 | 3,640 | 400 | 250 | 10,000 | 32,808 | 1,100 | 680 | 1 | 2 mg |
| 7.21 | 23.7 | 2.79 | 9.2 | 1,530 | 3,370 | 299 | 186 | 9,000 | 29,525 | 600 | 370 | 1 | 2 mg |
| 7.53 | 24.8 | 3.25 | 10.8 | 1,790 | 3,946 | 470 | 292 | — | — | 627 | 389 | 1 | 2 mg; b (100 kg - 220 lb) |
| 8.83 | 29 | 3.27 | 10.9 | 2,048 | 4,515 | 495 | 308 | 11,170 | 38,500 | 1,200 | 745 | 1 | 2 mg; b (30 kg - 66 lb) |
| 7.56 | 24.8 | 3.26 | 10.9 | 1,671 | 3,684 | 434 | 270 | 9,800 | 32,150 | 1,200 | 745 | 1 | 2 mg; b (60 kg - 132 lb) |
| 9.02 | 27.8 | 3.05 | 10 | 2,410 | 5,313 | 534 | 322 | 10,000 | 32,808 | 3,105 | 1,930 | 1 | 2 g; 2 mg; b (60 kg - 132 lb) |
| 11.10 | 36.5 | 4.01 | 13.2 | 4,330 | 9,560 | 383 | 238 | 8,000 | 26,250 | 788 | 490 | 2 | 3 mg; b (500 kg - 1,100 lb) |
| 17.85 | 58.7 | 5.05 | 16.8 | 8,190 | 18,078 | 360 | 224 | 7,500 | 24,610 | 1,400 | 870 | 4 | 3 mg; b (1,000 kg - 2,200 lb) |
| 14.36 | 47.1 | 5.32 | 17.6 | 10,360 | 22,840 | 450 | 280 | 8,000 | 26,250 | 1,700 | 1,056 | 4 | 3 mg; b (1,800 kg - 3,960 lb) |
| 18.78 | 61.8 | 5.40 | 17.8 | 8,750 | 19,290 | 260 | 162 | 5,800 | 19,029 | 1,200 | 745 | 4 | 3 mg; b (1,000 kg - 2,200 lb) |
| 15.79 | 51.8 | 4.55 | 14.9 | 8,590 | 18,930 | 410 | 255 | 8,200 | 26,900 | 1,160 | 721 | 4 | 6 mg; b (1,000 kg - 2,200 lb) |
| 18.19 | 59.8 | 5.03 | 16.6 | 14,980 | 33,070 | 515 | 320 | 7,500 | 24,600 | 2,300 | 1,430 | 4 | 5 mg; 1 g; b (2,000 kg - 4,410 lb) |
| 16.39 | 53.9 | 4 | 13.1 | 14,000 | 30,865 | 405 | 252 | 8,500 | 27,900 | 2,060 | 1,260 | 5 | 6 mg; b (2,495 kg - 5,501 lb) |
| 17.30 | 56.9 | 6.60 | 21.8 | 9,100 | 20,065 | 365 | 220 | 5,500 | 18,040 | 3,350 | 2,080 | 3 | 2 mg; b (1,500 kg - 3,300 lb) |
| 11.07 | 36.4 | 3.91 | 12.8 | 4,190 | 9,250 | 224 | 139 | 3,260 | 10,700 | 879 | 546 | 2-3 | 2 mg; 1 t |
| 15.87 | 52.1 | 4.72 | 15.6 | 4,895 | 10,792 | 388 | 241 | 7,160 | 23,500 | 1,690 | 1,050 | 3 | 2 mg; b (455 kg - 1,000 lb) |
| 12.11 | 39.9 | 4.65 | 15.3 | 5,700 | 12,566 | 259 | 161 | 6,300 | 20,700 | 1,500 | 930 | 3 | 3 mg; 1 t |
| 11.66 | 38.3 | 4.09 | 13.5 | 3,452 | 7,610 | 219 | 136 | 4,570 | 15,000 | 725 | 450 | 2 | 2 mg; 1 t |
| 10.72 | 35.2 | 3.68 | 12.1 | 3,651 | 8,050 | 245 | 152 | 5,000 | 16,400 | 1,005 | 625 | 2-3 | 2 mg; 1 t |
| 17.67 | 58 | 5.33 | 17.6 | 7,655 | 16,876 | 228 | 142 | 6,400 | 21,000 | 1,500 | 900 | 4 | 3 mg; b (1,300 kg - 2,800 lb) |
| 16.33 | 53.7 | 4.55 | 14.9 | 8,508 | 18,756 | 409 | 254 | 6,920 | 22,700 | 3,034 | 1,885 | 4 | 6 mg; b (1,815 kg - 4,000 lb) |
| 21.36 | 70.1 | 6.33 | 20.9 | 26,274 | 57,924 | 426 | 265 | 6,950 | 22,800 | 3,000 | 1,860 | 7 | 6 mg; b (5,890 kg - 13,000 lb) |
| 13.59 | 44.7 | 3.79 | 12.5 | 9,630 | 21,228 | 426 | 265 | 5,050 | 16,500 | 2,575 | 1,600 | 4 | 4 mg; 1 t |
| 12.12 | 39.9 | 2.99 | 9.8 | 5,670 | 12,500 | 428 | 260 | 8,315 | 27,280 | 1,810 | 1,125 | 3 | 2 mg; b (454 kg - 1,000 lb) |
| 11.96 | 39.3 | 3.76 | 12.4 | 5,028 | 11,100 | 367 | 228 | 10,000 | 32,808 | 1,786 | 1,100 | 2 | 2 mg; b (905 kg - 2,000 lb) |
| 11.48 | 37.8 | 4.47 | 14.8 | 3,855 | 8,500 | 251 | 156 | 5,180 | 17,000 | 1,015 | 630 | 2 | 1 t or b (1,000 kg - 2,200 lb) |
| 19.68 | 64.7 | 5.31 | 17.5 | 12,910 | 28,500 | 378 | 235 | 5,500 | 18,000 | 1,930 | 1,199 | 6 | 6 mg; b (2,000 kg - 4,500 lb) |
| 21.49 | 70.6 | 4.57 | 15 | 12,792 | 28,200 | 357 | 222 | 5,365 | 17,600 | 2,655 | 1,650 | 5 | 5 mg; b (3,175 kg - 7,000 lb) |
| 26.60 | 87.3 | 6.93 | 22.9 | 31,752 | 70,000 | 418 | 260 | 5,180 | 17,000 | 3,100 | 1,926 | 7-8 | 10 mg; b (6,350 kg - 14,000 lb) |
| 10.97 | 35.9 | 3.10 | 10.3 | 6,750 | 14,900 | 490 | 304 | 8,000 | 26,200 | 1,640 | 1,019 | 2 | 4 mg; b (1,000 kg - 2,200 lb) |
| 15.60 | 51.2 | 4.60 | 15.8 | 10,500 | 23,180 | 430 | 267 | 7,000 | 23,000 | 1,900 | 1,180 | 6 | 4-5 mg |
| 17.80 | 58.3 | 4.30 | 14.1 | 10,505 | 23,190 | 340 | 211 | 7,000 | 23,000 | 1,800 | 1,119 | 6 | 6 mg; b (2,000 kg - 4,400 lb) |
| 16.10 | 52.8 | 4.30 | 14.1 | 9,900 | 21,850 | 432 | 268 | 9,000 | 29,525 | 3,000 | 1,860 | 5 | 3 mg; b (1,600 kg - 3,257 lb) |
| 18.47 | 66.1 | 5.22 | 17.1 | 13,621 | 30,029 | 456 | 283 | 8,400 | 27,559 | 2,000 | 1,243 | 5 | 4 mg; b (1,100 kg - 2,430 lb) |
| 19.24 | 63.1 | 7.46 | 24.5 | 12,400 | 27,337 | 364 | 226 | 7,500 | 24,606 | 2,745 | 1,700 | 5 | 4 mg; b (1,200 kg - 2,650 lb) |
| 13 | 42.8 | 5 | 16.5 | 5,000 | 11,030 | 285 | 177 | 6,800 | 22,300 | 2,750 | 1,710 | 3 | 2-3 mg; b (600 kg - 1,329 lb) |
| 9.68 | 31.9 | 3.30 | 10.8 | 3,526 | 7,773 | 319 | 198 | 7,300 | 23,950 | 1,260 | 782 | 3 | 2 mg; b (700 kg - 1,543 lb) |
| 12.92 | 42.5 | 5.08 | 16.8 | 8,560 | 18,872 | 445 | 276 | 6,000 | 19,685 | 1,500 | 932 | 4 | 3 mg; b (2,580 kg - 5,688 lb) |
| 9.65 | 31.9 | 3.17 | 10.6 | 4,995 | 11,023 | 479 | 298 | 8,500 | 27,900 | 1,350 | 840 | 2 | 1 g; 1 mg; b (400 kg - 880 lb) |
| 12.56 | 41.2 | 5.14 | 16.8 | 4,330 | 9,546 | 300 | 180 | 6,000 | 19,685 | 1,500 | 932 | 2-3 | 3 mg; b (670 kg - 1,447 lb) |
| 16.20 | 53.2 | 3.88 | 12.9 | 5,950 | 13,115 | 310 | 193 | 10,000 | 32,808 | 1,200 | 745 | 4 | 5 mg; b (900 kg - 1,980 lb) |
| 17.17 | 56.4 | 5.23 | 17.2 | 11,385 | 25,133 | 494 | 307 | 9,000 | 29,525 | 2,300 | 1,430 | 4 | 1 g; 2 mg; b (2,000 kg - 4,400 lb) |

# Technical Data

| Page | Aircraft | Nation | Manufacturer | Type | Year | Engine | Wingspan m | ft |
|------|----------|--------|--------------|------|------|--------|-----------|-----|
| 85 | Bloch 210 | F | SNCASO | Br | 1935 | 2 x Gnome-Rhône 14N 950 hp (r 14 cl) a.c. | 22.80 | 74.8 |
| 85 | Bloch 131 | F | SNCASO | Br | 1938 | 2 x Gnome-Rhône 14N 870 hp (r 14 cl) a.c. | 20.27 | 66.6 |
| 85 | Amiot 143 | F | SECM | Br | 1935 | 2 x Gnome-Rhône 14Kirs 870 hp (r 14 cl) a.c. | 24.51 | 80.4 |
| 85 | Amiot 354 | F | SECM | Br | 1940 | 2 x Gnome-Rhône 14N 1060 hp (r 14 cl) a.c. | 22.83 | 74.9 |
| 85 | Farman F.222 | F | SNCAC | Br | 1937 | 4 x Gnome-Rhône 14N 950 hp (r 14 cl) a.c. | 36 | 118.1 |
| 86 | Keystone B-4A | USA | Keystone Aircraft Co. | Br | 1932 | 2 x Pratt & Whitney Hornet 575 hp (r 9 cl) a.c. | 22.78 | 74.9 |
| 86 | Martin B-10B | USA | Glenn L. Martin Co. | Br | 1935 | 2 x Wright Cyclone 775 hp (r 9 cl) a.c. | 21.49 | 70.6 |
| 86 | Curtiss A.12 Shrike | USA | Curtiss Aeroplane and Motor Co. | A | 1934 | Wright Cyclone 690 hp (r 9 cl) a.c. | 13.41 | 44 |
| 86 | Douglas B-18A | USA | Douglas Aircraft Co. | Br | 1937 | 2 x Wright R-1820-53 Cyclone 1000 hp (r 9 cl) a.c. | 27.28 | 89.6 |
| 86 | Douglas TBD-1 Devastater | USA | Douglas Aircraft Co. | TB | 1937 | Pratt & Whitney R-1830-64 Twin Wasp 900 hp (r 14 cl) a.c. | 15.24 | 50 |
| 86 | Northrop A-17A | USA | Northrop Co. | A | 1936 | Pratt & Whitney R-1535-13 Wasp 825 hp (r 9 cl) a.c. | 14.55 | 47.9 |
| 86 | Ilyushin Il-4 | USSR | State Industries | Br | 1940 | 2 x M.88B 1100 hp (r 14 cl) a.c. | 21.44 | 70.4 |
| 86 | Petlyakov Pe-8 | USSR | State Industries | Br | 1940 | 4 x Mikulin AM.35A 1350 hp (12 cl V) l.c. | 39.94 | 131 |
| 87 | Tupolev TB-3 | USSR | State Industries | Br | 1931 | 4 x M.17F (B.M.W.) 730 hp (12 cl V) l.c. | 39.50 | 129.5 |
| 87 | Tupolev SB-2 | USSR | State Industries | Br | 1936 | 2 x Klimov M.100A 830 hp (12 cl V) l.c. | 20.33 | 66.8 |
| 87 | Sukhoi Su-2 | USSR | State Industries | Br | 1940 | Elvetsov M.82 1400 hp (r 14 cl) a.c. | 14.30 | 46.9 |
| 87 | Kalinin K-7 | USSR | State Industries | Br | 1933 | 6 x M.34F 750 hp (12 cl V) l.c. | 53 | 173.8 |
| 87 | Mitsubishi B2M1 | J | Mitsubishi Jukogyo K.K. | TB | 1932 | Hispano-Mitsubishi 600 hp (12 cl V) l.c. | 15.22 | 49.9 |
| 87 | Mitsubishi Ki-2 | J | Mitsubishi Jukogyo K.K. | Br | 1933 | 2 x Napier Kotobuki 570 hp (r 9 cl) a.c. | 19.96 | 65.6 |
| 87 | Mitsubishi Ki-51 | J | Mitsubishi Jukogyo K.K. | A | 1940 | Mitsubishi Ha-26-II 940 hp (r 14 cl) a.c. | 12.10 | 39.8 |
| 87 | Mitsubishi G3M2 | J | Mitsubishi Jukogyo K.K. | Br | 1937 | 2 x Mitsubishi Kinsei 41 1075 hp (r 14 cl) a.c. | 25 | 82 |
| 87 | Kawasaki Ki-32 | J | Kawasaki Kokuki Kogyo K.K. | Br | 1938 | Ha-9-IIb 850 hp (12 cl V) l.c. | 15 | 49.2 |
| 87 | Aichi D3A1 | J | Aichi Kokuki K.K. | Br | 1940 | Mitsubishi Kinsei 43 1000 hp (r 14 cl) a.c. | 14.36 | 47.1 |
| 87 | Nakajima B5N2 | J | Nakajima Hikoki K.K. | TB | 1940 | Nakajima NK1B Sakae11 1000 hp (r 14 cl) a.c. | 15.51 | 50.9 |
| 92 | Junkers Ju.52/3m g3e | D | Junkers Flugzeuge und Motorenwerke AG. | Br | 1934 | 3 x B.M.W. 12A-3 725 hp (r 9 cl) a.c. | 29.95 | 95.9 |
| 92 | Bücker Bü.131B Jungman | D | Bücker Flugzeugbau GmbH | T | 1936 | Hirth HM504 100 hp (4 cl) a.c. | 7.40 | 24.3 |
| 92 | Blohm und Voss Bv.141A | D | Blohm und Voss Schiffeswert Abteilung Flugzeugbau | Rc | 1940 | B.M.W. 132N 865 hp (r 9 cl) a.c. | 15.45 | 50.8 |
| 92 | Arado Ar.196 A-1 | D | Arado Flugzeugwerke GmbH | Rc | 1939 | B.M.W. 132K 960 hp (r 9 cl) a.c. | 12.40 | 40.8 |
| 92 | Arado Ar. 96 B-1 | D | Arado Flugzeugwerke GmbH | T | 1940 | Argus As.410A 450 hp (12 cl V) l.c. | 11 | 36.1 |
| 92 | Arado Ar.240 | D | Arado Flugzeugwerke GmbH | Rc | 1940 | 2 x Daimler Benz DB601E 1175 hp (12 cl V) l.c. | 13.34 | 43.9 |
| 92 | Dornier Do.18D-1 | D | Dornier Werke GmbH | Rc | 1938 | 2 x Junkers Jumo 205C 600 hp (6 cl) l.c. | 23.70 | 77.9 |
| 92 | Henschel Hs.126B-1 | D | Henschel Flugzeugbau GmbH | Rc | 1939 | B.M.W. Bramo 323 A-1 850 hp (r 9 cl) a.c. | 14.50 | 47.7 |
| 92 | Fieseler Fi 156 C-2 | D | Gerhard Fieseler Werke GmbH | Rc | 1939 | Argus As.10C-3 240 hp (8 cl V) l.c. | 14.25 | 46.9 |
| 92 | Focke Wulf Fw.189A-1 | D | Focke Wulf Flugzeugbau GmbH | Rc | 1940 | 2 x Argus As.410 A-1 465 hp (12 cl V) l.c. | 18.39 | 60.4 |
| 92 | Focke Wulf Fw.200C-1 Condor | D | Focke Wulf Flugzeugbau | Br/Rc | 1940 | 4 x B.M.W. 132H 830 hp (r 9 cl) a.c. | 30.86 | 101.2 |
| 93 | Avro Tutor Mk.I | GB | A.V. Roe & Co. Ltd. | T | 1932 | Armstrong Siddeley Lynx IVC 240 hp (r 7 cl) a.c. | 10.36 | 34 |
| 93 | Avro Anson Mk.I | GB | A.V. Roe & Co. Ltd. | Li | 1936 | 2 x Armstrong Siddeley Cheetah IX 350 hp (r 7 cl) a.c. | 17.22 | 56.6 |
| 93 | Bristol Bombay Mk.I | GB | Short & Harland Ltd. | Tr/Br | 1939 | 2 x Bristol Pegasus XXIII 1010 hp (r 9 cl) a.c. | 29.18 | 95.9 |
| 93 | de Havilland Tiger Moth Mk.II | GB | de Havilland Aircraft Co. Ltd. | T | 1932 | de Havilland Gipsy Major 130 hp (4 cl) a.c. | 8.94 | 29.4 |
| 93 | de Havilland Dominie Mk.I | GB | de Havilland Aircraft Co. Ltd. | T | 1939 | 2 x de Havilland Gipsy Six 200 hp (6 cl) l.c. | 14.63 | 48 |
| 93 | Supermarine Walrus Mk.I | GB | Saunders-Roe Ltd. | Rc | 1936 | Bristol Pegasus II M2 775 hp (r 9 cl) a.c. | 13.97 | 45.8 |
| 93 | Miles Master Mk.IA | GB | Miles Aircraft Ltd. | T | 1939 | Rolls-Royce Kestrel XXX 715 hp (12 cl V) l.c. | 11.88 | 39 |
| 93 | Fairey Seafox | GB | Fairey Aviation Co. Ltd. | Rc | 1937 | Napier Rapier VI 395 hp (16 cl H) a.c. | 12.19 | 40 |
| 93 | Airspeed Oxford Mk.I | GB | Airspeed Ltd. | T | 1937 | 2 x Armstrong Siddeley Cheetah IX 350 hp (r 7 cl) a.c. | 16.25 | 53.4 |
| 93 | Westland Lysander Mk.I | GB | Westland Aircraft Ltd. | Li | 1938 | Bristol Mercury XII 890 hp (r 9 cl) a.c. | 15.24 | 50 |
| 93 | Short Sunderland Mk.I | GB | Short Brothers Ltd. | Rc | 1938 | 4 x Bristol Pegasus XXIII 1010 hp (r 9 cl) a.c. | 34.35 | 112.9 |
| 93 | Breguet 521 | F | Breguet | MR | 1935 | 3 x Gnome-Rhône 14 Kirs 900 hp (r 14 cl) a.c. | 35.13 | 115.2 |
| 93 | Bloch 174 | F | SNCASO | Rc | 1940 | 2 x Gnome-Rhône 14 1140 hp (r 14 cl) a.c. | 17.90 | 58.9 |
| 93 | Dewoitine D.720 | F | SNCAM | Rc | 1939 | 2 x Renault 12R 500 hp (12 cl V) a.c. | 14.90 | 48.9 |
| 93 | Hanriot Nc-530 | F | SNCAC | Rc | 1933 | M.17 680 hp (12 cl V) l.c. | 13.40 | 43.9 |
| 96 | Beriev MBR-2 | USSR | State Industries | Rc | 1933 | M.17 680 hp (12 cl V) l.c. | 13.40 | 43.9 |
| 96 | Beriev KOR-1 | USSR | State Industries | Rc | 1938 | M.25 750 hp (r 9 cl) a.c. | 10.99 | 36.1 |
| 96 | Tchetverikov ARK-3 | USSR | State Industries | Rc | 1936 | 2 x M.25V 750 hp (r 9 cl) a.c. | 19.90 | 65.3 |
| 96 | Tchetverikov MDR-6 | USSR | State Industries | Rc | 1939 | 2 x M.63 1100 hp (r 9 cl) a.c. | 19.78 | 64.9 |
| 96 | Polikarpov R.5 | USSR | State Industries | Rc | 1931 | M.17 680 hp (12 cl V) l.c. | 15.50 | 50.8 |
| 96 | Letov S.328 | CS | Letov | Rc | 1934 | Bristol Pegasus II M.2 560 hp (r 9 cl) a.c. | 13.70 | 44.9 |
| 96 | Aero A.100 | CS | Aero Tovarna Letadel | Rc | 1934 | Avia Vr-36 735 hp (12 cl V) l.c. | 14.70 | 48.3 |
| 96 | Vought OS2U Kingfisher | USA | United Aircraft Corp. | Rc | 1940 | Pratt & Whitney R-985-48 Wasp Jr. 450 hp (r 9 cl) a.c. | 10.94 | 35.9 |
| 96 | Stearman PT-17 Kaydet | USA | Boeing Aircraft Co. | T | 1940 | Continental R-670-5 220 hp (r 7 cl) a.c. | 9.80 | 32.2 |
| 96 | Vultee BT-13A Valiant | USA | Vultee Aircraft Inc. | T | 1940 | Pratt & Whitney R-985-AN-1 Wasp Jr. 450 hp (r 9 cl) a.c. | 12.86 | 42.2 |
| 96 | Lockheed A-28 Hudson | USA | Lockheed Aircraft Corp. | Rc | 1939 | 2 x Wright R-1820-G 102A Cyclone 1100 hp (r 9 cl) a.c. | 19.96 | 65.6 |
| 97 | Imam Ro.43 | I | Industrie Meccaniche Aeronautiche Meridionali | Rc | 1936 | Piaggio P.XR 700 hp (r 9 cl) a.c. | 11.57 | 37.9 |

| Length | | Height | | Take-off weight | | Speed | | Ceiling | | Range | | Crew | Payload/armament |
|---|---|---|---|---|---|---|---|---|---|---|---|---|---|
| m | ft | m | ft | kg | lb | km/h | mph | m | ft | km | ml | | |
| 18.82 | 61.9 | 6.70 | 22 | 10,190 | 22,487 | 322 | 200 | 9,900 | 32,480 | 1,300 | 808 | 5 | 3 mg; b (1,600 kg - 3,527 lb) |
| 17.83 | 58.4 | 4.10 | 13.5 | 8,590 | 18,960 | 349 | 217 | 7,250 | 23,785 | 1,300 | 808 | 4 | 3 mg; b (800 kg - 1,760 lb) |
| 18.26 | 59.9 | 5.66 | 18.5 | 9,700 | 21,385 | 310 | 193 | 7,900 | 25,920 | 1,200 | 746 | 5 | 4 mg; b (1,300 kg - 2,870 lb) |
| 14.50 | 47.7 | 4.06 | 13.4 | 11,285 | 24,912 | 479 | 298 | 10,000 | 32,800 | 2,500 | 1,533 | 4 | 1 g; 2 mg; b (1,000 kg - 2,200 lb) |
| 21.44 | 70.4 | 5.19 | 17 | 18,675 | 41,226 | 315 | 196 | 8,000 | 26,250 | 1,500 | 932 | 5 | 3 mg; b (4,200 kg - 9,260 lb) |
| 14.88 | 48.8 | 4.80 | 15.9 | 5,992 | 13,200 | 195 | 121 | 4,267 | 13,999 | 1,376 | 855 | 5 | 3 mg; b (1,134 kg - 2,500 lb) |
| 13.63 | 44.9 | 4.70 | 15.4 | 7,429 | 16,400 | 343 | 213 | 7,376 | 24,199 | 965 | 600 | 4 | 3 mg; b (1,024 kg - 2,260 lb) |
| 9.83 | 32.3 | 2.84 | 9.4 | 2,672 | 5,900 | 282 | 175 | 4,620 | 15,150 | 724 | 451 | 2 | 5 mg; b (180 kg - 400 lb) |
| 17.63 | 57.8 | 4.62 | 15.2 | 12,552 | 27,672 | 364 | 226 | 8,275 | 27,150 | 1,931 | 1,200 | 6 | 3 mg; b (2,948 kg - 6,500 lb) |
| 10.67 | 35 | 4.60 | 15.1 | 4,624 | 10,194 | 332 | 206 | 6,000 | 19,500 | 1,150 | 716 | 3 | 2 mg; b (454 kg - 1,000 lb) |
| 9.65 | 31.8 | 3.65 | 12 | 3,421 | 7,543 | 354 | 220 | 5,900 | 19,400 | 1,180 | 732 | 2 | 5 mg; b (180 kg - 400 lb) |
| 14.80 | 48.5 | 4.20 | 13.9 | 10,000 | 22,406 | 410 | 255 | 10,000 | 32,800 | 4,260 | 2,647 | 3-4 | 3 mg; b (2,500 kg- 5,512 lb) |
| 22.47 | 73.7 | 6.10 | 20 | 33,325 | 73,469 | 438 | 272 | 9,750 | 31,988 | 5,445 | 3,383 | 11 | 2 g; 4 mg; b (4,000 kg - 8,818 lb) |
| 24.50 | 80.3 | 8.45 | 27.7 | 17,400 | 38,360 | 215 | 134 | 3,800 | 12,470 | 2,200 | 1,367 | 8 | 6 mg; b (2,200 kg - 4,800 lb) |
| 12.27 | 40.3 | 3.25 | 10.8 | 5,725 | 12,637 | 424 | 263 | 9,500 | 31,200 | 1,200 | 745 | 3 | 4 mg; b (600 kg - 1,320 lb) |
| 10.25 | 33.7 | 3.75 | 12.3 | 4,075 | 8,965 | 485 | 302 | 8,800 | 28,900 | 1,200 | 745 | 2 | 5 mg; b (600 kg - 1,320 lb) |
| 28 | 91.8 | — | — | 38,000 | 83,700 | 225 | 140 | 4,000 | 13,000 | 1,000 | 621 | 11 | 3 g; 6 mg; b (9,000 kg - 19,800 lb) |
| 10.27 | 33.8 | 3.21 | 10.5 | 3,600 | 7,900 | 213 | 132 | 4,500 | 14,700 | 960 | 600 | 2 | 2 mg; b (800 kg - 1,764 lb) |
| 12.60 | 41.4 | 4.64 | 15.2 | 4,550 | 10,040 | 255 | 158 | 7,000 | 23,000 | 900 | 560 | 3 | 2 mg; b (300 kg - 660 lb) |
| 9.21 | 30.2 | 2.73 | 8.9 | 2,798 | 6,169 | 424 | 263 | 8,270 | 27,130 | 1,060 | 660 | 2 | 3 mg; b (200 kg - 441 lb) |
| 16.45 | 53.9 | 3.68 | 12.1 | 8,000 | 17,637 | 373 | 232 | 9,130 | 29,950 | 4,380 | 2,722 | 7 | 3 mg; b (800 kg - 1,764 lb) |
| 11.64 | 38.2 | 2.90 | 9.6 | 3,539 | 7,802 | 423 | 263 | 8,920 | 29,265 | 1,300 | 808 | 2 | 2 mg; b (450 kg - 992 lb) |
| 10.19 | 33.5 | 3.84 | 12.7 | 3,650 | 8,047 | 386 | 240 | 9,300 | 30,050 | 1,472 | 915 | 2 | 3 mg; b (370 kg - 813 lb) |
| 10.30 | 33.9 | 3.70 | 12 | 3,800 | 8,378 | 378 | 235 | 8,260 | 27,100 | 2,000 | 1,237 | 3 | 1 mg; 1 t |
| 18.90 | 62 | 5.53 | 18.2 | 9,448 | 20,917 | 277 | 172 | 5,900 | 19,360 | 1,300 | 808 | 4 | 2 mg; b (500 kg - 1,102 lb) |
| 6.62 | 21.9 | 2.25 | 7.5 | 670 | 1,474 | 183 | 114 | 4,300 | 14,000 | 650 | 400 | 2 | — |
| 12.15 | 39.8 | 4.10 | 13.5 | 3,895 | 8,598 | 399 | 248 | 9,000 | 29,530 | 1,140 | 708 | 3 | 4 mg; b (200 kg - 441 lb) |
| 11 | 36.1 | 4.45 | 14.7 | 3,730 | 8,225 | 310 | 193 | 7,000 | 22,960 | 1,070 | 665 | 2 | 1 mg; b (100 kg - 220 lb) |
| 9.13 | 29.9 | 2.60 | 8.6 | 1,695 | 3,747 | 340 | 211 | 7,100 | 23,295 | 990 | 615 | 2 | — |
| 12.80 | 42 | 3.94 | 12.9 | 9,438 | 20,834 | 618 | 384 | 10,500 | 34,450 | 2,000 | 1,242 | 2 | 6 mg |
| 19.25 | 63.2 | 5.31 | 17.5 | 10,000 | 22,050 | 260 | 162 | 4,200 | 13,780 | 3,500 | 2,174 | 4 | 2 mg; b (100 kg - 220 lb) |
| 10.85 | 35.7 | 3.75 | 12.3 | 3,090 | 6,812 | 356 | 221 | 8,300 | 27,231 | 720 | 447 | 2 | 2 mg; b (150 kg - 330 lb) |
| 9.90 | 32.6 | 3.05 | 10 | 1,320 | 2,920 | 175 | 109 | 5,200 | 17,060 | 390 | 240 | 2-3 | 1 mg |
| 12.02 | 39.5 | 3.10 | 10.2 | 3,945 | 8,708 | 349 | 217 | 7,300 | 23,950 | 670 | 416 | 3 | 4 mg; b (200 kg - 441 lb) |
| 23.46 | 77 | 6.30 | 20.8 | 22,700 | 50,045 | 360 | 224 | 5,800 | 19,000 | 3,550 | 2,206 | 5 | 4 mg; 1 g; b (1,250 kg - 2,755 lb) |
| 8.04 | 26.6 | 2.92 | 9.7 | 1,115 | 2,458 | 196 | 122 | 4,938 | 16,200 | 402 | 250 | 2 | — |
| 12.88 | 42.3 | 3.99 | 13.1 | 3,630 | 8,000 | 303 | 188 | 5,800 | 19,000 | 1,270 | 790 | 3 | 2 mg; b (165 kg - 360 lb) |
| 21.10 | 69.3 | 6.07 | 19.9 | 9,060 | 20,000 | 309 | 192 | 7,600 | 25,000 | 1,415 | 880 | 4 | 2 mg; b (900 kg - 1,984 lb) |
| 7.29 | 23.9 | 2.66 | 8.9 | 802 | 1,770 | 176 | 109 | 5,180 | 16,995 | 482 | 300 | 2 | — |
| 10.52 | 34.6 | 3.12 | 10.3 | 2,491 | 5,500 | 253 | 157 | 5,000 | 16,404 | 930 | 580 | 5-6 | — |
| 11.45 | 37.7 | 4.65 | 15.3 | 3,261 | 7,200 | 217 | 135 | 5,650 | 18,500 | 965 | 600 | 4 | 2 mg |
| 9.27 | 30.5 | 3.05 | 10 | 2,412 | 5,328 | 364 | 226 | 8,500 | 27,887 | 800 | 500 | 2 | 1 mg |
| 10.80 | 35.5 | 3.68 | 12.1 | 2,459 | 5,420 | 200 | 124 | 3,350 | 11,000 | 708 | 440 | 2 | 1 mg |
| 10.51 | 34.6 | 3.38 | 11.1 | 3,447 | 7,600 | 298 | 182 | 5,946 | 19,504 | 1,545 | 960 | 3 | — |
| 9.29 | 30.6 | 3.50 | 11.6 | 2,685 | 5,920 | 369 | 229 | 7,900 | 26,000 | 965 | 600 | 2 | 3 mg |
| 26.11 | 85.6 | 10 | 32.1 | 20,000 | 44,092 | 338 | 210 | 5,500 | 17,900 | 4,800 | 2,980 | 13 | 7 mg; b (907 kg - 2,000 lb) |
| 20.33 | 66.6 | 7.48 | 24.5 | 16,000 | 35,320 | 243 | 151 | 6,000 | 19,700 | 2,100 | 1,305 | 8 | 5 mg; b (300 kg - 660 lb) |
| 12.22 | 40.1 | 3.54 | 11.6 | 7,150 | 15,784 | 530 | 329 | 11,000 | 36,100 | 1,650 | 1.025 | 3 | 7 mg; b (400 kg - 880 lb) |
| 10.49 | 34.5 | 3.73 | 12.3 | 3,817 | 8,426 | 360 | 224 | 8,400 | 27,560 | 1,530 | 950 | 3 | 3 mg; b (200 kg - 441 lb) |
| 11.35 | 37.3 | — | — | 5,095 | 11,244 | 410 | 255 | 8,500 | 27,890 | 1,800 | 1,118 | 3 | 3 mg; b (500 kg - 1,100 lb) |
| 9.28 | 30.2 | 5 | 16.5 | 4,240 | 9,359 | 248 | 154 | 6,000 | 19,700 | 1,200 | 746 | 4-5 | 2 mg; b (300 kg - 660 lb) |
| 8.25 | 27 | 3.81 | 12.6 | 1,126 | 2,482 | 240 | 149 | 7,000 | 22,965 | 500 | 311 | 2 | 2 mg; b (100 kg - 220 lb) |
| 14.50 | 47.7 | — | — | 5,243 | 11,574 | 320 | 199 | 8,500 | 27,890 | 1,500 | 932 | 5 | 2 mg; b (1,000 kg - 2,200 lb) |
| 14.68 | 48.2 | — | — | 6,790 | 14,991 | 360 | 224 | 9,000 | 29,530 | 1,200 | 746 | 5 | 2 mg; b (600 kg - 1,320 lb) |
| 10.55 | 34.8 | 3.25 | 10.8 | 2,955 | 6,515 | 288 | 142 | — | — | 800 | 497 | 2 | 2 mg; b (240 kg - 530 lb) |
| 10.40 | 34.1 | 3.40 | 11.1 | 2,640 | 5,820 | 280 | 174 | 7,200 | 23,600 | 700 | 435 | 2 | 4 mg |
| 10.60 | 34.9 | 3.50 | 11.4 | 3,215 | 7,099 | 268 | 166 | 6,500 | 21,325 | 920 | 570 | 2 | 4 mg; b (450 kg - 992 lb) |
| 10.31 | 33.7 | 4.59 | 15.1 | 1,815 | 4,000 | 264 | 164 | 5,950 | 19,500 | 1,300 | 805 | 2 | 2 mg |
| 7.63 | 25 | 2.79 | 9.2 | 1,232 | 2,717 | 199 | 124 | 3,415 | 11,200 | 812 | 505 | 2 | — |
| 8.76 | 28.9 | 3.75 | 12.5 | 1,980 | 4,360 | 295 | 183 | 5,030 | 16,500 | 826 | 516 | 2 | — |
| 13.51 | 44.4 | 3.60 | 11.8 | 7,983 | 17,500 | 396 | 246 | 7,620 | 25,000 | 2,400 | 1,500 | 5 | 5 mg; b (340 kg - 750 lb) |
| 9.72 | 31.8 | 3.51 | 11.6 | 2,400 | 5,300 | 303 | 188 | 7,200 | 23,622 | 1,092 | 678 | 2 | 2 mg |

# Technical Data

| Page | Aircraft | Nation | Manufacturer | Type | Year | Engine | Wingspan m | ft |
|------|----------|--------|--------------|------|------|--------|------------|-----|
| 97 | Imam Ro.37 | I | Industrie Meccaniche Aeronautiche Meridionali | Rc | 1935 | Fiat A.30 RA bis 550 hp (12 cl V) l.c. | 11.08 | 36.4 |
| 97 | Saiman 202 | I | Saiman | Li | 1936 | Alfa Romeo 110 120 hp (4 cl) a.c. | 10.75 | 35.3 |
| 97 | SIAI Marchetti S.M.82 | I | SIAI Marchetti | Tr/Br | 1940 | 3 x Alfa Romeo A.R.128 RC18 860 hp (r 14 cl) a.c. | 29.68 | 97.5 |
| 97 | SIAI Marchetti S.M.75 | I | SIAI Marchetti | Tr | 1939 | 3 x Alfa Romeo A.R.126 RC34 750 hp (r 9 cl) a.c. | 29.68 | 97.5 |
| 97 | Caproni Ca.311 | I | Società Italiana Caproni | Rc | 1939 | 2 x Piaggio P.VII RC35 470 hp (r 7 cl) a.c. | 16.20 | 53.1 |
| 97 | Cant Z.501 | I | Cantieri Riuniti dell'Adriatico | MR | 1934 | Isotta-Fraschini Asso XIRC15 900 hp (12 cl V) l.c. | 22.50 | 73.8 |
| 97 | Renard R.31 | B | Constructions Aéronautiques G. Renard | Rc | 1934 | Rolls-Royce Kestrel II-S 525 hp (12 cl V) l.c. | 14.40 | 47.3 |
| 97 | Commonwealth CA-3 Wirraway | AUS | Commonwealth Aircraft Corp. | T | 1940 | Pratt & Whitney R-1340 S1H1-G Wasp 600 hp (r 9 cl) a.c. | 13.10 | 43 |
| 97 | Mitsubishi K3M3 | J | Mitsubishi Jukogyo K.K. | T | 1939 | Nakajima Kotobuki 2KA12 580 hp (r 9 cl) a.c. | 15.78 | 51.9 |
| 97 | Mitsubishi C5M2 | J | Mitsubishi Jukogyo K.K. | Rc | 1940 | Nakajima Sakae 12 950 hp (r 14 cl) a.c. | 12 | 39.4 |
| 97 | Nakajima E8N1 | J | Nakajima Hikoki K.K. | Rc | 1935 | Nakajima Kotobuki 2KA1 580 hp (r 9 cl) a.c. | 10.98 | 36 |
| 97 | Nakajima G5N1 Shinzan | J | Nakajima Hikoki K.K. | Br | 1939 | 4 x Nakajima NK7A Mamoru 11 1870 hp (r 14 cl) a.c. | 41.14 | 138.3 |
| 97 | Yokosuka K5Y1 | J | Dai-Ichi Kaigun Koku Gijitsusho | T | 1934 | Hitaki Amazake 11 340 hp (r 9 cl) a.c. | 11 | 36.1 |
| 97 | Kawanishi H6K4 | J | Kawanishi Kokuki K.K. | Rc | 1940 | 4 x Mitsubishi Kinsei 43 1000 hp (r 14 cl) a.c. | 40 | 131.3 |
| 104 | Focke Wulf Fw. 190 A-3 | D | Focke Wulf Flugzeugbau GmbH | Fr | 1942 | B.M.W. 801 D-2 1700 hp (r 14 cl) a.c. | 10.50 | 34.5 |
| 104 | Focke Wulf Ta 152 H-1 | D | Focke Wulf Flugzeugbau GmbH | Fr | 1945 | Junkers Jumo 213 E-1 1750 hp (12 cl V) l.c. | 14.43 | 47.4 |
| 104 | Henschel Hs.129 B-1 | D | Henschel Flugzeugwerke AG. | A | 1942 | 2 x Gnome-Rhône 14 M 700 hp (r 14 cl) a.c. | 14.20 | 46.7 |
| 104 | Dornier Do.335 A-1 | D | Dornier Werke GmbH | Fr | 1944 | 2 x Daimler Benz DB603 E1 1800 hp (12 cl V) l.c. | 13.80 | 45.3 |
| 104 | Heinkel He.219 A-2/R1 | D | Ernst Heinkel AG. | NF | 1943 | 2 x Daimler Benz DB603 A 1750 hp (12 cl V) l.c. | 18.50 | 60.8 |
| 104 | Heinkel He.162A A-2 | D | Ernst Heinkel AG. | Fr | 1945 | B.M.W. 003 E-1 800 kg (1,764 lb) | 7.20 | 23.7 |
| 104 | Messerschmitt Me.163 B-1a | D | Messerschmitt AG. | Fr | 1944 | Walter HWK 509 A-2 1500 kg (3,307 lb) | 9.30 | 30.5 |
| 104 | Messerschmitt Me.410 A-1 | D | Messerschmitt AG. | FB | 1943 | 2 x Daimler Benz DB 603A 1750 hp (12 cl V) | 16.35 | 53.8 |
| 104 | Messerschmitt Me.262 A-1a | D | Messerschmitt AG. | Fr | 1944 | 2 x Junkers Jumo 004 B-1 900 kg (1,980 lb) | 12.48 | 40.9 |
| 104 | Bachem Ba.349 | D | Bachem-Werke GmbH | Ic/Fr | 1945 | Walter HWK 509 C-1 2000 kg (4,400 lb) | 3.99 | 13.1 |
| 104 | Saab 21 A | S | SAAB | Fr | 1943 | Daimler Benz DB 605B 1475 hp (12 cl V) l.c. | 11.60 | 38.1 |
| 104 | F.F.V.S. J 22 | S | F.F.V.S. | Fr | 1943 | Pratt & Whitney Twin Wasp 1065 hp (r 14 cl) a.c. | 10 | 32.8 |
| 104 | Myrsky II | SF | Valtion Lentokonetehdas | Fr | 1944 | SFA-Pratt & Whitney Twin Wasp 1065 hp (r 14 cl) a.c. | 11 | 36.1 |
| 104 | IAR 80 | R | Industria Aeronautica Romena | Fr | 1942 | I.A.R.-Gnome-Rhône 14K 940 hp (r 14 cl) a.c. | 10 | 32.8 |
| 105 | Hawker Typhoon Mk.IB | GB | Hawker Aircraft Co. Ltd. | FB | 1941 | Napier-Sabre IIA 2180 hp (24 cl H) l.c. | 12.68 | 41.7 |
| 105 | Hawker Tempest Mk.V | GB | Hawker Aircraft Co. Ltd. | FB | 1944 | Napier-Sabre II 2180 hp (24 cl H) l.c. | 12.50 | 41 |
| 105 | Hawker Sea Fury F.B.11 | GB | Hawker Aircraft Co. Ltd. | FB | 1947 | Bristol Centaurus 18 2550 hp (r 18 cl) l.c. | 11.71 | 38.5 |
| 105 | Fairey Firefly Mk.I | GB | Fairey Aviation Co. Ltd. | Fr | 1943 | Rolls-Royce Griffon IIB 1730 hp (12 cl V) l.c. | 13.56 | 44.6 |
| 105 | Supermarine Seafire Mk.IIC | GB | Supermarine Division of Vickers Armstrong Ltd. | Fr | 1942 | tj Rolls-Royce Merlin 45 1340 hp (12 cl V) l.c. | 11.22 | 36.8 |
| 105 | Supermarine Attacker F.1 | GB | Supermarine Divis. of Vickers-Armstrong Ltd. | Fr | 1947 | tj Rolls-Royce Nene 3 2313 kg (5,100 lb) | 11.25 | 36.9 |
| 105 | de Havilland Hornet F.3 | GB | de Havilland Aircraft Co. Ltd. | Fr | 1944 | 2 x Rolls-Royce Merlin 130 2030 hp (12 cl V) l.c. | 13.71 | 45 |
| 105 | de Havilland Vampire F.B.5 | GB | de Havilland Aircraft Co. Ltd. | FB | 1948 | tj de Havilland Goblin 2 1420 kg (3,100 lb) | 11.58 | 38 |
| 105 | Armstrong Whitworth Meteor N.F.11 | GB | Armstrong Whitworth Aircraft Ltd. | NF | 1950 | 2 x tj Rolls-Royce Derwent 8 1587 kg (3,500 lb) | 13.10 | 43 |
| 105 | Gloster Meteor Mk.III | GB | Gloster Aircraft Co. Ltd. | Fr | 1945 | 2 x tj Rolls-Royce Derwent 1 905 kg (1,997 lb) | 13.11 | 43 |
| 105 | Fiat CANSA | I | CANSA | A | 1941 | 2 x Fiat A.74RC38 840 hp (r 14 cl) a.c. | 16 | 52.6 |
| 105 | Fiat G.55 | I | Fiat S.A. | Fr | 1943 | Daimler-Benz DB.605A 1470 hp (12 cl V) l.c. | 11.85 | 38.8 |
| 105 | S.A.I. 207 | I | Società Aeronautica Italiana Ambrosini | Fr | 1943 | Isotta-Fraschini Delta RC40 750 hp (12 cl V) l.c. | 9 | 29.6 |
| 105 | Reggiane Re.2001 | I | Officine Meccaniche Reggiane S.p.A. | Fr/A | 1941 | Daimler-Benz DB.601/A-1 1175 hp (12 cl V) l.c. | 11 | 36.1 |
| 105 | Reggiane Re.2002 | I | Officine Meccaniche Reggiane S.p.A. | A | 1943 | Piaggio P.XIX RC45 1175 hp (r 14 cl) a.c. | 11 | 36.1 |
| 105 | Reggiane Re.2005 | I | Officine Meccaniche Reggiane S.p.A. | Fr | 1943 | Daimler-Benz DB.605A 1475 hp (12 cl V) l.c. | 11 | 36.1 |
| 105 | Macchi M.C.202 | I | Aeronautica Macchi S.p.A. | Fr | 1941 | Daimler-Benz DB.601/A-1 1175 hp (12 cl V) l.c. | 10.58 | 34.8 |
| 105 | Macchi M.C.205 | I | Aeronautica Macchi S.p.A. | Fr | 1943 | Daimler-Benz DB.605A 1475 hp (12 cl V) l.c. | 10.50 | 34.5 |
| 105 | Imam Ro.57 | I | Industrie Meccaniche Aeronautiche Meridionali | Fr | 1943 | 2 x Fiat A.74 RC 38 840 hp (r 14 cl) a.c. | 12.50 | 41 |
| 106 | Mikoyan-Gurevich MiG-3 | USSR | State Industries | Fr | 1941 | Mikulin AM.35A 1350 hp (12 cl V) l.c. | 10.28 | 33.9 |
| 106 | Mikoyan-Gurevich MiG-5 | USSR | State Industries | Fr | 1943 | Shvetsov M.82A 1600 hp (r 14 cl) l.c. | 10.30 | 33.9 |
| 106 | Mikoyan-Gurevich MiG-7 | USSR | State Industries | Fr | 1944 | Klimov M.107A 1700 hp (12 cl V) l.c. | 13 | 42.8 |
| 106 | Mikoyan-Gurevich MiG-9 | USSR | State Industries | Fr | 1946 | 2 x tj RD-20 (B.M.W. 003A) 800 kg (1,764 lb) | 10 | 32.8 |
| 106 | Mikoyan-Gurevich MiG-15 | USSR | State Industries | Fr | 1947 | tj RD-45 F (Rolls-Royce Nene) 2270 kg (5,005 lb) | 10.08 | 33 |
| 106 | Ilyushin Il-10 | USSR | State Industries | A | 1944 | Mikulin AM 42 2000 hp (12 cl V) l.c. | 13.90 | 45.6 |
| 106 | Yakovlev Yak-1 | USSR | State Industries | Fr | 1942 | Klimov M.105 PA 1100 hp (12 cl V) l.c. | 10 | 32.8 |
| 106 | Yakovlev Yak-3 | USSR | State Industries | Fr/A | 1944 | Klimov M.105 PF2 1220 hp (12 cl V) l.c. | 9.20 | 30.2 |
| 106 | Yakovlev Yak-9D | USSR | State Industries | Fr | 1943 | Klimov M.105 PF 1260 hp (12 cl V) l.c. | 10 | 32.8 |
| 106 | Yakovlev Yak-23 | USSR | State Industries | Fr | 1947 | tj RD-500 (Rolls-Royce Derwent D) 1600 kg (3.530 lb) | 8.69 | 28.6 |
| 106 | Lavochkin LaGG-3 | USSR | State Industries | Fr | 1941 | Klimov M.105 P 1100 hp (12 cl V) l.c. | 9.80 | 32.2 |
| 106 | Lavochkin La-5FN | USSR | State Industries | Fr | 1943 | Shvetsov M.82FN 1640 hp (r 14 cl) a.c. | 9.80 | 32.2 |
| 106 | Lavochkin La-7 | USSR | State Industries | Fr | 1944 | Shvetsov M.82FN 1775 hp (r 14 cl) a.c. | 9.80 | 32.2 |

| Length | | Height | | Take-off weight | | Speed | | Ceiling | | Range | | Crew | Payload/armament |
|---|---|---|---|---|---|---|---|---|---|---|---|---|---|
| m | ft | m | ft | kg | lb | km/h | mph | m | ft | km | ml | | |
| 8.62 | 28.3 | 2.95 | 9.9 | 2,390 | 5,269 | 325 | 202 | 6,700 | 22,000 | 1,650 | 1,025 | 2 | 2-3 mg |
| 7.70 | 25.3 | 2 | 6.6 | 930 | 2,050 | 230 | 143 | 5,000 | 16,400 | 700 | 435 | 2 | — |
| 22.90 | 75.1 | 6 | 19.8 | 17,820 | 39,340 | 370 | 230 | 6,000 | 19,690 | 3,000 | 1,865 | 4-5 | 4 mg; b (4,000 kg - 8,800 lb) |
| 21.60 | 70.8 | 5.10 | 16.9 | 13,000 | 28,700 | 363 | 225 | 6,250 | 20,500 | 1,720 | 1,070 | 4-5 | 1 mg; 18 p |
| 11.74 | 38.6 | 3.69 | 12.1 | 4,822 | 10,645 | 365 | 226 | 7,400 | 24,280 | 1,600 | 990 | 3 | 3 mg; b (400 kg - 880 lb) |
| 14.95 | 49 | 4.43 | 14.6 | 5,950 | 13,117 | 275 | 171 | 7,000 | 22,965 | 2,600 | 1,616 | 4-5 | 3 mg; b (640 kg - 1,411 lb) |
| 9.19 | 30.2 | — | — | 2,122 | 4,686 | 295 | 183 | 8,750 | 28,700 | — | — | 2 | 2-3 mg |
| 8.48 | 27.8 | 2.66 | 8.7 | 2,990 | 6,595 | 354 | 220 | 7,000 | 22,965 | 1,150 | 720 | 2 | 3 mg; b (135 kg - 298 lb) |
| 9.54 | 31.2 | 3.82 | 12.6 | 2,200 | 4,850 | 240 | 146 | 6,390 | 21,965 | 800 | 497 | 5 | 1 mg |
| 8.70 | 28.6 | 3.46 | 11.4 | 2,345 | 5,170 | 487 | 303 | 9,580 | 31,430 | 1,100 | 691 | 2 | 1 mg |
| 8.81 | 28.8 | 3.84 | 12.7 | 1,900 | 4,189 | 300 | 186 | 7,270 | 23,850 | 900 | 558 | 2 | 2 mg; b (60 kg - 132 lb) |
| 31.02 | 101.9 | — | — | 28,150 | 62,060 | 420 | 261 | 7,450 | 24,440 | 4,260 | 2,647 | 7-10 | 2 g; 4 mg; b (4,000 kg - 8,818 lb) |
| 8.05 | 26.5 | 3.20 | 10.6 | 1,500 | 3,307 | 212 | 132 | 5,700 | 18,700 | 1,020 | 633 | 2 | 2 mg |
| 25.62 | 84 | 6.27 | 20.7 | 17,000 | 37,478 | 340 | 211 | 9,610 | 31,530 | 6,080 | 3,779 | 9 | 1 g; 4 mg; b (1,000 kg - 2,205 lb) |
| 8.79 | 28.9 | 3.94 | 12.9 | 3,973 | 8,770 | 615 | 382 | 10,600 | 34,775 | 800 | 497 | 1 | 2 mg; 4 g |
| 10.70 | 35.1 | 3.35 | 11 | 4,744 | 10,472 | 759 | 472 | 14,800 | 48,550 | 1,215 | 755 | 1 | 3 g |
| 9.73 | 32 | 3.25 | 10.8 | 5,243 | 11,574 | 407 | 253 | 9,000 | 29,530 | 690 | 428 | 1 | 3 g |
| 13.85 | 45.5 | 5 | 16.5 | 9,585 | 21,160 | 763 | 474 | 11,400 | 37,400 | 2,060 | 1,280 | 1 | 2 mg; 1 g |
| 15.55 | 51 | 4.11 | 13.6 | 11,200 | 24,692 | 670 | 416 | 12,700 | 41,660 | 2,000 | 1,243 | 2 | 6 g |
| 9.04 | 29.8 | 2.59 | 8.6 | 2,690 | 5,930 | 838 | 521 | 12,000 | 39,370 | 975 | 606 | 1 | 2 g |
| 5.70 | 18.8 | 2.50 | 8.2 | 3,950 | 8,707 | 900 | 559 | 12,000 | 39,370 | — | — | 1 | 2 g |
| 12.47 | 40.9 | 4.27 | 14 | 9,638 | 21,276 | 624 | 338 | 7,000 | 22,965 | 1,690 | 1,050 | 2 | 4 mg; 2 g |
| 10.60 | 34.9 | 3.84 | 12.7 | 6,396 | 14,101 | 869 | 540 | 11,450 | 37,565 | 1,050 | 652 | 1 | 4 g |
| 6.02 | 19.9 | 2.24 | 7.4 | 2,230 | 4,920 | 997 | 620 | 13.996 | 45,920 | 58 | 36 | 1 | 24 rz |
| 10.43 | 34.3 | 3.98 | 13.1 | 4,132 | 9,110 | 640 | 398 | 11,000 | 36,000 | 750 | 466 | 1 | 1 g; 2 mg |
| 7.80 | 25.7 | 2.79 | 9.2 | 2,850 | 6,300 | 576 | 358 | 9,150 | 30,019 | 1,250 | 780 | 1 | 4 mg |
| 8.35 | 27.5 | 3 | 9.8 | 2,950 | 6,504 | 530 | 329 | 9,000 | 29,530 | 500 | 311 | 1 | 4 mg |
| 8.16 | 26.9 | 3.60 | 11.9 | 2,485 | 5,478 | 510 | 317 | 10,500 | 34,500 | 950 | 590 | 1 | 2 g; 4 mg; b (200 kg - 440 lb) |
| 9.73 | 31.9 | 4.65 | 15.3 | 5,170 | 11,398 | 663 | 412 | 10,700 | 35,200 | 1,500 | 932 | 1 | 4 g; b (900 kg - 1,984 lb) |
| 10.26 | 33.8 | 5.16 | 16.9 | 5,210 | 11,500 | 702 | 436 | 11,100 | 36,417 | 2,500 | 1,530 | 1 | 4 g; b (905 kg - 1,997 lb) |
| 10.56 | 34.8 | 4.82 | 15.8 | 5,670 | 12,500 | 740 | 460 | 10,970 | 36,000 | 1,130 | 700 | 1 | 4 g; 907 kg (2,000 lb) |
| 11.46 | 37.7 | 4.14 | 13.7 | 6,350 | 14,020 | 508 | 316 | 8,500 | 28,000 | 2,100 | 1,300 | 2 | 4 g |
| 9.14 | 30 | 3.41 | 11.2 | 3,170 | 7,000 | 536 | 333 | 9,750 | 32,000 | 1,215 | 755 | 1 | 2 g; 4 mg |
| 11.43 | 37.6 | 3.02 | 9.9 | 5,216 | 11,500 | 949 | 590 | 13,715 | 45,000 | 1,915 | 1,190 | 1 | 4 g |
| 11.17 | 36.8 | 4.32 | 14.2 | 20,900 | 46,077 | 759 | 472 | 10,670 | 35,006 | 3,000 | 1,864 | 1 | 4 g; b (907 kg - 2,000 lb) |
| 9.37 | 30.9 | 2.69 | 8.8 | 5,620 | 12,390 | 882 | 548 | 13,140 | 44,000 | 1,960 | 1,220 | 1 | 4 g; 907 kg (2,000 lb) |
| 14.78 | 48.6 | 4.24 | 13.9 | 9,088 | 20,035 | 960 | 579 | 12,192 | 40,000 | 1,480 | 920 | 2 | 4 g |
| 12.58 | 41.3 | 3.96 | 13 | 6,260 | 13,800 | 793 | 493 | 13,400 | 43,963 | 2,156 | 1,340 | 1 | 4 g |
| 12.18 | 39.9 | 4 | 13.2 | 6,320 | 13,950 | 420 | 261 | 7,350 | 24,110 | 1,150 | 715 | 2-3 | 3 mg; 1 g |
| 9.37 | 30.9 | 3.77 | 12.4 | 3,720 | 8,200 | 620 | 385 | 12,700 | 41,700 | 1,650 | 1,025 | 1 | 2 mg; 3 g |
| 8.02 | 26.4 | 2.40 | 7.8 | 2,415 | 5,330 | 625 | 388 | 12,000 | 39,370 | 850 | 528 | 1 | 2 mg |
| 8.36 | 27.5 | 3.15 | 10.4 | 3,170 | 6,989 | 563 | 349 | 11,000 | 36,000 | 1,100 | 684 | 1 | 4 mg |
| 8.16 | 26.9 | 3.15 | 10.4 | 3,240 | 7,150 | 530 | 329 | 10,500 | 34,448 | 1,100 | 684 | 1 | 4 mg; b (640 kg - 1,400 lb) |
| 8.73 | 28.8 | 3.15 | 10.4 | 3,610 | 7,970 | 644 | 400 | 12,000 | 39,370 | 1,250 | 780 | 1 | 2 mg; 3 g |
| 8.85 | 29.1 | 3.02 | 9.9 | 2,937 | 6,480 | 600 | 372 | 11,500 | 37,700 | 765 | 475 | 1 | 2 mg |
| 8.85 | 29.1 | 3.05 | 10 | 3,224 | 7,120 | 650 | 403 | 11,350 | 37,200 | 1,040 | 646 | 1 | 2 mg; 2 g |
| 8.80 | 28.9 | 2.90 | 9.6 | 4,055 | 8,950 | 516 | 320 | 9,300 | 30,500 | 1,200 | 746 | 1 | 2 mg |
| 8.15 | 26.9 | 2.61 | 8.5 | 3,485 | 7,683 | 655 | 407 | 12,000 | 39,370 | 820 | 510 | 1 | 3 mg; b (200 kg - 440 lb) |
| 7.92 | 26 | 2.79 | 9.2 | 3,200 | 7,055 | 595 | 370 | — | — | — | — | 1 | 4 mg; b (200 kg - 440 lb) |
| 9.50 | 31.2 | — | — | 3,750 | 8,270 | 691 | 429 | 12,500 | 41,000 | — | — | 1 | 1 g; 2 mg |
| 9.75 | 32 | — | — | 5,070 | 11,070 | 911 | 566 | 13,500 | 44,290 | — | — | 1 | 3 g |
| 11.05 | 36.3 | 3.40 | 11.2 | 5,700 | 12,566 | 1,070 | 664 | 15,200 | 50,000 | 1,960 | 1,220 | 1 | 2 g; 500 kg (1,100 lb) |
| 12.20 | 40 | 3.50 | 11.6 | 6,335 | 13,966 | 500 | 310 | — | — | 650 | 404 | 2 | 3 g |
| 8.48 | 27.9 | 2.64 | 8.8 | 2,820 | 6,217 | 585 | 363 | 10,000 | 32,800 | 700 | 435 | 1 | 1 g; 2 mg |
| 8.50 | 27.9 | 2.38 | 7.8 | 2,660 | 5,864 | 648 | 403 | 10,900 | 35,760 | 900 | 560 | 1 | 1 g; 2 mg |
| 8.55 | 28.1 | 2.44 | 8 | 3,115 | 6,867 | 600 | 374 | 10,000 | 32,800 | 1,300 | 808 | 1 | 1 g; 1 mg |
| 8.16 | 26.9 | 3 | 9.8 | 4,985 | 10,990 | 950 | 590 | 14,800 | 48,555 | 1,200 | 745 | 1 | 2 g |
| 8.86 | 29.1 | 2.69 | 8.8 | 3,190 | 7,032 | 560 | 348 | 9,000 | 29,527 | 650 | 404 | 1 | 1 g; 3 mg; b (200 kg - 440 lb) |
| 8.50 | 27.9 | 2.81 | 9.2 | 3,360 | 7,406 | 647 | 402 | 10,000 | 32,800 | 700 | 435 | 1 | 2 g; b (150 kg - 331 lb) |
| 8.50 | 27.9 | 2.79 | 9.1 | 3,400 | 7,496 | 680 | 423 | 10,500 | 34,450 | 635 | 395 | 1 | 3 mg; b (150 kg - 331 lb) |

# Technical Data

| Page | Aircraft | Nation | Manufacturer | Type | Year | Engine | Wingspan m | ft |
|------|----------|--------|--------------|------|------|--------|-----------|-----|
| 106 | Bloch MB-152 | F | SNCASO | Fr | 1939 | Gnome-Rhône A4N 1030 hp (r 14 cl) a.c. | 10.54 | 34.7 |
| 106 | Dassault M.D.450 Ouragan | F | Avions Marcel Dassault | Fr | 1949 | tj Hispano-Suiza Nene 104B 2270 kg (5,004 lb) | 13.16 | 43.2 |
| 108 | Mitsubishi J2M3 Raiden | J | Mitsubishi Jukogyo K.K. | Fr | 1943 | Mitsubishi MK4R-A Kasei 23a 1800 hp (r 14 cl) a.c. | 10.80 | 35.5 |
| 108 | Mitsubishi A7M2 Reppu | J | Mitsubishi Jukogyo K.K. | Fr | 1945 | Mitsubishi MK9A 2200 hp (r 18 cl) a.c. | 14 | 45.9 |
| 108 | Mitsubishi K-83 | J | Mitsubishi Jukogyo K.K. | Fr | 1944 | 2 × Mitsubishi Ha-211 Ru 2200 hp (r 18 cl) | 15.50 | 50.8 |
| 108 | Mitsubishi J8M1 Shusui | J | Mitsubishi Jukogyo K.K. | Fr | 1945 | Toko Ro.2 1500 kg (3,306 lb) | 9.50 | 31.2 |
| 108 | Nakajima A6M-2N | J | Nakajima Hikoki K.K. | Fr | 1942 | Nakajima NK1C-Sakae 12 940 hp (r 14 cl) a.c. | 12 | 39.4 |
| 108 | Nakajima Ki-84 Ia Hayate | J | Nakajima Hikoki K.K. | Fr | 1943 | Nakajima Ha-45 1900 hp (r 18 cl) a.c. | 11.23 | 36.8 |
| 108 | Nakajima Ki-44-IIb Shoki | J | Nakajima Hikoki K.K. | Fr | 1943 | Nakajima Ha-109 1520 hp (r 14 cl) a.c. | 9.45 | 31 |
| 108 | Kawasaki Ki-45 KAIa Toryu | J | Kawasaki Kokuki Kogyo K.K. | Fr | 1942 | 2 x Nakajima Ha-25 1050 hp (r 14 cl) a.c. | 15.02 | 49.3 |
| 108 | Kawasaki Ki-102a | J | Kawasaki Kokuki Kogyo K.K. | Fr | 1944 | 2 x Mitsubishi Ha-112-II Ru 1500 hp (r 14 cl) a.c. | 15.57 | 51.1 |
| 108 | Kawasaki Ki-61-J Hien | J | Kawasaki Kokuki Kogyo K.K. | Fr | 1943 | Kawasaki Ha-40 1175 hp (12 cl V) l.c. | 12 | 39.4 |
| 108 | Kawasaki Ki-100-II | J | Kawasaki Kokuki Kogyo K.K. | Fr | 1945 | Mitsubishi Ha-112-II Ru 1500 hp (r 14 cl) a.c. | 12 | 39.4 |
| 108 | Kyushu J7W1 Shinden | J | Kyushu Hikoki K.K. | Fr | 1945 | Mitsubishi MK9D 2130 hp (r 18 cl) a.c. | 11.11 | 36.5 |
| 108 | Kawanishi N1K Kyofu | J | Kawanishi Kokuki K.K. | Fr | 1943 | Mitsubishi MK4E Kasei 15 1530 hp (r 14 cl) a.c. | 12 | 39.4 |
| 108 | Kawanishi N1K1-J Shiden | J | Kawanishi Kokuki K.K. | Fr | 1943 | Nakajima NK9H Homare 21 1990 hp (r 18 cl) a.c. | 12 | 39.4 |
| 108 | Commonwealth CA-12 Boomerang | AUS | Commonwealth Aircraft Corp. | Fr | 1943 | Pratt & Whitney R-1830 S3C4-G Twin Wasp 1200 hp (r 14 cl) a.c. | 11.05 | 36.3 |
| 108 | Commonwealth CA-15 | AUS | Commonwealth Aircraft Corp. | Fr | 1946 | Rolls-Royce Griffon 61 2305 hp (12 cl V) l.c. | 10.97 | 36 |
| 109 | Bell-P-39D Airacobra | USA | Bell Aircraft Corp. | Fr | 1941 | Allison V-1710-35 1150 hp (12 cl V) l.c. | 10.36 | 34 |
| 109 | Bell P-63A Kingcobra | USA | Bell Aircraft Corp. | Fr | 1943 | Allison V-1710-95 1325 hp (12 cl V) l.c. | 11.68 | 38.4 |
| 109 | Bell P-59A Airacomet | USA | Bell Aircraft Corp. | Fr | 1944 | 2 x General Electric J-31-GE-3 907 kg (2,000 lb) | 13.87 | 45.6 |
| 109 | Lockheed P-38 J Lightning | USA | Lockheed Aircraft Corp. | Fr | 1943 | 2 x Allison V-1710-111 1475 hp (12 cl V) l.c. | 15.85 | 52 |
| 109 | Lockheed F-80CS Shooting Star | USA | Lockheed Aircraft Corp. | FB | 1948 | tj General Electric J33-A-23 2086 kg (4,600 lb) | 11.85 | 39.9 |
| 109 | Lockheed F-94C Starfire | USA | Lockheed Aircraft Corp. | Fr | 1950 | tj Pratt & Whitney J-48-P-5 3970 kg (8,792 lb) | 12.03 | 39.4 |
| 109 | North American P-51A Mustang | USA | North American Aviation Inc. | Fr | 1943 | Allison V-1710-81 1200 hp (12 cl V) l.c. | 11.28 | 37 |
| 109 | North American F-82G Twin Mustang | USA | North American Aviation Inc. | NF | 1946 | 2 x Allison V-1710 1600 hp (12 cl V) l.c. | 15.62 | 51.3 |
| 109 | North American F-86E Sabre | USA | North American Aviation Inc. | Fr | 1950 | tj General Electric J47-GE-13 2538 kg (5,595 lb) | 11.30 | 37.1 |
| 109 | Curtiss P-40B Warhawk | USA | Curtiss-Wright Corp. | Fr | 1941 | Allison V-1710-33 1040 hp (12 cl V) l.c. | 11.38 | 37.4 |
| 109 | Brewster F2A-3 Buffalo | USA | Brewster Aeronautical Corp. | Fr | 1941 | Wright R-1820-40 Cyclone 1200 hp (r 9 cl) a.c. | 10.67 | 35 |
| 109 | Vought F4U-1 Corsair | USA | United Aircraft Corp. | Fr | 1943 | Pratt & Whitney R-2800-8 Double Wasp 2000 hp (r 18 cl) a.c. | 12.50 | 41 |
| 109 | Ryan FR-1 Fireball | USA | Ryan Aeronautical Corp. | Fr | 1944 | Wright R-1820-72W Cyclone 1350 hp (r 9 cl) a.c. | 12.19 | 40 |
| 109 | Republic P-43A Lancer | USA | Republic Aviation Corp. | Fr | 1941 | Pratt & Whitney R-1830-49 Twin Wasp 1200 hp (r 14 cl) a.c. | 10.97 | 36 |
| 109 | Republic P-47C Thunderbolt | USA | Republic Aviation Corp. | Fr | 1943 | Pratt & Whitney R-2800-21 Double Wasp 2000 hp (r 18 cl) a.c. | 12.42 | 40.9 |
| 109 | Republic F-84G Thunderjet | USA | Republic Aviation Corp. | FB | 1950 | tj Allison J35-A29 2540 kg (5,600 lb) | 11.10 | 36.5 |
| 109 | Grumman F8F Bearcat | USA | Grumman Aircraft Engineering Corp. | Fr | 1946 | Pratt & Whitney R.2800-34W Double Wasp (r 18 cl) a.c. | 10.92 | 35.8 |
| 109 | Grumman F7F-3N Tigercat | USA | Grumman Aircraft Engineering Corp. | NF | 1946 | 2 x Pratt & Whitney 3-2800-34W Double Wasp 2100 hp (r 18 cl) a.c. | 15.69 | 51.6 |
| 109 | Grumman F6F-3 Hellcat | USA | Grumman Aircraft Engineering Corp. | Fr | 1943 | Pratt & Whitney R-2800-10 Double Wasp 2000 hp (r 18 cl) a.c. | 13.06 | 42.8 |
| 109 | Grumman F9F Panther | USA | Grumman Aircraft Engineering Corp. | Fr | 1947 | tj Pratt & Whitney J42-P-6 2270 kg (5,000 lb) | 11.58 | 38 |
| 109 | McDonnell FH-1 Phantom | USA | McDonnell Aircraft Corp. | Fr | 1945 | 2 x tj Westinghouse J30-WE-20 725 kg (1,600 lb) | 12.42 | 40.9 |
| 109 | Northrop P-61B Black Widow | USA | Northrop Aircraft Inc. | NF | 1944 | 2 x Pratt & Whitney R-2800-65 Twin Wasp 2000 hp (r 18 cl) a.c. | 20.11 | 66 |
| 110 | Aichi B7A2 Ryusei | J | Aichi Kokuki K.K. | Br | 1945 | Nakajima NK9C Homare 12 1825 hp (r 18 cl) a.c. | 14.40 | 47.3 |
| 110 | Yokosuka D4Y1 Suisei | J | Aichi Kokuki K.K. | Br | 1943 | Aichi AE1A Atsuta 1200 hp (12 cl V) l.c. | 11.50 | 37.9 |
| 110 | Yokosuka P1Y1 Ginga | J | Nakajima Hikoki K.K. | Br | 1945 | 2 x Nakajima NK9B Homare 11 1820 hp (r 18 cl) a.c. | 20 | 65.7 |
| 110 | Yokosuka Ohka 11 | J | Daichi Kaigun Kokusho | — | 1945 | 3 x rp Type 4 Mk.1 Mod.20 800 kg (1,764 lb) | 5.15 | 16.9 |
| 110 | Kawasaki Ki-48 | J | Kawasaki Kokuki Kogyo K.K. | Br | 1942 | 2 x Nakajima Ha-115 1130 hp (r 14 cl) a.c. | 17.45 | 57.3 |
| 110 | Mitsubishi Ki-21-IIb | J | Mitsubishi Jukogyo K.K. | Br | 1941 | 2 x Mitsubishi Ha-101 1500 hp (r 14 cl) a.c. | 22.50 | 73.8 |
| 110 | Mitsubishi G4M1 | J | Mitsubishi Jukogyo K.K. | Br | 1941 | 2 x Mitsubishi MK4A Kasei 11 1530 hp (r 14 cl) a.c. | 25 | 82 |
| 110 | Mitsubishi Ki-67-I Hiryu | J | Mitsubishi Jukogyo K.K. | Br | 1944 | 2 x Mitsubishi Ha-104 1900 hp (r 14 cl) a.c. | 22.5 | 73.8 |
| 110 | Nakajima Ki-49 Donryu | J | Nakajima Hikoki K.K. | Br | 1942 | 2 x Nakajima Ha-109 1500 hp (r 14 cl) a.c. | 20.42 | 67 |
| 110 | Nakajima B6N2 Tenzan | J | Nakajima Hikoki K.K. | TB | 1943 | Mitsubishi MK4T Kasei 25 1850 hp (r 14 cl) a.c. | 14.89 | 48.8 |
| 110 | Nakajima Kikka | J | Nakajima Hikoki K.K. | Br | 1945 | 2 x Ne-20 475 kg (1,047 lb) | 10 | 32.8 |
| 110 | Nakajima G8N1 Renzan | J | Nakajima Hikoki K.K. | Br | 1944 | 4 x Nakajima NK9K-L Homare 24 2000 hp (r 18 cl) a.c. | 32.54 | 106.9 |
| 111 | Vultee A-35A Vengeance | USA | Vultee Aircraft Inc. | Br | 1942 | Wright 2-2600-13 Cyclone 1700 hp (r 14 cl) a.c. | 14.63 | 48 |
| 111 | North American B-25A Mitchell | USA | North American Aviation Inc. | Br | 1941 | 2 x Wright R-2600-9 Cyclone 1700 hp (r 14 cl) a.c. | 20.60 | 67.7 |
| 111 | Martin Baltimore Mk.IV | USA | Glenn L. Martin Co. | Br | 1944 | 2 x Wright R-2600-29 Cyclone 1700 hp (r 14 cl) a.c. | 18.60 | 61.4 |
| 111 | Martin B-26B Marauder | USA | Glenn L. Martin Co. | Br | 1942 | 2 x Pratt & Whitney R-2800-41 Double Wasp 2000 hp (r 18 cl) a.c. | 19.81 | 65 |
| 111 | Consolidated B-24D Liberator | USA | Consolidated Aircraft Corp. | Br | 1942 | 4 x Pratt & Whitney R-1830-43 Twin Wasp 1200 hp (r 14 cl) a.c. | 33.52 | 110 |

| Length | | Height | | Take-off weight | | Speed | | Ceiling | | Range | | Crew | Payload/armament |
|---|---|---|---|---|---|---|---|---|---|---|---|---|---|
| m | ft | m | ft | kg | lb | km/h | mph | m | ft | km | ml | | |
| 9.10 | 29.8 | 3.95 | 12.9 | 2,676 | 5,908 | 515 | 320 | 10,000 | 32,800 | 600 | 373 | 1 | 4 mg |
| 10.74 | 35.3 | 4.14 | 13.7 | 7,900 | 17,416 | 940 | 584 | 13,000 | 43,000 | 920 | 570 | 1 | 4 g; 908 kg (2,000 lb) |
| 9.94 | 32.7 | 3.94 | 12.9 | 3,435 | 7,573 | 587 | 363 | 11,700 | 38,385 | 1,900 | 1,180 | 1 | 4 g; b (120 kg - 264 lb) |
| 11 | 36.1 | 4.28 | 14 | 4,720 | 10,406 | 627 | 390 | 10,900 | 35,760 | 920 | 570 | 1 | 2 g; 2 mg; b (500 kg - 1,100 lb) |
| 12.50 | 41 | 4.60 | 15.1 | 8,795 | 19,390 | 705 | 438 | 12,660 | 41,535 | 3,500 | 2,175 | 2 | 4 g; b (100 kg - 220 lb) |
| 6.05 | 19.8 | 2.70 | 8.8 | 3,885 | 8,565 | 900 | 559 | 12,000 | 39,370 | — | — | 1 | 2 g |
| 10 | 32.8 | 4.30 | 14.1 | 2,460 | 5,423 | 434 | 270 | 10,000 | 32,800 | 1,780 | 1,107 | 1 | 2 g; 2 mg; b (120 kg - 264 lb) |
| 9.92 | 32.6 | 3.38 | 11.1 | 3,613 | 7,965 | 631 | 392 | 10,500 | 34,450 | 1,695 | 1,053 | 1 | 2 g; 2 mg; b (500 kg - 1,100 lb) |
| 8.78 | 28.8 | 3.25 | 10.8 | 2,993 | 6,598 | 605 | 376 | 11,200 | 36,745 | 1,700 | 1,050 | 1 | 4 mg |
| 10.60 | 34.9 | 3.70 | 12.2 | 5,276 | 11,632 | 547 | 340 | 10,730 | 35,200 | 2,260 | 1,404 | 2 | 1 g; 3 mg; b (500 kg - 1,100 lb) |
| 11.45 | 37.7 | 3.70 | 12.2 | 7,300 | 16,094 | 580 | 360 | 10,000 | 32,800 | 2,000 | 1,204 | 2 | 3 g |
| 8.75 | 28.8 | 3.70 | 12.2 | 2,950 | 6,503 | 592 | 368 | 11,600 | 37,730 | 1,100 | 684 | 1 | 4 mg |
| 8.82 | 28.9 | 3.75 | 12.3 | 3,670 | 8,091 | 570 | 354 | 11,000 | 36,000 | 1,800 | 1,118 | 1 | 2 g; 2 mg; b (500 kg - 1,100 lb) |
| 9.66 | 31.8 | 3.92 | 12.8 | 4,928 | 10,854 | 750 | 466 | 12,000 | 39,370 | 850 | 529 | 1 | 4 g; b (120 kg - 264 lb) |
| 10.58 | 34.9 | 4.75 | 15.7 | 3,500 | 7,716 | 490 | 304 | 10,560 | 34,645 | 1,670 | 1,036 | 1 | 2 g; 2 mg; b (60 kg - 132 lb) |
| 8.88 | 29.2 | 4.06 | 13.4 | 3,900 | 8,598 | 584 | 363 | 12,500 | 41,010 | 2,540 | 1,578 | 1 | 4 g; 2 mg; b (120 kg - 264 lb) |
| 7.77 | 25.6 | 3.50 | 11.6 | 3,492 | 7,699 | 486 | 302 | 8,840 | 29,000 | 1,500 | 930 | 1 | 2 g; 4 mg; b (227 kg - 500 lb) |
| 11.03 | 36.2 | 4.34 | 14.3 | 4,882 | 10,763 | 721 | 448 | 11,890 | 39,009 | 1,850 | 1,150 | 1 | 6 mg |
| 9.19 | 30.2 | 3.60 | 11.8 | 3,720 | 8,201 | 592 | 368 | 9,785 | 32,102 | 1,290 | 802 | 1 | 1 g; 6 mg; b (226 kg - 5,000 lb) |
| 9.96 | 32.8 | 3.84 | 12.7 | 4,763 | 10,500 | 656 | 408 | 13,100 | 43,000 | 725 | 450 | 1 | 1 g; 4 mg; b (680 kg - 1,500 lb) |
| 11.84 | 38.8 | 3.76 | 12.4 | 6,124 | 13,700 | 665 | 413 | 14,100 | 46,200 | 845 | 525 | 1 | 1 g; 3 mg |
| 11.53 | 37.8 | 2.99 | 9.8 | 9,798 | 21,600 | 666 | 414 | 13,400 | 44,000 | 724 | 450 | 1 | 1 g; 4 mg; b (1,450 kg - 3,200 lb) |
| 10.51 | 34.6 | 3.45 | 11.4 | 7,646 | 16,856 | 933 | 580 | 13,030 | 42,750 | 2,220 | 1,380 | 1 | 6 mg; 907 kg (2,000 lb) |
| 13.56 | 44.6 | 4.55 | 14.9 | 10,977 | 24,200 | 941 | 585 | 15,670 | 51,400 | 1,930 | 1,200 | 2 | 48 rp |
| 9.83 | 82.2 | 3.70 | 12.2 | 3,992 | 8,800 | 628 | 390 | 9,550 | 31,350 | 1,200 | 750 | 1 | 4 mg; b (454 kg - 1,000 lb) |
| 12.92 | 42.5 | 4.21 | 13.8 | 11,608 | 25,591 | 741 | 461 | 11,860 | 38,910 | 3,600 | 2,240 | 2 | 6 mg; 1,814 kg (3,999 lb) |
| 11.43 | 37.6 | 4.47 | 14.8 | 7,419 | 16,357 | 1,086 | 675 | 14,720 | 48,300 | 1,260 | 765 | 1 | 6 mg; 907 kg (2,000 lb) |
| 9.68 | 31.9 | 3.23 | 10.7 | 3,450 | 7,600 | 566 | 352 | 9,875 | 32,400 | 1,500 | 940 | 1 | 4 mg |
| 8.02 | 26.4 | 3.66 | 12.1 | 3,247 | 7,159 | 517 | 321 | 10,120 | 33,200 | 1,553 | 965 | 1 | 4 mg |
| 10.16 | 33.4 | 4.60 | 15.1 | 6,350 | 13,999 | 671 | 417 | 11,250 | 36,900 | 1,635 | 1,015 | 1 | 6 mg |
| 9.85 | 32.4 | 4.24 | 13.9 | 5,285 | 11,651 | 650 | 404 | 13,135 | 43,100 | 2,600 | 1,616 | 1 | 4 mg |
| 8.68 | 28.6 | 4.27 | 14 | 3,600 | 7,935 | 562 | 349 | 11,580 | 37,992 | 1,290 | 800 | 1 | 4 mg |
| 11 | 36.1 | 4.31 | 14.2 | 6,770 | 14,295 | 697 | 433 | 12,800 | 42,000 | 885 | 550 | 1 | 8 mg; b (230 kg - 500 lb) |
| 11.61 | 38.1 | 3.83 | 12.7 | 10,670 | 23,525 | 1,001 | 622 | 12,340 | 40,500 | 3,220 | 2,000 | 1 | 6 mg; b (1,814 kg - 2,100 lb) |
| 8.61 | 28.3 | 4.21 | 13.8 | 5,972 | 12,947 | 677 | 421 | 11,800 | 38,700 | 1,780 | 1,105 | 1 | 4 g |
| 14.27 | 46.8 | 5.05 | 16.7 | 11,666 | 25,719 | 700 | 435 | 12,400 | 40,682 | 2,570 | 1,597 | 2 | 4 g |
| 10.24 | 33.7 | 3.99 | 13.1 | 5,162 | 11,381 | 605 | 376 | 11,700 | 38,400 | 1,750 | 1,090 | 1 | 6 mg |
| 11.35 | 37.3 | 3.45 | 11.4 | 8,842 | 19,452 | 846 | 526 | 13,600 | 44,600 | 2,180 | 1,353 | 1 | 4 g; 907 kg (2,000 lb) |
| 11.81 | 38.9 | 4.31 | 14.2 | 5,459 | 12,035 | 770 | 479 | 12,530 | 41,000 | 1,580 | 981 | 1 | 4 mg |
| 15.11 | 49.7 | 4.47 | 14.8 | 13,472 | 29,700 | 589 | 366 | 10,100 | 33,100 | 4,830 | 3,000 | 3 | 4 g; 4 mg; b ( 2,900 kg - 6,400 lb) |
| 11.49 | 37.8 | 4.07 | 13.4 | 5,625 | 12,400 | 566 | 352 | 11,250 | 36,910 | 3,000 | 1,888 | 2 | 2 g; 1 mg; b (800 kg - 1,764 lb) |
| 10.22 | 33.6 | 3.67 | 12.1 | 3,650 | 8,047 | 552 | 343 | 9,900 | 32,480 | 1,575 | 978 | 2 | 3 mg; b (310 kg - 683 lb) |
| 15 | 49.2 | 4.30 | 14.1 | 10,500 | 23,148 | 547 | 340 | 9,400 | 30,840 | 5,300 | 3,338 | 3 | 2 g; b (1,000 kg - 2,205 lb) |
| 6.06 | 19.8 | 1.16 | 3.8 | 2,140 | 4,718 | 648 | 403 | — | — | 37 | 23 | 1 | 1,200 kg (2,646 lb) |
| 12.75 | 41.8 | 3.80 | 12.6 | 6,500 | 14,330 | 505 | 314 | 10,100 | 33,153 | 2,400 | 1,491 | 4 | 3 mg; b (400 kg - 880 lb) |
| 16 | 52.6 | 4.85 | 15.9 | 9,710 | 21,467 | 486 | 302 | 10,000 | 32,810 | 2,700 | 1,680 | 5 | 6 mg; b (1,100 kg - 2,425 lb) |
| 20 | 65.7 | 6 | 19.8 | 9,500 | 20,994 | 428 | 266 | 8,840 | 29,000 | 6,030 | 3,748 | 7 | 1 g; 4 mg; b (800 kg - 1,764 lb) |
| 18.70 | 61.4 | 7.70 | 25.3 | 13,765 | 30,347 | 537 | 334 | 9,470 | 31,070 | 3,800 | 2,360 | 6-8 | 1 g; 4 mg; b (800 kg - 1,764 lb) |
| 16.5 | 54.1 | 4.25 | 13.9 | 10,680 | 23,545 | 492 | 306 | 9,300 | 30,510 | 2,950 | 1,833 | 8 | 1 g; 5 mg; b (1,000 kg - 2,205 lb) |
| 10.86 | 35.8 | 3.80 | 12.5 | 5,200 | 11,462 | 481 | 299 | 9,040 | 29,660 | 3,050 | 1,892 | 3 | 2 mg; b (800 kg - 1,764 lb) |
| 8.12 | 26.8 | 2.95 | 9.8 | 3,500 | 7,716 | 712 | 443 | 12,000 | 39,370 | 950 | 586 | 1 | b (800 kg - 1,764 lb) |
| 22.93 | 75.3 | 7.20 | 23.7 | 32,150 | 70,897 | 592 | 368 | 10,200 | 33,465 | 7,500 | 4,639 | 10 | 6 g; 4 mg; b (4,000 kg - 8,818 lb) |
| 12.12 | 39.9 | 4.67 | 15.4 | 7,439 | 16,400 | 449 | 279 | 6,800 | 22,300 | 3,700 | 2,300 | 2 | 5 mg; b (907 kg - 2,000 lb) |
| 16.48 | 54.1 | 4.80 | 15.8 | 12,292 | 27,000 | 507 | 315 | 8,230 | 27,000 | 2,170 | 1,350 | 3-6 | 5 mg; b (1,360 kg - 3,000 lb) |
| 14.78 | 48.6 | 5.41 | 17.9 | 10,250 | 22,600 | 515 | 320 | 7,500 | 24,600 | 1,530 | 950 | 3 | 7 mg; b (907 kg - 2,000 lb) |
| 17.75 | 58.3 | 6.05 | 19.8 | 15,422 | 34,000 | 510 | 317 | 7,200 | 23,500 | 1,850 | 1,150 | 7 | 6 mg; b (1,360 kg - 3,000 lb) |
| 20.22 | 66.4 | 5.46 | 17.9 | 27,216 | 60,000 | 488 | 303 | 9,750 | 32,000 | 4,585 | 2,850 | 8-10 | 10 mg; b (4,000 kg - 8,818 lb) |

# Technical Data

| Page | Aircraft | Nation | Manufacturer | Type | Year | Engine | Wingspan m | ft |
|------|----------|--------|--------------|------|------|--------|:---:|:---:|
| 111 | Boeing B-17E Flying Fortress | USA | Boeing Aircraft Co. | Br | 1942 | 4 x Wright R-1820-65 Cyclone 1200 hp (r 9 cl) a.c. | 31.62 | 103.9 |
| 111 | Boeing B-29 Superfortress | USA | Boeing Aircraft Co. | Br | 1944 | 4 x Wright R-3350 Cyclone 2200 hp (r 18 cl) a.c. | 43.05 | 141.3 |
| 111 | Grumman TBF-1 Avenger | USA | Grumman Aircraft Engineering Corp. | TB | 1942 | Wright R-2600-8 Cyclone 1700 hp (r 14 cl) a.c. | 16.51 | 54.2 |
| 111 | Douglas SBD-3 Dauntless | USA | Douglas Aircraft Co. | Br | 1941 | Wright R-1820-52 Cyclone 1000 hp (r 9 cl) a.c. | 12.65 | 41.6 |
| 111 | Douglas A-20G Havoc | USA | Douglas Aircraft Co. | Br | 1942 | 2 x Wright R-2600-23 Cyclone 1600 hp (r 14 cl) a.c. | 18.69 | 61.4 |
| 111 | Douglas A-26B Invader | USA | Douglas Aircraft Co. | Br | 1944 | 2 x Pratt & Whitney R-2800-27 Double Wasp (r 18 cl) a.c. | 21.33 | 70 |
| 111 | Douglas Boston Mk.III | USA | Douglas Aircraft Co. | Br | 1942 | 2 x Wright GR-2600-A5B Cyclone 1600 hp (r 14 cl) | 18.69 | 61.4 |
| 111 | Curtiss SB2C-1 Helldiver | USA | Curtiss-Wright Corp. | Br | 1943 | Wright R-2600-8 Cyclone 1700 hp (r 14 cl) a.c. | 15.16 | 49.9 |
| 114 | Heinkel He.177A-1 | D | Ernst Heinkel AG. | Br | 1942 | 2 x Daimler-Benz DB.606 2700 hp (24 cl V) l.c. | 31.42 | 103 |
| 114 | Arado Ar. 234 B-2 | D | Arado Flugzeugwerke GmbH | Br | 1944 | 2 x Junkers Jumo 004B 900 kg (1,984 lb) | 14.10 | 46.3 |
| 114 | Junkers Ju.188 E-1 | D | Junkers Flugzeuge und Motorenwerke AG. | Br | 1943 | 2 x B.M.W. 801D-2 1700 hp (r 14 cl) a.c. | 22 | 72.2 |
| 114 | Mistel 1 | D | Junkers Flugzeuge und Motorenwerke AG. | Br | 1944 | 2 x Junkers Jumo 211J-1 1340 hp (Ju.88) Daimler-Benz DB.601E-1 1350 hp (Bf 109) | 20 | 65.7 |
| 114 | Yakovlev Yak-4 | USSR | State Industries | A | 1940 | 2 x Klimov M.105R 1100 hp (12 cl V) l.c. | 13.99 | 45.9 |
| 114 | Petlyakov Pe-2 | USSR | State Industries | Br | 1941 | 2 x Klimov M.105R 1100 hp (12 cl V) l.c. | 17.16 | 56.3 |
| 114 | Ilyushin Il-2M3 | USSR | State Industries | A | 1942 | Mikulin AM.38F 1770 hp (12 cl V) l.c. | 14.60 | 47.8 |
| 114 | Ilyushin Il-28 | USSR | State Industries | Br | 1948 | 2 x tj Klimov VK-1 2740 kg (6,040 lb) | 21.45 | 70.4 |
| 114 | Tupolev Tu-2 | USSR | State Industries | Br | 1943 | 2 x Salmson M.82 1850 hp (r 14 cl) a.c. | 18.85 | 61.8 |
| 115 | Fairey Barracuda Mk.II | GB | Fairey Aviation Co. Ltd. | TB | 1943 | Rolls-Royce Merlin 32 1640 hp (12 cl V) l.c. | 14.99 | 49.2 |
| 115 | Blackburn Firebrand T.F.5 | GB | Blackburn Aircraft Co. Ltd. | TB | 1946 | Bristol Centaurus IX 2500 hp (r 18 cl) a.c. | 15.62 | 51.3 |
| 115 | Avro Lancaster Mk.I | GB | A.V. Roe & Co. Ltd. | Br | 1942 | 4 x Rolls-Royce Merlin XX 1460 hp (12 cl V) l.c. | 31.09 | 102 |
| 115 | Avro Lincoln B-1 | GB | A.V. Roe & Co. Ltd. | Br | 1944 | 4 x Rolls-Royce Merlin 85 1750 hp (12 cl V) l.c. | 36.57 | 120 |
| 115 | English Electric Canberra B-2 | GB | English Electric Co. Ltd. | Br | 1950 | 2 x tj Rolls-Royce Avon 101 2948 kg (6,500 lb) | 19.49 | 63.9 |
| 115 | Saab 18A | S | Saab | Br | 1944 | 2 x Pratt & Whitney Twin Wasp 1065 hp (r 14 cl) a.c. | 17 | 55.9 |
| 115 | Commonwealth CA-11 Woomera | AUS | Commonwealth Aircraft Co. | Br | 1944 | 2 x Pratt & Whitney R-1830-S3C3-G Twin Wasp (r 14 cl) a.c. | 18.03 | 59.2 |
| 115 | SIAI Marchetti S.M.84 | I | SIAI Marchetti | Br | 1941 | 3 x Piaggio P.XI 1000 hp (r 14 cl) a.c. | 21.13 | 69.3 |
| 115 | CANT Z.1018 | I | Cantieri Riuniti dell'Adriatico | Br | 1943 | 2 x Piaggio P.XII 1350 hp (r 18 cl) a.c. | 22.50 | 73.8 |
| 115 | Piaggio P.108B | I | S.A. Piaggio & C. | Br | 1942 | 4 x Piaggio P.XII RC 35 1350 hp (r 18 cl) a.c. | 32 | 105 |
| 116 | Fiat RS 14 | I | CMASA | Rc | 1942 | 2 x Fiat A.74 RC38 840 hp (r 14 cl) a.c. | 19.54 | 64.1 |
| 116 | Fiat G.12 | I | Fiat S.A. | Tr | 1941 | 3 x Fiat A.74 RC42 800 hp (r 14 cl) a.c. | 28.60 | 93.8 |
| 116 | Nord 2501 Noratlas | F | SNCAN | Tr | 1950 | 2 x SNEMCA Hercules 730 2040 hp (r 14 cl) a.c. | 32.5 | 106.7 |
| 116 | Arado Ar.231 | D | Arado Flugzeugwerke GmbH | Rc | 1941 | Hirth HM501 160 hp (6 cl) a.c. | 10.16 | 33.4 |
| 116 | Blohm und Voss Bv.138 B-1 | D | Blohm und Voss Schiffswerft Abteilung Flugzeugbau | Rc | 1941 | 3 x Junkers Jumo 205 880 hp (6 cl) l.c. | 26.92 | 88.4 |
| 117 | Junkers Ju.290 A-1 | D | Junkers Flugzeuge und Motorenwerke AG. | Tr/Rc | 1942 | 4 x B.M.W. 801L 1600 hp (r 14 cl) a.c. | 42 | 137.9 |
| 117 | Junkers Ju.352 A-1 | D | Junkers Flugzeuge und Motorenwerke AG. | Tr | 1944 | 3 x B.M.W. 323 R-2 1000 hp (r 9 cl) a.c. | 34.20 | 112.2 |
| 117 | Junkers Ju.388 L-1 | D | Junkers Flugzeuge und Motorenwerke AG. | Rc | 1944 | 2 x B.M.W. 801 TJ 1800 hp (r 14 cl) a.c. | 22 | 72.2 |
| 117 | Arado Ar.232 | D | Arado Flugzeugwerke GmbH | Tr | 1941 | 2 x B.M.W. 801 1600 hp (r 14 cl) a.c. | 31.80 | 104.3 |
| 117 | Messerschmitt Me.323 D-1 | D | Messerschmitt AG. | Tr | 1942 | 6 x Gnome-Rhône 14N 1140 hp (r 14 cl) a.c. | 55 | 180.5 |
| 117 | Siebel Si.204D | D | Siebel Flugzeugwerke GmbH | T | 1942 | 2 x Argus As.411 600 hp (12 cl V) l.c. | 21.33 | 69.9 |
| 117 | Dornier Do.24 | D | Dornier Werke GmbH | Tr | 1941 | 3 x B.M.W. 323 R-2 1000 hp (r 9 cl) a.c. | 27 | 88.7 |
| 117 | Blohm und Voss Bv.222A | D | Blohm und Voss Schiffswerft Abteilung Flugzeugbau | Rc | 1942 | 6 x B.M.W. 323 R-2 1000 hp (r 9 cl) a.c. | 46 | 150.9 |
| 118 | Armstrong Whitworth Albemarle Mk.I | GB | Armstrong Whitworth Aircraft Ltd. | Tr | 1943 | 2 x Bristol Hercules XI 1590 hp (r 14 cl) a.c. | 23.47 | 77 |
| 118 | de Havilland Mosquito Mk.IV | GB | de Havilland Aircraft Co. Ltd. | Br | 1942 | 2 x Rolls-Royce Merlin XXI 1250 hp (12 cl V) l.c. | 16.51 | 54.2 |
| 118 | Tachikawa Ki-54c | J | Tachikawa Hikoki K.K. | Tr | 1941 | 2 x Hitachi Ha-13a 450 hp (r 9 cl) a.c. | 17.90 | 58.9 |
| 118 | Kyushu Q1W1 Tokai | J | Kyushu Hikoki K.K. | Rc | 1944 | 2 x Hitachi GK2C Amakaze 31 610 hp (r 9 cl) a.c. | 16 | 52.6 |
| 118 | Kyushu K11W1 Shiragiku | J | Kyushu Hikoki K.K. | T | 1943 | Hitachi GK2B Amakaze 21 515 hp (r 9 cl) a.c. | 14.98 | 49.2 |
| 118 | Aichi E13A1 | J | Aichi Kokuki K.K. | Rc | 1941 | Mitsubishi Kinsei 43 1060 hp (r 14 cl) a.c. | 14.50 | 47.7 |
| 118 | Aichi E16A1 Zuiun | J | Aichi Kokuki K.K. | Rc | 1942 | Mitsubishi MK8D Kinsei 54 1300 hp (r 14 cl) | 12.81 | 42 |
| 118 | Nakajima J1N1-C Gekko | J | Nakajima Hikoki K.K. | Rc | 1942 | 2 x Nakajima NK1F Sakae 21 1130 hp (r 14 cl) a.c. | 16.98 | 55.8 |
| 118 | Yokosuka E14Y1 | J | K.K. Watanabe Tekkosho | Rc | 1941 | Hitachi Tempu 12 340 hp (r 9 cl) a.c. | 11 | 36.1 |
| 118 | Kokusai Ki-76 | J | Nippon Kokusai Koku Kogyo K.K. | Li | 1942 | Hitachi Ha-42 310 hp (r 9 cl) a.c. | 15 | 49.2 |
| 119 | de Havilland Chipmunk T.10 | GB | de Havilland Aircraft Co. | T | 1949 | de Havilland Gipsy Major 8 145 hp (4 cl) a.c. | 10.46 | 34.4 |
| 119 | Avro York Mk.I | GB | A.V. Roe & Co. Ltd. | Tr | 1944 | 4 x Rolls-Royce Merlin XX 1280 hp (12 cl V) l.c. | 31.09 | 102 |
| 119 | Supermarine Sea Otter Mk.I | GB | Saunders-Roe Ltd. | Li | 1944 | Bristol Mercury XXX 850 hp (r 9 cl) a.c. | 14.03 | 46 |
| 119 | Handley Page Hastings C-1 | GB | Handley Page Ltd. | Tr | 1947 | 4 x Bristol Hercules 106 1675 hp (r 14 cl) a.c. | 34.44 | 113 |
| 119 | Mitsubishi Ki-46-II | J | Mitsubishi Jukogyo K.K. | Rc | 1941 | 2 x Mitsubishi Ha-102 1050 hp (r 14 cl) a.c. | 14.70 | 48.3 |
| 119 | Mitsubishi Ki-57-II | J | Mitsubishi Jukogyo K.K. | Tr | 1942 | 2 x Mitsubishi Ha-102 1080 hp (r 14 cl) a.c. | 22.60 | 74.2 |
| 119 | Mitsubishi F1M2 | J | Mitsubishi Jukogyo K.K. | Rc | 1941 | Mitsubishi Zuisel 13 875 hp (r 14 cl) a.c. | 11 | 36.1 |
| 119 | Kawasaki Ki-56 | J | Kawasaki Kokuki Kogyo K.K. | Tr | 1941 | 2 x Nakajima Ha-25 990 hp (r 14 cl) a.c. | 19.96 | 65.6 |
| 119 | Nakajima C6N1 Saiun | J | Nakajima Hikoki K.K. | Rc | 1944 | Nakajima NK9H Homare 21 1990 hp (r 18 cl) a.c. | 12.50 | 41 |
| 119 | Kawanishi H8K | J | Kawanishi Kokuki K.K. | Rc | 1940 | 4 x Mitsubishi Kinsei 43 1000 hp (r 14 cl) a.c. | 40 | 131.3 |
| 120 | Lockheed C-56 Lodestar | USA | Lockheed Aircraft Corp. | Tr | 1941 | 2 x Wright R-1820-71 Cyclone 1200 hp (r 9 cl) a.c. | 19.96 | 65.6 |
| 120 | Lockheed PV-2 Harpoon | USA | Lockheed Aircraft Corp. | Rc | 1944 | 2 x Pratt & Whitney R-2800-31 Double Wasp 2000 hp (r 18 cl) a.c. | 22.83 | 74.9 |

| Length | | Height | | Take-off weight | | Speed | | Ceiling | | Range | | Crew | Payload/armament |
|---|---|---|---|---|---|---|---|---|---|---|---|---|---|
| m | ft | m | ft | kg | lb | km/h | mph | m | ft | km | ml | | |
| 22.50 | 73.8 | 5.84 | 19.2 | 24,040 | 53,000 | 510 | 317 | 11,150 | 36,000 | 3,220 | 2,001 | 9 | 10-13 mg; b (7,985 kg - 17,600 lb) |
| 30.18 | 99 | 9.02 | 29.7 | 63,958 | 141,000 | 576 | 358 | 9,700 | 31,850 | 6,600 | 4,100 | 10 | 1 g; 10 mg; b (4,100 kg - 9,038 lb) |
| 12.19 | 40 | 5 | 16.5 | 7,215 | 15,905 | 436 | 271 | 6,800 | 22,400 | 1,950 | 1,215 | 3 | 3 mg; b (725 kg - 1,600 lb) |
| 9.96 | 32.8 | 4.14 | 13.7 | 4,717 | 10,400 | 402 | 250 | 8,260 | 27,100 | 2,164 | 1,345 | 2 | 4 mg; b (544 kg - 1,200 lb) |
| 14.63 | 48 | 5.36 | 17.5 | 12,338 | 27,200 | 545 | 339 | 7,800 | 25,800 | 1,750 | 1,090 | 4 | 8 mg; b (1,180 kg - 2,601 lb) |
| 15.24 | 50 | 5.64 | 18.6 | 15,876 | 35,000 | 571 | 355 | 6,750 | 22,145 | 2,250 | 1,398 | 3 | 10 mg; b (1,815 kg - 4,000 lb) |
| 14.32 | 47 | 4.83 | 15.8 | 11,325 | 25,000 | 490 | 304 | 7,400 | 24,250 | 1,650 | 1,020 | 4 | 6 mg; b (905 kg - 1,995 lb) |
| 11.18 | 36.8 | 4.01 | 13.2 | 7,537 | 16,616 | 452 | 281 | 7,650 | 25,100 | 1,785 | 1,110 | 2 | 2 g; 2 mg; b (907 kg - 2,000 lb) |
| 20.40 | 66.9 | 6.38 | 21 | 29,960 | 66,139 | 510 | 317 | 7,000 | 22,966 | 1,200 | 745 | 5 | 5 mg; 1 g; b (2,400 kg - 5,290 lb) |
| 12.65 | 41.5 | 4.30 | 14.1 | 8,410 | 18,541 | 742 | 461 | 10,000 | 32,800 | 1,630 | 1,013 | 1 | 2 g; b (1,500 kg - 3,300 lb) |
| 14.94 | 49 | 4.44 | 14.7 | 14,491 | 31,989 | 499 | 310 | 9,350 | 30,665 | 1,950 | 1,210 | 4 | 3 mg; 1 g; b (3,000 kg - 6,614 lb) |
| 14.40 | 47.3 | — | — | 14,815 | 32,700 | 482 | 300 | 760 | 2,500 | 770 | 480 | 1 | b (3,800 kg - 8,380 lb) |
| 10.16 | 33.4 | — | — | 5,200 | 11,465 | 566 | 352 | 11,900 | 39,040 | 1,600 | 994 | 2 | 3 mg; b (600 kg - 1,323 lb) |
| 12.66 | 41.6 | 4 | 13.1 | 7,680 | 16,931 | 541 | 336 | 8,800 | 28,900 | 1,500 | 932 | 3 | 5 mg; b (1,000 kg - 2,645 lb) |
| 11.65 | 38.2 | 3.40 | 11.2 | 5,510 | 12,147 | 404 | 251 | 6,000 | 19,690 | 600 | 372 | 2 | 2 g; 3 mg; b (600 kg - 1,325 lb) |
| 17.65 | 57.9 | 6.70 | 22 | 21,000 | 46,300 | 900 | 559 | 12,300 | 40,355 | 1,135 | 715 | 3 | 4 g; 3,000 kg (6,613 lb) |
| 13.80 | 45.3 | 4.20 | 13.7 | 12,800 | 28,219 | 550 | 342 | 9,500 | 31,200 | 2,500 | 1,553 | 4 | 2 g; 3 mg; b (3,000 kg - 6,613 lb) |
| 12.12 | 39.9 | 4.59 | 15.1 | 6,115 | 13,481 | 463 | 288 | 5,000 | 16,600 | 1,100 | 686 | 3 | 2 mg; 1 t |
| 11.86 | 38.9 | 4.55 | 14.9 | 7,938 | 17,500 | 563 | 350 | 8,690 | 28,500 | 1,200 | 746 | 1 | 4 g; 1 t |
| 21.18 | 69.6 | 6.10 | 20 | 31,752 | 70,000 | 462 | 287 | 7,500 | 24,500 | 2,670 | 1,659 | 7 | 10 mg; b (9,980 kg - 22,000 lb) |
| 23.85 | 78.3 | 5.25 | 17.3 | 34,020 | 75,000 | 513 | 319 | 9,300 | 31,500 | 2,365 | 1,470 | 7 | 6 mg; 6,350 kg (14,000 lb) |
| 19.96 | 65.6 | 4.78 | 15.8 | 21,185 | 44,500 | 917 | 570 | 14,630 | 48,000 | 4,274 | 2,656 | 3 | 2,722 kg (6,000 lb) |
| 12.23 | 43.5 | 4.35 | 14.3 | 8,140 | 17,946 | 465 | 289 | 8,000 | 26,250 | 2,200 | 1,367 | 3 | 3 mg; b (1,500 kg - 3,307 lb) |
| 12.06 | 39.7 | 5.53 | 18.2 | 10,109 | 22,287 | 454 | 282 | 6,700 | 21,981 | 3,570 | 2,220 | 3 | 2 g; 6 mg; b (1,450 kg - 9,200 lb) |
| 17.93 | 58.8 | 4.59 | 15.1 | 13,288 | 29,330 | 432 | 268 | 7,900 | 25,900 | 1,830 | 1,137 | 5 | 4 mg; b (2,000 kg - 4,400 lb) |
| 17.60 | 57.9 | 6.10 | 20 | 11,500 | 25,400 | 524 | 325 | 7,250 | 23,800 | 1,335 | 830 | 4 | 5 mg; b (2,000 kg - 4,400 lb) |
| 22.92 | 75.2 | 7.70 | 25.2 | 29,885 | 65,970 | 420 | 261 | 8,050 | 26,400 | 3,520 | 2,190 | 6 | 7 mg; b (3,500 kg - 7,700 lb) |
| 14.10 | 46.3 | 5.63 | 18.6 | 8,470 | 18,700 | 390 | 242 | 6,300 | 20,669 | 2,500 | 1,550 | 4-5 | 3 mg; b (400 kg - 880 lb) |
| 20.10 | 65.9 | 4.90 | 16.1 | 15,000 | 33,100 | 390 | 242 | 8,500 | 27,900 | 2,300 | 1,430 | 4 | 2 mg |
| 21.96 | 72 | 6 | 19.8 | 22,000 | 48,500 | 440 | 273 | 7,500 | 24,600 | 2,500 | 1,553 | 5 | 45 p or 8,458 kg (18,646 lb) |
| 7.80 | 25.7 | 3.10 | 10.1 | 1,050 | 2,315 | 170 | 106 | 3,000 | 9,840 | 500 | 310 | 1 | — |
| 19.85 | 65.1 | 5.90 | 19.4 | 14,390 | 31,724 | 390 | 242 | 4,200 | 13,779 | 3,880 | 2,411 | 5 | 2 mg; 2 g; b (300 kg - 661 lb) |
| 28.63 | 93.9 | 6.83 | 22.5 | 41,900 | 90,323 | 439 | 273 | 6,000 | 19,685 | 5,280 | 3,281 | 7-9 | 1 mg; 6 g |
| 24.60 | 80.8 | 5.75 | 18.8 | 19,570 | 43,144 | 370 | 230 | 6,000 | 19,685 | 3,000 | 1,864 | 3-4 | 1 g |
| 15.19 | 49.8 | 4.34 | 14.3 | 13,793 | 30,450 | 616 | 383 | 13,450 | 44,126 | 2,275 | 1,414 | 3 | 2 mg |
| 23.52 | 77.2 | 5.69 | 18.8 | 21,102 | 46,522 | 338 | 210 | 6,900 | 22,640 | 1,335 | 830 | 2-5 | 2 mg; 1 g |
| 28.50 | 93.6 | 9.60 | 31.6 | 43,510 | 95,923 | 232 | 144 | 4,000 | 13,120 | 1,300 | 810 | 5-7 | 6 mg |
| 11.95 | 39.2 | 4.25 | 13.9 | 5,600 | 12,346 | 368 | 230 | 7,500 | 24,600 | 1,800 | 1,118 | 2 | 8 p |
| 22.04 | 72.4 | 5.74 | 18.8 | 16,180 | 35,715 | 331 | 206 | 7,500 | 24,600 | 4,700 | 2,920 | 4-5 | 2 mg; 1 g |
| 36.50 | 119.9 | 10.90 | 35.9 | 45,540 | 100,390 | 310 | 193 | 6,500 | 21,325 | 7,000 | 4,350 | 11 | 3 mg; 3 g |
| 18.26 | 59.9 | 4.75 | 15.7 | 10,240 | 22,600 | 426 | 265 | 5,500 | 18,000 | 2,100 | 1,300 | 4 | 2 mg |
| 12.34 | 40.6 | 4.65 | 15.2 | 9,720 | 21,462 | 611 | 380 | 8,000 | 26,246 | 2,200 | 1,367 | 2 | b (905 kg - 1,995 lb) |
| 11.94 | 39.2 | 3.58 | 11.9 | 3,897 | 8,591 | 376 | 234 | 7,180 | 23,556 | 960 | 597 | 2 | 8 p |
| 12.08 | 39.8 | 4.11 | 13.6 | 4,800 | 10,582 | 322 | 200 | 4,490 | 14,730 | 1,342 | 834 | 3 | 1 g; 1 mg; b (500 kg - 1,102 lb) |
| 10.24 | 33.7 | 3.93 | 12.8 | 2,640 | 5,820 | 230 | 143 | 5,620 | 18,440 | 1,760 | 1,093 | 5 | 1 mg; b (60 kg - 132 lb) |
| 11.30 | 37.1 | 7.40 | 24.2 | 3,640 | 8,025 | 376 | 234 | 8,730 | 28,640 | 2,090 | 1,298 | 3 | 1 mg; b (250 kg - 550 lb) |
| 10.83 | 35.6 | 4.79 | 15.8 | 3,900 | 8,598 | 439 | 273 | 10,000 | 32,810 | 2,400 | 1,504 | 2 | 2 g; 1 mg; b (250 kg - 550 lb) |
| 12.18 | 39.9 | 4.56 | 15 | 6,890 | 15,190 | 530 | 329 | 10,300 | 33,795 | 2,700 | 1,678 | 3 | 1 mg |
| 8.54 | 28 | 3.80 | 12.4 | 1,450 | 3,197 | 246 | 153 | 5,420 | 17,780 | 880 | 548 | 2 | 1 mg; b (60 kg - 132 lb) |
| 9.56 | 31.4 | 2.90 | 9.6 | 1,530 | 3,373 | 178 | 111 | 5,630 | 18,470 | 750 | 466 | 2 | 1 mg; b (120 kg - 264 lb) |
| 7.82 | 25.8 | 2.16 | 7.1 | 907 | 2,000 | 222 | 138 | 4,880 | 16,000 | 480 | 300 | 2 | — |
| 23.93 | 78.6 | 5.03 | 16.5 | 31,075 | 68,597 | 480 | 298 | 6,500 | 21,325 | 4,345 | 2,700 | 5 | 24 p |
| 12.01 | 39.5 | 4.93 | 16.2 | 4,530 | 10,000 | 241 | 150 | 4,900 | 16,000 | 1,200 | 725 | 3-4 | 3 mg |
| 25.19 | 82.8 | 6.85 | 22.6 | 36,288 | 80,000 | 560 | 348 | 8,080 | 26,500 | 6,840 | 4,250 | 5 | 50 p |
| 11 | 36.1 | 3.88 | 12.9 | 5,050 | 11,133 | 604 | 375 | 10,720 | 35,170 | 2,474 | 1,537 | 2 | 1 mg |
| 16.10 | 52.8 | 4.68 | 15.3 | 8,173 | 18,018 | 470 | 292 | 8,000 | 26,246 | 3,000 | 1,865 | 4 | 11 p |
| 9.50 | 31.2 | 4 | 13.1 | 2,550 | 5,622 | 370 | 230 | 9,440 | 30,970 | 740 | 460 | 2 | 3 mg; b (60 kg - 132 lb) |
| 14.90 | 48.8 | 3.60 | 11.8 | 8,025 | 17,692 | 400 | 249 | 8,000 | 26,246 | — | — | 4 | 2,400 kg (5,290 lb) |
| 11 | 36.1 | 3.96 | 12.9 | 4,500 | 9,928 | 610 | 379 | 10,470 | 35,326 | 5,300 | 3,300 | 3 | 1 mg |
| 25.62 | 84 | 6.27 | 20.7 | 17,000 | 37,478 | 340 | 211 | 9,610 | 31,530 | 6,080 | 3,779 | 9 | 1 g; 4 mg; b (1,000 kg - 2,205 lb) |
| 15.18 | 49.8 | 3.37 | 11.1 | 7,938 | 17,500 | 407 | 253 | 7,100 | 23,300 | 2,574 | 1,600 | 2-3 | 17 p |
| 15.85 | 52 | 3.63 | 11.9 | 16,330 | 36,000 | 453 | 282 | 7,285 | 23,900 | 2,880 | 1,790 | 4-5 | 9 mg; b (1,360 kg - 2,998 lb) |

# Technical Data

| Page | Aircraft | Nation | Manufacturer | Type | Year | Engine | Wingspan m | ft |
|------|----------|--------|--------------|------|------|--------|-----------|-----|
| 120 | Curtiss SO3C-1 Seamew | USA | Curtiss-Wright Corp. | Rc | 1942 | Ranger V-770-6 600 hp (12 cl V) l.c. | 11.58 | 38 |
| 120 | Curtiss SC-1 Seahawk | USA | Curtiss-Wright Corp. | Rc | 1944 | Wright R-1820-62 Cyclone 1350 hp (r 9 cl) a.c. | 12.50 | 41 |
| 120 | Consolidated PB4Y-2 Privateer | USA | Consolidated Aircraft Corp. | Rc | 1944 | 4 x Pratt & Whitney R-1830-94 Twin Wasp (r 14 cl) a.c. | 33.53 | 110 |
| 120 | Consolidated PBY-5A Catalina | USA | Cosolidated Aircraft Corp. | Rc | 1941 | 2 x Pratt & Whitney R-1830-92 Twin Wasp (r 14 cl) a.c. | 31.70 | 104 |
| 120 | Consolidated PB2Y-3 Coronado | USA | Consolidated Aircraft Corp. | Rc | 1941 | 4 x Pratt & Whitney R-1830-88 Twin Wasp (r 14 cl) a.c. | 35.05 | 115 |
| 120 | Martin PBM-3 Mariner | USA | Glenn L. Martin Co. | Rc | 1942 | 2 x Wright R-2600-12 Cyclone 1700 hp (r 14 cl) a.c. | 35.97 | 118 |
| 120 | Grumman J2F-5 Duck | USA | Grumman Aircraft Engineering Corp. | Li | 1941 | Wright R-1920-50 Cyclone 850 hp (r 9 cl) a.c. | 11.89 | 39 |
| 120 | North American T-28A Trojan | USA | North American Aviation Inc. | T | 1949 | Wright R-1300-1 Cyclone 800 hp (r 7 cl) a.c. | 12.21 | 40 |
| 120 | North American AT-6A Texan | USA | North American Aviation Inc. | T | 1941 | Pratt & Whitney R-1340-47 Wasp 600 hp (r 9 cl) a.c. | 12.80 | 41.9 |
| 120 | Stinson L-5 Sentinel | USA | Consolidated-Vultee Aircraft | Li | 1942 | Lycoming 0-435-1 185 hp (4 cl) a.c. | 10.36 | 33.9 |
| 120 | Piper L-4 Grasshopper | USA | Piper Aircraft Corp. | Li | 1941 | Continental 0-170-3 65 hp (4 cl) a.c. | 10.74 | 35.2 |
| 121 | Lockheed C-69 Constellation | USA | Lockheed Aircraft Corp. | Tr | 1944 | 4 x Wright R-3350 Cyclone 2200 hp (r 18 cl) a.c. | 37.49 | 122.9 |
| 121 | Cessna AT-17 | USA | Cessna Aircraft Co. | T | 1942 | 2 x Jacob R-775-9 245 hp (r 7 cl) a.c. | 12.78 | 41.9 |
| 121 | Cessna L-19A Bird Dog | USA | Cessna Aircraft Co. | Li | 1950 | Continental C-470-II 213 hp (4 cl) a.c. | 10.97 | 35.9 |
| 121 | Curtiss C-46A Commando | USA | Curtiss-Wright Corp. | Tr | 1943 | 2 x Pratt & Whitney R-2800-51 Double Wasp 2000 hp (r 18 cl) a.c. | 32.94 | 108 |
| 121 | Fairchild C-119G Boxcar | USA | The Fairchild Engine and Aeroplane Corp. | Tr | 1950 | 2 x Wright R-3350-85 Cyclone 3500 hp (r 18 cl) a.c. | 33.32 | 109.3 |
| 121 | Beech UC-43 Traveler | USA | Beech Aircraft Corp. | Li | 1942 | Pratt & Whitney R-985 AN-1 Wasp Jr. 450 hp (r 9 cl) a.c. | 9.75 | 31.9 |
| 121 | Beech C-45B Expediter | USA | Beech Aircraft Corp. | Tr | 1942 | Pratt & Whitney R-985-AN Wasp Jr. 450 hp (r 9 cl) a.c. | 14.53 | 47.6 |
| 121 | Douglas C-47B Skytrain | USA | Douglas Aircraft Co. | Tr | 1941 | 2 x Pratt & Whitney R-1830-92 Twin Wasp 1200 hp (r 14 cl) a.c. | 29.10 | 95.6 |
| 121 | Douglas C-54A Skymaster | USA | Douglas Aircraft Co. | Tr | 1942 | 4 x Pratt & Whitney R-2000-7 Twin Wasp 1290 hp (r 14 cl) a.c. | 35.81 | 117.4 |
| 121 | Douglas C-124 Globemaster II | USA | Douglas Aircraft Co. | Tr | 1949 | 4 x Pratt & Whitney R-4360-63A Wasp Major 3800 hp (r 28 cl) a.c. | 53.08 | 174.1 |
| 122 | Ilyushin Il-12 | USSR | State Industries | CTr | 1946 | 2 x Shvetsov Ash-82FN 1650 hp (r 14 cl) a.c. | 31.70 | 104 |
| 122 | Antonov An-2 | USSR | State Industries | LT | 1947 | Shvetsov Ash-621R 1000 hp (r 9 cl) a.c. | 18.18 | 59.6 |
| 122 | Yakovlev Yak-16 | USSR | State Industries | CTr | 1948 | 2 x Shvetsov Ash-21 750 hp (r 7 cl) a.c. | 20 | 65.6 |
| 122 | Sud-Ouest SO-30P Bretagne | F | SNCASO | CTr | 1947 | 2 x Pratt & Whitney R-2800-B43 Double Wasp 1620 hp (r 18 cl) a.c. | 26.87 | 88.1 |
| 122 | Sud-Ouest SO-95 Corse | F | SNCASO | LT | 1947 | 2 x Renault 12 S-02-201 580 hp (12 cl V) a.c. | 18.01 | 59 |
| 122 | Sud-Est SE-161 Languedoc | F | SNCASE | CTr | 1945 | 4 x Gnome-Rhône 14N 1150 hp (r 14 cl) a.c. | 29.38 | 96.3 |
| 123 | Sud-Est SE-2010 Armagnac | F | SNCASE | CTr | 1949 | 4 x Pratt & Whitney R-4360 Wasp Major 3500 hp (r 28 cl) a.c. | 48.95 | 160.5 |
| 123 | Latécoère 631 | F | Société Industrielle d'Aviation Latécoère | CTr | 1942 | 6 x Wright GR-2600 A5B Cyclone 1600 hp (r 14 cl) a.c. | 57.43 | 188.4 |
| 123 | Convair 240 | USA | Convair Division of General Dynamics Corp. | CTr | 1947 | 2 x Pratt & Whitney R-2800-CA18 Double Wasp 2400 hp (r 18 cl) a.c. | 27.98 | 91.7 |
| 123 | Martin 2-0-2 | USA | Glenn L. Martin Co. | CTr | 1946 | 2 x Pratt & Whitney R-2800-CA18 Double Wasp 2100 hp (r 18 cl) a.c. | 28.42 | 93.2 |
| 124 | Boeing 314A Yankee Clipper | USA | Boeing Aircraft Co. | CTr | 1941 | 4 x Wright GR-2600 Cyclone 1660 hp (r 14 cl) a.c. | 46.33 | 151.9 |
| 124 | Boeing 377-10-26 Stratocruiser | USA | Boeing Aircraft Co. | CTr | 1947 | 4 x Pratt & Whitney R-436B-6 Wasp Major 3500 hp (r 18 cl) a.c. | 43.05 | 141.2 |
| 124 | Consolidated PBY-5A Catalina | USA | Consolidated Aircraft Corp. | CTr | 1941 | 2 x Pratt & Whitney R-1830-92 Twin Wasp 1200 hp (r 14 cl) a.c. | 31.70 | 104 |
| 125 | Lockheed L-749 Constellation | USA | Lockheed Aircraft Corp. | CTr | 1947 | 4 x Wright R-3350-C18-BA3 Cyclone 2200 hp (r 18 cl) a.c. | 37.49 | 122.9 |
| 125 | Douglas DC-4 | USA | Douglas Aircraft Co. | CTr | 1942 | 4 x Pratt & Whitney R-2000 Twin Wasp 1450 hp (r 14 cl) a.c. | 35.81 | 117.4 |
| 125 | Sikorsky VS-44A | USA | Sikorsky Aircraft | CTr | 1942 | 4 x Pratt & Whitney R-1830-S1C3G Twin Wasp 1200 hp (r 14 cl) a.c. | 37.80 | 124 |
| 125 | Hughes H-4 Hercules | USA | Hughes Aircraft Co. | Tr | 1947 | 8 x Pratt & Whitney R-4360 Wasp Major 3000 hp (r 28 cl) a.c. | 97.54 | 320 |
| 126 | Airspeed A.S.57 Ambassador 2 | GB | Airspeed Division of de Havilland Aircraft Co. Ltd. | CTr | 1948 | 2 x Bristol Centaurus 661 2625 hp (r 18 cl) a.c. | 35.05 | 114.9 |
| 126 | de Havilland D.H.104 Dove 1 | GB | de Havilland Aircraft Co. Ltd. | LT | 1945 | 2 x de Havilland Gipsy Queen 70-3 300 hp (6 cl) a.c. | 17.37 | 56.9 |
| 126 | Miles M.57 Aerovan 1 | GB | Miles Aircraft Ltd. | LT | 1945 | 2 x Blackburn Cirrus Major 3 155 hp (4 cl) a.c. | 15.24 | 49.9 |
| 126 | Short S.A.6 Sealand | GB | Short Brothers Ltd. | LT | 1948 | 2 x de Havilland Gipsy Queen 70-3 340 hp (6 cl) a.c. | 18.75 | 61.6 |
| 126 | Percival P.50 Prince 1 | GB | Percival Aircraft Ltd. | LT | 1948 | 2 × Alvis Leonides 501/4 520 hp (r 9 cl) | 17.07 | 56 |
| 126 | Bristol 170 Freighter | GB | Bristol Aeroplane Co. Ltd. | CTr | 1946 | 2 x Bristol Hercules 632 1675 hp (r 14 cl) a.c. | 29.87 | 98 |
| 127 | Airspeed A.65 Consul | GB | Airspeed Ltd. | LT | 1946 | 2 x Armstrong Siddeley Cheetah 10 395 hp (r 7 cl) a.c. | 16.25 | 53.3 |
| 127 | Avro Tudor 1 | GB | A.V. Roe & Co. Ltd. | CTr | 1945 | 4 x Rolls-Royce Merlin 621 1770 hp (12 cl V) l.c. | 36.58 | 120 |

| Length | | Height | | Take-off weight | | Speed | | Ceiling | | Range | | Crew | Payload/armament |
|---|---|---|---|---|---|---|---|---|---|---|---|---|---|
| m | ft | m | ft | kg | lb | km/h | mph | m | ft | km | ml | | |
| 10.59 | 34.7 | 4.31 | 14.2 | 3,233 | 7,105 | 269 | 168 | 5,030 | 16,500 | 1,030 | 640 | 2 | 2 mg; b (295 kg - 650 lb) |
| 11.07 | 36.4 | 4.88 | 16 | 4,082 | 9,000 | 504 | 313 | 11,400 | 37,300 | 1,000 | 621 | 1 | 2 mg; b (340 kg - 750 lb) |
| 22.73 | 74.7 | 9.17 | 30.1 | 29,485 | 65,000 | 381 | 237 | 6,300 | 20,700 | 4,500 | 2,800 | 11 | 12 mg; b (4,717 kg - 10,399 lb) |
| 19.45 | 63.8 | 6.14 | 20.2 | 16,066 | 35,420 | 281 | 175 | 5,520 | 18,100 | 3,780 | 2,350 | 7-9 | 5 mg; b (1,814 kg - 4,000 lb) |
| 24.16 | 79.3 | 8.30 | 27.6 | 30,845 | 68,000 | 343 | 213 | 6,130 | 21,111 | 2,400 | 1,491 | 10 | 8 mg; b (5,443 kg - 12,000 lb) |
| 24:38 | 80 | 8.38 | 27.6 | 26,310 | 58,000 | 319 | 198 | 5,150 | 16,900 | 3,440 | 2,137 | 9 | 7 mg; b (907 kg - 2,000 lb) |
| 10.36 | 34 | 4.60 | 15.1 | 3,144 | 6,711 | 302 | 188 | 8,230 | 27,000 | 1,255 | 780 | 2 | — |
| 9.75 | 31.9 | 3.86 | 12.7 | 2,887 | 6,365 | 455 | 283 | 7,300 | 23,950 | 1,600 | 994 | 2 | — |
| 8.84 | 29 | 3.55 | 11.6 | 2,404 | 5,300 | 335 | 208 | 7,325 | 24,032 | 1,205 | 749 | 2 | 2 mg |
| 7.34 | 24 | 2.41 | 7.9 | 916 | 2,019 | 209 | 130 | 4,815 | 15,797 | 675 | 419 | 2 | — |
| 6.70 | 21.9 | 2.03 | 6.8 | 553 | 1,219 | 137 | 85 | 2,835 | 9,301 | 305 | 190 | 2 | — |
| 29 | 95.1 | 7.21 | 23.6 | 32,660 | 72,003 | 530 | 329 | 7,620 | 25,000 | 3,860 | 2,399 | 4-6 | 60 p |
| 9.98 | 32.7 | 3.02 | 9.9 | 2,400 | 5,291 | 314 | 195 | 6,700 | 21,981 | 1,200 | 745 | 1-2 | 4 p |
| 7.85 | 25.7 | 2.21 | 7.2 | 1,088 | 2,399 | 243 | 151 | 5,640 | 18,504 | 850 | 528 | 2 | — |
| 23.27 | 76.3 | 6.63 | 21.7 | 25,400 | 55,997 | 433 | 269 | 8,400 | 27,559 | 1,930 | 1,199 | 4 | 50 p |
| 26.36 | 86.4 | 8 | 26.2 | 38,556 | 85,000 | 350 | 217 | 7,285 | 23,900 | 2,850 | 1,770 | 4 | 40 p |
| 7.98 | 26.1 | 3.12 | 10.2 | 2,132 | 4,700 | 319 | 198 | 6,100 | 20,013 | 805 | 500 | 1 | 4 p |
| 10.44 | 34.2 | 2.95 | 9.6 | 3,960 | 8,730 | 338 | 210 | 6,100 | 20,013 | 1,130 | 702 | 1 | 6-8 p |
| 19.43 | 63.7 | 5.18 | 16.9 | 11,793 | 25,999 | 370 | 230 | 7,315 | 23,999 | 2,574 | 1,599 | 2-3 | 27 p |
| 28.60 | 93.8 | 8.33 | 27.4 | 28,125 | 61,993 | 426 | 265 | 6,700 | 21,981 | 6,275 | 3,099 | 4 | 50 p |
| 39.62 | 129.9 | 14.73 | 48.3 | 88,225 | 194,502 | 370 | 229 | 5,600 | 18,372 | 6,480 | 4,027 | 8 | 200 p or 31,070 kg (68,498 lb) |
| 21.31 | 69.9 | 8.07 | 26.4 | 17,250 | 38,030 | 350 | 217 | 6,700 | 21,981 | 2,000 | 1,243 | 4-5 | 27 p |
| 12.95 | 42.4 | 4.20 | 13.7 | 5,500 | 12,125 | 200 | 124 | 4,350 | 14,271 | 905 | 562 | 2 | 10 p |
| 14.50 | 47.5 | 3.60 | 11.8 | 6,400 | 14,110 | 290 | 180 | 5,000 | 16,404 | 1,000 | 621 | 2 | 10 p |
| 18.95 | 62.1 | 5.89 | 19.3 | 20,126 | 44,370 | 438 | 272 | 5,300 | 17,388 | 1,270 | 789 | 2 | 30-37 p |
| 12.32 | 40.4 | 4.30 | 14.1 | 5,600 | 12,346 | 330 | 205 | — | — | 1,300 | 808 | 2 | 10-13 p |
| 24.25 | 79.5 | 5.13 | 16.8 | 22,941 | 50,576 | 405 | 252 | 7,200 | 23,622 | 1,000 | 621 | 4 | 33 p |
| 39.63 | 130 | — | — | 77,500 | 170,858 | 454 | 282 | 6,800 | 22,309 | 5,120 | 3,181 | 4 | 84-100 p |
| 43.46 | 142.5 | 10.10 | 33.1 | 71,350 | 157,299 | 297 | 184 | — | — | 6,035 | 3,750 | 5 | 46 p |
| 22.27 | 73 | 8.22 | 26.9 | 18,972 | 41,826 | 432 | 268 | 9,150 | 30,019 | 2,880 | 1,790 | 3-4 | 40 p |
| 21.74 | 71.3 | 8.66 | 28.4 | 18,098 | 39,899 | 460 | 286 | 9,150 | 30,019 | 1,022 | 635 | 3 | 40 p |
| 32.31 | 106 | 8.41 | 27.5 | 37,422 | 82,501 | 294 | 183 | 4,085 | 13,402 | 5,630 | 3,498 | 10 | 77 p |
| 33.63 | 110.3 | 11.66 | 38.2 | 64,434 | 142,052 | 547 | 340 | 10,000 | 32,810 | 6,760 | 4,200 | 5 | 55-100 p |
| 19.45 | 63.8 | 6.14 | 20.1 | 12,701 | 28,000 | 209 | 130 | 4,480 | 14,698 | 1,046 | 650 | 2-4 | 22 p |
| 29 | 95.1 | 7.21 | 23.6 | 48,534 | 107,000 | 504 | 313 | 7,620 | 25,000 | 3,637 | 2,260 | 6 | 44-64 p |
| 28.62 | 93.8 | 8.38 | 27.4 | 33,475 | 73,800 | 365 | 227 | 6,800 | 22,309 | 3,444 | 2,140 | 4 | 44-86 p |
| 24.16 | 79.2 | 8.41 | 27.5 | 26,082 | 57,501 | 257 | 160 | 5,790 | 18,996 | 5,790 | 3,598 | 9 | 26-47 p |
| 66.60 | 218.5 | 24.15 | 79.2 | 181,436* | 399,997* | 281 | 175 | — | — | 5,633* | 3,500* | 5 | 500-700 p |
| 24.99 | 81.9 | 5.74 | 18.8 | 23,814 | 52,501 | 463 | 288 | 10,500 | 34,448 | 885 | 550 | 3 | 47-55 p |
| 11.99 | 39.3 | 3.96 | 12.9 | 3,855 | 8,499 | 322 | 200 | 6,100 | 20,013 | 805 | 500 | 2 | 8 p |
| 10.97 | 35.9 | 4.11 | 13.4 | 2,676 | 5,899 | 177 | 110 | 4,040 | 13,254 | 724 | 450 | 1 | 8 p |
| 12.85 | 42.1 | 4.57 | 15 | 4,128 | 9,100 | 272 | 169 | 6,400 | 21,000 | 845 | 525 | 2 | 7 p |
| 13.06 | 29.9 | 4.90 | 16.1 | 4,835 | 10,659 | 288 | 179 | 7,160 | 23,491 | 1,515 | 941 | 2 | 8-10 p |
| 20.83 | 68.4 | 6.60 | 21.8 | 16,783 | 37,000 | 262 | 163 | 6,705 | 22,000 | 482 | 300 | 3 | 34 p |
| 10.77 | 35.3 | 3.38 | 11 | 3,742 | 8,250 | 251 | 156 | 5,790 | 19,000 | 1,448 | 900 | 2 | 6 p |
| 24.23 | 79.4 | 6.37 | 20.8 | 32,205 | 71,000 | 338 | 210 | 7,925 | 26,000 | 5,840 | 3,629 | 4 | 24 p |

# Technical Data

| Page | Aircraft | Nation | Manufacturer | Type | Year | Engine | Wingspan m | ft |
|------|----------|--------|--------------|------|------|--------|------------|-----|
| 127 | Avro Tudor 2 | GB | A.V. Roe & Co. Ltd. | CTr | 1946 | 4 x Rolls-Royce Merlin 621 1770 hp (12 cl V) l.c. | 36.58 | 120 |
| 127 | Avro 683 Lancaster 1 | GB | A.V. Roe & Co. Ltd. | CTr | 1944 | 4 x Rolls-Royce Merlin T24 1640 hp (12 cl V) l.c. | 31.09 | 102 |
| 127 | Avro 685 York | GB | A.V. Roe & Co. Ltd. | CTr | 1942 | 4 x Rolls-Royce Merlin 502 1610 hp (12 cl V) l.c. | 31.09 | 102 |
| 127 | Avro 691 Lancastrian 1 | GB | A.V. Roe & Co. Ltd. | CTr | 1945 | 4 x Rolls-Royce Merlin 502 1610 hp (12 cl V) l.c. | 31.09 | 102 |
| 127 | Scottish Aviation Prestwick Pioneer 2 | GB | Scottish Aviation Ltd. | LT | 1950 | Alvis Leonides 501/3 520 hp (r 9 cl) a.c. | 15.16 | 49.9 |
| 127 | Bristol 167 Brabazon 1. | GB | Bristol Aeroplane Co. Ltd. | CTr | 1949 | 8 x Bristol Centaurus 20 2500 hp (r 18 cl) a.c. | 70.10 | 230 |
| 128 | Vickers Viscount 700 | GB | Vickers-Armstrong Ltd. | CTr | 1950 | 2 x tp Rolls-Royce Dart R.Da.3 505 2540 hp | 28.55 | 93.8 |
| 128 | Handley Page H.P.81 Hermes 4 | GB | Handley Page Ltd. | CTr | 1948 | 4 x Bristol Hercules 763 2100 hp (r 14 cl) a.c. | 34.44 | 113 |
| 128 | Handley Page H.P.70 Halifax | GB | Handley Page Ltd. | CTr | 1946 | 4 x Bristol Hercules 100 1675 hp (r 14 cl) a.c. | 31.60 | 103.6 |
| 128 | Handley Page H.P.R. 1 Marathon | GB | Handley Page (Reading) Ltd. | CTr | 1946 | 4 x de Havilland Gispy Queen 70-3 340 hp (6 cl) a.c. | 19.81 | 65 |
| 128 | Short S.25 Sandringhan | GB | Short Brothers Ltd. | CTr | 1946 | 4 x Pratt & Whitney R-1830-90C Twin Wasp 1200 hp (r 14 cl) a.c. | 34.37 | 112.9 |
| 128 | Short S.45 Solent 2 | GB | Short Brothers Ltd. | CTr | 1946 | 4 x Bristol Hercules 637 1690 hp (r 14 cl) a.c. | 34.37 | 112.9 |
| 129 | Vickers Viking 1B | GB | Vickers-Armstrongs Ltd. | CTr | 1946 | 2 x Bristol Hercules 634 1690 hp (r 14 cl) a.c. | 27.12 | 88.9 |
| 129 | CASA-201B Alcotan | E | Construcciones Aeronauticas S.A. | CTr | 1949 | 2 x Enma Sirio S-VII 500 hp (r 7 cl) a.c. | 18.40 | 60.4 |
| 129 | de Havilland DHC-2 Beaver 1 | CDN | de Havilland Aircraft of Canada Ltd. | CTr | 1947 | Pratt & Whitney R-985-SB3 Wasp Jr. 450 hp (r 9 cl) a.c. | 14.64 | 47.9 |
| 129 | Canadair C-4 | CDN | Canadair Ltd. | CTr | 1947 | 4 x Rolls-Royce Merlin 626 1760 hp (12 cl V) l.c. | 35.80 | 117.5 |
| 129 | SAAB 90 A-2 Scandia | S | SAAB | CTr | 1946 | 2 x Pratt & Whitney R-2180-E1 Twin Wasp 1800 hp (r 14 cl) a.c. | 28 | 91.8 |
| 129 | SIAI Marchetti S.M.95 | I | SIAI Marchetti | CTr | 1946 | 4 x Bristol Pegasus 48 900 hp (r 9 cl) a.c. | 34.28 | 112.5 |
| 129 | Macchi M.B. 320 | I | Aeronautica Macchi | CTr | 1947 | 2 x Continental E.185 185 hp (6 cl) a.c. | 13 | 42.7 |
| 129 | Fiat G.212 CP | I | Fiat S.A. | CTr | 1947 | 3 x Pratt & Whitney R-1830-S1C3-G Twin Wasp 1065 hp (r 14 cl) a.c. | 29.34 | 96.3 |
| 129 | Breda B.Z.308 | I | Società Italiana Ernesto Breda | CTr | 1948 | 4 x Bristol Centaurus 568 2500 hp (r 18 cl) a.c. | 42.10 | 138.1 |
| 134 | Dornier Do.27Q-1 | D | Dornier AG. | LT | 1955 | Lycoming GO-480-B1A6 270 hp (6 cl) a.c. | 12 | 39.4 |
| 134 | Dornier Do.28A-1 | D | Dornier AG. | LT | 1959 | 2 x Lycoming 0-540-A1D 250 hp (6 cl) a.c. | 13.80 | 45.3 |
| 134 | L-200A Morava | CS | State Industries | LT | 1959 | 2 x M.337 210 hp (6 cl) a.c. | 12.30 | 40.3 |
| 134 | Aero 145 | CS | State Industries | LT | 1958 | 2 x M.332 140 hp (4 cl) a.c. | 12.24 | 40.2 |
| 134 | MR-2 | R | V.R.M.V.-3 | LT | 1956 | 2 x Walter Minor 6-III 160 hp (6 cl) a.c. | 14 | 45.9 |
| 134 | Grumman G-159 Gulfstream 1 | USA | Grumman Aircraft Engineering Corp. | LT | 1958 | 2 x tp Rolls-Royce Dart 529 2105 hp | 23.93 | 78.6 |
| 135 | Convair 540 | USA | Convair Division of General Dynamics Corp. | CTr | 1955 | 2 x tp Napier Eland 504A 3500 hp | 32.10 | 105.3 |
| 135 | Convair 880 | USA | Convair Division of General Dynamics Corp. | CTr | 1959 | 4 x tj General Electric CJ805-3 5080 kg (11,200 lb) | 36.58 | 120 |
| 135 | Aero Commander 560 | USA | Aero Design and Engineering Service | LT | 1954 | 2 x Lycoming GO-480-B 270 hp (6 cl) a.c. | 13.42 | 44 |
| 135 | Boeing 707-120 | USA | Boeing Aircraft Co. | CTr | 1957 | 4 x tj Pratt & Whitney JT3C-6 6124 hp | 39.87 | 130.8 |
| 135 | Boeing 720 | USA | Boeing Aircraft Co. | CTr | 1959 | 4 x tj Pratt & Whitney JT3C-7 5443 kg (12,000 lb) | 39.87 | 130.8 |
| 135 | Boeing 707-320 | USA | Boeing Aircraft Co. | CTr | 1959 | 4 x tj Pratt & Whitney JT4A-3 7167 kg (15,800 lb) | 43,41 | 142.4 |
| 138 | Lockheed L-1049 G Super Constellation | USA | Lockheed Aircraft Corp. | CTr | 1954 | 4 x Wright R-3350-DA3 Turbo Compound 3500 hp (r 18 cl) a.c. | 37.49 | 122.9 |
| 138 | Lockheed 188A Electra | USA | Lockheed Aircraft Corp. | CTr | 1958 | 4 x tp Allison 501-D13A 3750 hp | 30.18 | 99 |
| 138 | Douglas DC-6B | USA | Douglas Aircraft Co. | CTr | 1951 | 4 x Pratt & Whitney R-2800-CB16 Double Wasp 2400 hp (r 18 cl) a.c. | 35.81 | 117.6 |
| 138 | Douglas DC-7C | USA | Douglas Aircraft Co. | CTr | 1955 | 4 x Wright R-3350-18EA1 Turbo Compound 3400 hp (r 18 cl) a.c. | 38.80 | 127.2 |
| 138 | Douglas DC-8-20 | USA | Douglas Aircraft Co. | CTr | 1958 | 4 x tj Pratt & Whitney JT4A-3 7167 kg (15,800 lb) | 43.41 | 142.5 |
| 139 | Breguet 763 Provence | F | Société Anonyme des Ateliers d'Aviation L. Breguet | CTr | 1951 | 4 x Pratt & Whitney R-2800-CA18 Double Wasp 2400 hp (r 18 cl) a.c. | 42.98 | 141 |
| 139 | Sud-Aviation SE.210 Caravelle III | F | Sud-Aviation | CTr | 1959 | 2 x tj Rolls-Royce Avon 527 5171 kg (11,400 lb) | 34.30 | 112.6 |
| 139 | Nord M.H. 260 | F | Nord Aviation | CTr | 1960 | 2 x tp Turboméca Bastan IV 986 hp | 21.93 | 71.9 |
| 139 | PZL MD-12 | PL | Pantswowe Zaklady Lotnicze | CTr | 1959 | 4 x Nanakiewicz WN-3 330 hp (r 7 cl) a.c. | 21.31 | 69.9 |
| 139 | I.A. 35-X-III | RA | DIFNIA | LT | 1960 | 2 x I.A.R. 19-C El Indio 840 hp (r 9 cl) a.c. | 19.60 | 64.3 |
| 139 | I.A. 45 Querandi | RA | DIFNIA | LT | 1957 | 2 x Lycoming 0-320 150 hp (4 cl) a.c. | 13.75 | 45.2 |
| 139 | Peking | TJ | Istituto di Ingegneria Aeronautica di Pechino | LT | 1958 | 2 x Ivchenko AI-14R 260 hp (r 9 cl) a.c. | 17.50 | 57.5 |
| 139 | Piaggio P.136-L1 | I | Industria Aeronautica e Meccanica Rinaldo Piaggio S.p.A. | LT | 1955 | 2 x Lycoming GO-480-B1A6 270 hp (6 cl) a.c. | 13.53 | 44.4 |
| 139 | Pilatus PC-6 Porter | CH | Pilatus Flugzeugwerke AG. | LT | 1959 | Lycoming GSO-480-B1A6 340 hp (6 cl) a.c. | 15.20 | 49.8 |
| 139 | Fokker F.27-100 Friendship | NL | Fokker-VFW N.V. | CTr | 1958 | 2 x tp Rolls-Royce Dart 511-7 1710 hp | 29 | 95.1 |
| 140 | de Havilland D.H.114 Heron 2 | GB | de Havilland Aircraft Co. Ltd. | LT | 1952 | 4 x de Havilland Gipsy Queen 30-2 250 hp (6 cl) a.c. | 21.79 | 71.6 |
| 140 | Armstrong Whitworth A.W.650 Argosy 100 | GB | Armstrong Whitworth Aircraft Ltd. | CTr | 1959 | 4 x tp Rolls-Royce Dart 526 2100 hp | 35.05 | 115 |
| 140 | Scottish Aviation Twin Pioneer 1 | GB | Scottish Aviation Ltd. | LT | 1955 | 2 x Alvis Leonides 514/8 560 hp (r 9 cl) a.c. | 23.32 | 76.6 |
| 140 | Bristol 175 Britannia 102 | GB | Bristol Aeroplane Co. Ltd. | CTr | 1954 | 4 x tp Bristol Proteus 705 3870 hp | 43.36 | 142.3 |
| 140 | de Havilland DHA-3 Drover 3 | GB | de Havilland Aircraft Co. (Hawker Siddeley Group) | LT | 1960 | 3 x Lycoming 0-360-A1A 180 hp (4 cl) a.c. | 17.37 | 57 |

| Length | | Height | | Take-off weight | | Speed | | Ceiling | | Range | | Crew | Payload/armament |
|---|---|---|---|---|---|---|---|---|---|---|---|---|---|
| m | ft | m | ft | kg | lb | km/h | mph | m | ft | km | ml | | |
| 32.18 | 105 | 7.39 | 24.3 | 36,288 | 80,000 | 378 | 235 | 7,790 | 25,557 | 3,750 | 2,330 | 2-4 | 60 p |
| 21.18 | 69.4 | 6.10 | 20 | 29,484 | 65,000 | 338 | 210 | 7,500 | 24,606 | 2,270 | 1,659 | 4 | 11,350 kg (25,022 lb) |
| 23.93 | 78.6 | 5.03 | 16.6 | 31,075 | 68,509 | 338 | 210 | 6,500 | 21,325 | 4,345 | 2,700 | 4 | 18-21 p |
| 23.42 | 76.8 | 5.94 | 19.4 | 29,684 | 65,000 | 370 | 230 | 7,770 | 25,492 | 6,680 | 4,151 | 4 | 9-13 p |
| 10.59 | 34.9 | 3.10 | 10.1 | 2,630 | 5,800 | 195 | 121 | 7,010 | 23,000 | 675 | 420 | 1 | 4 p |
| 53.95 | 177 | 15.24 | 50 | 131,542 | 290,000 | 402* | 250* | 10,500 | 34,500 | 8,850* | 5,500* | 12 | 100 p |
| 24.94 | 81.8 | 8.46 | 27.7 | 22,680 | 50,000 | 508 | 316 | 8,380 | 27,500 | 1,530 | 951 | 3-4 | 47 p |
| 29.51 | 96.8 | 9.12 | 29.9 | 39,009 | 86,000 | 428 | 266 | 7,500 | 24,606 | 3,220 | 2,001 | 5 | 40-78 p |
| 22.43 | 73.5 | 6.91 | 22.8 | 30,845 | 68,002 | 418 | 260 | 6,400 | 21,000 | 4,070 | 2,530 | 3 | 10 p; 3,629 kg (8,000 lb) |
| 15.88 | 52.1 | 4.29 | 14.1 | 8,276 | 18,245 | 323 | 200 | 5,500 | 18,044 | 1,500 | 932 | 3-5 | 18-22 p |
| 26.29 | 86.3 | 6.96 | 22.8 | 25,400 | 56,000 | 356 | 221 | 6,500 | 21,325 | 3,880 | 2,410 | 5 | 30 p |
| 26.72 | 87.8 | 10.44 | 34.3 | 35,380 | 77,999 | 393 | 244 | 5,180 | 16,995 | 2,900 | 1,802 | 7 | 30 p |
| 19.86 | 65.2 | 5.94 | 19.4 | 15,422 | 34,000 | 338 | 210 | 7,240 | 27,753 | 2,735 | 1,700 | 5 | 24-36 p |
| 13.80 | 45.3 | 3.95 | 12.9 | 5,500 | 12,125 | 310 | 193 | 5,600 | 18,372 | 1,000 | 621 | 2 | 8-10 p |
| 9.98 | 32.7 | 3.18 | 10.4 | 2,300 | 5,071 | 230 | 143 | 5,486 | 18,000 | 1,190 | 735 | 1 | 7 p |
| 28.60 | 93.8 | 8.40 | 27.5 | 37,300 | 80,200 | 523 | 325 | 9,000 | 29,527 | 6,240 | 3,878 | 4 | 40-55 p |
| 21.30 | 69.9 | 7.08 | 23.2 | 16,000 | 35,274 | 391 | 243 | 7,500 | 24,606 | 1,480 | 920 | 4-5 | 24-36 p |
| 24.77 | 81.3 | 5.70 | 18.7 | 22,000 | 48,502 | 315 | 196 | 6,800 | 22,300 | 2,000 | 1,250 | 5 | 38 p |
| 8.66 | 28.5 | 3.19 | 10.6 | 2,500 | 5,511 | 252 | 171 | 5,600 | 18,372 | 1,600 | 994 | 2 | 4 p |
| 23.40 | 76.7 | 8.14 | 26.7 | 18,000 | 39,683 | 320 | 199 | 7,500 | 24,606 | 2,500 | 1,554 | 5 | 26-30 p |
| 33.52 | 109.9 | 7.20 | 23.6 | 46,500 | 102,515 | 441 | 274 | 7,350 | 24,114 | 7,700 | 4,785 | 3-4 | 80 p |
| 9.60 | 31.6 | 3.50 | 11.4 | 1,850 | 4,078 | 175 | 109 | 3,300 | 10,825 | 800 | 497 | 1 | 6-7 p |
| 9.18 | 30.1 | 2.80 | 9.2 | 2,450 | 5,400 | 235 | 146 | 5,700 | 18,700 | 1,150 | 715 | 1 | 6-7 p |
| 8.61 | 28.3 | 2.22 | 7.2 | 1,950 | 4,300 | 293 | 182 | 5,700 | 18,700 | 1,770 | 1,100 | 1 | 3-4 p |
| 7.77 | 25.6 | 2.31 | 7.6 | 1,600 | 3,257 | 249 | 155 | 5,900 | 19,360 | 1,697 | 1,055 | 1 | 3-4 p |
| 10.90 | 35.9 | 2.76 | 91.1 | 2,080 | 4,585 | 275 | 171 | 4,900 | 16,000 | 1,100 | 685 | 1 | 5 p |
| 19.40 | 63.8 | 6.95 | 22.8 | 15,240 | 33,598 | 573 | 356 | 10,570 | 35,006 | 3,780 | 2,349 | 2 | 10-19 p |
| 24.13 | 79.1 | 8.57 | 28.1 | 24,131 | 53,200 | 523 | 325 | 9,150 | 30,000 | 2,606 | 1,619 | 3-4 | 44 p |
| 39.42 | 129.4 | 11 | 36 | 85,957 | 189,503 | 930 | 578 | 12,600 | 41,338 | 5,150 | 3,200 | 5 | 84-110 p |
| 10.44 | 34.2 | 4.49 | 14.9 | 2,722 | 6,001 | 320 | 200 | 6,706 | 22,000 | 1,770 | 1,100 | 1 | 4-5 p |
| 40.04 | 144.6 | 11.79 | 38.8 | 116,576 | 257,000 | 919 | 571 | 9,980 | 32,414 | 4,950 | 3,075 | 4 | 121-179 p |
| 41.68 | 136.7 | 11.56 | 37.9 | 103,875 | 229,000 | 967 | 601 | 11,735 | 38,500 | 8,430 | 5,240 | 4 | 108-165 p |
| 46.60 | 152.8 | 12.67 | 41.7 | 141,523 | 312,000 | 972 | 604 | 11,340 | 37,200 | 7,450 | 4,630 | 4 | 131-189 p |
| 34.65 | 113.6 | 7.56 | 24.8 | 68,100 | 150,135 | 526 | 327 | 7,620 | 25,000 | 7,440 | 4,623 | 6 | 66-95 p |
| 31.85 | 104.6 | 9.78 | 32 | 52,618 | 116,003 | 652 | 405 | 8,230 | 27,000 | 4,458 | 2,770 | 5 | 66-99 p |
| 32.20 | 105.6 | 8.66 | 28.4 | 45,400 | 100,090 | 494 | 307 | 7,620 | 25,000 | 6,270 | 3,896 | 3 | 68-107 |
| 34.23 | 112.3 | 9.37 | 30.7 | 63,106 | 139,124 | 486 | 302 | 8,656 | 28,339 | 9,616 | 5,975 | 5 | 62-95 p |
| 48.87 | 150.6 | 12.91 | 42.3 | 125,190 | 276,000 | 946 | 594 | 9,150 | 31,019 | 6,888 | 4,280 | 5 | 112-173 p |
| 28.94 | 94.9 | 9.65 | 31.8 | 51,600 | 131,758 | 336 | 209 | 7,315 | 23,999 | 2,290 | 1,423 | 4 | 107 p |
| 32.01 | 105 | 8.72 | 28.6 | 46,000 | 101,413 | 779 | 484 | 12,000 | 39,370 | 1,640 | 1,019 | 4 | 64-99 p |
| 17.60 | 57.7 | 6.59 | 21.6 | 9,400 | 20,723 | 380 | 236 | 8,000 | 26,246 | 1,500 | 932 | 2 | 23 p |
| 15.80 | 51.8 | 5.82 | 19.1 | 7,500 | 16,534 | 280 | 174 | 5,200 | 17,060 | 700 | 435 | 2 | 20 p |
| 14.17 | 46.6 | 4.70 | 15.5 | 6,200 | 13,670 | 307 | 191 | 6,500 | 21,225 | 1,500 | 932 | 3 | 10 p |
| 8.91 | 29.3 | 2.79 | 9.2 | 1,800 | 3,968 | 245 | 152 | 7,500 | 24,606 | 1,100 | 685 | 1 | 4 p |
| 12.98 | 42.7 | — | — | — | — | 261 | 162 | 4,800 | 15,750 | 1,070 | 665 | 2 | 8 p |
| 10.80 | 35.5 | 3.75 | 12.3 | 2,720 | 5,996 | 273 | 170 | 5,600 | 18,370 | 1,150 | 715 | 2 | 3 p |
| 10.20 | 33.5 | 3.20 | 10.6 | 1,800 | 3,968 | 217 | 135 | 7,300 | 23,950 | 1,200 | 750 | 1 | 5-7 p |
| 23.50 | 77.1 | 8.50 | 27.8 | 17,690 | 39,000 | 428 | 266 | 8,840 | 29,000 | 1,250 | 775 | 2-3 | 40-52 p |
| 14.78 | 48 | 4.75 | 15.7 | 6,124 | 13,700 | 294 | 183 | 5,640 | 18,500 | 1,470 | 913 | 2 | 15-17 p |
| 26.44 | 86.9 | 8.23 | 27 | 39,917 | 88,000 | 486 | 302 | 6,890 | 22,605 | 3,220 | 2,000 | 2-3 | 84 p |
| 13.79 | 45.3 | 3.73 | 12.3 | 6,350 | 13,999 | 190 | 118 | 5,180 | 16,995 | 1,080 | 671 | 2 | 16 p |
| 34.75 | 114 | 11.17 | 36.8 | 70,308 | 155,000 | 603 | 375 | 7,315 | 24,000 | 6,310 | 3,921 | 8 | 74-90 p |
| 11.12 | 36.4 | 3.27 | 10.7 | 2,948 | 6,500 | 225 | 140 | 6,100 | 20,013 | 1,450 | 901 | 1 | 7 p |

## Technical Data

| Page | Aircraft | Nation | Manufacturer | Type | Year | Engine | Wingspan m | Wingspan ft |
|---|---|---|---|---|---|---|---|---|
| 141 | de Havilland Canada DHC-3 Otter | CDN | de Havilland Aircraft of Canada Ltd. | LT | 1951 | Pratt & Whitney R-1340-S1H1-G Wasp 600 hp (r 9 cl) a.c. | 17.69 | 58 |
| 141 | de Havilland Canada DHC-4 Caribou | CDN | de Havilland Aircraft of Canada Ltd. | CTr | 1958 | 2 x Pratt & Whitney R-2000-7M2 Twin Wasp 1450 hp (r 14 cl) a.c. | 29.13 | 95.5 |
| 141 | Canadair CL-44D-4 | CDN | Canadair Ltd. | CTr | 1960 | 4 x tp Rolls-Royce Tyne 515-10 5730 hp | 43.37 | 142.2 |
| 141 | Avro 748 Series 1 | GB | A.V. Roe & Co. Ltd. (Hawker Siddeley Group) | CTr | 1960 | 2 x tp Rolls-Royce Dart 514 1740 hp | 30.02 | 98.6 |
| 141 | de Havilland D.H. 106 Comet 4 | GB | de Havilland Aircraft Co. Ltd. | CTr | 1958 | 4 x tj Rolls-Royce Avon 524 4763 kg (10,500 lb) | 35.05 | 114.8 |
| 141 | Saunders-Roe S.R.45 Princess | GB | Saunders-Roe Ltd. | CTr | 1952 | 10 x tp Bristol Pegasus 600 3780 hp | 66.90 | 219.6 |
| 142 | Ilyushin Il-14P | USSR | State Industries | CTr | 1953 | 2 x Shvetsov ASh-82T 1900 hp (r 14 cl) a.c. | 31.70 | 104 |
| 142 | Tupolev Tu-104A | USSR | State Industries | CTr | 1957 | 2 x tj Mikulin AM-3M 8700 kg (19,180 lb) | 34.54 | 113.4 |
| 142 | Tupolev Tu-124V | USSR | State Industries | CTr | 1960 | 2 x tj Soloviev D-20P 5400 kg (11,905 lb) | 25.55 | 83.8 |
| 142 | Antonov An-12B | USSR | State Industries | CTr | 1960 | 4 x tp Ivchenko AI-20K 4000 hp | 38 | 124.8 |
| 142 | Antonov An-14 Pchelka | USSR | State Industries | LT | 1958 | 2 x Ivchenko AI-14RF 300 hp (r 9 cl) a.c. | 21.99 | 72.1 |
| 143 | Antonov An-24V | USSR | State Industries | CTr | 1959 | 2 x tp Ivchenko AI-24 2880 hp | 29.20 | 95.9 |
| 143 | Antonov An-10A | USSR | State Industries | CTr | 1957 | 4 x tp Ivchenko AI-20K 4000 hp | 38 | 124.8 |
| 143 | Ilyushin Il-18V | USSR | State Industries | CTr | 1957 | 4 x tp Ivchenko AI-20K 4000 hp | 37.40 | 122.8 |
| 143 | Tupolev Tu-144 Rossiya | USSR | State Industries | CTr | 1957 | 4 x tp Kuznetsov NK-12MV 12,500 hp | 51.10 | 167.7 |
| 146 | de Havilland Venom N.F.3 | GB | de Havilland Aircraft Co. Ltd. | NF | 1953 | tj de Havilland Ghost 104 2245 kg (4,950 lb) | 12.70 | 41.8 |
| 146 | Gloster Javelin F.A.W.7 | GB | Gloster Aircraft Co. Ltd. | Fr | 1956 | 2 x tj Armstrong Siddeley Sapphire 203 4990 kg (11,000 lb) | 15.80 | 52 |
| 146 | English Electric Lightning F.1 | GB | English Electric Aviation Ltd. | Fr | 1959 | 2 x tj Rolls-Royce Avon 210 6545 kg (14,430 lb) | 10.61 | 34.8 |
| 146 | Hawker Hunter F.6 | GB | Hawker Aircraft Co. Ltd. | Fr | 1954 | tj Rolls-Royce Avon 203 4536 kg (10,000 lb) | 10.26 | 33.8 |
| 146 | Hawker Siddeley Sea Vixen F.A.W.1 | GB | Hawker Siddeley Aviation Ltd. | Fr | 1957 | 2 x tj Rolls-Royce Avon 208 5102 kg (11,248 lb) | 15.24 | 50 |
| 146 | Supermarine Scimitar F.1 | GB | Supermarine Division of Vickers-Armstrongs Ltd. | Fr | 1957 | 2 x tj Rolls-Royce Avon 202 5105 kg (11,254 lb) | 11.33 | 37.2 |
| 146 | FFA P-16 | CH | Flug & Fahrzeugwerke AG. | FB | 1955 | tj Armstrong Siddeley Sapphire 200 4990 kg (11,000 lb) | 11.15 | 36.7 |
| 146 | Saab J32B Lansen | S | SAAB | Fr | 1957 | tj Svenska Flugmotor RM6 6890 kg (15,190 lb) | 13 | 42.8 |
| 146 | Saab J35A Draken | S | SAAB | Fr | 1958 | tj Svenska Flugmotor RM6 6804 kg (15,000 lb) | 9.40 | 30.8 |
| 146 | Yakovlev Yak-25A | USSR | State Industries | Fr | 1952 | 2 x tj Mikulin AM.9B 2600 kg (5,730 lb) | 11 | 36.1 |
| 146 | Mikoyan-Gurevich MiG-21F | USSR | State Industries | Fr | 1957 | tj Tumansky RD-11F 5750 kg (12,676 lb) | 7.15 | 23.6 |
| 146 | Sukhoi Su-7B | USSR | State Industries | FB | 1955 | tj Lyulka AL-7F TRD-31 10.000 kg (22,045 lb) | 9.25 | 30.4 |
| 147 | North American F-86D Sabre | USA | North American Aviation Inc. | Fr | 1951 | tj General Electric J47-GE17B 3402 kg (7,500 lb) | 11.91 | 39.1 |
| 147 | North American F-100D Super Sabre | USA | North American Aviation Inc. | FB | 1956 | tj Pratt & Whitney J57-P-21A 7711 kg (17,000 lb) | 11.81 | 38.9 |
| 147 | North American FJ-4B Fury | USA | North American Aviation Inc. | A | 1956 | tj Wright J65-W-16A 3493 kg (7,700 lb) | 11.91 | 39.1 |
| 147 | Convair F-102A Delta Dagger | USA | Convair Division of General Dynamics | Fr | 1954 | tj Pratt & Whitney J57-P-23 7711 kg (17,000 lb) | 11.61 | 38.1 |
| 147 | Vought F7U-3M Cutlass | USA | Chance Vought Division of United Aircraft Co. | Fr | 1951 | 2 x tj Westinghouse J46-WE-8A 2086 kg (4,600 lb) | 11.78 | 38.8 |
| 147 | Northrop F-89D Scorpion | USA | Northrop Aircraft Inc. | Fr | 1951 | 2 x tj Allison J-35-A-35 3266 kg (7,200 lb) | 18.18 | 59.8 |
| 147 | Douglas F4D-1 Skyray | USA | Douglas Aircraft Co. | Fr | 1954 | tj Pratt & Whitney J57-P-2 4400 kg (9,700 lb) | 10.21 | 33.6 |
| 147 | Douglas F3D-2 Skynight | USA | Douglas Aircraft Co. | Fr | 1951 | 2 x tj Westinghouse J34-WE-36 1542 kg (3,400 lb) | 15.24 | 50 |
| 147 | LTV F-8C Crusader | USA | LTV Aerospace Corp. | Fr | 1958 | tj Pratt & Whitney J57-P-20A 4854 kg (10,701 lb) | 10.72 | 35.2 |
| 147 | McDonnell F2H-4 Banshee | USA | McDonnell Aircraft Co. | Fr | 1953 | 2 x tj Westinghouse J34-WE-38 1633 kg (3,600 lb) | 13.66 | 44.8 |
| 147 | McDonnell F3H-2 Demon | USA | McDonnell Aircraft Co. | Fr | 1955 | tj Allison J71-A-2E 4400 kg (9,700 lb) | 10.77 | 35.4 |
| 147 | McDonnell F-4J Phantom II | USA | McDonnell Aircraft Co. | FB | 1966 | 2 x tj General Electric J79-GE-10 8120 kg (17,900 lb) | 11.70 | 38.5 |
| 147 | Republic F-105D Thunderchief | USA | Republic Aviation Corp. | FB | 1959 | tj Pratt & Whitney J75-P-19 12.020 kg (26,500 lb) | 10.64 | 34.9 |
| 147 | Lockheed F-104 Super Starfighter | USA | Lockheed Aircraft Corp. | FB | 1960 | tj General Electric J79-GE-11A 7167 kg (15,800 lb) | 6.68 | 21.9 |
| 147 | Dassault Mystère IV-A | F | Avions Marcel Dassault | FB | 1952 | tj Hispano-Suiza Verdoun 350 3497 kg (7,710 lb) | 11.12 | 36.6 |
| 147 | Dassault Super Mystère B-2 | F | Avions Marcel Dassault | FB | 1956 | tj Snecma Atar 101G 4500 kg (9,920 lb) | 10.07 | 33 |
| 147 | Dassault Etendard IV-M | F | Avions Marcel Dassault | Fr | 1958 | tj SNECMA Atar 8 4400 kg (9,700 lb) | 9.60 | 31.6 |
| 147 | Dassault Mirage III-C | F | Avions Marcel Dassault | Fr | 1960 | tj SNECMA Atar 9B 6000 kg (13,228 lb) | 8.22 | 27 |
| 150 | Douglas AD-5 Skyraider | USA | Douglas Aircraft Co. | Rc | 1951 | Wright R-3350-26W Cyclone 2700 hp (r 18 cl) a.c. | 15.24 | 50 |
| 150 | Grumman A-6A Intruder | USA | Grumman Aircraft Engineering Corp. | A | 1960 | 2 x tj Pratt & Whitney J52-P-8A 4218 kg (9,300 lb) | 16.15 | 53 |
| 150 | Grumman S-2A Tracker | USA | Grumman Aircraft Engineering Corp. | A | 1952 | 2 x Wright R-1820-82WA Cyclone 1525 hp (r 9 cl) a.c. | 21.23 | 69.8 |
| 150 | Sud-Ouest SO-4050 Vautour II B | F | SNCASO | Br | 1954 | 2 x tj SNECMA Atar 101E-3 3500 kg (7,716 lb) | 15.11 | 49.7 |
| 150 | Breguet Br. 1050 Alizé | F | Société des Ateliers d'Aviation Louis Breguet | A | 1956 | tp Rolls-Royce Dart Da.21 2100 hp | 15.60 | 51.2 |

| Length | | Height | | Take-off weight | | Speed | | Ceiling | | Range | | Crew | Payload/armament |
|---|---|---|---|---|---|---|---|---|---|---|---|---|---|
| m | ft | m | ft | kg | lb | km/h | mph | m | ft | km | ml | | |
| 12.75 | 41.8 | 3.83 | 12.5 | 3,629 | 8,000 | 222 | 138 | 5,730 | 18,800 | 1,520 | 945 | 1 | 9-14 p |
| 22.13 | 72.7 | 9.68 | 31.7 | 12,928 | 28,501 | 293 | 182 | 7,560 | 24,803 | 600 | 373 | 1-2 | 24-30 p |
| 41.73 | 136.9 | 11.80 | 38.7 | 95,256 | 210,000 | 508 | 316 | 9,144 | 30,000 | 4,625 | 2,875 | 3 | 28,700 kg (63,272 lb) |
| 20.42 | 67 | 7.57 | 24.8 | 17,237 | 38,000 | 414 | 257 | 7,470 | 24,500 | 885 | 550 | 3 | 40-50 p |
| 33.99 | 111.6 | 8.99 | 29.4 | 75,483 | 166,411 | 809 | 503 | 12,800 | 42,000 | 5,190 | 3,225 | 4 | 81 p |
| 45.11 | 148 | 16.99 | 55.9 | 149,690 | 330,009 | 579 | 360 | — | — | 8,480 | 5,269 | 6 | 105 p |
| 21.31 | 69.9 | 7.80 | 25.7 | 38,581 | 85,056 | 350 | 217 | 7,400 | 24,278 | 1,200 | 745 | 4-5 | 24 p |
| 38.85 | 127.5 | 11.90 | 39 | 76,000 | 167,550 | 800 | 497 | 11,500 | 37,730 | 3,100 | 1,926 | 5 | 70 p |
| 30.58 | 100.4 | 8.08 | 26.6 | 37,500 | 82,673 | 870 | 540 | 11,700 | 38,385 | 1,250 | 776 | 3-4 | 56 p |
| 33.10 | 108.7 | 10.53 | 34.6 | 61,000 | 134,480 | 600 | 373 | 10,200 | 33,465 | 3,400 | 2,110 | 5 | 20,000 kg (44,092 lb) |
| 11.36 | 37.3 | 4.63 | 15.2 | 3,600 | 7,936 | 175 | 109 | 5,000 | 16,400 | 650 | 404 | 1 | 6-8 p |
| 23.53 | 77.2 | 8.32 | 27.3 | 21,000 | 46,297 | 500 | 311 | 9,000 | 29,525 | 650 | 404 | 3 | 50 p |
| 34 | 111.6 | 9.80 | 32.1 | 54,000 | 119,050 | 680 | 423 | 11,000 | 36,000 | 1,220 | 758 | 5 | 100 p |
| 35.90 | 117.9 | 10.16 | 33.4 | 61,200 | 134,922 | 650 | 404 | 10,750 | 35,268 | 4,800 | 2,980 | 5 | 84-110 p |
| 54.10 | 177.6 | 15.50 | 50.8 | 17,500 | 38,580 | 770 | 478 | 12,000 | 39,370 | 8,950 | 5,560 | 10 | 170 p |
| 11.17 | 36.8 | 1.98 | 6.6 | 7,166 | 15,800 | 1,013 | 630 | 15,000 | 49,200 | 1,610 | 1,000 | 2 | 4 g |
| 17.20 | 56.9 | 4.80 | 16 | 19,578 | 43,165 | 1,130 | 702 | 15,850 | 52,000 | 1,530 | 950 | 2 | 2 g; 4 msl a.a. |
| 16.84 | 55.3 | 5.97 | 19.7 | 18,915 | 41,700 | 2,414 | 1,500 | 18,920 | 60,000 | 1,440 | 895 | 1 | 2 g; 2 msl a.a. |
| 13.98 | 45.8 | 4.01 | 13.2 | 8,051 | 17,750 | 1,142 | 710 | 15,700 | 51,500 | 3,085 | 1,900 | 1 | 4 g; 907 kg (2,000 lb) |
| 17 | 55.7 | 3.30 | 10.9 | 14,061 | 30,999 | 1,050 | 650 | 14,630 | 48,000 | 965 | 600 | 2 | 4 msl a.a.; 907 kg (2,000 lb) |
| 16.87 | 55.4 | 4.65 | 15.3 | 18,144 | 40,000 | 1,143 | 710 | 15,240 | 50,000 | 966 | 600 | 1 | 4 g; b (1,814 kg - 4,000 lb) |
| 14.24 | 46.9 | 4.10 | 13.5 | 11,700 | 25,795 | 1,100 | 685 | 14,000 | 46,000 | 1,000 | 621 | 1 | 2 g; 2,000 kg (4,400 lb) |
| 14.50 | 47.7 | 4.65 | 15.3 | 13,517 | 29,800 | 1,142 | 710 | 16,000 | 52,500 | 3,220 | 2,000 | 2 | 4 g; 4 msl a.a. |
| 15.34 | 50.4 | 3.88 | 12.9 | 8,255 | 18,200 | 1,910 | 1,188 | 18,000 | 60,000 | 1,300 | 800 | 1 | 2 g; 4 msl a.a. |
| 15.67 | 51.4 | 3.80 | 12.5 | 9,900 | 21,826 | 1,015 | 631 | 14,000 | 45,931 | 2,000 | 1,243 | 2 | 2 g; 50 rp |
| 13.46 | 44.2 | 4.50 | 14.9 | 7,575 | 16,700 | 2,000 | 1,243 | 20,000 | 65,610 | 560 | 350 | 1 | 2 g; 1,200 kg (2,646 lb) |
| 18.37 | 60.3 | 4.90 | 16.1 | 13,700 | 30,200 | 1,700 | 1,057 | 15,150 | 49,700 | 1,450 | 900 | 1 | 2 g; 2,500 kg (5,500 lb) |
| 12.27 | 40.9 | 4.47 | 14.8 | 9,060 | 19,974 | 1,113 | 692 | 15,164 | 49,750 | 1,238 | 769 | 1 | 4 msl a.a. |
| 14.32 | 47 | 4.57 | 15 | 15,800 | 34,832 | 1,390 | 864 | 13,720 | 45,015 | 2,415 | 1,500 | 1 | 4 g; 3,402 kg (7,500 lb) |
| 11.07 | 36.4 | 4.24 | 13.9 | 10,750 | 23,700 | 1,094 | 680 | 14,265 | 46,800 | 3,250 | 2,020 | 1 | 4 g; 1,360 kg (3,000 lb) |
| 20.83 | 68.4 | 6.45 | 21.2 | 14,288 | 31,505 | 1,327 | 825 | 16,460 | 54,000 | 2,170 | 1,350 | 1 | 6 msl a.a. |
| 13.48 | 44.3 | 4.45 | 14.7 | 14,353 | 31,642 | 1,094 | 680 | 12,190 | 40,000 | 1,060 | 660 | 1 | 4 g; 4 msl a.a. |
| 16.40 | 53.8 | 5.36 | 17.7 | 19,160 | 42,241 | 1,023 | 636 | 14,995 | 49,200 | 2,200 | 1,370 | 2 | 52 rp |
| 13.92 | 45.8 | 3.96 | 13 | 11,340 | 25,000 | 1,118 | 695 | 16,760 | 55,000 | 1,930 | 1,200 | 1 | 4 g; 1,814 kg (4,000 lb) |
| 13.86 | 45.6 | 4.87 | 16 | 12,179 | 26,850 | 965 | 600 | 12,190 | 40,000 | 1,930 | 1,200 | 2 | 4 g |
| 16.61 | 54.4 | 4.80 | 15.9 | 15,422 | 34,000 | 1,802 | 1,120 | 17,680 | 58,000 | 1,770 | 1,100 | 1 | 4 g; 2,268 kg (5,000 lb) |
| 12.24 | 40.2 | 4.42 | 14.6 | 10,120 | 22,312 | 856 | 532 | 13,650 | 44,800 | 2,370 | 1,475 | 1 | 4 g; 454 kg (1,000 lb) |
| 17.95 | 58.8 | 4.44 | 14.7 | 15,377 | 33,000 | 1,041 | 647 | 13,000 | 42,650 | 2,200 | 1,370 | 1 | 4 g; 2,995 kg (6,600 lb) |
| 17.76 | 58.3 | 4.96 | 16.3 | 24,765 | 54,600 | 2,389 | 1,485 | 18,900 | 62,000 | 1,450 | 900 | 2 | 7,257 kg (16,000 lb) |
| 19.58 | 64.3 | 5.99 | 19.8 | 21,954 | 48,395 | 2,280 | 1,417 | 15,850 | 52,000 | 3,220 | 2,000 | 1 | 1 g; 6,350 kg (14,000 lb) |
| 16.68 | 54.9 | 4.11 | 13.6 | 12,250 | 27,011 | 2,494 | 1,550 | 16,765 | 55,000 | 1,110 | 680 | 1 | 1 g; 1,814 kg (4,000 lb) |
| 12.85 | 42.2 | 4.40 | 14.5 | 7,500 | 16,535 | 1,120 | 695 | 13,715 | 45,000 | 917 | 570 | 1 | 2 g; 908 kg (2,000 lb) |
| 14.04 | 46.1 | 4.60 | 15.1 | 10,000 | 22,046 | 1,200 | 750 | 17,000 | 55,750 | 870 | 540 | 1 | 2 g; 908 kg (2,000 lb) |
| 14.40 | 47.3 | 4.30 | 14.1 | 10,200 | 22,486 | 1,099 | 683 | 15,000 | 49,200 | 1,700 | 1,056 | 1 | 2 g; 1,360 kg (3,000 lb) |
| 14.77 | 48.6 | 4.25 | 13.9 | 11,800 | 26,014 | 2,230 | 1,336 | 16,500 | 54,135 | 1,200 | 745 | 1 | 2 g; 1,360 kg (3,000 lb) |
| 12.21 | 40.1 | 4.82 | 15.8 | 11,340 | 25,000 | 501 | 311 | 8,230 | 27,000 | 2,080 | 1,294 | 3 | 2 g |
| 16.64 | 54.7 | 4.75 | 15.7 | 27,500 | 60,626 | 1,102 | 685 | 12,700 | 41,660 | 5,190 | 3,225 | 2 | 8,165 kg (18,000 lb) |
| 12.87 | 42.3 | 4.95 | 16.3 | 11,930 | 26,300 | 461 | 287 | 7,010 | 23,000 | 1,450 | 900 | 4 | 2,181 kg (4,810 lb) |
| 15.84 | 52 | 4.95 | 16.2 | 20,700 | 45,635 | 1,102 | 685 | 15,000 | 49,200 | 2,575 | 1,600 | 4 | 2,400 kg (5,300 lb) |
| 13.86 | 45.6 | 5 | 16.5 | 8,200 | 18,078 | 470 | 292 | 6,100 | 20,000 | 2,850 | 1,785 | 3 | 1,360 kg (3,000 lb) |

229

# Technical Data

| Page | Aircraft | Nation | Manufacturer | Type | Year | Engine | Wingspan m | ft |
|------|----------|--------|--------------|------|------|--------|-----------|-----|
| 151 | Douglas AD-6 Skyraider | USA | Douglas Aircraft Co. | A | 1952 | Wright R-3350-26W Cyclone 2700 hp (r 18 cl) a.c. | 15.24 | 50 |
| 151 | Douglas A-4E Skyhawk | USA | Douglas Aircraft Co. | A | 1961 | tj Pratt & Whitney J52-P-6 3855 kg (8,500 lb) | 8.38 | 27.6 |
| 151 | Convair B-36 | USA | Consolidated Vultee Aircraft Corp. | Br | 1952 | 6 x Pratt & Whitney R-4360-53 Wasp Major 3800 hp (r 28 cl) | 10.10 | 33.1 |
| 151 | Convair B-58A Hustler | USA | Convair Division of General Motors | Br | 1959 | 4 x tj General Motors J79-GE-5 7075 kg (15,598 lb) | 17.32 | 56.8 |
| 151 | Boeing B-47E Stratojet | USA | Boeing Aircraft Co. | Br | 1953 | 6 x tj General Electric J47-GE-25 2721 kg (6,000 lb) | 35.35 | 116 |
| 151 | Boeing B-52G Stratofortress | USA | Boeing Aircraft Co. | Br | 1958 | 8 x tj Pratt & Whitney J57-P-43W 6248 kg (13,750 lb) | 56.38 | 185 |
| 151 | North American A-5A Vigilante | USA | North American Aviation Inc. | Br | 1958 | 2 x tj General Electric J79-GE-4 7325 kg (16,150 lb) | 16.15 | 53 |
| 152 | Vickers Valiant B-1 | GB | Vickers-Armstrongs Ltd. | Br | 1953 | 4 x tj Rolls-Royce Avon 204 4536 kg (10,000 lb) | 34.85 | 114.4 |
| 152 | Handley Page Victor B-1 | GB | Handley Page Ltd. | Br | 1956 | 4 x tj Armstrong Siddeley Sapphire 202 4990 kg (11,000 lb) | 33.53 | 110 |
| 152 | Fairey Gannet AS.4 | GB | Fairey Aviation Co. Ltd. | A | 1956 | tp Armstrong Siddeley Double Mamba 101 3035 hp | 16.50 | 54.1 |
| 152 | Hawker Sea Hawk F.G.A.6 | GB | Hawker Aircraft Ltd. | A | 1955 | Rolls-Royce Nene 103 2359 kg (5,200 lb) | 11.89 | 39 |
| 152 | Hawker Siddeley Buccaneer S.1 | GB | Hawker Siddeley Aviation Ltd. | A | 1958 | 2 x tj de Havilland Gyron 101 3220 kg (7,100 lb) | 13.41 | 44 |
| 152 | Avro Vulcan B.1 | GB | A.V. Roe & Co. Ltd. | Br | 1955 | 4 x tj Bristol Olympus 101 4990 kg (11,000 lb) | 30.18 | 99 |
| 153 | Tupolev Tu-16A | USSR | State Industries | Br | 1954 | 2 x tj Mikulin AM-3M 9500 kg (20,940 lb) | 32.93 | 108 |
| 153 | Tupolev Tu-20 | USSR | State Industries | Br | 1954 | 4 x tp Kuznetsov NK-12MV 1500 hp | 48.50 | 159 |
| 153 | Tupolev Tu-22 | USSR | State Industries | Br | 1960 | 2 x tj 12.250 kg (27,000 lb) | 27.70 | 90.8 |
| 153 | Myasishchev Mya 4 | USSR | State Industries | Br | 1953 | 4 x tj Mikulin AM-3D 8700 kg (19,180 lb) | 50.48 | 167.7 |
| 156 | Grumman E-1B Tracer | USA | Grumman Aircraft Engineering Corp. | Rc | 1957 | 2 x Wright R-1820-82WA Cyclone 1525 hp (r 9 cl) a.c. | 22.05 | 72.4 |
| 156 | Grumman SA-16B Albatross | USA | Grumman Aircraft Engineering Corp. | Rc | 1958 | 2 x Wright R-1820-76A Cyclone 1275 hp (r 9 cl) a.c. | 24.38 | 79.9 |
| 156 | Grumman E-2A Hawkeye | USA | Grumman Aircraft Engineering Corp. | Rc | 1960 | 2 x tp Allison T56-A-8A 4050 hp | 24.56 | 80.7 |
| 156 | Grumman OV-1 Mohawk | USA | Grumman Aircraft Engineering Corp. | Rc | 1959 | 2 x tp Lycoming T53-L-3 1005 hp | 12.80 | 42 |
| 156 | Douglas RB-66B Destroyer | USA | Douglas Aircraft Co. | Rc | 1954 | 2 x tj Allison J71-A-13 4536 kg (10,000 lb) | 22.10 | 72.6 |
| 156 | North American T-2A Buckeye | USA | North American Aviation Inc. | T | 1958 | tj Westinghouse J-34-WE-36 1542 kg (3,400 lb) | 10.97 | 35.9 |
| 157 | Fairchild C-123B Provider | USA | The Fairchild and Aeroplane Corp. | Tr | 1953 | 2 x Pratt & Whitney R-2800-99W Douglas Wasp 2300 hp (r 18 cl) a.c. | 33.53 | 110 |
| 157 | Lockheed C-130E Hercules | USA | Lockheed Aircraft Corp. | Tr | 1961 | 4 x tp Allison 756-A-7 4050 hp | 40.41 | 132.7 |
| 157 | Lockheed U-2A | USA | Lockheed Aircraft Corp. | Rc | 1955 | tj Pratt & Whitney J57-P-13 5080 kg (11,200 lb) | 24.38 | 80 |
| 157 | Lockheed P2V-7 Neptune | USA | Lockheed Aircraft Corp. | Rc | 1954 | 2 x Wright R-3350-32W Cyclone 3500 hp (r 18 cl) a.c.; 2 x tj Westinghouse J-34-WE-34 1542 kg (3,400 lb) | 31.65 | 103.8 |
| 157 | Republic RF-84F Thunderflash | USA | Republic Aviation Corp. | Rc | 1953 | tj Wright J65-W-7 3540 kg (7,800 lb) | 10.24 | 33.7 |
| 157 | Douglas C-133A Cargomaster | USA | Douglas Aircraft Co. | Tr | 1957 | 4 x tp Pratt & Whitney T34-P-WA 6500 hp | 54.76 | 179.8 |
| 158 | Fokker S.14 | NL | Fokker-CFW N.V. | T | 1951 | tj Rolls-Royce Derwent 8 1574 kg (3,470 lb) | 11.89 | 39 |
| 158 | Yakovlev Yak-18A | USSR | State Industries | T | 1957 | Ivchenko Al-14R 260 hp (r 9 cl) a.c. | 10.60 | 34.9 |
| 158 | Fouga C.M.175 Zéphyr | F | Potez Air-Fouga | T | 1956 | 2 x tj Turboméca Marboré IIB 400 kg (880 lb) | 12.15 | 39.8 |
| 158 | Hispano Saeta HA-200A | E | Hispano Aviacion S.A. | T | 1955 | 2 x tj Turboméca Marboré IIA 400 kg (880 lb) | 10.42 | 34.2 |
| 158 | L-29 Delfin | CS | State Industries | T | 1959 | tj M-701 870 kg (1,920 lb) | 10.08 | 33.1 |
| 158 | TS-11 Iskra | PL | State Industries | T | 1960 | tj SO-1 1000 kg (2,204 lb) | 9.98 | 32.8 |
| 158 | Fiat G.91 R-3 | I | Fiat S.p.A. | Rc/CIS | 1959 | tj Bristol Siddeley Orpheus 801/02 2270 kg (5,000 lb) | 8.56 | 28 |
| 158 | Aermacchi M.B.326 | I | Aeronautica Macchi S.p.A. | T | 1957 | tj Bristol Siddeley Viper 11 1134 kg (2,500 lb) | 10.60 | 34.9 |
| 159 | Avro Shackleton M.R.3 | GB | A.V. Roe & Co. Ltd. | Rc | 1955 | 4 x Rolls-Royce Griffon 57A 2450 hp (12 cl V) l.c. | 36.53 | 119.9 |
| 159 | Folland Gnat T.1 | GB | Folland Aircraft Ltd. | T | 1959 | tj Bristol Siddeley Orpheus 101 1920 kg (4,230 lb) | 7.32 | 24 |
| 159 | Hunting Percival Provost T.1 | GB | Hunting Percival Aircraft Ltd. | T | 1950 | Alvis Leonides 126 550 hp (r 9 cl) a.c. | 10.71 | 35 |
| 159 | Supermarine Swift F.R.5 | GB | Supermarine Division of Vickers-Armstrongs Ltd. | Rc | 1955 | tj Rolls-Royce Avon 114 4285 kg (9,450 lb) | 9.86 | 32.4 |
| 159 | Auster A.O.P.9 | GB | Auster Aircraft Ltd. | Os | 1954 | Blackburn Cirrus Bombardier 203 180 hp (4 cl) a.c. | 11.10 | 36.5 |
| 159 | Blackburn Beverly C.1 | GB | Blackburn and General Aircraft Ltd. | Tr | 1955 | 4 x Bristol Centaurus 237 2850 hp (r 18 cl) a.c. | 49.38 | 162 |
| 159 | Hunting Percival Jet Provost | GB | Hunting Percival Aircraft | T | 1958 | tj Bristol Siddeley Viper ASV.8 794 kg | 10.72 | 35.2 |
| 159 | Fuji T1F-2 | J | Fuji Jokogyo Kobushiki Kaisha | T | 1958 | tj Bristol Siddeley Orpheus 805 1814 kg (4,000 lb) | 10.49 | 34 |
| 159 | Canadair CL-28 Argus 2 | CDN | Canadair Ltd. | Rc | 1957 | 4 x Wright R-3350-32W Turbo Compound 3700 hp (r 18 cl) a.c. | 43.77 | 142.3 |
| 168 | MBB HFB 320 Hansa | D | MBB | LT | 1964 | 2 x tj General Electric CJ610-9 1406 kg (3,100 lb) | 14.49 | 47.6 |
| 168 | Ilyushin Il-62 | USSR | State Industries | CTr | 1963 | 4 x Kuznetsov NK-8 10,500 kg (23,148 lb) | 43.20 | 142 |
| 168 | Sud Aviation SE-210 Super Caravelle | F | Sud Aviation | CTr | 1964 | 2 x Pratt & Whitney JT8D-1 6350 kg (14,000 lb) | 34.30 | 112.6 |

| Length | | Height | | Take-off weight | | Speed | | Ceiling | | Range | | Crew | Payload/armament |
| m | ft | m | ft | kg | lb | km/h | mph | m | ft | km | ml | | |
|---|---|---|---|---|---|---|---|---|---|---|---|---|---|
| 11.83 | 39.2 | 4.77 | 15.8 | 11,340 | 25,000 | 518 | 322 | 8,690 | 28,500 | 1,840 | 1,143 | 1 | 4 g; 3,628 kg (8,000 lb) |
| 12.21 | 40.1 | 4.62 | 15.2 | 11,113 | 24,500 | 1,102 | 685 | 14,935 | 49,000 | 1,480 | 920 | 1 | 2 g; 3,719 kg (8,200 lb) |
| 49.40 | 162.1 | 14.22 | 46.8 | 185,976 | 410,000 | 661 | 411 | 12,160 | 39,900 | 10,940 | 6,800 | 15 | 12 g; 36,000 kg (86,000 lb) |
| 29.49 | 96.9 | 9.58 | 31.5 | 72,576 | 160,000 | 2,228 | 1,385 | 19,500 | 64,000 | 8,248 | 5,125 | 3 | 1 g; 8,820 kg (19,450 lb) |
| 33.47 | 109.8 | 8.50 | 27.8 | 93,759 | 206,700 | 975 | 606 | 12,345 | 40,500 | 6,435 | 4,000 | 3 | 2 g; 9,072 kg (20,000 lb) |
| 48.03 | 157.7 | 12.40 | 40.8 | 221,500 | 448,000 | 1,062 | 660 | 16,765 | 55,000 | 13,680 | 8,500 | 6 | 4 mg; 30,000 kg (66,000 lb) |
| 22.33 | 73.3 | 5.92 | 19.5 | 28,232 | 62,000 | 2,228 | 1,385 | 20,420 | 66,994 | 5,150 | 3,200 | 2 | 1 b; 2,270 kg (5,000 lb) |
| 32.99 | 108.3 | 9.80 | 32.2 | 63,504 | 140,000 | 912 | 567 | 16,460 | 54,000 | 5,550 | 3,450 | 5 | 9,525 kg (21,000 lb) |
| 35.05 | 114.9 | 8.59 | 28.1 | 81,650 | 180,000 | 1,030 | 640 | 16,765 | 55,000 | 4,345 | 2,700 | 5 | 15,876 kg (35,000 lb) |
| 13.10 | 43 | 4.16 | 13.8 | 10,208 | 22,506 | 481 | 299 | 7,620 | 25,000 | 1,510 | 943 | 3 | 907 kg (2,000 lb) |
| 12.08 | 39.8 | 2.79 | 8.8 | 6,253 | 13,785 | 901 | 560 | 13,560 | 44,500 | 1,191 | 740 | 1 | 4 g; 907 kg (2,000 lb) |
| 19.33 | 63.5 | 4.95 | 16.3 | 20,865 | 46,000 | 1,158 | 720 | 12,190 | 40,000 | 3,700 | 2,300 | 2 | 3,630 kg (8,000 lb) |
| 29.60 | 97.1 | 7.95 | 26.1 | 77,112 | 170,000 | 1,030 | 640 | 16,765 | 55,000 | 4,830 | 3,000 | 5 | 9,525 kg (21,000 lb) |
| 34.80 | 114.2 | 10.80 | 35.6 | 68,000 | 149,906 | 945 | 587 | 13,000 | 42,650 | 5,760 | 3,580 | 7 | 6 g; 9,000 kg (19,800 lb) |
| 47.50 | 155.8 | 11.78 | 38.8 | 154,000 | 340,000 | 805 | 500 | 13,400 | 44,000 | 12,550 | 7,800 | 10 | 6 g; 11,304 kg (25,000 lb) |
| 40.53 | 132.8 | 5.18 | 17 | 83,902 | 184,970 | 1,480 | 920 | 18,000 | 59,000 | 2,250 | 1,400 | 3-5 | 1 g; 9,070 kg (20,000 lb) |
| 47.20 | 154.8 | 14.10 | 46 | 160,000 | 352,740 | 900 | 560 | 13,000 | 42,650 | 11,000 | 6,835 | 6 | 10 g; 10,000 kg (22,000 lb) |
| 13.82 | 45.4 | 5.13 | 16.8 | 12,247 | 27,000 | 466 | 290 | 7,010 | 23,000 | 1,450 | 900 | 4 | — |
| 18.49 | 61 | 7.39 | 24.2 | 12,281 | 27,075 | 382 | 237 | 6,550 | 21,489 | 4,345 | 2,706 | 5-6 | — |
| 17.17 | 56.4 | 4.88 | 18.4 | 22,453 | 49,500 | 595 | 370 | 9,660 | 31,700 | 3,060 | 1,900 | 5 | — |
| 12.50 | 41 | 3.86 | 12.8 | 4,728 | 10,423 | 510 | 317 | 10,670 | 35,000 | 2,700 | 1,680 | 2 | — |
| 22.91 | 75.2 | 7.19 | 23 | 31,752 | 70,000 | 955 | 594 | 13,100 | 43,000 | 3,220 | 2,000 | 3 | 2 g |
| 11.78 | 38.7 | 4.50 | 14.9 | 4,536 | 10,000 | 795 | 494 | 12,950 | 25,000 | 1,550 | 963 | 2 | — |
| 23.08 | 75.9 | 10.38 | 34.1 | 32,205 | 71,000 | 330 | 205 | 8,840 | 29,000 | 2,365 | 1,470 | 2 | 61 p |
| 29.79 | 97.9 | 11.68 | 38.4 | 70,308 | 155,000 | 579 | 360 | 10,060 | 33,000 | 6,145 | 3,820 | 5 | 92 p or 16,194 kg (35,700 lb) |
| 15.11 | 49.7 | 3.96 | 13 | 7,834 | 17,270 | 804 | 500 | 21,340 | 70,000 | 4,180 | 2,600 | 1 | — |
| 27.83 | 91.4 | 8.94 | 29.4 | 34,246 | 75,500 | 555 | 345 | 6,700 | 22,000 | 3,540 | 2,200 | 9-10 | — |
| 14.52 | 47.7 | 4.57 | 15 | 12,700 | 28,000 | 1,092 | 679 | 14,020 | 46,000 | 3,540 | 2,200 | 1 | 4 mg |
| 48 | 157.4 | 14.70 | 48.3 | 124,740 | 275,000 | 482 | 300 | 5,915 | 19,400 | 6,395 | 3,975 | 10 | 200 p |
| 13.30 | 43.8 | 4.67 | 15.4 | 5,352 | 11,775 | 716 | 445 | 11,125 | 36,500 | 900 | 560 | 2 | — |
| 8.35 | 27.5 | 3.25 | 10.8 | 1,326 | 2,901 | 263 | 163 | 5,060 | 16,600 | 710 | 441 | 2 | — |
| 10.21 | 33.6 | 2.95 | 9.6 | 3,400 | 7,496 | 649 | 403 | 11,000 | 36,088 | 770 | 478 | 2 | 2 mg; b (100 kg - 220 lb) |
| 8.88 | 29.2 | 3.26 | 10.8 | 3,173 | 6,995 | 700 | 435 | 12,000 | 40,000 | 1,700 | 1,056 | 2 | 2 mg |
| 10.82 | 35.6 | 3.10 | 10.2 | 3,509 | 7,736 | 179 | 422 | 12,100 | 39,700 | 1,290 | 800 | 2 | 454 kg (1,000 lb) |
| 11 | 36 | 3.30 | 10.9 | 3,952 | 8,712 | 800 | 497 | 12,000 | 39,400 | — | — | 2 | — |
| 10.29 | 33.9 | 4 | 13.2 | 5,670 | 12,500 | 1,090 | 677 | 13,260 | 43,500 | 1,850 | 1,150 | 1 | 2 g; 680 kg (1,500 lb) |
| 10.66 | 35 | 3.72 | 12.3 | 3,430 | 7,561 | 815 | 506 | 12,500 | 41,000 | 1,090 | 680 | 2 | — |
| 26.62 | 87.33 | 7.11 | 23.4 | 45,360 | 100,000 | 486 | 302 | 6,100 | 20,000 | 6,780 | 4,215 | 10 | 2 g; 4,536 kg (10,000 lb) |
| 9.65 | 31.9 | 3.20 | 10.6 | 3,742 | 8,250 | 1,026 | 636 | 14,600 | 48,000 | 1,900 | 1,180 | 2 | 454 kg (1,000 lb) |
| 8.73 | 28.6 | 3.70 | 12 | 1,995 | 4,399 | 322 | 200 | 7,620 | 25,000 | 1,040 | 650 | 2 | — |
| 12.88 | 42.3 | 4.11 | 13.6 | 9,702 | 21,400 | 1,102 | 685 | 7,620 | 25,000 | 772 | 480 | 1 | 2 g |
| 7.21 | 23.8 | 2.56 | 8.5 | 966 | 2,130 | 204 | 127 | 5,640 | 18,500 | 395 | 246 | 2-3 | — |
| 30.30 | 99.5 | 11.81 | 38.9 | 64,865 | 143,000 | 383 | 238 | 4,880 | 16,000 | 2,090 | 1,300 | 4 | 94 p or 20,412 kg (45,000 lb) |
| 9.73 | 31.9 | 3.86 | 12.8 | 2,654 | 5,850 | 530 | 330 | 9,450 | 31,000 | 793 | 493 | 2 | — |
| 12.11 | 39.8 | 4.06 | 13.4 | 4,840 | 10,670 | 926 | 575 | 14,630 | 48,000 | 1,950 | 1,200 | 2 | 1 mg; 680 kg (1,500 lb) |
| 39.09 | 128.3 | 11.20 | 36.9 | 67,130 | 148,000 | 507 | 315 | 8,840 | 29,000 | 9,495 | 5,900 | 15 | 7,076 kg (15,600 lb) |
| 16.61 | 54.6 | 4.94 | 16.2 | 9,200 | 20,280 | 825 | 513 | 12,200 | 40,026 | 2,370 | 1,473 | 2-3 | 7-12 p |
| 53.12 | 174.3 | 12.35 | 40.6 | 162,000 | 357,148 | 900 | 559 | 13,000 | 42,650 | 6,700 | 4,165 | 8-10 | 86 p |
| 33.01 | 108.3 | 8.72 | 28.6 | 52,000 | 114,640 | 835 | 519 | 12,000 | 39,370 | 2,650 | 1,646 | 4 | 68-105 p |

## Technical Data

| Page | Aircraft | Nation | Manufacturer | Type | Year | Engine | Wingspan m | ft |
|------|----------|--------|--------------|------|------|--------|-----------|-----|
| 168 | Dassault Mystère-Falcon 20 | F | Avions Marcel Dassault | LT | 1963 | 2 x tj General Electric CF700-2C 1900 kg (4,500 lb) | 16.30 | 53.6 |
| 169 | Tupolev Tu-134A | USSR | State Industries | CTr | 1970 | 4 x tj Soloviev D-30 6800 kg (14,990 lb) | 29 | 95.1 |
| 169 | Fokker F.27-500 Friendship | NL | Fokker-VFW N.V. | CTr | 1967 | 2 x tp Rolls-Royce Dart 532-7 2250 hp | 29 | 95.2 |
| 169 | McDonnell-Douglas DC-9-10 | USA | Douglas Aircraft Co. | CTr | 1965 | 2 x tj Pratt & Whitney JT8D-5 5556 kg (12,249 lb) | 27.25 | 89.5 |
| 169 | Douglas DC-8-63 | USA | Douglas Aircraft Co. | CTr | 1967 | 4 x tj Pratt & Whitney JT3D-7 8618 kg (19,000 lb) | 45.23 | 148.4 |
| 169 | Convair 990 Coronado | USA | Convair Division of General Dynamics Corp. | CTr | 1961 | 4 x tj General Electric CJ805-23B 7302 kg (16,098 lb) | 36.58 | 120 |
| 170 | Swearingen SA-226TC Metro II | USA | Swearingen Aviation Corp. | LT | 1969 | 2 x tp Garrett-AiResearch TPE331-3UW-304G 940 hp | 14.10 | 46.3 |
| 170 | Boeing 737-200 | USA | Boeing Commercial Airplane Co. | CTr | 1967 | 2 x tj Pratt & Whitney JT8D-15 7030 kg (15,500 lb) | 28.35 | 93 |
| 170 | Cessna Citation 500 | USA | Cessna Aircraft Co. | LT | 1969 | 2 x tj Pratt & Whitney JT15D-1 998 kg (2,200 lb) | 13.32 | 43.7 |
| 170 | Lear Jet 24B | USA | Gates Learjet Corp. | LT | 1966 | 2 x tj General Electric CJ610-6 1340 kg (2,950 lb) | 10.84 | 35.7 |
| 171 | Grumman Gulfstream II | USA | Grumman Aircraft Engineering Corp. | LT | 1966 | 2 x tj Rolls-Royce Spey Mk.511-8 5170 kg (11,400 lb) | 21.87 | 71.9 |
| 171 | Boeing 727-200 | USA | Boeing Commercial Airplane Co. | CTr | 1967 | 3 x tj Pratt & Whitney JT8D-9A 6580 kg (14,500 lb) | 32.92 | 108 |
| 171 | Boeing 747-200 | USA | Boeing Commercial Airplane Co. | CTr | 1970 | 4 x tj Pratt & Whitney JT9D-7/3a 21,319 kg (41,000 lb) | 59.64 | 195.8 |
| 171 | Aero Spacelines SGT Guppy 201 | USA | Aero Spacelines Inc. | CTr | 1970 | 4 x tp Allison 501-D 22C 4912 hp | 47.62 | 156.2 |
| 173 | Lockheed L-1011-200 Tristar | USA | Lockheed Aircraft Corp. | CTr | 1976 | 3 x tj Rolls-Royce RB-211 524 21,770 kg (47,995 lb) | 47.34 | 155.3 |
| 173 | McDonnell-Douglas DC-10-30 | USA | McDonnell-Douglas Corp. | CTr | 1972 | 3 x tj General Electric CF6-50A 22,230 kg (49,009 lb) | 50.41 | 165.3 |
| 173 | Ilyushin Il-62 | USSR | State Industries | CTr | 1963 | 4 x tj Kuznetsov NK-8 10,500 kg (23,148 lb) | 43.20 | 141.7 |
| 174 | Piaggio P.166-B Portofino | I | Industria Aeronautica e Meccanica Rinaldo Piaggio | LT | 1962 | 2 x Lycoming IGS0-540-A1C 360 hp (6 cl) a.c. | 14.25 | 49.6 |
| 174 | de Havilland Canada DHC-6 Twin Otter 300 | CDN | de Havilland Aircraft of Canada Ltd. | LT | 1969 | 2 x tp Pratt & Whitney PT6A-27 625 hp | 19.81 | 65 |
| 174 | Hawker Siddeley Trident 1E | GB | Hawker Siddeley Aviation Ltd. | CTr | 1964 | 3 x tj Rolls-Royce RB.163-25 Mk.511-5 Spey 5170 kg (11,400 lb) | 28.96 | 95 |
| 174 | BAC One-Eleven 500 | GB | British Aircraft Corp. | CTr | 1967 | 2 x tj Rolls-Royce Spey Mk.512 5692 kg (12,550 lb) | 28.50 | 93.6 |
| 175 | Pilatus Britten-Norman BN-2A Islander | GB | Britten-Norman Ltd. | LT | 1966 | 2 x Lycoming O-540-E4C6 260 hp (6 cl) a.c. | 14.94 | 49 |
| 175 | Britten-Norman BN-2 Trislander | GB | Britten-Norman Ltd. | LT | 1970 | 3 x tp Avro Lycoming 0-540-E4C5 264 hp | 16.15 | 53 |
| 175 | Vickers-Armstrongs Vanguard 953 | GB | Vickers-Armstrongs Ltd. | CTr | 1961 | 4 x tp Rolls-Royce Tyne 512 5545 hp | 35.97 | 118 |
| 175 | BAC Super VC10 | GB | British Aircraft Corp. | CTr | 1964 | 4 x tj Rolls-Royce Conway RC43 10,200 kg (22,500 lb) | 44.55 | 146.2 |
| 175 | Handley Page H.P.R.7 Herald | GB | Handley Page (Reading) Ltd. | CTr | 1961 | 2 x tp Rolls-Royce Dart 527 2105 hp | 28.88 | 94.9 |
| 175 | Short Skyliner | GB | Short Brothers Ltd. | CTr | 1967 | 2 x tp Garrett AiResearch TPE 331-201 715 hp | 19.79 | 64.9 |
| 176 | Antonov An-72 | USSR | State Industries | LT | 1977 | 2 x tj Lotarev D-36 6500 hp | 25.83 | 84.9 |
| 177 | BAC Aérospatiale Concorde | F/GB | BAC-Aérospatiale | CTr | 1969 | 4 x tj Rolls-Royce SNECMA Olympus 593 Mk.610 17,260 kg (38,050 lb) | 25.56 | 83.8 |
| 177 | Tupolev Tu-144 | USSR | State Industries | CTr | 1968 | 4 x tj Kuznetsov NK-144 20,000 kg (44,090 lb) | 28.80 | 94.6 |
| 177 | Tupolev Tu-154B | USSR | State Industries | CTr | 1973 | 3 x tj Kuznetsov NK-8-2U 9500 kg (20,944 lb) | 37.55 | 123.2 |
| 178 | McDonnell-Douglas F-15A Eagle | USA | McDonnell Corp. | MrFr | 1974 | 2 x tj Pratt & Whitney F100-PW-100 10,800 kg (25,000 lb) | 13.05 | 42.8 |
| 178 | McDonnell-Douglas F-18 Hornet | USA | McDonnell-Douglas Aircraft Co. | A | 1978 | 2 x tj General Electric F404-G2-400 7258 kg (16,000 lb) | 11.43 | 37.6 |
| 178 | Northrop F-5E Tiger II | USA | Northrop Corp. | Fr | 1972 | 2 x tj General Electric J85-GE-21A 2268 kg (5,000 lb) | 8.13 | 26.8 |
| 178 | Grumman F-14A Tomcat | USA | Grumman Corp. | MrFr | 1972 | 2 x tj Pratt & Whitney TF-30-P-412 A 9480 kg (20,900 lb) | 19.54 | 64.2 |
| 178 | General Dynamics F-16A | USA | General Dynamics Corp. | MrFr | 1976 | tj Pratt & Whitney F100-PW-100 10,800 kg (25,000 lb) | 9.45 | 31 |
| 178 | Dassault Mirage F.1C | F | Avions Marcel Dassault | Fr | 1973 | SNECMA Atar 9K 7200 kg (15,873 lb) | 8.40 | 27.7 |
| 178 | Dassault Super Mirage 4000 | F | Dassault-Breguet | MrFr | 1979 | 2 x tj SNECMA M53-5 9000 kg (19,840 lb) | 11 | 36.1 |
| 178 | Aeritalia-Macchi-Embraer AMX | I-Br | Aeritalia-Macchi-Embraer | A | 1983 | tj Fiat Spey Mk.807 5000 kg (11,023 lb) | 8.88 | 29.1 |
| 179 | Yakovlev Yak-36MP | USSR | State Industries | MrFr | 1976 | tj 7935 kg (17,495 lb) + 2 x tj 360 kg (795 lb) | 7.50 | 24.7 |
| 179 | Sukhoi Su-15 | USSR | State Industries | Fr | 1967 | 2 x tj Tumansky R-11 F2-300 6200 kg (13,671 lb) | 9.15 | 30 |
| 179 | Sukhoi Su-19 | USSR | State Industries | MrFr | 1974 | 2 x tj Lyulka AL-21F8 12,000 kg (26,460 lb) | 17.15 | 56.3 |
| 179 | Mikoyan-Gurevich MiG-23S | USSR | State Industries | MrFr | 1970 | tj Tumansky 10,000 kg (22,050 lb) | 14 | 46 |
| 179 | Mikoyan-Gurevich MiG-25S | USSR | State Industries | Fr | 1967 | 2 x tj Tumansky R-266 12,300 kg (27,300 lb) | 13.95 | 45.9 |
| 179 | Saab AJ37 Viggen | S | SAAB | A | 1971 | tj Volvo Flugmotor RM8A 11.800 kg (26,000 lb) | 10.60 | 34.9 |
| 179 | IAI Kfir C2 | IL | IAI | MrFr | 1976 | tj General Electric J79-GE-17 8120 kg (17,900 lb) | 8.22 | 26.9 |

| Length | | Height | | Take-off weight | | Speed | | Ceiling | | Range | | Crew | Payload/armament |
| m | ft | m | ft | kg | lb | km/h | mph | m | ft | km | ml | | |
|---|---|---|---|---|---|---|---|---|---|---|---|---|---|
| 17.15 | 56.3 | 5.32 | 17.5 | 12,000 | 28,660 | 860 | 536 | 12,800 | 42,000 | 3,050 | 2,080 | 2 | 8-10 p |
| 37.10 | 122.6 | 9.02 | 29.5 | 47,000 | 103,616 | 870 | 541 | 12,000 | 39,370 | 2,400 | 1,491 | 5 | 76-80 p |
| 25.06 | 82.2 | 8.71 | 28.5 | 20,412 | 45,000 | 518 | 322 | 9,000 | 29,527 | 1,075 | 668 | 2-3 | 52-56 p |
| 31.82 | 104.5 | 8.38 | 27.6 | 35,245 | 77,700 | 903 | 561 | 10,675 | 35,023 | 1,601 | 995 | 4-5 | 90 p |
| 57.13 | 187.4 | 13.23 | 43.4 | 158,760 | 350,000 | 965 | 600 | 9,150 | 30,000 | 7,240 | 4,499 | 5 | 259 p |
| 42.50 | 139.9 | 12.04 | 39.6 | 110,765 | 244,195 | 1,006 | 625 | 12,500 | 41,000 | 6,308 | 3,920 | 5 | 96-121 p |
| 18.10 | 59.4 | 5.12 | 16.7 | 5,670 | 12,500 | 473 | 294 | 8,230 | 27,000 | 1,102 | 685 | 2 | 19-20 p |
| 30.40 | 99.7 | 11.28 | 37 | 49,435 | 108,885 | 915 | 569 | 9,145 | 30,000 | 3,555 | 2,209 | 5 | 115-130 p |
| 13.43 | 44 | 4.36 | 14.3 | 4,695 | 10,351 | 644 | 400 | 11,704 | 38,400 | 2,124 | 1,320 | 2 | 6 p |
| 13.18 | 43.2 | 3.84 | 12.7 | 5,897 | 13,000 | 860 | 536 | 13,720 | 45,000 | 2,045 | 1,271 | 2 | 6 p |
| 24.36 | 79.9 | 7.47 | 24.6 | 29,711 | 65,500 | 936 | 582 | 13,100 | 43,000 | 6,625 | 4,117 | 3 | 19 p |
| 49.69 | 153.1 | 10.36 | 34 | 83,820 | 184,791 | 953 | 592 | 10,060 | 33,005 | 4,260 | 2,647 | 6-7 | 189 p |
| 70.66 | 231.8 | 19.33 | 63.5 | 332,900 | 733,918 | 910 | 565 | 13,715 | 45,000 | 8,000 | 4,971 | 10-13 | 400 p |
| 43.84 | 143.8 | 14.78 | 48.4 | 77,110 | 170,000 | 463 | 288 | 7,620 | 25,000 | 4,700 | 2,920 | 4 | 24,494 kg (54,000 lb) |
| 54.17 | 177.7 | 16.87 | 55.3 | 216,363 | 476,998 | 982 | 610 | 12,800 | 42,000 | 6,820 | 4,238 | 13 | 256-400 p |
| 55.50 | 182 | 17.70 | 58.1 | 256,280 | 565,000 | 908 | 564 | 10,180 | 33,400 | 11,580 | 7,196 | 13 | 255-380 p |
| 53.12 | 174.3 | 12.35 | 40.6 | 162,000 | 357,148 | 900 | 559 | 13,000 | 42,650 | 6,700 | 4,165 | 8-10 | 86 p |
| 11.90 | 39 | 5 | 16.5 | 3,800 | 8,377 | 359 | 223 | 8,870 | 29,100 | 2,410 | 1,500 | 2 | 6-9 |
| 15.77 | 51.9 | 5.66 | 18.5 | 5,670 | 12,500 | 338 | 210 | 8,138 | 26,700 | 1,198 | 744 | 2 | 20 p |
| 34.98 | 114.8 | 8.23 | 27 | 60,780 | 133,997 | 972 | 604 | 9,450 | 31,000 | 3,934 | 2,445 | 7-8 | 115 p |
| 32.61 | 107 | 7.47 | 24.6 | 47,400 | 104,500 | 871 | 541 | 10,670 | 35,000 | 2,720 | 1,690 | 4-5 | 119 p |
| 10.86 | 35.8 | 4.18 | 13.8 | 2,993 | 6,598 | 257 | 160 | 4,025 | 13,205 | 1,153 | 716 | 1 | 9 p |
| 15.01 | 49.3 | 4.32 | 14.2 | 4,536 | 10,000 | 241 | 150 | 4,450 | 14,600 | 1,610 | 1,000 | 1 | 17 p |
| 37.45 | 122.8 | 10.64 | 34.8 | 66,452 | 146,500 | 684 | 425 | 9,150 | 30,000 | 2,945 | 1,830 | 7 | 97-139 p |
| 52.32 | 171.8 | 12.04 | 39.6 | 151,950 | 335,000 | 935 | 581 | 12,800 | 42,000 | 7,600 | 4,723 | 6-8 | 163-174 p |
| 23.01 | 75.4 | 7.34 | 24 | 19,500 | 42,990 | 442 | 275 | 10,060 | 33,005 | 2,830 | 1,759 | 3 | 56 p |
| 12.21 | 40.1 | 4.60 | 15 | 6,214 | 13,700 | 327 | 203 | 6,858 | 22,500 | 1,115 | 693 | 1-2 | 19 p |
| 26.57 | 87.2 | 8.23 | 27 | 30,500 | 67,241 | 720 | 447 | — | — | 1,000 | 621 | 3-5 | 32 p or 7,500 kg (16,535 lb) |
| 62.10 | 203.9 | 11.40 | 37.5 | 185,065 | 407,994 | 2,179 | 1,354 | 18,290 | 60,000 | 6,580 | 4,089 | 8 | 144 p |
| 65.70 | 215.6 | 12.85 | 42.2 | 180,000 | 396,830 | 2,500 | 1,554 | 18,000 | 59,054 | 6,500 | 4,040 | 8 | 140 p |
| 49.70 | 157.1 | 11.40 | 37.4 | 94,000 | 207,234 | 900 | 559 | 12,000 | 39,370 | 3,200 | 1,988 | 8 | 168 p |
| 19.43 | 63.9 | 5.63 | 18.5 | 25,401 | 56,000 | 2,701 | 1,678 | 30,500 | 100,000 | 1,600 | 995 | 1 | 1 g; 7,620 kg (16,800 lb) |
| 17.07 | 56 | 4.66 | 15.4 | 19,960 | 44,000 | 2,125 | 1,320 | 15,240 | 50,000 | 740 | 460 | 1 | 6,214 kg (13,700 lb) |
| 14.68 | 48.2 | 4.06 | 13.4 | 11,187 | 24,664 | 1,705 | 1,060 | 15,790 | 51,800 | 2,863 | 1,779 | 1 | 2 g; 3,175 kg (7,000 lb) |
| 18.86 | 61.8 | 4.88 | 16 | 31,880 | 70,280 | 2,548 | 1,584 | 21,000 | 68,900 | 930 | 578 | 2 | 1 g; 7,250 kg (15,985 lb) |
| 14.52 | 47.8 | 5.01 | 16.5 | 14,968 | 33,000 | 2,123 | 1,319 | 15,420 | 50,000 | 925 | 575 | 1 | 1 g; 4,763 kg (10,500 lb) |
| 15 | 49.2 | 4.50 | 14.9 | 14,900 | 24,030 | 2,335 | 1,450 | 20,000 | 65,600 | 900 | 560 | 1 | 2 g; 4,000 kg (8,800 lb) |
| 18.70 | 61.3 | 6 | 19.8 | 20,000 | 44,100 | 2,650 | 1,650 | 20,000 | 65,600 | 861 | 536 | 1 | 2 g; 6,000 kg (13,200 lb) |
| 13.57 | 44.5 | 4.58 | 15 | 12,000* | 26,445* | 1164* | 723* | — | — | 965* | 599* | 1 | 1 g; 3,800 kg (8,378 lb) |
| 16 | 52.6 | 4.30 | 14.1 | 13,000 | 28,660 | 1,250 | 772 | — | — | 560 | 348 | 1 | 900 kg (1,958 lb) |
| 20.50 | 67.2 | 5.79 | 18.9 | 16,000 | 35,280 | 2,445 | 1,519 | 19,800 | 64,963 | 725 | 450 | 1 | 2 msl a.a. |
| 21.29 | 69.8 | 6.20 | 20.4 | 30,850 | 68,024 | 2,608 | 1,621 | 19,000 | 62,339 | 1,950 | 1,211 | 2 | 1 g; 7,500 kg (16,537 lb) |
| 16.15 | 53 | 3.95 | 13 | 17,200 | 37,925 | 2,123 | 1,319 | 15,250 | 50,035 | 1,000 | 621 | 1 | 2 g; 4 msl a.a. |
| 22.30 | 73.2 | 5.60 | 18.4 | 36,200 | 79,820 | 3,380 | 2,100 | 24,400 | 80,056 | 1,130 | 702 | 1 | 2 g; 4 msl a.a. |
| 16.30 | 53.6 | 5.60 | 18.4 | 16,000 | 35,275 | 2,135 | 1,320 | 18,300 | 60,000 | 1,000 | 621 | 1 | 6,000 kg (13,200 lb) |
| 15.55 | 51 | 4.25 | 13.9 | 14,600 | 32,188 | 2,442 | 1,517 | 16,000 | 52,495 | 1,300 | 807 | 1 | 4,000 kg (8,800 lb) |

# Technical Data

| Page | Aircraft | Nation | Manufacturer | Type | Year | Engine | Wingspan m | Wingspan ft |
|------|----------|--------|--------------|------|------|--------|------------|-------------|
| 179 | Hawker Siddeley Harrier GR. Mk.1 | GB | British Aerospace | A | 1967 | tj Rolls-Royce Bristol Pegasus Mk.101 8602 kg (19,000 lb) | 7.70 | 25.3 |
| 179 | Hal HF-24 Mk.1 Marut | IND | Hindustan Aeronautics Ltd. | Fr | 1967 | 2 x Rolls-Royce Orpheus 703 2200 kg (4,850 lb) | 9 | 29.6 |
| 179 | MRCA Tornado | D-GB-I | Panavia | MrFr | 1979 | 2 x tj Turbo Union RB.199-34R-04 6120 kg (13,495 lb) | 13.90 | 45.7 |
| 179 | Sepecat Jaguar S | GB-F | Sepecat | MrFr | 1972 | 2 x tj Rolls-Royce Turbomeca Adour 102 3313 kg (7,305 lb) | 8.69 | 28.6 |
| 180 | Aeritalia G.91Y | I | Aeritalia S.p.A. | A | 1966 | 2 x tj General Electric J85-GE-13A 1850 kg (4,080 lb) | 9.01 | 29.6 |
| 180 | Pucarà IA-58 | RA | FMA | A | 1974 | 2 x tp Turbomeca Astazou XVIG 1022 hp | 14.50 | 47.7 |
| 180 | Lockheed S-3A Viking | USA | Lockheed Corp. | A | 1974 | 2 x tj General Electric TF34-GE-2 4207 kg (9,275 lb) | 20.93 | 68.8 |
| 180 | Fairchild Republic A-10A | USA | Fairchild Republic Co. | A | 1975 | 2 x tj General Electric TF34-GE-100 4207 kg (9,275 lb) | 17.53 | 57.6 |
| 181 | Mikoyan-Gurevich MiG-27 | USSR | State Industries | A | 1973 | 1 x tj 10,000 kg (24,500 lb) | 14 | 46 |
| 181 | Tupolev Tu-26 | USSR | State Industries | Br | 1970 | 2 x tj Kuznetsov NK-144 22,000 kg (48,500 lb) | 34.45 | 113 |
| 181 | Dassault Mirage IV-A | F | Avions Marcel Dassault | Br | 1963 | 2 x tj SNECMA Atar 9K 7000 kg (15,432 lb) | 11.84 | 38.8 |
| 181 | BAe 167 Strikemaster | GB | BAe | A | 1967 | tj Rolls-Royce Viper Mk.535 1547 kg (3,410 lb) | 11.23 | 36.8 |
| 181 | Cessna A 37 | USA | Cessna Aircraft Co. | A | 1967 | 2 x tj General Electric J85-GE-17A 1293 kg (2,850 lb) | 10.93 | 35.8 |
| 181 | General Dynamics F-111F | USA | General Dynamics | A | 1973 | 2 x tj Pratt & Whitney TF30-P-100 11,385 kg (25,100 lb) | 19.20 | 63 |
| 181 | Rockwell International B-1 | USA | Rockwell International | Br | 1974 | 2 x tj General Electric F101-GE-100 13,600 kg (30,000 lb) | 41.67 | 136.9 |
| 182 | de Havilland DHC-5D Buffalo | CDN | The de Havilland Aircraft of Canada Ltd. | Tr | 1976 | 2 x tp General Electric CT64-820-4 3133 hp | 29.26 | 96 |
| 183 | Boeing E-3A Sentry | USA | Boeing Aerospace Co. | Rc | 1977 | 4 x tj Pratt & Whitney TF33-P-7 9525 kg (21,000 lb) | 44.42 | 145.9 |
| 183 | Lockheed P-3C Orion | USA | Lockheed Aircraft Co. | Rc | 1968 | 4 x tp Allison T56-A-14 4910 hp | 30.37 | 99.8 |
| 183 | Lockheed C-141A Starlifter | USA | Lockheed Aircraft Corp. | Tr | 1963 | 4 x tj Pratt & Whitney TF-33-P7 9525 kg (21,000 lb) | 48.80 | 160.1 |
| 183 | Lockheed C-5A Galaxy | USA | Lockheed Aircraft Corp. | Tr | 1968 | 4 x tj General Electric TF39-GE-1 18,600 kg (41,000 lb) | 67.88 | 222.9 |
| 183 | Beechcraft T-34C | USA | Beech Aircraft Corp. | T | 1973 | tp Pratt & Whitney PT6A-25 400 hp | 10.16 | 33.3 |
| 184 | Hal HJT-16 Mk-IA Kiran | IND | HAL | T/CIS | 1964 | tj Rolls-Royce Viper 11 1134 kg (2,500 lb) | 10.70 | 35.1 |
| 184 | Aero L-39 Albatros | CS | Aero | T | 1968 | tj Walter Titan 1720 kg (3,792 lb) | 9.46 | 31.1 |
| 185 | Ilyushin Il-76-T | USSR | State Industries | Tr | 1971 | 4 x tj Soloviev D-30KP 12,000 kg (26,445 lb) | 50.50 | 165.8 |
| 185 | Antonov An-22 Antei | USSR | State Industries | Tr | 1965 | 4 x tp Kuznetsov NK-12MA 15,000 hp | 64.40 | 211.4 |
| 185 | Tupolev Tu-126 | USSR | State Industries | Rc | 1968 | 4 x tp Kuznetsov NK-12MV 14,795 hp | 51.20 | 168 |
| 185 | Beriev Be-12 | USSR | State Industries | Rc | 1961 | 2 x tp Ivchenko Al-20D 4000 hp | 32.91 | 108 |
| 186 | Alpha Jet E | F-D | Dassault-Breguet/Dornier | T | 1973 | 2 x tj Snecma/Turbomeca Larzac 04-C5 1350 kg (2,976 lb) | 9.11 | 29.9 |
| 186 | Transall C-160T | F-D | Arbeitsgemeinschaft Transall | Tr | 1967 | 2 x tp Rolls-Royce Tyne RTy.20 Mk.22 6100 hp | 40 | 131.3 |
| 186 | Breguet 1150 Atlantic | F | Breguet Aviation | Rc | 1965 | 2 x tp Rolls-Royce Tyne RTy.10 Mk.21 6105 hp | 36.30 | 119.9 |
| 186 | Aermacchi M.B.339 | I | Aeronautica Macchi | T | 1976 | tj Rolls-Royce Viper Mk.632-43 1815 kg (4,000 lb) | 10.86 | 35.8 |
| 186 | Aeritalia G.222 | I | Aeritalia | Tr | 1970 | 2 x tp General Electric T64-GE-P4D 3400 hp | 28.70 | 94.2 |
| 186 | SIAI Marchetti S.M.1019A | I | SIAI Marchetti | Li | 1971 | tp Allison 250-B15 G 317 hp | 10.97 | 36 |
| 186 | SIAI Marchetti SF 260W | I | SIAI Marchetti | T/CIS | 1972 | Lycoming 0-540-E45A 260 hp (6 cl) a.c. | 8.35 | 27.5 |
| 187 | Kawasaki C-1 | J | Kawasaki Jukogyo Kabishi Kaisha | Tr | 1970 | 2 x tj JT8D-M-9 6577 kg (14,500 lb) | 10.60 | 100.5 |
| 187 | Shin Meiwa PS-1 | J | Shin Meiwa Industry Co. | Rc | 1968 | 4 x tp Ishikawajila T64-H11-10 2850 hp | 32.8 | 107.3 |
| 187 | CASA C-101 Aviojet | E | CASA | T/CIS | 1977 | tj Garrett-AiResearch TFE731-2-25 1588 kg (3,500 lb) | 10.60 | 34.8 |
| 187 | BAe SA-3 Bulldog T Mk.1 | GB | BAe | T | 1973 | Lycoming 10-360-A}B6 200 hp (4 cl) a.c. | 10.06 | 33 |
| 187 | BAe Hawk T.Mk.1 | GB | BAe | T/CIS | 1974 | tj Rolls-Royce Turboméca RT172-06-11 Adour 151 2422 kg (5,340 lb) | 9.39 | 30.8 |
| 187 | Short Belfast C. Mk.1 | GB | Short Brothers & Harland | Tr | 1964 | 4 x tp Rolls-Royce Tyne RTy.12 5730 hp | 48.42 | 158.9 |
| 188 | VFW-Fokker 614 | D | VFW-Fokker | LT | 1971 | 2 x tj Rolls-Royce M 45H Mk.501 3302 kg (7,280 lb) | 21.50 | 70.6 |
| 188 | Fokker F 28 Mk.2000 Fellowship | NL | Fokker VFW B.V. | CTr | 1971 | 2 x tj Rolls-Royce RB.183-2 Spey Mk.155-15 4468 kg (9,850 lb) | 23.58 | 77.4 |
| 188 | Aérospatiale S.N.601 Corvette | F | Aérospatiale | LT | 1972 | 2 x tj Pratt & Whitney of Canada JT15D-4 1134 kg (2,500 lb) | 12.87 | 42.2 |
| 188 | Dassault Mercure 100 | F | Dassault-Breguet | CTr | 1971 | 2 x tj Pratt & Whitney JT8D-15 7030 kg (15,500 lb) | 30.55 | 100.2 |
| 189 | BAe 146-100 | GB | BAe | CTr | 1981 | 4 x tj Avco Lycoming ALF 502R-3 3039 kg (6,700 lb) | 26.34 | 85.5 |
| 189 | Hawker Siddeley 125-700 | GB | BAe | LT | 1976 | 2 x tj Garrett AiResearch TFE731-3-1H 1680 kg (3,700 lb) | 14.33 | 47 |
| 189 | Airbus A-300 | F-D-GB-E | Airbus Industries | CTr | 1974 | 2 x tj General Electric CF650C 23,135 kg (51,400 lb) | 44.84 | 147.1 |

| Length | | Height | | Take-off weight | | Speed | | Ceiling | | Range | | Crew | Payload/armament |
| m | ft | m | ft | kg | lb | km/h | mph | m | ft | km | ml | | |
|---|---|---|---|---|---|---|---|---|---|---|---|---|---|
| 13.87 | 45.6 | 3.43 | 11.3 | 9,979 | 20,000 | 1,186 | 737 | 15,200 | 50,000 | 3,700 | 2,300 | 1 | 2 g; 2,270 kg (5,000 lb) |
| 15.87 | 52.1 | 3.60 | 11.8 | 10,908 | 24,048 | 1,112 | 691 | 12,200 | 40,000 | 1,000 | 621 | 1 | 4 g; 1,815 kg (4,000 lb) |
| 16.70 | 54.9 | 5.70 | 18.9 | 17,700 | 39,020 | 2,125 | 1,320 | 17,500 | 57,415 | 1,300 | 808 | 2 | 2 g; 5,500 kg (12,125 lb) |
| 16.83 | 55.2 | 4.89 | 16.1 | 15,500 | 34,000 | 1,593 | 990 | — | — | 1,315 | 818 | 1 | 2 g; 4,535 kg (10,000 lb) |
| 11.67 | 38.2 | 4.43 | 14.6 | 8,700 | 19,180 | 1,110 | 690 | 12,500 | 41,000 | 611 | 380 | 1 | 2 g; 1,814 kg (4,000 lb) |
| 14.25 | 46.9 | 5.36 | 17.7 | 3,600 | 14,991 | 500 | 310 | 10,000 | 32,810 | 3,042 | 1,890 | 2 | 2 g; 4 mg; 1,620 kg (3,571 lb) |
| 16.26 | 53.4 | 6.93 | 22.9 | 19,277 | 42,500 | 834 | 518 | 12,200 | 40,000 | 3,705 | 2,303 | 4 | 3,500 kg (7,715 lb) |
| 16.26 | 53.4 | 4.47 | 14.8 | 21,500 | 47,400 | 722 | 449 | — | — | 1,000 | 621 | 1 | 1 g; 7,257 kg (16,000 lb) |
| 16.15 | 53 | 3.95 | 13 | 17,750 | 39,130 | 2,123 | 1,320 | 15,250 | 50,000 | 1,000 | 621 | 1 | 1 g; 4 msl a.t. |
| 40.23 | 132 | 10.06 | 33 | 122,500 | 270,000 | 2,445 | 1,520 | 18,920 | 60,000 | 5,475 | 3,570 | 4 | 1 g; msl |
| 23.41 | 76.8 | 5.40 | 17.7 | 31,600 | 69,665 | 2,340 | 1,454 | 20,000 | 65,600 | 1,240 | 770 | 2 | 7,257 kg (16,000 lb) |
| 10.27 | 33.8 | 3.34 | 10.9 | 5,215 | 11,500 | 774 | 450 | 12,200 | 40,000 | 1,166 | 725 | 2 | 2 mg; 1,360 kg (3,000 lb) |
| 8.93 | 29.3 | 2.70 | 8.8 | 6,350 | 14,000 | 816 | 507 | 12,730 | 41,765 | 740 | 460 | 2 | 1 mg; 2,450 kg (5,400 lb) |
| 22.40 | 73.5 | 5.22 | 17.1 | 45,359 | 100,000 | 2,335 | 1,450 | 18,000 | 59,000 | 5,093 | 3,165 | 2 | 1 g; 14,290 kg (31,500 lb) |
| 45.78 | 150.3 | 10.24 | 33.7 | 176,810 | 389,800 | 2,125 | 1,320 | 18,300 | 60,000 | 9,815 | 6,100 | 4 | 52,164 kg (115,000 lb) |
| 24.08 | 79 | 8.73 | 28.8 | 22,316 | 49,200 | 467 | 290 | 9,450 | 31,000 | 1,112 | 691 | 3 | 41 p or 8,164 kg (18,000 lb) |
| 46.61 | 152.9 | 12.93 | 42.5 | 151,315 | 333,600 | 886 | 550 | 11,885 | 39,000 | 12,000 | 7,475 | 17 | — |
| 35.61 | 116.8 | 10.29 | 33.8 | 61,235 | 135,000 | 761 | 473 | 8,625 | 28,300 | 3,825 | 2,383 | 10 | 8,735 kg (19,250 lb) |
| 44.20 | 145 | 11.98 | 39.3 | 143,600 | 316,600 | 917 | 570 | 12,800 | 42,000 | 10,370 | 6,445 | 4 | 154 p |
| 75.54 | 247.8 | 19.85 | 65.2 | 348,810 | 769,000 | 919 | 571 | 10,360 | 34,000 | 6,033 | 3,749 | 5 | 345 p or 100,228 kg (220,967 lb) |
| 8.75 | 28.8 | 3.02 | 9.7 | 1,978 | 4,360 | 464 | 288 | 9,145 | 30,000 | 1,205 | 748 | 2 | — |
| 10.60 | 34.9 | 3.64 | 11.9 | 4,100 | 9,039 | 695 | 432 | 9,150 | 30,000 | 745 | 463 | 2 | 453 kg (1,000 lb) |
| 12.32 | 40.5 | 4.72 | 15.5 | 5,270 | 11,618 | 700 | 435 | 11,500 | 37,730 | 1,600 | 994 | 2 | 1,100 kg (2,425 lb) |
| 46.59 | 152.9 | 14.76 | 48.5 | 170,000 | 374,785 | 800 | 497 | 9,000 | 29,527 | 5,000 | 3,100 | 3 | 40,000 kg (88,185 lb) |
| 57.80 | 189.7 | 12.53 | 41.1 | 250,000 | 551,160 | 740 | 460 | — | — | 10,950 | 6,800 | 5-6 | 80,000 kg (176,350 lb) |
| 55.20 | 181.1 | 15.50 | 50.8 | 170,000 | 376,900 | 770 | 478 | 12,000 | 39,370 | 8,950 | 5,560 | 10-15 | — |
| 29.18 | 95.9 | 6.68 | 21.9 | 29,500 | 65,035 | 610 | 379 | 12,285 | 40,000 | 4,000 | 2,485 | 5-6 | 10,092 kg (22,250 lb) |
| 12.29 | 40.4 | 4.19 | 13.9 | 6,100 | 13,448 | 1,000 | 621 | 15,000 | 49,200 | 440 | 273 | 2 | 1 g; 2,250 kg (4,960 lb) |
| 32.40 | 106.3 | 11.65 | 38.5 | 16,000 | 35,270 | 536 | 333 | 8,500 | 27,900 | 4,558 | 2,832 | 4 | 93 p or 16,000 kg (35,270 lb) |
| 31.75 | 104.2 | 11.33 | 37.2 | 43,500 | 95,900 | 658 | 409 | 10,000 | 32,800 | 9,000 | 5,590 | 12 | t; msl; b |
| 10.97 | 36 | 3.99 | 13.1 | 5,895 | 13,000 | 898 | 558 | 14,630 | 48,000 | 1,760 | 1,093 | 2 | 1,815 kg (4,000 lb) |
| 22.70 | 74.5 | 9.80 | 32.2 | 26,500 | 58,422 | 540 | 336 | 7,620 | 25,000 | 2,220 | 1,380 | 3 | 8,500 kg (18,740 lb) |
| 8.52 | 27.9 | 2.38 | 7.8 | 1,270 | 2,800 | 250 | 155 | 6,000 | 19,685 | 1,225 | 760 | 2 | 227 kg (500 lb) |
| 7.10 | 23.4 | 2.41 | 7.9 | 1,300 | 2.866 | 315 | 196 | 4,665 | 15.300 | 556 | 345 | 2 | 300 kg (661 lb) |
| 29 | 95.2 | 9.99 | 32.9 | 45,000 | 99,210 | 806 | 501 | 11,580 | 38,000 | 3,353 | 2,084 | 5 | 60 p or 7,900 kg (17,415 lb) |
| 33.5 | 109.9 | 9.7 | 31.8 | 39,400 | 86,862 | 547 | 340 | 9,000 | 29,500 | 2,168 | 1,347 | 10 | t; b; msl |
| 12.25 | 40 | 4.25 | 13.8 | 5,600 | 12,345 | 676 | 420 | 12,495 | 40,500 | 1,176 | 730 | 2 | 2,000 kg (4,400 lb) |
| 7.09 | 23.3 | 2.28 | 7.6 | 1,066 | 2,350 | 241 | 150 | 4,875 | 16,000 | 1,000 | 621 | 2-3 | 290 kg (640 lb) |
| 11.17 | 36.8 | 3.99 | 13.1 | 7,755 | 17,097 | 1,000 | 621 | 15,240 | 50,000 | 1,038 | 645 | 2 | 1 g; 900 kg (2,000 lb) |
| 41.69 | 136.5 | 14.30 | 47 | 104,300 | 230,000 | 566 | 352 | 9,145 | 30,000 | 8,530 | 5,300 | 5 | 150 p or 35,000 kg (78,000 lb) |
| 20.60 | 67.7 | 7.84 | 25.8 | 19,950 | 43,982 | 704 | 438 | 7,620 | 25,000 | 1,204 | 748 | 2 | 44 p |
| 29.61 | 97.1 | 8.47 | 27.9 | 29,485 | 65,000 | 849 | 528 | 10,670 | 35,000 | 1,213 | 754 | 4-5 | 79 p |
| 13.83 | 45.4 | 4.23 | 13.8 | 6,600 | 14,550 | 760 | 472 | 12,500 | 41,000 | 1,555 | 967 | 2 | 13 p |
| 34.84 | 114.3 | 11.36 | 37.3 | 54,500 | 120,152 | 932 | 579 | 10,000 | 32,800 | 1,772 | 1,101 | 6-8 | 162 p |
| 26.16 | 85.8 | 8.61 | 28.3 | 33,840 | 74,600 | 778 | 483 | 9,145 | 30,003 | 1,760 | 1,093 | 2 | 88 p |
| 15.46 | 50.8 | 5.36 | 17.7 | 10,977 | 24,200 | 808 | 502 | 12,500 | 41,000 | 4,318 | 2,683 | 2-3 | 8 p |
| 53.62 | 175.9 | 16.53 | 54.3 | 165,000 | 363,762 | 878 | 546 | 10,675 | 35,020 | 4,263 | 2,649 | 8-10 | 253 p |

# Technical Data

| Page | Aircraft | Nation | Manufacturer | Type | Year | Engine | Wingspan m | ft |
|---|---|---|---|---|---|---|---|---|
| 191 | Boeing 767 | USA | Boeing Commercial Airplane Co. | CTr | 1981 | 2 × Pratt & Whitney JT9D-7R4D 21,773 kg (47,700 lb) | 47.55 | 159.2 |
| 191 | Boeing 757 | USA | Boeing Commercial Airplane Co. | CTr | 1982 | 2 × Rolls-Royce RB211-535 16,965 kg (37,400 lb) | 37.95 | 124.6 |
| 191 | McDonnell-Douglas MD-80 | USA | McDonnell-Douglas | CTr | 1980 | tf Pratt & Whitney JT8D-209 8392 kg (18,500 lb) | 32.9 | 107.8 |
| 192 | Piaggio GP-180 | I-USA | Rinaldo Piaggio/Gates | LT | 1985 | 2 × tp Pratt & Whitney PT6A-66 1400 hp | 13.84 | 45.4 |
| 193 | Aérospatiale ATR-42 | I-F | Aeritalia/Aérospatiale | LT | 1984 | 2 × tp Pratt & Whitney PW120 1800 hp | 24.57 | 80.7 |
| 193 | Airbus A-320* | F-GB-D-E | Airbus Industries | CTr | 1988 | tf CFM 56-4 10,500 kg (23,000 lb) | 33.9 | 111.2 |
| 193 | Airbus A-310 | F-GB-D-E NL-B | Airbus Industries | CTr | 1982 | tf General Electric CF6-80-A 22,680 kg (50,000 lb) | 43.9 | 144 |
| 194 | Chance Vought XF5U-1 | USA | Chance Vought Division of United Aircraft Corp. | ExFr | 1946 | 2 × Pratt & Whitney R-2000-2 Twin Wasp 1600 hp (r 14 cl) a.c. | 7.20 | 23.6 |
| 194 | Northrop B.35 | USA | Northrop Aircraft Inc. | Ex | 1946 | 4 × Pratt & Whitney R-4360 3000 hp (r 28 cl) a.c. | 52.43 | 172 |
| 194 | Bell X-1 | USA | Bell Aircraft Corp. | Ex | 1946 | Reaction Motor XLR-11-RM-3 2721 kg (6,000 lb) | 8.53 | 28 |
| 194 | Bell X-2 | USA | Bell Aircraft Corp. | Ex | 1955 | Curtiss-Wright XLR-25-CW-3 6804 kg (15,000 lb) | 10.59 | 34.7 |
| 194 | Bell X-5 | USA | Bell Aircraft Corp. | Ex | 1951 | tj Allison J45-A-17A 2222 kg (4,900 lb) | 10.21 | 33.4 |
| 194 | Douglas X-3 Stiletto | USA | Douglas Aircraft Co. | Ex | 1952 | 2 × tj Westinghouse XJ34-WE-17 1905 kg (4,200 lb) | 6.90 | 22.8 |
| 194 | North American X-15A | USA | North American Aviation Inc. | Ex | 1959 | rz Thiokol XLR-99M-2 31,752 kg (70,000 lb) | 6.70 | 22 |
| 194 | North American XB-70A Valkyrie | USA | North American Aviation Inc. | Ex | 1964 | 6 × tj General Electric YJ93-GE-3 14,060 kg (31,000 lb) | 32 | 105 |
| 195 | de Havilland D.H.108 | GB | de Havilland Aircraft Co. | Ex | 1946 | tj de Havilland Goblin 4 1701 kg (3,753 lb) | 11.89 | 39 |
| 195 | Boulton Paul P.111 | GB | Boulton Paul | Ex | 1950 | tj Rolls-Royce Nene 2313 kg (5,100 lb) | 10.21 | 33.6 |
| 195 | Armstrong Whitworth A.W.52 | GB | Armstrong Whitworth Aircraft Ltd. | Ex | 1947 | 2 × tj Rolls-Royce Nene 2270 kg (5,000 lb) | 27.43 | 90 |
| 195 | Fairey F.D.2 | GB | Fairey Aviation Ltd. | Ex | 1954 | tj Rolls-Royce Avon RA.28 4548 kg (10,027 lb) | 8.18 | 26.8 |
| 195 | Avro 707 A | GB | A.V. Roe & Co. Ltd. | Ex | 1951 | tj Rolls-Royce Derwent 5 1587 kg (3,500 lb) | 10.40 | 34.1 |
| 195 | Handley Page H.P.115 | GB | Handley Page Ltd. | Ex | 1961 | tj Bristol Siddeley Viper 862 kg (1,900 lb) | 6.10 | 20 |
| 195 | Bristol Type 188 | GB | Bristol Aircraft Ltd. | Ex | 1962 | 2 × tj Bristol Siddeley Gyron Jr DGJ.10R 6350 kg (14,000 lb) | 10.69 | 35.1 |
| 195 | Martin Marietta X-24A | USA | Martin Marietta | Ex | 1969 | rz Thiokol XLR-11 3625 kg (7,992 lb) | 4.16 | 13.8 |
| 196 | Space Shuttle | USA | Rockwell International | | 1977 | 3 × rz Rocketdyne SSME 213,192 kg (470,000 lb) | 23.79 | 78 |

# INDEX (Numbers in italic refer to illustrations)

| Length | | Height | | Take-off weight | | Speed | | Ceiling | | Range | | Crew | Payload/armament |
|---|---|---|---|---|---|---|---|---|---|---|---|---|---|
| m | ft | m | ft | kg | lb | km/h | mph | m | ft | km | ml | | |
| 48.51 | 159.2 | 15.85 | 52 | 136,080 | 300,000 | Mach 0,8 | | 11,920 | 39,100 | 5,058 | 3,143 | 6-8 | 211-289 p |
| 47.32 | 155.3 | 13.56 | 44.6 | 108,600 | 240,000 | Mach 0,8 | | 11,703 | 38,395 | 4,336 | 2,695 | 6-8 | 178-233 p |
| 45.06 | 147.8 | 9.05 | 29.7 | 67,813 | 149,500 | 879 | 546 | 10,678 | 35,000 | 3,219 | 2,000 | 6-7 | 137-172 p |
| 14.17 | 46.5 | 3.93 | 12.9 | 4,445 | 9,800 | 740 | 460 | 12,500 | 41,000 | 3,965 | 2,464 | — | 7 p |
| 22.7 | 80.7 | 7.95 | 26 | 14,715 | 32,440 | 513 | 319 | 7,620 | 25,000 | 1,300 | 808 | 2-3 | 42 p |
| 36.8 | 120.7 | 11.8 | 38.7 | 64,000 | 141,096 | 800 | 497 | — | — | 3,340 | 1,800 | 7 | 158-179 p |
| 46.67 | 153.1 | 15.81 | 51.8 | 132,000 | 291,000 | 667 | 414 | 11,275 | 37,000 | 5,300 | 2,850 | 9-11 | 195-282 p |
| 8.72 | 28.6 | 4.50 | 14.9 | 7,260 | 16,006 | 811 | 504 | 9,750 | 31,980 | 1,465 | 910 | 1 | 6 mg; 907 kg (2,000 lb) |
| 16.18 | 53.1 | 6.09 | 19.9 | 70,308 | 155,003 | 629 | 391 | 12,200 | 40,000 | 16,000 | 10,000 | 15 | |
| 9.45 | 31 | 3.30 | 10.8 | 5,443 | 12,000 | 1,545 | 960 | 21,340 | 70,012 | — | — | 1 | |
| 13.84 | 45.5 | 3.58 | 11.9 | 11,300 | 25,910 | 3,369 | 2,094 | 38,465 | 126,200 | — | — | 1 | |
| 10.16 | 33.3 | 3.65 | 11.9 | 4,479 | 9,874 | 1,134 | 705 | 12,800 | 42,000 | 1,206 | 750 | 1 | |
| 20.34 | 66.9 | 3.81 | 12.6 | — | — | 1,045 | 649 | 10,670 | 35,006 | — | — | 1 | |
| 15.24 | 50 | 3.96 | 12.9 | 15,105 | 33,300 | 6,692 | 4,159 | 95,935 | 314,744 | 442 | 275 | 1 | |
| 59.64 | 196 | 9.14 | 30 | 240,400 | 529,991 | 3,185 | 1,979 | 24,400 | 80,051 | 12,000 | 7,457 | 4 | |
| 8.17 | 26.8 | — | — | — | — | 900 | 559 | — | — | — | — | 1 | |
| 7.95 | 26.1 | 3.82 | 12.6 | 4,354 | 9,000 | 1,000 | 621 | — | — | — | — | 1 | |
| 11.38 | 37.4 | 4.39 | 14.5 | 15,490 | 34,150 | 804 | 500 | 15,240 | 50,000 | 2,414 | 1,500 | 2 | |
| 15.72 | 51.5 | 3.35 | 11 | 6,018 | 13,267 | 1,911 | 1,187 | 12,200 | 40,000 | 1,335 | 830 | 1 | |
| 12.90 | 42.4 | 3.53 | 11.7 | 4,309 | 9,500 | — | — | — | — | — | — | 1 | |
| 13.72 | 45 | — | — | 2,268 | 5,000 | — | — | — | — | — | — | 1 | |
| 21.64 | 71 | 4.06 | 13.4 | — | — | 1,931 | 1,200 | — | — | — | — | 1 | |
| 7.47 | 24.6 | 3.15 | 10.4 | 4,990 | 11,000 | 1,686 | 1,048 | 21,760 | 71,390 | — | — | 1 | |
| 37.26 | 122.2 | 17.25 | 56.5 | 70,805 | 156,098 | 28,325 | 17,601 | — | — | — | — | — | — |

# Index

240